AN EDUCATIONAL HISTORY OF THE WESTERN WORLD

AN EDUCATIONAL HISTORY OF THE WESTERN WORLD

Second Edition

ADOLPHE E. MEYER, PH.D.

Emeritus Professor of Educational History
New York University
Member of the Authors League of America

McGRAW-HILL BOOK COMPANY

New York   St. Louis   San Francisco   Düsseldorf   Johannesburg
Kuala Lumpur   London   Mexico   Montreal   New Delhi   Panama
Rio de Janeiro   Singapore   Sydney   Toronto

An Educational History of the Western World

Library of Congress Catalog Card Number 79-178930

07-041740-7

1 2 3 4 5 6 7 8 9 0 D O D O 7 9 8 7 6 5 4 3 2

This book was set in Press Roman by Creative Book Services, division of McGregor & Werner, Incorporated, and printed and bound by R. R. Donnelley & Sons Company, Inc. The designer was Creative Book Services, division of McGregor & Werner, Incorporated. The editor was Robert C. Morgan. Ted Agrillo supervised production.

TO ADOLPH, MY SON

UP TO RECENT TIMES

The first edition of this book came into being in May, 1965, after a prolonged period of gestation during which I professed educational history at New York University. Its reception was gratifyingly cordial both in the professional journals and in the organs of lay opinion. Like its predecessor, the present edition aspires to do two things. For one, it seeks to delineate the salient events of Western education as it winds its path from a remote and grizzly antiquity into the domain of the recent past. For another, it undertakes to relate them as adroitly and agreeably as candor and decorum permit, and in a prose which will be free from the curse of professional fustian. This purpose I see no reason to surrender, and so it remains unchanged.

The presuppositions which underlie the present volume are the same which grounded its parent, namely, that educational history at bottom is social history, and that always there is some connection between education and society—that the one reflects the other, and as the one changes significantly, so—given ample time—does its attendant reflection. Do these assumptions make sense, then it follows that an understanding of educational history presumes an understanding of the society of which it is a part. For this reason I have been at pains to present my tale of the educational past by standing it at all times before the cultural mirror.

Though my objectives and assumptions remain unaltered, this does not mean that putting the present volume into its new dress has been simply a matter of rendering it up-to-date or repairing insidious errors. There have been a number of changes both in form and substance. Every chapter has undergone careful search; new and pertinent matter has been brought in, and old, superfluous stuff has been discarded. Not only has the book undergone the revision aforesaid, but some of its parts have been accorded the labor of an entirely fresh composition. Such has been the case, to confine examples, with the Catholic Reformation and some of the trailblazing European educational progressives. In fact, to get even a sampling of the latter on paper grew to such a gigantic dimension that a brand-new chapter ensued.

Like its *avant coureur* of 1965, the present volume offers its pages to anyone who knows how to read, but they are addressed especially to collegians enrolled for good or ill in courses in educational history, or in courses concerned with the foundations of education, wherein a study of the educational past is generally regarded as an unavoidable necessity. As in the first edition, I have eschewed the use of footnotes. Where their material might be helpful to the understanding, I have enclosed their essence in the body of the text itself, and where it is simply documentary, I have sentenced it to the bibliography. Like its antecedent in the previous volume, it is not content to show itself as a mere checklist, but seeks rather to serve as a useful and instructive commentary.

Although, as I have given notice, I support the historian's confidence in the cultural-reflection premise, it is no more than proper to let it be understood that I hold some qualifying *ifs, buts,* and *whereases.* Educational history, I yield to the learned, is social history. Yet it is also the history of philosophy and psychology, of teaching methods, school organization, school support and maintenance, of race and religion, of politics and law, and what seems to be more and more the forgotten low man on the totem pole in the whole enterprise, the art and science of pedagogy. Nor should it be overlooked that at bottom it involves not only inexorable social forces, but also the hopes and strivings of people, particularly those involved in its innumerable concerns, whether as consumers or dispensers, peers or plain folk, and especially its immortal great, its weavers of dreams—aye, even its seers. It scarcely needs saying that an educator, whatever his standing in educational chronicles, is never just an educator. He is also a husband, a family man, a lover. He consumes food and imbibes fluids, whether spiritous or plain branch water. He is a winner in life or a loser, a believer or a renouncer, the residence of bacteria and complexes, all of which, for weal or woe, bear upon his work and thought. Only when we understand the man can we hope to understand his performance. It is in this vein that I have assembled the pages that follow—an educational history of all the Western people and the world in which they live and struggle and die.

In my prowls for information and my attempt to hold down slips in dates and names and suchlike bogies that forever lurk to trap and bedevil us, I have leaned often enough on countless readers, professional and profane. To name them all is, of course, beyond the bounds of possibility, and though here they must remain anonymous, my gratitude to them is nonetheless sincere and immeasurable. But to some, on whose patience and benevolence I have depended more than a little, my debt is even greater. There is Professor Joe Burnett of the University of Illinois, a colleague when I still bedizened the academic cloth; Professor Janice L. Gorn, one of my former graduate students, and now bearing the torch in the ivied halls of N.Y.U.; Professor Harry K. Hutton of the Pennsylvania State University, a friendly man, but for all that, an objective critic, whose counsel, though I have sometimes spurned it, has been tremendously inspiring. Finally I am indebted to Thomas Edward Ratcliffe, Jr., librarian in charge of the vast reference repository of the University of Illinois and to associate librarian Dorothy Miller Black, both now enjoying the savory fruit of retirement. Without their unsparing help, this work would have been inordinately more difficult to compose.

Adolphe E. Meyer

ANCIENT TIMES

CHAPTER 1

GREECE

For all the glitter of her achievement, ancient Greece, even in her finest moments, was but a handful of land. A dwarf among countries, she measured only half the space of current Illinois, and Attica, her largest state and the home of Athens, for centuries the shining star of Western culture, was smaller even than Rhode Island. Except for her northern border, Greece, or as the word has always been to her people, Hellas, is a sea-surrounded land, breaking out from the continent into the Mediterranean and Aegean. It is a country fretted with gulfs and bays and innumerable inlets, like Norway or Maine. A large flotilla of islands anchors all around, from mere specks of earth in a world of water to Crete, the largest and the longest, stretching out for more than 150 miles. The Grecian terrain is rough, bestrewn with mountains of which the tallest is Olympus, once the residence of the fabulous gods, and so lofty in its reach that even in the heat of summer it sports a glistening bonnet of ice and snow. Firs and pines huddle up the hillside, while farther down the fig tree flourishes, as do the olive and the vine. Save only in the plains and along the river's edge, the soil is inhospitable to husbandry, and so Greece was not celebrated like Mesopotamia and Egypt for the fatness of her granaries. But the olive offset this shortcoming. A Hellenic staple, it offered oil and food, and furthered trade among nations. The grape too did its part. Mixed with resin, its fermented juices made a heady drink, the delight and glory of Dionysus the wine god, the inspirer of carnival and clown shows and doubtless not a little more.

Despite their beauty, Grecian streams were not always friendly—often, indeed, they caused deep distress. In the springtime, when the clouds emptied out their heavy rains, rivers soon boiled over, far beyond their banks, perennially washing away land and habitations. Later, when the heat became infernal, the waters receded into a mere trickle, so small and shallow that one could step from shore to shore with ease. But no engineers rose up, as in Egypt, to tame the fickle flow, and so for months on end the inland waterway was lost to navigation.

A shred of land like Greece, so confined in its geographic latitude, could scarcely hope to entertain a variety of climate. On the whole it was of good temper. Winters were not long, and though chill winds blasted down from northern Thrace, they were not intolerable. When spring's rains had spent themselves, Greeks stirred out of doors. Presently the winds would drift in from northern Africa, and a long sojourn of sunblessed weather would ensue. Herdsmen now headed their flocks up to the mountain's higher greenery, while farmers turned the sod. Ships, snuggled during the winter months in the safety of their harbor, ventured forth once more upon the sea. Even armies came out of hibernation to resume their wars where some months earlier they had bogged in the gray gloom of winter. With the advance of fall the tide of events reversed. Shepherds returned, ships hurried to shelter, and armies settled into dormancy.

3

Other interests now emerged. Festivals, especially man's perennial homage to the culling of the grape, were aplenty. The theater reopened, and lawsuits, suspended in spring, were resumed.

The early Greeks were not opulent. Amongst them there was no empty show, at least not in the sense of the Orient's gaudiness or the splash of imperial Rome. There was little material comfort, either for the rich or for the poor. Their food and their garments were plain at best. Even in their greatest days their homes were mere huts of sun-baked clay, drab shelters with little ventilation and primitive sanitation. But Greek poverty came not from idleness, but from a want of resources. It was a sparsity that brought contentment without humiliation. "He alone is disgraced," said Thucydides, "who makes no effort to avoid poverty."

Greece never rolled up a large population. Even so, despite the smallness of their number, her inhabitants never managed to unite under the standard of a single nation. The hard barrier of geography with its vast wall of mountain, its moody rivers, and its islands, scattered near and far, worked against unity, and so did the proud self-love and provincialism of the separate states. Instead of welding themselves into one nation, sturdy and indivisible, the Greeks rent themselves into an assortment of communities, the so-called city-states, each free and independent. The smallest like the largest lived under its own laws, minted its own coin, and maintained its own army and navy, ready at all times to uphold its jealously guarded rights.

The origin of the Greeks is veiled in mist. Reaching back to the first days of human history, they are doubtless a blend of several parts of which two, at least, are vaguely discernible. There existed, for one thing, a native stock, dark in hair and feature, who dwelt along the Mediterranean's northeastern reaches. As the years ran on, they mixed with a fair-haired and blue-eyed folk who hailed from the steppes of the Asiatic west. The dark-domed chaps apparently had a flair for art, while their lighter brethren excelled in sports and in feats of arms. In sum, the Greeks were of Aryan stock, blood brothers to the Indo-European and the blond-topped Teuton who on some faraway tomorrow would come rumbling down from Europe's north to butcher the Roman legions.

Like most self-respecting people of antiquity, the Greeks took a much more high-toned view of their beginnings. The way they told it to their offspring, they were the heirs and descendants of Deucalion and Pyrrha, the sole survivors of the flood waters unleashed by Zeus in his ire against the human race, a flood so devastating it ranks second only to God's similar handiwork in the Holy Bible. The couple's first born was named Hellen, and in honor of this eponym the Greeks called their land Hellas and themselves Hellenes. Though all this is a transparent myth, and though the later Greeks were not unaware of its fictitious nature, as an idea it was as real and solid as Mt. Olympus itself. The distant ancestor of all Greeks, Hellen represented not only a common origin, but a frail filament of unity among a people torn apart by separatism and by the fierce power of their rivalry. Did the Hellenes fail to forge a united nation? Then, for all that, they were proudly aware of their common kinship. Non-Greeks were called barbarians, and whether they were superbly civilized or merely savages, a gloating sniffishness was reserved for them.

2

As common to Greece as its waters and its mountains were its great athletic spectacles. Four stood above the rest—the Pythian, Nemean, Isthmian, and Olympian—and the Olympian towered above all the others. The earliest Olympics are dimmed in the dark abysm of the unrecorded past. One does not even know for certain when they first were held, though the Greeks credited them to 776 B.C., when the Spartan ruler and lawgiver, Lycurgus, is said to have given them their characteristic form and substance. There is no doubt, however, that the games were run off at Olympia in the Peloponnesus, the native fastness of the pugnacious Spartans. As the years increased in number the games took on an enormous significance not only for the Spartans, but for all the Greeks. The Olympics were not merely an occasion for a colossal display of athletic powers; they were also a social and religious show, and though the Greeks shied away from national union, their Olympics had all the air of a national holiday.

Held every fourth year, the contests were for men only, women being barred from the scene both as contestants and as spectators. However, this is not to say that they were not present behind the scenes, particularly those of easy virtue, who for a fee dispensed their professional favors. Men swarmed to Olympia in a tremendous crowd. They made their way from the remotest nooks and crannies, and they swept in from all directions, some afoot and some by boat, while a few privileged ones rode in on horse. Every social rank graced the games, and so did every occupation. There were peasants and herdsmen and fishermen; but there were also writers, poets, orators, musicians, and metaphysicians. Most of them were on hand simply to feast their eyes and ears, but not a few were there to snare the elusive Olympic crown. To attain it made one a man of great distinction, and city vied with city to produce a winner. Competitors matched their skill not only on track and field. Some flaunted their talents in poesy; others recited their concoctions in prose. Tonemasters chanted their tunes and strummed their lyres. In time there were also drinking matches—even, indeed, contests in manly beauty.

The Olympic festivals were jammed, like cards in a pack, into five short days, but since they pulled in their participants, lay and competitive, from the outermost regions of the Hellenic world, and exacted a trip that was often long and sometimes even hazardous, a holy truce was declared throughout Greece to lighten the trek to and from Olympia. Consecrated to Zeus, the ruling chief executive of the Greek cast of gods and goddesses, the games opened and closed on a religious note, with sacrifices to please and placate divinity, and with especially cordial notices to Zeus himself. All this was interspersed with long and lusty gulps of the fermented grape. The festival was under the eye of a board of overseers who ruled on such puzzlements as a contestant's eligibility, his fitness for competition, and the like. The events themselves came under the jurisdiction of selected officials who, in tribute to their office, alone had the right to sit down. All others, spectators and competitors—save a boxer who had taken too many bumps—were expected to remain on their feet.

The games comprised short and long foot races, wrestling, and boxing. To these time added the ferocious pancratium, a rough-and-tumble free-for-all wherein two contestants could resort to almost any means to exact a triumph. In the passing years chariot and horse racing were introduced, but since Greece was not a horsy land, such enterprise confined itself to a very few. Ever sensitive to balance and harmony in the makeup of man, the Greeks put great stock in the all-round athlete. To bring him out they featured the pentathalon, wherein he wrestled, leaped, and ran, besides heaving the discus.

The Olympic contests reflected themselves in art and education. The artist's delicate tracery still lingers to charm and astound present-day admirers. Recurring frequently enough to keep alive the appetite for victory on some bright and unforgettable tomorrow, the games inflamed youth with heroic dreams. More important, however, than this lure of glory was its incentive to physical fitness, and the ready willingness it incited in the young to submit to the demands of discipline and training imposed upon them by their gymnasts.

Today's Olympic games are no longer singularly Greek; instead, they are international. To commemorate his achievement, their current victor acquires a gleaming medal. Sometimes, to supplement his usufruct, he gets a royal handshake from a sovereign. In our own fair republic, and in other advanced civilizations as well, his features bespangle the sports page; and if his triumph is of more than ordinary mark, he is sometimes flattered with an opportunity to edify the rest of us by showing himself on television. By contrast, the ancient Olympic conqueror obtained no medal, but a simple crown of olive leaves. But his gaud meant a great deal, and unlike his present-day successor, he was of an immortality which was, so to say, more than merely transient. His true reward was the glow and respect of his fellow citizens. In his honor they ripped out a section of the city wall—for with such a walking arsenal of power in its midst, the city obviously needed no wall in its defense. Sometimes the hero's likeness was hammered and chiseled out of marble to add a touch of beauty to a city street. For the poets it was, of course, a field day, and for the music makers too. What incentive, after all, could better quicken their creative muse than the unsurpassable feats so marvelously wrought by their very own Olympic hero?

The games themselves, as has been said, were of short duration—less than a week of breathtaking activity and they were over. The last victor received his crown, the last cheer melted into silence, the final rites were consummated in honor of Zeus, greatest of all Olympian gods, and now the horde of youths and men betook themselves to their scattered and faraway homes to pick up once more their everyday existence. A month—perhaps a little longer—and the solemn

Hellenic truce expired. With it severed the tender thread which had joined all Greeks, so briefly but so magnificently. And now some of the very men who but a short while before had thrilled to the common Hellenic grandeur might seize their shields and broadswords to grapple with one another in mortal combat. Such was the strange enigma of Greek unity and division.

3

If Greeks were linked by their games and by the ties of a common ancestry, then they also did business with the same gods. Although certain deities vouchsafed special aid and protection to certain cities—for example, Athena to Athens and Apollo to Delphi—this is not saying that they had no time to help and serve the other Greeks. They were the gods of all the Greeks, and the holy places were open to all at all times and everywhere.

There was, of course, more than one Greek religion—not so many, it is true, as in the present era of enlightenment, but more than one just the same. The most common, and the best known by far, is that depicted in the works of Homer. It had evolved over many hundreds of years, partly out of the fancy of the Greeks themselves but also out of plentiful pilferings and adaptations from outside sources. It came to its fullest flower on the eve of the Grecian heyday, but already by the fifth century B.C. it was showing signs of modification, and even a flash of novelty. Its ceremonials, for example, were on the increase, and so was its inclination to showiness and public revelry. At the same time there was a steady growth of free speculation, with the result that, under the philosopher's professional eye, some of the gods were viewed somewhat doubtfully—indeed, some of them and their transactions, discredited altogether, were elbowed from the scene of real existence into the limbo of fable.

Greek religion in its Homeric form is closely intertwined with education. It was grist for the literary mill. It made its way into music. And it fed the general fancy. Conceiving their gods in the image of themselves and their surroundings, whose mystery they could not fathom, the Greeks deified the forces and objects of nature, their human heroes, and even their birds and beasts. They endowed their gods with all the human qualities, capacities, and powers. Time for the gods was as infinite as space, for they were immortal. And not doomed to an inevitable grave, they could afford to shrug off every fear of death. Their home adorned the upper floors of Mt. Olympus. There, with Father Zeus to lead them, they engaged in life on a gorgeous scale. There they consumed delectable food and beverage, made love, politicked, quarreled, and sometimes fought like alley cats. There they spun their plans, contriving at times to be of use and comfort to man, but more often being merely sinister and destructive. Occasionally they roamed the earth, calling on mortal man at his fireside or workshop, or in the vast stretches of his outdoor world. Like all dark and mysterious powers of the air, they commonly entertained themselves with mischief, broadcasting fire, flood, and famine. Because of their japes a wife found herself sterile, milk turned to curd, and the cost of living climbed. The gods were jealous of mortal men—of great men especially. Witness, for example, Ulysses and everything that befell the badgered man between the covers of the *Iliad* and the *Odyssey*, simply because Poseidon, the sea god, hated him powerfully. As for their morals, they were on a par with the veneries of England's second Charles and France's fifteenth Louis. The gods excelled in murder, robbery, rape, adultery, and all the other accomplishments in human vice, not only aloft in their Olympian cloudswept heights, but in the human vale below.

Most gods—in fact, the vast majority—happened to be male. Each was in charge of certain specialties. Zeus was the father of the clan and its ruler. Myiagros, a minor fellow, was his flycatcher, charged with shooing off the flies when they gathered around his sacrifices. Poseidon was the admiral of the ocean and everything that went with it, from whales to sardines, tempests to typhoons. Seafaring men were careful to court his friendship. Poseidon's liegeman was Achelous, the river god. The father of innumerable nymphs, he enjoyed the kinship of more than 3,000 brothers.

The most industrious god of all, and also the most versatile, was Apollo. The handsomest of Olympians, he was the god of beauty, and therefore of all its art and mystery. He was also in charge of youth and human energy and mental enterprise. The dean of physical culture, he was advertised as the first Olympic winner. From his gymnastic concern, Apollo advanced as a matter of course into the more somber business of war. He was also in charge of the department of fortune telling, and his oracle at Delphi was never at a loss for business. And when he had the time, he urged and protected the interests of music and poetry, both of which he was said to have invented.

The foremost goddess—or at all events the one receiving the greatest public notice—was Athena. Patroness of Athens, she was of course the Athenian favorite. More important to the pursuers of knowledge is that she ran the department of wisdom. The owl perched on her shoulder is testimony to her expertness in this role. To most Greeks, and particularly to the multitudes whose minds were empty, a more diverting deity was Aphrodite, the lady divinity in charge of love. Or perhaps their favorite might have been Dionysus, the wine god, who inspired carnalities unmatched even in Hollywood. Less flamboyant than this loud and loutish fellow was Hestia, who forwarded domestic felicity and was worshipped in every home and hearth, where a friendly flame was kept alive in her honor at all times. Every city reserved a suitable place of veneration dedicated to the promotion of her cordiality.

All in all there were a dozen major deities. But their labors were supplemented and fortified by a herd of lesser potentates who presided over such important everyday affairs as the connubial relationship, bearing the young, planting the grain, and the chase in field and stream. Religion irradiated every Greek activity, and no important occasion was allowed to pass without a fitting salute to the divine professors on Olympus. Greek life thus consumed itself in a steady round of services and sacrifices, interspersed ever so often with calls for counsel and guidance from the holy oracle. Nearly every chamber in the home had its officiating deity, and so did every school and gymnasium and every public edifice.

From the Greeks, however, religion brought forth no milk of human kindness. Nor was it conducive to meekness, or even charity. The Greeks were not exhorted by their gods to love one another—instead when Greek met Greek there was likely to be a tug of war. Did Greek religion engender none of the homely virtues? Then, on the other hand, it spurred the manly ones of courage and alertness of mind and body, and it evoked a concern for beauty such as the world has seldom seen again. To the virtuous Greek the blackest of all wrongs was an arrogance of spirit, a haughtiness which dared to trespass beyond the bounds set by Olympus. Prometheus, for example, defied the gods and made off with their precious fire to give it to mortal man, an affront so blasphemous that Prometheus was wracked and battered almost beyond endurance. At the other pole stood the virtue of reverence or, at all events, great respect for one's parents and for the aged.

The Greek priesthood, such as it was, was not organized or professional or hereditary. The sacerdotal influence, hence, was never as powerful as, say, in Egypt or India. Consequently, the Greeks escaped the curse of priestcraft. Their creative genius enjoyed a freedom unknown to their contemporary world, and even to generations who roamed the earth centuries later. For fashioners of arts and letters, and even for iconoclastic philosophers, the field was wide open. A major concern to Greek life, such enterprise was pursued frankly, boldly, and not uncommonly with infinite beauty.

With all their crimes and misdemeanors, the Greek gods were not always base. In their nobler moments one glimpses the idea of Greek yearning, and idealization of human qualities, especially of grace and strength and beauty. In Apollo one meets them in their perfected combination. Orchestrated against that god's agility of mind, they represent, as we shall presently see, the ideal of Greek education, the cultivation of a harmonious alliance of body, mind, and spirit.

4

There were many city-states, but two rose above all others—Sparta and Athens. For generations they were leaders of Hellas, the one a totalitarian soldier state, where discipline and obedience reigned as the highest good, and where the faintest breath of nonconformity was promptly snuffed out; the other a free-functioning political entity, sometimes called a democracy, whose citizens were encouraged to enjoy the boon of self-expression. The difference between the two modes of living, as might be expected, put its mark upon the theory and practice of their education. Bitter rivals ever, Sparta and Athens became deadly foes, so deadly, in truth, that their antagonism finally destroyed them both.

Let us come to cases first with Sparta. The very name is suggestive. To be a Spartan is to be strong and hardy, physically fit, terse of speech, austere, self-effacing, and valorous to the last beat of a proud heart. In their prime the Spartans dominated southern Greece, the Peloponnesus, which, but for the slender strip of its attachment to the Grecian mainland, would have been an island roughly twice the size of Crete. The Spartans, who never accounted for more than 30,000 head, were conquerors. A fierce, relentless folk, they hammered their way out of their mountainous fastness in the north, destroying whoever blocked their course and subjugating the survivors, first the inhabitants of Laconia, then those of Messina. As the years unfolded, they clamped their shackles on some 300,000 souls, a number ten times greater than their own.

Known commonly as Dorians, this handful of conquerors settled in Laconia. None save this master class could be citizens. They alone made the laws; they alone held office; and in time of war they alone commanded.

A notch lower than the Dorians stood the Perioeci, of whom estimates say there were about 120,000. Free men, which is to say they were neither slaves nor serfs, they dwelt in scattered mountain villages or on the fringe of Laconia, where they performed the ancient tasks of farmers and herdsmen or even those of minor tradesmen. They were levied upon, and in war, which was not infrequent, they were put upon to bear arms. But, as has been hinted, they had no voice in making the laws under which they lived, and to maintain the Spartan blood pure and uncorrupted, they were forbidden to marry into the Dorian master class.

At the bottom of the social pile lumbered the Helots, some 220,000, or almost twice the number of Perioeci. Half slave, half serf, the Helot was attached to the land. He had no rights, though he could not be sold. Sometimes he operated as a domestic; sometimes he tilled the land. If he wished, he might enter connubial bliss, though should his heart toward a Dorian maid incline, he soon found out that the penalty for such madness might well be death. Even so, he was not completely miserable. Generally he had the pleasure of having a roof over his head, and so long as he got no false ideas, he was in no great peril. But encircled as they were by a horde ten times vaster than their own, the master class could afford to take no risks. Between Dorian and Helot there was actually a perpetual state of war. Not only did the Dorian secret cops spy upon the Helots constantly, but if a Dorian put an end to a Helot, whether deliberately or otherwise, then his act was never murder, but merely a simple and even laudable deed of war.

Sparta is not hailed, as is Athens, for its Socrates or Plato, or even for one of a dimmer candlepower. No deathless lyrics warbled from the Spartan throat. In the arts and sciences there was nothing but a desert. There was a time, it is true, before the Spartans had embraced their fateful regimented role, when the Muses dwelt amongst them, and when, like their fellow Greeks, they entertained a lively interest in the arts. Yet for all its promise, it never rooted. The fact is it was deliberately scotched by a self-assumed totalitarianism, begotten, it is said, by Lycurgus. Though nine-tenths of him is no more real than Rip van Winkle,

Lycurgus has come down the corridors of time as Sparta's salient lawmaker, its Moses, as it were, and the author of its political and social institutions. The truth, in greater likelihood, is that these issued from a transformation which ran through the seventh and sixth centuries B.C. During these years a revolt blazed up against the master Dorians, and though in the end it was put to death, its threat had been so frightening as to cause the Spartan rulers to put on a violent brake. All cultural traffic ground to a halt. Citizens—namely, Dorians—were forbidden to engage in trade, and to make it hard—nay, impossible—to lay up any store, private property was in effect abolished, and all lawful coin was minted in the form of heavy iron bars. Thus, all private initiative was put under the heel of state necessity. In the end it was Sparta's blood and not its Muse that transported its message.

In all affairs which freight human life, the state was the prime mover, and the citizen was merely its obedient mechanism. No sooner had the babe made entrance into the world than he was borne by his father to confront a council of elderly inspectors. Was the new arrival well formed, in good health, impeccable and full of promise? Then the councilors granted him their approval and acceptance. Was he on the other hand sickly and brittle, or otherwise of dubious prospect? Then let him be flung into space from the mountaintop to be dashed on the rocks below.

If accepted, the child was returned to the maternal nest. There, if he was a boy, his mother fed and tended him for seven years, rearing him in the grimmest austerity, exhorting him everywhere and always to be brave, and taking infinite pains to break his childish will to the stern glory of Spartan discipline. At seven the child bade farewell to the hearth to make his residence in the public barracks where he was promptly articled not only to the first tasks of schooling, but to his military regiment. He now fell under the eye and ear of a *paidonomos*, the barracks youth commander and drillmaster. Presently, if the lad showed himself of more than ordinary competence, he became a sort of captain over the fellows of his class. It was their duty to render him strict and unqualified obedience, and whenever they fell short of his ordinances, he had the authority to deal out the severest punishment.

All education—if one may stretch the meaning of the term several miles—was overladen with a heavy martial note. Games were played, it is true, but to harden the human apparatus, not primarily to unburden the animal spirits. Nude as man's First Father, boys were spurred to let go with all their might, to run and jump, to wrestle and box, to pitch stones, the javelin, and the discus, and to engage in military drill; but always everything they did was under relentless watch. They were incited at all times to come into contest and to lay on with fists, and when one showed signs of timidity or cowardice, he was roughly handled. Time was to bring the boy the capacity to endure all pain and hardship. To this end he was frequently flogged, and every year a dozen lads were singled out to be scourged publicly before the alter of Artemis until the stones ran red with blood. Did they bear it without a whimper? Then they were well regarded.

Did they flinch? Then they were upbraided by their leaders and mocked and taunted by their comrades. At twelve a boy surrendered his underwear—henceforth he was to have but one light garment for the year. Unlike his American successor, the Spartan boy rarely tubbed, water being regarded as a menace to health and morals. Nor did the Spartan yield himself to the charm and comfort of a mattress or even a simple blanket: winter and summer he laid himself on the hard outdoor ground. If he disported himself fittingly, he was allowed to mess with the inner circle in the communal hall—not to show himself off, of course, but to hearken to the conversation of his elders.

On his eighteenth birthday the Spartan received his military greetings—he was old enough now to become a recruit at arms, suffering, as usual, from his sergeants and developing his proficiency in the art and science of war. Two years later he found himself a soldier in full equipment, serving his ten-year term wherever the fates ordained.

Until he was thirty the Spartan male had passed his peacetime hours in the barracks. Of domestic bliss he was a complete and utter ignoramus. He had learned his primer ABCs, but for him reading and writing were a bore, and he seldom resorted to them. On the other hand, he was privy to the fatherland's every law, not from learned books to be sure, but from firsthand contact. He had been taught to keep himself sober, again not by hollow moralizing, but by the power of example. For this purpose Helots were regularly forced into their cups to make a mock and scandal of themselves, and thus serve as an everlasting lesson to the Spartan young. Although he was free from the thrall of drink, he was an accomplished liar and a thief, so that as a soldier in time of war he could live off the country and bamboozle the enemy with false information. Conditioned from early childhood to the importance of being well and strong, he had learned to keep himself fit at all times. Though Spartans ate sparingly, now and then their glands became heretical, and a man began to get roomy. But in Sparta fat men were not popular—indeed, if their spaciousness grew unduly, they were accosted by the police and forced to puff and sweat in a campaign of hard and relentless exercise.

Although at thirty the Spartan was freed from the fetters of actual soldiering, there now loomed another threat. For under Doric jurisprudence every able-bodied Spartan, having managed to survive thirty years, was now esteemed fit and ready to take himself a spouse. He had had some practice in love, it is true, with both men and women, for in such matters the Spartans had no qualms. But now the job at hand was to propagate offspring, and for this end the state commanded him to take a mate. Did he hold back for any reason? Then he and others like him were incarcerated in a room filled with darkness and unwed women, and when presently he emerged his bachelorhood was history. On rare occasions some stray and heedless male ventured to prolong his single blessedness. But not for long. For not only did he lose the privilege of warming to the festivals of youth, where the young, male and female, danced and paraded in the utter altogether, but if he persisted in his disloyalty, the knave was exiled from Laconia.

At bottom, though, wedlock thrust no halter upon the married male. Most of his day he passed at the barracks, eating and sleeping there, and overseeing the young. By the same token his time at home was short and seldom, and his children scarcely knew him. When on occasion he actually made an appearance, then usually his business was to share the connubial couch. Next to the tort of celibacy stood that of physical incompetence. A childless father soon became the subject for public raillery, and if his misfortune persisted, he was put upon to engage a substitute, say, a brother or some other qualified volunteer, to aid his wife to fulfill her natural and patriotic function.

Girls, like boys, were subject to state control. If, as newborn people, they got by the council of inspectors, they were brought back home to be kept under their mother's constant vigilance. They were never immured in barracks, but whatever they did was under iron supervision. In their games they played as roughly almost as the boys, running, throwing, pitching darts, and even wrestling. Always they were under order to maintain themselves in health and strength, so that by their twentieth birthday they would be prepared to bear formidable progeny. They were not immune to the tonal art, but their singing was not the free and easy twitter of childhood, but the robust airs of patriotism and the solemn hymns intoned to the departed brave. Like the boys, they engaged in festive parades and dances, capering publicly as per custom in the nude. Needless to say, reading and writing, sparsely meted out to the male, were not wasted at all on the female.

In the main Spartan women fared better than their frailer sisters elsewhere. Spartan girls, says Plutarch, were bold and masculine, but he adds that not uncommonly they were beautiful. For their time they enjoyed a great many rights. They could, for example, hold property, such as it was, and they could bequeath it, a boon which even in our own glorious democracy was not generally granted to the ladies until past the mid-nineteenth century. Their marriage, compulsory and unromantic though it usually was, was nonetheless secure. There was almost no adultery, and prostitution was unknown. Divorce was so rare as to be singular—indeed, even a king was fined when he ventured to rid himself of his wife for a younger and comelier creature.

In human chronicles Sparta is the first eugenic state of which we have any news. There, doubtless, the professional medicos would have had sparse pickings, and so also would the doctors of the psyche. Health and strength were not merely a national slogan—they actually flourished, and so did obedience and discipline, and a deep and unswerving love of country. The Spartan way caught the fancy of the outland sages, and especially of Plato, in whose *Republic* there are discernible traces of Spartan influence, and who, though he enjoyed himself as a bachelor—or, maybe, because he did—offered the women of the *Republic* privileges and prerogatives the ladies of Athens had only vaguely heard of, but of which a number were in actual Spartan practice. It is true the Spartans were free; at the same time they were under the yoke of remorseless duty, and they were ever the slaves of their laws. Their army, which was their justifiable pride, was the envy of all Greeks, though not all Greeks by any means aspired to such military potency at the gruesome price it put upon the citizen—the surrender, that is, of nearly all his personal liberty. The roster of Spartan virtues is long, but its entries are nearly always civic. The Spartan's personal qualities, putting aside his severe simplicity, were few. He was, like Nietzsche's superman, a prodigy of coldness and brutality, an excellent soldier and an obedient citizen, but beyond that little else, a creature without mercy and without soul.

5

Hardly a day's trek from Sparta lay Athens—a place full of flaws, to be sure, and sometimes even of palpable injustice. But it was also open to new ideas, flexible in time of peace, and flexible even in time of war, with a surprise ever around the corner, a civilization deferential to individual rights, enlightened, complex, varied, fanciful, tolerant, and boldly skeptical. It was, in sum, a land of free people.

Athens was the foremost municipality and the fortress, so to say, of Attica, sprawling over a peninsula just to the north and east of Sparta. It was the largest of the city-states, and by all odds the richest. Like so many other enlightened folk, the Athenians took great pride in their mean beginnings, and they talked gravely of having "sprung from the soil." More likely they stretched back to the Ionians, a people of great versatility and enterprise, and who at one time inhabited the mysterious reaches of the Near East. As the years ran on, the Athenians advanced themselves from a primitive rusticity through monarchy and tyranny until, by the fifth century B.C., they were thriving under a considerable degree of self-rule. Had it not been for their fleet, they would certainly have starved to death, for their land was insufficient for their needs. Consequently they flourished by their brisk trade overseas, joining in the process the greatest importers of their time, and extending their business into the Mediterranean to Sicily and the neighboring islands, southward into Egypt, northward into Thrace, up the Danube line, and even beyond into the cold and clammy bleakness of Russia. When, at length, they lost their grip on the waters, their slide down the chute of fortune was swift and beyond repair.

The social scale of Athens was baldly simple. At the top stood the citizens, male and native, and even at the pinnacle of their fame never more than 100,000. Below them were the aliens, free but barred from the full enjoyment of civic right and privilege, and numbering about 40,000. At the bottom were the slaves, not necessarily inferior of person and attainment, but mainly the victims of the caprices of war. Overwhelmingly they were the property of private hands, but some were the property of the state, and served as guardians of the public peace, various clerks, and street cleaners. In their high day they accounted for some 200,000.

The frontier between the classes was plainly marked. Citizens, for example, were forbidden to engage in the affairs of trade or business, for it was a cardinal article of patriotic faith that such doings were degrading. Commerce hence was the pursuit mainly of foreigners. To them fell the tasks of the artisan and the chores of keeping shop. Though they were excluded from citizenship, and hence from access to the ballot and important political jobs, there is no blinking the fact that some of them enjoyed an excellent life. Like the citizen, however, they were subject to the levies of the tax gatherer, and in time of war they were put under arms to fight side by side with the natives. For its part, the free citizenry consumed most of its time in public service, giving its attention to the political talk in the marketplace or in the general assembly, executing the functions of the higher civic offices, or issuing commands in the army or navy. On the slaves, as usual, fate forced the tasks nobody wanted, though their labors were not always without dignity, nor were they necessarily menial. The slave's condition was not generally harsh, save when he was put to sweating in the state-owned silver mines where his life was usually short and dreadful. Actually, one may think of the generality of Athenian slaves as somewhat akin to servants with the assurance of lodging and regular commons, but without wages, and bereft, of course, of the right to vote. If things went well for them, there was always the hope that on some tomorrow their master might set them free, and thus open the way for them in the class above.

Only in the army was there a trace of the privilege of property. A horse owner, for example, assigned himself to the cavalry. One of lesser fortune, but sufficiently well heeled to own a suit of armor, served his time in the heavy infantry. Less august fellows operated as light foot soldiers or pulled oars in the fleet.

With so much interest in the practice of public affairs, it was only natural that Athens should grace itself with a number of political institutions which made life within its walls much more tolerable than in austerity-ridden Sparta. To begin, there was an assembly which, forgetting the disfranchised, embraced every citizen, whether high or low, rich or poor. From it nine leaders, or archons, were chosen, but their powers, once very great, had been pruned, and they amounted to very little. When the assembly convened in full congress, it was, at bottom, a vast public meeting. Its potency ran to great length, reaching into lawmaking, the running of the state, and even the administering of justice. In ordinary times the assembly held its meetings monthly, though it could be summoned into special session at any time. Any man managing to get the floor was free to address his comrades, and he could propose any measure, however stupid, provided it contained itself within the limits of the prevalent moral opinion and the constitution. Even though the assembly failed to fetch all the citizens to its deliberations at any single time, its size was too unwieldy to enable it to carry on the business of everyday governance. Hence it was given the aid of a number of smaller bodies. There was, for one, a council of five hundred. Made up by lot, it prepared the agenda for the assembly, and directed its attention to matters of immediate concern. Lower down the scale was a council of fifty, a sort of steering committee for the larger group. With a new chairman every day, it sat in session during the rainy season, which is to say a couple of months or so at best.

The execution of justice, as has been said, fell upon the general assembly. But Athens had no professional judiciary, and it was spared the presence of attorneys, either for the prosecution or for the defense, the general idea being that an aggrieved one should voice his complaint directly to his hearers, and that the defendant should be put upon to answer it in the same forthright manner. For petty cases there were local courts, but for the major abuses, whether criminal or civil, the trial scene was always Athens. The jury which gave ear to such matters might range from 101 to 1,001, the smaller bodies reserving their attention for the lesser breaches, and the larger ones for the baser and more serious offences. There was no trial judge; instead, a foreman or chairman was picked to exercise his talents. Plaintiff and defendant pleaded their own causes, though each was allowed the services of a scribe; after his logic was arranged and ornamented by the scribe, he learned it by heart and proceeded to reproduce it orally. When the speechmaking was over, the jury disgorged its verdict, and the law's machinery began its inexorable grind.

By some connoisseurs of political science Athens has been counted as a democracy. If democracy means that all the people participate in the affairs of government, then plainly the Athenians fell far from the mark, as must also every other state, whether old or young. But if democracy means that every citizen takes an active part in government, then Athens made the grade. From making policy to carrying it out, the governance of Athens was in the hands of nonprofessionals—men who loved politics no less than they did their city-state, and for whom involvement in civic affairs was as natural and necessary as food and air. Before an Athenian left this earth to mingle with the eternal shades, he might find lodgment in any public post, from juryman to chairman of the council of fifty, an office which, if the assembly happened simultaneously to be in session, elevated him for twenty-four hours to the rank of dignity of titular head of state.

If the Athenian male permitted himself a spacious freedom, then his womenfolk by contrast were hedged in by restraints and prohibitions on every side. There was a time, it is true, when their part in everyday life was conspicuous, but by the fifth century B.C. it had subsided into a mere memory. The female was, by Aristotelian sagacity, a sort of third-rate male. Romance brushed her cheeks but seldom, and in marriage it eluded her almost entirely. Her mating, consummated not uncommonly as early as her fifteenth birthday, issued from negotiations conducted between her father or a marriage broker and her prospective spouse, who in all likelihood had never set eye upon her, the whole transaction being forwarded by the lure of a rewarding dowry. For the run of Greeks, whether of the Spartan or Athenian variety, the reason behind wedlock was not love or even the comfort of domesticity, but the propagation of the masculine line. To supplement the services of a wife, a husband was allowed to keep a concubine, but the children of such a union were not to be regarded as lawful. "We have courtesans for pleasure," observed Demosthenes, "concubines for our everyday physical health, and wives to bear us legal offspring, and to be the loyal custodians of our homes." Did a man engage in a little extracurricular wenching? Then moral rectitude was not against him, nor was the law. On the other hand, did his wife stray onto a rival's couch? Then without ado she might be divorced or even put to death.

The rights a woman enjoyed were almost nil. Her spouse might emblazon her with gems, but she could not inherit his property. She could make no contracts; nor could she indebt herself beyond a trifling sum; nor could she sue in the courts, no matter how grave her injury. By the moral lights of her day she was expected to abstain from public appearance, save to attend to her religious devotions or to visit the theater, when she was decorously veiled and properly squired. On all other occasions she was to cut herself off from the world, sequestering herself in her quarters in the rear of her home. But, for all the discrimination against her, in her domestic domain she was not without honor. Her husband, it is true, charged himself with all the household marketing. On the other hand, she was the stewardess of her home, overseeing its help and contributing to the administration and execution of its affairs.

Though husbands were generally anesthetic to the companionship of their wives, this is not saying they were immune to feminine charm and wile. Ladies of obliging affability thrived in Athens, as they did in all Greece, save, of course, in Sparta. For such ladies, indeed, there were even special seminaries, run commonly by retired houris, the first trade schools, as it were, to show themselves in the Western world. The most celebrated Greek courtesans were the *hetaerae*. Living a life of almost feminist boldness, they displayed themselves at large in gaudy raiment, flashing not only their studied pulchritude, but their concern for culture as well. Not a few of them were literate, and some are still remembered for their wit. No man, said Plutarch, was ashamed to be seen with them. In truth, even Socrates consorted with them, and so did Plato, and the great Pericles even married one.

6

Athenian education sorts itself into two main varieties, the one which flourished before the rout of the Persian invaders in 490 B.C., and the other which took shape thereafter. The older Athenian education grounded itself, as in Sparta, mostly on tribal convention, but as their Doric rivals proceeded to lock themselves into their ironclad totalitarianism, the Athenians, as has been observed, allowed themselves to bubble in a lively self-expression. As a result, their youth enjoyed a fuller and far more liberal tutoring, one which essayed to cultivate in them the quality of urbane habit and easy utterance, and to enable them, when they were of age, to participate freely in the city's brisk communal life.

In Athens, as in Sparta, the newborn babe was subject to adult approval and acceptance, though in this case the decision of life or death resided solely in the father. A boy's chances, as one might expect in Athens, ran somewhat better than a girl's, though if a family happened to be crowded, even a boy's fortune could run out, and he might be left to die and rot on some lonely wayside. If the infant was granted his life, then on his fifth day he was formally consigned to the care and custody of the household gods. Another five days and the father publicly acknowledged the child as his own, identified it with a name, and declared himself responsible for its rearing.

For seven years the boy remained under the family roof. Though he was subject to the jurisdiction of his father, his care fell mainly to his mother, assisted, if she was lucky, by a nurse, who frequently was a slave. They stood sentinel over his character, endeavoring to make him strong, healthy, and decent. Meanwhile, the small fry, male and female, yielded most of their time to play, leaping and prancing, as in their immemorial way, chasing one another at tag, hiding, seeking, leapfrogging, and in general letting loose their brimming energy. Even then girls babied dolls, and boys knuckled marbles.

At seven life became more grave. Though no law said so, the time had come for a boy to be articled to school. Its daily sessions were long, from the rise of the morning sun to its evening fall. His sister however, confronted no such hardship, for there was a disinclination to waste knowledge on girls, and most of them grew up innocent of reading and writing. Instead, they were kept at home, where they were introduced to the perennial household knacks, from spinning and weaving to sewing and cooking. Some of them made their way into music and the dance.

The schoolboy was assigned to the care and keeping of a *paidogogos*, once probably an active slave but now too far gone in years for hard practice. The function which befell this footman was to assure the safe delivery of his ward at school and, later in the day, at home, and to hold his skylarking along the road within proper bounds. As the boy increased in years, the *paidogogos* graduated into a sort of male duenna, counseling his charge in the intricacies of manners and morals, and striving at all times and everywhere to keep him out of trouble.

The boy's first school was privately run, usually by a person of low estate—not uncommonly, in fact, by a liberated slave seeking to make an honest but precarious living. For all the high worth in which they wreathed their learning, the Athenians held their schoolmasters in slight respect. Indeed, to call an ordinary man a teacher was to offer him an affront. A man reported missing, so the Athenians used to jibe, must be either dead or a schoolmaster.

In school the boy was put to nurse at his ABCs. To this end he served his time under a special master, the so-called grammatist, who directed his first steps into literacy. For Greeks learning to read was a forbidding business, requiring infinite diligence and no little suffering. No beauteous picture books bedazzled the learner's interest; instead he applied himself to his teacher's barren script. There was no class system among the letters, all of them being capitals. Nor, unhappily, was there a traffic system to guide one through a sentence, all letters being linked together JUSTLIKETHISLETTERFORLETTER in a gigantic literary chain without benefit of commas or periods, or even spaces to mark off the words. Is today's Johnny sometimes said to be a stranger to the reading art? Then surely his ancient forerunner, had he been equally deficient, might have pleaded at least a plausible excuse.

Hand in hand with reading went writing. The future penman launched himself by tracing his letters in sand, after which he was put to carving them with a stylus, a sharply pointed, pencil-shaped instrument, into a waxen tablet which he secured on his knee, desks being then unheard of. As he grew in skill, he was occasionally trusted with ink and papyrus, or if he was of sufficient pocket, with the more expensive parchment.

Learning to cipher was even more ghastly than learning to read. For Greeks, having no numbers, employed letters in their place, so that even the simplest problem became an exercise of overpowering difficulty. As a consequence, Greeks tallied with their fingers, and the more facile and eager ones sometimes with their toes as well. Even so, being a virtuoso in arithmetic was generally regarded with bilious eyes. Practical in its essence, it was for tradesmen and such lowly commoners, and not for the free and liberally educated. In the Athenian school, hence, arithmetic was consigned to a minor place.

Meanwhile, his reading, having passed beyond the point of mystery, fixed its attention more and more on the development of an excellent expression. But still there were no books. Instead, the master read, and the pupils labored to copy what he said, or they learned his words by heart. Thus they introduced themselves to Homer and Hesiod and the rest of the literary greats. From them they acquired their taste in letters, besides an understanding of their geography and history, an intimate glimpse of their pantheon of gods and goddesses, and even, in fact, a guide to everyday virtue.

As reading was brought to terms, the boy made acquaintance with music. The tonal art was to serve him throughout his life, in the notices he transmitted to his divinities, in the drama that stirred him in the theater, in the parades that swept down the street of a holiday afternoon, and most of all, as a sign to all the world that he was a truly educated Athenian, a man not merely civilized with learning, but with a love of beauty as well. To be a stranger to music was, indeed, to be an alien. To initiate the boy in the art of tone was the work of a specialist. From him he learned to sing and to strum the lyre, a great-grandfather among the strings. The flute, though occasionally resorted to, was not well regarded. Like the waltz, when it was first disclosed in public, it was suspected of indecency. Music, as has been hinted, was not altogether an autonomous art. It underlay nearly all bodily expression, from gymnastics to the dance. The handmaiden of all poetic utterance, it constituted with poetry a single art, the most honored of them all.

But the Athenian boy, his elders agreed, was not merely a blend of brain and beauty—brawn too was important. Hence the importance of cultivating him physically. For this purpose the gymnasts spoke with authority. The boy's first exercising was light—some games, a bit of running and jumping, and perhaps some dancing and swimming. But as he acquired size and sturdiness, his effort took on more heft and power. He ran farther, and he played more fiercely, and he hurled the discus and the spear. Already he was dreaming of snaring an Olympic crown.

The schools themselves were usually of a lowly sort, in strange and startling contrast to the colossal and costly palaces which gloss the current world of learning. Suffering on backless benches, boys confronted neither desks nor tables. Ventilation and lighting were of the meanest kind. What ameliorated the pupils' lot somewhat was that on fair days, which were, of course, numerous, much of their enterprise was carried on outdoors. Their morals were under constant vigilance. In fact, to safeguard boys from any untoward advances, the presence of any adult male on the academic premises, except only the schoolmasters and their sons and brothers, was under heavy prohibition. To insure the full effectiveness of its watch, the state placed a policeman of morals in the schools. Under the circumstances discipline, as one might guess, was rigorous, and the corrective lash was applied fiercely and frequently.

Schooldays came to an end for most boys when they turned thirteen or fourteen. By having granted them some education their fathers obtained a measure of security for their own faraway future, when the fire of their middle years had burned itself out and they could maintain themselves no longer, for by Athenian law a son thus educated was required to support his father when the years had done him in. Youths aspiring to exercise their full civic function were made to submit to yet more training. For them the state provided a couple of public gymnasiums. Nestled in a stately grove just beyond the city limits, these "palaestra," as they were called, were sumptuously appointed with steam rooms, rubdown parlors, a variety of playing fields, two stadiums, one of them sheltered for bad weather, and with reserved seats at all times for rhetoricians, philosophers, and similar worthies. In truth, but for the absence of Christian endeavor, they might well have fired the envy of any current YMCA. In the palaestra the youth trained and developed his full physical prowess. He not only ran and leaped and hurled as before. He also punched the heavy, weighted bag. He boxed and wrestled. And if he had any talents, the Olympics now beckoned more earnestly than ever. Finally, he learned the use of rudimentary arms and to ride on horse. When this day arrived, he was on the border of eighteen, which is to say, on the brink of his two-year military obligation.

He now became an *ephebos*, a sort of militiaman and apprentice citizen. Now under complete state control, he was shorn of his long locks, thrust into a black uniform, equipped with shield and sword, and residenced in the municipal barracks. With his comrades he publicly vowed allegiance to the state, promising solemnly that he would never disgrace his arms and that he would fight for the temples and the public property everywhere and at all times, both alone and with others. "I will transmit my fatherland," he swore, "not only not less, but greater and better than it was transmitted to me." He went on to bind himself to obey the laws of the land and to honor the faith of his fathers.

Under the tireless eye of his superiors, he was encouraged to ape his elders, organizing, like them, into assemblies and councils, convening in meetings, assaulting the air with speeches, and giving his support to endless resolutions. Meanwhile, he lent his ear to a steady flow of lectures on the prevalent arts and sciences, and on the moral and civic opinion of the day. His rights and prerogatives were numerous. A reserved seat awaited him at the theater. On holidays he and his fellows marched in parades. Periodically, he exhibited himself in athletic tournaments.

Thus his first ephebic year. At nineteen he was shifted to the forlorn and faraway frontier, where for the ensuing twelve months he continued to exercise his alertness on behalf of his country. He made an unsparing study of the lay of the land, the roads and shoreline, and the mountain passes, and he assisted in the enforcement of the laws. When his services came to an end, he was freed from the parental mantle, a citizen at long last in his own right, with all the charms and usufructs of citizenship but not without its duties and obligations and, unhappily, at times its nuisances.

Such was Athenian education in its older style. Starting out in rusticity as frontiersmen, its proponents, a virile and imaginative people, refined themselves in the flow of many centuries into one of the most civilized folk this planet has ever seen. Moral scientists, it is true, decry their blemishes, their fettering, for example, of their women, their practice of slavery, and their almost total void of human tenderness. Unlike their Spartan neighbors, however, the Athenians conferred upon their citizen the right to function freely, and in pretty nearly all departments of human life. Surrounded by a vast array of democratic organizations, he was expected to acquaint himself at firsthand with public affairs and to engage therein to his full capacity. To this end, however, the state imposed on him the prerequisite of education. Indeed, without it the gate to citizenship was securely bolted. Yet, save in its last and higher stages, such education was neither compulsory nor state-controlled, the overwhelming portion of it being private and at the father's choice and expense. So simple were its offerings, they defy the modern understanding—reading and writing, a slight dash of arithmetic, followed by splurgings in literature and music, and the cultivation of the body, strong, healthy, and handsome. There were no special lessons in history and geography, or even in religion and virtue. But Athenian youth was familiar with them just the same, for they lurked all about—in the daily talk he encountered on every side, in the imperial and sonorous verses of his poets, and particularly in the lively effervescence that was Athens everywhere. Though in his early days he was given to a good deal of imitating and memorizing, as he grew to manhood he was expected to teach himself in action. Thus he gave training to his body and cultivation to his mind and spirit, engaging in free palaver, making music, soliciting and placating his divinities, practicing politics, soldiering on the front, at home, and at the border, until at twenty he unfolded into the full flower of his citizenship. Thus he learned to be himself and at the same time to do his duty for the state. It was not much, perhaps, when judged by modern values; but in its heyday it was without a peer—nay, it was without a rival.

7

In the year 490 B.C. a handful of Greeks, led by the Spartans and the Athenians, succeeded in chasing a vastly larger horde of invading Persians back to their

Oriental lair. Their victory was calculated to astound the world, and from the Pillars of Hercules to the remote reaches of Syria men gaped at its wonder. For Hellas it was a powerfully reassuring tonic, but especially for Athens, whose gorgeous vitality now unloaded itself at a dizzy pace to fashion in the course of time a thoroughly cosmopolitan culture.

While the trade and commerce of Athens boomed, foreigners, lured by the town's wonderful opportunities, streamed in from all directions and in ever-increasing number. Granted, a great many of them were self-seekers, pushful adventurers aspiring to quick and easy riches. But a few of them were men of incandescent talent who in the centuries ahead were to become an everlasting glory to their adopted land. There was, to come to cases, the father of medicine, Hippocrates, who hailed from coastal Asia Minor; there was Thales, the reputed founder of Greek philosophy, from the same region; and finally, there was the greatest of them all, Aristotle, who issued from Stageirus, a tiny settlement in Thrace.

But whether high or low, the newcomers were the bearers, often enough, of novel and striking views, drawn into service from the remotest quarters of the globe, from the Mediterranean's western end to Egypt and Mesopotamia—even from places as far away as India and China. For many Athenians, and particularly for those who had risen in their material estate, hobnobbing with the New Thought took on the air of a pleasant dalliance, and since not a few of the ideas were alluring, the precepts and values which had served so many generations of Athenians fell under challenge. Out of the collision between the old and the new there rose up a tidal wave of skepticism which presently rolled over both the sacred and the earthly spheres, and which manifested itself everywhere, from the comedies of Aristophanes to the caustic queries of the dog-faced Socrates. Under its powerful sweep the gods fell from their airy elevation to descend in the passage of time into mere literary figures. Morality, disrupted from its authority of revelation, remained either with nothing to give it mooring, or with reason alone. In politics the old stress on blood and birth, once indispensable to one's status, yielded to wealth, with a swarming of plutocratic job holders, both military and secular. Meanwhile, Athenian youth, seduced by the new order's promise of personal aggrandizement, chafed under the restraint put upon it by the old ideal of communal service. As a result, the old educational views fell into disrepute, and when new ones appeared from around the corner, young Athens was ready to give them attention.

Known as Sophists or wise men, the new teachers were mainly aliens, touring academicians, as it were, who during the fifth pre-Christian century set themselves up in Athens to sell their scholarly wares. They taught only a handful of students at a time, and they kept no schools as such. Instead, they plied their ancient art in whatever place was handy, in the marketplace or some convenient plaza or, in the rainy season, in the shelter of an inn. A great many of them, doubtless, were merely clever, adroit spinners of gossamer subtleties, and they were more concerned with raking in drachmas than with the enlightenment of the young. Aristophanes, a virtuoso in the concoction of everlasting badinage, branded them as cheats and liars. The scholarly Isocrates charged them with gulling students with lofty promises. Even Plato, suspending for a moment his flight to the bristling peaks of absolute and eternal verity, derided them as crafty mountebanks who conned men of wealth and place with bogus learning as their lure. For all such outcry, however, the truth is that a number of Sophists were actually first-rate men of learning. One of them was the famous Hippias of Elis, a veritable walking university. Orator, poet, musician, he discoursed familiarly on literature, morals, and politics. In addition, he dabbled in history and diplomacy, besides tailoring his own clothing.

No less extraordinary was Gorgias, who was born about 483 B.C. at Leontini in Sicily. A familiar of rhetoric and politics, he served his people as ambassador to Athens. His chief talents, however, lay in speechmaking wherein he was master of every trick. A perambulating orator, he excited much wonder, executing his spell in one place after another, and wherever he spoke young Greeks buzzed around him not only to give him an ear, but to beg him for lessons in the arcana of his art. For a substantial stipend, he gladly acceded. He was still a powerhouse in his seventies—in fact, in 407 B.C., speaking at the Olympic Games, he transported his listeners to the pinnacle of ecstasy when he urged them to cease their eternal fratricide and join their Hellenic hands to face the common threat of a revived and vengeful Persia. Like most professors, Gorgias deposited his genius in several books, of which *On Nature* was the most important and certainly the most intrepid. Nothing, he argued therein, exists beyond the senses. And even supposing it did, he went on, his head chasing his tail like a dog's, we would not be able to know it because knowledge comes through the senses. Finally, if it were knowable, we could not talk about it, since all communication depends upon the senses. Of Gorgias's numerous writings, these lines constitute the sole survivor. It is a scanty fragment of what was once a full and spacious body. Even so, in the intellectual's war on assumptions ungrounded in human experience, resorted to especially by metaphysicians and theologians, it has proved to be an indispensable weapon. Gorgias died, it is said, holding to his conviction, a grizzled patriarch of more than a hundred years. But before he took off—befitting his agnosticism—he had the forethought to lavish upon himself the bulk of his tremendous fortune.

The grand archon of them all, and to conservatives the most frightening—not counting Socrates, of course—was Protagoras of Abdera. He stands out among Sophists not only for the brilliance of his mind, but for the staggering fees he was able to subtract from his clients—as much, it has been said, as $10,000 from a single student. Even Plato, who was not given to squandering kind words on the Sophists, esteemed Protagoras as a man of sterling quality. The creator, in all likelihood, of the so-called Socratic dialogue, Protagoras is also the father of European grammar and philology; he enriched our lives with three genders of nouns, besides breeding a number of tenses and begetting moods for verbs. Like the relentless Gorgias, he laid down the dogma that our only means for attaining knowledge is seated in the senses. This view, after centuries of Christian enlightenment, was given heavy reinforcement by England's Locke and still flowers lushly in certain contemporary philosophical gardens. Of philosophical absolutes Protagoras made a blazing bonfire. Justice, goodness, beauty, even truth—all, he insisted, are relative and transitory, for being man-made, they change as man changes. "Man," he proclaimed, "is the measure of all things." Immensely audacious, his skepticism led him in time onto the ghostly plane. "As for the gods," he was heard to say at the home of the playwright Euripides, an agnostic in transcendental matters, "I know not whether they exist . . . or what they are like. Many things prevent our knowing; the subject is obscure; and brief is the span of our mortal life." This was a derisive challenge so abhorrent to devout right-thinkers in the Athenian assembly that they drummed Protagoras out of town and ordered all his books to be seized for a public burning in the marketplace. The victim departed hurriedly for Sicily, but the gods, it is reported, intercepted him before he got there and saw to it that he was drowned.

In their opinions about the Sophists the youth of Athens differed powerfully from their elders, so strongly, in fact, that their disagreement may well be the first massive generation gap in the history of Western parental-filial relationships. The new propositions, though denounced as deceptive and dangerous by old-time Athenians, were regarded by the young as full of charm and, more important, as the key to personal fame and fortune. In consequence, they thronged to the newcomers, seeking them out for instruction not only in the New Thought, but in the technique which spawned and forwarded it. Under Sophist tutoring young Athens applied itself to the mastery of a persuasive utterance, then as now the recommended way to win friends and influence people. In addition, it made a thorough study of the grammatical and rhetorical art and science. The substance of its discourses no longer centered in the doings of the spooky gods, whether for good or evil, but rather in the pragmatism of everyday living, and especially in politics and ethics, all to the end of money-making and personal success.

With so much weight put upon individual gain, the visits to the gymnasiums began to slacken, and exercises, once bent on producing a fit and stouthearted Athenian, grew less and less exacting. Instead of seeking to stiffen the national muscle, Athenians now made their hearts leap with the pleasures to be had from play and recreation and making the body beautiful. Meanwhile, the older generation called for the intervention of Zeus and the police.

Among the Sophists, no doubt, there were quacks aplenty. For a fee, which in some instances soared to dizzy heights, some were agreeable to teach almost anything, from public speaking in all its intricacy to art and music, mnemonics, military tactics, and household management. Charged with making "the worse appear the better cause," some ventured, for example, to assert that a lie well told is as good as true, that a crook is better than an honest man, that adultery is not improper, and even, indeed, that murder can be a moral virtue. But such nonsense was not the common Sophist baggage, and the reputable ones among them more than made up for the wayward ones. There is no doubt that, taking the good with the bad, they left their mark on learning, especially in its higher reaches. Under their impact the pursuit of knowledge not only broadened; it also quickened. To bridge the gulf between the dying Athenian order and its emerging successor, they struck a blow at the old school's conventional stock-in-trade, satisfactory, it is true, for innumerable generations, but now fraying around the edges. They introduced Athenians to the art of speech in all its branches, from the exotic and delirious exudation of the polished orator to the devious argument of a supplicant for public office. Hand in hand with the spoken art went grammar, rhetoric, and logic, which, as the centuries bore on, intrenched themselves in learning and which still serve us today. Where the demand showed itself, some Sophists were ready to give light in philology, geometry. and astronomy—even, in fact, in statecraft—which are all more or less specialized and, in a measure, vocational, and hence at odds with Athenian liberal tradition.

To their craft the Sophists brought a tremendous and oftentimes irreverent skepticism which rocked the vaunted Athenian values, but which enkindled the light of reason, a sanction they had scarcely known and which, though it was to flicker and even vanish in the progress of time, was never entirely to waste and die. Without the Sophists, in truth, there might have been no Socrates.

8

What we know of Socrates directly is very little, for, like Jesus, he wrote nothing, and he left no records. Most of our early information has come to us secondhand, mainly from Plato, his student and biographer, and Xenophon, also his student, and a writer of history sometimes accurate and sometimes fanciful. Socrates's father was a sculptor, in Athens a respectable endeavor, and his mother a midwife, one of the few feminine callings bespoken favorably by Athenian men. Though his interests were overwhelmingly cerebral, Socrates found time to exercise daily, and to the end of his days he enjoyed robust health. In the army he was in practice in the heavy infantry, and he contributed to a number of gory battles, in one of which he distinguished himself for valor. Married to Xanthippe, a shrewish woman, given to wrangling and shrilling, he nonetheless found wedlock to his taste; at all events when, for a spell, Athens legalized polygamy, he permitted himself the luxury of maintaining an additional spouse. He was evidently absent when Apollo, the beauty god, was dealing out virile handsomeness—so homely, indeed, was Socrates that at the battle of Delium he was reported to have frozen the Spartans in their tracks merely by glaring at them, thereby saving himself, gargoyle face and all. His wants were simple. Not gnawed by any desire to savor the world, he passed most of his days in his hometown, except now and then when he took off to call upon a distant oracle. Whenever he worked, which was as little as possible, he labored as a stonecutter. His clothes were of the meanest sort—often they were next door to shabbiness, a prevision, perhaps, of the present-day student's disrelish for his sartorial appearance. At the same time, good wine and victuals were music to his palate, and when the rich courted him with summonses to share their commons, he was rarely known to issue a refusal.

A sharp and contentious fellow, Socrates gravitated toward philosophy, and as early as his nonage he fell under the spell of the Sophists. Most of their eminent practitioners he met at some time or other—Protagoras, Hippias, Gorgias, and several more. He embraced some of their specialties—for example, their skepticism, their argumentative trickery, and their confidence in logic. But rhetoric he dismissed as useless, and he had no interest in the natural sciences, except to warn his listeners against them. From the Sophists, very likely, he obtained his logical artillery, the so-called "dialectic." It became his custom to challenge men's opinions, to disrobe them, as it were, bit by bit, until they stood naked in all their lacks and limitations and, not uncommonly, their absurdity.

"What is courage?" he would casually ask a soldier.

"Courage is holding your ground when things get rough."

"But supposing strategy required that you give way?"

"Well, in that case you wouldn't hold—that would be silly."

"Then you agree that courage is neither holding nor giving way?"

"I guess so. I don't know."

"Well, I don't know either. Maybe it might be just using your head. What do you say to that?"

"Yes—that's it; using your head, that's what it is."

"Then shall we say, at least tentatively, that courage is presence of mind—sound judgment in time of stress?"

"Yes."

Thus Socrates operated wherever he could snare a promising quarry, in the marketplace, in the stores and workshops, in the palaestras, anywhere and everywhere. Thus he hoped to set up his booth even as a postmortem shade, "to find out who is wise and who pretends to be wise, and who is not." His was the self-elected task—his demon, he called it—of clarifying ideas, first by demolishing false and shaky opinions, and then by aiding to rebuild them with the rivets of reason—the essence, in short, of his philosophical function. His opponents, as is not unusual, berated him for his irony, his mental shiftiness, and his unwillingness to state his answer to his own question. "I know nothing," he would dodge when pressed, by which he probably meant he entertained no cocksure certainty, no dogmas, and no facile generalizations. He was, he vouchsafed, not the author of knowledge, but simply an intellectual midwife giving a hand to delivering knowledge into the world.

A middle-of-the-roader, like Plato and Aristotle, between the Athenian Old Guard on the one side and the radical Sophists on the other, Socrates supported the Sophist premise that of all things man is the measure. But if this be so he added, then it behooves man to know himself, for thus alone is wisdom given to him. Only the wise man, he insisted, can do no wrong—which is to say, it is psychologically impossible for him to do evil. Socrates's confidence in wisdom as the one sure way to virtue led him inevitably to search for truth, the truth on which all wise men, regardless of their individual differences, will agree. To this end he employed his method.

In the field of morals that method was chiefly analytical, that is, it took ethical opinions apart to see what made them plausible. Yet it was not mere curiosity that gave it being, but hope. Even so, the method, of which a part devoted itself to the devastation of false and unclear notions, got Socrates more enemies than friends. His students, it is true, loved him dearly. But the vast number of plain men he made uneasy. By his questioning, for all the sincerity behind its search for wisdom and virtue, he seemed to be mocking the homely goods most of them cherished as, for instance, matrimony, democracy, and above all, religion. Like Protagoras, he had been heard to say that about the gods he knew nothing. At the same time he was cautious to make no public assault on the established religious customs—indeed, he himself was a believer in dreams as emanations from on high, and like all decorous Greeks, he resorted to oracles and gravely accepted their communiques. Even so, the tide against him steadily rose. Where once he had been regarded merely as a logic chopper and a nuisance, in the advancing years he came to be thought of as a suspicious character, and finally as a public enemy. When the state summoned him to answer its complaint, the bill of its particulars credited him with inciting youth to disrespect its elders, with unsettling morality, and with being atheistic. Found guilty by a majority of 60 votes out of 502, in 399 B.C. the old man was put to death. For all her tongue and temper, Xanthippe wept. But time made her husband a martyr and even a saint, and the faith which he enkindled in wisdom and virtue never perished. In the hands of his protégé, the admiring Plato, and in those of Aristotle, the effort to liberate the human mind was to receive still further promotion, even more formidable and much more sophisticated, though, unhappily, not altogether successful.

9

Plato was not, like Socrates, of humble ancestry. In him coursed the blood of aristocracy—even, indeed, of kings. His actual name was Aristocles, but nature had invested him with a powerful structure, and soon everybody was calling him Plato—literally, the broad-shouldered one. As handsome as Socrates was ugly, he enjoyed an easy access to women, and to men as well. His talents as a wrestler were highly touted, and so was his bravery as a soldier. He lived high and was a yachtsman of distinction and an admirer of fine horses. Conviviality delighted him, and to his closing secular moments he relished fine food and something more than well water to wash it down. He was on easy terms with mathematics, besides rhetoric and music. But his genius he fed mostly to the Muses as a composer of tragedy in the classic style and as a maker of lush and ardent verse.

Plato was scarcely out of his teens when Socrates entered his life. For the youth the old man had a powerful enchantment. So taken, in fact, was Plato by his teachings that presently he burned his rhymes and plays, and turned his back on sports and women, to absorb himself instead in the pursuit of wisdom.

In 404 B.C.—Plato was then twenty-three—the discontent which had Athens in its grip erupted into a revolution. Led by Plato's kinsmen, it ran its sanguinary course, displacing the old regime with a dictatorship of its own, only to be itself done in with the restoration of democracy, its leaders dead and in the end Socrates tried and destroyed, a casualty not only to his iconoclasm, but to politics as well.

Dashed and dismayed by the world's brutality, Plato turned his back on Athens. For a while he wandered about seeking to erase his sorrow in study and contemplation, but the fates still hounded him, and he succumbed to hostile hands who sold him into slavery. In a sense his misfortune turned out to be lucky, for when his cronies heard about it, they not only raised the required ransom, but wooed him back to Athens. They obtained for him a suburban recreation park, complete with buildings, tranquil lanes, and sheltered walks. There Plato founded the Academy, a seminary of the higher learning. Its students paid no fees, for Athenians still cherished an active aversion for such matters. Instead they preferred to make donations. But if Plato made a concession here to the public prejudice, then on the other hand he refused to bow to its attitude toward women. The frailer sex, if they had the brains and stamina, he admitted on equal terms with men at all times to all the academic rights and privileges. The Academy, at bottom, was something of a religious brotherhood, devoted, like the monasteries at a later time, to the cultivation of the good life and the furtherance of learning. Far from being selfless, however, its inmates exulted their ego with caps, walking sticks, and a flowing academic livery. To gain access to the Platonic learning, one had to be acquainted with at least the rudiments of geometry. The Academy's mathematical course was the most prized of all its offerings. Grounded on the theory of numbers, it made its way into astronomy, with side trips into music, letters, history, and jurisprudence, and heavy doses of philosophy.

As a teacher, Plato was something of a virtuoso. Sometimes he practiced his art through discourse, going after false thinking, like Socrates, with a stick, less ironically, perhaps, but more guilefully. Sometimes he exercised the student mind with problems. And sometimes he lectured. His harangues, however, were not his most brilliant performance. Usually they were technical, and not uncommonly they got lost in the labyrinth of a phrasal metaphysics. On a few of his more formidable students, however, they left a wide mark, on Demosthenes, for example, on Xenocrates, and particularly on Aristotle, the most gifted of them all.

Plato is often hymned for the merit of his literary art, which sometimes is lovely and bedazzling, but sometimes also vague and labored. Exhibited in his thirty-six *Dialogues*, it ascends to its summit in the *Symposium* with its glimpse of an alcoholized Alcibiades, an Aristophanes sagging away from the festive board and hiccuping, and the most unforgettable of all, that hammer of folly and stupidity, the incurable scoffer, Socrates. The most famous of the *Dialogues* is doubtless the *Republic* which after all these centuries is still being printed and fingered wherever ideas continue to leap and flame.

The *Republic* contains the fullest statement of the Platonic philosophy and its consequences for pedagogy. Plato launches himself by accepting his master's dictum that knowledge is virtue. But Plato has scarcely started to get up steam when he pauses, as per the immemorial custom of logicians, to pry into the meaning of the term knowledge. It is, he finally satisfied himself, that which conforms to reality. But the answer merely breeds another question, namely, what is reality? To begin, the test of reality is not, as the Sophists were contending, in the world of sense, nor is it what an individual makes it out to be, for no single man is ever, as Sophists asserted, the measure of all things. Instead, knowledge is attainable only through Ideas, which is to say, the generalized image which organizes our welter of sensations into a concept. The variety of details existing, say, among the herd of tables which we perceive, we arrange according to their similarities into a class. The result is not an actual table which catches our eye and under which we can stretch our legs; it is a table existing not in the realm of sense, but in the realm of thought. Even so, as an Idea it is unchangeable and indestructible. Tables are made to serve and please us, but time wills them to their eventual grave; yet our generalized image, or Idea, of tables will survive to the end of time. What holds for tables holds for all perceptible things, from dogs and fleas to parallelograms, democracy, and justice. The highest-valued of all Ideas is Goodness, which Plato vaguely identifies with God, thus furnishing some rather luscious food for thought for Christendom's first theologians.

To transcend the world of sense perception and lift one's self into the ethereal space of pure Ideas requires a capacity for ratiocination which is not given the common stock of men. What is needed is some super sense which will enable one to distinguish the real from the merely apparent, to separate the diamond, so to say, from the rhinestone, a property which, Plato contended, escapes all men save philosophers. This is not to say that they alone can lead an upright life, but rather that they alone can truly grasp the full nature of perfect and absolute Goodness.

These are the main premises on which Plato erects his model Republic. On it lies the heavy hand of state control, with a place for everyone and everyone in his place. Although it took its cue largely from Old Athens, schooling in the Platonic paradise flaunts a number of salient innovations. For one thing, it is completely and utterly under the hand of the state, and it is mandatory for all the young, whether male or female, up to their twentieth anniversary. For another thing, its offerings, scrutinized by a hawk-eyed censor, have been purged of all untoward reference. Not only have the myths about the ancient gods been laundered, but they have been supplemented with new ones sweetly scented with the homely virtues, especially that of obedience to the state. By the same token, music, cleansed of all seductiveness, has been given a tonal chastity, all to the end of uplifting morality, individual as well as communal. Between the education of boys and girls there is no whit of difference. Not only do girls apply themselves to the mastery of the same subjects; they also carry on with their brothers in the gymnasium, running, jumping, and hurling with them, and without a stitch of clothing to impede them—indeed, with boys they even engage in military training, for in war they too will have to fight.

At twenty the Republic's youth are sifted through a network of physical, mental, and moral tests. The vast majority to whom thinking is a closed art are destined, of course, to miss the target, and accordingly they will be mustered out of the academic world once and for all. Born for a life of toil, they will become the Republic's artisans, its tailors, and its tubmakers, its farmers and its men of business. Vouchsafed a bit of property, they are free—within limits—to pursue their enterprise. Even so, the penalty of their failure weighs upon them, for, like a corpse sealed forever in its vault, they are doomed to remain where they are.

The lucky ones who survive their first tests are in for ten more years of schooling and training to submit, at thirty, to a second series of tests. Again all but a few will succumb, to be combed out to serve the rest of their mortal span in the army of the Republic. The handful who survive their second trial go on to devote their thinking for the five ensuing years to "divine philosophy," in all its branches, from logic. politics, and law to mathematics, astronomy, and music. At thirty-five they will enter the Republic's exalted order of officialdom to serve their country as it deems fit. Do they linger on earth until they are fifty? Then at long last they reach their zenith: thenceforward, until rigor mortis claims them, they will ponder the elusive reality of pure Ideas. Philosophers, they adorn the Republic's highest caste, not only in the acuity of their mind, but in their influence and power. For in Plato's Republic philosophers alone shall be kings, and kings philosophers. Yet for all their elevation, they are fenced in by taboos on every side. They possess neither money nor property. Not even their wives are strictly their own, for they must share them "with the best as often as possible." When they mate is determined by public need, and should they, at nature's urging, propagate nonetheless, then a child thus begotten is doomed to be destroyed. Their legitimate children they know only while they are at nurse; thereafter all infants are transmitted to the communal barracks to begin their progress to their predestinate place in the service of the Republic.

The Republic, of course, never saw the light of day. Even its creator was under some doubt about its perfection, and on various occasions he undertook to amend and overhaul it. Commissioned at sixty to give enlightenment to Dionysius the Younger of Syracuse, Plato started off his royal patron with the study of geometry. Alas, after a flash of transient gusto, the sovereign lost his taste for circles, squares, and triangles, and Plato's dream of setting up a philosopher-king in actual practice ran aground.

Although the Republic's pedagogy never got beyond the line of theory, this is not saying that in the pursuit of knowledge Plato played a minor part. His Academy, though not the first promoter of the higher learning to appear upon these scenes, was destined for an enduring and meritorious place in human annals. For all the informality of its methods, its lack of system and compulsion, and the easygoing ways of its students, it served powerfully to shake and stimulate the reason, and to make thought a primary concern of man. Aristocrat in blood, Plato held, as did Hamilton and Jefferson after him, for a political leadership of brains. Metaphysician, he sought to transcend the everyday world of sense for the extraterrestrial domain of Ideas, pristine, absolute, and everlasting, thereby fathering the philosophy of Idealism which in various incarnations has persisted to the very present. Feminist, Plato went all out for equal rights for women, in addition to equal duties and responsibilities. Eugenist, he called for a sexually regulated state whose citizens should produce their offspring by the ponderable laws of nature, and ever mindful of the needs of the state. Though at heart he was an artist, and his prose is full of song, Plato was also a puritan, and hence suspicious of the snares of beauty. The scissors of his censor would surely have cut Beethoven to shreds, and Brahms and Schubert too, and all the other great immortals—in truth, not even Plato's own youthful poesy would have escaped. Though, like Socrates, his teacher, and Aristotle, his pupil, Plato failed to arrest the schisms and deceits which harried Athens, he continued just the same to do the things he liked, to write, to teach, to reason, and to relish life until, while at a wedding feast, a white-haired octogenarian, he was summoned by death.

10

Unlike Socrates and Plato, Aristotle was a non-Athenian. Born to the north in Thrace, he was the son of a court physician who, it is reported, introduced him to the rudiments of anatomy before packing him off for study in the Platonic grove. Aristotle was endowed with a quick and curious mind, and he soon marked himself as the Academy's most brilliant scholar. Indeed, in many ways he was destined to surpass his teacher. His impact on the thought of the Middle Ages was colossal, and for a time his teachings, purified of their more unseemly paganism, were all the rage of Christian scholarship. To schoolmen of that remote age he was The Philosopher, but his intellectual interest swept over the whole dominion of knowledge. His researches were of a staggering heft, and so were his writings, though only a part of them remains. Biologist, physicist, economist, psychologist, moralist, logician, metaphysician, and a critic of the arts, he was antiquity's "master of those who know."

Early in life Aristotle was summoned to Philip's Macedonian palace to give instruction to Alexander, then a youth full of fire and ambition and concentrating on sowing his princely oats, yet destined to be set down in the pages of history as "the Great." Back in Athens after a few years, Aristotle founded the Lyceum. It was sequestered, like the Academy, in the stillness of the woodland, amidst gardens and rambling walks to give it an investiture of peace and charm. The school's first professor and chief executive was an extremely busy man. During the morning hours he labored with his students, lecturing at times, and, more to his liking, parleying with them intellectually as he made his daily round about the campus. Later in the day it was his practice to bestride the lecture platform to distill his learning for the general public.

Although the Lyceum had started life as a promoter of rhetoric and philosophy, it presently betook itself in the direction of science. Toward this end Aristotle stocked his seminary not only with a vast library, but with a museum of natural history and even a zoo. But if he peopled the Lyceum with beasts and birds, he granted no such concession to women. They, he insisted, were inferior and on them silence was more becoming than freedom. Like the Sophists Aristotle viewed the senses as the source of our knowledge, though he went to great lengths to chide these schoolmen for fabricating their theories of the universe without taking a close look at its natural manifestations. Like Plato, he gave his countenance to the power of reason, but unlike his teacher, he dismissed mere intellectual ponderings as insufficient to the advancement of our knowledge. What was needed in addition was a diligent and unsparing scrutiny of all observable phenomena. For such purpose Aristotle put upon his students to make forays into every realm of knowledge from, say, the cultures of primitive folk to the nature and distribution of the flora and fauna. Such data he had his learners gather and arrange in orderly concert to make them useful and agreeable to lovers of knowledge. As sometimes happens in the academic world, The Philosopher did not shrink from borrowing from such findings to implant them, sometimes to his subsequent blushful discovery of mistakes, in his own innumerable acres of written exposition.

It should not be necessary to have to add that under the leader's rein the Lyceum thrived. Its fame radiated everywhere, and soon intellectuals were placing it on a plane with Plato's older Academy. Between the two there presently arose a sort of Yale and Harvard rivalry, and their respective student bodies treated one another with grandiloquent disdain. The Academy men, it is true, were mostly of rank and blood, while the Lyceum's clientele sprang mainly from the middle class, a social cleavage which doubtless added to the student difference of opinion. Whatever the cause, the rivalry did not relent until the two schools clearly marked off separate spheres of interest, the Academy declaring itself for mathematics, metaphysics, and politics, and the Lyceum for natural science.

Aristotle was a fertile writer though, lacking Plato's light and graceful splendor, he wrote with a drab and leaden hand. At least twenty-seven dialogues issued from his pen, but many of them have vanished into the darkness of oblivion—a casualty very likely, to the conquering Roman sword. What remains is for the most part technical and abstruse, and at times full of tedium. But the man's sweep remains truly amazing. From logic it bore into science, thence into metaphysics, esthetics, ethics, and politics.

It is in the latter two that Aristotle turns his thoughts to pedagogy. His *Nichomachean Ethics* is the first systematic and comprehensive theory of morals of which we have any record, and his *Politics,* though it has wandered down to us only in fragmentary substance, is the first formal treatise on comparative government. In consonance with Plato, Aristotle beheld education as a branch of politics. It is, he contended, a state function, and its nature, in essence, is a reflection of the society which it serves to protect and preserve—a view which, though under heavy assault by various posses of contemporaneous philosophers, is still, after more than two thousand years, full of plain sense.

Yet, though Aristotle holds that education should carry on to conserve the established order, this is not saying that he intends it to be cold to the qualities which lie fallow in every human being. Such a course is doomed to be uncreative and inadequate to its ultimate end, which is the making of an upright person. But for Aristotle goodness is not, as Socrates had it, almost entirely wisdom. This may be the most lustrous of all human values, but beside it range many others, from low to high, some of them modest and even a little homely. Nor, in any remote degree, is virtue to be attained merely through the filter of philosophic meditation, for at bottom virtue rests not on knowledge, but on deeds. Nor, finally, are there any rigid absolute goods—indeed, exaggerated and pushed too far, a virtue can become a curse. What every man needs is moderation, temperance, common sense—qualities, in short, which enable him to steer the course of his daily life in the middle lane between the extremes that lurk on either side. The archwrongdoer, hence, is the one who fails to live up to his natural dowers, or the man who, by the same yardstick, functions excessively or not sufficiently.

Aristotle, like Plato, declared for a human nature which is in part rational, but in even larger part irrational. To the fruition and direction of these elementals all education is harnessed. In a sense the process is put to work even before a man makes his advent in life, for—like Plato again—Aristotle, seeking to insure the birth of a healthy infant, called for a controlled and sanitary marriage, with instruction and a dietary regime for the expectant mother. Should her babe, nonetheless, be malformed or sickly, then, as per the familiar custom, let it be done away with.

To the female as might be expected, Aristotle granted little learning. Deficient in rational capacity, she is doomed to drink the bitter cup of inferiority. Her natural setting, said Aristotle, was the fireside, the bedroom, and the nursery, and to help her function properly therein, she was to make acquaintance with the usual ins and outs of the household enterprise. Like the Spartan girl, she was to keep herself well and physically proficient so that at eighteen she would be ready to gratify a spouse, who was, of course, the complete and absolute lord of the whole connubial domain. To obey him, to please him, and to bear him a squadron of healthy successors such was the essence of her function. It was a view which men admired extravagantly, and which later was translated into Christendom. Its early moral experts not only gave it support; they even extended it to mean that not only is the female inferior, but she is also the root of all evil. Augustine, indeed, expressed amazement that women should have been created at all. As a matter of fact, as late as 1595, not quite twelve centuries after the saint's translation from this earth, professors at the University of Wittenberg were heating the air in formal academic debate over whether or not women could be considered human beings. Unluckily, the problem proved too baffling for even their great minds to solve.

Under the "master of those who know," the males, of course, fared vastly better. In fact, for even the nethermost men—forgetting the ones in slavery— Aristotle set aside no less than twenty-one years of training and schooling. The process got under way, as it had in Old Athens, in the home which, despite the sour notes of Plato, Aristotle continued to prize. There, under the parental hand, the boy was exercised and conditioned for a manhood of health and virtue. The problem, in the long run, was to enable him to function according to his natural capacity, for only then could he be expected to snare life's elusive happiness. Since by nature a boy was still in the dark cave of irrationality, he was to be guarded at all times against work and study until he was safely over the border of seven. Then his instruction was bespoken by the state which undertook to groom him in health and strength and morality.

His burden at school was to be neither too heavy nor too light but, true to the Aristotelian formula, somewhere in between. He was not to be a mere listener, but a doer as well. Hence the teachings of his pedagogues were to be fortified at all times by practice in daily living, for what counted in the making of an upright, contented man was not the stockpile of his accumulated theories, but the armament of his good habits. Virtue, Aristotle let it be known, is not merely an act: it is a habit. At fourteen, and for the four years following, the pupil adventured into reading and writing besides music and drawing. What he derived therefrom, however, reserved itself always for a leisurely and liberal end, the enhancement, that is, of life's joys and gratifications, and contra, never for mere vocation and moneymaking, for such endeavors were the hallmark of the mean man and not the free one. Gymnastics of the formal sort remained unbidden until the youth turned eighteen when they burst upon the scene fortissimo to continue for the next three years, not so much to prepare for eventual military practice, but rather for full and vigorous health, for self-control, and for athletic skill and pleasure.

Thus Aristotle's program for man's nonrational side. His prescription for the intellectual side, unfortunately, has escaped the world. Either he never tackled it or, if he did, it has long since slid into the murky shades. Still, from his own practice in the Lyceum one may infer that he would have put his main pressure on the pursuit of the natural sciences and on politics, with gentle but persistent undertones in clear thinking.

Rather interestingly, student participation in determining the school's educational policies, one of the multitudinous issues inflaming higher learning

throughout the contemporary world, was an established practice in the Aristotelian Lyceum. Not only did the older students elect their representatives to
state their case in deliberations of the school's policies, they also had a say in
compounding the school's curriculum. True to their headmaster's philosophic
outlook, moreover, at all times they encouraged practical action and experience.
But if ever they resorted to the strategy of confrontation, or even gave such a
tactic a thought, the record thereof is bare.

The influence of Aristotle on his own time, like that of Plato, was almost nil.
The old city-state was too far gone to fetch it back, and with its passing the
ancient ideal of the citizen-man was embalmed in the pages of history. For
Athenians it was now dog eat dog and every man for himself, a situation which
was to be brought to terms only by the imposition of a powerful external
authority.

In time, though, the winds of destiny shifted, and after the fifth century
Aristotle began to be noticed again. But the knowledge of him was anemic, and
it was not till many hundred years later that a fuller glimpse of this extraordinary Greek was afforded the studies of the Arabs who had long since been
his admirers. To Christian savants his secular knowledge appeared staggering.
Presently, when it became apparent that at many points his secular knowledge
collided with their own sacred teachings, resolving the differences, as will be
noted in pages hereinafter, became the object of assiduous examination and
study by some of the most powerful minds theology has ever known. As a result
The Philosopher took his place side by side with the saintly Fathers, the familiar
par excellence of universal knowledge and its undisputed arbiter. By 1250 his
teachings had risen to such high renown that they were interwoven with the
official philosophy of Holy Church. Professed in all universities of Europe, they
gave light and guidance to academicians for centuries yet unborn. But his
tremendous fame and circumstance were to cost him dearly, for with the onrush
of the Renaissance and its aftermath he was not only impeached and unseated
by a newer scholarship, but he was even damned for having been in error all his
life.

Even so, the range of the man's intellectuality was stupendous. Medieval
schoolmen gaped at it, but they prized especially his deductive logic, forgetting
all the while his partisanship of induction. Indeed, in historical afterlight it seems
not a little strange that some of his teachings should have reaped such a high
tolerance. His *Ethics*, for example, he launched by casting out all a priori
dogmatizing, and insisting on an inductive approach to the study of ethical
behavior. In his study of the world of nature, he dismissed the power of
inscrutable, supernatural agents, and relied instead on explanations based on
natural causes and effects. To this end he directed his powers of observation, and
in this spirit he turned his senses on the clouds, the fog and the dew, thunder
and lightning, even the rainbow and the meteor. Man he beheld as a rational
animal—rational, to be sure, but an animal. The ape he hailed as a link between
Homo sapiens and the rest of the mammalian order; and the earth, his habitat,
he was certain, was a sphere. Aristotle was not immune, of course, to error.

Some of his bobbling was tremendous, and sometimes even comic. For example, he held for the spontaneous generation of the eel. The human female, he declared, entertained fewer ribs than the male. And, flirting with the theological doctrine of design, he convinced himself that man was adorned with a bottom, round and cushioned because, having but two legs, he needed such physiological equipment in order to sit himself comfortably down.

It is easy to laugh at such puerilities—in truth, there was a time in this republic when every high school senior possessed better information. But Aristotle, after all, was a trailblazer, and hence he suffered from the usual infirmities and handicaps. He had to sweat out his own methodology, and he worked without the boon of instruments, without a glass or thermometer, without even a shred of litmus paper. For all his stumbling, he furnished science and philosophy a terminology they still find useful today. Sometimes he even raised the curtain on doctrines which did not get firmly on their legs until the late nineteenth century. He reached, for example, the front yard of evolution, and like current sages and scientists, he conceived of the universe as perpetually dynamic.

In pedagogic theory his impact was of a minor force. His views on womankind, unhappily, bedazzled and beguiled his male successors, and it was not until the nineteenth century, under the pounding of a vastly changed industrial and scientific order, that women's gradual emancipation began. Aristotle's teaching that there is a connection between the school and the society which it adorns and serves has become an everyday axiom. And so, finally, has his doctrine that to flourish and benefit the general populace, education must be not a private but a public enterprise.

Aristotle's declining years, like those of Socrates, ended on a melancholy note. His Lyceum, for all its great renown, was badgered and berated by rival schools. Patriots, decrying his alien origin, denounced him as a traitor and a spy. Presently even his books were under onslaught. They were, the town's moral element let it be heard, full of subversion, unfriendly to decency, and hostile to religion. While his foes thus beset him, Aristotle, unwilling, as he remarked, to give Athens a second chance to sin against philosophy, migrated to other parts. It was just as well, for the Athenians levied the death sentence against him. But the fates did not support them, and for a few months at least The Philosopher was safe. Then, in his sixty-third year, he died, the victim, it is said, of a stomach ailment

11

Even before Aristotle's passing, Athens, the city-state of older days, once bubbling with pride and freedom and an infinite self-confidence, had itself succumbed, and so, in fact, had nearly all Greece. The beginning of the end darkened the younger days of Plato when, for almost thirty years, Athens and Sparta embraced in a suicidal war. So spent were these archrivals from their vast and drawn-out effort that when the Macedonians presently rolled down upon them from the north, first under Philip, then under his son, the great Alexander, they could not stay them.

Their collapse, however, was largely political. For out of the ashes of their defeat, Hellenic learning swept far beyond its first horizon. The old ephebic training, it is true, having lost its reason for being, decayed and died. Military training yielded to philosophy—before long, in fact, hearkening to the professors of philosophy became an article of compulsion, and in time their schools even acquired a measure of public support. Meanwhile, the rhetoricians were not idle. They had attracted notice, it will be recalled, with the coming of the Sophists, and as they grew in force and following, one of them, Isocrates, founded the first rhetorical school in Athens. Highly regarded, it was well attended—soon, in fact, its intellectual traffic matched that of the Lyceum and the Academy. For a spell a brisk rivalry prospered among these groves, with altitudinous and even astounding claims for their respective enlightenment. But as the years passed, the booming and boosting gradually simmered down, and by the second century before Christ's coming their academic industry coalesced into what has since become known as the University of Athens, with a course of study running from six to seven years, a staff of paid professors, and students with all the vices and virtues of their latterday successors. The citadel of the ancient learning in Athens continued to prosper well into Christian times until, specifically, the year 529 when Justinian, a Roman emperor and a partisan of Christ, wrenched and uprooted it for its heathenry.

Meanwhile, under Alexander, the Hellenic culture had followed in the track of his conquering armies toward the East. Greeks swarmed everywhere, in Egypt and Persia, as far away as India, and up the shoreland of the Black Sea and the Caspian Sea—merchants and builders, philosophers, artists, and scientists, all looking for the main chance, and all eager to settle down. Wherever they established themselves, Greek cities arose, and with them a civilization partly Hellenic and partly Oriental. The Greek tongue, once the instrument of a mere handful, burst its hoary bounds to become the universal utterance of the learned. With the rise of more and more cities, new centers of learning presently came upon the scene. There were Tarsus and Pergamum in Asia Minor, Antioch in Syria, Rhodes at the Aegean's southern end, and Alexandria on the delta of the Nile.

The city of Alexandria issued from the brain and fancy of Alexander the Great, but the actual job of putting it into being he left to Dinocrates, his architect. Planned and laid out from its start, it was revised and improved over the years to become the most up-to-date municipality to grace the Hellenic world. Its main street, a colonnaded concourse a hundred feet wide, ran through the town from end to end, some fifteen miles, while a similar one three miles long bisected it at right angles. All the important thoroughfares were paved and lighted, and for that far-off time they enjoyed a capital degree of sanitation. The place thronged with public edifices, gymnasiums, and temples to a galaxy of gods and goddesses. Its museum was world-renowned, and so was its library. The town abounded in parks and gardens. There was an excellent beach, a stadium, a racetrack, and just beyond the city limits lay the City of the Dead, the last earthly tenement for departed Alexandrians. Glossed sometimes as the City of Aphrodite, the love goddess, Alexandria boasted of its luxurious mansions of which some of the finest were the property of ladies who took their virtue as easily as they did their fees. The town effervesced with commercial enterprise. More than a thousand shops and markets lined its streets, and through them streamed not only Greeks and Macedonians, but Egyptians, Persians, Syrians, and Arabs, besides Jews and Negroes.

The University of Alexandria was the work of the Ptolemies, the first, second, and third of the clan. They lavished money and affection upon it to make it in the course of time the peer and, maybe, even the superior of the University of Athens. Started as a museum and a library about 300 B.C., it gradually took on a greater substance. Its store of manuscripts became the largest then known to civilization, with about 700,000 stored cheek to jowl in its cases. In addition the university possessed a first-rate botanical garden, an observatory, lecture chambers, and quarters for scholars as well as books. Dedicated to the Muses, it was inspirited with a religious undertone. Its savants were becomingly frocked and whiskered, and technically their head man executed something of a priestly role. The professors, who were nearly always Greeks, were hired by the throne, and their wages came out of a royal fund. Their duty, however, was not the common one of giving illumination to the young, but rather to cull, classify, and if possible, advance knowledge.

To this purpose men of learning flocked to the Alexandrian cloisters from near and far, philosophers, grammarians, mathematicians, scientists, writers, and sometimes even a hopeful schoolmaster. Some of these men attained an everlasting fame. At Alexandria, Euclid unraveled his geometric science, while Galen explored in medicine and Archimedes in physics. Hipparchus scanned the heavens, studying the heavenly bodies, laboriously counting them, and organizing them into constellations. Herophilus was a wonder worker in anatomy and surgery, while Aristarchus, a grave and industrious man, now almost forgotten, unearthed the eight grammatical parts of speech which still work their havoc on schoolboys the world around. At Alexandria archeology was born, and so was the first lexicon. In the groves of Alexandria the Hebrew Scriptures were rendered into Greek for the benefit of the Hellenized Jews, who had long since forgotten the language of their ancient fathers. From Alexandria's research halls issued the famous Ptolemaic system of the universe, false and full of error to be sure, but nevertheless powerful—so powerful, in truth, that it was not successfully challenged until the sixteenth century when Copernicus tore it from its hallowed groundwork.

Though it made its advent in a pagan world, Alexandria was destined to serve the cause of learning until the fourth century when its library and museum fell prey to an incendiary's torch. A momentous event in the annals of arson, it was thought for long years to have been the handiwork of the Muslim Caliph Omar. But time has found this charge to be slanderous, and today's experts incline to lay the blame on the excesses of certain Christian fanatics.

While Greeks were winging their way into their golden, discordant glory, on the Adriatic's western edge another folk, also of Aryan stock, had begun to fashion a new civilization. Pitched on seven hills hard by the Tiber's silty mouth, Rome reaches back in history to the ninth century B.C., when wandering bands of herdsmen and tribesmen settled in that region. More precisely Rome herself celebrated her beginnings as of the year 753 B.C. Twelve centuries of history were to be her destiny. The tiny settlement on the hills was to expand into a massive, imperial colossus, only to disintegrate and in the end to plunge into collapse and chaos. Six centuries before Christ's advent Rome was an up-and-coming town under a king. Another hundred years or thereabouts, and the monarchy was overthrown, and the affairs of state put under the sovereignty of a republic. Two and a half centuries more, and practically the entire Italian peninsula was under its sway, and 150 years after that the city had made herself mistress of the Mediterranean. Thus she was steadily to increase until, during the reign of Trajan, the Emperor from 98 to 117, Rome's dominions stretched from the bogs of Britain to the deserts of the Sudan, and from Portugal's Atlantic shoreline to the towering majesty of the faraway Caucasus. Her bulk, then in its heyday, was about two-thirds that of the continental United States while her populace numbered less than half of ours.

Unlike the Greeks, the Romans kept their feet on solid ground. A practical, pragmatic people, they absorbed themselves not in airy speculation, but in the successful management of their everyday affairs. Rome's architects built no Parthenons; her dramatists wrote no masterpieces; and her thinkers pale and shrink before the Grecian great. On the other hand, the Romans expressed their gifts in the art of practical governance. Under their standard they welded into a single nation not only their Italian neighbors, but an immense and disparate populace, flung over the earth in all directions. Save only in the Mediterranean east, where Greek refused to be uprooted, the Roman language became the instrument of common interparlance; her coins circulated far and near; her civil service was everywhere the same; and so was her law. The Romans, indeed, were the first to elevate law to the honor and dignity of a science, and they were the first to enshrine its propositions in the permanence of the written word.

The Roman social order arranged itself, as usual, into the high and the low, the one being known as patrician, the other as plebeian. But time and experience melted most of their important differences, and as the Republic advanced into its early maturity, they were often indistinguishable. The law's mantle spread its stern and implacable mandates upon both of them alike. When plebeians were soldiers, they could aspire to the officer's regalia, and when they practiced as civilians, they could attain the highest office in the land. By the midfifth century B.C. marriage between the two estates became legally permissible, and thenceforward the frontier which separated them, though not always hospitable, was at least open to a crossing.

With the conquest of the Mediterranean this agreeable condition altered—in time, indeed, it was to vanish altogether. As the Romans circulated between peace and conquest, an enormous prosperity engulfed the land. Things moved briskly in the world of trade and commerce, and especially among its bankers and brokers, its realtors, builders, and contractors, its importers and exporters, its suppliers of the army, and not the least, of course, its tax gatherers. The upshot was the rise of a small class of super rich, living amidst their pomps and vanities, with country estates and town houses in Rome ornamented in marble, with gold-encrusted ceilings, voluptuous furnishings, gardens, swimming pools, carriages, costly horses, and not uncommonly, even more costly mistresses. There is plain evidence here of what the economic brethren call an uneven distribution of wealth, and with it there ensued a serious social chasm with all the familiar distempers and discontents—one which was to fret and harass the Romans to the end, and which, for all their practicality, was to become a salient factor in their ultimate undoing.

By the time Caesar was upon the scene, Rome had become a tremendous city. Its original handful of ruralized inhabitants had swollen into a million head—a figure New York was not able to muster until a little more than a century ago. As cosmopolitan as any modern municipality, the town swarmed not merely with Latins, but with Greeks and Syrians, besides Celts and Germans and miscellaneous Asiatics. About a quarter of the populace was slave, but by the standards of the time, their lot was not unduly onerous. They slaved to be sure, and they were subject to the lash, and they might even be made to meet death in the arena, but they were also allowed to own property and to store up money, and when they had enough of it, they could bargain for their freedom.

To house and clothe so vast a people and to keep them at all times properly diverted and content represented a major enterprise. The rich graced their usual grandiose villas. For the middle classes there were apartment houses of brick and stone, eight to ten stories high. And for the poor there were the slums, the rookeries of dirt and disease, and an early grave. There was not enough grain in Italy to feed so many mouths; in consequence, some of it had to be hauled in from overseas. But Roman husbandry, using the most up-to-date methods, fared very well. The production of the olive was big business and the source of no little wealth, and so was that of the vine which sometimes reaped investors as much as eighteen cents on every dollar. Water, always a problem in a city of so many folk, was tapped from springs and aqueducts into an army of gushing fountains. The Romans were industrious bathers—probably the most washed people known to ancient history, saving, possibly, the Egyptians. For the lower orders there were numerous municipal baths, while the very rich, of course, luxuriated in pools of their own. There were public markets in plenty with the government's eye and challenge fixed upon them at all times for cheats and chiselers. The Roman highway, as everyone knows, was a masterpiece of construction, and where traffic thickened into undue bulk, its snarls were put to rout under effective regulation. At the same time numerous streets bordered on the primitive. The boon of nocturnal lamplight was unknown; nor was there any public transportation—nor even a patrolman to guard the common security.

2

Thus the broad outline. Its essence shows itself, as usual, in education. Did the Romans launch themselves, for example, in modest manner, a plain and practical people, awed by law and order, honoring their gods, their family, and their fatherland? Then so did their early education. Did the Romans break forth from their primitive seclusion to rub shoulders with alien folk, and notably the Greeks? Then so, again, did their education. And, finally, did the Romans burst their republican dam to turn into a vast and overflowing empire, held within bound by common currents, but full of diversity just the same, and in the end even treacheries and schisms? Then, as Rome climbed and stumbled and fell, so did her education.

By youth's common law, life for a Roman boy should have been blessed abundantly. At all events for four hundred years at least, there was not a single school to give him grief, and to the Empire's last gasp its education remained in the main a private enterprise. This is not saying, however, that parents neglected their duties to their children, and that the young floated into manhood in the bliss of ignorance. On the contrary, growing up in early Rome was a stern and regulated matter, and if no school existed, then there were other ways of carrying on its business.

The school's foremost substitute was the home, with reinforcement, as the boy grew to youth, from the ever-active market square, the forum, and the army barracks. Unlike the Greeks, the early Romans put a sturdy pride and confidence in the potency of the home. Its dean and commander was the father whose powers were next to absolute. By virtue of his office he could flog and incarcerate his wife and progeny—indeed, if he willed, he could even slay them. Ambassador to the gods, he was their domestic priest. He alone summoned them, sweetening them with sacrifices, bargaining with them for their interest and assistance, and agreeing to do for them if they did for him. Yet despite his awful powers, the head of the house was usually a man of common rectitude. In old Rome the matrimonial cord was generally secure—in truth, interwoven with religious sanction, it was regarded as something of a sacred contract. As a result, both within her home and beyond it walls, the Roman matron enjoyed a pleasant respect, far greater, by a long shot, than her less lucky sisters across the Adriatic.

The yardstick of Roman life was not theory but practice, not learning but utility. Thus bottomed, the common rearing of the young directed itself toward practical ends, the father enlisting his effort in preparing his son for everyday living, and the mother in making her daughter an efficient mistress of the home, soothing and obedient to her future husband, and the bearer of a lusty and useful brood. Preparing the young to serve their land and family, to do their job, and to live in harmony with the inscrutable gods—such, in sum, was the mission of education. No spacious ideas fed its fire. Virtue, courage, earnestness, piety, concern for duty, and love of country—such was its rugged loftiness. These, said Pliny, were riveted into the young at all times and everywhere, "not only through the ears, but through the eyes," and one might add, through deeds as well.

Some fathers taught their sons an ordinary familiarity with simple letters, not, however, to transmute them into book eaters on some tomorrow, but to help them in their daily practice as efficient Romans. There was no great hankering to master the mystery of Roman numerals, for like the Greek ones, they were a curse. But if their difficult and incommoding operation floored the boy, then he became adept in reckoning with his fingers—in fact, in digital arithmetic the Romans had no peer. The Latin youngster made no formal bow to the study of the past, but from his father's lips he was moved to a living intimacy with his history, and particularly with the deeds, both real and imaginary, of his country's salient heroes. Very early in life he was introduced to the law, both civil and sacred. After 450 B.C., when the Romans inscribed their jurisprudence in their Twelve Tables, the boy was set to grappling with torts, real and personal property, summonses and judicial proceedings, and fittingly enough, the rights of a father. The articles of the Twelve Tables became the substance of his common reading and writing, and before he was done with them, he had settled most of them for all time in the folds and creases of his memory. Thus, contended Cicero, he was to "comprehend how our ancestors excelled all other nations in wisdom."

Unlike the musical Greeks, the early Romans found no joy in the art of tone, and save when it served to heat their patriotism and to give their regards to their divinities, they gave it but little notice. What went for music went also for the dance—even for gymnastics, particularly of the Grecian kind. "What an absurd system of training the young! . . . " exclaimed Cicero. "What a frivolous preparation for the labors of war!"

As the boy took on years, he went with his father, if he was a farmer, to the fields where, by hard and diligent practice, he introduced himself to the ancient rustic art. Did he happen, on the other hand, to dwell in town? Then he accompanied his father on his public tours, to the market and the shops, and to the courts and forum, wherever Romans transacted the affairs of their daily living. Thus under parental counsel and direction, and by keeping his eyes and ears cocked constantly, he was to learn not only what was afoot, but presently to be ready himself to carry on. When the time came to decide on a means of livelihood, the preparation, again, was direct and practical. If the youth happened to be of rank and blood, then in all likelihood he was destined for some profession. But if he was from lower down, then his destination was probably trade or business, or some practical art or craft. In either case, he attached himself in service to some practitioner, usually a kinsman or some family friend, under whose tutelage and guidance he was put to mastering the tricks and secrets of his specialty, not from books, but from actual practice.

3

War, as the Romans practiced it, was a form of business. It not only increased their land and resources; it also added enormously to the individual pocket. From the soldier to the general, men braved the hazards of combat with an eye ever ready for loot and booty. A single triumphant campaign, to illustrate, yielded Caesar enough to unsaddle himself from a debt of nearly three million dollars, pay his troops a princely bonus, and still reserve a prodigious bit of change for himself. The impact of victory not only made Rome vaster and wealthier; it also changed her ways. Once of an almost stoic simplicity, her people presently enjoyed lush and pleasant circumstances. Even the lowly thrived—not uncommonly, in fact, they commanded the help and service of a slave. The citizens, wailed the hidebound Cato, "no longer listen to good counsel, for the belly has no ears." Such transformations, as nearly always, showed themselves in education.

When, in the second century B.C., Rome made herself sovereign of the Mediterranean, it was not long before she was under the stimulus of the Hellenic spell. Even before, there had been a small but steady infiltration of Greeks into Italy. As early as the sixth century B.C., for example, Greek merchants were drumming up trade in Sicily, and from the island to the peninsula was but a hop. On the heels of commerce followed the Greek language and culture, even, in truth, the Greek pantheon of gods and goddesses. By the third century some Roman senators knew Greek well enough to make speeches in it, while even common folks were able to relish an occasional Greek pun. Afterward, when Greece went down before the Roman sword, thousands of her people were brought to Italy in servitude. As was slaves' wont of old, they toiled at all things, from low to high, and not a few of them, much more learned than their owners, were put upon to give instruction to the young. One such fellow was Livius Andronicus, whose translation of Homer into Latin marked the advent of the literary art in Rome. The work fell on fertile ground and sprouted into a large and steady circulation—in fact, for at least a couple of centuries it was as indispensable to the Roman schoolboy as his waxen tablet, his stylus, and his lunch. So well was the work esteemed that its author presently was accorded his freedom. Though Andronicus was doubtless a busy man, he was able, even so, to compose a number of Latin dramas, both comic and tragic, a feat which so gratified the civic fathers that they proffered him and his fellow literati the right to incorporate.

From the Greeks the Romans got their first schools. The earliest appeared close to the end of the third century B.C., and the first schoolmaster of whom we have any word was Spurius Carvilius, a retired slave. His venture into pedagogy was entirely private, though in deference to Roman taste, he charged no fees, relying instead on the liberality of his patrons. Apart from its Hellenistic tinge, the Roman's early schooling remained more or less what it had been when it was conducted under the paternal roof. Known to Latins as a *ludus* which to Romans connoted "play" or "exercise," the elementary school received its beginners, girls as well as boys, when they were seven, and it proceeded much in the manner of the Athenians to dose them formidably in the fundamentals. Such frilly things as music and dancing, however, were cautiously held at bay, for, as in the old days, the stress in Roman learning continued to be predominantly practical.

The schoolday ran from dawn to dusk, but since there were frequent public festivals to gods and country, children were gladdened by numerous furloughs from the academic grind. To keep them reasonably decorous and free from harm, the Roman young, like their Grecian models, were made to trek from home to school in the custody of a *paedagogus*. Fair days usually saw the academic ritual carried on outdoors, or at all events on a porch which nearly always adorned the school. In those innocent days, of course, little was known of the teaching art—indeed, to the general run of masters the idea of gracing their performance with charm and interest would have been unthinkable; instead they resorted to threat and bluster, and to a frequent and ferocious fanning of their charges. "A man who has not been flogged," ran the Latin saying, "is a man not trained."

Except for the sons of the rich, the Romans put away their books when they were eleven or twelve years old. For the handful whose parents ordained that they go on, there was a grammar school. In the beginning its instruction centered in Greek, but as time ran on, a Latin facsimile appeared. True to its name, the grammar school, whether of Greek or Roman strain, trafficked heavily in grammar, its declensions, and its conjugations of normal and abnormal verbs, besides syntax and composition. Literature followed grammar. The standard work, as has been hinted, was Homer, but in time he was joined by Aesop, and as the Romans produced some meritorious writers of their own, by Horace, Virgil, and several others. The student busied himself with lovely letters not merely to gain culture and enlightenment from literary style, but also to benefit from reference to history, geography, mythology, religion, and the various Roman virtues. For this purpose he was put to analyzing lengthy passages, both in writing and in speech, until he could rattle them off from memory, correctly and with dispatch. Sometimes there were rehearsings in arithmetic, and sometimes in geometry. But these were in a minor key, and always their end was as practical as, say, the plotting of a piece of land, or laying down the groundwork of a house. In general the sciences were ignored, and the Romans did little to advance them.

The Roman equivalent of the American college was the rhetorical school. The offspring of its Grecian namesake, it stretches back to the days of the Sophists. Like its Hellenic ancestor, it endeavored to make its clients adept in the art of public address, and thereby to ease their way to higher preferment in law, politics, and the public service. Sumptuous rewards awaited the practiced speaker, and in consequence Rome teemed with professional rhetoricians. For a fee some of them appeared in court to plead their client's case; some specialized in writing speeches for men of affairs, too busy or too stupid to do it themselves; and a good many frequented the lecture trail, roving from town to town, where they gave light and diversion to their hearers with literary, philosophical, and political harangues. Not a few offered private counsel in the secrets of their craft, and some even ran flourishing schools. Since their custom came almost wholly from the rich, their fees, as might be expected, were often high—more altitudinous even than the ones which harry American collegians today.

Students commonly began their apprenticeship in rhetoric when they were sixteen, and most of them hauled up some four years later. Women were admitted to the Roman higher learning on equal terms with men. They sought its boon usually after marriage, and they dallied with its revelation not for professional purposes, as did most of the males, but chiefly to while away their superfluous idle hours.

The most important tool in the rhetorician's kit was, of course, the spoken word. To promote ease and power in his oral utterance, the rising rhetorician was relentlessly drilled until he was at home in all its forms. As day followed day, he exercised himself in oratory, declamation, and debate. He practiced posturing and pronouncing. To put melody into his voice he studied music. He devoted himself to the techniques of tricking and cozening his audience to make it sob or smile as he desired. To make preparation for law, he dissected hypothetical cases, and to render himself truly versatile, he furnished his advocacy to both plaintiff and defendant. To sniff out lurking fallacies, he applied himself to logic, and to applaud and defend the right, he tackled ethics. Finally, to equip himself with a wide knowledge so that he might discourse with ease on almost any subject, he reviewed literature and grammar, arithmetic and geometry, philosophy, and what then passed for astronomy. For all this vast diligence he piled up no credits, and he obtained no letters, either academic or athletic. But if he was dowered with a fair capacity, and if he was also a little lucky and ready, in addition, to be ruthless, then his way to success was open. So Caesar was trained, and so, likewise, Cicero—so, indeed, nearly all the Roman worthies.

The upsurge of Hellenic culture was not always pleasantly regarded. Older citizens, especially, conceived a vast aversion toward it. Not only was it unforgivably alien, but since many of its professors were men of skeptical tastes, it was also suspect as antireligious. "Wherever that nation (Greece) shall bestow its learning," said Cato, the apostle of virtue, but scarcely its practitioner, "it will corrupt all things." In 161 B.C. the senate, seeking a way to stop the rising "Greeklings," ordained that henceforth "no philosophers or rhetoricians shall be permitted in Rome." But for once the Latin's talent for law enforcement deserted him. The philosophers and rhetoricians not only stayed; they came in an everswelling number.

As time rolled into the imperial epoch, the grammar and rhetorical schools had so augmented that Vespasian ordered a subsidy for their head professors. Thus that sagacious ruler not only reaped their gratitude, but in a measure also their subservience. Other benefits gradually followed. Emperor Trajan, for example, reserved scholarships for youths heavy in brains but light in purse. Hadrian, himself a concocter of verse and the father of a book on grammar, brought comfort to senescent teachers with the security of a pension. In the year 150, or thereabouts, Antoninus elevated certain dignitaries of the higher learning into the paradise of senatorial privilege by freeing them from the levies of the tax gatherer and from service in the military. Gratian followed in 376 with a salary scale for teachers throughout the Empire. Another half century, and the establishment of schools became a state prerogative, but the chance to put a national school system on its legs had gone, for the barbarian was already within the gates, and Rome herself was doomed.

Those Romans who wanted to occupy their minds with the highest learning usually betook themselves to one of the Hellenic groves. Caesar, for instance, served his time at Rhodes, and Brutus and Horace at Athens, while Cicero attended first one and then, for good measure, the other. Some seventy years after the coming of Christ, Vespasian enriched the Eternal City with its first public library. Like the library of Alexandria, which it sought to imitate, it became the rendezvous for scholars, and again like its sister on the Nile, it presently arrayed itself with sumptuous edifices and facilities of every sort, to become the so-called "Athenaeum." It was not long, of course, before men of learning undertook to give instruction, and from these beginnings there arose a curriculum in law, architecture, engineering, and medicine, all concerned more or less with the practical. Though Rome's professors graced the public payroll, and some of them even enjoyed a great price, their art had none of the lambent fire of the imaginative Greeks. Indeed, in the Romans' heavy hands what the Greeks had done so well so long ago descended not uncommonly into mere wordmongering.

As might be expected, the Romans, being what they were, put the soft pedal on the advancement of scientific theory. In this respect not even medicine was an exception. The old Romans, like all primitive folk, whether ancient or modern, relied on their deities to rid them of their croups and bellyaches. As a result, quacks and soothsayers did an excellent trade. Until imperial times, when the medical brethren were put under rule and order, almost anybody could set himself up as an expert in the healing art. Indeed, not infrequently barbers and cobblers and woodworkers engaged in it briskly and profitably. When Greek medicos, the most advanced then known to civilization, appeared in Rome, they were suspect and resented. "They have sworn to slay all foreigners by the use of medicine," warned the vigilant Cato, "and this very thing they do for pay! ... " Thus conditioned, the dwellers on the seven hills continued generation after generation to succor the blind with the Emperor's saliva and the lame with the touch of the imperial foot.

For all their prejudice, however, the Romans found medicine of interest, not in the advancement of its theory, to be sure, but in its ability to heal and cure. By Caesar's time more and more Romans were investing their confidence and their cash in laic doctors—in fact, when that mighty man himself happened to fall into a low state, even he sought the help of the Greek Asclepiades, whose success with malaria, the curse of swamp-encircled Rome, had lifted him in the public eye to something of a miracle man. It was Caesar who vouchsafed the medical profession the state's first official sanction, and Augustus, his successor, who granted its practitioners the boon of tax exemption. But it was Asclepiades who got medical education on its feet by summoning students into his company, taking them on his rounds, and introducing them to the knacks and knowledge of his craft. When he succumbed to an ailment that not even he could cure, his apprentices organized themselves into a union with regular sessions in what they called a medical school. Later, under Vespasian, this simple beginning blossomed into a program of instruction under full professors, mostly Greeks, who drew their fees from the public till. When the academic enterprise reached its end, the student became *medicus a republica*, a sort of ancestral M.D., and legally he alone could engage in practice. As usual in Roman learning, women were not debarred from the pursuit of such advances. There were, indeed, a number of female medicos, and one of them even compiled a handbook, much consulted, on the technique of abortion.

Despite all this progress, of course, fakes and frauds still abounded, as they have ever since. But their traffic was no longer entirely free and easy. Did a patient, for example, leave this earth to translate himself into an eternal shade? Then the law demanded an explanation, and if his healer was found careless or ignorant, whether he was *medicus a republica* or not, he was held accountable.

Absorbed in practical action, the generality of Roman doctors were not greatly given to research and experimentation. Their writings, thus, were in the main expository and descriptive, a medical blueprint, as it were, for everyday practice. There were a number of such works, but far and away the most important issued from Aurelius Cornelius Celsus, a gatherer of knowledge, and one of the first encyclopedists in human annals. Save for the writings of Hippocrates, his *De Re Medicina* is the oldest surviving classic in the field. It was embedded in a vast compendium of knowledge running from agriculture and war to rhetoric and metaphysics, and by a whim of fate it is the only part of that colossal collection which remains. By another caprice of fortune, it was not only thorough, but also full of life and charm—in truth, so rare in its class was the purity and elegance of its Latin that Celsus became known as the Cicero of the medicos. With the fall of Rome this extraordinary work disappeared from sight, only to bob up in the fifteenth century, just in time, it almost seems, to lend a ready hand to man's effort to recapture his ancient classical legacy. Cast into print before either Hippocrates or Galen, the book was destined to give a powerful stimulus in a later day to the overhauling and amelioration of the physician's art and science—in fact, much of Celsus' technical terminology is still in current medical usage.

The best-educated and most distinguished doctor in Rome was a Greek. Galen by name, he came from Pergamum in Asia Minor, and for a while he taught in Alexandria. Hailed everywhere as a wonder worker, Galen treated many of the high and mighty, including the Emperor Marcus Aurelius. But he had something more than an ingratiating bedside manner. When the Romans invited him to lecture on anatomy and physiology, he eagerly accepted. Circumstances compelled him to demonstrate his science with goats and swine, for the Romans, who took infinite delight in slaughtering people for fun in the Coliseum, turned thumbs down at the notion of human dissection for the promotion of scientific knowledge. To mention Galen is to recall at once his knowledge of anatomy. An explorer of the human frame, he charted its unknown regions, so well, in fact, that in more than one particular his observations still hold. His writings on the pulse embrace seventeen chapters, but he was not above dealing with burns and sniffles—even, indeed, with warts and the lowly corn. Throughout his life Galen craved surety and finality, and for his science he sought the exactitude of geometry. Yet for all his hope and confidence in the attainment of precise knowledge, he yielded not infrequently to mystical vapors. "There is nothing useless or inactive in the body," he announced, "and all parts . . . have been endowed by the Creator with specific powers," a declaration clearly at odds with the skepticism of Hippocrates, the father of medicine. "Science and faith," said the latter, "are two things—the first begets knowledge, the second ignorance."

4

Despite her twelve centuries of history, Rome produced few writers on pedagogy. Cicero, it is true, nodded gravely at the subject, and so did Tacitus and Suetonius, but the propositions they laid down are brief, and they devote themselves mainly to the higher learning, and particularly to the training of the public speaker. The most momentous of Roman writers on education, and the only practicing professor in their ranks, was Marcus Fabious Quintilian. He was born some time during the mid-thirties of the first Christian century in Calagurris on the Ebro, currently designated as Calahorra, a town in northern Spain, celebrated in Roman annals for the glitter of its culture, especially in the domain of letters. Son of a rhetorician, who for a while also offered instruction in his specialty, Quintilian followed in the paternal trail. He was still in his nonage when he made ready for a career in law by serving as an apprentice to Domitius Afer, a successful juridic pleader of the time. Returned to his native haunt, young Quintilian engaged in legal practice and mixed a bit in politics, but after a decade of such endeavor he transferred his major activity from the courtroom to the classroom. The next time we have any important word about him falls around the year 68, when he appeared in the Eternal City to run a school where he sat as a teacher of rhetoric besides practicing occasionally as a pleader in the courts. The Romans regarded his talents favorably, and some of his students were destined to make an impressive splash in history. He gave knowledge to the younger Pliny, and possibly Tacitus and Juvenal, all of them big wigs in intellectual and cultural chronicles. Even the empurpled Vespasian fell to the charm of this suave and handsome man. The Emperor not only committed his adopted sons to Quintilian for special counsel and instruction, but in 78 A.D. he elevated him to Rome's first professorship in rhetoric with a lifetime reservation on the public payroll. For a score of years or so, Quintilian performed his work as teacher, lawyer, writer, and public speaker not only under Vespasian, but also under his successors Titus and Domitian. Time saw the professor feted as Rome's foremost teacher of the rhetorician's art and science and heaped with no end of gauds and honorifics, including senatorial rank with all the special majesty and prerogatives thereunto appertaining. Nevertheless, in the year 88—he was then in his early fifties—Quintilian turned his back on the lectern to spend his remaining years in contemplation and writing. He elected, as he said, "to retire honorably from teaching and from speaking in the Forum while my services were still in demand."

A man so hymned and anointed, one would think, should have enjoyed a life of unremitting bliss. Alas, this was not the case. Death took his wife when she was not yet twenty. His two sons, to whose education he had directed his major literary effort, died before they were men. It is no cause for wonder, hence, that the fear of death haunted him—though not in the ordinary sense of being afraid to die, for he was too much a Stoic for that. What he dreaded was being cut off from his work before it was done. In consequence, he wasted no time, writing in high gear far into the hush of the night, incessantly and laboriously—sometimes all too hurriedly—until, after two years, his script was ready for its publisher.

The work for which Quintilian is remembered is his *De Institutio Oratoria*, or in plain English, *The Education of an Orator*, or in less plain English, *The Institutes of Oratory*. It is an expansive treatise, comprising a dozen books or sections, each running some seventy-five pages. Despite the limitation suggested by its title, it wanders into broader fields, with glimpses into the future orator's childhood years at home, his hours on the schoolboy's bench, the art and science of rhetoric, the pursuit of its mystery in the rhetorical school, the development of oratorical skill, from its soft and mellifluous play on the strings of human emotion to its shouts and bellows and waving of the arms, and finally in book twelve, a penetrating discourse on literary taste and criticism.

For a man enmeshed in the practical business of hatching and maturing accomplished orators, Quintilian was a man of wide cultural inclination, a man who not only knew his Greek, but who admired and recommended it as a primary diet to aliment the higher professional education. So important did Quintilian regard the mastery of the Hellenic tongue that he made it his pupil's first medium of instruction. There is no sound reason, he insisted, why that instruction should be put off until the boy's seventh birthday—the Roman practice at the time. Let him, instead, face his books and master as soon as he is ready, which is to say, the professor explained, echoing an Aristotelian caution, when learning will lay no untoward burden upon his sprouting powers. Unlike so many Romans of a spacious pocket, Quintilian put no store in tutorial education. Although even the best school is doubtless far from perfect, yet its merits, he contended, outweigh its faults. There is no satisfactory alternative, he went on, for a lad's mixing with numerous others, and being alone day upon day with even the most exemplary preceptor is at best a poor replacement for the social give and take to be had in school. Isolation under the paternal roof can be a dangerous thing: all too often it may bear a gross and ignoble brood, in instance, apathy, conceit, shyness, and suchlike threats to human well-being. Not only is the healthy rivalry afforded in a school a magnificent spur to individual effort; it is also a tonic to the teacher, and the larger his audience, the greater the challenge to his artistry.

For an old-time schoolman, and above all a Roman one, Quintilian was a man of extraordinary tenderness. He believed, for example, as did Froebel, the author of the kindergarten, nearly eighteen hundred years later, that play can be educative, and that the learning which is unbearable can be made tolerable and even attractive, when masked with badinage. In a day when teaching was in a low and decrepit state, and learning was hence a torture, Quintilian exhorted his brethren to swathe their dull and forbidding offerings with soft allurement, even with a sort of velvet charm, so that not only will a boy be enticed to bend over his books, but that "he will not reserve a dislike for what once had given him a pain"—a notion which pedagogic lingo nowadays speaks of as "motivation," and which is, of course, a cardinal article in the contemporary teaching canon. At a time when the common run of schoolmasters clubbed their pupils into line like so many jail keepers, Quintilian urged upon them an understanding of the young and humane treatment of them in school. Unhappily, his recommendation was not to be granted serious application until fairly recent times.

Quintilian needed no psychologist to tell him about individual differences. His long engagement in the grove, on the playground no less than in the classroom, had brought him face to face with every shade of student nature. Some students, he had observed, inclined to laziness; others bore an aversion to being told what to do; yet others fell easy prey to fear or disheartenment. Unfailingly some were grain, while just as unfailingly others were chaff. In any case, despite his fixed addiction to large classes, Quintilian was at pains—as was Rousseau some seventeen centuries later—"to know the pupil," for only on such a footing could he be taught effectively. The best student of the lot, the selected seed corn, so to say, was the lad "who rouses when he is praised, who profits when he is encouraged, and cries when he is defeated." Such a lad, contended Quintilian, would be fired with ambition and, with a little bit of luck, he is marked for success and maybe even glory. But let him bear in mind that eloquence is not a vendible commodity. Even a lawyer, the author of the *Institutio* insisted—blowing a friendly kiss to Cloud Nine—should be impervious to accepting pay, save only if his privy purse happens to be lean.

When Quintilian wrote down his thoughts on the making of the complete orator—a man, as he said, "possessed of every moral virtue"— he undertook not only to give guidance and counsel to his instructors, but also to restore the art of speechmaking to the lofty and influential place it had held in the pre-imperial times of Cicero, in whom the professor discerned all the attributes of the perfect orator. To obtain his end, he relied on the services of the traditional schools, mellowing their methods, as has been told, with a benignity which in those rough-and-ready times was pedagogically so unseemly that it abraded the ideals of right-minded rattanners, causing them anguish and not a little horror.

To lay the groundwork in reading and writing Greek and Latin became the business of the elementary *ludus*. Once the learner had these under reasonable rein, he moved into the grammar school which instructed and rehearsed him in grammar so that he would learn to speak and write without a flaw, made him intimate with the writings of the great poets besides, as was then commonly but erroneously accepted, enabling him to hone and strop his mind to a razor's edge. To give extra help in putting the budding Cicero on the right path to successful oratory, he was made to apply himself to the study of philosophy, geometry, music, and astronomy. But the philosophy he pondered was scarcely the robust discipline with its theories of knowledge, value, reality, and the like, admired and pursued by Plato and Aristotle and their infinite horde of successors. The truth is that of the generality of practicing philosophers, Quintilian held a rather low opinion, and if he allowed himself to concede a place to their mystical gurglings, it was largely for the practical purpose of casting light on the emanations of the poets, which not infrequently were shrouded in the haze of philosophic meaning. Did the rising orator study music? Then it was not to gain competence as a tonal artist, but rather, among other things, to cultivate his speaking voice, to develop a sense of tone and tempo, and to ease the strain which life persisted in laying upon the psyche. One may well wonder why a prospective speechmaker should bother himself with geometry. Again the purpose was preeminently practical. Getting into sweat over the Euclidian mystery, with its heavy recourse to deductive reasoning, can go a long way, Quintilian was sure, to exercising and fortifying a student's ability to frame convincing and conclusive arguments. Like grammar, moreover, geometry was held to be a magnificent grindstone to sharpen the human mind. Even astronomy can be made to serve a utilitarian oratorical end. A knowledge of the heavenly bodies and other celestial phenomena is not only useful and impressive material in the orator's intellectual garderobe, but, supported and upheld by geometric calculations, it serves to help him to invest the mystery of the universe with meaning.

True to its title, *The Education of an Orator* shines the better part of its telltale light on the culminating period of his confection, his training, that is, in the rhetorical school. There is no suspension here of his traffic in general learning. He continues to commune with beautiful letters, their poesy and their prose, and their lessons to improve and uplift his moral character. He gives his attention to rhetoric and composition, to logic and professional ethics. He also examines the historical past, not to pigeonhole its salient events and dates, but rather to give them animation, and to draw upon them on some tomorrow, should the need arise, for apt and telling illustrations to fortify his harangues. In addition, of course, there is the inescapable professional training, involving every aspect of the speaking craft, from enunciation and pronunciation, gesture and facial expression to style and delivery. The student learns how to render a simple address; he pleads for an imaginary client; and he fills the air with oratorical wind music. Finally, he is made privy to every trick in the lawyer's kit of flimflammery, for, true to the juridic ethics of his time, Quintilian held that an advocate may resort to any means, however dubious and deplorable, in order to win a case.

When Quintilian died, probably in the year 95, his fame was neither mute nor inglorious. Poets and essayists garlanded him with eulogy. He was, said Martial, himself a Spanish Roman, "the best of guides for unstable youth." The satirist Juvenal, who seldom found occasion to pronounce praise on anything, declared Quintilian to be "wise, noble, and high-minded." The one chink in his marmoreal stature, his craven and degrading foot-kissing of the Emperor Domitian—second in Roman annals in his satanry, perhaps, only to Nero—was graciously overlooked. Quintilian's treatise was given a warm reception during his lifetime, and long after its author had gone to rest, though it was aped and pirated, it remained without any serious challenge. Then, like an April shower, it suddenly disappeared, with only fragmentary relics of it existing here and there. Lost apparently forever, it came out of hiding in 1416 when Poggio Bracciolini and three companions, aprowl for errant manuscripts, found a full copy of it in the dark and musty recesses of the abbey of Sankt Gallen in Switzerland. Hand-copied in hurry-scurry by its finder in a few weeks, it presently found employment in the groves of knowledge for another several hundred years. Wherever it went, Quintilian's ideas on pedagogy tagged along. To the common stock of schoolmasters most of the wisdom of those ideas was patent nonsense, but to a stray reformer here and there the food it offered was delectable, and often it was irresistible. The advanced pedagogues of the Renaissance in the fourteenth century and thereafter gave Quintilian's precepts a cordial embrace, and some of the teachers of the era—in illustration, the eminent Vittorino da Feltre—struck their colors to their potency, and even ventured to try some of them in their everyday practice. In fact, in his school at Mantua, Vittorino not only adapted some of the views of the ancient Roman to the prevailing Italian culture, but in his teaching he was Quintilian come alive again. Thus the professor's ideas continued to filter into educational thought down the boundless trail of time, and though their author is overlooked and sometimes never even heard of by the common classroom practitioner, today many of them have fixed themselves as settled principles in modern education.

Although the bulk of Quintilian's educational theory has escaped time's fearful laceration, this is not to suggest that its immunity has been perfect. For example, Quintilian's view of the operation of the human mind, the so-called faculty psychology, though it was still sacrosanct as late as the mid-nineteenth century, has since fallen from scientific grace. With the knell of its passing, there occurred still another casualty, the theory, that is, that through formal discipline the mental faculties—whatever they may be—can be trained. Rome's most famous schoolmaster, as has been said, was no philosopher, at least not in the usual sense that he cerebrated systematically over the vast and engulfing problems of the cosmos. Devoid of the metaphysician's itch to speculate about universal riddles, Quintilian confined his thinking to the world in which he lived. An unremitting utilitarian, high-minded, no doubt, as Juvenal had depicted him, he envisaged education in its social and practical context. The orator, as he protrayed him, is the consummation of Roman social attainment. He was, as has been noted, a cultivated person, but the culture he had acquired during his long years of preparation was designed not to give his life enrichment or enjoyment, but to serve him usefully in the practice of his profession. For Quintilian the pursuit of culture was for the sake of utility. It was, in sum, the prerequisite to successful pleading. But let the fact not be overlooked that for all his Roman proclivity for the practical, Quintilian was not anesthetic to dreaming. "I only hope," he wrote, "that, at some future day, the perfect orator who is to come will appropriate to himself the study of philosophy. . . . The ideal orator will raise it once more to a place of honor. Like one who recovers stolen goods, he will assign it again to its proper position in the field of eloquence."

5

In the pursuit of knowledge, Rome's contribution lies not in the advancement of education itself, but in the furtherance of the conditions which prospered it, and especially in the variety of its application. She had an extraordinary affinity for law and government—indeed, in these matters during her time she had no equal. Conqueror of the Mediterranean world, she bent it to her requirements, exploiting it shamelessly, as she did all her fallen foes. Yet for two centuries she brought that troubled space order and prosperity, a peace of stability far beyond even the wildest poetic visions. Rome acquired the Hellenic learning like a garment readymade, and though she altered it to suit her need and taste, its finest features remained, at bottom, Hellenic. Rome not only absorbed the ancient legacy—she preserved it; and after two more centuries of time, before she fell at length to the barbarian, as low as once she had been high, she had transmitted it to the West—without her, in truth, all this magic which still enchants the world might have been lost.

Although Rome did not fire the world with new ideas, she had no disinclination to take in the ones she found. Those to which she gave her countenance she put to work with an inexhaustible industry and a skill which sometimes rose to genius. With her sword she hammered the nations of the earth into the unity of a single empire, a world state destined to excite the dreams of ambitious rulers ever since. At the same time she bestowed upon that realm an abiding and unexampled peace, the like of which mankind still longs to revive. To secure that peace she formulated a body of law whose majesty even the barbarian came to recognize and respect, and from whose roots sprang the Medieval Church's canon law. When, during the twelfth and thirteenth centuries, the study of secular law, so long dormant, suddenly flared anew, it was to Justinian's ancient code that men turned for help and guidance. Thus Rome's juridic legacy was to give light once more to the protection of life and property. Its long arm was to reach down the centuries far beyond the Middle Ages to illuminate the Napoleonic Code. Its influence, in fact, is still a power.

To the world Rome bequeathed her alphabet and her speech. Latin lingers in the works of her own writers, of course, in Virgil's sonorous strophes, in Cicero's stately prose, in Livy, Horace, Marcus Aurelius, and several more. It survives in the Middle Ages in the written utterance of its scholars. And though in recent years it has given ground to younger living tongues, it still resounds in the intonations of Mother Church, both in her ritual and in her hymnody. It lurks in the phraseology of every law book, it shows itself in the terminology of the natural sciences, and it runs through the doctor's everyday prescription. Latin has borne a host of children. All the Romance languages are its progeny, and no speaker of English could express himself without its discernible traces.

Rome advanced the practice of city government. The incorporated municipality and its charter of rights and privileges are ancient Roman hallmarks. The idea which underlies governance by checks and balances, so esteemed currently by free democracies, is of Roman provenance. Even the structure of Holy Church was patterned at the outset on Roman lines, the one universal Christian church, maintained and ruled by a hierarchy of prelates from the pontiff supreme down the scale to the parish priest, and with all ecclesiastical roads leading to the Eternal City.

Wherever Rome applied her gifted hand, there usually man's everyday knowledge and performance inclined to improve. The farmer she introduced to novel and better tools, a superior tillage, and a horde of new trees, shrubs, and plants, most of which she had come upon in the vanquished East. She laid down almost imperishable roads, joining them all to the nation's capital. She charted and traversed new sea routes, linking land and water to the markets of the world. She begot the early form and substance of capitalism with practical and vigorous devices to promote banking and investment. She drained marshes and developed public sanitation, and she organized medicine and established hospitals. Her architects and engineers erected the world's tallest buildings, colossal coliseums, and vast triumphal arches. They conceived innumerable reservoirs and fountains, and hundreds of bridges, which even in their moldering afterlife, still manage to astonish and amaze us. These men worked not so much for beauty as for use—even so, for all their stupendous practicality, in the end their labors combined to transform their country into a fair and civilized land.

In education the story runs in a similar vein. The Romans did not, like the Greeks, entertain the ideal of a liberal education. The concept of the all-round man, cultivated harmoniously in body, mind, and spirit, was beyond their appreciation. Grecian learning they embraced, but true to their utilitarian temper, they denuded it of its lofty spirit. To warm a freeman's son to the charms of living beauty, to make him musical as a gratification of his daily living, to enhance the physical graces—all this left the Romans cold. But if they extinguished the candles on the altar of art, and if the instruction of their young descended often into the hollow and dogmatic, then at least they compensated somewhat by organizing and developing what they took from the Greeks on a scale the world had never seen before. The curriculum they favored survived the Romans to pass through the halls of endless time into the Middle Ages where it became the Seven Liberal Arts, and from which it flowed, altered, to be sure, and sophisticated and enlarged, into later times.

The arrangement of the Roman educational system into lower, middle, and higher schools has, of course, never left these scenes, though the manner in which these divisions have been welded into a single unity is comparatively new. It is, in fact, the creation of our own republic, as distinctively American as ice-cream soda and ham and eggs. Although the Romans were large-scale borrowers, they were not totally void of invention. They were the first, for instance, to put their young to the study of foreign tongue so that it could serve them, when they grew up, both usefully and ornamentally. In the West, and probably also in the East, they were the first to tolerate women in the shrines of learning—not as schoolma'ams, it is true, but as students. They admitted the fair ones to all their schools, from the bottom to the top, and they allowed them to function, like men, in some of the professions.

As Rome plummeted from her zenith to her nadir, the pursuit of knowledge became, like the Empire, a mere shell of its former self. But before she went down the dreadful chute of history, Rome caught at least a glimpse of what has since become a commonplace. As emperor followed emperor, education became more and more a province of the state. The wages of Rome's established schoolmen were put under regulation, and they were drawn from the public purse; her houses of learning fell more and more under imperial vigilance; and finally even the right to establish them was claimed as the emperor's exclusive prerogative. Although in practice this never came to pass, nevertheless it was a foreshadowing of things to come. When the eighteenth-century Prussian sovereigns ordained that all schools, public and private, are children of the state, subject to its control, always and everywhere, they were merely putting into deed what the last Roman emperors had cherished in their hearts, and what has since become the general rule in all civilized lands, whether Eastern or Western.

CHAPTER 3

AFTER ROME

During the first two centuries after the advent of Christ, Rome unfolded in her full florescence. For some two hundred years her empire exulted in peace—a spectacle never witnessed in history before and never again since. In the country the earth was fat, the sheds and granaries full; and everywhere a general prosperity caressed the nation. The middle classes, piling up their riches faster than ever, disported themselves more and more like lords, while their cities increased not only in number and magnitude, but in splendor and public works. The new stability allayed unrest and even lessened crime, and as bandits and pirates went on furlough, travelers ventured forth on land and water, sometimes to drum up trade, but often enough as tourists idling on a holiday. There were other boons besides. The law, once so stern and even harsh, showed itself mellowing, and in the process it became more humane and tolerable. There was a surge in private philanthropy. The number of sanatoriums augmented. The domain of letters and ideas flourished, and so did the pursuit of knowledge. And, to cap it, there was a ponderable improvement in the power and circumstance of woman, in both her domestic and her public relationships. "Every day," rhapsodized Tertullian, "the world becomes more beautiful, more wealthy, more splendid. . . . Recent deserts bloom. . . . Forests give way to tilled acres. . . . Everywhere are houses, people, cities. . . . " Such in substance was the Pax Romana, the Roman peace.

But as with all our happy days, it was not granted the Golden Age to last forever. It attained its brightest luster in the reign of Marcus Aurelius, who died in the year 180. Thereafter, the torch of progress sputtered, and the days of peace and plenty, which had come to be taken for granted, presently succumbed to gloom and foreboding. Everywhere calamities and scandals scourged the land. There were plagues and floods, followed by famine and starvation. Government, once a Roman hallmark, fell into the hands of base and cynical men, and a people so long overladen with order and confidence gave way to doubt and discontent. Corruption polluted high places—even, indeed, the imperial palace. The extremely rich, attended by their hordes of slaves, grew richer, while the ranks of the poor and workless became steadily larger. For the assurance of bread and shelter peasants were willing to become serfs, and hardpressed craftsmen and shopkeepers threw in their lot with the city rabble. Meanwhile, the Christians, preaching their homely virtues and promising the Kingdom of Heaven to all believers, were leading more and more converts to their fold. At first the Romans had thought of them as somewhat daft, but as the years proceeded, they began to regard them suspiciously—even as subversive to the Roman way and a menace to the nation. Yet, for all the attempt to put them down, the Christians persisted—indeed, they actually gained in force and momentum—until the day came when the cross won even an emperor, the great Constantine.

Beyond the Rhine and Danube, meanwhile, the flare of barbarian campfires was drawing closer. The Roman garrisons had always been able to hold the

Teuton within bond, but years of voluptuous peace had dulled the Latin sword. When this became manifest even to high politicoes, they resorted to appeasement, letting in some Germans now and then, granting them access to the army and even to positions of state, and hoping to keep out the horde by absorbing the few. But the outlanders, who were themselves being pressed by the advancing Huns, would not be stayed forever, and before long they were falling upon the Empire. They poured in from all directions, out of the north and from the east, not only Germans, but Goths, Visigoths, and Ostrogoths, and in the lengthening years still others, all surging onward inexorably and irrepressibly, like a demented river to the sea. In 378, close by Constantinople, the Visigoths killed the Emperor and shattered his army. A few years more and they were in Greece, and in the century's final year they were pitching camp in northern Italy. Another decade and they were in the capital itself, for eight hundred years impervious to every foe, but now flayed and pillaged, its people palsied, and the Empire in the palm of the invader's hand.

The Teutons who felled the Romans were a people of great pugnacity. Tall, blue-eyed blonds, they were a fierce and brawling lot, and to the Romans one of appalling prowess. They had issued, it is believed, from the chilblained reaches of the north, prowling during the centuries to the regions toward the south, inhabiting the gloomy fastness of the forest, and feeding themselves off the country. They had a rude sort of government, mostly of a tribal sort. Over the years they had invested themselves with numerous gods, male and female, who, like their pagan celebrants, were a strong and scandalous lot with their war god, Wotan, as executive-in-chief. The Teutons entertained some notions of a life beyond the grave, but their Valhalla, a warrior's paradise, reserved its ghostly glamor for those who had come to a hero's end in battle.

With the collapse of Rome, the peoples of Europe passed into a long period of confusion. The translation, however, was gradual, for the invasions bridged many years—the years, in fact, stretched into decades, and the decades into centuries. Yet, even before the final plunge, the fire had gone out of Rome's vitality. Bankrupt and almost incoherent, the once-proud Empire was showing all the signs of decaying from within. The barbarian avalanche did not launch the process; it merely brought it to its last phase. Time saw the conqueror gradually tamed, and as his rampages came to an end, he settled himself in a rudimentary sort of farming. But authority had dwindled and crumbled, and everywhere there was violence and disintegration. Roads and bridges fell into disrepair; ships rotted in their harbors; trade stood still; work generally stopped; and intercommunication, the mother of change and progress, was almost obsolete. Even cities, not only Rome, but Antioch, Corinth, Ephesus, Lyons, and dozens more, once the wonder and the glory of the Roman world, and great even by current standards, were presently wilting in the aching chaos—some, indeed, caved in completely.

The maladies infesting the state spared nothing. They not only devoured the material things which make people rich and powerful; they struck at things which transcend the fleeting moment, things of the heart and mind, the wonderful works of civilized man which illuminate the lives of not just a single people, but all of us throughout the ages. The arts and sciences wasted away. Apart from a handful of monks and clerics, scarcely anybody sought surcease and explanation in literature, whether in reading or writing it. As a result, the Latin language, become vagrant and disorderly, strayed from its vaunted classical course into a variety of spoken corruptions, the forerunners of a later day's Latin, our so-called Romance languages. Learning, formal or informal, all but stopped. For a while, the Roman schools attempted to carry on, but they were accorded little more than apathy, and in 529 Justinian's imperial fiat shut them down. Thereafter, save for the scattered and restricted enterprise of monastic and cathedral schools, education was in collapse.

There is always tragedy, and there is always hope. The havoc which enshrouded Western civilization extended to her farthest corner. Yet, for all the woe and trouble, the disaster was not total. Underneath the wreckage there lingered the substance of long and indissoluble experience. The Empire, after all, was not a mere aggregation of discordant and far-flung parts, riveted into place by the might of arms. Rome was an organic unity, a pulsing, breathing way of life, nourished and sustained by the common blood of language, law, government, and tradition. Granted, there were differences among Britons, Gauls, Illyrians, and all the others that composed the Roman state; yet despite the array of their diversity, at bottom they were a unified and coordinated civilization, predominantly and pervasively Roman. In the cities, where the barbarians were outnumbered, some of the old forms and substances of life remained. It was in the city that the crafts continued to subsist after they had foundered everywhere else. It was in the city that, even under the Teuton's disarrayed and awkward rule, an embodiment of the old government survived, and that a Roman, if he was lucky, could plead his grievances under the cloak of Roman law. And finally, it was in the city that the Roman schools carried on until at length they too gave way under the impingement of events.

2

The supreme fact amid Europe's tears and curses was not the direful barbarian, but the growing force of Christianity. Its devotees had started out in Palestine, a feeble, motley handful, addressing themselves to all men, but most beguilingly to those of low estate, the vast and wretched multitude whom fortune had so palpably forgotten. Proclaiming the essential dignity of human life and of man's equality before God—for all the inequities which beset him here below—they proffered the hope of happiness, perfect and unending, in the world beyond the grave. The first converts were simple folk, and it needed no prodigality of evidence to convince them. The promise of postmortem bliss apparently sufficed not only to win them, but to buoy them up as their days on earth whiled by.

This does not mean, however, that none but the lowly offered themselves for baptism. On the contrary, as the years increased, the new religion reached out far beyond its native haunt until it lodged in the Empire—even, indeed, in its very capital. Early in the fourth century Constantine granted Christianity a legal status, and in 337, on his deathbed, he himself yielded to baptism. Thus, befriended and protected, the faithful emerged from their dank and creepy catacombs. They not only executed their holy enterprise in the plain sight of the public eye, but to give themselves a greater puissance and proficiency, they organized themselves into a church with Rome, the city of the Caesars, destined to become the seat of the vicar of Christ. What had started so auspiciously at the century's beginning came to its triumphant climax toward the century's end when another emperor, Theodosius by name, outlawed all practice of heathenry within the limits of the Empire, thereby assuring the new faith a promising future.

When the Empire faded out at last, Holy Church, having fashioned her administration in the Roman style, constituted, as it were, a state. The sole organized entity of any scope and consequence, she assumed the burden of recapturing some of the repose and order of a vanished yesterday. Throughout the wide Roman world—even, indeed, beyond it in the barbarian's very lair—she set herself to work with infinite diligence to arrest the general decay, and to make life tolerable once more for civilized man. To Christianize the pagan her experts journeyed far and wide, from the dreary mists of Scotland to the forested depths of Germany, and as the years coalesced into centuries, even into the forlorn marshes of the Baltic. Her emissaries were adroit and venturesome men, and some of them, like Patrick and Augustine—to confine examples—later arose as saints. Let it not be forgotten, however, that theirs was a difficult operation, and although many spoke with tongues of eloquence, their words did not always fall on receptive ears—in sad truth, some of them were banged, beaten, and even butchered for their pains. But in the long run they exerted their influence, if not to melt the barbarian heart, then at least to mellow his behavior.

To God's tortured world the Church imparted a sense of right and order, and as time went on, she was able to restore some of life's bygone gratifications and half-forgotten enterprise. It became her lot not only to preach the virtues of an upright and godly life, but through her strength and solicitude to steer the ship of civilization back onto its course. On earth she was God's appointed surrogate, invested with the interpretation of His holy ordinances and the execution of His will and purpose. To this end her vision swept from Rome, like a searchlight, in all directions and at all times. Nothing escaped it, not even the meanest hamlet or the tawdriest wayside chapel. Her mandates embraced everyone, whether in purple or in rags. She received man as a newborn babe and baptized him at the altar of God. She heard his confessions; she meted out his penance; she refreshed and exalted him in the miracle of communion. She sanctified and ennobled his marriage, permitting him but one wife, and exacting from the couple the vow of lifetime devotion and fidelity. She gave him aid and comfort when he was depressed; she succored him when he was stricken. And when at life's end he left this tumorous vale, she covered him with the mantle of her hallowed earth and prayed for the repose of his everlasting soul.

For her missionary work Mother Church relied very heavily on her monks. Their provenance is shrouded in the mystery of the faraway past, but very likely they came into being in the East, the scene of so many other pious events. In the Western world two of them were sighted as long ago as the year 340. A century and a half later their ranks had swollen many thousand times, and their sacred edifices were to be found all over Christendom. Renouncing the everyday world with all its snares and menaces to life eternal, they settled in out-of-the-way retreats—in some forlorn enclave, for example, by the sea, hard by a secluded marshland, or in the cloistered thickness of the forest. Though they shunned the world, and even cherished an aversion toward it, it became their ironical fate to be mustered by the church to labor in her cause. They were her most assiduous servants, putting the soft pedal on a loutish world, not only by the power of their evangel, but as much also by the force of their exemplary life and practice. The inheritors of civilization, they nursed and maintained it during Europe's enraged and chaotic hours, and by their art and instruction passed it on in the course of a long lifetime to the barbarian. The monks were the foremost farmers of their time, its finest artisans, its builders, its architects—even its brewers and winemakers. Their monasteries became hospitals for the sick, almshouses for the needy, and the safest shelter for the traveler. And in an age when learning was in rack and ruin, these holy men cultivated and preserved the written word.

3

Thus the framework of the time and its circumstance. Out of their necessities education, as usual, took its shape and substance. Actually, its early phases showed themselves in Rome's more spacious days before the rise of the barbarian flood, when Christianity was throwing out its first lure for converts. They were, as has been recounted, a simple and unschooled folk. Of learning they knew nothing—in fact, they generally regarded it suspiciously, and even somewhat disdainfully. Nevertheless, to start them off for baptism, and hence, on their way to celestial eternity, they were in need of at least some rudimentary tutoring. For such purpose they and their children gathered at regular intervals with a priest or some other familiar of Christian belief, who taught them its leading postulates, its moral mandates, and the fundamentals of its worship. To prepare for baptism usually required about two years, but as time ran on, and the procession of candidates steadily lengthened, especially in the number of its junior recruits, the period of training was doubled. Informal in the beginning, it presently acquired a degree of organization, and in the passing time, as the circle of its attendants grew ever wider, it even accorded itself the dignity of a name, the catechumenal school, the first to devote itself purely to Christian ends, or at any rate, the first of which we have any news.

During the first two centuries the catachemenal schools sufficed unto the general Christian needs, which is to say, the moral and religious edification of the lower classes. But as the next century loomed, the new revelation was beginning to attract a more elegant and substantial type of pagan. Often bred to the ancient learning, he had little taste for the artless offerings laid before the ordinary run of converts. Consequently, as a practical matter, when the time came to put his boy to books, he dispatched him to a conventional Roman school, safeguarding him at home betweenwhiles against false steps with powerful doses of moral and religious enlightenment. Leaders of the faithful, it is true, took a rather dubious view of such a situation, loaded as it was with peril to the soul, but until something better offered itself, it had to be endured.

The solution, happily, was not long in coming. For as the Christian clientele increased in quality as well as quantity, its speculations began to receive the scrutiny of Rome's men of higher learning. Some of them, estranged by the irrational and often hazy mysticism of the new faith, plied it with derision and dismissed it on grounds of reason. Others, of a less skeptical and more flexible turn of mind, granted it ratification, and presently some of them were even joining the church. Before long a number of such converted academicians undertook not only to furnish Christian youths with a wholesome and superior schooling, but also to supply the necessary sophistication to enable at least the brighter ones to take the field against the pagan intelligentsia, now engaged in a fullarmed critical assault on Christian doctrine.

To attain this end the new educators sought to confront their adversaries on their own ground by teaching the heathen's own stock of knowledge, his grammar and literature, for example, besides his rhetoric, and the whole range of Greco-Roman philosophy. These were broached as thoroughly as in the foremost groves of pagan thought, and to them students were expected to apply their fullest diligence. But to ensure the students at all times against exposure to the omnipresent false thinking, their learning was subjected to a throughgoing Biblical purging. Private at first, and somewhat casually arranged, such endeavor soon became a refined and organized part of the Church's cultural labor, the so-called catechetical school, an unmellifluous name to be sure, but signifying merely that its instruction based itself on a system of spoken questions and prefabricated answers. Some of its teachers were men of high intellectual stature—in illustration, Pantaenus, a Stoic metaphysician, who taught at Alexandria during the second century, and Clement and Origen, who followed him in the third. At its start the catechetical school opened its chambers to all young men of Christian conscience; but as the new religion settled into a state of permanence, it gradually reserved its instruction for those of clerical aspiration. It thus transformed itself into a kind of Christian divinity school, the first of any consequence to be recorded in human chronicles.

When, in the early fourth century, Christianity was accorded the honor and dignity of an official religion, it was no longer the simple creature of its nonage with its trusting, childlike appeal that had captured the hopes of the first believers. It had been invaded on the lower intellectual plane by facile stories and gaudy assurances, and by wonders and superstitions that had served, usefully no doubt, to convince the barbarian of the new God's awful and overwhelming powers, and to bring him into the communion of the faithful. Even on the higher level among the illuminated the new doctrine had undergone alteration. Subjected to the critical search and skepticism of men of culture, the body of Christian belief had been given amendments and qualifications in the light of Greek philosophical speculation. The effort to Hellenize Christianity and thereby make it tolerable to thinking and urbane men, prospered especially in the East, in Alexandria and Edessa and Antioch, and most vigorously in the hands of some of the eminent fathers of the early church. The friendliness thus granted to Hellenic learning in the East was not similarly extended by the theologians of the West. Although many of them had graced professorships in pagan schools before their enlistment in the ranks of Christ, time had rendered them increasingly hostile to the ancient learning. Some of them, in fact, went so far as to hint that there was something wicked and illicit about it, and displeasing, hence, to the Heavenly Father. Saint Jerome, in his younger days a hearty drinker from the pagan's intellectual spigot, lived to regret his heathenish flings, and to feel an acute disrelish for his early days. And what went for the good saint went also for many of his brethren.

The difference between East and West led to a long and intensive contest wherein, as is not uncommon in such strife, each faction thunderously upbraided the other. But the Western fathers, led by the incomparable Augustine, commanded the votes, and though their everyday protests availed them naught, they were able, when the church gathered her magnificoes in council at Carthage in 401, to put the pagan authors on an official blacklist. Henceforth, it was solemnly resolved, no one, not even the holy clergy, was to resort to the ancient writers. Thus heavily hobbled, Greek learning fell on drab days in the West. It subsisted for another couple of centuries among the Spaniards, and for a somewhat longer period among the Irish, a free-spirited people then as now. But presently it could maintain itself no longer, and everywhere it gave way to slumber. It was not to awake from its frosted coma for many hundred years, and when at least it began to stir, shy, faltering, and not a little strange, the world had changed, and time was standing on the threshold of a dazzling classical revival, the so-called Renaissance.

In 325, soon after Constantine had sanctioned Christianity as the state's official religion, the Council of Nicea addressed itself to the task of putting the ecclesiastical realm under efficient rule and management. To effect this purpose the holy clerks were organized into a hierarchy, tautly woven with strands of steel and reaching from the parish priest to the bishop of the diocese, with Rome as its natural center. The main strength of the early church, needless to say, concentrated itself in the cities. As was only right and proper, the bishop was usually resident in one of the bigger and more prominent municipalities, which became his episcopal seat and from which he directed his ecclesiastical affairs.

To the episcopal duties there was presently added the business of attracting promising young men to the church's sacred personnel and of providing them with the necessary light and instruction. As long as the catechetical school was fulfilling its reason for being, the bishop had no problem. But as year passed after year, these divinity shrines began to lag, and after a while there was a perceptible dwindling of their number. As this came to pass, the practice obtained of offering instruction in the bishop's church. Sometimes His Excellency himself performed this pedagogical service, but as more and more duties pressed upon him, the function was turned over to a master especially appointed for its execution. By this route evolved the cathedral school, or as Easteners spoke of it, the bishop's or episcopal school. After the senescent pagan schools were at last done in by Justinian's imperial mandate in 529, the cathedral schools were left to fill the breach, and in the centuries following, not a few of them (York, for instance, and Canterbury, and Rheims and Chartres, and notably Notre Dame in Paris) were to become vastly celebrated—luxuriant oases, so to say, in an immense and engulfing desert of ignorance. The differences in the work of monastic and cathedral schools were only slight, and they are of no great consequence to anyone today, save, possibly, antiquarians. Hence, since to study the one is to know the essentials of the other, we shall concern ourselves mainly with the monastic schools, which we shall examine in the pages soon to follow.

Of the Christian fathers, the greatest and, excepting possibly Saint Thomas Aquinas, also Holy Church's most formidable theologian was Aurelius Augustine. He originated in 354 in the town of Thagate in Roman North Africa, the offspring of a pagan father and a Christian mother who, like her son, is now celebrated in the calendar of saints as Saint Monica. Despite the superlative example of his mother's piety, her son clung to his paganism, sampling now one brand, now another, from Manichaeism to Neoplatonism, until at length in his early thirties while he was in Milan, the powerful evangelistic voltage of Saint Ambrose, whom Augustine had come "to damn," but "stayed to praise," jolted him, and he presently submitted to baptism. As sometimes happens in the progress of a sanctified holy man—witness the cases, for example, of Saint Benedict and Saint Ignatius Loyola—Augustine enjoyed a wild and flaming youth, given, as he relates in his *Confessions*, to sinister and sinful doings, but his conversion, happily, made an end of such dereliction once and forever.

Although his father was a man of slender means, yet he was at pains to stretch his budget to give his heir a good education, that is, the usual groundwork in the elementals, executed in a strictly no-nonsense atmosphere, and fortified within copious beatings of the boy's behind. Thus entertained and motivated, the future saint had little taste for the lower learning. "One and one are two, and two and two are four was a baleful song to me," he lamented in his later years. Fortunately, his lessons in the secondary school proved somewhat more agreeable. There, indeed, he even generated a liking for lovely letters, especially the poesy of Virgil. "The wooden horse full of armed men and the burning of Troy . . . ," he glowed, "were a most pleasant spectacle of vanity." The altruism of a fat-pursed patron enabled the youth to attend the sessions of a rhetorical school at Carthage. There, while cultivating himself in the liberal and professional learning, he also entered the teaching practice. Looking back on his academic yesterdays in his *Confessions*, Augustine let it be understood—modesty was obviously not one of his excesses—that "whatever was written on rhetoric or logic, music or arithmetic, I understood without any great difficulty, and without the teaching of any man."

Following his conversion, Augustine entered the sacerdotal ranks, serving God and the Church with an eager zeal and a high competence, not only as a working priest, but as a missionary, propagating the gospel in faraway and sometimes very unfriendly places. Like Luther, a millennium or so later, Augustine was fond of disquisition and argument. Time, indeed, saw him pour forth some of his most eloquent objurgations upon the Manichaeans, who held that in our disturbed and wearied world evil was a principle ruling in its own right, and of God entirely autonomous—a teaching with which during his pagan heyday Augustine had hobnobbed, but which the light of Jesus now clearly revealed to be fallacious. In the same way he took the floor to denounce the wrong-thinking Donatists, who ventured to argue that unless a priest led a high and blameless life, the sacraments he administered went for naught. Finally, he did execution on the Pelagians, for whose insistence that human nature was not inevitably evil, he relished an intense dislike. For her son's long and praiseworthy service Mother Church was not ungrateful; indeed, as was only right, when the chance beckoned, she elevated him to episcopal grandeur, as Bishop of Hippo in North Africa.

Saint Augustine has come down the ages as the "father of Christian philosophy," a designation which, despite the blightings time has laid upon some of his theorems, he nevertheless deserves. Propagated intellectually from a hybrid Platonism, the so-called Neoplatonism, which for the nonce enjoyed a bit of a vogue among some of the Empire's intelligentsia, the Augustinian doctrine, grafted, needless to say, on sturdy Christian stock, was laid down in a horde of discourses—the labor of the literary Hercules—and most notably in the saint's two books, the *Confessions* and the *City of God*. Both works still enjoy the distinction of a classic, though for its significance, the latter clearly outshines the former. Launched on the heels of the barbarous Alaric's ravening of Rome in the year 410, and especially in response to the widespread wail that Rome's collapse was the consequence of her neglect of the altars of the ancient deities, the *City of God* was some thirteen years in its composition. There are, its author asserts, two kinds of states, the one earthly and man-made, the other heavenly and divine. The first secular state was the work of Cain, while Rome was given its start by Romulus, who, like his predecessor in Holy Writ, was an assassin. Conceived in sin, the earthly state is damned to suffer all the horrors and evils ever heard of, and some, doubtless, still to be heard from. By contrast, the City of God, founded in Eden, but translated, after Adam's fall, to extraterrestrial space, is the perfect state, the home of the good, the true, and the beautiful, and, of course, utter and everlasting happiness. Although Augustine warns that only a few of us will ever attain the perfect bliss on high, yet while we go about our appointed rounds on earth, it behoves us to establish the Heavenly City here below, thus preparing a place which will be fit and wholesome for the Savior when at long last the Second Coming is upon us.

Not a little of Augustine's meditation on right and wrong emanates in one way or another from his own experience. Does he hold, for example, that God allows the existence of evil in order to make the good more alluring to man, that God, as the bishop put it, "judges it better to bring good out of evil than to suffer no evil to exist?" Then it is because, during the gay days of his heathenry, having tasted the Manichaean postulate that evil is not the mere absence of good, but an active principle operating independently of God, Augustine's conversion to the holy cross opened his eyes to that pagan fallacy. Does the saint express doubts and misgivings about sex? Then it is because, given to asceticism, he finds sex offensive to his pruderies, and in consequence, he equates it with carnality. The most exalted earthly existence, the bishop permits himself to believe, is the one which renounces the pleasures and gratifications of life, the existence, say, of a friar abstaining from mundane delights, sensing the thorns rather than the fragrance of the rose, in order to enhance and sublimate his soul. If it is Augustine's conviction that man is naturally depraved, and that without the light of divine grace he is forever doomed to be a practitioner of evil, then let us not forget the conditioning effect of the bishop's long apprenticeship as a free-and-easy libertine preceding his submission to Christ, an event which, as the years moved on, he had the comfort of knowing was all that spared him from the everlasting flame and fume of Hell.

A minority of men—God's so-called elect—Hippo's bishop believed, the Heavenly Father had predestined for a glorious resurrection in the vaulted blue; the overwhelming rest, even before they drew their first breath, he reserved for an eternity of postmortem incineration. The doctrine, with its somber bull fiddle tone, proved too lugubrious for most of the latter medieval divine scientists, who amended or rejected it. But in Luther, an admirer of Augustine, the theory of human depravity inspired awe and respect, and he accepted it wholeheartedly, and so also did Calvin, the archfather and head architect of Puritanism. Time witnessed a revival of the doctrine even in the Catholic Church in the sacred exudations of the seventeenth-century Dutch Bishop Jansen, whose views and exploits are embroidered in later pages. But the Church put them under the heavy fist, and their author as well, whom it pronounced a heretic and, to safeguard the general spiritual hygiene, it had arrested and quarantined in a common dungeon.

Augustine bottomed his educational theory on the same Platonic dualism which he employed in the *City of God*, namely the world wherein we dwell and from which we draw our knowledge more or less through our senses, and the imperceptible world of ideas which lies tantalizingly beyond. The one reeks with error, illusion, wrong thinking, and dangerous opinions, while the other, as in the City of God, is the habitat of perfect ideas, eternal and immutable truth, wisdom, and justice.

To rise to the majestic plane of true knowledge is difficult, and for most persons impossible, but it is not altogether hopeless. Let the seeker, questing his grail, begin his search by putting himself in the hands of God the Father, all-wise, all-knowing, and all-true. Let him abandon his dependence on his eyes and ears and his other senses, for too many times they are unreliable and delusive. Let him not even confide in reason, for this too may cajole and deceive him. To break through the trammels imposed upon us by the world of sense, there remains but one recourse, namely faith—which is another way of saying belief in something which is not known. Do only a handful of us possess the necessary attributes to enable us to transport ourselves from the illusory world of sense to the lofty alp of true knowledge? Then, happily, the overwhelming rest of us can avail ourselves of the blessings God has heaped upon us by hearkening to the teachings of Mother Church, the Almighty's representative on earth. Not only will she illuminate mankind with the beacon of the heavenly truth, but as the Good Lord's designated earthly deputy, she is also empowered to induce his children to accept it, or if they cannot be made virtuous by persuasion, then let them be damned. If such be the Church's divinely ordained role, then obviously the task befalls her to teach what man needs to know in order to enable him to repair and rectify his false thinking and to lead him therefrom to God's absolute and eternal truths. To such an end Augustine would direct all education.

Such learning, needless to say, is not for its own sake; nor is it to enable its possessor to make a splash among his friends and associates. The kind of education Augustine would settle for is pretty much the sort he himself endured when he wore himself out in the schoolboy's bench in Africa, namely, a basic bedding in reading, writing, and counting, followed with a top-dressing of grammar, rhetoric, philosophy, and nature study. Over the importance of the latter the bishop made a considerable fuss, not, however, for any of the profane reasons currently being advanced by deep-thinking materialists, but rather for purely sacred ones. For, Augustine believed, a knowledge of nature was indispensable to the clarification of some of the hidden and elusive meanings secreted in God's Holy Word. In fact, Augustine's personal observation of nature had even enabled him, as he gravely reports in the *City of God*, to catch a glimpse of a headless man with eyes in his breast.

Although to the end of his years upon this twirling globe His Grace bemoaned the countless blisterings he had suffered at the hands of his birchmasters, yet at no time did he incline to disavow their necessity. For children, no less than their elders, are the inheritors of Adam's sin. Thus, naturally dowered in depravity, they must be granted no quarter. To curb and control their native wickedness, and to bring forth any goodness which might fortuitously lurk within their innermost recesses, the stick is the one certain and unfailing instrument.

Rather strangely, the propagator of Christian philosophy and one of Christendom's foremost students of moral theology, and hence, one would gather, a man of some intellectual puissance, put little stock in the power of human reason. So potent is man's proclivity for sinning, that all too often his intellect, which, like his liver and lights, is part of his physical makeup, will play him false. Far better, therefore, for a man not to reason why, but rather to accept and resign himself to the dogmas of God's Holy Church.

Although Augustine had drunk heavily from the spring of pagan literature, as the years edged on he began to regard the ancient writings with considerable disquiet. To be sure, about their literary merits no doubts accosted him—in this respect, in fact, he readily and unapologetically granted that the bulk of the ancient literary lights stood head and shoulders above their Christian successors. Yet, the fact that they were pagans is ineffaceable, and hence, howsoever graceful and magnetic their word music might be, all too frequently their heathenry befouled their thinking, to the detriment of the principles of the Church. For a spell Augustine inclined to straddle: he would permit the reading of those pagan writers whose words did the Christian tenets no serious damage, in illustration, the works of their specialists in grammar and rhetoric. To uphold his concession, the bishop volunteered the opinion that these subjects enjoyed biblical sanction—a bit of episcopal casuistry, no doubt, but which, because of the authority behind it, was effective nevertheless. Even so, despite the prelate's blessing, the crusade against pagan letters failed to subside. Time, in truth, saw the Church's guardians of purity gain in force and stridency, until, at length in 401, led by no less than the Bishop of Hippo himself, who, by now had apparently undergone a change of mind, the Council of Carthage, as has already been mentioned, put the ancient writings under proscription. Henceforward, Christians—not excepting even their consecrated fathers—were forbidden to lay eyes on any of the pagan confections. Thus the Church bolted an iron door on the ancient humanistic legacy. There would be an occasional Peeping Tom, of course, stealing a furtive glance, but for most of the several medieval centuries, the grand classics of antiquity were more dead than alive. Oddly enough, the sterility which crept over medieval scholarship, with its ban on the free exercise of the mind, which characterized so long a part of this era, is due in no small measure to the overriding power and influence of the "father of Christian philosophy."

Yet, when set in the frame of historical prespective, the saint stands forth as one of the Church's giants. Despite his denigration of human reason and his willingness to hamper and hobble the freedom of its functioning, Augustine himself looms as one of the Church's foremost intellects. As a Latinist, he wrote with grace and power. Among Romans, he alone can stand comparison with the Athenian Plato. His myriad dealings with the human horde, men of every shade and stature, high and low, good and bad, made him shrewdly privy to their ineffable ways, whether for weal or woe—a capacity which has impelled some of his latter-day admirers to eulogize him as the "father of modern psychology." Augustine's theology dominated most of the Middle Ages. His stress on man's total depravity and humankind's almost certain predestined commitment for burning in the pits of Hell was accepted, as has been pointed out, by Luther and Calvin, both prophets and paladins of the Protestant Revolt, and the progenitors of an infinite army of yes-men. It scarcely needs saying that Augustine, in conformance with the wisdom of his time, believed in witches, male and female, and although he did not cause them to be slain as bidden by Holy Writ (Exodus XXII, 18), yet he went to great lengths to excoriate them and the infamous practices of their trade. Like huge numbers of Homo sapiens, who enrich and enliven our present era of enlightenment by their presence, the bishop put a great store in the powers of the stars, not, however, for their unfailing aid in the furtherance of any personal fame and fortune, but rather as a means for helping man to fathom God's inscrutable will. Like all the Christian fathers, Hippo's spiritual leader was committed to the notion that work is necessary, if not as an atonement for the original sin, then at least as a safeguard against the blandishments of that ever-lurking beguiler Beelzebub. Although Augustine cast his ballot for the necessity of work on moral grounds, he also gave his approval to slavery, justifying it as God's punishment of the sinful. Then as now such moral delinquents must have been in plenty—in fact, so late as the sixth century the great Pope Gregory enjoyed possession of the largest array of slaves of any potentate in Christendom, sacred or otherwise. Finally, it should come as no surprise that Augustine, like his comrade males, whether in the holy shroud or in plain unhaloed garb, regarded women with grave distrust, like so many creatures of a subhuman order, imperfect, debauched, and impure. In fact, as was mentioned earlier, the bishop once expressed public amazement that the Omnisicient had ever bothered to invent them at all.

MEDIEVAL TIMES

CHAPTER 4

THE CONSERVATION OF KNOWLEDGE

The first monks of whom we have any knowledge were hermits. They came from all the human walks. Some had been plowmen, and some shepherds; some had fished or cobbled or baked; others had risen in commerce or in law or as officers in the army, and some even as statesmen of high repute. For the most part they were frightened men—frightened by the immoral pressures and temptations of everyday life, and the dreadful burden these things put upon the struggle to save one's soul. To protect themselves, they cut themselves off from civilization, seeking refuge in seclusion in some remote and out-of-the-way retreat. Here they immersed themselves in the meanest austerity, living in ascetic sparseness, fasting, praying, and suffering all things to exalt and glorify their souls under the universal eye of God. To gratify the Omnipotent, many went to fantastic lengths; and yet, though it was a simple matter for most of them to renounce sin, it was not easy to maintain themselves apart from the last shred of human fellowship. Hence it should be no cause for wonder that as the years followed one another into the past, these fugitives from evil should seek each other out to merge their common interest in collective endeavor. Thus was born the first monastery.

Europe's first monasteries were much like its first bishops, which is to say, they were their own bosses, defining their own ends, inventing their own rules, and managing their affairs as they deemed fit and decent. Thus, inevitably they differed from place to place, some being grave and strict, and others more or less easygoing. So things rested until the sixth century when Benedict of Nursia, now a saint, appeared upon the scene. Born to wealth and family, Benedict attended school in Rome, but the free sinning of the place appalled him, and he fled to the neighboring hills. There he strove to lead a simple, solitary life, full of piety and self-denial. Alas, he attained such a high degree of holiness that presently sightseers swarmed in upon him from every side to the ruin of his peace of mind and the peril of his soul. Thus menaced and beset, he headed southward to Monte Cassino where in 528 he founded his famous monastery.

Benedict was, by all odds, a man of acumen, endowed with a sense of order, and wily in the ways of men. To run his monastery with economy and competence, he formulated a set of regulations, the so-called Rule of Benedict. It ran to seventy-three articles, and so effectively did it come to grip with its task that for several centuries it set the standard for monastic life and governance all over Europe. Turning their backs on the delusive rewards of the material world, Benedict's monks subordinated themselves to what they conceived to be the diligent service of God. To this purpose they walled themselves off from the world, and none of them, except by the abbot's expressed affirmation, was ever to stray into the mundane space which lay beyond.

From start to finish the Benedictine day was arranged: six hours for work, four for prayer, and three for sacred reading. Launched in the watches of the night when the brothers assembled to chant their vigils, the day ran its course with solemn intonations at regular hours until, with the singing of the vespers, sundown drew its veil and darkness came. All activity was rigorously laid out like a timetable. The monk rose with the sun, and presently he went to mass, whereupon he repaired to the chapter house to be assigned his work for the day. Sometimes there might be a sermon, and generally confession was heard, after which ensued a high mass. At midday, at long last, the brother sat down to his first meal. The rest of the day went for work, reading, a variety of holy enterprise, a second meal—except during Lent—and as night settled, a long and, one hopes, carefree slumber.

Benedict took a rather unkindly view of asceticism—his drift, by contrast, was toward moderation. Even so, under Benedictine jurisprudence every abbot was to exact strict obedience from his friars, and in cases of witting violation he was free to apply the rod. Solemnly vowed to chastity, the monk renounced all claims of amour. He was, as Jesus said, among those "that have made themselves eunuchs for the Kingdom of Heaven's sake" (Matthew XIX, 12). Nor, for all his sweat and toil, was he allowed to lay up any store in this world: sworn to personal poverty, he was to possess nothing—"neither a book, nor tablets, nor a pen—nothing at all." And since, as the Rule insists, "idleness is the enemy of the soul," every brother was made to work. Not only did it credit him with serving and pleasing God; it also helped to keep his mind off carnality and other wicked matters.

Benedict's concern for learning was at best slim, and it was never his desire to make Monte Cassino a seat for scholars. Even so, as the years went on, monasteries became prime movers in the world of knowledge, and some of them attained a high excellence therein. Benedict was not yet laid to his final rest, when already it was becoming clear that to read for even a minute—not to say three hours, as the Rule ordained—a monk had to be literate in Latin. To assure such proficiency, some instruction became essential, not only for the youth who aspired someday to make the cloister his permanent abode, but also for those already in the fold, but who, because of their previous condition, happened to be strangers to the written word. To give them aid and accommodation, certain monasteries undertook to introduce them to reading and writing, a knowledge of reckoning to help them calculate the time of the religious festivals, and a sufficient familiarity with the tonal art to enable them to carry a religious tune. Here and there such boons were extended to the sons of the laity. Designated as externs, or outsiders, they entertained no longing to take the vows, and they were confined to special quarters, away from the regular students. In the course of time such instruction became fairly general indeed, monastic schools became more or less the rule.

2

It was not Benedict but one of his younger contemporaries, Cassidorus, who planted the seeds from which flowered the finest monastery learning. Bred to the law, he rose rapidly, reaching the topmost heights as a sort of secretary and counselor to Theodoric, King of the Ostrogoths. Though the Council of Carthage had shut the door on pagan learning, it had not securely locked it, and the King's secretary was able to maintain a flirting relationship with it, cultivating and enjoying it, and even in a manner extending it with a composition of his own, a *History of the Goths*. When, at sixty, the years began to weaken his grip, he left the King's service to seek surcease in the serenity of country retirement, but all the while projecting great plans in the kingdom of books. He was, in his way, a connoisseur of learning, and though a fervid Christian, he never quite rid his inner consciousness of the imprint of his early Roman boyhood.

The blood of the booklover flowed in Cassidorus. At a time when books were running rapidly toward extinction, he not only declared for their conservation, but he even undertook to devise the means to such an end. A ravenous seeker of ancient manuscripts, he scoured Italy and North Africa for Greek and Latin writings. What he gathered he stored in a monastery which he founded close by his country home at Apulia in Italy. There he passed the rest of his ninety-three years amidst his holy brethren, counseling and assisting them as they pondered and copied his many treasures. "Of all the works which can be done with manual labor," he confided, "none pleases me so much as the work of the copyists"—if only, he went on, they will copy correctly. To spread his encouragement still further, he compiled a little book, the *Institutes*, a work which current experts would set down as a handbook or, at all events, a study guide. Besides casting out hints on how to copy manuscripts with becoming accuracy and neatness, it offers a plan for the study of the ancient writings, whether sacred or profane. In addition it carries a detailed discussion of musical instruments, from percussion to wind, and an analysis of fifteen tonal keys. The *Institutes* was accorded a long and hospitable reading, especially by the Benedictines—in fact, it was still being studiously fingered some five centuries after its appearance.

Cassidorus, like Benedict, was a man of great persuasiveness and, like the saint, he blazed a memorable trail. Because of him the gathering and copying of books developed into a major and respected monastic occupation, and before long a library and a writing chamber became as essential to the operation of a first-class monastery as its bakery and its brewery. There had been libraries before, of course, in the younger and grander days of Rome—for a time, indeed, the business of publishing had burgeoned with great prosperity. But those days, like Rome itself, were gone, and save for Cassidorus and the monkish copyists who followed him, there would have been no one to make books. Theirs, it is true, was not the high desire of creation; rather, it was the simpler one of preserving and transmitting what already existed. Even so, but for the infinite industry of these patient men, most of the old writings might well have slid into oblivion, lost perhaps forever.

Today, when books thrust themselves upon us at every side, it is difficult to conceive how great and many were the tasks which beset the monks. There was no stationer around the corner to give them aid, and no supply house to give them stock. In truth, from start to end, the brothers themselves had to produce everything which passed into the making of a book. They wrought their own parchment, usually out of the skin of a sheep or goat, cleaning and scraping and treating it, stretching it to its utmost thinness, then rubbing and smoothing it, until at length it attained its perfected finish, satiny, creamlike, and glistening. They made their inks; they ruled the pages; and sometimes they embellished them in a delicate border of reds and golds and heavenly blues. When these pages were inhabited at last with words, the monks made the binding to contain them. If the completed volume chanced to be of a great scarcity, there remained the necessity to chain it to something solid and immovable, and to inscribe a malediction against the long-fingered knave who, for all the measures of precaution, might still be tempted to make off with it.

The writing room, or in monk's Latin, the scriptorium, was the scene of the actual labor of transcription. Sometimes it was a mere cell, drafty and dimly lighted, where the friar, huddled over his desk and copyholder, toiled alone. At other times, especially in the more flourishing and spacious abbeys, it was a larger chamber where monks, a dozen or so, worked in concert, shaping their letters into the design of the words as one of their comrades dictated. At one stroke they thus made a dozen copies while the solitary brother in the cell confected merely one—an accomplishment which, in the framework of its time, bordered on the miracle of mass production. Doubtless it is true that some monks were a great deal less interested in the meaning of what they copied than in the actual labor of copying. They thus not only begot mistakes, but occasionally a stray and elfish one amongst them, his devotion corrupted by his fancy, took it upon himself to alter and, perhaps, improve the original—a venture which reaped him no thanks, but only scorn and censure from scholars of generations later. As the centuries toiled on, copying attained a degree of art—indeed, one still delights in the stained-glass beauty of the majestic initial capitals and the trim, black rows of letters marching across the page.

The monks worked hard and, all things considered, many hundreds of hours went into their effort in order that a single piece of early writing might endure. From their copy rooms issued an interminable flow of writing, both religious and secular, from missals, catechisms, prayer books, and moral homilies, to poetry, allegories, and nearly all the texts and manuals that served the medieval world of learning. A good part of their output the brothers placed upon their library shelves; some of it they exchanged for works they did not have; and some they sent away, with compliments, to fellow friars, in abbeys elsewhere. Thus the preservation of some of the old writings was accomplished. It was at best a slow and tedious process, and the collections which gradually came into being were never large. In today's light they were dwarfs, scarcely ever running beyond two or three hundred volumes. In fact, as late as the sixteenth century, when the Middle Ages had all but gone to seed, the largest library—and by long odds—was in Germany in the cloisters of Fulda which claimed the celebrity of harboring 700 volumes in its stacks.

Though the brothers lent and traded their treasures to their frocked comrades in other parts, one literary concoction which was peculiarly their own, and which was rarely available to outside eyes, was their daily chronicle. A log of thousands of day-by-day occurrences, it traffics largely in the commonplace, in the humdrum matters that beclog so much of every man's existence. Yet, when eyed collectively and in retrospect, these journals, so seemingly insignificant when they were inscribed, irradiate the enveloping darkness in which the everyday life of the Middle Ages might otherwise rest. Without these countless mirrors of their words our knowledge of the plain people of that faraway day would surely be impoverished.

3

Because the number of monks was so large and the part they enacted in Christendom so enormously impressive, it is easy to forget that monasticism embraced women as well as men. Like the brethren, not a few of the sisters fled the world for its wickedness and corruption. But at a time when the male was the acknowledged lord of creation and when women had scarcely any rights, a good many of them were attracted to the veil not merely for its great boon of grace, but also because to them the convent offered a rich and satisfying life, one which in addition bore the mark of public approbation. Not a few sisters originated in high society, and some of them were of a magnificent talent, intellectually, artistically, and otherwise. Their practice generally parallels that of the men, which is to say, they spent their day in worship, reading, and work. They labored at all things, in the shops and in the kitchen, behind the loom and spinning wheel, in the writing room and in the library. As springtime passed into summer, and summer faded into fall, they turned the earth, planted the seed, nurtured and tended it, and in just reward gathered in the harvest—as many of them still do to this very day. Some of their art and industry, however, was singularly feminine. Men might do the heavy muscle work, draining the marsh-land and grappling with trees and boulders. They could swing the ax and anvil hammer. But to women alone was it given to trace the lacy delicacy of the altar cloth and the silken loveliness of the priestly vestments.

Like the monastery, the nunnery engaged in instructing its novices not only in virtue and religion, but in reading—in Latin, of course—and in lettering and figuring, besides music, needlework, and some of the common household knacks. Like the monastery, once more, it opened its doors to the worldly outsider. In this respect the convent fulfilled a far more pressing need than its monkish counterpart. For in those far-off times the chance for the frailer sex to obtain even the rudiments of learning was almost nil. As a result, it became the inclination and the custom of families of the middle and upper orders, as it still is in certain Catholic quarters today, to send their daughters to the sisters for light and learning not only in the domains aforesaid, but also in good manners and decorum. Thus, until at least the thirteenth of the Christian centuries, the convent fostered and encouraged a fine feminine talent which otherwise might have remained mute and, perhaps, altogether indiscernible.

4

Instruction in the monastic school was carried on in Latin, but it was no longer the vehicle familiar to the ancient classic world, and even a magnifico like Cicero would have been sorely puzzled by some of its novelties and aberrations. On the other hand there were plenty of things to put him in mind of his own days at school. The holy clerk, for example, began his reading by memorizing his letters, as thousands of Roman schoolboys had done before him; and like them, he ventured into writing by scratching his letters onto a waxen tablet with his sharply pointed stylus. Arithmetic still languished under the pall of the cumbersome Latin numbers, and until something better was devised, tallying on one's fingers remained the favorite practice. From the first there had been a copious training in music, both singly and in chorus, not of course to give the young postulants a personal delight and exhilaration, but rather that in their later years they might intone the sacred songs to which God's ear was tuned. Once the alphabet and simpler words had been safely weathered, the pupil made his way into his first reader, usually a Latin psalmbook, faltering and stumbling through its pages, until at length he could not only read it but had even learned it by heart. To give him ease and assurance in the art of talk, he was put to endless rehearsings in pronunciation and in dialogues, specially composed, which dealt with the familiar things of everyday, and which ranged from cowherds and wheelrights to the charms of the seven psalms and litanies, to exhortations on the benefits to be reaped from living a good and godly life.

Although Jesus had loved children, and had even manifested a rare tenderness for them, in this respect neither the brothers nor the sisters emulated him. Rather they accepted the popular principle of their time, namely, that children had no rights, with the result that not uncommonly a kind of instinctive antagonism reigned between the teacher and his learners. Unless spoken to they were to remain silent, and when addressing the abbot they were to make a knee. Never were they to fidget, or scratch themselves, or drape themselves against the wall, or seat themselves unbidden. Against such misdemeanors, and others equally unseemly, the teacher stood sentry, and when, for all his care and admonition, they occurred nonetheless, he was quick to swing his ever-ready switch. "Learn or depart," Winchester warned its newcomers, "a third choice is to be flogged." During the seventeenth century the school reserved Saturday for this rite, flogging so many of its boys they called it "the bloody day."

Apart from the monastic and cathedral schooling for the run of youth, the prospect of getting an education was dim unless, as sometimes happens, a lad possessed the gift of song. For him Mother Church maintained a special school—a song school it came to be called—where she trained him for choral singing and other church service, besides vouchsafing him an introduction to the simpler secular learning. But such illumination was special, and though the church sought to sweeten it with free board and lodging, its lure was for the few.

The cornerstone of medieval learning, whether high or low, was Latin, and so it was to remain until the sixteenth century, when Protestant reformers, suspicious of its Romish tinge, made an end of it in the elementary school. But higher up, in the secondary and university tiers, its vogue was far more hardy. There, though time was to bring many and startling changes to the world, Latin continued, like an unimpressed barnacle, to cling to its hoary primacy. Without an understanding of the ancient tongue, no one could aspire to cross into the kingdom of knowledge. For practicing lawyers and men of God it remained, as ever, indispensable. Sheriffs composed their reports in the language, and merchants their accounts—even navigators resorted to it when they plotted their voyages.

The modest tutorings in Latin which had their beginnings in the monastery and cathedral classroom grew in the passing years into something more spacious and substantial. Referred to in the lexicon of pedagogy as the "trivium"— because of its threefold aspect—it dealt with grammar, rhetoric, and logic. Grammar then did not confine itself to the anatomy and physiology of language as it does today, but included also its behavior, which is to say its operation in the prose and poesy of the vanished masters—a formidable assignment in any age. There were, it is true, the usual hand-to-hand battlings with definitions and classifications, with nouns and verbs and moods and cases, and the rest of the grammatical legion; yet in the main its mission was to help the learner to garnish his utterance with grace and clarity. "It is," said Rabanus Maurus, one of its foremost familiars, "the art which qualifies us to speak and write correctly."

To such an end rhetoric marched side by side with grammar. Were the erudite Maurus still in circulation, he would salute it, without a doubt, as the art of effective communication, both on paper and in speech. But its main engagement was with written composition which it sought to reduce to rule and order. Conceived by the ancient Aristotle as a liberal art, rhetoric was not supposed to be of any tangible utilitarian value. A few more turns of the wheel of time, however, and this notion underwent modification—in fact, by the eleventh century the rhetorician's art had become substantially enhanced. Its professors, content no longer to reveal the plain facts about mere writing, were now, in addition, initiating their apprentices in the compounding of bills of sale, wills and testaments, and similar useful instruments in the letters of law and commerce.

The third member of the trivium, logic, was calculated to develop the power of correct and nimble thinking, and per contra, the capacity to ferret out error and fallacy. For a long time its importance was subordinate to that of grammar. But as theology advanced to become something of a rational science, familiarity with the ways and byways of logic became immensely useful, and for an aspiring theologian to deny himself its services would have been to assume an unnecessary handicap. The increased importance of logic was a boon, naturally, to its student appeal, and a joy to its professors. To give it an even greater attraction and reinforcement, some men of learning began presently to include theological problems in its drill and exercise, a practice which prospective experts in divine science admired vastly, and which gradually became the rule. Logic, its connoisseurs now advertised, was "the science of the sciences."

For several centuries the trivium maintained itself an undisputed master in the educational drill halls—indeed, it had not even a rival. Nevertheless, there existed also a "quadrivium," to wit, arithmetic, geometry, music, and astronomy, which, when arrayed with the trivium, were spoken of, somewhat grandiloquently, as the Seven Liberal Arts. So highly were they regarded that cathedrals now and then carved their names into stone where, weathered and worn, they still linger vaguely discernible. The quadrivium was not really liberal, nor was it truly of the arts—if anything, it inclined toward science.

Arithmetic, as indicated a few pages back, was still in the clutches of the Roman numerals, and until it was emancipated, there could be no progress. Some slight help came in the tenth century when Gerbert of Aurillac devised an abacus which, though simple, helped to accelerate and extend the ordinary arithmetic calculation. A man of great intellectual caliber, Gerbert was afflicted with a powerful thirst for knowledge—to quench it he even braved the unchristian citadel of Moorish Spain. So full was this man with rare and esoteric learning that he was rumored at one time to have tapped the forbidden files of Satan, a charge which turned out to be gross and without warrant, for subsequently Gerbert was elevated to the papal throne to reign over Christendom as Sylvester II. What really helped to promote arithmetic and to give it power and momentum was the introduction in the twelfth century of the Arabic system of numbers—a system which, its ancient vintage notwithstanding, is still in useful service today.

If the medieval schoolboy's knowledge of arithmetic was conspicuously smaller than that of his twentieth-century successor, this is not saying that its burden was inordinately light. On the contrary, he had to attend to matters of which today's schoolboy is innocent—at least in his official classroom capacity. In that age of miracles and monsters, numbers were not the cold and bloodless symbols of quantity that mathematicians currently would have us believe. Instead, they bore all sorts of occult and disconcerting powers, propitious at times, but all too often sinister and dangerous. All such concerns, naturally, had to be apprehended, and so instead of wearing out his brain trying to figure out the number of square feet in a rug 3 miles long and $5\frac{1}{8}$ yards wide, the medieval novice in arithmetic devoted himself to learning that the number two symbolizes diversity, three totality, four perfection and solidarity, and five—but here we had better put on the brakes.

Like arithmetic, the study of geometry was bogged in a lack of tools. True, the propositions of Euclid's plane geometry—the very ones which still knit the brows of high school boys and girls today—were on hand; but unluckily, in the chaos following Rome's collapse their solutions had gone astray. For a long time, consequently, geometricians were at a loss to teach their specialty, and once again it was not until the twelfth century, when the Arabs, having managed to preserve intact the venerable Euclid, presented him to Europe, that professors could properly teach his mystery. Thereafter, geometry quickly increased its pace and power, and the learner, then as now, could be put to wondering over the remarkable qualities and tangents, trapezoids, and parallelograms, and even the equality of vertical angles and that of the alternate interior ones made by a transversal of two lines parallel.

Unlike either arithmetic or geometry, the subject of music obtained a greater sumptuousness. From early times it had served Holy Church admirably in her varied enterprise, and for a man of learning, however slight, to be a stranger to its significance is surely assuming a great deal. Many illustrious schoolmen gave it an energetic examination, and several even worked out a number of treatises on it. But in the classroom, as in schoolbooks, much of the treatment accorded the subject was abstruse and academic, and presented in a tone one usually reserves for a consideration of the streptococci or the lesser shellfish. Yet, for all the obstacles of pedantry, the tonal art, though dampened, was not extinguished, and in certain schools, for example, at Metz in Alsace and at Sankt Gallen in Switzerland, the teaching of music prospered. Somehow church music, both vocal and instrumental, continued to be written, and some of it, glorious and unforgettable, still lives to lift our hearts today, a strange and touching testament to beauty in a world consumed more and more by ugliness.

The most popular study in the quadrivium was astronomy. It had come to Europe out of the East, and as of old, it occupied itself not only with the study of the simpler planetary motions, but also with such public affairs as the changing of the seasons and, more especially, the movable days of religious note, such as Easter and the forty Lenten days before it. The subject was, of course, dreadfully hampered by the lack of instruments and the requisite mathematics, and by the theological assumptions which befogged it. A good part of its business, moreover, was not astronomical at all but astrological, specializing in the casting of horoscopes, both for individuals and for entire nations. An early chapter in the history of human guidance, astrology counseled a man when to plant his turnips, how to deal successfully with warts and gallstones, and even how to pick the proper conjugal mate. Many moons were to wax and wane before astronomy finally rid itself of its dubious partner—in fact, as late as the seventeenth century the great astronomer and mathematician, Johann Kepler, was still casting horoscopes to earn himself some pocket pfennigs. Today, of course, astrology has been ostracized from the groves of serious learning, but over and beyond them its executants still thrive in greater number, indeed, than ever, both in our own fair land and in other havens of enlightenment.

5

Wherever considerable knowledge has to be brought to terms, there books of one sort or other will usually be found. The Middle Ages had its textbooks too, but their number was small—so small that they were not employed, as they are today, by students but by their masters. But even they seldom merchanted their knowledge directly from an author's complete and untransformed work, but rather from a compendium, not unlike the outlines which currently crowd the shelves of every well-stocked campus bookstore. From his manual the teacher dictated, spreading his words, slowly and deliberately, before his listeners, while they labored to imprison them in their tablets. Once edited and corrected, these notes were put between the covers of a little parchment volume to become, when packed from end to end, a visible testimony to the student's diligence and a permanent repository of his knowledge.

The first texts of any consequence made their advent in learning's most important subject, grammar. They were composed in the fourth century by Aelius Donatus, the teacher of Jerome who gave Catholics their official Bible, and who has since been canonized. Donatus wrote two books, the *Ars Grammatica Minor* for beginners and the *Ars Grammatica Major* for the advanced. Both works acquired a tremendous usage—in fact, so familiar became Donatus's name in the realm of learning that in time's course it worked itself into several languages as a common designation for any Latin grammar whatsoever. No grammatical work in the Western world has ever enjoyed a greater audience, nor has there ever been another whose influence proliferated so vastly into later times. For two hundred years Donatus had no competition at all; then, when Priscian came out with a book to breathe upon his heels, Donatus matched him step by step, rivaled perhaps, but never overtaken. His grammars continued to instruct and edify the young for over a thousand years, and when at length age began to wear them down, the newcomers which rose to oust them frcm their long dominion bore many of the older books' familiar marks. In truth, even today, 1,600 years or so since Donatus passed into the shadows, the grammatical nomenclature which he favored, with its indicatives and imperatives, its perfects, imperfects, and pluperfects, and all the rest—all of them are still at large to trip the tongues and puzzle the minds of youngsters wherever grammar continues to be taught.

Another work of no little dazzle in its time was *The Marriage of Mercury and Philology*. Put together in the fifth century, it issued from the pen of Martianus Capella, by birth a North African. Despite its arresting title, the book is actually a pedagogical discourse in the false face of an allegory on what later was to become the standard curriculum of the Middle Ages, the so-called Seven Liberal Arts. Confessing the scholar's immemorial bent, Capella shoveled detail after detail into his treatise, some true but many dubious, to tell the world about the illustrious Seven, what they were and what they promised to be in the domain of learning. Yet for all the drone of its interminable utterance, the book actually managed to convey very little information. True, there is buried in its cargo the assertion that our earth is round, and that the sun is the center of the universe, a notion borrowed unthinkingly by some of Capella's successors, but one which at the time was so patently absurd as to escape any serious consideration. Following the literary mood of his generation, Capella frequently cantered into verse, a practice much to the pleasure of the student, for his dithyrambs possessed a rocking-horse lilt, and like those of present-day singing commercials, they sneaked readily into the memory.

By some current masterminds Capella's work has been dismissed as a work of utterly no importance—but surely such a judgment is somewhat beside the mark. The book suffers, of course, from its pendantry, and perhaps even more from the change in literary taste which today makes its art not only spurious but indigestible. Yet in the academic circles of its own era it was esteemed as a very toothsome bit of pastry—so delicious in point of fact that scholars and students continued to savor it long after Capella and the Middle Ages had left the earth, as late, indeed, as the sixteenth century.

The century following Capella saw the coming of yet another writer, Boethius by name and a colleague of Cassidorus, and like him in the royal service of Theodoric. He was, for his era, a gentle and cultivated man, a devotee of the ancient learning, a logician and a rhetorician, and something of a wonder in Greek in a generation which was rapidly forgetting its Greek. Like Cassidorus, he dreaded the loss of the ancient legacy, and he set himself the duty of helping to conserve it. "I am glad," he declared, "to assume the remaining task of educating our present society in the spirit of Greek philosophy." To this purpose he undertook to put all Plato and Aristotle into Latin, a project so prodigious that, even had he not had a whit else to do, its accomplishment would have run into enormous difficulty. But in addition he dallied in writings of his own, including texts on arithmetic, geometry, and music, besides a couple of tracts directed against the heresies which were causing no end of trouble to the theologians of his time. His labor of translation, hence, never got beyond a couple of Aristotle's logical treatises and a commentary thereon. But skimpy though this was, until the twelfth century it represented all that was known of Aristotle in Western Europe.

Boethius's most memorable work is his *Consolation of Philosophy.* Written after he had fallen from royal favor and while he was languishing in a cell in the shadow of his impending execution, it speculated on the meaning of life, its joys and satisfactions rather than its sorrows and tears. There is in it no fear and no repining, no mention of Jesus, not even the slightest hint of life eternal—to Boethius death was apparently a matter of indifference. The slender little book came to being just before its author's end, when he was not quite fifty.

Boethius has been celebrated as the Schoolmaster of the Middle Ages, an honor he undoubtedly merits. His texts on arithmetic and geometry, paltry and insufficient though they were, were the best to be had until the twelfth century when the Arabs gave these subjects a much-needed shot in the arm. His book on music—*De Institutione Musica* was its name—not only served tone makers in Europe's middle years, but was still being honorably employed at Oxford in the eighteenth century about the time of Benjamin Franklin. Boethius's translations of Aristotle spun the delicate strand by which the schoolmen of Europe hung on to the ancient master besides, in a later period, providing its Scholastic philosophers with a working Latin vocabulary and a method by which they sought to harmonize faith and reason. But the work which was the most admired was the *Consolation.* Few books have ever had so distinguished an audience. Dante was familiar with it, and so were Shakespeare and Milton, and England's first

Elizabeth, and all of them quoted freely from its lines. In the ninth century it was rendered into Anglo-Saxon by Alfred the Great. Two centuries following, it was put into German, and two after that into French—and so on down the road of time. It is not a truly great book, even when judged by a kindly standard; its glory rather is the honesty and clarity of its expression on a theme that will engross pensive men as long as life remains an art and a mystery.

It is said that in his youth Isidore of Seville, upbraided for his lack of brightness, ran away from home. If so, before he died in the seventh century, he atoned for it. For not only did he serve Christendom some thirty years as Bishop of Seville, but by compiling an encyclopedia, he succeeded in achieving what not even Aristotle, that pigeonholer extraordinary, had been able to accomplish. The bishop was not, like Cassidorus and Boethius, a true lover of the ancient learning, nor did he, like them, take occasional flight in thought. "We are not allowed," he warned, "to form any belief of our own will. . . . We have God's apostles as authorities." For monks he laid down the rule that it was better for them to be ignorant than to burn forever in the flames of Hell for having read the works of pagans and heretics. Luckily for medieval scholarship, Seville's ecclesiastical primate was a somewhat pliant man, and when he undertook to put together his own books of knowledge he found it possible to take a holiday from this dogma, it being his purpose, as he explained, to catalog all information, sacred and otherwise, about everything "that ought to be known." The result was his *Etymologies and Origins.*

Though Isidore was scarcely more than an ordinary man, when he sprigged himself in the toga of a man of learning, he was relentless. His encyclopedia, hence, was a vast armory of knowledge, filling nine hundred pages, arranged not alphabetically but topically, and running from the liberal arts to God, the saints, and the angels, to men and monsters, food, drink, furniture, and yet much more. Its author grounded himself in all the hidden meaning of nature's mystery and all the common sights and sounds of superstition. Satyrs existed and so did unicorns, and Satan, that scoundrel, walked abroad. Crows could change their sex; twelve onion rings foretold the annual rainfall; and to meet a pregnant woman of a morning foreboded a dreadful calamity.

Isidore's bemused reflections must be judged, not in the contemporary afterlight, but rather by their inherent intention. To store all knowledge and to bend it to moral principle was the bishop's aim, and for the Christian world which he adorned it was apparently enough. His volume, despite its empty showiness, its nonsense, and its prejudice, was highly esteemed, and before long it was storming every citadel of learning. For six hundred years it remained the only one of its kind. Not until the thirteenth century was it challenged and unseated by a rival, the *Speculum* of Vincent of Beauvais.

Thus the age's most notable makers of texts. The impulse to deride them as mere embalmers of old and sometimes worn-out knowledge is ever strong, since save for rare and fleeting moments none of them stepped outside the familiar patterns. Yet to brush these men aside as of slight account is to forget the huge odds against which they toiled. In a world of blind and ugly ignorance they reached out to let in some light. But for their effort Europe might well have become what, erroneously, it has been said to have been, namely, a world of complete and utter darkness. They were high-minded men, all of them, patient, searching, and not a little impressed by the worth of learning. But how curbed and circumscribed they were by the accident of time! The surprising thing is not that they produced so little, but rather that that little was so much. It is true their works abound in error and superstition. Yet it is also true that, despite the obstacles which confronted them at every turn, they were able in the end to conserve and transmit a lingering residue of knowledge, so hard won in history.

CHAPTER 5

TWO SOVEREIGNS AND CHIVALRY

Despite the high hopes of Boethius and Cassidorus, the years which followed their passing saw a steady decay in the ancient learning, and by the seventh century its visible remains were few. The fact is, to the guardians of Christian conscience the old classics had become suspect. Even the great Pope Gregory, an able and intelligent man, and one versed in the ancient learning, filled with anger at the thought of subjecting the words of the Heavenly Oracle to the rules of grammar. "The same mouth," he warned, "cannot say the praise of Christ and the praise of Jupiter." Save in Ireland and in parts of England, the knowledge of Greek had all but withered away, while the rest of the old culture had passed into the sterile Sahara of the Seven Liberal Arts, a bedraggled relic of a mind once infinitely vigorous, but now manacled by the demands put upon it by Christian faith and rectitude. But even the Seven might have been tolerable— at least under the assumption which gave them merit—had their chief custodians lived up to their early promise. Unluckily, as monasticism increased in years, it increased also in material estate, and in the process the commandments of the sage Benedict were frequently forgotten. For more and more monks reading became a pain, and copying an accomplishment alien to their inclination. But for a few exceptions, their libraries gathered dust, and their copy rooms wasted in idleness. Meanwhile, the mood of intellectual apathy grew and spread, so much, in fact, that to hear of an ignorant cleric presently was neither singular nor novel.

Such in essence was the situation when the stupendous figure of Charlemagne broke upon Europe. On the brink of thirty when he became King of the Franks, he ruled until his time ran out in 814, not quite five decades later. Nature had been lavish to him in her gifts. He was large and well proportioned, of incredible strength and vigor, intelligent, imaginative, and in his prime, not a little handsome. German blood ran in him, and so did German ways. His speech was a Frankish German, but he could talk a fair Latin, and he is reported to have understood some Greek. For a king his tastes were modest. Plain food sufficed, and a little wine taken in the company of his family, while minstrels played in the background. He wore the rough garment of the Frank except on regal occasions when he let himself be robed and crowned—a dazzling sight, indeed, and every inch of his 6 feet 4 inches a sovereign. Married four times, he was devoted to each of his wives. Yet, good Christian though he was, he could not resist a sightly ankle, and since the ground rules for monarchs then were not too rigid, he allowed himself half a dozen mistresses. He loved them as he loved his wives. Love, indeed, overwhelmed him, and in the passing years it rewarded him with more than a score of progeny. Basically, he cherished a warm affection for his fellow man, provided, of course, he was a Christian. But when aroused, he could be wild and stormy. He wept for his friends when they were injured, but he thought nothing of ordering the death of several hundred Saxons on the eve of Christmas, and then proceeding to church to celebrate the birth of the Prince of Peace.

Charlemagne took an almost boyish delight in war, and during his lifetime carnage was a constant enterprise, one which carried the advantage, in his eyes at least, of letting him combine his love for battle with his love for Christ. Early in his reign he undertook to Christianize the Saxons, and when they resisted he flung his hordes upon them in swift and terrible fury. He was a fair man, however, and when at length they yielded, he gave them the chance to be baptized or die. Yet custom can be stubborn, and every year these hellish people rose in wild revolt, and it required more than thirty years and many thousand lives before they finally agreed to be enlightened. During the long rule of this most Christian monarch there were more than fifty-odd campaigns, more than a war a year, and sometimes there were several raging full blast and all at once. Yet, when in the years of his decline the King looked back, he faced no specter of regret; for war had brought him the largest dominion the West had known since Rome fell into its slumberous wonder. From the Pyrenees it reached out to the wind-swept Baltic, and from almost the full length of the Atlantic seaboard to the shoreline of the far-off Vistula. As for Charlemagne, he too had risen in the world. No longer a mere king, he had grown into an emperor, the Holy Roman Emperor, the successor of the Caesars, crowned and anointed by the papal hand in 800 A.D., and the acknowledged protector of the One Holy and Apostolic Church.

2

Though the eagle perched upon his shoulder, the sovereign was no stranger to the dove. A master in war, Charlemagne was also a master in peace. He administered his far-flung realm with an exuberantly dexterous talent, not unlike a benevolent despot, humoring, cajoling, and cozening his subjects, and always ready to unleash his flintlike will. Under his force and character, his land—for all its inner disaffections, its proud localisms and clashing cultures—acquired a governance and unity such as Europe had not witnessed since the Roman heyday. Though he could envision large and transcendental designs, he kept a sharply vigilant eye on detail. To this end he maintained a flock of royal emissaries—the *missi dominici*—whom he dispatched to every quarter of his empire to protect "the Church, the poor, and wards and widows, and the whole people" against the evils and malpractices that emanate from the complex web of human relationships. His laws and his communiques touched every phase of human endeavor, from farming to industry, politics, education, religion, and morality. At a time when trade and commerce were in a sickly state his laws ordained the control of prices and the frequent inspection of weights and measures, and they brought an anarchistic currency under rule and stability. They ordered the building of new roads and bridges and the proper maintenance of the old ones. For the multitudes of poor they contrived a system of relief, making the clergy and nobility their trustees, and taxing these worthies accordingly. The free peasantry they undertook to secure against the spread of a malignant serfdom, but here, unhappily, they were face to face with forces they could not fathom and could not curb. And finally, through his acts and edicts Charlemagne invested the enormous power of his authority in the labor of dredging learning out of its stagnant apathy and restoring it, as of old, to a high and laudable dignity.

Charlemagne launched himself as an educational reformer by laying plans to overhaul and improve the school of the royal palace at Aachen. An heirloom from his father, it had been conceived to lead and instruct the courtly young, but its performance had been insufficient to its purpose, and it had long since passed into the murky shadows. To direct the work of resurrection, the sovereign obtained the services of Alcuin, a holy clerk in practice at the cathedral school of York, and one of the most renowned teachers in Britain. With him Alcuin brought the reinforcement of three minor experts, a bundle of manuscripts, and a confidence in the power of knowledge which was surpassed only by his eagerness to advance and spread it.

Though the Palace School was in a sorry state, its condition was not beyond rescue if only for the reason that behind it lodged the talent and potency of an inexhaustibly dogged king. Did the school, for example, lack students? Then Charlemagne proceeded to people it, dragooning every available male and female in the palace, whether elderly or young, to attend its sessions. When he could steal some leisure, he sat in the learner's bench himself. As a student he bubbled with all the fervor of a proselyte. His torrential spirit fell upon learning with the same delirious and unsparing eagerness with which it consumed an enemy's territory. It is said that he learned to read Latin, but writing it floored him, and he never mastered it. He wanted to know all about the moon, particularly its phases and positions, so that he might calculate the coming of the Easter feast all by himself. Whether he ever managed it has eluded our chronicles. But if he failed, then surely he should have felt some compensation by his knowledge of the four winds. He understood not only much of their complex character, their beginning, their middle, and their end, but he even honored them with names— the very ones, in fact, they still bear today. For all his hobnobbing with the scholar's Latin, in his heart the King stayed loyal to his maternal German. He enjoyed it immensely, and he spoke it whenever possible. He compiled a Frankish grammar—not without some friendly aid, to be sure. And—albeit skeptics view this somewhat doubtfully—he set his emissaries in pursuit of all existing German verse, dispatching them in all directions in the hope of preserving the verses forever between covers.

3

Under the galvanic student-king the palace became a bustling place of study. But into the tapestry of its success there was also woven the skill and devotion and

the monumental diligence of its headmaster, the rare and mysterious inter-
twining of talented executive and understanding teacher, Brother Alcuin. He was
not a man of great learning as was, say, Boethius or Seville's omniscient Isidore.
His stock of knowledge issued from some forty books, which he had pondered
meticulously from end to end, and most of which, following the custom of his
time, he had memorized. Grammar was his academic favorite, and in it he strove
to excel not only because of the challenge of its art and science, but more
especially to enlist its service in the improvement of the prevailing Latin style. In
his own case, sad to say, the grammarian swallowed the stylist—at least in his
professional handiwork. Only in his letters do we catch a fleet and wandering
glimpse of the man himself, a grave man, it is true, but a man also of repose and
tenderness, and if not of laughter, then at least of an incipient smile.

But it was in teaching that Alcuin was supreme. Up at dawn, he wrote down
the questions and answers which later in the day he would dictate to his charges,
and which in time they would be expected to know by heart. Sometimes he
engaged his apprentices in discourse, not, however, in the sly manner of the
ancient Socrates to waken some dormant thought, but simply to take account of
what was deposited in their vaults of memory. Some pupils, he soon found out,
were swift of mind, and some were slow, while the bulk ranged in between.
Whatever they were, he met each according to his own capacity, softening a bit
here and pressing somewhat there, now with honey, now with vinegar—a practice
currently approved by psychological science, but for many hundreds of years to
be dismissed by the masters of pedagogy as a plain absurdity. Though Alcuin was
immune to mirth, at least in his general practice, now and then he permitted
himself a strategic jest. The glib he trapped into false answers with spurious
questions, and the cocky he put to endless panting on problems that were
unsolvable. If, as is sometimes said, teaching is an art, a gift, as it were, from the
angels, then Alcuin was richly favored. He loved the feel of the classroom, the
daily jousting with his flock, and long after its members had passed for the last
time from his presence he still retained them in his thoughts. On occasion he
wrote them, inquiring about their recent doings, praising them for this, reproach-
ing them for that, but bidding them always to honor knowledge, to help man,
and to love God.

No sooner had the Palace School been transformed into a live and going
concern than Charlemagne bethought himself of the state of learning throughout
his realm. In 787, in a directive to the men of God, he commended them for the
prayers they were sending aloft in his behalf; but he also let it be known that he
had noticed all too often that their language was uncouth and their tongues
unlettered. This displeased and distressed him no little, for among his clerics he
could bear no ignorance. To remedy matters, let them have a change of heart—in
short, let the holy men bestir themselves "to advance the cause of learning which
has been almost forgotten. . . . " To such a goal Charlemagne extended a generous hand, even, indeed, going so far as to summon learned monks from abroad,
especially from Italy, and assigning them to his principal abbeys to give instruction in arithmetic and grammar. Other directives presently followed, one in 789,

which bade the clergy to establish schools in every monastery and cathedral, and another two years later, which urged every freeman to put his son to school "until he should become well instructed in learning."

The harvest of all this exhortation was depressingly lean. For once not even the iron will of a Charlemagne sufficed, so far was the land gone in ignorance. But if the general yield fell short of the sovereign's expectation, it did not play him completely false. One cleric, at least, gave the monarch ear. Theodulf by name, he was bishop of Orleans and, like the King, full of friendly words for learning. By the adept use of his ecclesiastical power, Theodulf undertook to bring about the establishment of a school in every parish, thereby not only bowing to his master's wishes, but distinguishing himself at the same time in the annals of learning as the first to make an attempt toward the establishment of universal schooling.

4

It is easy to overestimate the intellectual accomplishments of the reign of Charles—to call it, as some have done, a renaissance. The truth is that its attainments were meager. The light which it let in was frail—indeed, the fierce brilliance of the Arabic learning, as we shall see, reduced it by comparison to a pale and unsatisfying candlelight. The period produced no writers of gay and lovely words, whether in poetry or in prose. Alcuin, for all his sensitivity to the teaching art, is full of the clichés of his craft. Theodulf the bishop took flight in verse, but time has been sufficiently gentle to transfer it to a well-earned oblivion.

In Charlemagne's rule of almost half a hundred years, only one literary name stands out, that of Eginhard. Prepared in the cloister of Fulda, he preferred to efface himself, a bit deceptively to be sure, as "a barbarian very little versed in the Roman tongue." In the court he was omnipresent, as industrious as an ant, an energetic little man, forever toting books, parleying with Alcuin or even with the King himself. He soon eased his way into the royal confidence, serving in the advancing years as steward to the Crown, its treasurer, the supervisor and, not unlikely, in certain instances the designer of some of its more audacious architectural enterprises. Despite his self-disparagement—or maybe because of it—Eginhard was able to ensnare the royal heart, and he became not only the King's servant, but his friend and counselor as well, and more important, as time proceeded, his biographer. The memorable moments in the monarch's life the intrepid Eginhard set down much in the manner of the classical Suetonius in his *Lives of the Caesars*—sometimes, indeed, he even allowed himself the liberty of burgling Suetonius's very phrases. How much of Eginhard's account is truth and how much is fancy is hard to say—nor is it a matter of the utmost importance. For beneath its obvious gilding and glossing, its trifles, and its chitchat, there resides the spectacle of a great king and a great reign, much of whose lively charm would have been lost to us without Eginhard to record it.

Meanwhile, there remains the extraordinary Alcuin. After fourteen years his palace service came to an end when his master, in recognition of its excellence, elevated him to the abbacy of St. Martin of Tours. Eight more years on earth were granted Alcuin, and these he passed as in the early manner, a bit less strenuously perhaps, but no less eagerly, in the furtherance of knowledge, virtue, and piety. He still yielded some of his time to teaching, but the interest which captivated his heart lay in the enclosure of the copy room. There, amidst his scrivening friars, he spent endless hours, directing their writing, reading copy to them, correcting, explaining, exhorting—all to the end that the world might have better and lovelier books. Out of this immense concentration of industry there emerged a new mode of handwriting, the so-called Carolingian miniscule, its letters rounded and delicately joined, its small and capital letters differentiated, its words discreetly separated, a book hand neater and more readable than man had ever known, and the blood ancestor of our contemporary script.

Under Alcuin's benign and tireless care the monastery of Tours attained a high renown, and through the contagion of his inspiration and the influence of some of his former students, a few other places presently fevered with the same high mission. Viewed in the long perspective of history, their achievement in the sphere of letters, slight though it was comparatively, may well have been the nearest Charlemagne got to the fulfillment of his hope for a vast upsurge of learning. When the Emperor passed from these scenes in 814, he had at least the contentment of knowing that the most active centers of learning were no longer in Britain and Italy, but in his own widespread domain, at Tours, Orleans, and St. Denis in France, at Fulda beyond the Rhine, and at Sankt Gallen in the shadow of the Alps.

5

Inevitably Charlemagne's achievements bring to mind those of another, Alfred the Great, King of the Anglo-Saxons. He ascended the throne in 871, a tender prince, barely over the frontier of twenty, at a time when his people were reeling under the fury of the invading Viking. Between the English King and his Frankish counterpart there is a marked resemblance—often, indeed, fate seems to have cast them in similar roles. Champions both of Christ, they worked throughout their lives, now by force of arms, now by the eloquence of words, to subdue His heathen foes. Both men possessed high gifts as warriors, statesmen, and students. Both consolidated and extended their dominions; both rebuilt towns and cities; both improved the law and reformed the administration of its justice; both took legal steps to give aid and protection to the poor; and both strove by precept and personal practice to awaken learning from the fearful sleep of ignorance.

Though his life was bedeviled by frequent war and the never-ending perplexities of welding a diverse and factious people into the substance of a powerful unity, Alfred was a sickly man—probably an epileptic—a man inclined to the pursuits of peace, and by temperament a scholar. In his boyhood the churches prospered. They thronged, he tells us, with worshipers, and they were laden with treasures and books. But by his early manhood they lay everywhere in ruin, the charred and battered relic of the marauding Norsemen. So low had learning sunk among the English that very few of their clergy could understand the Latin in which they sang the mass, or render even a simple letter from Latin into the everyday speech.

To repair this damage, Alfred followed more or less in the track of his Frankish predecessor—some of his ideas, no doubt, had sprouted originally in the soil across the Channel. Thus, like Charlemagne, he founded a palace school, fetching teachers from abroad to proffer the gift of knowledge not only to the courtly in his residence, but beyond the palace walls, to the sons of the upper laymen to fit them for the burden of executing a wise and efficient governance. Alfred got his grip on reading somewhat late in life, but he was able to vanquish the mystery of putting words on paper. He thus succeeded where the great Charles had failed, and his scholarship accordingly must be graded a notch or so higher. His respect and admiration for his native tongue accepted no limits. In fact, in a day when the Continent's men of learning tilted their noses in high disdain of the vernacular, Alfred not only resorted to its vigorous idiom in his common affairs, but even ventured to employ it as an instrument for scholarly communication. On the upper intellectual level the man's accomplishments remain enormously impressive. By his translation from Latin into Anglo-Saxon of a variety of treatises, philosophical, theological, and geographic, and especially of Bede's *Ecclesiastical History of England*, he became, in a manner of speaking, the father of English letters; and by ordering the maintenance of an account of the important day-by-day occurrences of his reign—the so-called *Anglo-Saxon Chronicle*, the King sponsored the compilation of the first written historical record known to us in English.

Fortune, which had granted Charlemagne and Alfred so many triumphs, was not at their side in education, a constant and ever-ready helpmate. The one ruled almost fifty years, the other thirty. Yet the pall which blanketed learning was far too thick and too engulfing to be lifted within a single lifetime. Great and opulent though their talents undoubtedly were, neither monarch was able to bring to learning more than a faint pallor of its ancient luster. Yet even this little represented at least a hope. It marked the end of the night, and though it failed to catch a glimpse of the sun rising in all its blazing promise, at least it bore witness to a faintly discernible thinning of the enveloping darkness. With Alfred and Charles the Dark Ages, so-called, reach the beginning of their end.

6

In spite of his genius in putting together his empire and sustaining it for almost half a century, Charlemagne failed to build enduringly. After death took him off, his domain disintegrated, and the rule and order he had brought to his people began to drift away. Invasion and strife wracked his land, while turmoil and dilapidation mounted, and everywhere the sword became the arbiter of dispute. Out of this sorrowful mess there evolved what came to be known as "feudalism," a system whereby peasants, workers, and ordinary folk aligned themselves with a neighboring nobleman, seeking the security of his protection in exchange for some of their labor, a share of whatever it produced, and when they were called upon, which was frequent, their military service.

It is not necessary here to negotiate feudalism's long and baffling labyrinth; for its twists and turns are uncountable, and they vary without end from place to place and from age to age. Established on military grounds, feudalism made war its central concern. Fighting was its rule, peace its exception. Its main values ring with a martial clang—strength, endurance, valor, glory—and to these and related ones it directed the training of the young. Feudalism's salient figure was the knight, a riding armored fortress, so to say, who executed his main business while in the saddle. Coming into being in the tenth century, organized knighthood, or to give it its more elegant name, chivalry, attained its peak in the thirteenth century, but in another hundred years or so, gunpowder and cannon were blowing it up.

To be received into the fraternity of knighthood, a youth's blood had to run blue as well as red. In addition, he had to submit to a long term of training, as long almost as that consumed currently by an American who makes his way into the Bachelor's cap and gown. His pedagogical inauguration came at seven or eight when, as a page, he was inducted into service in a castle. Most of his learning hours he spent with the lady of the manor, which is to say the lord's wife, who grounded him in the elementary axioms and theorems of his craft. She watched over his faith and morals. She kept a searching eye on his manners, instructing him in the fine points of decorum and courtesy, and the sinuous ways and byways of palace etiquette. She quickened his sense of gallantry and honor. She taught him to play chess, to make music, to sing of love and war, and in general to make himself an attractive and desirable ornament in the courtly circle.

His intellectual fare, by contrast, was light, a mere mouthful, as it were: a little reading and writing, and in rare and unusual instances a bit of Latin. On the other hand, unlike any other learner of those times of earnest Christian conscience, he was made mindful of his body, and to build and fortify it became a sort of vocational obligation. And so, as of old among the pagans, he was made to run and jump, to box and wrestle and ride and swim. He perfected himself in fencing and archery, and he hawked and hunted. When, at length somewhere around the age of eleven or twelve he was judged of sufficient bulk and stamina, he was initiated in the rudiments of combat.

Meanwhile, the lord had not forgotten his page. Under his tutelage the lad was guided into the meaning of service, both its philosophy and its practice, but mostly the latter. He executed his master's elementary errands, bearing his messages, tending him at table, making his bed, and in a general way ameliorating and gratifying his personal comfort.

At the turn of fourteen the page became a squire. He still tendered service to his lady, but his duties now shifted more and more toward his lord. He was his valet and bodyguard, ministering to his every want in peace and combat. At night he extracted him from his clothes and helped him into bed, and on the morrow he reversed the process. He stuck to his master's side always and everywhere, at table, in battle, in travel, in the hunt, and in the sickroom. He looked after his noble boss's wardrobe and his arsenal of military hardware. And he waited on his master's favorite horse, cleaning and rubbing and slicking him, as befits a lordly nag. Betweenwhiles, he busied himself in the tiltyard. This was, in a sense, his laboratory. Here in simulated combat, he applied himself to the mastery of his battle tools, until the day came, single and unforgettable when he unhorsed his first antagonist, and thereby met triumphantly the test of strength and skill and courage, the supreme test of all his training.

His palette was not always grave—sometimes it was even gay. After the shadows fell and work had gone to rest, he gladdened himself occasionally in social flittering, gaming and frolicking, and best of all, making himself charming to the ladies. Once over the border of twenty, he singled out a lady love. She might be older than he and wed, and perhaps not even comely. No matter—to her he pledged his everlasting service and devotion even though later he walked another to the altar.

At twenty-one, which, as life spanned in those unsanitary days, put the squire into his middle years, he was ready to be knighted—that is, if he had the means. It was an event of great ceremonial awe. Prefaced by a bath, it was followed by fasting, prayer, self-examination, confession, and communion. The investiture itself was consummated in a cathedral in the presence of the high and mighty, both lay and ecclesiastic. Here at God's sacred altar the candidate vowed to be ever truthful, to defend Mother Church, to help the poor and weak, and to rain calamity on all heretics and infidels. To his lord he pledged unstinting feudal loyalty; to women eternal protection; and to his comrade knights mutual courtesy and assistance. Thereupon a priest blessed his sword, and knights and ladies arrayed him in his armor, piece by piece, down to his golden spurs. Finally, his lord, tapping him thrice with the flat of his sword, and summoning God, St. Michael, and St. George as witnesses, dubbed him knight.

Thus, in brief, the chivalric ideal. But let us not be duped by its cosmetic. The Galahads and Lancelots and all the others over whom romanticists have made so much fuss, existed only in the bubble land of fancy, and the actual run of knights were generally of a grosser sort. The Church, it is true, tried to hold them to their vows. She forbade tournaments, and she ventured repeatedly to pacify the more pugnacious amongst them by getting them to lay down their arms for at least a transient peace. But for all her power and influence here below and above, she had but moderate success, and the knights continued in the main to be a rough and brawling lot. Yet, though Holy Church failed to tame them, she at least put them under some regulation and restraint, and in this respect civilization doubtless was the gainer.

In education chivalry was not without significance. Intellectually, it was, of course, anemic. On the other hand, its stress on the physical, on health and strength, and on the polite arts and social graces outlasted chivalry itself. In the long run these things were to make their way into the education of the nobility and the gentry, and thence, in newer and richer incarnation, into the prep and finishing schools of the high-toned where, as everyone knows, they are still cherished today.

LIGHT FROM ISLAM

While the Christian West was snoozing in its intellectual half-light, in the Near East things were somewhat better. There, under the benign attitude of the Eastern Church, ancient Greek continued to be read and even translated into a variety of tongues, especially Syriac. There the dye of Greek thought ran deep—so deep, in truth, that it tinged the intellectual activity of the foremost groves of Christian sapience, as witness Antioch, Ephesus, and Alexandria. From their lecture halls it seeped into Christian theological speculation, and before long it was even tinting the views of Nestorius, the patriarch of Constantinople, a man of no slight consequence and a ponderable following. His fall from theological impeccability so affrighted his more conservative associates in divine science that in 431, the church, abandoning her free and easy forebearance, put the teachings of the heretical patriarch under ban. Rather than surrender their Hellenized Christianity, Nestorius and his fellow believers took to their heels, fleeing to Syrian cities beyond the reach of the ecclesiastical arm. There they continued to carry on their forbidden traffic in Greek science and philosophy. For this purpose they founded schools, some of them of a rather high luster; they made translations and they wrote commentaries; and in general, more than all Western Europe's men of learning put together, they contributed to the conservation of the ancient learning.

It was with this learning and with that of Babylonia and Egypt that the Moslems collided as they came out of their Arabian haunts to storm down upon the Mediterranean's east, thence westward through northern Africa toward the Atlantic seaboard, and eventually across Gibraltar's narrow strait into Spain and France, where in 732 at Tours, Charles Martel, King of the Franks and the father of Charlemagne, put the brake on their phenomenal rampage.

We know very little of them before the arrival of their prophet, Mohammed. They were of Semitic blood, a roving people, untamed, poor, living off the country, with a hungry eye for plunder, as is natural among such folk. Of education, save only in its crudest form, they were innocent—indeed, even their prophet appears to have been only vaguely familiar with reading and writing. It is true they were given to making gorgeous verse, but they rendered it orally, and they imprisoned it not on paper but in their heads; so it was even with their sacred book, the Koran, which for generations had passed from the old to the young by word of mouth before it was finally preserved on paper.

If the early Arabs wasted in ignorance, their descendants, after Mohammed, were quick to let in some light. As they rubbed shoulders with civilization they took delight in its amenities; at the same time they made it their business to become literate, and as the years advanced, some of them obtained a rather high degree of erudition. The ancient Greeks and the even more ancient Hindus and Persians became their masters, and as they pondered the works of their mentors, the mission gradually devolved upon the Moslems not only to absorb and maintain much of the old learning, but also to enlarge and enrich it with achievements of their own, and when the time was ripe, to tender it to the lagging West.

Though he himself was but sparsely tutored, in the confidence and encouragement he gave to the pursuit of knowledge, Mohammed was indomitable. It should thus be no cause for wonder that the faithful took a high pride in their zeal for learning. A generation, in fact, had hardly lapsed since their seer's passing when the first important school showed itself in 653 in the city of Medina. Two and a half centuries more, and this event had multiplied itself many times over, and throughout Moslem's far-flung realm pretty nearly every city possessed a school of one sort or another. Wherever a mosque made its appearance, there instruction in at least the rudiments would almost invariably sprout, and to it, from the fifth year on, every boy and girl was expected to submit. Executed by a tutor, such schooling was not free, but the fees which were exacted were usually small—so small as to be comparative trifles. But where, for all their slightness, they might still cause hardship, they were not insisted upon.

The accent in learning, as was then the common rule, was on religion. What makes a first-rate Moslem and how to grow up to be one—such was the overwhelming concern of education. For this purpose the young were introduced to good Arabic, both in reading and in writing. At the same time they exercised their spirit, learning, for example, Allah's ninety-five most lovely names. Gradually they worked their way into the Koran, studying its innumerable mandates, copying its simpler verses, and filing formidable passages of it in their memory. The study of numbers was put off for later years, but of the common children not many managed to break through its mystery. When, for all that, it came to pass, then nearly always they were boys, and their occupation with it was suffused, once more, with a religious undertone, namely, to enable them someday to calculate their inheritance by the rules laid down in the Koran.

2

For those disposed to climb somewhat higher on the ladder of learning, some of the more important mosques offered a sumptuous fare, including algebra, logic, biology, law, theology, some history, and the usual generous portions of grammar. As time moved on, it became the practice for men of money to establish schools not only for the young of their own exalted class, but also to give enlightenment to the more promising offspring of those lower down on the social scale.

Like the Christians, the Moslems put a high premium on theology, and for those seeking to master its propositions the larger mosques usually reserved special and advanced instruction. At a date long since buried in anonymity, some of these seminaries were put under governmental hand. At the same time, their monetary lot was eased with a small subvention and with gratuities from social-minded and well-to-do philanthropists. Thus enriched in goods and dignity, they became Islam's first purveyors of the higher learning, its madrasahs, or colleges. Needless to say, they soon widened the scope of their academic operation, offering instruction without the charge of a single penny not only in the aforesaid divine science, but in mathematics, astronomy, and logic as well, and in the Arabic tongue in all its luxuriant odds and ends, from its philology and rhetoric to its grammar and literature, in both prose and poesy. As time closed in, such intellectual shrines were to be found all over the Moslem world, in Baghdad, Mecca, Damascus, Cairo—even, indeed, in its far-off Spanish reaches, in Cordova, Seville, Granada, and Toledo. Scholars tracked to them from all directions not to embellish themselves with a degree, for of such gauds there then were none, but rather to obtain the prized endorsement of some scholar of surpassing excellence. Under the circumstances learning did a lively trade. Everywhere in Islam it was vastly admired, and by the year 900 those engaged in its transactions, whether as students or as professors, enjoyed an agreeable public approbation.

3

Hand in hand with the vigorous thrust for knowledge went the making and gathering of books. From the Far East the Moslems had picked up the knack of making paper which, because it was cheaper than parchment, propagated a brisk demand. The first paper plant to greet customers made its appearance in Baghdad toward the end of the eighth century. The availability of paper in cheap and steady supply was a powerful stimulus to the book trade, and pretty soon the larger municipalities were teeming with book vendors. By 900, in fact, Baghdad was being served by more than a hundred of them. Nearly all the mosques prided themselves on their libraries, and it was not long before up-and-ready cities were accommodating readers with free libraries, some of which in the passage of time attained not only a remarkable bulk, but more important, a high and far-reaching reputation. Meanwhile, there were the usual private connoisseurs, men of wealth with collections so large it required several hundred head of camel to transport them—a prime camel then being able to carry a load of about 300 pounds. But whether public or private, libraries, as always, were the natural grazing grounds for men of learning. They swarmed to them from everywhere, logicians, rhetoricians, and grammarians, intimates of natural and divine science, even poets and writers, all panting to know, bending over their scripts, memorizing here, copying there, all in the hope of giving birth some day to yet another book.

4

The Moslems were prodigious borrowers of knowledge, but this does not mean that they were empty of imagination, or that they merely borrowed. They got their geometry from the Greeks and Hindus, and from the latter their algebra. But they gave algebra an exactness it had never known before, and what they gleaned from trigonometry they refined and extended in both its plane and its spherical sectors. They applied their knowledge in divers ways: they mapped the land, they charted the seas, they plotted the sky. The so-called arabic numbers they imported from the Hindus. Immensely superior to the ungainly Roman variety, they not only edged these out of everyday use, but they themselves never left the scene, and they continue to render us meritorious service to this moment. Almost single-handed the Moslems transformed chemistry into something of an experimental science. Out of their labs emanated an amazing procession of discoveries, from potassium, silver nitrate, and corrosive sublimate to a variety of acids and alkalis, and yet much more. They analyzed alcohol and gave it its name, though they were under prohibition to savor it. Chemistry's cousin, pharmacy, they enriched with syrups, juleps, elixirs, analgesics, and embrocations, dozens of oils, love potions, and a herd of other boons to the human race. Meanwhile they continued to exert themselves diligently in alchemy, searching for the mysterious philosopher's stone by which they aspired to transmute such commoners of the metal world as iron or lead into the peerage of gold and silver.

And so they labored in other sciences, borrowing, enlarging, and putting them to work to suit their need and taste. Did Christians dream of becoming angels? Then Moslems relied instead on the service of a professional medico. Their doctors were probably the best to be had. Their knowledge of anatomy and physiology, it is true, had serious limitations, for their faith forbade them to dissect animals, whether higher or lower, and so their progress in surgery suffered. But in certain other respects they knew no betters. They were the familiars of hygiene, and they recommended frequent bathing, at times in water, but often in steam. They stilled the agony of an operation with anesthetics, and they tranquilized the suffering with sedatives. The world's first pharmaceutical school was their invention. Their dispensaries and hospitals were numerous, and so were their drugstores. While Christendom was levying its ban on the practice of medicine, Islam busied itself with the founding of medical colleges, mainly in hospitals. All doctors were subject to state examination, and to engage in practice they had to be licensed, and so did barbers and druggists. Even in those days medical bills ran high, but then as now, doctors inclined to good works, treating the poor without fees, and even extending their gratuitous service to the residents of jails and madhouses.

The Moslems ranked high not only in science and learning, but in many other things as well. In the world of letters they were of an infinite industry, especially in poetry, and their works of fancy, often voluptuous, were sometimes truly beautiful. Masters of the song of love, they were the ancestors of the minne-singers and troubadours who, in later years, were to warble their amorous tunes all over Europe. Their feeling for beauty the Mohammedans implanted in their handicrafts, fashioning a myriad of objects of rare and tender delicacy. Their glassware and pottery were often masterpieces, and so was the hand tooling of their leather. Finally, in music they caught a glimpse of theoretical acoustics, and they introduced themselves to the measured length of strings, and even the pale beginning of harmony. They gave us the lute, the mandolin, and the drum, and for extra measure they added the conductor's baton.

The roll of Moslem learning glistens with illustrious names: Al-Birini in geography, Jabir in chemistry, Haitham in optics. Al-Razi, known to us as Rhazes, was the greatest doctor of the Middle Ages, and the foremost clinician of the era. Finally, there was Al-Husein ibn Sina, or as Europe preferred to call him, Avicenna, Islam's supreme philosopher, its outstanding writer on medicine, and the author of one of the few autobiographies to come down from the Arabic past.

Avicenna's life was a curious compound of triumph and disaster. Schooled in the liberal arts, he made the acquaintance of medical science without any special instruction. The greenness of youth was still upon him when he cured the Sultan of Bokhara. His rise thereupon was swift, and in time he was rewarded with a public office. But his fall was even faster. He was plummented out of favor, his home plundered and wrecked, and a price put upon his head. While in hiding, he launched himself as a writer. Snared by his foes and thrown into the lockup, he nevertheless continued his literary excursion. Presently the winds of hazard reversed themselves. He escaped, and after a hurricane of adventures, some real and some imaginary, he made his way to the Emir of Isfahan where, in the company of scientists and philosophers, he was able at last to bring his chaotic odyssey to a tranquil halt.

Thus, at any rate, it says in Avicenna's self-story. More important, no doubt, is the fact that, for all his troubles, he was able somehow to maintain his literary industry. When he departed this world at the age of fifty-seven, he had composed a trunkful of essays besides two colossal major works, *The Book of Healing*, an eighteen-volume encyclopedia on the arts and sciences, and the *Canon of Medicine*, wherein he incarcerated more than a million words. A systematizer of the first order, he was full of the schoolmaster's proclivity for classification and definition, a quality which was to endear him to Europe's medieval schoolmen, and which later fetched him the title Father of Scholasticism. In addition, however, he was dowered with a lucid and graceful utterance which helped to spare him from the clutch of pedantry. His *Canon*, heavily bethumbed for centuries, was translated into Latin and presently became the leading text in Europe's medical schools—indeed, as late as the seventeenth century it was still required reading for nascent healers at both Louvain and Montpellier.

Avicenna's reputation as a medico was rivaled only by his fame as a philosopher. As a young fellow he had worked his way into Aristotle, particularly the *Metaphysics,* which, he confessed, he read from end to end more than thirty times before it made sense, an experience which is reported to have befallen others. To the end of his time he venerated the ancient Stagirite—The Philosopher he called him, a term which among the men of learning of the Middle Ages was to become synonymous with Aristotle. His own philosophy, however, was flavored with a dash of Plato. He held, for example, that general ideas existed before things (*ante res*) in the mind of the Omnipotent. The idea of man, to illustrate, was present in God's mind before man. Next, when God brought forth man, the divine idea took shape and existence in the thing (*in rebus*), which is to say, in man. Finally, as man observed the likenesses common to all men, he himself arrived at the abstract generalization, or in Platonic lingo, the idea after the thing (*post res*).

Like many of his fellow Moslem thinkers, Avicenna believed that philosophy could be made to support religious revelation; but he also felt that the glare of reason should be made to penetrate even such matters as are generally accepted on faith alone. As a result, a number of his views flew in the face of orthodox teaching. With Aristotle, for example, he held for the eternity of the world, that is, a world without beginning and without end, and thus he scoffed at the notion of its special creation by God. Prayer, he gave notice, availed us naught, for the Heavenly Father did not bother himself with man's personal affairs—a contention which later on was given support by Voltaire and other Deists. Finally, to make sure he would have no friends at all among the faithful, and particularly among their ordained ambassadors of God, he dismissed the idea of personal immortality as pious piffle, a wishful dream, as it were, ungrounded in the slightest shred of reason.

5

The cream of Moslem civilization, as might be expected, lay in the cities. Damascus, the first upon the scene, was gray with years even before its occupation by the Arabs. It abounded, like all ancient cities, in clamor and stench and urban busyness. Pitched on a spot where five streams merge, it was blessed with a handy access to the sea, and so it rose swiftly as a center of commerce and trade, and in consequence, of wealth and culture.

Larger and richer, and more important intellectually, was Baghdad. It was founded in 760, but slightly more than two hundred years later some 800,000 inhabitants were cluttered within its limits, and in the number of its people the city stood second only to Constantinople. It too lay hard by the sea, and its trade and industry harvested a staggering fortune. Its public services, for its time, bordered on the miraculous. Its main streets were paved and regularly swept, they were policed, and after dusk they were lighted. The city enjoyed an ever-flowing supply of fresh water which was conducted in large conduits to its public squares and into some of its houses. In consequence, its fountains and lovely gardens flourished, and so did its public baths, which were more numerous, indeed, than even its mosques of which they were several hundred.

Early in its history, under the deft hand of its Caliph Haroun-al-Rashid, Baghdad began to attract a far-flung notice for its energetic cultural enterprise. The place thronged with schools and libraries and learned associations. Its House of Wisdom, to cite only a single example, became the intellectual wonder of its days, and scholars streamed to it from everywhere. Founded in 830 at a cost of almost a million dollars, it was of a princely spaciousness, serving its clients as both a university and a research center. Its library ranked among the finest, and its scientific equipment and observatory knew no superior. Besides instructing students in its various arcana which ranged from rhetoric and logic to theology, medicine, and surgery, the House of Wisdom employed a staff of professional translators and even paid them handsomely out of the public purse.

To support their city folks the Moslems developed an expert agronomy. First-class farmers, they husbanded their land with care and ingenuity. Whatever the nature of the soil, they tailored their crops to its demands, stimulating growth with fertilizers and irrigation. They waged successful war against insect pests and plant disease. They were connoisseurs of cattle and horseflesh, and they were not unfamiliar with some of the mysterious requirements which underlay the improvement of their stock. Europe they introduced to the culture of rice, buckwheat, and sugar, and a whole store of table delicacies from pomegranates, strawberries, and cherries to oranges, lemons, and bananas. They enhanced our gastronomic happiness with spinach, asparagus, and artichokes. They raised cotton and hemp, and to keep their silkworms contented they grew mulberries. They even cultivated the grape, and though the faithful were forbidden to drink its fermented juices, they made money, nevertheless, by hawking them to men whose consciences were less powerful than their thirsts.

6

Wherever the Moslems settled they carried their culture. They bore it to Sicily and, more significant, to Spain where, after the hemorrhage of their wars had finally ceased, they fashioned the most fair and civilized land then to be encountered in the Western world. Admittedly, their emirs and caliphs were often cynical and cruel, but they were probably no worse than their Christian counterparts, and their despotism was tempered often enough with magnanimity and benovelence. Taking one with another, they possessed a knack for governance, and on the whole, they ruled with a wise and competent hand. The laws they issued were reasonable in the main, and their execution was generally just and efficacious. In local affairs they granted the vanquished Spaniard a free and generous rein even in the making of the ordinances which governed him and in the selecting of his officials. There was a high religious tolerance, and until the twelfth century, when Moslem liberalism succumbed to an obscurant conservatism, Jews and Christians enjoyed a considerable privilege. A good many, indeed, were so impressed by the agreeable enlightenment of their conquerors that presently they turned their back on their paternal faith for the glories and promises of the Moslem God. But the coin had its tawdry side. Were Christians courteously treated and fairly free? Then their organized church was not. Many a Christian shrine went up in smoke to the Moslem torch, and the erection of new ones was under stringent interdict. Moslem rulers reserved the right to appoint Christian bishops, and not infrequently their choice fell to the highest cash bidder. As for the church's common cleric, he was regarded with contempt. The victim not uncommonly of public mockery and affront, he had no recourse to law.

As in the Middle East, the Moslems in Spain took a great interest in learning. All their salient cities—Granada, Toledo, Seville, and especially Cordova—palpitated with activity in the pursuit of the arts and sciences. Seville flourished in music, Cordova in the amassment of books, and all of them sustained schools. Elementary ones were all about, and as in Araby both girls and boys frequented their classrooms. Colleges bedizened the larger towns, and in Cordova the highest learning bloomed luxuriantly. Sprawled over the whole town much in the manner of some of its current American urban successors, it was bound rather loosely together, and it ran its sessions in the city's leading mosques. As a result, the place arrayed itself with scholarly men, from philologists and lexicographers to the usual host of rhetoricians, grammarians, metaphysicians, jurists, and theologians. Some of them were of a capital brilliance—collectively, indeed, they knew a great deal more than their Christian equivalent. They were superior mathematicians; they excelled in the physician's art, especially in their grasp of the pathology of the eye; they were on friendly terms with biology, a science which in the rest of Europe had sunk into nothingness; and they had a fuller and stronger grip on geography, then still regarded as something of an intruder in the halls of learning. Above everything, however, they bristled with daring and fascinating speculations about man and his place in the universe.

7

The most outstanding intellect in their midst, and the one who cast the greatest spell on the medieval Christian mind, was Abu al-Walid Muhammed ibn Rushd, known to Europe simply as Averroës. Privy to law and medicine, he rose to the office of chief justice, first at Seville, then at Cordova, where his father and grandfather had served similarly before him. Later, as his prowess as a healer attracted a higher and higher esteem, he was summoned to the emir's court to act as its head house doctor. He was, in all certainty, one of the ablest performers of his time, the first to unravel the function of the retina, and the first to realize that an attack of smallpox, one of the deadliest of killers in those days, bestowed a subsequent immunity upon its sufferer. His views on medicine Averroës put together in an encyclopedia, which was given acclaim not only in the East, but even in the backward West, where for several centuries after the passing of its author it continued to be pondered by university students.

But it was in philosophy that Averroës made his deepest mark. Early in his life he had convinced himself that Aristotle was the greatest philosopher of all time—"the wisest of all the Greeks"—and that during the fifteen hundred years following his death no one had "been able to add anything to his writings" or even to find any error therein. Armed thus with ardor—somewhat disingenuous, to be sure, when weighed by current standards—Averroës attempted a thorough-going probe of the ancient sage, compiling as he went along an immense and authoritative treatise on his subject, so excellent that all through Europe its author came to be celebrated as The Commentator. Besides hatching this enormous output, Averoës managed somehow to find time to express himself on subjects of every imaginable kind, on logic, grammar, psychology, metaphysics, law, theology—even physics and astronomy. It was his opinion that philosophy and religion should coexist, that one should throw its light on the other, and to bring this about he worked with a bulldog tenacity. Alas for him, he had tasted too deeply the philter of skepticism. The world, he let it be known, has ever been, and it will ever be; creation is a myth; the Lord gives no heed to individuals; and life everlasting is utter nonsense. For all its disposition to be courteous, Moslem Spain couldn't put up with such delirium, and in 1194 it vanished the court physician from Cordova. He was pardoned some four years later and recalled, but in the same year he died.

Arabic learning in the East attained its high mark in the labors of Avicenna. For three centuries, from the eighth through the eleventh, it had risen steadily, overflowing in the course of time its original banks, and flooding northern Africa, Mediterranean Sicily, and even the Spanish outpost on the European mainland. But now, its exuberance spent and its daring stilled, it teetered on the brink of extinction. Harried and hampered by the orthodoxy of the theological brethren, who despised and feared it with the fullness of their fanatic hearts, it had never rested on the pillow of easy assurance. By the mid-eleventh century its hopes dimmed yet more when the Seljuk Turks overran much of the Near East. Only recently out of the wilderness of heathenry, they had accepted the Mohammedan revelation, but they were drawn to it not for its element of enlightened liberalism, but for its element of conservative dogmatism. Islam's learning, hence, came to an abrupt brake, and its leading representatives, wherever they could, took off for other parts. Many found sanctuary in Spain and the surrounding region where things were more tolerable, and where, for a while at least, they continued to work for enlightenment. On the heels of the Seljuks came the much more ferocious Mongols, lovers of uproar and utterly unfriendly to learning. Thereupon the promise of cultural progress in the East came to a harrowing halt: where the Seljuks had merely retarded it—vastly to be sure—the Mongols almost uprooted it.

8

While Islamic savants were enjoying the fruit of their Golden Age, their European comrades in learning were confining their activities to the narrows of the Seven Liberal Arts. They were not stupid men, of course, nor were they lacking in scholarly diligence. Some of them, as was observed a few pages back, were of a very high intellectual caliber, devoted and persevering. But unlike their fellow scholars to the east, they were nearly always clerics, and their scholarship, such as it was, had to subordinate itself to their Christian theological assumptions. The skeptical meditations which fevered among Moslem sages were anathema in the West. There the Age of Reason was still in the womb of time, and so was the Age of Science.

But curiosity lurked, nonetheless, and as tidings of Spain's new learning began to trickle beyond the Pyrenees, a few of the Continent's more enlightened men yielded to its temptation. The first Christian to venture into the land of the Moslem heresy and to study there, as may be recalled, was Gerbert, a strange, almost incongruous amalgam of skeptic and believer, who was later enthroned as Pope Sylvester II.

After him came others, and by the tenth century, Latin translations of Arabic writings made their advent. Another hundred years, and Constantine, a resident in Italy, put out a Latin version of a Hebrew-Arabic monograph on fevers. His effort was followed in the twelfth century by the translations of Adelard, an Englishman from Bath. After putting in some years in Spain and Sicily, Adelard produced Latin renderings on arithmetic wherein he amazed and delighted Europe's specialists in the third *R* with the revelation of Arabic numbers. In addition, he came out with a popular compilation of Moslem science, in which there are discernible signs of his contamination as a Christian thinker. "Nothing," he announced, "is surer than reason," for which, he added, "authority is a halter." After Adelard came Robert of Chester. Something of a man of parts, he fused his interests in science and in religion by writing Latin works on alchemy and algebra, and by making a translation of the Koran, the first glimpse of the Prophet's sacred lucubration to be available to Latin Christian eyes. The most industrious translator of them all, however, was Gerard of Cremona. Active in the twelfth century, he is credited with the translation of some ninety-odd Greek and Arabic treatises, including the *Almagest* by Ptolemy and the almost endless *Canon of Medicine* by Avicenna.

For the most part, Europe's men of learning were scornful of Moslem science. They adopted its system of numbers, to be sure, and they succumbed to the meretricious lure of its alchemy. But beyond that their interest was negligible; often, indeed, it was actively hostile. What they desired in the main was to stock and refurbish the hazy and hollow spaces in their own texts of the earlier classical writers—materials, in sum, which would repair and improve the faulty content which comprised the Seven Liberal Arts. Their primary need centered in the recapturing of Aristotle whose gigantic cargo, lost to Christendom because of the embargo put upon pagan authors by the Church fathers, had strayed from Greek into Syriac, thence into Arabic and Castilian, to compete the circle of its wandering with its translation into Latin. In the restoration of Aristotle to a place of importance in the West, the Easterners, and especially Averroës, were enormously useful. The brightest minds in Europe sang his praise, and some of them, notably Albertus Magnus and Thomas Aquinas, show visible signs of his thinking. Though their works and those of others would have been consummated, maybe, without his cerebration, with it their task was made immeasurably less difficult.

CHAPTER 7

FAITH AND REASON

T he early Christians, as has been said, were generally common folk unburdened by schooling who embraced their new beliefs with a childlike simpleness. Later, as Christianity reached into higher ranks to convert the educated, its evangelists, seeking an instrument to penetrate their skeptical reserve, injected a measure of sophistication into their homely message. Time and experience brought the new teachings a certain crude coherence; still, their underlying mystification remained, and so did their inconsistencies and contradictions. For more than a thousand years Holy Church had no great reason to reduce her propositions to order and harmony, and to put them under the light of reason. Did doubts arise to torment a perplexed mind? Then to put them down the fiats of popes and councils sufficed. Did they, in stubborn cases, linger just the same? Then, as per the Augustinian formula, let the doubter yield to faith, for it transcends reason—in short, let him believe or let him be damned.

So things hung more or less until the twelfth century when a combination of circumstances induced Mother Church to take a fresh look at her ancient teachings. For one thing, the European scene reposed in a moment of relative quiet. The devastations from the north had ceased, and so had those of the Moslems. The Germans, once the terror of the mainland, had submitted to Jesus, and had eased themselves into domestic tranquility. Under the Church's might even the bellicose nobility was holding itself in some slight check. Meanwhile, Moslem learning had begun trickling into Europe, on the one hand from the Greek academies in the East, and on the other from its Arabic settlements in Sicily and Spain. The New Thought moved slowly, it is true; even so, it was full of subversive possibilities. For to men of an inquiring mind it represented a mint of fascinating ideas—ideas which were not found in Christian writing and which oftentimes stood in provocative challenge to doctrines held dear by the Holy Catholic Church.

To lay this wave of intellectual and religious menace the Church turned to her nimblest minds, her philosophers and theologians, her logicians, and even her politicians. Their task was to restate and fortify Catholic faith and doctrine, to cement it with a degree of order and consistency, and where possible, to reconcile its unshatterable sureties with the newer ways of thinking. To this end, logic was an indispensable instrument. In the academic cloister, where so long it had played second fiddle to grammar and rhetoric, it now leaped to the fore, the most important subject of its time, saving only that congeries of subjects, theology.

Logic's conspicuous authority, of course, was Aristotle. At one time Holy Church had held his teachings under suspicious eye, and twice at least she had put them under formal ban. But they were dipped into, nevertheless, along with the works of his leading partisans, Averroës and Avicenna. With the tide for Aristotle towing so strongly, the Church, true to her perennial prudence, undertook in the thirteenth century to direct the making of an official Latin version of the ancient pagan's works, but to take care, at the same time, that they be "purged of all suspicion of error." Thus the corpse, so to say, got up and made merry. Rendered respectable, Aristotle rose not only to eminence, but to high medieval authority, a sort of associate in the Holy Trinity, from which he was not to be dislodged for another several centuries.

The Church's effort to organize and systematize her sacred teachings, and to embroider their fabric with the strands of reason, came to be known as Scholasticism. Come into being in the twelfth century, it rose to its apogee during the hundred years following, whereupon, apparently done in, it slid downward rapidly. Its practitioners were nearly always academicians who, true to their timeworn manner, were quick to bog themselves in a wallow of words. From their contentions issued two warring metaphysical parties, one the Realists, the other the Nominalists. The Realists, led by Anselm of Canterbury, were something of a Platonic second coming, holding with the ancient Athenian that ideas alone constitute real existence. The senses, they went on, are deceptive, revealed truth alone being reliable, and reason and experience permissible only to give it support and strength. The Nominalists, for their part, took their cue from Aristotle. With Roscellinus, a canon of Compiègne, and their principal advocate, they insisted that reality consists of individual, concrete things, that ideas, or concepts, are but names we bestow on the generality of things, and that the truth thereof is ascertainable only through investigation and reason. Roscellinus's bold innovation of applying reason to the nebulous region of revelation, as might be expected, got him into hot water with his ecclesiastical superiors, to whom his views seemed next door to atheism. And so, for all its kinship to Aristotle, the Nominalist cargo was dumped overboard, and its sponsor made to recant. Even then, the hapless man was stoned almost to death, and had to flee for England.

2

The controversy over the relationship between reason and faith mustered some of the world's most supple minds. There is no occasion here to rehearse them all—suffice it to confine ourselves to their most prominent exemplars. Towering over them all was Thomas Aquinas. But there was also his archrival, the Venerable John Duns, a Scotsman; more important, his teacher, Albertus Magnus; and before him, Peter Abelard.

Of noble stock, Abelard came to life in Brittany, near Nantes, in 1079, and he died sixty-three years later in the Priory of St. Marcel, near Châlons. He has come down to us as a man of numerous and remarkable gifts. He was handsome, audacious, brilliant; yet he was also vain and cocky, a disturbing and turbulent man, philosopher, poet, and teacher, whose adherents ran into the thousands, but whose enemies were legion. Of a strong and restless mind, he was still in his teens when he made for Paris to equip himself in logic and metaphysics in the school of Notre Dame. His rise there was swift—so swift that by and by he was bedeviling his teacher, correcting the poor man's blunders, real and imaginary, and making a public mock of him, a brashness which rejoiced Abelard's mates, but which certainly failed to endear him to his professor. Fresh out of Notre Dame, the youth set himself up as a schoolmaster in the outskirts of Paris beyond its noise and stink. There, in his sleek, insinuating manner, he continued to take potshots at his former prof, scoffing at his lack of competence, stealing his students, and promising someday to usurp even his job, a prediction which before long he fulfilled.

Soon Abelard became the idol of the Latin Quarter. No teacher before him, and not many after him, have addressed themselves to so many students in so short a time. They thronged to his classes in massive packs, peers and com-moners, in velvet and in rags, from many lands, and from all directions. They stopped him in the corridors; they halted him in the streets; wherever he turned, there students crowded. All the qualities that put spirit in the young gathered within this man. A scholar of vast knowledge, he talked to his audience in the gusty language of youth; at the same time he would have no paltering with ignorance. In an age of faith his was the bright light of reason; in a world shackled to authority, he was a skeptic, mild and gingerly to be sure, but a skeptic nevertheless. Yet despite his stupendous learning, he was at bottom something of a showman, a pleaser of crowds without a doubt, but still an artist of infinite industry, who delighted in molding the substance of his thought with the lure of beauty, and giving it the embellishment even of joy and laughter. A specialist in logic, philosophy, and theology, he was a dead shot in debate, clamoring an interminable defiance to his brother schoolmen, and challenging them, like an eager child, for a chance to bring them down in public disputation. His students spoke of him admiringly as the Wizard, the Giant, the Dragon, and even the Rhinoceros Indomitable. Most of his academic horde, as it must ever be, passed from his eyes into forgotten anonymity. But a few climbed the heights. Some turned into writers, some into scholars, and not a few ascended in statecraft—one, indeed, was Eleanor of Aquitaine, the queen of France. A score at least rose to the cardinal's robe and hat, and more than fifty were boosted into bishoprics.

For all his huge acclaim, Abelard ran into considerable woe, professional and otherwise. Smitten in his nonage by the beautiful Eloïse, his pupil, he introduced her not only to philosophy, but to lovemaking as well. When she became pregnant, he married her in secret. But when the truth leaked out, he was seized and castrated by the hired hoodlums of the girl's uncle. His wild and cyclonic onslaughts on his academic brethren brought him inevitably into scandal and disrepute. His intellectual waspishness repulsed many of his contemporaries, and acquired for him the powerful rancor of a number of archbishops, and in time, even Pope Innocent II, from whose decree of excommunication he was spared only by the help of Peter the Venerable, the very wise abbot of Cluny. His last years he eked out in the friar's frock, a tired, disenchanted man, seeking what repose remained in the quiet lanes and gardens of his abbey.

Like most professors, Abelard was a writer of books. But his output was restrained: a work on the Holy Trinity, an informal one on the comparative qualities of Judaism and Christianity, another on *The History of My Misfortunes*, a sad and tear-stained self-accounting, and one which has been food for poets ever since. His most famous composition was the *Sic et Non* (*Yes and No*), a textbook for ascending theologians. Put together in the manner of the canon lawbooks, it raised such questions as "Is God one or three?" "Is Adam buried in Calvary?" and "Is it worse to sin openly than secretly?" Crafty teacher that he was, Abelard listed the arguments for and against each proposition, but furnished no gratuitous final answers; their formulation he left to the thinking of his students, a practice which, because of the possibility of their arriving at heretical conclusions, shocked many of his contemporaries, and for which he was roundly denounced. Peter Lombard, his pupil, took no such chances. His book *The Sentences* Lombard modeled on the *Sic et Non,* but for every query he propounded, he was careful to supply the one true and orthodox response. As a result, the volume raised itself above suspicion, and for two hundred years running it thrived, the standard and required textbook for every novice in divine science.

Metaphysically, Abelard was neither Realist nor Nominalist, but what he styled as a Conceptualist. As such, he declared against the Realist contention that ideas have objective existence, and against the Nominalist view that ideas are merely names. Instead, he insisted that ideas, or concepts, represent the sum total of qualities common to a number of objects. Though to one of a non-philosophic mind, all this may seem as so much twaddle, in Abelard's time the academic circle was heavily buffeted by just such wind. As a matter of fact, as year succeeded year Abelard's Conceptualism gathered force and momentum, and by the thirteenth century it underlay the thinking of some of the world's most powerful intellects, notably Albertus Magnus and Thomas Aquinas.

Not all Abelard's thinking inspired such respect. His view, for example, that reason must precede faith was assailed as academic bolshevism, and it fetched him reprimands from right-thinking churchmen everywhere. The notion ran through his *Sic et Non,* of course, and it flowed through most of his thinking. Yet for all its skeptical boldness, it maintained itself always within the harbor of his surrounding culture. He believed in divine revelation and in the Good Book without reservation, and from cover to cover. There is no doubt, however, about the weight of his influence on Paris. The power of his fine teaching made Notre Dame the magnet of philosophical Europe. When presently the cathedral school burst its ancient seams to become the first university in France, the credit and the honor in large share must go to Peter Abelard.

3

Not so scintillating as a teacher, but a scholar of insistent diligence and no little incandescence was Albertus Magnus. He too was of noble lineage, and like Abelard, he was educated in the best schools available in the thirteenth century. While still in youth, he took the friar's oaths, joining the Dominicans, a brotherhood which then stood out for its high interest in learning. Talented in pedagogy, he was presently assigned to classroom service in the order's various German strongholds, and eventually in Paris. Convinced—almost fanatically—that Aristotle was the world's greatest authority in science and philosophy, he made it his business not only to examine all Aristotle's available works, but in addition, to square their ideas with Christian thought. To this purpose he plowed through the bulk of Aristotle and all his important commentators, especially the Moslems, Averroës and Avicenna, and on occasion the Jewish Maimonides. The task consumed the better part of his seventy-nine years, and is today stored in twenty-one formidable volumes. Meanwhile, Albertus advanced in worldly reward and responsibility. He was made provincial of his order for Germany, and in 1260 he was elevated to bishop of Ratisbon. But he continued to study and write as vigorously as ever; indeed, in the history of learning he remains almost singular—an administrator whose scholarship remained undimmed even under the pressure of executive duty.

The first Scholastic to come to such passionate grips with The Philosopher, Albertus is also the first and, in all likelihood, the only scholar to pass down the ages honored permanently, like some rare and exalted monarch, as "the Great." It was Albert's monumental labor that made Aristotle the kingpin of the later Middle Ages; and from the great reservoir of his accumulation of pagan, Hebrew, Moslem, and Christian thinking issued the clear and penetrating system put forth later by his famous pupil. Without the great Albert's hard preliminary toil, Thomas Aquinas would have found his enterprise infinitely more difficult.

Though, like all Scholastics, he specialized in fathoming the divine will, Albertus stands apart from most of them for his attachment to science. He was, to be sure, in thrall to the book science of Aristotle, and he endorsed most of his dogmas, even when they were nonsensical; yet within him smoldered a curiosity about the world of nature, with all its mysterious challenge, which made him, when he could spare the time, a ravenous observer. He betook himself deep into the earth into mines to study the various metals; he gathered the flora of Germany; he studied the shells of the sea. "The origin of our knowledge," he confessed—somewhat riskily—"is in sense. . . . " Inevitably, in the end he compiled a treatise on the qualities of plants which, for all its lacks when viewed through current eyes, is marked with unmistakable traces of the scientific spirit. And yet, within the same man there huddled much of the credulity of his time. He believed in the possibilities of magic, astrology, and divination. He was awed by dreams, not in the racy Freudian sense, but as instruments of prophecy. And in his *Praise of the Blessed Virgin Mary* he permitted himself to remark, humorlessly, that in her grasp of the Seven Liberal Arts, from grammar to logic to astronomy, she was perfect.

4

The greatest of all Scholastics was Thomas Aquinas. Now a saint, he was born, like Abelard and Albertus, of the nobility. He was, even in youth, a pious and studious lad, and like his teacher, the great Albert—albeit against his parents' wishes—he took the Dominican vows. Following in his master's footsteps as a cherisher of Aristotle, he presently overtook him in the knowledge of the ancient philosopher, and wherever he taught, whether at Paris or Cologne or Rome, he drew an ever-widening crowd of students. For the task of fitting Greek thought, which is to say Aristotle, into Christian theology he was superbly equipped. He knew no Greek, it is true, but he had read its leading writers, besides those of the Jews and Moslems, in Latin translation. Versed in all the Seven Liberal Arts, he had few betters in scholastic disputation. When the Franciscans pressed him into the combustible controversy over the possibility of reconciling faith and reason, Aquinas overran their arguments, one by one, gently, astutely, completely.

Few men have written so much, and fewer still have written more. His output flowed like the wind. His most important work, the *Summa Theologica*, though unfinished, resides in a mansion of twenty-one volumes. In its totality his published writing stands in 10,000 double-columned folio pages, and in magnitude it equals that of Albert, though Thomas inhabited the earth only half as long. He surveyed the whole intellectual dominion: logic, metaphysics, psychology, ethics, politics, religion, and of course, theology. His performance in prose, unhappily, is more learned than sparkling, and reading him, despite the vigor of his ideas, is not particularly cheerful. But this is not saying that he was void of literary grace. When the mood lay on him to compose hymns and prayers, for example, he could fashion poetry of the most exquisite delicacy. Indeed, a small portion of it—*O Salutaris Hostia*—is still sung at the benediction of the Sacrament.

With all his extraordinary qualities, Aquinas was a self-effacing man, high-minded and gentle, save in matters of principle, when he could be of granite. It was inevitable that so unusual a figure should catch the papal eye. In 1274 Gregory X called upon him to attend the Council of Lyons. Simultaneously he proffered Aquinas an archbishopric which he declined. Soon afterward he took to his bed in a Cistercian monastery in Italy where, though he was not yet fifty, he succumbed.

In his *Summa contra Gentiles*, Aquinas set apart faith and reason in two separate intellectual domains. In reason the mind may exercise freely with whatever data it brings to hand, but in faith its operations are hedged within the limits set by divine revelation. Between these two spheres there may be an interchange of data. The evidence of the senses may be marshaled to support revelation; but in the absence of such testimony, or where it chances to be at odds with revelation, what has been divinely revealed must, nevertheless, be accepted as an objective fact. Some articles of faith—in illustration, such cardinal ones as the Holy Trinity, redemption, the Last Judgment—cannot be proved by reason. In such instances man must put aside his finite speculations and count on faith alone. In its way faith is knowledge—it is, indeed, a higher kind of knowledge than reason, for it grounds itself on revelation. Though faith may have the support of reason, in the last analysis its definition and interpretation must be the business of authority, and in the matter of the truth eternal regarding faith and morals, the sole repository of authority is the Holy Roman Catholic Church.

Not all Scholastics followed Aquinas in his attempt to synthesize Greek thinking and Christian theology. His most powerful rival was a Franciscan, John Duns by name, a Scotsman, more usually known to us as Duns Scotus. A man of great brains, Duns gagged at the marriage of faith and reason, and during the better part of his short sojourn on earth—he died at forty-two—he labored his utmost to annul it. One may, he argued, prove the existence of Almighty God by reason, but beyond that the mind runs into a dead end, and the rest of the Christian journey must be made over the path of faith alone. As the Dominicans threw their collective weight behind their Brother Thomas, so the Franciscans rushed to the aid of their comrade John. There ensued a long and dinful metaphysical combat wherein both adversaries generated much heat, but in which neither took the trouble to look its assumptions in the face. Noah existed for them all, and so did the ark with all its tourists from the elephant to the flea, male and female. Like all such hubbub, the dispute abounded in indecorum and animosity. It was Scholasticism at its worst, a laborious logic-chopping which served, as the years proceeded, to sicken the schoolman's vogue, and finally to bring it to its grave. Duns, himself an expert in such vaporings, earned the not too enviable title of "Doctor Subtilis." His followers, who took the same quibbling tactic, and in its employment outdid even their leader, became known as "Dunsmen," a name which later was to stroll into everyday speech, where it has since obtained the meaning of "dunce."

Although Aquinas had opposition, there was, at bottom, no successful resistance to his reasoning. It served apparently to satisfy the needs of the faithful, both high and low, as it still suffices today for a countless multitude. More important, perhaps, it brought a measure of reconciliation to Christian theology and Greek thought—the latter purged and antisepticized, to be sure, of its pagan festerings. Thereby Aquinas's reasoning not only made Greek thought tolerable to men of culture; it also arrested the raids of skeptical freebooters. Once reason had a foot inside the door, it was unwilling to stand interminably by. As the years spun on, the senses and the reason began to polarize new doubts; in fact, in the long run not content to remain mere upholders of the sempiternal certitudes of revelation, they insisted on examining them, so to say, under the glass, and where they were found wanting, not to accept them for all that, but even to cast them out. Thus the Age of Faith slowly glided into memory. Its main contentions were disrupted, as we shall see, by the Renaissance and by the Age of Reason, and again after them by the Age of Science. Though it lingers, and its devotees are actually more numerous than even in its salad days and more widespread over this planet than ever, its intellectual hegemony, once also solitary, has nonetheless declined.

This is not saying, of course, that the work of Thomas Aquinas, like that of so many other Scholastics, hangs on today as but the shrunken remains of an outworn past. Time has done its relentless work, no doubt; but its touch on the whole has been mild and not unkind. Honors and titles have piled on Aquinas from every quarter. He was hailed in his own day as the Leader of the Scholastics, and posterity has made him the Angelic Doctor and even the Seraphic Doctor. His earthly remains are venerated in numerous shrines. His right arm, for example, has been preserved as a sacred relic in the Eglise de St. Jacques at Paris, and other parts of him are similarly revered at Naples and Rome. In 1323 he was canonized, thereby attaining recognition not only for his own saintly merit, but also for the Dominicans, the order he had so assiduously served. At the Council of Trent in the sixteenth century his *Summa Theologica* was placed on God's holy altar along with the Decretals and the Bible. In the same century, in 1567, his festal day was marked for tributes and honors which heretofore had been reserved solely for Ambrose, Jerome, Augustine, and Gregory, the four illustrious Latin fathers. And, finally, in 1879 Pope Leo XIII ordained that Aquinas's teachings, though not necessarily without error, be accepted as authoritative by all Catholic theologians. They thus became Mother Church's official philosophy. They are taught at all Roman Catholic colleges, and they underlie, of course, all current Catholic education, as will be noted in later pages.

5

Not all the intellectual power of the day made its way into philosophy and formal logic. Some of it, indeed, showed itself much more tenderly in the pursuit not of the word, but of the elusive beauty and benignity it conveyed. As early as Abelard there was manifest, for example, at the schools of Orleans, Laon, and Chartres a Humanistic rather than a philosophic approach to Christian verity. Led by the illustrious John of Salisbury, a practicing don at Chartres, these Humanists devoted themselves to perfecting the art of cultivating beautiful Latin in both its prose and its poetry. Their star was not Aristotle but Plato, with light now and then from Augustine. Suffused with a mystic strain, they looked askance at mere logic, and like the Quakers of a later time, they sought to bring themselves to God not over the highroad of the intellect, but rather over that of the heart. Most of them regarded the Scholastic endeavor as a waste of time. Unluckily, in their concentration on the literary classics they made more enemies than friends. But in their modest way they were a portent, pallid perhaps, but a portent nevertheless, of the flaming sunburst which someday was to break upon the world in the great classical revival of the Renaissance.

Did the Middle Ages perceive the flutterings of an incipient Humanism? Then they were also witness to stirrings in the natural sciences. They were not so powerful or so abundant as in the world of Moslem learning, and they never broke loose from their moorings in religion. Nearly always, in fact, the promoters of science were of the sacred cloth. Hence, their industry, like that of the metaphysicians and theologians, was overborne by Christian doctrine, and not uncommonly it directed itself to the solution of some pious problem, say, the exact whereabouts of Paradise, the cubic measurement of the ark, or the depth and temperature and public relationships of Hell. Even so, behind this effort, so solemn and so curiously immaterialistic, there lay the beckoning of human curiosity, and though its glimpse of truth was only hazy, in the annals of knowledge it has come down to us as the first frail step of Christendom toward what later was to emerge more resolutely as the Age of Science.

The first one of any prominence to apply his mind to scientific matters was Robert Grosseteste, an Englishman. He served God as a Franciscan, and so ably did he work for Him that in his later years he was made bishop of Lincoln. Still in his early teens when he took his degree in divinity, he remained in professional scholarship for the bulk of his more than eighty years. Like most men of his craft in those remote days, he was at ease in any number of occupations. He not only labored as a theologian; he was also a lawyer, a doctor, and a scientist. He busied himself with social reform; and he made eloquent assaults on the practice of evil, particularly in high places, whether sacred or secular.

But it was in teaching that he performed to his best effect. He began practice at Oxford, his alma mater, then but newly sprung up, but by the end of the thirteenth century without a peer in England and as an intellectual oasis second only to Paris. There he promoted the cause of Greek and especially its great adornment, Aristotle. But he also gave a hand to the study of Hebrew—with a view, albeit, of bringing the Jew repentent on his knees to Christ. His study of science, though festooned with the usual bows to Aristotle, led him nonetheless into some observations of his own and thence to the conviction that for the advancement of knowledge experimentation is desirable. Adept at physics, particularly in its domain of optics, he was familiar with the mystery of the magnifying lens. He was at home in mathematics, enjoying it with more than ordinary delight, and holding that not only is a knowledge of it essential, but without it there can be no science. For all his weighty erudition, he was well regarded as a teacher—so well that his classes bulged with students, not, to be sure, in the manner of the vast, wholesale assemblies that gave ear to Abelard, but large enough at all events to bring about his ascension to what current Americans might well designate as the presidency of Oxford.

6

Grosseteste nurtured several excellent minds, but the best of them, and certainly the most renowned, was Roger Bacon. Like his professor, Bacon was a Franciscan, and again like his sponsor, he was animated by a powerful affinity for knowledge. But he was also a restless, striving nature, scattering his academic attendance over a wide space, now at Oxford, now at Paris, now somewhere in Italy. He was within easy reach of forty when his scholastic wandering came to an end, and he returned to the motherland to settle into lecturing at Oxford. There for fifteen years he performed the familiar professorial tasks, from reading and ruminating to teaching and writing, whereupon, his health apparently done in, he withdrew from his labors and for the following decade evaporated into obscurity.

Bacon's scholarly output was not so large as that of Albertus Magnus or Aquinas, but its prose danced with an easy grace—sometimes it even raised itself to eloquence. His chief convictions are interred in three books, the *Opus Maius,* or *Larger Work*, the *Opus Minus*, or *Smaller Work*, and the *Opus Tertium*, a general summary. They concerned themselves, as any full and vigorous scholarly work was then supposed to, with the totality of knowledge, from A to Z, including discourses on nature, inventions, optics, the causes of error, faith and reason, the necessity of moral science, and yet much more. Bacon's scholarly fancy, he confessed, ran to mathematics, the sciences, and the languages. He hired Jews to teach him Hebrew and to steer him through the Old Testament; he knew Greek well enough to compile a lexicon; and he had at least a bowing acquaintance with Arabic.

For the professional metaphysician, so highly touted by his contemporaries, he showed no awe. The controversy between Realists and Nominalists he dismissed with a wave of the hand. "A universal," he vouchsafed, "is nothing but the similarity of several individuals," and "one individual has more reality than all individuals put together." Nor was he taken in by the logicians' knack of twisting meaning to suit their purpose. He was equally disdainful of his contemporaries in philosophy. Their writings, he complained, were a mass of sentimental reasoning, and were grounded on weak and faltering assumptions. Aquinas's grave examination of the habits, powers, and intellect of angels moved Bacon to a polite cough. Not even Aristotle escaped the riddle of his fire. That fellow's books, he let it be known, he would cause to be reduced to ashes, so empty were they of value—a pronouncement which doubtless must be taken with a pinch of salt, but which by the fourteenth century, when the Renaissance came to flower, was to be given a grave acceptance.

The road to knowledge, declared this castigating friar, is not logic or metaphysics, but mathematics and experiment. Like his later namesake, the celebrated Francis Bacon, Roger called for the careful observation of particulars wherefrom we may arrive at our generalizations—in other words, what today's parlance calls the inductive process. Like Francis again, the earlier Bacon exhorted men of money to donate freely from their hoard to render assistance to learning for the purchase of books and instruments, the establishment of laboratories, the maintenance of records, and the employment of competent personnel.

Despite his eloquence on behalf of experimentation, his own industry therein was slight. Perhaps he was preoccupied with his literary compositions, or perhaps he was too busy formulating the principles which underlie science's quest for truth. Whatever it was, when he left this vale in 1294 at almost eighty he had to his laboratory credit only a handful of ventures into optics, most of which, he freely conceded, were little more than an elaboration of work done by others. Though Bacon permitted himself to scoff at some of the methods of the saintly Thomas, this is not to say that he himself was without his own preconceptions. Did he argue against the "ineffable falsity" of Scholastic premises? And did he cast doubt on the prevailing reliance on authority? Then let it not be forgotten that he also believed that the one perfect wisdom resides in Holy Writ, and that he was ever careful not to disclaim "that solid and sure authority which . . . has been bestowed on the Church." The science for which he pleaded so earnestly was often no more than an effort to nail down Scriptural assertions, to promote Biblical geography, to correct sacred chronology, and always, in the end, to battle the Antichrist.

Bacon, no doubt, has suffered from fortune's strange and inscrutable caprice. Born into an age when the spirit of the times ran heavily against him, he was veiled for a long time in mystery. The derogatory shafts which he directed at the morals of high prominenti brought him into disfavor. For this untowardness, it was believed that for a time he was stored in jail, but the testimony is slight and inconclusive. It was also the general view that he transacted with the dark and mysterious powers of the air, that, in fact, he threw a bridge over the English Channel, and after crossing it, caused it to vanish—but again the corroborative evidence is not at hand. Subsequently, in a era more friendly toward the experimental pursuit of knowledge, Bacon's star began to shine, and he was credited, erroneously, with scientific attainments which clearly were not his. The zeal is understandable, but surely it is superfluous. To foreshadow, as he did, an intellectual movement which, as the years unfolded, was destined to change the world—certainly, this should be a sufficient accomplishment for any mortal man.

7

Bacon's doctrine that the rich should grant aid and encouragement to the pursuit of knowledge fell for the most part on barren soil. In truth, a few more centuries were to turn before its germ was to give any visible sign of life. Meanwhile, far beyond the ramparts of Oxford, in Sicily, in the palace of Frederick II, the Holy Roman Emperor, there flourished a strange and almost miraculous exception. A child of the Age of Faith, Frederick was also of a sharply skeptical mind—his enemies, in fact, credited him with atheistic leanings. A crusader in the Holy Land, he was, nonetheless, feared and hated by the popes, and when his political ambitions settled in their vested Italian domain, they sought to unhorse him with their most corrosive anathemas, and for most of his adult years they badgered him with war, and even excommunication.

Frederick was the richest monarch in Europe, and he was also the best-educated. He could parley in half a dozen tongues, and hold his own in three more at least. The *Stupor Mundi* he was called—the Wonder of the World. Animated with a belief in the potency of the arts and sciences, the emperor encircled himself with scholars, artists, and literary figures, Jews, Christians, Moslems, from every quadrant of the compass. His coterie of court philosophers and astrologers was drawn from diverse lands, one from Scotland, for example, another from Pisa, and a third from the East. Their composite investigations took then into every imaginable field. They wrote treatises on meteorology, zoology, and the volcanoes of the Lipari Islands. They compounded prescriptions for the imperial court. They discoursed on mathematics, on hygiene, on the care of dogs. They studied the flora and fauna, and to give them tangible aid, *Stupor Mundi* provided them with gardens and a zoo, peopled with rare and exotic birds and beasts. Employed mostly to satisfy the curiosity of learning, they occasionally took to the road with the Emperor, thereby spreading pleasure and edification among Germans and Italians.

All this tremendous endeavor was not only sponsored but dominated by the Emperor. He himself exchanged thoughts with the world's most eminent minds on religious, philosophical, and scientific matters. He was also something of a poet, hatching verses in Italian, his favorite language. With Bacon he shared a kindred belief in experimentation. To ascertain whether the soul departed before the body, he is reported to have caused a man to be sealed in a cask until he was dead. To determine whether a child's first language might be Hebrew, or even Latin, Greek, or Arabic, he had several youngsters reared in complete silence. And to study the effects of fatigue on the human body, he ordered that a couple of tired men be disemboweled. But these are probably the inventions of fabulists; in any event, save for their touch of irony, they produced precisely nothing.

More solid was Frederick's own study of hawks. His book *On the Art of Hunting with Falcons* issued from a long and assiduous searching. Flouting Aristotle, "who," declared the emperor, "never hunted with birds," it sprang from Frederick's personal observation and experience. Time, of course, has wrinkled some of its information, but when the fire of youth blazed within its eye, it was beyond compare, the first penetrating study in its field. By an odd stroke of fate, a copy of it may still be seen in all its charm and beauty in the very citadel of its author's former foes, in the great library of the popes in the Vatican.

To encourage learning among the young, as well as to give some ponderable permanence to the imperial passion for new knowledge, Frederick founded the

University of Naples in 1224. He manned his faculty with the outstanding scholars of his time, and he paid them the highest wages. He established scholarships for the poor, and he ordered that the youth of his realm might attend no rival seat of learning. The first medieval university to be chartered out of the secular hand and without the papal sanction, Naples is inscribed in the annals of learning as Europe's first state university.

8

That scholars of the thirteenth century, with their thirst for summaries, should have entranced themselves with the making of encyclopedias is surely no reason for wonder. There still circulated, of course, that perennial grab bag of learning, the *Etymologies and Origins,* filled by Isidore of Seville some six hundred years earlier, but continuing, nevertheless, to make its rounds in the more distinguished houses of learning. Yet its progress in life was coming to its end—the advent of the Moslem enlightenment and the new glamor of Aristotle had made it all but inescapable. As early as the twelfth century competitors had arisen to challenge its monopoly—Hugo of St. Victor, for example, and Bernard Sylvester and Hildegard of Bingen. But these were folk of tender sentiment, poets and mystics who let their hearts lead their heads, and for the earnest searcher after knowledge their works, which were conceived in a misty allegory, were almost devoid of sustenance. Other surveys presently ensued—*The Origin of Things*, put together by a couple of Englishmen and a Frenchman, and Bartholomew of England's *On the Property of Things*, a smaller study but broader in scope and not unpleasantly garrulous. By middle century Brunetto Latini, a Florentine living in France, put out his *Treasure of Books*, and for the first time Isidore's primacy was in danger. It was a modest survey of history, government, science, and morality, but it carried the advantage of being up to date. In fact, more than half a thousand years later, and half a hundred after the publication of Diderot's and D'Alembert's historically unforgettable *Grande Encyclopédie*, Napoleon was still sufficiently attached to Latini's work to ponder ordering its reincarnation in the French language.

What finally played out Isidore's time-tattered *Etymologies* was the *Speculum.* Compiled by Vincent of Beauvais and a small squadron of writers and editors, it essayed to gather excerpts from some four to five hundred Greek, Latin, and Arabic authors, an editorial practice still regarded favorably by publishers and college professors everywhere. The idea was to cull the material from the library of Louis IX so as to make its enormous content fit for His Majesty's all too human assimilative capacity. The *Speculum* was a tremendous wave of forty stout volumes, and when it rolled over Isidore, he was ready at last for the grave. Three parts, one on nature, a second on doctrine, and a third on history, composed its essence, but it extended to pretty nearly every other department of life, from its manifestations in art, music, commerce, and industry to agriculture and government, besides a well-stocked store of odds and ends. A fourth part on virtue appeared after Vincent's promotion to his post-mortem reward, but its content was largely kidnapped from the pages of Thomas's more substantial *Summa.*

Although Vincent protested that he "did not know a single science," and that much of his knowledge of the universe came forth "from the light of specula-tion," in the eyes of his readers, this did not dim his qualifications as an encyclopedist. In his labor of twoscore tomes, the wonders of science and theology coalesce, as do those of magic and superstition. Needless to say, the work soared like an atomic flash to a high pinnacle of favor. Among books of knowledge it became the established standard. Though the more energetic and sophisticated pursuit of knowledge and science in later centuries outmoded much of its eminence, no other encyclopedia conceived on such a spectacularly majestic scale appeared until the eighteenth century.

9

Thus the thirteenth of the centuries. Its hundred years project the high mark of the Middle Ages. Faith still sounded the pervasive chord, and a blissful celestial eternity was still man's supreme and overwhelming aspiration. But from the Greek and Arabic East had come the bewitching murmur of reason. To establish its relationship to faith and to effect some sort of working concordat between the two became the mission of the Christian Scholastics. They were, said Carlyle reproachfully, so many intellectual dervishes. The phrase is more apt, perhaps, than meets the eye. For, in a manner of speaking, dervishes they were. Even the cleverest of them worked almost fanatically to the end of advancing knowledge not a whit. They compiled it, and they pigeonholed it in a mass of neverending compendiums, summas, and encyclopedias. They defined, they classified, they corroborated—but always their conclusions were the same as their beginnings. In short, despite their furious cerebral bustle, they got exactly nowhere.

All the same, let it not be forgotten that their activity was powerfully intellectual. The problems which consumed them were the great and con-spicuous ones of their own day, the problems which began and ended in God whose will was unchallengeable. Tethered at all times to the teaching and authority of Mother Church, the schoolmen were not free to graze in un-orthodox pastures, so alluring but forbidden. They took a high pride in matters of the mind, and their foremost representatives were, beyond a doubt, a tremendous stimulus to learning. Without them, indeed, there might have been no bridge between antiquity and modern times. In Scholasticism itself, however, lurked the very causes of its downfall. Preposterously bookish and wordy, it sought its truths in the hocus pocus of formal, deductive logic, bound to the delusion that its premises, as long as they issued from authority, need be neither plausible nor even impartial. Already within its own times it was confronted by critics—Humanists, for example, like John of Salisbury, who shrugged off the whole Scholastic business as a waste of time, and more important, the new scientists who sought the key to knowledge in the senses. So preeminent was the Scholastic vogue in its heyday that the fact is easily overlooked that the age which produced an Albertus and an Aquinas also bred a Bacon and a Frederick II.

CHAPTER 8

SECULAR STIRRINGS

The great spiritual event of the Age of Faith, and very likely its gaudiest and most glamorous, was the effort to wrest the Holy Land from the infidel Moslem. Overrun by the Arabs in the seventh century, this hallowed spot continued to remain open to Christian pilgrimage for another four hundred years, and then it fell to the Seljuk Turks. These people, far more ferocious than their predecessors, not only barred their domain to Christian access but, planting themselves astride Constantinople, threw a hungry shadow over the whole of Eastern Christendom. To make an end of this appalling business, Pope Urban II exhorted all Christians, high and low, to put aside their internal strifes, and in a vast and devastating operation to fall upon "the unclean nations . . . irreverently polluting" the Holy Land, and to seize it "from that wicked breed, and subject it to yourselves." Thus in the year 1095 was hatched the First Crusade.

It is not necessary to rehearse the many details of these pilgrimages. Suffice it to observe that there were seven in all, one following the other through several generations, the final one coming to its end toward the close of the thirteenth century. In their first assault on the infidel the crusaders were successful, and Jerusalem fell to them in 1099, only to slip presently from their grip, and by 1244 to be irrevocably lost.

Though the crusaders fell short of their mission, they produced several results of deep and vital importance. Gone, for one, was the isolation which had blanketed Europe ever since the fall of Rome. Shaken too was the facile credulity in the words of those in high ecclesiastical office. They had portrayed the enemy as an intolerable savage whom the infinite justice of the Christian cause would quickly rout. Instead, the soldiers of the cross encountered a brave and gallant foe who, in moments of truce, showed himself as a decent and affable fellow, whose amenities of life were often immensely superior to anything ever heard of in Christendom. So surprised and enchanted, in fact, were some of the Westerners with Moslem life that they promptly put Christ out of their mind, submitted to circumcision, and yielded themselves to the Prophet for conversion.

Those returning home bubbled over, as wanderers commonly do, with tales of the new wonders, some true but many merely fanciful. But whether true or false, their accounts served to untap a stream of curiosity and expectation, and it was not long before a scattering of bold men began to turn their backs on their native roost to set out for strange and far-off places in China, India, and even Japan. The vast majority, of course, remained as before, fettered to their mean little shacks, waging their everlasting struggle for food and shelter. But this is not saying that they were entirely oblivious to the unfolding new world, and that when they stole an odd moment to hope, their thoughts drifted, as they once invariably had, to the glories that would await them beyond the Pearly Gates. Instead, more and more of them permitted their dreams to be caressed by the agreeable possibilities of life here on earth.

Many crusaders never came home again. Some, as has been made evident, settled in the East. Others fell victim to the interminable bloodletting among themselves, but many thousands more succumbed to a cruel climate and to pestilence ever lurking. Yet, as history progressed, their wholesale exit turned out to be a boon. A rough and tornadic lot, they had persistently throttled the consolidation of the rising royal power. Their removal from these scenes not only strengthened the sovereign hand, but by weakening feudalism, especially in England and France, it set the stage for the coming of the national state. Even greater and more sweeping than any of these developments, however, was the revival of trade and commerce, the concomitant rebirth of a vigorous town life, and the rise to power of a new estate of city people, composed of merchants and craftsmen and their retinue of brokers, insurers, and money lenders.

2

Medieval towns sprouted in various ways. Some, rooted in the ancient past, were the lineal descendants of once-flourishing Roman ancestors. Others arose and spread out of the activity which issued from the bishop's church or sometimes from a monastery. But a great many more had their beginning on the manor of a feudal lord. A wall-environed enclave, the town afforded a measure of defense to its residents and the neighboring country people against the raids of ravenous lords and against the enemy in time of war. Generally speaking, the early towns suffered from overcrowding, but circumstances worked to keep them small—in fact, before the year 1200 only London and Paris could count ten thousand head. Save for the marketplace there were few open spaces, no arenas and public baths as in Rome, and no gorgeous fountains and gardens as in Islam. Streets, such as they were, were badly kept, ambling aimlessly from end to end, as if lost. Houses were usually several-storied, some timbered or half-timbered, but the better ones were of stone and mortar, sturdy and thick-walled and often enough they were striking and beautiful. Filth was all about, and so was stench. Every nook offered its invitation as a public toilet, and every street as a catcher of the communal rubbish, from the rot and garbage of everyday to the slaughterer's castout. Death bore cruelly upon the townsmen, especially their children, of whom but a tiny handful could expect to escape an infant's grave.

Travel was onerous and a risk to limb and life, and so the earliest towns enjoyed little intercourse, whether social or economic. Like the manor from which so many had sprung, they were sufficient unto themselves, producing all they needed, saving only their farm products which were toted in from the adjacent countryside. Even though the burghers secured themselves behind their city walls and maintained themselves in industry rather than farming, they were scarcely more than underlings. They were levied upon regularly by the lord of the neighborhood, as their ancestors had been before them, as exactingly and unsparingly as ever. That they pined for a better life is no cause for wonder, but until conditions changed such evils had to be endured.

3

Change began to be manifest by the eleventh century with the multiplication of trade and with the townsman's desire to satisfy something more than his gross needs. The first medieval traders of whom we have any account were itinerant peddlers, trekking from bishop to abbot and from lord to commoner, hawking their wares for whatever they could snare. Their goods in the main were novelties fetched oftentimes from distant regions and not to be obtained locally, and so the trade they drove was commonly brisk. The more successful prodigies of commerce gradually settled down, buying and selling as their successors do today, though naturally on a less Olympian scale. Like them, they needed facilities for storage and transport, and like them again, they kept a watchful eye on business opportunities. To the older residents these newcomers appeared as a novel breed, amazing adventurers bobbing up from parts unknown and earning their keep not by their hands but by trade alone. To the veteran townsmen, and particularly to the petty craftsmen and tradesmen, the advent of these personages portended the dawn of a better day, for the more the latter augmented, the greater was the former's promise for self-improvement. Local industry thus came to stand on firmer legs, and where once it had merely crawled, it now began to move with a bold and resilient stride.

But before there could be such an advance in worldly rewards, some alterations had to be made in the burghers' semiservile condition. Their discontent runs through these years like a recurrent refrain, and not infrequently they rose against their overlords in insurrection. As the years increased, the practice obtained not only of granting the townsmen certain specified rights and privileges, but of guaranteeing them in a written charter, drawn up in lawyer's Latin, properly witnessed, signed, and sealed. Sometimes, where the lord chanced to be of more than everyday sagacity, he would bestow such rights and prerogatives of his own free will. In certain lands, especially in England, where the zeal for bargaining ran high, it was not unusual for an affluent town to buy its charter. But more commonly this treasured writ had to be wrung from its grantor by compulsion.

As townsmen succeeded in bringing their lords to terms, a host of unaccustomed problems plucked them by the sleeve. Somehow they had to master the essential ground rules of government. They had to protect their hard-won rights and franchises with walls and militia, and to this end they had to lay taxes for the commonweal. To safeguard their mutual interests, which were overborne often enough with a strong and recurrent economic note, some towns banded together as nations do today in alliances, for instance, the Lombard League of northern Italy, the Spanish League, and the largest and foremost union of them all, the Hanseatic League, composed in its heyday of some seventy German towns. For all this cordial handshaking, however, towns were given to a gusty rivalry not only in the affairs of commerce, but in those of civics as well. There were boosters and boomers then as now. Did town X, for example, ornament itself with a new city hall? Then Y, not to be outdone, must needs erect a bigger and better one. Even today there still remains a tinge of this provincialism, and one still hears men lauding their merits as Hamburgers or Frankfurters rather than merely as Germans.

To advance and protect their interests the town's merchants and artisans knitted themselves into associations, the one into a corporation of tradesmen, the other into one of a variety of craft guilds. The first such union of which we have any notice was founded as early as 1061 by the chandlers of Paris. It was not long, however, before pretty nearly every form of human industry was similarly organized, from tailors, pastry cooks, and chimney sweeps to cobblers, pewterers, and fishmongers—even, indeed, song writers. Guilds varied a great deal from place to place, but their existence was always grounded on the same objective, namely, to keep anyone outside the fold from the practice of a trade. Some guilds were large and rolled up a vast fortune. Their town hall, in just recognition of their place in society, was often a lavish and resplendent edifice, a laic shrine, so to say, erected to the majesty of mammon.

As guildsmen increased in riches, so naturally did their prestige and popularity. They hobnobbed with peers and prelates—often their rights and usufructs were under the guarantee of the King himself. As the years edged on, they shouldered their way into political potency. Sometimes they were elevated to high public office, and frequently they rendered counsel on important matters of state. In the mounting struggle between monarchs and their feudal satraps, they gave their support to the former, not without self-interest, of course, but in the hope of attaining a measure of governmental stability and thereby a greater prospering of trade and industry. Though they still devoutly hoped on some tomorrow to flutter celestial wings, nevertheless their material interests and especially their desire for an unhampered freedom of enterprise brought them increasingly into collision with trade and economic principles set down by Holy Church.

Some townsmen, and particularly those more adroit at making money, were cultivated people. They resided in sumptuous dwellings, and they encompassed themselves with things of charm and beauty. Not a few were literate, and they read and wrote not only Latin, but even the language of everyday. Indeed, for their enjoyment a vernacular literature was conjured into being, and the book business, once the monopoly of monks, transferred itself more and more into secular hands.

4

As usual when there is a powerful social change, the rise of the merchants and craftsmen in status and influence mirrored itself in education. Preeminently practical, the men of commerce had no appetite for the usual academic table d'hôte provided by the Seven Liberal Arts. What they wanted for their sons was a schooling which would serve them in their daily living, and particularly in the advancement of their business interests—in other words, the three Rs, some bookkeeping, a bit of law, perhaps even a slight dash of Latin, for the Roman lingo remained the favored instrument of international parlance, whether in trade or otherwise. To impart this knowledge some fathers made arrangements with a tutor. Sometimes a guild maintained such a service. As commonly happens, the more resourceful guild schools gradually enlarged and extended their industry, teaching not only the elements of business, but even the grammatical and rhetorical formulas of the older schools. Some of these seminaries were well regarded, and their reputation sometimes soared to snowy heights, as witness the Stationers School and the Mercers School, both of London, and the most talked-of of them all, the Merchant Taylors School, which is of the same town and still in active and successful practice.

In consonance with their high place in municipal affairs the merchants were able to pave the way for the first town schools. These came on the scene during the twelfth century, but for at least a couple of hundred years their increase was sluggish. Even so, inasmuch as they were laic establishments, they are the foreshadowing of the wisdom then still buried in the distant future.

They existed in two varieties, the one a Latin school, the other a reading and reckoning school. As might be expected, they were resorted to mainly by the heirs of the merchants and the well-to-do. Occasionally, the lower school would reserve a bench or two for the fair sex, but the much more common policy was to show the girls the door. As for the Latin school, we need only skirt its rim, for save that its fortunes rested usually in the keeping of a municipal council, and that its masters were of the laity, it differed only slightly from its historic ecclesiastical forerunners, the cathedral and monastic schools. On the other hand, the writing and arithmetic school offered its hospitality to something new. Concentrating on subjects of a higher practical worth, it introduced its young not only to their letters and numbers, but to a primitive accounting and to the arithmetic of business as well. Great value was put on the mastery of a fair and sightly hand, and many of its alumni turned their talents to earning their livelihood as professional scribes. They kept books, maintained records, and set down guild and municipal minutes, and not a few of them went into practice as free-lance scriveners for the horde of unlettered, whose correspondence they penned for a few coins.

The new schools, as has been hinted, came into their own but slowly. The local clergy, discommoded by the threat to their long-standing educational monopoly, belabored them with antagonism. But the townsmen, bursting with their newborn puissance, went above their august clerics, appealing oftentimes to the Pope himself, who usually in such disputes sided with the burghers. Thus, in a way, the holy father gave aid and comfort to an institution which, as human values grew more and more worldly, was to become a liege of the state, in most instances utterly bereft of churchly sway.

As the budding merchant was accorded his special training, so the future craftsman was tendered his. It was in the main a guild affair, subject to guild regulation and supervision, but differing from town to town and from guild to guild. Starting out as an apprentice, a lad was attached to a master who for a fee contracted not only to introduce him to the knacks and secrets of the craft, but in addition to keep him fed and lodged and decently clothed. The term of apprenticeship varied. Usually it ran for seven years. Sometimes, though, as in the simpler and homelier trades, two years sufficed. On the other hand, to promote oneself into a goldsmith required almost as much time as to metamorphose into a doctor of theology. Like the articles made, the apprentice's instruction was conducted in the shop, where the master performed as a sort of head dean and full professor. The earliest of such endeavor was strictly vocational, with no literary trimmings to speak of. But as the world gained in experience and enlightenment, the more enterprising guilds gave their novices an acquaintance with numbers and letters together with a spacious drill in the theory and practice of rectitude.

Once his boot training had run its course, the apprentice's days of servitude were over. To attest to his training and competence he received a certificate which raised him to the rank and style of journeyman. He now enjoyed the freedom to work for wages, but not, unluckily, to set up his own shop. Reserved strictly for a master, this right and dignity was not always easy to come to. Sometimes it was confined to the master's sons and others of his blood, and always it depended on time and money, and specifically, on the confection of a masterpiece, recognized and approved by the craft's fraternity of established masters.

The medieval workshop was the first technical school to break into human society. The faraway sire of the current industrial and vocational training, it developed a program that was to hold for centuries. Not until the coming of the mill and the machine did its powers begin to wane. Here and there one may still glimpse the guildsmen's lovely halls, and on certain festive days one may even behold their dwindling members bedecked, as of old, in their bright-hued robes parading down the streets in stately pomp as their ancestors were wont to do in the vast backward of vanished time. But they are just a wan reminder of the glorious yesterday. As an active force in everyday life the guild has long been done for. Replaced by the labor union, it has gone the way of all earthly things into the reservoir of the past.

CHAPTER 9

THE HIGHER LEARNING

Out of the intellectual stirrings of the twelfth and thirteenth centuries there came an institution which in purpose and machinery was unknown to the ancients, but which, despite the alteration imposed upon it by time and circumstance, has somehow managed to preserve its essence to the present. We do not know exactly when the first universities were sighted, for they were not founded deliberately as they are now with money, buildings, a tract of land, and the vision of grand things to come. Our earliest universities, in truth, started planlessly—one might even say unwittingly. They emerged for a variety of reasons, and not uncommonly, out of special conditions. The University of Paris, for example, is the child of the cathedral school of Notre Dame, which because of the magnetism of some extraordinary teachers, especially in logic and divinity, soared beyond its rudimentary confines into the sphere of higher learning.

Even before the advent of the University of Paris in the twelfth century, Italy was adorned with a number of energetic medical schools. The foremost stood at Salerno, a town hard by Naples and touted throughout civilization for its miracles as a health resort. The natural gathering place for practicing medicos, it was also a likely spot for aspiring future healers to seek acquaintance with the physician's art and science. To give them light and counsel medical men proffered instruction—an endeavor which, as it acquired shape and strength, presently grew into the University of Salerno.

Meanwhile, northward many miles, at Bologna, where a young man's professional fancy veered not to medicine but to jurisprudence, there existed a flourishing school of law. There, in the eleventh century, under Irnerius, an expert on Roman law, and his student Gratian, the first to codify ecclesiastical law—both powerful professors of their specialties—the University of Bologna took form.

Not all our early universities began quite so casually. In England, in the country above London, where the Thames flowed so low and narrow that an ox could easily ford it, we hear so early as 1117 of "a master of Oxenford," and of advanced instruction some years following. But it was not until some fifty years later that a university got on its legs when a group of English scholars at the University of Paris, recalled to the motherland by their king and expelled from France by Louis VII, uprooted themselves from their Gallic haunt to establish themselves more satisfactorily at Oxford. The first university to be deliberately planned and launched appeared in 1224 at Naples, the handiwork, as has already been said, of Frederick II.

2

The early higher learning began in the starkest simplicity. Sometimes there was a specific site; sometimes there was not. There were no buildings, no labs, no campus, no coliseum. Only the essence was there—a parcel of students who desired knowledge and a few professors who, for a modest fee, were ready and willing to instruct them.

By the thirteenth century the higher academic enterprise had become a sufficiently large and going concern for its participants to give some thought to organization. In Italy, where students were generally on in years—not uncommonly they were grave and whiskered men of thirty and sometimes even forty—they linked themselves into a sort of students' union, or as the word was then, a guild. Founded ostensibly to protect its members against the frauds and extortions of prehensile townsmen, particularly the tradesmen and the providers of food and lodging, the association presently undertook to regulate the professors. The men of learning were charged to begin their lectures on time and to bring them to an end on time. They were to stick closely to the text, and they were to expound it clearly without the fiddle-faddle of a long and tedious introduction. There were to be no omissions, no dalliance with empty word music, and positively no side trips into the pleasant but futile paths of irrelevancy. The professor was to grant himself no holidays—a day was allowed for his honeymoon—but otherwise there was not to be another, whether in sickness or in health, save by the guild's expressed consent. And to ensure that there would be no professorial finagling, the man was required to advance a yearly bond of about ten dollars—a lot of money in those days, especially for a professor.

When summer's respite came at length, the guild refunded him his due. Not unusually it contributed to his wages—more commonly, though, they were paid him directly by his students. Under the circumstances he inclined, no doubt, to bathe them in his approval, and reports have it that sometimes he even adjusted his standards to suit his paying clientele.

But there was no solace for the inept or mule-headed prof who flouted the students' union. The stubborn and incompetent teachers it fined and boycotted, and even caused to be dismissed. Near the thirteenth century's end, when the advantage of having a university in a town began to penetrate the skulls of Italy's civic fathers, Bologna undertook to pay a couple of its professors out of the municipal till—but the selection of the professors remained, as before, a student prerogative.

That the professors should establish an association of their own—if only in self-defense—was perfectly natural, particularly in an age when the interests of nearly every craft and trade were given to the care and keeping of some sort of guild. As the years passed, the professors' and students' guilds coalesced, and out of their fusion issued the University of Bologna, as we came to know it later on, a corporation full-feathered and on the wing, with instruction not only in law, but in the liberal arts and medical science, and after some delay and haggling, in theology. By the thirteenth century Bologna was sufficiently advanced to admit women to its sessions—a first, very likely, in the higher learning—and a century later it was permitting them to be professors, a practice which moral opinion in the Western world then regarded as extremely risky.

Not all student collectives were as strong and assertive as that of Bologna. At Paris, where enrollment was infinitely larger and where a great number of students were foreigners, the students were also a great deal younger. Upon them, hence, the reins of self-government did not sit so well. The professorial guild which sprouted at Paris grew in time into a stalwart plant, comprising the four schools, or faculties, of the arts, canon law, medicine, and theology, each headed by a dean elected by the teaching masters—a practice which still prevails in many European universities, but which in democratic America has long since curled up and expired.

At Paris the professors' main task was not to officer and regulate their students, though in that rough-and-ready age keeping them within bounds was always a prime concern. The professors' chief woe was grounded on their desire for a decent measure of academic freedom. Let it not be overlooked that Paris was not, like Bologna and Salerno, under secular influence. The offspring of Notre Dame, it specialized in theology. Scan the roster of its professional illuminati and you will find the greatest assemblage of experts the divine science has ever known—Abelard, John of Salisbury, Albertus Magnus, Thomas Aquinas, Roger Bacon, Duns Scotus, and at least a dozen more. The university's chief executive was the cathedral's chancellor, a man of God, of course, and he alone had the right to bestow degrees, which is to say in those days, to license graduates to teach and practice anywhere in Christendom. Though Parisian professors never quite succeeded in ridding themselves of their ecclesiastical apron strings, they did manage to attain at least an elementary autonomy. Eventually the dean of the arts faculty became the head of the university. Known as the rector, he directed its affairs in fact as well as name. The friends of popes for years, the professors of Paris found it possible to countenance and support their causes in logic, devious and even spurious on occasion, but serviceable nevertheless. Yet in the flow of time they grew wary of the papal tinge, and as kings mounted in power, they found it possible to side with the sovereigns in their disputes with the pontiffs. In truth, as early as the year 1222 the University of Paris chided the Pope for volunteering opinions without a degree in theology.

3

The first universities drew their students from many lands. So numerous, in fact, were the outlanders, that it was not long before they were flocking together for sociability and mutual protection in some sort of regional association. In Italy they were content to arrange themselves into those who came from the near side of the Alps and those who issued from the far side. Parisian students cast themselves into four nations—French, Norman, Picard, and English. The University of Orleans did much better—indeed, with ten organized nations in its midst it was in this respect the champion. Although the student body was international in composition, it was hardly international in its heart. The French were berated by others as sissies; the English were old rummies doomed to early graves; the Germans were arrogant and sniffy—and so on down to the treacherous Bretons and the fiendish and lascivious Sicilians. Everywhere the national temperatures ran high—so high that turmoil and bloodshed, and even loss of life, were not infrequent.

To get into a higher cerebral center was much simpler in those days than in these. The baggage which flaunts itself at every turn in the academic world today was then happily unknown. There were no formal admission requirements, no psychological tests, no letters of reference—not even an interview. All that was asked of the prospective student was that he be able to handle Latin—a requirement which, at bottom, made plain sense. His lectures, after all, were in Latin, and so were his textbooks—in fact, Latin was compulsory in every form of student interparlance, whether in the university or in the world which lay beyond.

Once enrolled, the freshman—or as the phrase went then, the yellow beak—nursed himself on grammar, rhetoric, and logic, consuming, if all went well, about four or five years to raise himself into a bachelor of arts, a degree which among guildsmen corresponded to a journeyman, but which academically was of no great account. For a master's degree in arts he plowed on another three years or four, completing the Seven Liberal Arts and putting his main weight on Aristotle. For a doctor's degree in one of the professions he grappled with the works and commentaries of his specialty. Of all courses theology was the most insistent. At Paris it was possible to make oneself a master of its mystery in eight years, but the results were not altogether meritorious, and so, as the years moved on, the process of ripening into a theologian was stretched out over a period of no less than fourteen years. No student, it was then ordained, could aspire to the doctorate in holy science until he was safely over the frontier of thirty-five.

Besides being sufficiently aged, the doctoral candidate was put upon to make a public defense of his thesis. Launched at six in the morning, the inquest was carried on by a succession of examiners, and ordinarily it lasted at least half a day. If he sustained himself successfully, he proceeded to plume himself in cap and gown, the uniform, so to say, of his trade, and if in Paris, he journeyed to the cathedral, where he was formally admitted into the kingdom of teaching masters. His sponsor deposited upon his cheeks a public kiss and sang his benediction thrice. Whereupon, at the candidate's expense, there followed a banquet for the assembled masters, of whom some had been gratified earlier by the courtesy of a bath, paid and provided for, once more, out of the candidate's personal pocket. But examinations, then as now, did not always end in joy. Sometimes the candidate succumbed, a casualty to his ignorance. Sometimes he was rejected not on intellectual but on moral grounds. In such events there ensued no feast, of course, and if the professors tubbed at all, then they did it with money out of their own pocket. But their persons, at least, were fairly safe, for the candidate had been made to pledge upon his oath that if he failed, he would refrain from assailing his examiners with knife or dagger.

4

When there was no special building, classes gathered now in cathedral cloisters, now in houses huddled together in the neighborhood, and now even in a room rented by the professor. The tolling of the tower bells summoned students to class, as it still does in countless shrines of learning the world around. Most classes were early starters, assembling soon after sunrise, save those in law which held back their labors till nine, thus affording the jurists of tomorrow a little extra practice in their art of professional procrastination. Not even the simplest amenities were known. Decent light was at a premium—fortunate, indeed, was the student who found himself a place close by a window. Ventilation in those glad days of old was not even a hypothetical question. The eternal draught of old buildings lurked everywhere, and not uncommonly students clustered in their benches cloaked and hatted as for the street, a practice which may have soothed against the winter's clammy chill, but which in a day when bathing was still unfailingly a luxury, often overbore the air with pungent aromas. At first there were not even chairs, and students squatted on stone floors, making their knees into impromptu desks. Later, when the luxury of benches was introduced, they were long and narrow, not unlike pews in a church, all too hard and crowded to inflame any lingering passion for learning. Towering over his audience in his lofty rostrum, like a sailor perched atop some high-pooped vessel, rested the professor, remote and impressive, in the august elegance of his professional regalia.

The professor lectured, which generally meant that he read material from his text which, of course, was in Latin. Only his comments and elucidations were spoken freely off the cuff—again in the inevitable Latin. Some of his hearers pursued his words in books of their own, but these were scarce and extremely dear, and their possession was denied to many. Usually the bookless student attempted to copy the master's utterance, inscribing his words after the ancient fashion on a waxen tablet. Later he would fill his memory with his notes, and when he happened to be in sufficient purse, he emptied them onto a treasured piece of parchment. Student guilds ventured to tell professors how fast to speak—to set their verbal speed limit as it were. But in this department there was no unanimity. At Bologna, where students craved the full measure for every penny of their tuition, they required their professor to speak fast—"bringing out his words as rapidly as if no one were taking them down." By contrast, the Parisians insisted on a leisurely pace, and when, in due time, the authorities ordered some verbal acceleration, the learners not only howled and clamored, but threatened to go on strike.

More important, doubtless, and more exhilarating than the lecture and the notetaking, were the student reviews and discussions. When the day was done, or on weekends, the young academicians would gather in small circles to parley on the subjects but recently heard in the lecture hall. Formal at times, in the vein of the approved Scholastic style, these disputations served them not only to vent their excessive steam, but by sharpening their wits in action, they prepared themselves for that longed-for day when, in defense of their thesis, they would confront their professorial inquisitors. "Nothing," declared Robert of Sorbon, "is known perfectly which has not been masticated by the teeth of disputation."

5

It is from the same Robert that the Sorbonne, an integral part of the present-day University of Paris, obtained its name. In 1257 Robert of Sorbon, who was chaplain to St. Louis, the King, endowed a house to furnish food and lodging for sixteen theological students—a house which in the gathering years was to honor him by bearing his name. To Robert's outlay the sovereign added money from the royal vaults, and as the years followed, nobles, prelates, and opulent burghers began to emulate the King's example. Since their charity was nearly always well advertised, their act was begotten often enough by vanity rather than devotion, a visible testimony to their wealth and importance.

As the number of such houses augmented, the practice gradually established itself of maintaining a master with the students. A sort of policeman of their virtue, he became in time a tutor who, besides vouchsafing moral homilies to his charges, also afforded them instructional aid and counsel. By the fourteenth century the tutor had worked himself into a full-fledged teacher, and what had begun as a free dormitory and commons for a few selected poor now became a college. As its advantages became more clearly discernible, the college multiplied rapidly, and in some places it proceeded to devour its parent, the university. Students were made to reside within its walls, a faculty was assigned to it, and all instruction was executed on the college premises. Henceforth the university's special function shrank into that of conducting examinations and granting degrees. The new fount of higher learning flourished especially in England, as of course it still does today, and whence in the seventeenth century it was imported into colonial America. On the Continent too it prospered, at least until the French Revolution, after which it was generally abandoned.

6

Though the student's nose was on the academic grindstone, his life was eased by a number of useful gratifications. He was exempt from bearing arms; he paid no taxes; and at Oxford and Cambridge he obtained parliamentary representation, a prerogative he still enjoys today. Since shaving his head like a monk and assuming a few other burdens served to put him in the clerical class, he was allowed to enjoy some of its special benefits. Hence, when he broke the public peace, he was tried not under civil but under church law. As clerics, students were required to lead a celibate life. Did some hussy beguile one, nevertheless, to fall from single blessedness? Then he could continue his studies, but he lost his privileges, and he could receive no degree. Obviously the penalty was draconian—too harsh, indeed, to prosper honest virtue.

For all his clerical affiliation, the medieval student was no angel. Perhaps he reflected his age of blood and uproar, or perhaps the Old Adam within him was too potent to be decently subdued. At any rate, the accounts of the day glut with his crimes and misdemeanors. When drinking water was a hazard and the boon of coffee not yet known, he reconciled himself with wine and beer. Taverns clung to the university's environs like barnacles. With wine went women and gambling. Students, lamented the good Sorbon, are more familiar with dice than with their text on logic. At Oxford armed students roved the streets at twilight "and assaulted all who passed by." Not to be outdone, their Roman counterpart passed from tavern to tavern "committing manslaughter, thefts, robberies." Leipzig students were fined for pitching stones at their professors. And at Paris they were booked and later excommunicated for shooting dice on the altars of Notre Dame. "They counted fornication no sin," sobbed the disturbed Friar Jacques de Vitry in 1230. So filled with this vice was Paris that "in one and the same house there were classes above and a brothel beneath."

Such onslaughts on the decencies may have been the exception rather than the rule, and for one knave there may have been dozens of quiet and diligent lads, content with more decorous pastimes and devoting their greater time to the earnest pursuit of knowledge. But whatever their way of life, on one thing students were in general accord: townsmen, at bottom, were scoundrels and fit only to be despised. In consequence, town and gown were at constant odds, and costly antagonisms, even riots, were not uncommon—an earlier manifestation perhaps of the mass free-for-alls which currently follow the spectacle of a great victory in football. To maintain and bolster virtue, authorities resorted to the familiar device of curbing joy of any kind. Oxford outlawed chess as "noxious," and playing with bat and ball it decreed "insolent." Needless to say, the more joys of this sort it interdicted, the more students enjoyed them, and the merrier they seemed to get.

The merriest of them all, at least so far as the historians of jocosity have recorded, were poets. Reaching their flood height in the early twelfth century, they ran for about a hundred years. Most of them were migrant clerics, students, former students, even professors, passing from town to town and sometimes from university to university, often as mendicants, gnawed by restlessness, and sometimes in search of learning. As poets they were neither mute nor inglorious, though most of them today are nameless, and many of them no doubt were rogues. "They go about in public naked," mourned the Council of Salzburg in 1281; and "they frequent taverns, games, harlots." Most of their poesy has a dulcet ring and a strongly mischievous hint. They mocked the prejudices and imbecilities of the world, and especially its reverend men of God whose psalms and prayers they often parodied, and for which they earned not the laureate's wreath, but only public reprobation. Named for the wholly imaginary Bishop

Golias, "a parasite notorious for his intemperance," whose disciples they professed to be, they called themselves Goliards and their warblings Goliardic. "In
our wandering," they let it be known, [we are] "blithesome and squandering."
They

> Eat to satiety
> Drink with propriety. . . .
>
> Laugh till our sides we split
> Rags on our hides we fit. . . .
>
> Jesting eternally
> Quaffing infernally.

"In the public house to die," clamored another, "is my resolution."

> Let wine to my lips be nigh
>   At life's dissolution!
> That will make the angels cry
>   With glad elocution,
> "Grant this toper, God on high,
>   Grace and absolution."

In their spare moments European students still intone an occasional Goliardic
favorite. In Germany, indeed, no academic *Bierfest* would be meet or complete
without the jaunty *Gaudeamus Igitur*, whose hoary strains have even reached the
waxed recording and may now be heard in the American family room along with
Brahms and Beethoven.

Not all the Goliard's airs were merely voluptuous. Some were gravely sober.
Here, to cite a single case, is a Goliard who aspired to

> Seek a better mind;
> Change, correct, and leave behind
> What I did with purpose blind;
>   From vice sever, with endeavor
> Yield my soul to serious things;
> Seek the joy that virtue brings.

With the passing of the Goliards, Latin verse fell on gloomy times. The great
minds sought surcease not in lovely rhymes but in the mazes of metaphysics and
theology. In the universities the classics were shouldered into a minor anteroom.
Finally, in the thirteenth century, when Dante and Petrarch ventured to cloak
their verse in a lush and lyrical Italian, the requiem of the ancient tongue as a
literary instrument began its intonation.

7

Though it has been the style to think of the Middle Ages as a time of minor intellectuality, nevertheless, as the years went on the universities augmented and spread. By the end of the period, in fact, some eighty have been accounted for. The early higher learning modeled itself after the fashion of either Paris or Bologna, the southern representatives following the latter, and the northern ones the former. Spanish universities were singular. Though, like nearly all their European sisters, they were the handmaidens of the Church, at the same time they were founded and chartered by the Crown, and they even submitted to a gentle governmental control; yet their financing and supervision remained an ecclesiastical prerogative. The luxury of the higher learning did not show itself in Germany until late. Prague, the first university on the central European scene, was established in 1347 under the imperial charter of Charles IV. Heidelberg, the first to appear in what is now West Germany, was brought forth in 1385 by Ruprecht, the Elector Palatine of the Rhine.

Not all universities endured. Some, congenitally frail, struggled only to perish. Some, like Salerno, flashed brilliantly for quite a while, and then faded and passed away. Others, like Oxford and Cambridge, Paris, Montpellier, Bologna, and Salamanca—to name only a handful—increased in strength and influence to survive the havoc of time, and to continue in service to the present. Like some of their modern successors, several of our first universities attracted fame for their specialties. Paris rose to the top in theology, the acknowledged queen of medieval learning. Montpellier superseded Salerno in medicine. Orleans drew attention for its classical and literary studies, and during the thirteenth century it stood second only to Bologna in the teaching of civil and ecclesiastical law. And, to make an end, in the world of Spanish learning Toledo and Seville stood out for their instruction in Arabic and Hebrew.

Of the institutions which have made the long trip from the Middle Ages into modern times—forgetting for the moment the Roman Church—the university bears the closest resemblance to its ancient forbear. It is still, as it was then, an organization of students and professors, dedicated to the pursuit of the higher learning. It is the inheritor of the basic medieval degrees, the bachelor's, the master's, and the doctor's, though these have spawned in colossal variety, and sometimes with no little absurdity. To attain them students are still put upon, as of old, to master a curriculum of subjects, and they are still tested by examination. And should any of them be eager for the doctor's hood, he is still made to compose a thesis, and in certain places he is still called upon to stand up in its oral defense, sometimes even in public. The gowns we flaunt at academic ceremonials have their beginning in the medieval period, though Thomas Aquinas, for all his brain and fancy, would scarcely recognize any of them. On the other hand he would be on familiar terms with the faculty of arts and the professional schools of law, medicine, and theology. Deans, rectors, and chancellors the good saint would probably remember, though their current duties and responsibilities, and the method of their selection would doubtless flabbergast him.

The rights and privileges students once enjoyed have long since slid down the drain of time. Today, like the rest of us, a good many of them shoulder arms and pay taxes, and when they break the law and are caught, they are tried and sentenced by the secular arm, though their diploma still talks, as of old, of conferring on them "all the rights, privileges, and immunities. . . ."

The medieval students' practice of hiring and, if need be, of firing their men of learning, and of holding them to the line in their manner of presenting their subject, has apparently vanished, though of recent years by uproar and insurrection, students in this and other great and enlightened lands, have managed to exert sufficient pressure upon university governance to effect a somewhat similar end, which is to say that sometimes their collective insistence has brought about a professor's—aye, even a president's—dismissal or resignation. By the same procedure they have been able now and then to save a worthy man of learning from being unjustly cashiered. As for the students' right to have a say in making the rules under which they have to live, until a short time ago this too had apparently gone with the dodo. But again by resorting to collective action, vigorously, and sometimes even riotously executed, here and there they have regained some semblance of a power their early medieval antecedents took for granted. In truth, several centers of the current higher thought, have made students voting members on their governing boards—a concession which, though bordering on revolution, appears at the moment to be gaining in favor.

One hears complaint often enough, particularly in our own land, that today's higher learning is anti-intellectual and that its offerings are heavily freighted with vocationalism, a charge which is not altogether without ground. Yet underneath its courses in stocks and bonds, its dissertations on dishwashing, laundering, and women's lingerie, the university still harbors a lingering residuum of its old tradition, the earnest and nonmaterialistic concern for the advancement of man's knowledge and learning.

TRANSITION

CHAPTER 10

THE RENAISSANCE

The age which followed Rome's collapse was dark, but it was not wholly dark. There was an intellectual glimmer, of course, in the monastic and cathedral schools. They bore the torch for the Seven Liberal Arts, an heirloom from antiquity, but purged with Christian purpose, and bruised not a little by the long centuries of barbarian carnage. For all their title, the Seven were neither liberal nor art. What passed for learning was little more than a memorizing of the accepted knowledge. Whatever its nature, it was executed only with the consent of the Church, and it was always under her sharpest vigilance. Her mission, it should not be forgotten, was not to enlarge and extend the existing fund of knowledge, but rather to defend and uphold it. Under the circumstances there could be no free journeying of the mind, and until conditions changed, the pursuit of knowledge was heavily shackled.

Nor were the arts bogged in sterility, particularly among the northern French whose musicians were prospering the tonal art, and whose poets were bursting into verse with a new and eager vigor, not only in Latin, but in the mother tongue. Similarly, in the building art a fresh boldness was introducing itself. The venerable Romanesque vogue, with its solid vaults and rounded arches, was already yielding to the challenge of newer Gothic, with its pointed arches, its jutting ribs of brick and stone, and its windows of infinite colored beauty.

As the twelfth century ran into the thirteenth these manifestations increased in potency and proportion. Indeed, the thirteenth has been cited by some as the greatest of the Christian centuries. The quintessence of the Age of Faith, it reached its peak in the *Summa* of St. Thomas Aquinas and in the sonorous strophes of Dante. But there were counterforces too. Behind the outer drapery there were perceptible murmurs of skepticism and secularism—even of nationalism, soft, it is true, and only faintly audible, but destined to swell into an immense and insistent roar.

2

When Petrarch was born in 1304 the Middle Ages were playing out; when he died, seventy years later, Europe was in the first flushes of the Renaissance. It was in many ways a disturbed and exigent century. Heavy troubles weighed on the papacy—for long years, in fact, even its existence trembled in doubt. In 1377, for example, when the Church's woes boiled over in the Great Schism, there were actually two popes, one in Rome, the other in Avignon, France, each declaring himself to be Peter's true and rightful successor. Meanwhile, from every side discontent and criticism rained upon the Holy See, from William of Ockham to Marsiglio of Padua, from England's Wycliffe to Bohemia's Huss, and even from the Florentine Dante. By the middle years of the century France and

England had locked themselves in what was to become the Hundred Years' War, but its hemorrhage was slight when compared with the slaughter of the Black Death which presently was stalking from door to door across the Continent.

Yet, where there are shadows there is also light. It glowed most palpably in Italy. There the earlier Nicola Pisano's passion for the classics became, in time's course, the animation of a new interest in art and music, and in letters. There was fresh light in England too, as witness, the philosophy of Ockham, the music of Dunstable, and, most enduring of all, the poetry of Chaucer.

The fugleman of the new age was a Florentine, Francesco Petrarca by name, or as he is known to us, Petrarch. So much of the Middle Ages did this man renounce, its Scholasticism, for example, its obsession with Aristotle, the quackeries of its astrologers and its medicine men, that admirers have saluted him as the First Modern Man, a title which, of course, is dubious, and which has also been hung on several others. Petrarch was still in his twenties when chance brought him a couple of Ciceronian writings, cobwebbed by the many centuries and long since strayed from human memory. It was a startling find, and it fevered Petrarch with an immense yearning. "My own age," he confided, "has always repelled me, so that, had it not been for the love of those dear to me, I should have preferred to have been born in any other period than our own." What he wanted was to see and absorb the whole classical legacy, to dredge it from obscurity, and to restore its vanished grandeur. He became in the process a relentless tracker of forgotten manuscripts—in truth, as the years chased on, his frenzy infected others, and soon the sight of grave and grown-up men digging into the recesses of moldy buildings in search of some hoary manuscript ceased to be a novelty. By this route many an ancient writing was rescued from oblivion, though a great many others, not so lucky, have strayed from these scenes presumably for good.

Petrarch's hope to learn Greek never fructified, but with Latin he got along handsomely. Virgil and Cicero were his models, the one for his own flights into serious verse, the other for his concoctions in scholarship, of which today the bulk is scarcely ever looked at. But when Petrarch stepped outside the conventional patterns to sing with his heart to his beloved Laura, he resorted not to Latin, but to Italian. His lyrics were not meant, of course, for the vulgar eye, and Petrarch shrugged them off as of no consequence. His estimate, as it turned out, was wrong. His sonnets have not only never been forgotten, but their wonderful essences remain as fresh as when they were first distilled.

For all Petrarch's virtuosity, he was not without his faults, but in him at times even these attain a measure of significance. He was ignorant of art, and history was to him a blank. Disdainful of philosophy and innocent of science, he yielded himself to the blandishment of words, lovely at times, to be sure, but at bottom only words. In consequence, he enthroned the ornamented Cicero, but dismissed the more prosaic Aristotle. He raged at Scholastics for their traffic in intellectual flyspecks and their lack of Latin luster. But he overlooked that without these men the light of knowledge might have flickered even lower. In an age of authority and conformity Petrarch dared to be critical, and even more, he ventured to be himself, though he remained steadfast in the faith, and he quoted the early fathers familiarly and approvingly. Nonetheless, he preferred pleasure to self-denial. Inordinately vain, he entertained a delight for flattery, roving from one place to another in quest of adulation, and gloating in a series of letters to the great men of antiquity that he was without a doubt their peer. But for all that, by his resolute roundup of ancient manuscripts, and by the fire he set for classical studies, Petrarch was able to give aid to what afterwards blazed into an ever-growing interest in letters, and especially the glittering legacy of Greece.

Petrarch's mantle fell upon his friend Boccaccio. Like the one, the other took an almost boyish delight in digging out the classic past. He brought back to circulation a number of its salient figures, and he found a tutor to pilot him into Greek, thereby becoming, it is said, the first Westerner to master its mystery since John Scotus Erigena, who lived and died in the ninth century. Like Petrarch again, Boccaccio was a worldly fellow, but where the former remained in cautious piety, the latter was of a perambulating conscience, and though in after years the Church was able to retrieve him from his errors, for much of his span on earth he lolled in the spacious paganism of Greece and Rome. Like his friend, Boccaccio fathered a number of scholarly dissertations which he rated very highly, but which have long since gone to the graveyard. He too was brushed by the wings of fancy—indeed, next to Chaucer he was probably the finest teller of tales the world has ever known. His *Decameron*, racy and rambunctious, and to the pure forbidden, still brings chuckles to its audience.

By the fifteenth century the zeal for the old-time Greeks and Romans had assailed new heights, and for every Petrarch and Boccaccio there were now dozens of successors. They were to be found in every up-and-doing town, and most abundantly in Florence, Venice, and Rome, where wealthy and influential patrons jostled one another to give them support and comfort. When Petrarch was still on earth, instruction in Greek was scarce and hard to come by, but now its familiars were all about. One of the first and one of the most noticed was a Greek, Manuel Chrysoloras, who appeared in Florence in the fourteenth century. So brisk was the demand for his instruction that presently he went into regular service, expounding his knowledge privately, but also flaunting it publicly before large audiences in lectures on Greek literature.

For young men equipped in the classics the times bubbled with opportunity. Everywhere men who stood high in the world besieged them for help and advice. The Medici of Florence hired them in squads, and so did Cardinal Bessarion, and so also the municipal fathers of Venice. They engaged these Humanists, as they were now known, to ferret out lost manuscripts, to build up libraries, to compose erudite works, to translate the writings of Greek antiquity into Latin, and not uncommonly, to bring tone and glamor to their social standing. For such ends Pope Nicholas V collared the best classical brains in Christendom. One of them was Lorenzo Valla, a shining scholar, but like so many others of the Humanistic order, vainglorious and not a little bawdy. Even so, the Holy Father summoned him to Rome, piled him with honors, and put him to work. There ensued a procession of translations from Herodotus to Thucydides to Demosthenes, all of the first chop, and the envy everywhere of rival patrons and connoisseurs. Despite his papal tie, Valla was not always Holy Church's dutiful and obedient son. In truth, if posterity still favors him with attention, it is not for his labors of translation, but for his destruction of the authenticity of the *Donation of Constantine*, a document whereon the papacy had grounded, at least in part, its claim to secular power and authority. So masterful was Valla's dissection and devastation of this ancient writ that he has gone down in chronicles as a faraway ancestor of the present-day scientific historians.

3

The old schools did not, of course, immediately curl up and give way to the new classicism; instead, for a long time they stayed in service, carrying on as of old in the familiar medieval manner. But by the early fifteenth century there were unmistakable signs of a changing wind. One of its first heralds was the discovery in Switzerland of Quintilian's *Institutes of Oratory*. Copied copiously and eagerly bethumbed, it became the model everywhere for pedagogic liberals who worked its principles not only into their professional treatises, but more important, into their schoolroom practice.

The schooling which now came upon the scene was not, of course, for those of common substance, who remained as before in stupefying ignorance. Instead, it offered its benefits to the well-born and to those of high preferment, which is to say, the issue of the aristocracy, the bankers, and the successful merchants. Not a little of it was dispensed by private tutors, but before long schools appeared. Known as court schools, they were the work, usually, of some thriving blue blood, who not only gave his countenance to the world's new spirit, but sought to inject it into his offspring, girls as well as boys. Most of these lordly sires have long since passed from the halls of recollection, but the memory of their schools, and especially of the men who ran them, still lingers in testimony to their excellence and devotion.

Among them two stand out—Guarino of Verona, who cast his teaching spell for more than thirty years in a court school at Ferrara, and Vittorino of Feltre, who performed similarly at Mantua. Of the two, Vittorino stands somewhat the higher. A doctor from the groves of Padua, he was on the brink of forty when he launched himself in schoolmastering by enrolling a number of private pupils under his roof to introduce them to the ancient classics. He was an intelligent and kindly man who picked his students from high and low, exacting stiff fees from the wealthy, but instructing the poor for nothing. His fame spread swiftly, and pretty soon fathers were packing off their sons to him from all over Italy, even, indeed, from beyond its boundaries. As the years toiled on, Vittorino's reputation caught the ears of Gonzaga, a successful tyrant who was bent, like so many of that company, on immortalizing his name by glorifying the arts and sciences. To advance his chances, he bespoke Vittorino to settle in his palace to lead and teach the ducal young, a position Vittorino accepted reluctantly, but in which, once he was installed, he functioned until he died in 1446, almost a quarter of a century later. What began as a group of princely fledglings soon reached out beyond the court to draw in some of the children of the neighbor-hood—in fact, in its palmiest moments Vittorino's teaching extended to a band of more than seventy.

Most of Vittorino's ideas and practice take their cue from Quintilian. Like the ancient Roman, Vittorino contended that the school ought to be soothing to the psyche. His own school he called the Happy House, the *Casa Gioiosa*, which, because it might be mistaken for another kind of house, had better not be translated literally. Its chambers were large, bright, and springlike, overborne with an always imminent joy. In the world outside, meadows environed the house, a stream pirouetting through their greenery, past tree-lined lanes and scattered playing fields. The Happy House, like so many of its current incarna-tions, was a world where learning was living, and living was an adventure. Very likely it was the world's first secular boarding school, and it may well have been its first progressive one.

For its time its discipline was highly civilized—in fact, though the phrase had not yet been minted, it enjoyed a modest measure of self-government. In a day of decaying morals Vittorino put his first stress on character, and though he adored the classics, he fused his love of learning always with his love of God. Like Quintilian, Vittorino recognized that children, being people, differ no end, and that therefore it is an absurdity to try to cast them from a single mold. The fact is often forgotten that centuries before Rousseau expressed it, his Italian forerunner urged teachers to study their pupils before they undertook to instruct them. Contrary to the established medieval principle, it was Vittorino's contention that schoolwork should be fun, that in truth, even the drab and direful, when blazoned with the teacher's art, can be made alluring. In this vein he taught the classics, becoming in the process, like all beloved teachers of the young, a child himself again, earnest when called upon, but reserving time aplenty for play and sport to leap and howl with his charges, and with a laugh ever ready up his sleeve.

4

The new education, like its medieval antecedent, based itself on the Seven Liberal Arts. But logic no longer ruled the roost, as it had in its Scholastic salad days, having been dispossessed by grammar and rhetoric. Pursued, however, not for their own selves, they were to lay the groundwork for an assured and easy fluency in written and spoken Latin, which was to serve in the long run as a sort of second mother tongue, and was the sign to all the world of a refined and educated gentleman. Once the learner was of sufficient competence, he was ushered into the great writings of the ancients, their wonder workers in prose and poetry, their philosophers and historians, chiefly, of course, in Latin, but also, as the youth took on years, in Greek. As for the rest of the Seven, the quadrivium, that is, they too continued to be pondered. The boy studied the stars and planets, their names, habits, and behavior; he set his heart thumping to the magic of tune; he dallied with numbers, with squares, triangles, parallelograms, and the other hair-raisers in the Euclidian closet. Now and then the student applied his mind to algebra, but such engagement was the exception rather than the rule. Overwhelmingly, the stress fell on language and letters, or as the idiom of the learned expressed it then, the "humane learning and good literature." Yet if the lad remained innocent of science and the higher peaks of mathematics, then he could take heart in other gratifications. Out the window, for example, went the bookishness of medieval schooling, its diet of verbal straw, its logic-mincing, its laying up of facts and definitions, its yes-smirking to so-called authority, its astigmatic pedagogues with their obscure profundities and their ever-ready sticks. What the new education proposed was the cultivation of the person, integrated in body, mind, and spirit, a man of poise, of urbane and graceful habit, of confidence and self-control, and on excellent terms with himself and the world—in fine, the ideal of ancient Athens.

To capture this elusive prize, the young were trained not only in mind but in manners and morals, and in the faith as well. For the first time since apostolic times—forgetting transiently the practice of the knights—the body was accorded a meet and decent respect. In consequence, a boy exercised not only his brain, but also his nerves and muscles. As of old in Athens, he ran and leaped, and he hurled and wrestled. But he also fenced and danced, and he played an early form of football—occasionally, in fact, certain schools matched their skill and prowess in competition, not a little like their present-day successors.

Such an education was naturally of a price, far and away beyond the range of the ordinary purse. Reserved, hence, in large measure for the well-heeled, its felicities were administered to those who could endure an education, usually by hired tutors seasoned in the classical lore, and reinforced now and then by gymnasts, dancers, tone artists, and similar aesthetic gentlemen. As the classics firmed their grip on European learning, schools presently appeared to give them accommodation, in illustration, the Latin grammar school in Britain, the *collège* in France, and the *Gymnasium* in Germany. All of them are still alive and in helpful service, and in one way or another, some of the ideas which bred their blood and bones found their way into America's colonial education.

5

As early as the late fourteenth century the Humanistic movement was beginning to make its way beyond the Alps into Germany and France, and across the

Narrow Seas into England. It was transplanted into its new setting chiefly by scholars who had come upon it while studying in Italy. Occasionally some touring merchant, home from his pilgrimage of trade in Italy, helped to give it added notice. And in the case of France, her military, back from their aborted occupation of Naples, Milan, and Florence, gave a useful hand to its furtherance. But what really served to put the New Learning on its feet in France was the hearty encouragement it got from Francis I, who assumed his kingship in 1515.

In form and substance the learning which now unfolded was akin to that of its Italian predecessor. There was, for one, its palpably aristocratic air and the eager patronage it got from court and peerage. There was the familiar culling of manuscripts, the creation of presses to multiply their number, and the founding of libraries and classical lectureships. And, finally, there were blasts in plenty against the older learning, its sacrosanct assumptions, its verbosity, its isolation from worldly interests, and, in particular, the preoccupation of so many of its academicians with gossamer nothings.

The foremost among the French Humanists was Guillaume Budaeus (born Budé). A gifted and imaginative man, he had a taste for books, and for numerous years he attended them faithfully as the King's librarian. At the same time he planted his field in the world of learning, perfecting a fine scholarship therein. His study of Roman coinage, a work over which he steamed and sweated the better part of nine years, arouses a modest handclapping even today. Like nearly all the later Humanists, Budaeus was an eager partisan of Greek, and he preferred it at all times to the cruder and less flexible Latin. Through him, in fact, Hellenistic studies made themselves at home in Paris, where for the next two hundred years they remained, a rich and flourishing mine of classical scholarship.

As might be expected, the schools which rose out of the new culture were heavily classical. Sometimes, as had been the case in Italy, they came into being under princely auspices, and sometimes from the strivings of successful and ambitious merchants, who, as is common enough, were a power in municipal affairs. Out of the royal hand of Francis, for example, issued the Collège de France. Devoted to the pursuit of Greek and Latin, the Collège was hospitable also to the study of Hebrew, and rather curiously, to that of mathematics. In southern France, Humanism's most famous stronghold was the Collège de Guyenne, which was brought to being in 1534 by the city fathers of Bordeaux. Montaigne, its most dazzling alumnus, attended its sessions from 1539 to 1546, and some thirty years following he served as chairman of its board. It was, as might be guessed, a tuition school, and its custom came from the upper classes. Open to boys when they were six or thereabout, it kept them busy for a decade, belaboring them powerfully during this time with Latin and Greek. There were some slight concessions to arithmetic, including the tracking down of square and cube roots and the elements of simple proportion. During the boy's first three years behind his desk he was permitted the use of his mother tongue—in fact, he was even drilled systematically therein, both in speech and writing. But each endeavor was always in a lesser tone, and as he grew older his use of French fell under prohibition.

6

In Teutonic lands the Humanistic revelation lit its candle not on the altar of esthetic feeling but on that of moral uplift. There the new learning impressed itself not so much on the refinement of the person as on the promotion of social reform. As a result, twilight did not close down, as in Italy, on the older Christian writings. Bracketed with the works of the ancient pagans were those of the church fathers, and side by side with Greek and Latin, though somewhat less sprightly, marched Hebrew.

Its foremost expert was Johannes Reuchlin, a professor at Heidelberg and Tübingen, and celebrated in intellectual history as the Father of Modern Hebrew Studies. A sedulous student of the Old Testament, he commented upon it freely and adventurously, and also, while he was about it, upon the Talmud and Caballa. His superb insistence on his right to teach and learn without restraint brought him into collision with the powerful Dominicans of Cologne who undertook not only to silence him, but even to burn him at the stake. Luckily for Reuchlin, their flayings fell short of their mark. From all directions men of learning rallied to the professor's defense, and in the end, instead of throttling their man, the Dominicans succeeded only in advertising his views.

The flagman of the northern Humanists and their most distinguished representative was Erasmus of Rotterdam. Of illegitimate birth and orphaned during his early youth, he was taken in hand by the Brethren of the Common Life, an association of pious, gentle-hearted men, which was dedicated, among other things, to the education of boys. With aid from the brothers, Erasmus took his first steps in Latin, a language he was to cherish, and which he practiced constantly, until in the end he became the most accomplished Latinist of his generation, the finest, it has been asserted, since St. Augustine. He was the most traveled of all the Humanists—one might think of him, in truth, as a man without a country. His studies took him to Paris, and his lectures to Cambridge. He spent years at Louvain, several more in South Germany, at Freiburg, and yet more across the Rhine in Switzerland. Even now his bones rest not in his native Holland, but somewhere in the soil of Basel, in Switzerland, where he died, a syphilitic, the current medical science suspects, in 1536 at the age of seventy.

Erasmus was preeminently of the scholar's disposition. A lover of life's serenity, he avoided, so far as possible, the cockpit of its controversies. An upholder of reason, he disdained the facile sureties of dogmatists of every breed, and throughout his life he endeavored to steer his bark in the free and uncharted waters that range in between the antagonistic opposites. It was an unpopular position, of course, with the solid citizen, and one which in the fume and frenzy of the Reformation estranged him from both Catholic and Protestant. Holy Church eyed him suspiciously, and Luther lashed him with public vituperation. But through it all Erasmus stuck to his tenuous autonomy. The pontiff could not daunt him, and as for Luther—"I should wish you a better disposition," Erasmus wrote him, "were you not so marvelously satisfied with the one you have."

In the realm of scholarship Erasmus' most laudable accomplishment was his Greek-Latin edition of the New Testament. He worked on it for long and tedious years, scanning the texts of early manuscripts, noting their variations, their spurious interpolations, their errors and contradictions, until in 1516 he was able at last to behold the fruit of his effort in print. For its deviation from the official Catholic version the work, needless to say, was roundly castigated. Nevertheless, in the long perspective of history, the integrity of its maker becomes at once apparent. Since then enormously superior editions have been wrought, but in one sense that of Erasmus is the parent of them all. The first critical edition of this Christian holy work, his New Testament marks the foreshadowing of modern higher Biblical scholarship.

Erasmus was not a prolific writer, but what he wrote rippled with charm and wit; as a result he was vastly read—his audience was by all odds the largest of his time. His most arresting book was *The Praise of Folly*, which he inscribed to Thomas More, one of the most ravishing satires ever conjured up, and still a favorite. Cast in the form of a harangue which Folly disgorges in eulogy of herself, the work salutes man's inveterate and awful silliness from his highest representative on earth to his meanest, secular as well as sacred. The performance was doubtless more scintillating than learned. But it was also smooth and insinuating, offensive to Luther, and to the shrewd eyes of the Church not a little subversive.

If *The Praise of Folly* was something of a best-seller for its time, then the *Colloquies* fared even better. A schoolbook on Latin style, it ran from the rudimentary to the advanced, throwing out as it rolled along a generous bit of religious and moral enlightenment together with satirical potshots at some of the prevalent social practice. Despite the gravity of its textbook purpose, Erasmus undertook to flavor it here and there with a delectable drollery. As a consequence, the *Colloquies* won the thanks of schoolboys everywhere, and sometimes even of their schoolmasters. In fact, even Luther, for all his sourness toward Erasmus, gave parts of the volume his blessing and recommended its use in Protestant schools. The years, of course, have blown away the *Colloquies*—though not altogether. Like *Uncle Tom's Cabin*, the work still makes an occasional appearance, much abbreviated to be sure, and sandwiched between the editor's introduction at one end and his notes and illuminations at the other. Even so, it still springs and prances, and among such works of instruction it remains a rare delight.

Erasmus' views on pedagogy may be found in his *Liberal Education of Children*, which was put between covers in 1529. For their greater part they echo the Italian Vittorino who, in turn, echoed the faraway Quintilian. Most of the familiar propositions are given notice, in illustration, the educational merit of play and games, the need for penetrating the complex and often mysterious character of the learner, the removal of burdens and restraints upon his capacities, and the great value to be derived from giving him a cordial and civilized treatment. The primary function of a liberal education, Erasmus argued, is to produce a man who not only knows, but who thinks and feels as well. Education should direct its mission not to the furtherance of utility, but to humanity. To this end the pupil should soak himself in the classics, not just Cicero and similar standbys, but a vast pool of others in whose collective thinking run civilization's perennial great ideas. Thus conceived, the business of education can be directed toward social progress. Molded in the cultural crucible of its time, it offered itself not to all the children, of course, but only to the few whom fortune had befriended. But Erasmus permitted the fair sex within this circle—indeed, like the ancient Plato, he even urged upon them the same educational opportunities as those enjoyed by their brothers.

In the north, as in the south, the classical upsurge presently put its grip upon the schools. The first to take note of it, and also the most numerous and far-flung, were the Brethren of the Common Life. They had established themselves in the late fourteenth century at Deventer in Holland, but as the years followed, they had gone into service in various places in the Low Countries, in northern France, and in Germany. They professed the simple Christian virtues, and in putting them into good works they began to give instruction in Latin, and in piety and virtue. At a time when the science of social justice was unheard of the brothers extended a helpful hand not only to the poor, but even to those of a slow and tardy mind, whom the Muses had cast aside, and for whom learning was filled with pain and grief. To encourage and help the backward, their mentors abandoned the schoolroom's rigorous formulas to broaden its offerings and to flex its procedures. The Brethren made it their business to master their teaching craft not only by bolstering their performance with knowledge, but even more important, by giving it the enchantment of a high art. Not all their pupils were of the lower orders, nor were they always of meager talent, Some of them, indeed, soared to wind-swept heights, for instance, Thomas à Kempis, Nicholas of Cusa, Sturm of Strassburg, and the most astounding of them all, Erasmus of Rotterdam.

For those whom the fates had put in high estate, there were the usual seminaries of place and privilege, the palace or court schools, or as German parlance puts it, the *Fürstenschulen.* Their purpose, as in Italy, was to confect a full-fledged man, comfortable in the classics, but at the same time a person of high character, sturdy in body and lofty in spirit, a man, in short, ready to serve competently in the princely calling or, at all events, in the higher public service.

The most famous German center of classical learning was the *Gymnasium.* Similar in purpose to the French *collège*, it volunteered, for a modest fee, to give training to its flock in Latin and Greek, and like its neighbor on the Rhine's western bank, it is still in everyday operation, though the passing centuries, naturally, have worked their slow but inexorable changes. The creation of the laity, the *Gymnasium* found its natural habitat in the municipalities. There were a number of such schools, and they ranged from Bremen to Frankfurt to Danzig, but the most conspicuous, at least in the long, backward glimpse of history, was at Strassburg, in those days the property of the Germans and a flourishing center of their commerce. Though the school was under municipal control and care, time saw it run aground, and in 1537 the city summoned Johann Sturm to reorganize and revive it.

Sturm had fallen under the Humanistic spell as a student in the halls of Louvain, and later he taught logic and the classics at Paris. His Humanism was not the unfettered Italian variety, nor was it the deftly critical Erasmian kind. His erudition, however, was stupendous—almost, indeed, rabbinical—and his name was respected far beyond the city walls. From all over Christendom worthies trooped to his door, and when they could not engage him in face-to-face parley, they fustigated him with mail. As a result, his correspondence, like that of Erasmus, grew like a tapeworm. Nevertheless, despite his high qualities, there drifts from him from time to time an unmistaken whiff of pedantry. Sturm ran his school for almost half a century, and during this time he composed a mountain of schoolbooks and several scholarly works as well. For one of such an academic cast of mind, the man was an extraordinarily successful organizer. When he mounted the bridge of his Strassburg school, it registered a mere handful of pupils; pretty soon they numbered several hundred; and before he relinquished his command, they tallied several thousand. His fame had carried to the four winds—indeed, for their *Gymnasium* the Strassburgers had become almost as eminent as for their goose liver and their cathedral.

The *Gymnasium*, after Sturm overhauled it, embraced ten classes, each running a year, and each under the eye and hand of a special master. All ten years were consecrated to the mastery of Latin in all its phases, both useful and ornamental, while six of the ten years, in addition, were reserved for Greek. From the boy's first wobbling to the day of his triumphant academic consummation his classroom language was Latin—save only when he wrestled with his catechism, in which case his native guttural was permissible. Though Sturm's school stood out for the excellence of its instruction and the robust quality of its scholarship, at bottom its industry was almost entirely intellectual—a hallmark which was to affix itself to all *Gymnasiums*, and which was to endure, but slightly altered, into the present century. For Sturm, who favored an almost gloomy gravity, the school's purpose directed itself grimly and overwhelmingly to brains. There was no place in this cerebral sweathouse for the cultivation of the body; no place for the making of a mannerly man; and certainly no place, as Quintilian had moved so long ago, and Vittorino and Erasmus had seconded, for frolic and jocosity. The end sought was not the high and full-blown classical ideal, an integrated and cordial alliance, that is, of body, mind, and spirit. Instead, said Sturm, it was "piety, knowledge, and the art of speaking." It was, of course, a confined and delusive Humanism, a denial of its early spirit and a betrayal of its promise.

Unlike Italy's wealthier merchants, their German counterpart had little fancy for the New Learning. Apparently, the northerners were more concerned with moneymaking than with the Muses. Here and there, it is true, a father flattered his household with a tutor to edify his son with classical enrichment. Later, when the *Gymnasium* had fixed itself into the German academic way, it was not uncommon to find the sons of merchants in attendance at its sessions. Principally, however, the men of commerce invested their confidence and their money in the burgher schools, where their heirs and successors were rehearsed in the language of everyday, in both reading and writing. Usually, also, the nascent Gimbels and Wanamakers were put upon with arithmetic so that some day they could keep their books and correctly calculate their gains and losses. Now and then they made acquaintance with the ABCs of business law, and sometimes with the elements of commercial Latin.

7

In England the New Learning was pretty much the same as on the Channel's eastern edge. It showed itself first in the fifteenth century at Oxford, where Linacre, Grocyn, and especially Colet, transported by its glitter, sought to give it some promotion. Not long afterward Cambridge invited Erasmus to grace its gray-stoned cloisters. There, from 1510 to 1514, he lectured and wrote, initiating his scholars in Greek, repairing their barbarous Latin, and, more important, carrying on shrewdly and prodigiously to bring the Humanistic cause to flower. There were, of course, the usual antagonisms from the inevitable and inescapable corps of implacables—Scholastics, monks, and cocksure obcurantists—who sought to hobble Humanism at every turn. But, despite their feverish industry, its vitality proved too potent, and in the end they could not stay it.

The New Learning progressed, and in time it projected itself not only within the walls of Academe, where one would naturally expect to find it, but even into the royal court. Its most sparkling representative in ermine without a doubt was the great Elizabeth. Endowed with an agile mind and a fine memory, she excited the prideful wonder of her tutor, the learned and beloved Roger Ascham, once a professor at Cambridge. He escorted his royal pupil into Latin and Greek, both of which Elizabeth learned to write and speak, and in which she continued to seek improvement even after she had become queen. Just as sure-tongued in the modern languages, she was strikingly articulate in French, Italian, Spanish, and German. She was adept on horse; she could bring an arrow surely to its mark; on the dance floor she could hold her own with anyone; and in the art and mystery of politics she possessed a skill which surpassed, if possible, even that of her celebrated father, the eighth Henry. She was, in a word, the personification of the fullest expression of the English Renaissance.

It was not in the higher learning, but in its secondary and preparatory substations, the so-called Latin grammar schools, that the Humanists made their strongest strike. Some of these establishments were of a white-haired age as long ago as the twelfth century, having started out as monastic or cathedral schools merchanting the Seven Liberal Arts, but now brought into accord with the newer classical fashion. Sometimes the grammar school was the work of some friend of learning, and sometimes—in illustration, the grammar school of

Sandwich–it arose from a communal effort. Not their whole weight, of course, fell on the classics. Piety was omnipresent, and so were manners, morals, and manliness. Nor was music overlooked. As early as the fourteen hundreds the English were regarded as the best tune makers of Europe. Every tavern had a ready lute, and so did every barbershop. "The English," said Erasmus, "may claim to be the most musical of all people." Without song, hence, the education of a gentleman, whether in some private salon or in school, would have been gravely deficient.

The most famous cradle of secondary schooling in the early days, and one destined to become the fountainhead of several hundred successors, was St. Paul's at London. It had begun as a cathedral school, and as the years increased, it had come to prosper as one of the finest of its kind. Nevertheless, time brought it neglect, and it gradually withered and wasted away.

In 1510 it was given renovation by John Colet, the dean of St. Paul's Church, and also an ardent Humanist and admirer of Erasmus. To St. Paul's Colet gave not only his heart, but also his purse. Just as useful, no doubt, was the help and counsel of friendly Humanists, and notably Erasmus and William Lily. The one donated lavishly of his time and sagacity, composing texts, luring students, and even seeking first-class masters to shepherd the young into a refined and sophisticated manhood. The other, who had sipped his Humanism at its Italian springhead, served the school as its first principal, or as the English were wont to say, its high master. He too was the father of a well-known text, *Lily's Latin Grammar*. More heavily freighted than the *Colloquies* of Erasmus, and much less adroit, it became, nevertheless, the most widely circulated Latin grammar in the English-speaking world, not only in the motherland, but even in colonial America. Renamed the *Eton Latin Grammar* in 1758, it continued in use at Eton for another century. It is credited with over a hundred incarnations, the last one appearing in 1945 in New York, with an introduction by Vincent J. Flynn.

St. Paul's is still in active operation, and so are a herd of other grammar schools, all laden with age and liveried in tradition. Some are as advertised as Heidelberg or the Sorbonne, or to come to our own shores, Harvard or Vassar. To run their roll is to summon Eton, Rugby, Harrow, Winchester, Charterhouse, and so on and on. Time and conditions, of course, have brought them a measure of modernness, snail-like in its progress until, at any rate, after the mid-nineteenth century, when the pace of change began to quicken. Their curriculum, though still deferential to the ancient classics, now harbors such contemporary intruders as the sciences and the modern languages and their various literatures. Of late their doors have opened somewhat wider so that their enlightenment is no longer the singular prerogative of the high and moneyed. But their academic industry still grounds itself, as of old, not on the practical and utilitarian, but on the liberal arts. Hence they have been challenged by younger rivals, un-ivied and unsung, but more in touch with the needs of the large generality of men, which is to say, their scramble to make a living. Even so, in Britain's heart the grammar schools are enshrined, a monumented testimony to their liberal ideal in a world which is succumbing more and more to the pressure of utilitarian necessity.

8

The year that saw Columbus plant the flag of Spain in the New World was witness also to the birth at Valencia of Juan Luis Vives. In him streamed the blood of aristocracy; better still, nature had favored him with a mind of more than ordinary candlepower. His education befit his caste, which is to say, its beginnings were conducted privately under the domestic roof, and—by way of exception—they were directed by his mother, a lady, evidently, of some intellectual luster. Raised along the constricted lines of Scholasticism, with its usual massive infusions of Latin, logic, grammar, and rhetoric, he made his way in the passing years to the University of Paris, where he ran head on into the new and fevered interest in the Humanistic learning to which he presently succumbed. Time saw him divest himself of his Scholastic raiment and betake himself to Louvain. There he attended classes at the university, only to find himself commissioned before long to cast some light of his own, especially on his favorites, the Messrs. Virgil and Cicero.

At Louvain, Vives made the acquaintance of the touted Erasmus, a man more than a quarter century his senior, but destined to become his friend and counselor, and in some respects, his admirer. Though, as say the French, to compare is not to prove, yet the impulse to stand Vives and Erasmus side by side, and under the glare of powerful lights, to take their respective measures, is strong. Between the two there was much in concert. As scholars, both sat at the first table, and both wrote and spoke a sleek and polished Latin, but as a literary figure, the Dutchman clearly held the edge. A minter of the fresh and glittering phrase, he had a fine hand for humor as well, and was given on occasion to incite one to mirth with a bold and saucy mot. As a scholar, the Spaniard was the better read; in point of fact, the length and breadth of his verbal intake was truly gargantuan. No less diligent was his zeal with pen and ink—his literary output in education was by all odds the most spacious of his era. But while Vives wrote prodigiously, Erasmus, though by no means parsimonious in setting down his thoughts on paper, worked his quill more selectively, and by the collocation of his superior gifts, he managed to hold the attention of the largest reading audience of his time.

Like the Rotterdammer, the Valencian made the journey across the Channel, and in 1522 (on the continent the Protestant insurrection was already raging in its fifth year), we see Vives in London, consorting with Sir Thomas More and other more or less high-toned bearers of the Humanistic torch. Betweenwhiles, the Spaniard disgorged a learned tract on Saint Augustine's *City of God*, which some secret inner voice whispered to him to inscribe to Henry VIII. Whether the sovereign ever read beyond the words of presentation is, of course, hard to tell, nor does it greatly matter. The fact is that whatever hopes their author had placed in his work were more than amply realized. Oxford, for one, discovered him to be a scholar of rare and exceptional quality, worthy even of its doctoral toga, and to demonstrate its high confidence in his merit, it invited him to irradiate its lecture halls with his philosophic incandescence. Meanwhile, Henry's wife—the first of a train of five successors—the hapless Catherine of Aragon, bespoke her countryman to take charge of the education of her daughter, later to mount the throne as Mary Tudor. He introduced the girl to the fountainhead of Humanistic learning, taking care all the while, however, that her deep-seated Catholicism suffered no pagan defilement, so that when she grew to woman-hood, she would lead a fine and blameless life.

The princess proved herself an admirable pupil, eager and amiable, a veritable joy, if one may accept her master's confidence without the proverbial grain of salt. True to the scholar's not unusual way, Dr. Vives maintained an accounting of his thoughts, stowing the details assiduously in his memoranda and, in 1523, after ordering and ornamenting them as becomes a master of the literary art, he had them set into type in Latin as *Two Letters on a Plan of Study for Youth*, one wherein he formulated a scheme for the instruction of Princess Mary, and the other to the same end in behalf of the son Lord Mountjoy. Other writings were to follow, the bulk of them on education, but some, as will be rehearsed in pages to follow, on subjects of no less consequence.

Vives's presence in England fell into the period when the connubial partner-ship between Henry and Catherine was skidding badly. When the monarch took steps to persuade the Holy Father to dissolve the marriage tie, Vives, an implacable Catholic and a Spaniard to the core, sided with the queen who had befriended him, thereby igniting the King's moral indignation, and fetching Vives a notice to get out of the country at once. He departed for Bruges in the Low Countries, where he soon stood forth not only for the breadth and brightness of his classical erudition, but also for the piquancy of his potshots at Scholasticism, in particular, its adoration of the Aristotelian deductive dialectic.

So much for the man and his more notable doings. Let us now beam our attention at some of his educational ideas. They lie at rest in his most important work, which appeared in 1531. Compounded in Latin, it embraced a dozen books, or, as the expression is nowadays, "sections," under the general title *Concerning the Teaching of the Arts*. A substantial portion of the work—its first seven books, to be precise—concerns itself with crying down the faults and follies of the prevalent educational practice, its bookishness, for example, its stress on learning by rote rather than by observation, its flatulent school-mastering, its immense amount of talk without action, and so on and on.

Is Vives given to the vice of pulling down? Then he is also given to the virtue of building up. The rest of his treatise, in fact, he devotes to driving home his ideas on what constitutes a meet and worthwhile education. There is in them the bright light of other forward-thinking pedagogic artists, some long previously furloughed to eternity, as, in instance, Plutarch and Quintilian, but some still on their legs and wide awake, as witness, Erasmus. But there is also much in it that bears the hallmark of Vives himself.

It was Vives's conviction that a child's development of the understanding should get under way while he was still a toddler. In this endeavor both parents were to exercise their influence. As lord and master of the hearth, the father was in command of policy, its direction and execution. His better half, on the other hand, who watched and tended their offspring during the day's greater part, was the child's mentor and counselor, the safekeeper of his manners and morals, and, of course, his godliness—she was, in actuality, his first teacher. When, at the age of seven or thereabout, the youngster had outgrown his rompers, and had entertained the foresight also to have been born a male, he was packed off for school, sometimes nearby but more often at a distance. He was to dwell, if possible, with relatives or family friends, but not in any case in a dormitory, which Vives believed was all too commonly the incubator of carnal desires and other incendiary shenanigans. The boy's teacher, who was to be picked with surpassing care, was to be exemplary in every department of life, sound in mind and body, a man of rectitude and learning, and, needless to state, a subscriber to all the prevalent orthodoxies, whether sacred or secular.

Unlike the general mass of pedagogues, Vives turned thumbs down on the aged and bedraggled practice of fitting the schoolboy into a prefabricated curriculum. Instead, the doctor laid upon the teacher the task of making a searching study of his pupil, scrutinizing his humors and his vapors, his general and particular strengths and weaknesses, and his special needs, and thus outfitted with data, to tailor a curriculum that fit him snuggly and comfortably like a finely customed glove. From time to time the master was to engage in discourse with his colleagues to confer with them on the progress of the pupils, and to adjust his teaching accordingly.

Vives addressed his main pedagogical pondering to those of average mind and capacity. The truly bright and competent, he believed, came, like all good things, in sparse supply, and they alone, he insisted, should be allowed to frequent the seances of the higher learning. Finally—and far and away ahead of his time—Vives held the view that education should be a public responsibility, and that whatever wages, benefits, and perquisites a schoolmaster might draw should be supported out of the communal till.

As a Humanist, the author of *The Teaching of the Arts* naturally laid a heavy hand on the importance of mastering the ancient classics. Not only were they the key to human wisdom and grandeur, but as models of the literary art, they were beyond compare. Even so, Vives shared the Erasmian scorn of the growing adulation and the consequent aping of Cicero as the ultimate in literary perfection—"Ciceronians," as Erasmus derisively lampooned this guild of degenerate Humanists in one of his famous satires. Nor was Vives inspired by the notion that all the snowy peaks of human knowledge and wisdom had been scaled by the ancients, that, in other words, there was little possibility of amending or rejecting or transcending their superb achievement. He was in this respect a foreshadower of those who, numerous generations later, were to bring forth the doctrine of progress, to which most Americans, as every connoisseur of constructive idealism well knows, are still immensely devoted.

For all his esteem of the ancient tongues and letters, Dr. Vives cherished a lavish affection for the native language. Although he died a few years before the birth of Cervantes, the originator and propagator of the incomparable Don Quixote, Vives nevertheless was on these scenes early enough to appreciate the spectacle of a mounting respect for the Spanish language and literature. In Spanish memoirs, in fact, his natal year—brushing aside, for a second, Columbus and his monumental feat in the same year—is regaled with pomp and circumstance not only for the advent of Vives upon this earth, but also for the publication of the world's first textbook on Castilian grammar. Designed to yield its light to young senoritas fluttering in no less than the fifth heaven of the Spanish court, the book for many years was the only one of its kind, so before long its pages were being turned by meaner but no less aspiring hands. The ascending interest in the vernacular among cultivated Spaniards sat well with the Humanistic Vives, so well, indeed, that despite his predilection for the writings of the great literary lions of an older time, he proclaimed that "it is the duty of every parent and master to take pains that children speak the maternal tongue correctly." In order to bring this about, Vives realized that to be effective their teacher needed to be familiar with every in and out of the native idiom. For only by having resort to the "right words with the matter with which he is dealing will he be certain not to mislead them." Not only would efficiency in the use of the vernacular help a youth immeasurably in participating successfully in the pageant of his everyday life, but it would also profit him as a basic training for his subsequent grappling with Latin.

The doctor's insistence on the attainment of correctness and fluency in the usage of the native lingo was not, of course, a novel idea. Long ago, when Christendom was still in infancy, the Roman rhetorician Quintilian had given tongue to a somewhat similar sentiment, but the passing centuries had dealt it a heavy stroke. However, when in a very different world Vives reincarnated it, the idea, so long bogged in desuetude, appeared fresh and springlike, and despite its collision with all the settled principles and practices of the established pedagogues, from a fragment of the enlightened laity it gathered a warm and dulcet applause.

In the melting sunlight of his short sojourn on earth—he went to his reward, wherever it was, before he was fifty—Vives set down his thoughts on the workings of the learner's mind, thereby unwittingly opening a thin and precarious path to what has since expanded into the immensely traveled concourse of educational psychology. When learning by rote was the fashion, the general run of pedagogic thinkers had little need to explore the dark and baffling subcellars of the learning process, and so they directed their chief attention to the matter which was to be learned, with little, if any, concern for how the business could be most efficaciously transacted. Against this lack of consideration for a better understanding of the learning process, Vives issued a flat objection. That process, experience had told him, hinges not on the subject at hand, but on the nature of the learner's wit and attitude. Like Comenius in a latter age, and Rousseau in an age later still, Vives contended that "our senses are our first teachers." Rousseau, typically enough, went so far as to declaim that "our first teachers are our feet, our hands, and our eyes."

The doctor's disrelish for Scholastic Aristotelianism rested not so much on an aversion to the teachings of the old-time sage, but rather on the undue stress academicians were wont to put on the ancient philosopher's deductive reasoning, with its stagnant, sacrosanct assumptions. Like the Anglo-Saxon Bacon some generations later, Vives put his trust in firsthand observation as the primary source of new knowledge. "The course of learning," the Spaniard let it be known, "is from the senses to the imagination, and from that to the mind ... and so progress is made from solitary facts to groups of facts, from solitary facts to the universal"—*in piccolo*, the inductive process.

Although Vives generalized freely on the nature of learning, yet at all times his capital concern bore on a respect for the cultivation and preservation of a pupil's individuality. To accommodate a child's education to his special require-ments, the doctor turned his back, as allusion has already been made, to the ready-to-wear curriculum, the same everywhere for one and all regardless of any personal differences or idiosyncracies. By the same token, this man of sensitive heart began to wonder what could be done educationally, if anything, for those whom nature had sorely damaged, as, in instance, the blind, the deaf, the mute, the mentally deficient, and other dispossessed children of the earth. Here Vives ran into a walled-off realm, for such afflictions Christendom then generally regarded, like fleas on a dog, as God-ordained, and even the mere thought of meddling therewith was deemed an affront to the wisdom of the Creator. Though the doctor's reflections on these themes advanced him precisely nowhere—the waters of several centuries were to flow underneath the bridge of social progress before some far-out thinkers began to convert the dream of Vives into actual realization—still in human annals the name of Vives must be put in nomination for the distinction as a seer, if nothing more, who caught a glimpse, however enigmatic, of the possibility of bettering the lot of the handicapped through education.

If Vives marched in the procession of the Humanists, he broke their measured tread not only when he made a plea for the vernacular as a fit and essential subject for learning, but also when he insisted that any education which pays no heed to the facts of everyday living is unfailingly inadequate. "The student," he declared—in defiance of the aristocratic corpuscles which ran in him—"should not be ashamed to enter shops and mills and ask craftsmen questions and get to know the details of their work."

A man so alert to the challenges of the world he adorned and enriched and which, for all his ardor for the hoary classics, he was bent on fathoming and even improving, could scarcely be expected to be numb to some of the bedevilments which preyed upon the masses. It was in this vein that, in 1526, Vives put forth his book *On the Relief of the Poor*. The first systematic treatment of the subject of which we have any knowledge, it made a bonfire of some of its most cherished syllogisms, namely, for one, that pauperism rests on God's inviolable ordinance, and that, per consequence, the poor, like Heaven and Hell, will be forever with us. Handing out alms, the favorite device in those days of pious human inequality, for lightening the burdens of the wretched poor, Vives rejected out of hand. Not only is such charity demeaning to its beneficiary, however great the pressure of his want, but in the long run it is bound to be futile. To be effectual the relief of the needy must be made a communal responsibility, and it must not merely give surcease to their sufferings; it must also develop a program for getting them out of the wallow of their degradation once and for all—and this at public expense.

So noble a marriage of heart and brain as proposed by Vives, needless to say, passed for the most part unnoticed not only among the general populace, but among the minority of cerebrals. The doctor's comrade Humanists, like the Renaissance from which they sprang, inclined to be sniffish of the nether folk whom, like the immortal Hamilton a lot later and in a different land, they dismissed as so much human slag. Per contrast, Vives, breaking step once more from his fellow intellectuals, insisted that, given a fair chance, even the lowly could rise to the heights.

No cloistered academician, tremendous book-eater though he was, Vives canvassed the world around him with sharp and sweeping eyes. "I see from the depths a change is coming," he said. "Amongst all nations men are springing up of clear, excellent, and free intellects, impatient of servitude, determined to thrust off the yoke of tyranny from their necks. They are calling their fellow-citizens to liberty." A wishful thought? Perhaps. But as the years winged on, and revolution followed revolution, Vives's preview took form and substance—in fact, even now it is still in the process of greater and greater fulfillment, an extraordinary testimony to this Spaniard's vision.

9

Thus the Renaissance. It was not, as was once almost unanimously believed, the fierce outbreak of a sudden sun on a period swathed for centuries in the shadows of the night. There had been intervals of light before, pale, to be sure, and tender, but light nevertheless. Against all these flickerings, however, there had always been the restraining curtain of Mother Church. But now her vigilance was allowed to ease somewhat, and before long, literate and imaginative men, kept for centuries on the paltry aliment of metaphysicians and theologians, were gorging themselves at the festive board of classical Greece and Rome. There they savored a culture enormously different from their own, one, indeed, of delight and no little instruction.

The Renaissance was more than a classical upsurge. Dozens of windowpanes reflected its light. Its luminaries were not always professional men of learning; some of them were critics; some released themselves in the literary art; and not a few dwelt on such mundane matters as business, politics, diplomacy, military science, and even social problems. A stimulant to self-expression, the Renaissance gave vigor and freshness to the creative arts. It spurred philosophers and men of science, though their enterprise, it must be said, was on a lesser scale and not so grand. The Renaissance gathered its greatest following amidst the substantial townsmen, and it ascended to its highest pinnacle in their urban habitat, the bustling jumble of homes and people, of marts and money, from Florence to Nürnberg, and to places far beyond their city walls. It was, of course, no movement of the masses, but in the stretch of a long time its spirit was engulfing, and though stayed and stemmed, it could not be stopped forever. Its concern lay not in the charm and contentment that beckoned from a celestial eternity, remote, beautiful, and glorious, but in the challenge of man's everyday world, a turbulent world and often a cruel and a wanton one, but at the same time, a world of infinite possibility.

Inevitably, the power of the Renaissance made its way into education. The vacuous bookishness of medieval learning, its endless engorging of facts and definitions, its mumbo jumbo of logic and wordmongering, its rigidity and its formalism—all this it swept into the garbage can to clean house for a liberal education. What it sought was a smooth and working concert of body, brain, and soul, a person, in other words, of urbane habit and expression, polished and cultivated, and able to face the world with equanimity. Toward such an end the classics were brought to bear—Latin and Greek, and after a while Hebrew—but so also were manners, virtue, piety, and manliness. In the process, not a few masters unbent, their methods relaxed, and learning, once regarded, like measles and whooping cough, as an experience necessarily baleful and so by God ordained, began to glow with pleasure and forebearance.

It was, needless to say, an ideal. Reserved for a lucky handful, the new education sought at first to work its magic through hired tutors and special schools. Later, when the movement's youth was gone, its early yearning spent, it hardened and narrowed into Europe's classic secondary schooling, the *collège*, that is, of France, the *Gymnasium* of Germanic lands, the grammar school of Britain. All of them are still alive and in helpful service, and in one way or another some of the ideas which bred their blood and bones found their way into colonial America.

CHAPTER 11

THE PROTESTANT REVOLT

Once the Renaissance swept a man into its arms, he was never again quite the same. Its touch exhilarated, and it fed his dreams, but when they were done, and his eyes opened to the world around, his joy collapsed. The more the men of the Renaissance exulted over the civilization of Greece and Rome, the more some of them fretted with irritation for their own. At odds with its antiworldliness, they took the field against what they disdained—its pettiness, its renunciations and restraints, the follies of its people, the vast twaddle of its learning. Nothing could stay their critical sniping—not even Holy Church. In truth, as the years floated by, it befell the Renaissance not only to sustain and strengthen the new individualism and secularism, but even to train the gunfire of its brashness on the powerful Medieval Church.

Disturbance and dissension were no strangers to Mother Church. Heresies had plagued her oftentimes before. Yet always she had managed to bring her defiers to book, or if things came to their worst, to cremate them at the stake. But now the antagonism toward her was overwhelming. No mere affair of faith and virtue, it crowded upon her from every quarter—from the makers of national states whose political ambitions collided with those of Rome; from merchants eager for a commerce freed from ecclesiastical restriction; from land-starved peasants drooling for a morsel of her choice and immeasurable ground; and from people everywhere averse to the exactions of Peter's tithe taker. Motivated by men whose weather vane pointed nearly always to private, secular, and even materialistic ends, these forces, girded by religious and moral issues, now drew themselves together against the ancient church.

The contest started decorously—even unexpectedly—in 1517, when Martin Luther, an Augustinian monk and professor of sacred science, worried and worked up by some of the Church's fund-raising tactics, poured forth his concern in *Ninety-five Theses*, which he nailed to the door of the court church at Wittenberg. Though they hung there for all to see, only a few could make out their sense. Cast in Latin, they were addressed, as per medieval university custom, to the small fraternity of the learned, especially the ones in the ghostly craft, challenging one and all of them to engage in verbal combat with Luther. But the session of words and mild excitement the friar had expected soon burst the academic trammels. Put into the vernacular by some unknown meddler, the *Ninety-five* passed from soul to soul, and pretty soon they were flaunting themselves in the farthermost reaches of Europe. Presently what Luther had expected to be a conventional academic disputation surged over Europe in a torrential and far-flung controversy. As it gathered force and momentum, it poured into the sea of an outright insurrection, sweeping with it not only the clergy but the laity as well, and cleaving Christendom into a Protestant and a Catholic sphere.

The full force of Luther's defection fell squarely on the issue of scriptural authority. Is Holy Writ the Heavenly Father's inspired and infallible word? Then it is also his ordinance, and it alone and not the pontiff is the authority for Christian belief and behavior. Are the sons of Adam naturally and incorrigibly base, creatures corruptible, incapable of a single righteous act? Then priests and good works availed them naught. Let them rather throw themselves upon the mercies of God; for only by their faith can they attain an eternity of post-mortem bliss. It was Luther's belief that the baptized took on a sort of priestly capacity, and that guided by the Holy Spirit's ineffable hand, they would come to the biblical truth. Time, however, saw this simple view embroidered with the Protestant contention that with the Holy Ghost's illumination, a practicing Christian might also interpret the Bible's sacred meaning. But as this principle was put to work, it soon became apparent that one man's truth was another man's error, and that for all the chaperoning by the Holy Spirit, there could be as many interpretations as interpreters, some of them even at angry odds. There thus followed an immense multiplication of sects, a process which, though nowadays more relaxed, nonetheless has never ceased. As the years unfolded, Protestantism accounted not only for Lutherans, but a couple hundred other denominations as well, from Pilgrims, Puritans, and Presbyterians to Russellites, Groaners, and Come-outers, the Disciples of Christ, the Church of Daniel's Band, the International of the Foursquare Gospel, and the Holiness Church of God, Inc. Presently, in fact, certain devotees began to entertain some serious second thoughts about their original interpretations, as, for example, the Baptists, who proceeded to split into Regular Baptists, Duck River Baptists, Seventh Day Baptists, General Six Principle Baptists, Two-Seed-in-the-Spirit Baptists, and yet more.

The Reformation, as has been said, was bred in part from the critical spirit of the Renaissance. In fact, several of its outstanding insurgents—even Luther—had been nursed by the Humanistic learning. But as Christendom festered more and more with religious hostility, bigotry soon shut the door to reason, and for over a century the intellectual promise of the Renaissance suffered. The chasm lay not merely between Rome and Wittenberg. Dissension rioted even among dissenters. For all their divine inspiration in the Good Book, not uncommonly the various Protestant sects found themselves in cantankerous and even violent dispute. Against the warlock in the Vatican their gorges rose in unison, and it was easy for them to make a common cause; but when it came to wiping out the difference which separated, say, an Anglican from a Puritan, or a Puritan from a Quaker, their rancor boiled over, and they held themselves implacable. Although Luther had made an issue of religious freedom, he had no inclination to extend it generally, and certainly not to those so benighted as to advocate tenets which collided with his own. Reason, he began to suspect, is "a poisonous beast." It is, he wrote in the evening hours of his threescore years, "the Devil's harlot." It was a sentiment which well became the time, an angry and fanatical time, ridden by theological absolutism, whether biblical or papal, and unfriendly to the examination of the cosmos in rational terms, and inhospitable, hence, to a Copernicus or a Galileo.

If the age was inimical to the free functioning of thought, this is not saying that culturally it was stagnant. The first massive movement in human accounts to have been fought with the armament of the printed word, the Reformation unloosed a rousing cannonade of tracts and treatises, pasquinades and pronunciamentos. Most of them, of course, were of a rasping partisanship, and save for the sardonic humor their recollection has afforded some latterday historians of human imbecility, they have long since wasted in the literary boneyard. But there were also some works of high distinction—even, in truth, glowing and everlasting. From Luther's fancy, for example, soared "A Mighty Fortress is Our God," the battle hymn, as it were, of the Reformation, but sung today even in Catholic churches. Again, it was Luther who gave his followers their first satisfactory Bible, although with some discreet trimming, and irregularities aplenty. It is no more than fair to mention that in his work of translation Luther was flanked and helped by Melanchthon (born Schwarzerd), an expert in Greek, and Aurogallus (born Goldhahn), a master of Hebrew. Rendered into a form of virile peasant German, Luther's Bible attained a respectful merit to become in the passing years an abiding legacy. Luther's ascension into the German literary Valhalla was matched in French by Calvin with his *Institutes for the Christian Religion*, and in English by Tyndale with his translation of the New Testament.

2

Needless to say, for the vast human horde snagged in the coils of illiteracy, such pearls were out of reach—hence the insistence of Protestant standard-bearers on the necessity of teaching the faithful how to read, thus enabling them to immerse themselves in Holy Writ's unshatterable verities, and thereby improve their chances someday to join the angel host. To such an end Luther turned his genius for potent verbiage upon German Protestant rulers, praying them in a special encyclical—his *Letter to the Mayors and Aldermen of All the Cities of Germany in Behalf of Christian Schools*—not only to support elementary schools, but also to see to it that parents confided their offspring to their sessions. His ideas are simple enough. Instruction, he let it be known, "is a matter in which Christ and the whole world is concerned." German schools not only wallow in an appalling swamp; they are rapidly getting worse. Therefore, since the "welfare of the state depends on the intelligence of its citizens, Christian schools must be established and maintained." To this purpose the towns should give support, something which is now easy since Omnipotence "has released them from the exaction and robbery of the Roman Church." Such schools, Luther went on, should be free, and they should accommodate every child, whether in skirts or pants, rich or poor. Man's right to schooling is inherent—as inalienable as his right to breathe. But inasmuch as parents so often shrug off their educational responsibility, it behooved the state not only to provide schools, but to make attendance at their sessions mandatory, and thereby inescapable. Finally, lest his proposal might be held to be too costly, he let it be remembered that annually Germans "spend large sums on muskets, roads, bridges, dams, and the like. . . . " Why then, Luther wanted to know, "should we not apply as much to our poor neglected youth in order that they may have a skillful schoolmaster or two?"—a query which, of course, has been ringing down time's interminable hallway ever since.

As for instruction on the lowest plane, it should familiarize children with reading and writing, religion, the related thou-shalts and thou-shalt-nots, and hymnody, besides gymnastics. To this end an hour or so a day in the classroom would suffice. The rest of the day boys should pass at home to master some useful trade while their sisters devoted their talents to housekeeping. Thus equipped, Luther was sure, the Germans would cease to be "a nation of blockheads . . . useful to nobody."

3

Luther was much too busy directing his war on Rome to spend himself on the details of pedagogy. But in this sector he was ably represented by Johannes Bugenhagen and Philipp Melanchthon, both of whom had sweated with him in academic robes at the University of Wittenberg. The one toiled in Germany's northern flatlands, the other in its central and more southerly parts. Both men were freighted with learning, and both were ignited by the teaching zeal. Assigned to get the new Lutheran education on its feet, Bugenhagen put an elementary school in every parish. Hamburg he enriched with a Latin school, and Brunswick with two. He left his mark wherever he worked, from Bremen and Schleswig on one side of Germany to Pomerania on the other. Before he passed from this vale he was summoned by the King of Denmark to give a Lutheran overhauling to the national church and the schools. So meritorious was the man's performance that some Germans, more romantic perhaps than correct, still pay him tribute as the father of their primary school, the so-called *Volksschule*.

A devotee of the Humanistic classicism, Melanchthon (born Schwarzerd), had given long and assiduous service to its promotion in Germany. His pedagogic interest, hence, rested not so much in the lower and common learning as in the secondary and loftier variety. With Luther he had formally professed at Wittenberg, and when that center of wisdom switched to the new religion to make itself the first in the German higher learning to sever its Roman ties, Melanchthon became its specialist in the Lutheran theology. For his time and place he was something of an Abelard in Protestant regalia, less dashing, to be sure, and much less brilliant, but a magnetic master just the same, who pulled in students in droves, and from all directions. In the teaching world his merest hint was accorded grave respect. Protestant princes sought his guidance, and when he recommended someone for a job, it was almost automatically an appointment. Like most Humanists, he was a fertile composer of texts in Latin and Greek grammar, and in rhetoric, ethics, and logic. In Germany his works were highly prized, and time ran on long after he had gone before they were finally obsolete.

Melanchthon's greatest feat is dated 1527 when the Elector of Saxony bade him cast an eye upon its schools and make recommendations for their improvement. The Prince reaped an ample harvest, for by his *Book of Visitation* Melanchthon preserved not only himself but also his patron in pedagogic history forevermore. At bottom a school survey, the first of which we have any knowledge, it recommended the establishment of a Latin school in every Saxon town and village. Three classes were to adorn each school. Of these the first grounded its beginners in reading and writing, both in the language of everyday and in Latin, with extra grapplings in grammar and the Lutheran revelation, besides, of course, its prayers and sacred airs. In the second form Latin chased out the mother tongue, except only in religion. The following year reserved itself exclusively for Latin. Rome's literary magnificoes now fell under scrutiny, from Cicero to Virgil and from Horace to Livy, with side searching parties into rhetoric and logic.

Melanchthon was the most productive school planner of his time—one of the most fecund, indeed, the human race has ever known. So vast and widespread was his industry, and so fruitful his aid and advice to city after city and state after state, that history still salutes him as the Schoolmaster of Germany.

In the Saxony Plan the Reformation and the Renaissance coalesce, the one with its stress on the vernacular reading and writing and the essence of the Lutheran canon, the other with its splurging in the ancient letters. The scheme was only partially adopted, and its operation lay not in the hands of the state, but in those of the Evangelical Lutheran Church.

The first true state system of which we have any account made its appearance in 1559 in the Duchy of Württemberg. A comprehensive arrangement from end to end, it took its male and female recruits through the recognized Lutheran rudiments, sacred and secular, after which followed six years of classical training for competent and ambitious boys, whereafter, if they thirsted for the higher cerebration, the door was open to the university. For its day the Württemberg school system was something of a wonder, and before long other German states—or at any rate their rulers—began to parrot some of its features. Amended and ameliorated during several ensuing generations, it gradually established itself in the German pedagogical garden so that by the seventeenth century's middle years pretty nearly all the German states had given it their approval—in fact, even Bavaria, then as now a rugged pillar of Catholicism, had organized its schools in the Württemberg mode, with Roman overtones, of course, instead of Lutheran.

4

As year faded after year, Luther's plea for the education of the masses began to be given some heed, and before long elementary schools of one kind or another were bobbing up not only, as has been noted, in various German lands, but in other Protestant strongholds as well, especially where Calvinists had the say, as they did in Geneva, Holland, and Scotland. The reason for the coming of these schools was, of course, religious—in fact, without such a spur to rowel them, there is little doubt that their advent, like that of the Second Coming, might have encountered a long and sad delay. It is to Protestantism, hence, that we credit the rise of the vernacular elementary school. A cradle of faith when it started, it directed its tuition to what in those long gone days was counted as essential to the welfare and happiness of humankind, whether at large in this faulty world or aflutter in the glorious beyond. For this the Protestant prescription of reading and religion and its corollaries in moral science was resorted to, with fortifying bracers here and there of writing, ciphering, and gymnastics. When recourse to the art of tone was not frowned upon as a snare to the immortal soul—as it was, for instance, among the Quakers—the young were exercised in song. On occasion, in some of the larger Protestant enclaves, where Satan and his aids were known to work twenty-four hours every day, including Sunday, boys were put upon to foil their evil ends by employing their idle hours to master some useful trade, while their sisters were expected to perform prodigies of housekeeping.

Although the makers of the Reformation went to great lengths to provide instruction for the run of ordinary folk, their solicitude for the preparation of their future holy clerks was no less rapt. For this purpose they relied on secondary and higher learning. Developed during the Renaissance, the former, as reference has been made, had specialized in giving its clients a solid grounding in the ancient tongues, a training which in the case of an embryonic man of God was regarded as well-nigh indispensable not only for the high amperage it purportedly built into his brain, but also for its eventual professional usefulness. Though during the Reformation the stress on language outweighed all else, forgetting, of course, that put on religion and morality, a few secondary groves enhanced their linguistic exploits with music and physical culture, the simpler mathematical operations, and those revelations of rudimentary science which stood in accord with the awful truths of Holy Scripture in order, as Luther explained, to demonstrate once and for all the "wonders of divine goodness and the omnipotence of God." If, as has been said, the Reformation scored its secondary learning in the key of the ancient classics, this is not to suggest that it also piped its predecessors' fresh and buoyant air. The sorry truth is that even before that fateful day at Wittenberg in 1517, the pedagogic liberalism of the Renaissance had begun to stale. What had started as an educational aspiration to refine and humanize the individual, and in particular to free him from the bondage of Scholastic pedantry, had relapsed all too often into the mouthing of words, cramming the mind with facts and by the same blow smothering the freedom of its functioning. To the fair sex the secondary learning was fenced off. Not only could girls never serve God as pastors, but their ordained mission in life was to keep the home, and to people it with numerous progeny. Did a woman weary and even die from the perils and pains of high-pressure breeding? No matter, remarked Luther, let her "die from bearing, she is there to do it." Such was the reigning view, and it was not for centuries—not in fact, until the French Revolution—that it began to be put to serious challenge.

For young men of grand hopes and longings there were the universities. These had come to life, as has been narrated, in the Middle Ages. Once under way and fully formed, the founts of higher knowledge untapped their wisdom in law, medicine, philosophy, and theology, lecturing, drilling, and surveying their hopefuls in the arcana of their specialty, and in the end capping and gowning the lucky survivors. Like the larger world of which they were a part, some of them had adopted the Protestant revelation, and consequently the divine science they professed was that of the new religion. Though in Luther's times, as in ours, such training was not unfailingly necessary to make one's way into the holy calling, still it was helpful, and for a judicious young man seized by tremors to scale the loftiest professional crags, it made sense for him to suffer the higher academic discipline.

5

Luther's greatest rival was John Calvin. Born in 1509 in Picardy, he was raised in theology and law. His grip on Latin and Greek brought him to pondering the Bible which, like Luther, he presently recognized as "God's eternal decree," Christendom's singular and inerrant authority, its constitution, as it were, and the basis, rigid and to the letter, of its moral law. Forced to get out of France, Calvin took haven in Switzerland at Geneva, where he founded a church-state, so dour and oppressive that the Genevans expelled him. But soon he was back, and this time he stayed until his death in 1564, some twenty-five years later. His main work, *The Institutes of the Christian Religion*, a massive theological manual of some eight hundred pages, came out in 1536, and before long it was being put into one edition after another and into most of Europe's major tongues. The first lucid and systematic expression of the new faith, it exerted a powerful influence not only in Geneva, but far beyond the Alps, wherever Calvinism penetrated, in Holland, England, Scotland, even in Catholic France where the Huguenots were its partisans—even, indeed, in the wilderness Zion of colonial Massachusetts where the Puritans were its advocates.

At the heart of Calvin's doctrine stands the absolute and impregnable will of God. The source of all things, it underlies life's every act. Every thought, every word, and every feeling, however trivial, drapes itself in moral significance, and becomes subject, therefore, to ecclesiastic jurisdiction to which every mortal, whether in infancy or senility, bears bondage. With this in mind Calvin converted Geneva into a theocracy. Its divines studied God's hallowed ordinances, and its constabulary put them into execution. Under its tireless watch, the Genevan passed his days—and his nights—in a house of glass, forever in review and forever answerable for his thought and conduct. So close was the tie between church and state that an act against the public peace was an act against God. "He that shall be treacherous against the civil government," admonished the Puritan Urian Oakes, a Harvard president, and a man who ought to know, "is guilty of high treason to the Lord Jesus." Malefactors, in consequence, whether card players or cannibals, were harshly dealt with.

Like Luther, Calvin made the school the church's handmaid. "The liberal arts and good training," he proclaimed, "are aids to a full knowledge of the Word." They are, he urged, "a public necessity. . . . " In the Geneva Bible State the business of putting its leader's thought into practice was simple—much simpler, certainly, than in Germany which, despite Luther's repeated warnings, continued to swarm with papists. As a consequence, before long every Geneva parish armed itself with a school. It addressed its practice to the children of the plain folks, teaching them not only the three Rs and religion, but also the simple propositions of civil and moral science, and with stress aplenty on the terrors which await them, inevitably and almost without exception, in the eternal fireplaces of Hell.

Higher up was the familiar classical stronghold. Reserved for tomorrow's men of large affairs, it put its weight on mastery of Latin and Greek, with the usual elephantine dosings in grammar, rhetoric, and logic. To equip its attendants for the efficient execution of their professional duties later on, whether sacred or profane, the *collège* trained them heavily in public utterance, with particular concern for the oratorical art, from diction to enunciation to arm waving and noble phrase making. Twice a month every boy was put upon to raise the wind with a massive speech. Nor, as one might expect, were pupils pinched for instruction in moral theology. They memorized Calvin's catechism in both French and Latin; they ingested the New Testament in Greek; and they gave their ear to sermons, long, informative, and sometimes not a little grisly. On the whole, these schools were manned by capital teachers—one of them, in fact, was the illustrious Corderius (born Cordier), once in pedagogical harness in the Humanistic *collège* at Guyenne, in France, and the teacher there, by chance, of Calvin, then still an unreconstructed Catholic and too young to be a prophet.

Highly ranked in the academic world, but especially, of course, in its Calvinistic enclaves, the Geneva *collèges* attracted students from lands all over Europe to which in time's course they returned to lead their people as preachers, teachers, and assorted public servants. Like Calvinism itself, these institutions scoffed at the ravages of time. Several of them held on long after the theocracy had fallen apart, as witness, in particular, the Collège de Genève. Founded in 1559, it still swings its ancient doors, no longer captive, of course, to the cheerless dogma of its apostle, but up and doing in the world of current wonder, scarcely less efficient than of old, and everywhere politely respected.

6

The fireworks which Luther had set off on that fateful day in 1517 did not show themselves in England until something like a decade later. When they burst upon the scene their primal causes were not moral and religious, but dynastic and personal. Though King Henry VIII was—and to his dying gasp remained—a worshipping Catholic, his royal dander was aroused and he turned his back on Mother Church when she refused to liberate him from his marriage to Catherine, a union which the Queen had been unable to bless with the production of a prince. By the Act of Supremacy in 1534 Parliament rent the English faithful from their popish mooring, while Henry, once hailed and bemedaled by the Pontiff as the Defender of the Faith—the King had written a blast against the infamous Luther—undertook to head and defend the newborn English rival. The shift was not one of rite and dogma, but of authority and control. Even so, it was not until 1547, when Henry's nine-year-old son put on the Crown as Edward VI, that Protestantism became England's one legal and official faith. Two years following, in 1549, a *Book of Common Prayer* and a *Confession of Faith* were adopted, and to give them support, everybody, old and young, was made to accept them.

Following Edward's brief sojourn on the throne Catholicism returned. But its stay was only transient, though not a little tragic, and when Mary Tudor was succeeded by her sister, the first Elizabeth, the English were hauled back to Protestantism. By the Acts of Supremacy and Uniformity in 1558, the Anglican Church became the land's official church, with the sovereign as its executive head.

These measures brought quiet. But there was unrest beneath the surface. Catholics refused to crook their knee. Secretly they prayed and plotted, and they suffered and died to bring their church back to its former state and power. Nor, as usual, was there unanimity among Protestants. It was all very well, growled the Puritans, to cashier the Pope and to settle Protestantism upon the realm. But what was needed besides was an upheaval vastly more sweeping, a Protestantism chaste and undefiled, a Protestantism cleansed of even the faintest Catholic tinge. What was needed, in sum, was a national church tailored to a Calvinistic cut, the spiritual arm of the English body politic, and operated by God's appointed Puritan Elect. Another faction, the Separatists, gagged at the Established Church's "filthy traditions," which they found differed slightly from those of lascivious Rome. But unlike the Puritans, they would have no truck with such wormwood, and they divorced their church from the state completely.

Thus the broad pattern. There is no space here to embroider its many details. Framed in brutality and intolerance, they are sometimes more satanic than divine. As on the Continent, the uproar over ecclesiastic doctrine and practice, whether Catholic against Protestant or Protestant against Protestant, was no mere religious matter, but one which laid its hand on powerful secular concerns, the struggle, that is, for power and status, social, economic, political, and national. It was to enmesh its participants for long and sordid years. No settlement was to caress the land until 1689 when Parliament granted a measure of toleration to Protestant dissenters. But there was to be no respite for Roman Catholics; on the contrary, as the years moved on, more enactments were piled up against them. As a matter of fact, until the nineteenth century, when the discriminatory Test Acts succumbed to repeal, public offices, both state and municipal, were reserved for Anglicans.

Hatched from politics rather than religion, the English Reformation was not given, as was that of Luther and Calvin, to any great alteration in creed and practice. Taking them as they come, the same priests continued in office, Anglican now instead of Roman. True, they shepherded their flock in English, and their bishops were the sovereign's placemen and not the Holy Father's. Executed, moreover, by the governing class, Henry's Reformation never raised the voltage of the man of the multitude as did its predecessor across the Channel. Nor did it offer him the chance to attain celestial wings by the exercise of his faith and personal responsibility while he sweated and suffered here below. His religion, its tenets and its worship, issued from the Established Church. Let him cast no critical eye upon its mandates; instead, let him accept and conform.

7

The differences between the Lutheran and the Anglican Reformation exhibit themselves plainly enough in education. Did the former lift its voice in behalf of the universal education of boys and girls in at least reading and religion? Then the latter granted them but a nod. Did the former exhort the secular arm to give financial subsidy to the schooling of the common child, and to order and compel parents to send their young to school? Then the latter would brook no such dealings. Thus England had no Württembergs and it enjoyed no Saxonys. Instead, as the years unraveled, education became more and more the province of the Established Church. It alone licensed the nation's schoolmasters, male and female, exacting from them, before it acted, a vow of loyalty and conformity; it kept a relentless eye on all instruction, both lay and religious; and presently, it enjoined its teachers "to frequent the public prayers of the Church, and cause their scholars to do the same."

The government's educational abstinence took a deep and abiding hold. It bared itself wherever the English way held sway, not only in the motherland, but in the world beyond the sea, in Virginia, in New York, and New Jersey—at least for a spell—and in the West Indies. Only where the Calvinists were in the saddle, say, in theocratic Massachusetts, was the state bent on making its children literate as well as godly.

England's reluctance to give a hand to the schooling of its children bore heavily, of course, upon the lower orders. Before Henry repudiated the Vatican, their chances to snare at least the elements of knowledge had doubtless been no worse than anywhere else in Christendom. But when the King renounced the Pope, he also brought down his main purveyors of learning. In the struggle chantries succumbed, and so did the song schools and the ·hospital schools, and presently even the monasteries. With their exit disappeared the chief dispensaries of England's lower learning. They were replaced but slowly. Sometimes—and especially in the Elizabethan high day—a parish besought one of its men of God, now in Anglican frock, to give instruction. At other times the business fell to private enterprise. Commonly its chief executant was a woman—or as the word ran then, a dame—who assembled some of the local youngsters at her fireside where, besides performing her daily household chores, she labored to stuff the rudiments of faith and knowledge into her clients. That she expected some modest reward for her exertions, if not in the nation's jingling coin, then at least in some of its goods and sundries, was surely no more than fair. Known as dame schools, such seminaries did quite well, and when the English planted their flag in the New World, they introduced them over here, where they carried on until even after the Revolution.

As usual, those cruising in the upper social orbit cut a better figure. Young men of quality generally were tutored under the family roof or in the household of some prominent worthy, after which, not uncommonly, they were dispatched to Italy or France to refine themselves in courtly ways and manners. The lesser lords and gentry usually got along without the service of a private mentor, and obtained their learning instead in a Latin grammar school. To these groves Henry's revolt had not been kind, and under its blows a great many of them crumbled and passed away. But in the years, as the Reformation entrenched itself more firmly, some of the confiscated monasteries were reincarnated as churches with schools attached. Similarly, in a few of the larger municipalities some of the former schoolmasters, or their assigns and successors, returned to their former haunts to resume their abandoned practice.

The fortune of these schools varied with the shifting religious tides. They fell into their blackest steeps in the baleful days of Mary when scarcely twenty could be accounted for; but in the reign of her succeeding sister their increase was more than sevenfold; and toward the close of the seventeenth century, when the dreams of England's Roman Catholics were finally dashed, the grammar schools numbered over half a thousand.

Modeled after St. Paul's in London, they put their accent on Latin, not, however, in the free and florescent style of early Humanism, but in the more constricted manner of the Reformation. Cradles of the national orthodoxy, they brought up their young men to the Anglican God, disciplining them stiffly in piety and morality. Besides the usual effusion of nonentities, they managed somehow, in addition, to disgorge some first-rate graduates, men who rose to a respectable position, not only in church and state, but in the world of learning, letters, and law—even in trade, finance, and industry.

8

One of the laudable educational by-products of the period issued not from the clashes of religion—at least not directly—but from the tangled web of economics. The sixteenth century bore witness to staggering economic developments. The New World's gold and silver had given Europe a sorely needed transfusion. Minted into money and put into circulation, the precious metals raced the metabolism of the marketplace and thereby put forth the possibility for a man to lay up a princely store. At the century's end farming was still England's foremost occupation, but the making of woolens was on the rise and even bidding to become a national industry. Just about this time, moreover, the English had become partisan to the joint stock company, whose magic allowed men of moderate means to join their opulent betters in vast and breathtaking economic transactions. At the same time, since the country's wealth was being pumped more and more into its rising colonialism, this new creature, so full of lure and promise, was destined soon to play a vigorous part in the forwarding of England's imperial ambitions.

Unluckily, the gold and silver which poured so lushly from the New World into the Old did not wash its joys on all alike. Lovers of lucre—the bankers and brokers and the men of business—pocketed the greatest part, while men of a meaner caste got their hands on very little. Meanwhile, as the nation's pile of gold and silver mounted, the cost of living also mounted, while wages, as usual, could not match the dizzy pace. In consequence, there was a dreadful suffering. To aggravate the woe, the harvest was thin. Even worse was the landlords' new practice of fencing in their land as sheepfolds—"enclosing," they called it. But whether fence or enclosure, the system threw more and more farmhands out of work. In the old days, before Henry had broken up the monasteries, the monks had been the kingdom's almoners, but now they were gone, and their successors were not inclined to their warm and generous heart. When beggars came to town, some, we know, gave them bread, but many more sicked their dogs on them or laid on with the whip. And so misery bred discontent, and discontent begot peril.

To lessen such horrors and to succor the poor and unemployed, Parliament applied its corrective hand in a number of measures which culminated in 1601 in the Poor Law. Laying a levy on men of property within a given parish, the act sought to put an end to the hateful beggars, the terror of honest countryfolk ever since the days of Henry. By another stroke the statute attempted to reduce the national idleness, in those days a sin against the Heavenly Father and a crime against the commonweal. For this purpose it ordered the laying in of "a convenient stock of flax, hemp, wool, thread, iron, and other stuff to set the poor to work." Finally, lest the offspring of the poor grow up in admiration of their idle elders, it was ordained that they be put out as apprentices in workplaces where they were to learn some useful trade and, needless to say, piety and virtue. Engendered as much or, maybe, even more—from fear and hatred of the idle and unruly as from pity and a propensity, however vague, for good works, these principles cemented themselves in everyday practice; and subsequently, when the English crossed the sea to set themselves up in the Colonies, they introduced them over here. Massachusetts put them into law as early as 1642, and Virginia followed suit soon after.

9

The successor of the Renaissance, the Reformation displayed some of its familiar trappings. Like its antecedent, it put its stock in the study of original sources, biblical now rather than classical; and like the one, the other lit its torch in behalf of individual judgment. But in the daily practice the flare sometimes sputtered—indeed, on the precise meaning of the Scriptures, Protestants found themselves incessantly at odds. The Reformers were men of courage; and some of them were also men of brains; but they were not geniuses, nor were they skeptics. Intellectually, they based themselves in Holy Writ. Their finest exemplars were at ease in Latin and Greek, and not infrequently in Hebrew. But given to theological obsessions, they were averse to explaining the cosmic phenomena by looking them squarely in the face. Their roster glistens with men of God and men of learning, but always their test for ideas and truth was not plausibility, but the authority which gave sanction. Their *prominenti* are the Luthers, the Zwinglis, the Burgenhagens, and the Melanchthons, patrons all at the fount of surety; but in their lists one finds no Vallas, no Boccaccios, no Erasmuses, and no da Vincis, drinkers all of a bubbling skepticism, poisonous, to be sure, when taken too rashly, but emboldening too, and indispensable to the emancipation of the modern mind.

The supreme fact of the Reformation is its enthronement of the Bible as the sole guide of faith and conduct. It became, so to say, the Protestant Pope, or as some wag, probably Romish, put it, a "paper pope." This, bracketed with the fact that the Reformation, unlike the Renaissance, tendered its attraction not to an elite, whether talented or merely moneyed, but to the innumerable folk in the mass, became the springboard for Protestant education. Did a man's acquaintance with Holy Writ promise to ease his ascension to the Pearly Gates? Then obviously he ought to know how to read it. Not only did Protestant commanders urge the boon of literacy upon their faithful; some even sought to make its attainment mandatory; and some, going a step further, declared for the establishment of schools with aid and support from the civil arm. It is to Protestantism that we owe the rise and spread of the vernacular elementary school. Intended for the common children, it drilled and policed them in reading and religion, occasionally in writing, and always in the axioms of good and evil. Though various Protestant leaders were far from despising assistance from the governmental purse, this is not to say that they conceived their primary school as a servant of the state rather than of God.

As the years slipped on, Protestant primary schools slowly took shape and substance. They prospered especially in Calvinistic lands, not only in Geneva, but in Scotland and Holland, and in Puritan Massachusetts. But they found favor too in Germanic lands. In England, where the Reformation was much more worldly in its flavor than spiritual, they made heavy weather of it. Yet whatever their national or religious affiliation, on one point they were in accord, namely, that children are full of malicious animal spirits, and to fit them for the world here and beyond, flogging them fiercely and frequently is an inescapable obligation. Schoolmasters, hence, were esteemed not so much for their knowledge or for their talents in pedagogy as for their powers to clout and curb the young.

Though the Reformers recognized the need for instructing the common people, and even achieved wonders in giving the business at least a modest start, in the beginning of the Reformation they were even more concerned with keeping their churches stocked with competent pastors. Hence their traffic in the secondary learning, the *Gymnasiums, collèges*, and grammar schools which offered tomorrow's holy men their essential tools, the ancient languages, that is, some rhetoric, grammar, and logic, and gigantic draughts of religion and morality. For those aspiring to God's highest services, there were the universities, reformed and refurbished according to denominational specifications.

CHAPTER 12

THE CATHOLIC REFORMATION

Even before the Lutheran cataclysm a number of Catholics, lay as well as frocked, had been urging a moral housecleaning on Mother Church, but she gave no heed. The Reformation, in truth, was more than a quarter century on its way before the Church found herself in a mood to deal with her afflictions. For this purpose Pope Paul III summoned a council in 1555 in the Italian city of Trent. When, some eighteen years later—after the passing not only of Paul, but three of his successors as well—the congress issued from its deliberations, it had set in motion what has since been called the Catholic Reformation. Not only did it undertake to purge the Church of her most glaring contaminations; it also sought to clarify and reaffirm her venerable claims and doctrine. To nail down the results of its labor, the council—like the leaders of the new religions—reposed much of its hope in the power of education.

A number of organizations soon ventured to work toward such an end, and among them the Society of Jesus, or as common parlance prefers, the Jesuit Order, stood in the forefront. Founded in 1534 and granted papal approval six years later, the society was the work of Ignatius Loyola, a Spanish grandee and soldier, and today a blessed saint. Loyola's predilection for the military manner showed itself in the organization of the society which was welded together like an army, full of discipline and obedience, with a general in the high command and officers in descending order and responsibility down to the lesser privates in the ranks. Starting as missionaries to convert the Moslems, after Trent the Jesuits enlarged their endeavor, exerting themselves always and everywhere "for God's greater glory," to strenghten the Church and the Papacy, and by their teaching and preaching, and the spell of their rectitude, to induce the truant heretics to return to the ancient faith.

The order was under the rule of a constitution, of which the fourth part, the Ratio Studiorum, laid down the ordinance for Jesuit education. Put together with unsparing care, the Ratio came into being only after a prolonged scrutiny of the best educational practice then known to Europe and after years of trial and overhauling in Jesuit classrooms. It appeared in its first incarnation in 1586, but thirteen years came and passed before the Ratio attained its final form. From then on it maintained itself without alteration for almost 250 years until 1832 when, bowing to the facts of a more modern age, the society put a slightly augmented stress on the study of science and mathematics besides history and geography. Thus the Ratio remained until 1906 when its compulsory nature was relaxed, and every Jesuit province was allowed to bring its teaching into greater correspondence with local needs.

2

The Jesuit fathers addressed themselves to the preparation of boys in the secondary and higher learning, and except under very special circumstances, they did not concern themselves with the elementary variety. Their schools fell into two kinds, lower and upper, the former taking in its boys at the age of twelve or slightly more, and the latter from about sixteen on. A boy enrolled in a Jesuit academy might harbor the hope of wearing the Jesuit cloth himself some day, or he might content himself to remain an ornament of the laity. He might be rich or he might be poor. He might even be a Protestant. In any case, his education was the same, and from its beginning to its end it cost him not a penny. In an age when any learning beyond the barest elements was popularly regarded as a prerogative of the rich and the highborn, and as something beyond the need and right of the common folk, such a policy exerted an enormous charm, and attracted not only Catholics, but even heretics.

A boy seeking admission to a Jesuit school was expected to have at least a nodding acquaintance with Latin. Once enrolled, he was put upon, under peril of penalty, to speak Latin at all times, whether he chanced to be reciting in the classroom or working off steam on the playing field. Naturally, a great store was put on religion and virtue, and everything known to moral and theological science was done to ground him soundly for a happy life not only here but beyond the grave. From first to last his studies were prescribed, and so were his schoolbooks. During his first three years, besides introducing himself to Greek, he applied himself to studying Latin grammar "including all the exceptions and idioms. . . . " Meanwhile, he made his way into ancient letters, beginning warily with easy pieces from Nepos and proceeding, as he gained in information and confidence, to Virgil, Cicero, Catullus, and several others of that line. With grammar out of the way, he began to break ground for "eloquence." He now increased his erudition, and sampled his first precepts of rhetoric. The whole range of the classical literary art came under search and inspection, but the kingpin was Cicero, and no sun was allowed to set without the study of at least one of his prose passages. The last stage of the boy's schooling concentrated on making him an accomplished and polished virtuoso of the rhetorical art, in both its useful and its ornamental phases. Toward such a goal he drilled himself diligently in the refinements of a voluptuous utterance, with Cicero as his model, but with assistance from Tertullian and Aristotle.

For most boys the study of rhetoric marked the turning point in their chase for knowledge, and with its consummation, their schooldays came to an end. Those accepted as candidates for the order now passed into a two-year probationary period, the so-called "novitiate," during which, shut off from the pleasures and gratifications of everyday, and put under an iron discipline, they immersed themselves in spiritual and religious exercise. They were under constant watch and appraisal, and those whose qualities fell short of approval were dismissed. The survivors, after vowing to remain poor, to keep themselves chaste and celibate, and to obey their superiors no matter what, now confronted a three-year course in philosophy. Cicero's Humanistic hand was still plain to see—the Jesuit conditioning had been much too powerful for it ever to be dispelled. But it was Aristotle who now dominated the field, and where the Humanists had disowned him, and even piled him with abuse and contumely, the Jesuits extolled him, not only in the realm of moral philosophy, but in the physical sciences as well. "Never," cautioned the Ratio, "deviate from Aristotle in matters of any importance." Thus the fathers sought to perfect a blend of the ancient legacy which the Humanists had restored to its lost grandeur, and the Aristotelian tradition which for so many hundreds of years had held the medieval schoolman in the palm of its hand.

3

With the completion of his philosophical engagement the young man, now in his early twenties, was commissioned to teach grammar in one of the lower schools. Thus he might be made to serve the rest of his days on earth. But if he was designed for a loftier mission, his sufferings as a grammarian lasted only a couple of years until he was put upon to prepare himself for holy orders at a Jesuit university. When he came forth four years later, he was ready to be ordained for the priesthood. If he happened to be of a notable teaching talent, he was made to give another two years to study. At the same time he perfected himself in the pedagogic art and got set to teach in one of the Jesuit colleges. When that time arrived, the incipient professor found himself on the borderline of thirty, a little more, perhaps, or a little less. With such infinite care bestowed on his selection and training, with all the surveillance, the consultation, the testing and appraising that had gone into his making, the Jesuit teacher was not only in the *garde du corps* of his organization; he was also—and by long odds—the finest representative of his craft within the confines of Christendom.

As one might expect, the fathers gave sober thought to the manner in which teachers executed their ancient specialty in the classroom. Such an attitude, however, should not be taken for granted. True, even then the idea of teaching methodically and in accord with a body of plausible principles was no novelty. The ancient Quintilian, it will be recalled, had started the ball rolling, and Humanists and a few others had given it a fresh push. Even so, in general practice the idea was given little notice, and so, though the Jesuits were not the first to entertain the notion of employing a systematic teaching methodology, they were the first to put it into vigorous use, and on a scale which for its time was gigantic.

The Jesuits' instruction and the organization of their pupils went hand in glove. Every class, to cite cases, was cast into two opposing fronts, each vying to outdo the other in collective merit. Again, every class was divided into platoons of ten, each under the eye of a monitor, who not only heard his squadmen recite their memorized homework, but also reported on their various pathologies, mental, moral, scholastic, and miscellaneous. By boyhood's unwritten law such a fellow should have been judged reprehensible; rather curiously, he was not, and his monitorial office was even accorded a show of deference. In addition, every pupil had an appointed "rival" who, like a shadow, was always with him, yet who, unlike a shadow, was far from silent. Rather like a sentinel, he was ever on guard, hovering to ensnare his rival in error. If successful, he was under orders to expose the blunder and correct it straightway before the class and master assembled. Each class, finally, had its officers, but since the boon of suffrage had not yet been invented, at least not in schools, they were appointed by the teacher. Wisely, the Ratio laid down its caveat against the malpractice of favoritism, and so the offices usually went not to the politicians, nor even to the gladsome and brawny ones, but to the bright and shining lads who wrote the best Latin compositions.

As for the method itself, like all important things in Jesuit education, it had been carefully studied and combed, and its use was mandatory. Stressing an oral approach, it undertook to explain and clarify the matter under study. Gleaned from Cicero, it might run from a mere two lines to a couple of hundred words. It might be simple and transparent, or it might be knotty and profound—yet in every instance its source had to be Cicero. The professor began his assault on the selection by rendering it aloud. Then he explained its meaning as a whole. Then, like a customs officer, he sorted and sifted it, first sentence by sentence and finally word by word, pondering it as he went along, its grammar and structure, its history, geography, and literature, and if anything else popped up, he set upon that too. Meanwhile, his scholars, bending over their desks, gave him ear and scribbled notes. But it would be wrong to infer, as some have done, that the Jesuit schoolboy was a mere copyist, and that his questions were discouraged. Not only could he ask questions, but his master was expected to attend to them politely, and there were always discussions. Like all vivid explanations, those of the Jesuit teacher abounded in comparisons and apt allusions. This does not mean that he was to forego the subject at hand and wander garrulously, as professors have been reported sometimes to do, into whatever mazes his fancy swept him. His job, first and last, was to teach Ciceronian Latin. Nor does it mean that he was permitted the luxury of speaking his own thought. "Even in matters where there is no risk to faith and devotion," the ever-present Ratio warned him, "no one shall introduce . . . any opinion that does not have suitable authority without first consulting his superiors." His instruction hence was scarcely pliant, but corseted, and sometimes even politic.

The professor's untangling of the text was supplemented and fortified by the recitation. But it was only remotely like the recitations some of us recall. Much more than a verbal exchange between master and fledgling, it was played on the vibrant instrument of competition, with bold and frequent overtones from itching rivals. Finally, there were debates, or as the word was then, disputations. These were, so to speak, the sweetmeat that graced the more substantial table.

There was at least one debate a day, and it was witnessed by the entire school gathered in assembly. Some debates, however, were private. The more formal and elegant ones were reserved, as one might guess, for festive public occasions.

If, as the fathers liked to say, repetition is the mother of learning, then drill and review were its indispensable helpmates. They punctuated the schoolboy's calendar with a rhythmic regularity. Every school day was greeted with a reboiling of yesterday's learning, and the same day went to its sunset with a systematic second look at the new intellectual intake. There was a review every week and a special one every month, and there was a gala one every half year, and a de luxe one at the end of the year. The familiar query of contemporary students about whether the professor will bedevil his classes with a final examination was never raised in Jesuit circles. The test came, like death, inevitably and inexorably. No one escaped it, neither the brilliant nor the dull. And the inquest was always oral, conducted in the presence of all the students. Those who regarded themselves as potential Jesuits were required to pass with honors; the rest got off more easily.

Although the Jesuits never heard of the science of boy behavior—or misbehavior—which is well esteemed currently by enlightened nations everywhere, they had a sharp instinct, nevertheless, for some of its propositions. At a time, for example, when it was generally considered necessary to make learning effective by administering it in unpalatable doses, the fathers counseled moderation. Never was a boy—or even a teacher—to be badly used. The ordeal of study was to be relieved by sport and play—outdoors if the weather chanced to be friendly. In an age when the ambush of sickness and death was forever around the corner, the Jesuit teachers, for all their academic mark, were mindful of the needs of health, and they did their utmost to favor them. That individuals vary in everything which constitutes Homo sapiens was recognized in Jesuit quarters long before it became a contemporary commonplace. Though no boy was to abstain from anything which was required, if he happened to be endowed with some special talent, then his master was to furnish him extra help and advice. A lad could be promoted at any time, or he could be put back.

The Jesuits, it is common knowledge, were strict, but apparently they never forgot the old chestnut that boys will be boys. The boys were rewarded with prizes and honors when they were meritorious—even, indeed, with a fanfare of public acclamation. But when they were wicked, they were punished. To spare a teacher from his pupil's awakened rancor, only minor breaches of the peace were left under the master's jurisdiction. The rest became the business of a specialist. Although the official corrector was not a member of the Jesuit Society, he was equipped with what amounted to plenipotentiary powers. When he was called upon to do his duty, the Ratio bade him to execute his warlike enterprise with discretion. But where the evildoing was gross and flagrant, the sentence might be suspension, or even dismissal.

4

Looked at historically, Jesuit education is, of course, incommensurable with modern standards. Judged by the standards of its own time, however, it was doubtless of a high and uncommon caliber. "Consult the schools of the Jesuits," declared Francis Bacon, an Anglican, "for nothing better has been put into practice." To be sure, many of their freshmen dropped by the roadside, and they never reached commencement; but those who did were superbly schooled. They could speak and write Latin with ease and grace; they were familiars of the finest in ancient letters; and they were as learned and mannered as the best methods in the hands of the most adroit teachers could make them. It has been charged that they were ignorant of whole fields of human inquiry, that they were strangers to independent thinking, and that the ideas they flaunted were ready-made, cast in the mold of official Catholic doctrine. For the overwhelming run of Jesuit alumni this was doubtless the case, but it is not the whole case. Jesuit graduates, like those from any other grove, comprised a herd of inconsequentials; on the other hand—and perhaps merely by way of exception—their roll glistens with the names of Descartes, Corneille, Tasso, Calderon, and Molière—even, indeed, such infidels as Diderot and Voltaire.

The quality of Jesuit education, fortified by the colossal force and diligence of the fathers, brought their work a fine prosperity. There apparently was no lack of altruists eager to furnish the essential funds to erect and supply school buildings, the chapel which was their necessary partner, and the perpetual endowment for the maintenance of the staff and professors. The first Jesuit school, the Collegium Romanum, opened its doors in Rome in 1551, in the seventeenth year of the society's existence. A year later in the same city there followed the Collegium Germanicum. One observes their schools and missions not only gaining in number, but reaching out in all directions, to the east as far as Japan, and to the west into the remote marches of the New World, as time was dissolving into memory. Some half a hundred years after its advent, the society had founded not quite two hundred houses of learning; by 1640 it could muster almost twice as many; and by 1706, the sesquicentenary of Loyola's passing, their schools numbered a round eight hundred. After that the winds of fortune turned, and in 1760 the number had fallen to some 725.

It was in Europe, of course, that the Jesuits concentrated their most pressing effort. There, as God's commandos, they carried on a relentless campaign on behalf of the Counter Reformation, and if in certain lands the onrush of Protestantism was stalled, and sometimes even reversed, then in no small measure it was due to the industry of the fathers. Inevitably this sucked some of their number into the shadowy corridors of power politics where, sometimes, their devotion to the Church was corrupted by their zeal to promote her cause at any price. There is no blinking the fact that their methods, which were sometimes base and discreditable, brought them into bad repute. The historians of morality have duly noted that they were ousted from land after land. In time they alienated not only Protestants, but Catholics too, and in 1773 Pope Clement XIV, recognizing, as he said, "that for the welfare of Christendom, it were better that the Order should disappear," ordered its dissolution. In the Kingdom of Prussia, then under the scepter of the great Frederick, a despot, but also a guarantor of religious freedom, the papal order was flouted. "Since I am regarded as a heretic," the sovereign declared, with a Voltairean gloat, "the Holy Father can absolve me neither from keeping my promise nor from behaving as an honorable man and king." In Romanov Russia Catherine the Great reacted similarly.

When the society returned forty years later, the world had changed. The issue of the Reformation and the Counter Reformation which, during the order's heyday, had inflamed the entire civilized world of the West, though still faintly smoldering underneath its embers, was now mostly academic. This is not saying that the fathers were stranded without a purpose. They still toiled for God's greater glory, for the propagation of the faith, and for the Papacy. But their appeal, once so alluring, had lost its early magic. The fact is, time had left them standing still. Starting out in the mid-sixteenth century as the purveyors of the most thorough and efficient education then to be had in Europe, they had long since been overtaken by the more advanced and improved pedagogy of Comenius and Ratke, and of Rousseau and Pestalozzi. Nor did the competition they were getting from the rising secular schools ease their lot. Their Ratio Studiorum, for all its laudable qualities, was nevertheless a time-bound mechanism, and until its revision in the nineteenth century, and its general loosening-up in the twentieth, the fathers could not hope to cope with the demands of a civilization wherein skepticism and secularism were becoming a compelling, and in the years following, a commonplace, reality.

5

The Jesuits, as has been said, occupied themselves with the secondary and higher learning. It fell to others, and notably the Christian Brothers, to grapple with the problem of instructing the younger child. The Christian Brothers, or, to give it the dignity of its official designation, the Institute of the Brethren of the Christian Schools, was founded in 1684 by Jean-Baptiste de la Salle. Born into the upper orders, de la Salle, who is now a saint, was a man with plenty of money. In later years, however, when he took to good works, he renounced his riches, disbursing his money to the poor, and living, so to say, on the land. He was undoubtedly a man of high intellectual potency, not, of course, of the extraordinary caliber of his fellow saint, Thomas Aquinas, or even Roger Bacon, but of a great gift nonetheless. At the age of eight, when the generality of boys are enjoying dreams of becoming home-run kings or bank robbers, de la Salle was in attendance at the University of Rheims. Three years later he made his way through the initial ceremonial in his candidacy for the priesthood, and five years after that he was ensconced as a canon on the staff of the Rheims cathedral.

As happens not uncommonly, de la Salle came into teaching by accident, and it was only after many days and nights of prayer and self-examination that he was able to make up his mind. The truth is he had aspired to advance himself over the ecclesiastical route and become, if Providence was agreeable, a bishop, or maybe an archbishop, or even a pope. But fortune steered him off his course into the company of young schoolmasters. They were, in the main, a woebegone lot, full of meritorious aspirations, it is true, but insecurely grounded for their work, low of funds, and short of rations. De la Salle took pity on these men, and presently was attending them with food and lodgment, and a variety of practical counsel. They, for their part, inclined to gather round him, and in the course of time it was probably inevitable that they should look to him to lead them out of the wilderness. It is not necessary to detail the story of this bond. Be it enough to indicate that out of its loose and indeterminate beginning there emerged the Christian Brothers with de la Salle at the wheel as their full-time chief and counselor.

The brothers dwelt together under a common roof, and as in the case of the Jesuits, their lives and labors were regulated by stringent rule. They were a lay society, which is to say they were neither priests nor monks, though they robed themselves in long, black habits, and they swore the common monastic oaths. Even before the advent of the order the founder had evinced concern over the appalling ignorance of the lower classes, and especially the poor. Hence, when the brethren got under way, one of their primary purposes was to afford the boys of the underprivileged an easy access to elementary schooling and without cost. Needless to say, the way the cultural tide was running then, such learning was tinged heavily with religion and morality. The brothers burned, they let it be known, to preserve their pupils' innocence, that is, "where they have not already lost it," besides scaring them away "from the horror of evil." To such purpose the members of the society were to labor "by prayer, teaching, and vigilance."

Like the Jesuit schools, those of the institute were enormously successful. Starting at Rheims with a dozen brothers, they soon overran other parts of France, showing themselves in one municipality after another, and in the advancing years even on the Atlantic's western shore, where, of course, they are still in flourishing practice. Unlike the Jesuits, however, the brothers were predominantly French. When their order was suppressed and put under interdict in 1792 during the French Revolution, its enterprise extended to some 120 communities in France, and at least a half a dozen more in other places. At the time, some thirty thousand youngsters were wearing out its benches, taking their learning from about a thousand masters. It is not improbable, as some contend, that the work of the brothers marks the start of the common French boy's schooling in the mother tongue. Under the first Napoleon the ban on the society was lifted, and it was allowed to resume its Heaven-sent mission. In Catholic lands, considering one school with another, the education it offered the younger boy, though in no sense on a level with the best then on tap, was probably the best to be had by the nether folk right into the middle years of the nineteenth century.

6

Where the Jesuits relied educationally on their Ratio, the brothers served themselves with what they called the *Conduct of Schools*. Unlike the former, however, the *Conduct* was not compounded collectively and after several years of classroom trial, but was the work of de la Salle himself. It was, like the Ratio, a highly wrought educational declaration, and it dealt with education's every detail, from the content of subjects to the methods employed to impart them, and from the correction and improvement of penmanship to the penalties to be meted out to careless and wicked boys.

As a boy toiled up the steep hill of learning, he disposed of the common three Rs, besides spelling, penmanship, and composition. He introduced himself to reading by learning the ABCs from a large chart hung from the wall—a practice which still obtains in various parts of the world. Next, he tackled a simple reader, working his way through its mystery from one cover to the other. Once he managed to read aloud with an easy fluency and with suitable deference to commas, semicolons, and periods, his proficiency was pronounced satisfactory. Now he set himself on a Latin prayer book, but he merely skirted the outer rim, and he never did any execution on its grammar and syntax.

The brethren applied themselves with undivided earnestness to the teaching of penmanship, an art greatly esteemed in those days, but now fallen into a low state. They drilled and rehearsed their wards relentlessly in every detail, from the correct method of pen gripping and body stance to the actual fabrication of the letters themselves. After a boy had mastered this delicate knack, he was put to work copying everyday commercial forms, besides leases, deeds, mortgages, contracts, and similar writs of practical enlightenment.

The school day ran for seven hours, five days a week, with time off for religious holidays, and a month's sabbatical in September. At least half the program was devoted to sacred exercise, including hymnody and the study of the catechism. Mass was celebrated daily, and at all times children were exhorted to count their beads and offer frequent prayers to the Most High.

As was meet and proper, a great stress was laid on manners and decorum. There were bowings aplenty not only before the holy cross, as is to be expected, but before the presiding master. By the same token, the savant was expected to treat his pupils with courteous consideration. He was never to affront them with "unseemly motions," and he was never to embellish them with dubious titles, such as pig or donkey, even when they were worthy of such honors. To lighten a parent's task of bringing his young ones to heel in the first principles of a passable conduct, de la Salle provided them with a manual of arms, the *Règles de la bienséance et de la civilité chrétienne.* Such handbooks on the punctilios of human comportment were common enough—in fact, from the Middle Ages on learned men, including such high and mighty ones as Erasmus and Corderius, had been distilling them by the keg. What the father of the Christian Brothers offered was pretty much the same: a concoction, that is, which was calculated to induce a conscious rectitude in such things as manners, hairdos, posture, table address, and the like, for none of which from time out of mind the young had ever shown an appreciative respect. But, for all that, de la Salle's admonitory counsel bore the quality at least of being outspoken and understandable. "Take special care," it enjoined, "to see there is no vermin or stink. . . ." "It is shameful," it bore on, "to have dirty, filthy hands; this is tolerable only in the case of laborers and peasants." And in an age of deprivation, when comfort stations were unheard of, "when one needs to urinate, one should always retire to a secluded spot, and it is wrong to perform other natural functions except in places where one cannot be seen." Less conventional than Saint Jean-Baptiste's rules of etiquette were his views on discipline. The bastinado, to be sure, he did not ban; nevertheless, he deplored its all too frequent use. It is used, he said, "only out of bad temper or weakness. For the birch is a servile punishment, which degrades the soul even when it corrects, if indeed it corrects, for its usual effect is to harden."

In his *Conduct of Schools* de la Salle, who seems to have had a psychopathological horror of the merest decibel, put his taboo on unnecessary sound. The ideal classroom, hence, had all the muted stillness of a mortician's parlor. The young were bidden to tread "lightly and sedately," and they were to sit silently without wiggling and with no foot scraping. At bottom, the stress was on the written word, though some concessions had to be granted to its spoken cousin in learning numbers and the catechism, and of course, in reading aloud. To preserve quietude the brothers replaced speech with signals and gestures. Even punishment was to be delivered and received in silence. In such a tomblike atmosphere there was obviously no room for mirth. Play and recreation were outlawed not only within the school itself, but within its immediate neighborhood.

This does not mean that the brethren were harsh or barbaric. In fact, for the times in which they labored, they were comparatively enlightened, not, perhaps, as astutely as were the Jesuit fathers, but more, certainly, than the Calvinists who believed in the child's innate depravity, and whose specialists in divine science likened the young to rattlesnakes, alligators, and other guests of the zoological garden. De la Salle addressed himself assiduously to the subject of disciplining the young, and in the *Conduct* he was at pains to treat its psychology, morality, and sociology at great length. Some of his views, connoisseurs have granted, sit very well even in our own day of elaborate refinement. All punishment, for example, was to be moderate. It was to fit the crime, and it was always to be administered prudently, and with a high dignity. It was dispensed to all disturbers of the peace without exception, save only in the case of the sick, the stupid, and the incoming freshmen. Only major torts, moreover, called for the visitation of the lash, and even these were quantitatively regulated. There were to be so-and-so many whacks for fibbing, and so-and-so many for pilfering. Other punishable crimes were quarreling, brawling, acting irreverently in church, and the like. In any case, no matter what the misdeed, there were never to be more than five clouts per offense. These were to be applied solely to the palm. The school code prohibited any outcry from the condemned; nor was he even permitted to caress his outraged hand. Instead he was to regard the whole business as beneficial to the state of his soul. Where a boy proved unamenable to law and order, his sentence might incur dismissal. It is only fair to state that the brothers were quick to recognize virtue, and that they rewarded the righteous frequently.

For all their limitations, the Christian Brothers did education a good service. They not only provided instruction in the rudiments for the heirs of the lower classes; they also ran orphan homes, boarding schools, industrial schools—even, indeed, a reformatory for the wayward young. Their method of forwarding the art of handwriting did credit to their pedagogical resourcefulness—in fact, their method of teaching in general, whenever their insistence on silence did not hobble it, was in advance of the common practice. They sorted their pupils into categories, and gave them instruction as a group rather than operating on each of them singly, as was then the universal custom. Familiar to us as the homely class lesson, the scheme was put forward with great ardor by Jan Amos Comenius, a Protestant scholar and teacher who performed in the seventeenth century. However, with practicing schoolmasters it got precisely nowhere, and despite the excellent results it bore the Christian Brothers, the world continued to regard it apathetically until the nineteenth century, when it came at length into its own.

As for the training of teachers, the Jesuits had, of course, given the matter some conscientious reflection. Their quest, however, was not for instructors primarily, but for men of learning. It soon dawned on de la Salle that the two are not identical, and that teaching the very young required something more than a well-stuffed head, that, in truth, some insight into the elusive mystery of the boy's nature and behavior would be of help. To provide such training de la Salle founded a seminary for teachers in 1685 at Rheims. Though this was not the first attempt to introduce teachers to the secrets of their craft, yet it was the first school of its kind, and therefore it was also the faraway ancestor of the teachers college, now in full florescence everywhere. In 1950, on the fifteenth of May, Pope Pius XIII declared St. Jean-Baptiste de la Salle to be the "Celestial Patron of all teachers."

7

Besides the Jesuits and the Christian Brothers, several other teaching orders, as has been hinted, struggled to instruct young France in knowledge, morality, and the Christian religion. Of these only two stand forth, and though time has long since withered them, so meritorious was their service when they were in full bloom, that we needs must give them some of our time and thought. Of the twain the first on the scene was the Order of the Oratory of Jesus, or in the layman's terser talk, the Oratorians. Its ancestry reaches back to the sixteenth century when it was founded in Italy as a monastic community, without, however, the imposition of the friar's customary vows. Transplanted into France in 1611—the Society of Jesus was then already a grizzled seventy-seven—it shed its monkish trappings to become an independent teaching association of priests, specializing in preparing ambitious youths for the holy cloth. Before long, however, it found itself conducting a number of secondary schools for the edification of the laity, among them the heirs of aristocracy.

More liberal than the Ratio-shackled Jesuits, the Oratorians leaned not on the authority of the venerable Aristotle, but on the thinking of René Descartes, a mathematician and philosopher of their own time, and in the annals of thought a savant of the front rank. Although he had attended the sessions of the learned Jesuits and had been one of their most dazzling students, when Descartes came to his intellectual ripeness, he found no relish in the teachings of his masters. Of a quick and eager cast of mind, he demanded something more substantial than the mere say-so of a custom-made authority. To obtain the intellectual assurance he so sorely wanted, he proceeded to work out a method, whose principles he recorded in 1637 in his trailblazing *Discourse on Method*. Therein he embraced the proposition that in order to compound a body of logical and dependable knowledge philosophers, no less than scientists, must not only divest themselves of all preconceptions, however charming and admirable they may seem to be, but they must also rid themselves of the venerated authority of the ancients.

The first step, in a manner of speaking, was to clear the cerebral decks, stripping them for action of every shred of bias and presumption. This taken care of, one proceeded to refine and reduce every problem to its essential elements, stating them in their plainest and simplest form. Thereupon, step by logical step, one advanced from the simple knowledge which was clearly indisputable to a more complex and elaborate formulation. After that, one arranged one's thoughts and propositions in orderly progression. Then there followed a comprehensive analysis and review with a statement of the conclusion as a grand finale. The method is the familiar one of the mathematician. "You can substitute," Decartes once commented, 'the mathematical order of nature' for 'God' wherever I use the latter term." The fact is that for Descartes mathematics constituted the only relationship between the world and its innumerable parts, and he was convinced that in philosophy, as in science, it could be relied upon to bring forth the same unfailing certainty.

8

The relatively liberal outlook of the Oratorians is reflected in their pedagogy. Dear to their heart, for one thing, were the humanities, especially the ancient tongues and letters. For those of their clients who aspired someday to serve at the altar of God, a secure grounding in Latin and Greek was, of course, absolutely necessary. But for numerous others who were heading for a profaner way of life, the Oratory made concessions, offering them a chance to perfect themselves in such newer idioms as Spanish and Italian. In France the seventeenth century witnessed a surging pride in the national language. Intoned in the lofty strophes of its dramatists, the immortal Corneille and Racine, in plainer form, though clear and resonant, it became the vehicle for Descartes's scholarly treatise, a linguistic achievement which, had it been hazarded only a short time earlier, would have been excoriated as an affront to academic decorum. To this development the order was not insensitive. In fact, not only did its practitioners insist on a thorough mastery of the maternal tongue, but in their classes, for the first four years of a boy's schooling, it became the medium of his instruction, an innovation, if ever there was, in the halls of secondary learning in those days of long ago.

Like the Jesuits, though with ponderably less heat, the Oratorians laid an appreciable stress on the development of a gracious and powerful utterance, and for this reason they emphasized training in the spoken word over the written. The hospitality they accorded the vernacular in their course of study found a sympathetic echo in their recognition of French history as a meet and proper object of learning. It was a stand which took some daring, but which, unhappily, was not emulated by other centers of knowledge before the lapse of a considerable time. Not only did the Oratory surpass the Society of Jesus in its affirmation of the native culture, but by its offerings in chemistry, physics, and anatomy it tendered ocular proof of its acknowledgement of the anticipated importance of the natural sciences in the emerging Western world. Needless to say, a band of earnest and devoted masters who took their intellectual cue from the mathematics-breathing Descartes would be expected to make room for his specialty in their curriculum. "I know of nothing of greater use than algebra and arithmetic," glowed Father Lamy, one of their votaries, forgetting for a moment all about the mother tongue. As has already been said, in some of their schools—as witness, their *collège* at Juilly—the Oratorians were favored by the carriage trade, the sons, that is, of the nobility and the well-heeled. To help such worthies meet the exigencies life had forced upon them, the order thoughtfully enriched its catalogue of courses with the theory and practice of such fine arts as music, dancing, and horsemanship.

In their teaching the Oratorians were only slightly less advanced than in their renovation of the curriculum. Subscribers to the New Vision of Descartes, they not only revealed the essence of his philosophy in their classrooms, but true to his method, they undertook to illuminate their quest for truth with the light of reason—within the limits, of course, of the inarguable axioms of the Holy Church. Though their primary aim was religious, this did not prevent them from reading the works of the secular literati, so long as they conduced to virtue and piety. In a world where all too frequently book knowledge counted as education, the fathers of the Oratory caught a glimpse of the value of learning through the experience of the senses. What history they taught they interwove with the strands of geography, anticipating thereby what in the distant future was to go by the name of correlation. To vivify and reinforce the learner's understanding of science they feasted his eyes with classroom demonstrations and they set him to experimenting in the laboratory. In their chambers of learning they were the declared antagonists of dullness, and though the psychological doctrine of interest was still several centuries from its hatching, they strove at all times to make their teaching as charming and engaging as humanly possible. In consequence, they had no need to resort to threats and bluster. Discipline, indeed, yielded to sweetness and light; only in extremity did they summon assistance from the lash, and even then its application was moderate.

From the start the Oratorians basked in warm prosperity. Like the Jesuits, they cast their spell into other lands, though not as widely, it is true, nor as lavishly. Nor did they ever scale the dizzy heights of success attained by the liegemen of Saint Ignatius Loyola. The Jesuits, in truth, were their foes, philosophical and theological no less than pedagogical, and by their shrewd wire-pulling in high places, they did their utmost to hamper and harass them. But the Fates caressed the Oratorians with their smile—not, to be sure, without the usual ironic overtones. For in 1773, when the Society of Jesus received orders from the Vatican to close house and disband, it became the lot of the underdog Oratorians to fill the breach caused by the dissolution of their rivals. So the Oratory of Jesus conducted its numerous groves, working and spreading its light over the young, until they themselves fell prey to the caprice of fortune to find themselves done in and proscribed.

9

A quarter century or so after the Oratorians had settled in France another religious establishment made its abode in the vacated Cistercian nunnery of Port-Royal-des-Champs, on the outer skirts of Versailles at Chevreuse, which, though it was scarcely more than a cartographic flyspeck, was destined, nevertheless, to become the center of a furious theological rumble-bumble. The creation of Jean Duvergier de Hauranne, spoken of in chronicles more commonly as the Abbé of St. Cyran, or simply as St. Cyran, the Port-Royalists came into being as a sanctuary for men gnawed by their consciences, and panting to insulate themselves against the snares and seductions of a world far gone in sin in order to improve their chances, when the time came, for celestial ascension. To this end, they immersed themselves in study and hard work, supplementing and fortifying their industry with frequent sessions of prayer, fasting, and self-examination.

St. Cyran has passed through the long procession of the ages as a man of spotless probity, of the utmost piety, and a whole-souled friend and disciple of the Dutch Cornelius Jansen, who for a time lectured on sacred science at the University of Louvain, and who subsequently was invested with the episcopal cap and crook at Ypres. Time saw His Grace embrace some of Saint Augustine's gloomy dogma. With the cocksure Saint, for example, he committed himself to the doctrine that ever since Adam had invented sin, his descendants had been utterly and totally depraved. Born into this fretful world with Beelzebub already clutching their souls, humankind were predestined—saving a skimpy handful of God's Elect—to sizzle and crackle postmortem in a Hell of furious fire and suffocating fumes. Although Mother Church solaced her faithful with the assurance that baptism would purge the newborn babe of the stain of Adam's sin, yet St. Cyran insisted that so ingrained was man's depravity, the sacrament, for all its heavenly wonder, lacked the potency to confer more than an evanescent antisepsis, and that, left to his own devices, the baptized would unfailingly revert to sin. To counter this natural bent for wickedness, what was needed, besides the baptismal sprinkling, was to place the young under the steady watch and care, day and night, of dedicated Christian teachers. To such a purpose, in 1637, St. Cyran and his comrades undertook to instruct and oversee a small clutch of boys.

10

From the start the Jansenists fell afoul of the Jesuits, who harried and hindered them at every turn, but whose hostility the former reciprocated sometimes, in truth, with more than measure for measure. One of their advocates was Blaise Pascal. A young physicist and mathematician of great promise, but also a practitioner of a gay and even carnal life, he almost came to an abrupt end in a carriage accident. The mishap so shattered him that for months he teetered on the edge of a neurasthenic collapse. When, at length, he emerged from his traumatic haze under the conviction that his brush with death had been a heavenly portent, he straightway renounced his mundane activities, sober and otherwise, and withdrew to Port-Royal where, riven between hopes and fears, he sought to calm his quavering psyche through piety, work, and reflection. Time watched him climb to a towering height on the Jansenists' ladder, expounding and upholding their sacred theorems with all the frenzied eloquence of the evangelical Jonathan Edwards. Man's inherent sinfulness shocked and dismayed him, and to discharge an installment of personal expiation thereby, he became virtuous to the point of eccentricity. He resorted to recurrent prayer and fasting. He covered his skin with coarse hair shirts, and to make his penance still more onerous, he wore a cumbrous breastplate with iron spikes that rent his flesh. He died before he was forty, a casualty, no doubt, to his self-torment—a dotty genius if there ever was one.

But before he took off for his predestined eternity, Pascal emblazoned his name, probably forever, in the scroll of his country's literary history. Besides several fugitive pieces, two books issued from his pen, the *Pensées*, an apologia for Christianity, which he did not live to complete, and the *Lettres provinciales*, which Voltaire, despite his repugnance for Jansenist moral pathology, hailed as "the first work of genius in prose." Put together over a spread of several years, the *Lettres* constitute Pascal's counterblast against the Jesuits. The work is at once melodious, malicious, and merciless, a hypnotic arrangement of ridicule which pinned its victims to the pillory of an unsparing mockery. Although the Jesuits suffered a severe disfigurement of their public profile, still in the seats of the high and mighty they continued to exert a formidable puissance. The Jansenists could not match the Jesuits' political acumen. The Loyola clerks not only outnumbered the former; they also outmaneuvered them. When, in 1638, St. Cyran braved a public defense of Jansen's doctrines, under Jesuit elbowing and with the help of the powerful Cardinal Richelieu, who pronounced the abbé "more dangerous than six armies," the authorities cried him down as a heretic, and to protect the populace from his Hell-compounded toxins, they deposited him in a dungeon.

Pascal's dissertation did not stay the Jesuits; on the contrary, it only stirred their waspish fury. Consequently, as year chased year, and the Jesuits raised their pressure notch upon notch, the Port-Royalists began to buckle. In 1656 their chief schools were ordered padlocked, and four years later their few remaining ones suffered the same proscription Thus, after less than twenty years of life, the Port-Royalist schools of France vanished from sight.

11

Two motives impelled St. Cyran to turn his attention to pedagogy, the one theological, the other personal. Is Satan, that evil angel, forever hanging about our flanks? Then to outwit him, "the one thing necessary," said St. Cyran, is education. Let there be no dawdling in this matter, he insisted, for Old Horny, as everyone knows, wastes not a fraction of the wink of an eye. To vaccinate the young against his deadly pox, their education, as has been hinted, needs to be extended throughout their childhood, and the business must be executed under the incessant and laborious vigil and inspiriting example of devout and sensitive teachers. To make this possible, the Port-Royalists spared no effort to restrict their centers of learning to a modest dimension, never stocking them with more than fifty pupils, or, as was their more common wont, with no more than a score or thereabout. In truth, had St. Cyran been able to follow his inclination, he would have peopled a school with no more than an even six, whom he "would have chosen as it might please God"—though just how the divine pleasure manifests itself has baffled even our best historians, sacred and profane. Because of their pocket-sized enrollments the Port-Royalist seminaries came to be known as Little Schools, the first designation used by the French to denote a lower school, and one which was to remain in linguistic service for some generations to come.

To allow a master to stand sentinel over his fledglings at all hours, day and night, he was given custody of a flock which never exceeded a half-dozen members, a practice which stood out in startling contrast to the custom prevailing in the secondary schools where instructors were sometimes called upon to face a horde running as large as a hundred head in a single class. During the daytime the Port-Royalist master presided over young minds in the classroom; he monitored their speech and manners at their meals; and he squired them during their momentary jousts with leisure. In the dull of the night, when Hell's agents threw their throttle wide open, the boys shared their master's chamber. On him now fell the duty to pilot them securely through the nocturnal terrors, not only against the insidious powers abroad in the night air, but against the more discernible acts of indecency and indecorum and various and sundry boyish lapses.

Though St. Cyran subscribed to several articles in the Puritans' theological doctrine, notably, original sin, human depravity, and predestination, he looked askance at the dictum laid down by some of their foremost deputies of God, that the Heavenly Father abhorred children, that to him, indeed, they were as loathsome as crocodiles and cockroaches and similar representatives of the divine creation. Although the abbé granted that on some inescapable tomorrow, some nine of every ten children were predestined to populate the Brimstone Pit, still, not unlike the Son of God, he was intent on suffering the little ones to come unto him. "I wish," he remarked, "you would read in my heart the affection I feel for children." His passion for the young set him ablaze with a yearning to succor and save them, and though the odds against their ultimate redemption were staggering, it was to this purpose, nevertheless, that he and his colleagues set the sights of their educational enterprise, "whose chief end," they declared, "should be to save the children and ourselves with them."

In order to keep his protégés high-minded and pure, St. Cyran not only put them under a daily twenty-four-hour watch, including Sundays and holidays, but he also walled them off from all but a limited contact with the world outside. For, as he had observed, the mingling of saints and sinners sometimes sullied the saints. Since even parents, howsoever elevated their intentions, have been known to exert an untoward influence upon their brood, the abbé made it an inflexible rule to accept no child for his light and leading unless the child's propagators granted him plenipotentiary powers in his dealings with their offspring. Thus unencumbered by parental meddling, St. Cyran was free to oversee and direct the education of each of his charges as he saw fit. Did a lad, as sometimes happened, succumb to the charm and challenge of the secular subjects to the danger of his immortal soul? Then, in order to safeguard his imperiled spirit, the abbot ordered him henceforth to abstain from all intellectual intercourse, and to concentrate his thoughts exclusively on religion. Did a father, unmindful of his abdication of authority to the abbot, descend upon him with blood in his eye to protest against such an unheard-of noncerebral schooling? Then he was bidden to remove his heir to some other less scrupulous grove, even, if need be, to a house run by the infamous Jesuits.

Though St. Cyran strove to choose his pupils "as it pleased God," he was aware that his judgment, being all too human, might play him false, and that a boy, who at first glimpse appeared to be a prospect for angelic wings, might, once he was tucked within the Port-Royal fold, show all the qualities of a potential lifer in Hell. Such a fellow was usually fractious and insubordinate, a sworn enemy, as it were, of household peace and tranquility. Although such little dastards were usually a rarity, still should one of them manage to slide past the abbot's guard, then the Port-Royal director insisted that it should be within his right to wash his hands of him forthwith and forever, and "without those from whom he had received him bearing him a grudge for it."

For five years St. Cyran was the reluctant guest of his jailers at Vincennes. It was 1643, shortly after Richelieu's death, when they at length discharged him. His liberation, alas, was all too brief, for a few months following, he too departed from this melancholy world. The force of his impact on the Little Schools, though powerful when he was at large, was too short-lived to leave more than thin and fading trail.

It may well be that in the long run this fortuity was for the good. For though the Abbé of St. Cyran was inherently a kindly man, he was not always tolerant. In him, indeed, the theologian had consumed the pedagogue. In consequence, for all its high purpose, St. Cyran's educational outlook was starkly unimaginative, respectable but undistinguished. Upon his demise his work fell to younger hands. Not a whit less fevered over the Jansenist revelation than their martyred founder, the followers were none the less in closer concord with the bright new spirit then beginning to flare in France—the French sunburst in letters and thought, for example, and especially the newfound pride in the national tongue. Like the Oratorians, not a few of St. Cyran's successors had savored the writings of Descartes and had found them highly delectable. The upshot was a mellowing of their master's pedagogical austerity. Although they continued to tread the path which their leader had blazed to the end of preparing their pupils for the ultimate eternity of Christian bliss, they broadened and strengthened that trail upon a solid bedrock of Cartesian postulates and with a reinforcing overlay of national sentiment.

12

Even more than the Oratorians, the Port-Royalists made the mastery of the mother tongue a matter of capital concern. Indeed, in the protocol of their curriculum, their consideration for the native language was surpassed only by the primacy they bestowed upon religion and morality. Protestant schoolmen had, of course, long since done away with Latin as the instrument of learning and communication in their lower schools, but among Catholics, where the urgency of reading Holy Writ in the vernacular was practically nonexistent, the Roman parlance continued, as it had in the remote and hoary past, to be given deference as the language of the classroom—not counting such daring violations of tradition as those of the Christian Brothers and the Oratorians. To lighten the child's burden in learning to make sense of written French, Blaise Pascal furloughed himself transiently from his other secular pursuits to invent a phonetic method of teaching reading—an extraordinary achievement, when one considers the colossal mingle-mangle of French orthography. Did the Port-Royalists lay the groundwork of the three Rs in the familiar idiom of the child's everyday talk? Then they did it not only because to the learner it made sense, but also because, in its clarity and elegance among the living tongues, they were convinced it was beyond compare. So well was French regarded as the speech of politesse that even outlanders with any pretence to culture were straining to master it—in fact, as the seventeenth century oozed into the eighteenth, French had become the language of many a Continental court. Even that arch-Prussian, the great Frederick, parleyed preferably in French, reserving his staccato German, a language he declared barbarous, for his underlings—his lackeys and soldiers, that is—and his dogs, who, for all their Hohenzollern advantages, were never able to master French.

Although the Jansenists did not say it, they clearly acted on the premise that *"si ce n'est pas clair, ce n'est pas français,"* which means that if a statement fails to make plain sense, then it is not French. To teach their pupils to speak and write the national utterance with clarity and excellence thus became a devoir of supreme importance in every Port-Royal school. In this aspiration the masters may well have set an enduring example, for the high pride those long-since-ghostly gentlemen took in teaching their young how to write and speak a commendable French has permeated Gallic teaching to the present and, it may be added, with praiseworthy results—at all events until recent years, when school enrollments burgeoned so enormously that hard pressed teachers could no longer effectively fulfill their historic role.

Only after they had attained the required mastery of the mother tongue were pupils granted the right to proceed to the study of Latin. They were initiated into its mystery in accordance with the age-old rite, by making acquaintance with the rules, regulations, and bylaws which governed the Roman parlance, not forgetting, of course, the foul play of their numerous scofflaw exceptions. They studied the gender of nouns, surprised, doubtless, that unlike the French, the Romans did not conceive of things as either masculine or feminine—that, as a matter of odd fact, their word for war was, so to say, sexless. They learned that a Latin noun entertains more than a single ending, that, in truth, as far as suffixes are concerned, a Roman noun is, in a way of speaking, a polygamist. They found out too that verbs are tensive and that they have their moods, and so on and on, through all the other fauna in the Romans' lingual zoo. If the Port-Royal schoolboy suffered the usual migraines of having to jampack his head with the principles of Latin's grammatical jurisprudence, then, unlike the run of his generation, sweating and groaning in the conventional caverns of learning, he was at least spared the agony of having to learn them by heart in Latin, a language he was just beginning to ponder. For his relief, indeed, a Port-Royalist—his name was Lancelot—put together a brief Latin grammar written in French, thereby committing a deed of chivalry which not even his Round Table namesake could have hoped to match.

Once he had a fair grip on the ground rules of Roman speech, the boy was put to reading its representative literati, scrupulously disinfected, of course, of any heathen indelicacy. In this vein Port-Royal sanitized even the drolleries of Terence, putting into their pupils' hands an edition of the *Comedies of Terence made very decent while changing very little*, an act which epicures of bawdiness still rank as downright unspeakable. But the main stress fell on rendering the ancient writings, whether prose or poetry, into a stately French. The mood and style of the author was to be respected, and, whenever possible, this was to be maintained, but never was a translation to be slavishly literal. It should always be clear no less than accurate; at the same time it should be so confected as to pass for the work of an exemplary French writer. Thus conceived, translation ceased to be mainly an exercise of the mind: it became, even more, a work of art. Not until a boy had attained the requisite proficiency in metamorphosing Latin into lucid and fluent French was he set to composing his own pieces in Latin—a practice which was at sharp odds with the prevailing custom of putting schoolboys to Latin composition as soon as they had attained a passing acquaintance with the simple elements of grammar.

13

As might be expected from the followers of St. Cyran, whose heart overflowed for the little ones, in an age when beating and banging them was justified on the ground that such treatment was God-ordained, the Port-Royalists abstained from even the slightest use of the corrective stick, or any other form of public humiliation. Relying on honey rather than vinegar to mend the ways of the wicked, the masters were bidden "to speak little, endure much, and pray even more." With the banning of the birch, there also passed the ubiquitous monitor, a boy catchpole whose duty was to spy upon his mates and report their misdoings. If, for all that, their recourse to harps and psalteries availed them naught, and an errant boy proved a continual violator of Port-Royal's law and order, then in the interest of the commonweal, there was nothing left to do but to bid him a permanent adieu. Despite their probing of the elusive recesses of the child's nature, Port-Royal's preceptors, unlike the sagacious Jesuits, put down their collective foot on rivalry, whether intellectual or otherwise. They prohibited competition of any sort, and by the same score, they outlawed emulation. Under the circumstances rewards for merit were strictly taboo.

As Jansenists, the Port-Royalists laid first stress on the development of a virtuous character; as Cartesians, they naturally gave a high rating to clear and logical thinking. Jansenism and Cartesianism were, so to speak, the bright windows and the glittering chandeliers of learning, and without their light even the vastest erudition, their devotees believed, faded into a mere fatuity. Hence, they put little stock in the piling up of knowledge by rote, a method then riding in high favor in the common mills of knowledge. Nor did the Port-Royalists allow themselves to be taken in by prodigies who could spout a flood of memorized knowledge without understanding what it meant. Such fellows were instructed, perhaps; but they were not educated. Like the Oratorians, their fellow Cartesians, the Port-Royalists enlightened their neophytes in logic and geometry, and they paid some heed to science, though it was of a lesser depth and beam and, rather curiously, it was devoid of any supplementation of laboratory experience.

But in one respect the Port-Royalists clearly outsparkled the brethren of the Oratory, and that was in their striving to fathom the nature of the child. Though the prospect of the science of child study was then not even a pallid glimmer in some psychological smart aleck's eye, still in some of their discernments St. Cyran's successors were palpably digging into some of that science's virgin ground. As mentors of youth, they made it their resolve not only to reduce learning to its simplest terms, but to raise it at the same time to the breathtaking altitude of a vivid and unforgettable rapture. From their professional practice they had gathered that the squatters in the schoolboy's bench varied vastly in native assets and liabilities—no novelty, to be sure, if (in case it has fled your mind) you will turn back these pages to the gusty days of Marcus Fabius Quintilian. But the illustrious Marcus had entertained a passion for bulging classes, while the Jansenists cherished just the opposite. As a result, they were in a far better position to grapple hand-to-hand with their laboratory animals, to observe them at close range and with a greater keenness, and to render, as a result, a more accomplished judgment on the varied qualities of their students' dowerings. "Beyond a doubt," volunteered Coustel, one of their salient performers, "a schoolman should understand the different sorts of intellect he is expected to cultivate."

14

As has already been mentioned, in 1660 a royal fiat clamped the lid on the Little Schools in France, but this is by no means saying that it also put a quietus on the hounding of their sponsors. In 1710 Port-Royal's abbey was reduced to rubble, and in an outburst of demoniac madness the graves of their gracious dead were turned up and their bones tossed to the attending dogs. But life sometimes has a way of righting its wrongs. Some Port-Royalists managed to escape, and a few even crossed the ocean to begin life anew in a less hostile clime. For all its persecution in *la grande nation,* the society persisted, and it still provides. teachers in other lands, notably in French Canada. The dissolution of the Little Schools, rather curiously, turned out in the years ahead to be an unexpected blessing. Released from the tedium of their daily twenty-four-hour schedule of teaching and safeguarding their protégés against sin and indecorum, some of the uprooted masters turned to airing their educational views in print. Their output of texts and schoolbooks was truly prodigious. There was Varet with his *Christian Education*; Nicole with the *Education of a Prince*; Coustel with his *Rules for the Education of Christian Children*; and Arnauld, a layman, overflowing with Jansenist juices, with his trinity on *Logic, General Grammar,* and *Regulations on the Studies in the Humanities.* There was even a feminine antiphone, *Regimen for Children* by Jacqueline Pascal, sister of the hapless Blaise, and mistress of a Port-Royal school for girls. As precocious almost as her blighted brother, she introduced herself to the writer's creative art at the age of twelve with a lyrical effusion on the Queen's pregnancy. Though the mills of the gods have been found to grind slowly, through their endless book-writing, the Port-Royalist faithful have made certain that they grind surely: through their texts and treatises, they not only spread the seed of their pedagogic views, but by the same stroke they enjoyed the last laugh over their archfoes and would-be destroyers, the Jesuits.

CHAPTER 13

COLONIAL AMERICA

The rancors which Luther set ablaze in 1517 flamed long after he left this world, not quite thirty years later. During the following century Catholic and Protestant writhed in struggle, each determined to bring peace to a tortured Europe by obliterating the other. The full vigor of their butchery was reached in the seventeenth century in the Thirty Years' War. When the Peace of Westphalia made an end of it at last in 1648, Middle Europe was on its back, its land ravaged, its economy exhausted, and famine and pestilence triumphant. Worse yet, there was no end in sight; for already new wars were breeding, no longer, it is true, for creed and church, but for king and country, for materials and markets, for a national spot, in short, at the rich colonial trough.

It was in such gloom and foreboding that the Thirteen Colonies came into being. All except Georgia originated in the seventeenth century. Though time was to snuggle them under the British wing, they were peopled by a folk vastly varied, not only in personal power and circumstance, but even in such large matters as nationality and religion. All sorts of yearnings lured them across the ocean. Some itched for adventure; some hoped to make their fortune; some pined to Christianize the Indian. Not a few, of course, came to get away from harried Europe, the slings and arrows of its hardships, and especially its wars and religious tyrannies. But whatever their ends, whether solitary or several, the stamp of Europe was upon them. Their settlements, for all their variations, whether in New England, in the Middle Country, or in the South, were just another part of the mother country, the faraway projection of a proud and venerable civilization.

A long time had gone into the making of that civilization, and many threads composed it. Embroidered on the remnant of a faded Greco-Roman fabric, it was given freshness and strength by medieval Christendom, dominant and binding for hundreds of years, until the Renaissance and the Reformation introduced strands of a strange and discordant sort, clashing not a little with the familiar pattern, and marking it in the process with the insignia of an incipient modern age. Three elements suffused its tapestry—the individual, the middle class, and the national state—and in varying style and degree they were interwoven. These elements are visible in the colonists' way of living, their social ideals and enterprise, and their economic, political, and religious institutions. And one glimpses them, of course, in their educational ideals and practice.

Although education in the Colonies displayed much that was common to all, there were also some palpable differences. The likenesses, as anyone can guess, issued from the common Old World heritage, and the differences from the variations in nationality, religion, the local culture, and the power and influence of climate and geography, at times tender and propitious, but not infrequently harsh and hostile. From the interplay of these forces there evolved three distinct sorts of colonial education.

Put your eyes, for example, on Massachusetts Colony. Solidly Calvinistic, its reins of government in theocratic hands, the Bible State found it simple to direct the Colony's educational policy, and by legislation to seek its execution. Nor should you underestimate the educational significance of the New England village. Small, compact, and sufficient to most of its ends, it set its residents within eye and earshot of one another, thus facilitating their communication, and forwarding the interests of the commonweal. The combination of state, church, and tautly bound community made the town school almost natural and inevitable.

The religious solidarity so characteristic of the Commonwealth was absent in the Middle Colonies. There, in place of a single faith, official and all-embracing, one comes upon a crazy quilt of creeds whose Biblical interpretations, as usual, not only varied, but were often in sharp contention. Nor was there even the bond of a common language. Instead of a town school, hence, the people of the Middle Colonies relied on the parish school to give light to their young. For a spell, it is true, New Netherland's Calvinistic Dutchmen operated a few town schools, and even gave them a bit of help from the civil purse, but always held them, so far as was feasible, under the vigilance of the national Dutch Reformed Church. But after the Dutch lowered their flag to the conquering English such doings came to an end.

The Southerners did not, like the New Englanders, lodge themselves in compact, little villages, but dwelt instead on large plantations, separated from one another by a gulf of tremendous space. Under the circumstances, town life barely existed, and the South maintained no town schools. But even had things been otherwise, such seminaries would still have encountered heavy weather, for like their countrymen in the motherland, the Southern governing class had no hankering to school the young under the auspices of government. Instead, they regarded education, like a man's fancy in neckties or garters, as something delicately personal, and no business of the state. In consequence, education in the Southern Colonies was run pretty much in the easygoing manner of the homeland. With the pursuit of knowledge, so to speak, a matter of self-service, the planters with money edified their young with private tutors, or if no such fellow was to be had, they had recourse to private schools either here or overseas. For the generality of children there were, in time, a few free schools, but their offerings were scanty, and from the government they got not even a farthing. Down the human ladder on the nethermost rung, the chances to become literate were for a long time next door to nothing.

It is easy, especially for Anglo-Saxon eulogists, to forget that while the Thirteen Colonies were getting on their legs, flags of other lands were flapping beyond their borders. There too one sights efforts to throw light upon the darkness of ignorance, mainly by the Frenchman and the Spaniard, and in particular by their ordained representatives of God venturing to advance and spread the Catholic faith. Granted, the trail they tracked in American education was slight and has all but vanished. Nevertheless, underneath the external overgrowth a trace of it has been fortuitously preserved. One may behold it in a whole line of states from Florida to Louisiana, thence to Texas, New Mexico, and Colorado, and beyond to Arizona and California.

2

Nearly all the motives which made men take ship for the New World assailed the Puritans, but the most nagging of them all, doubtless, was religious. Their pleasant delusion that some day they would rid the Church of England of its "petty anti-Christs and paltry popes" was dashed by James I. Himself a fancier of theological speculation, the sovereign would brook no such talk, and he promised to make the Puritans conform or "harry them out of the land, or else do worse." Some took the hint and left for Holland whence, in 1620, a tiny contingent proceeded to America.

But another decade went by before the Puritan exodus started in earnest. Then, in 1630, the Year of the Great Migration, more than a thousand alighted on the Massachusetts shore. Doubtless a great many came because of the hard times at home where, they confessed, "the land grows weary of her inhabitants . . . and all towns complain of the burden of the poor. . . . " Even greater than their economic trouble was their longing to rid themselves of the Anglican yoke. In Massachusetts they hoped to found a church-state, an American Geneva, set aside by God, they were convinced, for those "whom He means to save out of the general calamity." By 1631 the Lord's Garden was well on its way.

True to their Calvinism, the Puritans entertained a high regard for learning. As early as the mid-thirties towns turned to the business of schooling their youth. The first attempt may well have been at Boston whose town fathers in 1635 recommended that a certain "Brother Philemon Pormort shalbe intreated to become scholemaster for the teaching and nourtouring of children among us." There is reason to believe that a school actually came upon the scene, and that it may have been the celebrated Boston Latin School. Unfortunately, our knowledge of its seedling days is disappointingly sparse—in fact, we are not even sure of the exact year of its advent, some memoirists placing it in 1636, while others, including those of the school itself, hold for the preceding year. There is no doubt, however, that the school was modeled after the grammar schools then prevailing in England. The archmother of America's secondary learning, Boston Latin is still in salubrious practice, modernized to be sure, though scarcely anesthetic to the pride and honor that befall its historic singularity. From its corridors has flowed an endless stream of illustrious men, not only in the Puritan sacred smock, but in respectable bourgeois suits, as witness John Hancock, Samuel Adams, Benjamin Franklin (who, however, was a dropout), and somewhat closer to our own times, Ralph Waldo Emerson, Charles Francis Adams, Henry Ward Beecher, and so on and on.

Taking its novices at an age of seven or thereabout, when they could read such simple declarations as "The cat ate the mouse," or vice versa, the original Boston Latin School belabored them with Latin grammar. Once they were broken to its rules and regulations and the swarm of their anarchistic exceptions, they were put upon adventuring with the salient authors of Latin letters from Caesar, Cicero, and Virgil to Pliny, Ovid, and several others no less redoubtable. After a half-dozen years of such industry the boys, now advanced into their middle teens, began their reconnoiterings in Greek, proceeding from their gropings in grammar to Homer, Hesiod, and the New Testament. Sometimes when a boy possessed the necessary wit and gumption, he was set to work on Hebrew. The idea behind it all was to instruct and inspire him in the humanities and lovely letters. But the compulsions of the Puritan's moral purpose chilled the teaching masters all too often to the beauty that was simply beauty, and made them declare instead for an art which conduced at all times to virtue, which is to say, the moral certitudes of Calvinism. Thus wooed, the study of the ancient writings lost the vibrant freshness of its Renaissance forerunner, and descended instead into packing a boy's intellectual warehouse with so many homilies on good and evil. Did the masters hold their literary and linguistic lessons steadfast to the rockbound theorems of Puritan moral science? Then they also counted on them to strengthen the youthful mind, a pedagogy which in after years was to be rationalized as the doctrine of mental discipline, but which current psychological science has rejected. What Boston Latin aspired to at its optimistic best was the making of a Harvard freshman, or some other creature equally incandescent, a lad, in short, who could stagger the human eye and ear with a gush of Latin and Greek, and who at the same time was sturdily bottomed in the moral and religious jurisprudence of the Puritan Jahveh.

The residuary legatee in America of the classical Humanistic tradition, but renovated and reworked to jibe with the pedagogy of the Reformation, the Boston Latin school was the most renowned of New England's grammar schools, a monument to the Puritan's intellectual pride and to his religious resolution. But let it not be forgotten that there were several other such nurseries of knowledge, and some of them were of a superlative cut, for instance, Cambridge, Dorchester, Roxbury, all of which, like neighboring Boston, have borne the torch of learning unto the present.

Save for their stress on the ancient classics, and on Puritan right-thinking and right-doing, and that they reserved their pedagogical talents for the male, these schools varied no end. Indeed, even the funds which gave them life came from different sources. Their bulk, as then was usual, came out of the parental pocket. Sometimes they were bolstered by subsidies extracted from the revenue from license fees, the fishing industry, or the town domain. Happily, then as now altruists adorned the country, and some of them occasionally pried open their money boxes to give a hand to learning. Finally, though grudgingly, some townsmen yielded to the curse of taxation.

3

Soon after the coming of the first Puritans, the General Court—the Colony's legislature—set aside £400 "towards a school or college." From this princely sum the first colonial college sprang—a building and a president who was put upon to practice as its faculty. Two years after, in 1638, when the Reverend John Harvard died and left his library and a windfall of £800, the college promptly christened itself after its benefactor, a practice which ever since has been a distinction of the American higher learning.

The gateway to high Puritan office and particularly to the pulpit, Harvard took in only those who could make sense of Cicero, or some similar classical celebrity, and who could speak Latin in verse and prose, spell and pronounce the easy words of Greek, and parse the component parts of such thoughts as "Alexander the Great had a horse." Once granted access to the college and safely residenced in its premises, the student was put upon strict and compulsory rations in grammar, rhetoric, logic, geometry, astronomy, ethics, ancient history, Greek, and Hebrew—astonishing, no doubt, to America's current collegians, and even alarming, but in those days the typical academic bill of fare of an English college. Those designed for the professional service of God armed themselves additionally in sacred science with special attention to the Good Book, which they were made to read fluently in the original languages, and from cover to cover. Besides his intellect the student's virtue was carefully exercised and guarded, and whenever corruption overcame him, he was dutifully rattanned. Those who met all requirements—an apt lad usually consumed four years—took their diplomas in July at a celebration graced by the presence of the Colony's loftiest magnificoes. Even in that primeval academic era a master's degree was available. To acquire it took another three years, and to have it threw open the portal of opportunity to the highest preferment to be had in the Commonwealth.

The first English college in America was not stampeded by a horde of applicants. For long years, in fact, its student body numbered but a handful. Economically, it leaned toward exclusiveness, for the instruction it purveyed ran from £50 to £75, a stupendous amount in those times, and beyond the reach of all save a lucky few. Even intellectually, the college merchanted its benefits to the few, designed as it was to serve a small but competent elite to steer the Puritan state on some tomorrow when its present rulers would be in the dust.

4

The Puritans' great concern for the education of men able to protect and advance the affairs of the Bible State inclined them to favor the secondary and higher learning. But this is not saying that they snorted at the lower kind, though the energy they expended on it was somewhat less extravagant. The main weight here, as per Protestant formula, fell on faith and morals and, of course, on reading. At first the business was conducted privily, parents doing the best they could, with proddings, when they lagged, from the pastor and his ever-ready watchers. As the years ticked on, dame schools appeared, and for a fee a parent could transfer his pedagogic burden to a schoolma'am. Another importation was the writing school. Its birchmasters were usually men, and its specialty was, of course, the teaching of a sleek and readable hand. Sometimes it belabored its audience with the mystery of simple numbers and, on a father's request, with reading. These seminaries, however, were not in great demand, and until the times changed, and the New Englanders succumbed to the lure of commerce, their number remained sparse.

In the ebb of time the parental educational endeavor fell more and more under misgiving. Surviving in the wilderness crowded a man's time, and for all their Calvinism, when it came to teaching their little Jonathans and Priscillas, some parents did a bit of wobbling. At length, in 1642, the Bible State declared against such scandal by ordering the town selectmen "to take account from time to time of all parents and masters of their children . . . especially of their ability to read and understand the principles of religion and the capital laws of this country." Did a youngster flounder in ignorance? Or did his elders refuse to render such account? Then they could be fined. Moreover, did some magistrate so decide, then the town fathers might thrust into apprenticeship the offspring of such persons not "able and fit to employ or bring them up," which is to say, devious and wicked fellows who scoffed the law.

Enacted, as it said, to combat "the great neglect of many persons and masters in training up their children in learning and labor," the 1642 law was a réchauffé of the English Poor Law of 1601. This, as may be recalled, had sought to give aid to the needy, and had made provision for the apprenticeship of pauper children. But the Bible State was gaming for a bigger pot. The blow it dealt was not merely one of economics and child maintenance as it had been in Elizabeth's England; at bottom the Law of 1642 represented the theocracy's first direct and deliberate attempt to nail down its Calvinism through the compulsory teaching of the rising generation. In operation till 1648, the statute was imitated throughout New England, except in infidel Rhode Island whose inhabitants insisted on keeping church and state apart.

The Law of 1642 required a knowledge of reading and religion; but it did not go so far as to press for schools. Just how its mandates were to be fulfilled was left to parental sagacity. In some places, as has been said, private instruction worked the wonder; here and there a town itself attempted some sort of schooling; and in certain cases parents discharged the duty. But there was also plenty of finagling. Finally, in 1647, the General Court took a stronger line by ordering every town of fifty householders to take steps to ensure instruction in reading and writing, it being, as the lawmakers observed, "the one chief project of the old deluder Satan to keep men from the knowledge of the Scriptures." To frustrate Old Horny even more powerfully, the law went on to require towns of

100 families to furnish instruction in Latin grammar to fit their youth for Harvard. Actually, the statute did not establish a school, though its net effect was pretty much the same. What it called for, specifically, was the appointment of "one ... to teach ... all such children as shall resort to him." Lest there might be doubts on the subject, he was to be paid either "by the parents or masters or by the inhabitants in general."

The Old Deluder Satan Act, as the law came to be called, evoked no vast handclapping. To the hard-pressed settler the law not only seemed harsh; it was also a burden. In the American wilderness, where hands were scarce, fathers needed their sons, and mothers their daughters, to help ease the endless labors which beset them. Vanquishing the ABCs was fair enough in theory, especially if it proposed to gratify Calvin's dour God; but in the everyday working world this meant that parents were doomed to double and even triple toil, a prospect not calculated to rejoice even the most industrious Puritan. Where a town happened to be so pinched that even an underpaid teacher strained its means, and parents were thus put upon to do their own schoolmastering, the hardship often sufficed to incommode the law's effective operation. For all the Bible State's power to bring troublemakers to book, floutings of the law flourished. Not only did magistrates have to put defiant fathers on the judicial carpet; sometimes they had to apply the corrective stick to the towns themselves. Indeed, some settlements, already subverted to Yankee foxiness, presently figured out that it was less costly to pay a fine than to engage the services of a first-class schoolmaster.

Not similarly executed, the law of 1647 was not even similarly interpreted. Take, for instance, the subject of girls. Some town Justinians contended that the term "children" as written into the law clearly did not embrace the fair sex. On the other hand, there were townsmen who tolerated no such shystering, and ordered their schoolmaster to shine his lamp on girls and boys alike. But such idealism was not the rule, and the number of town schools accommodating boys and girls on equal terms was small. Yet this is not to say that a young lady worthy of the name was reared in the bliss of ignorance. Through her parents and their tree of elderly relations, and the aid, maybe, of the resolute pastor or, if in service, a private schooldame, many a girl was saved from darkness to become, as she expanded, a literate and virtuous Puritan.

A variety of explanations have been laid upon the Law of 1647. Some experts have submitted it as testimony to the Puritan's passion for learning. Others have insisted that the statute was mostly a rainbow hope, and that it was only defectively respected. Some writers of history have sighted in the measure "the cornerstone of the American school system," while others, less romantic and more skeptical, regard it simply as "an effort to ... impose the Puritan creed upon the first generation of nativeborn New Englanders." Unluckily, in the case before the bench direct evidence is almost totally lacking, and save for demonstrating that today's historical science has not yet attained the lofty Matterhorn of objectivity of, say, algebra or stenography, one scholar's hazard is as good as another's. Still, as a matter of logic there is the fact that in 1647 Massachusetts, the Lord's Garden, was a theocracy, steel-like in its moral and religious grip, and almost overmastering in its power. Thus the Old Deluder Satan Act would scarcely make a fitting "cornerstone" for the edifice of the American state school system which was erected in the nineteenth century when this land was vastly different. Unlike the Puritan church-state, the states which later made up the Union kept themselves aloof from any religious tie. Secular rather than religious, they regarded schooling not as a ram to batter Satan, that rascal in red tights, but rather as an instrument to achieve ends which were usefully and sometimes charmingly earthly. Nevertheless, for all the meanings put upon it, the law was the first of its kind in this country. And despite the smoke and sputter it generated, its main principle received a wide acceptance—in fact, by 1671 all New England, aside from Rhode Island, had adopted some sort of compulsory education.

5

If New England's girls had fewer rights than boys, they were no worse off than their sisters elsewhere. Only beyond the grave did equality between the sexes beckon. On earth a Puritan, whether male or female, was a sinner, and like the one, the other was booked 9½ times out of 10 to be grilled and roasted in the fires of Hell. For a child the odds for such a postmortem end were overwhelming. For in the sight of God, declared Jonathan Edwards, children "are infinitely more hateful than vipers." Their very nature, observed Cotton Mather, another specialist in moral pathology, was "of Death, Hell, and Wrath." Under the circumstances, parents obviously faced a problem. Though their hearts bled for their little progeny, God nevertheless abhorred children. The remedy, though drastic, was simple. Not only was a child raised in a mass of shushing and flogging, but while he was still in tender bud, he was made familiar with the Bible, its truths and triumphs, and, even more, its taboos and terrors. Once he had the knack of reading, he was put to prowling through its pages, not merely as the mood befell him, but from Genesis I to Revelation XXII, and not just once, but again and again and again.

In the child's early stage, the Biblical disclosure was drummed into him by his parents and, of course, his pastor. Then, when he was sufficiently old and hardy, he was initiated in reading. Commonly he started with a "hornbook" which was not a book at all, but a paddle-shaped board with a sheet of paper whereon were printed the ABCs in letters small and capital, chased by the vowels and a herd of syllables from ab and ib to di and du. Thereupon followed the Lord's Prayer and, fittingly enough, the Benediction. To preserve the treasured paper from youth's unsanitary paws, a thin film of transparent horn, not unlike the present-day plastic, was tacked over the printed sheet—hence the name hornbook.

In school as at the fireside, the Bible, naturally, ranked over every other book, human and divine. But other writings presently appeared to fortify and supplement its lessons. One of the earliest was John Cotton's *Spiritual Milk for Babes Drawn out of the Breasts of Both Testaments*. But whether milk or something else, Cotton's compound must have been powerful, containing as it did discourses on Original Sin, the Trinity, the Last Judgment, and the ministry of the law.

The most famous schoolbook, by a long shot, was the *New England Primer*, a literary gnat of less than ninety pages. Put into covers in 1690, it continued to pour from the presses for the next century and a quarter to swell into a dinosaur, it is estimated, of more than three million copies. It was compulsory reading in church and school, and no Puritan home, however squeezed, was long without its woe and solace. Saving only the Bible, the *Primer* was America's first best-seller. Naturally it rang out its most flattering tributes in the Commonwealth where the faithful gave it deference as the Little Bible of New England. However, incarnated under such titles as *The Columbian Primer, The New York Primer*, and *The American Primer*, it enjoyed a brisk trade in other parts, even in such wicked seaports as Philadelphia and New York—indeed, slightly altered, it even served to achieve prodigies for the Lutherans. Like similar works of enlightenment in Europe, the *Primer* devoted itself to the advancement of reading and religion, and of course, the good life, in prose and verse. Good children must, it counseled,

Fear God all Day
Parents obey
No False thing Say
By no Sin Stray
Love Christ alway
In Secret Pray
Mind little Play
Make no Delay

For those inclined, just the same, to slide down the slippery hill it tolled a warning:

DEATH (SPEAKING)
No pity on thee can I show,
Thou hast thy God offended so,
Thy soul and body I'll divide.
Thy body in the grave I'll hide,
And thy dear soul in Hell must lie
With Devils to eternity.

As the years moved on, the *Primer*'s cargo underwent some modification. But always it carried the alphabet, in verse and picture, from A to Z. To almost its end it held that

In Adam's fall
We sinned all

and that

Xerxes the great did die
And so must you and I

and finally

Zaccheus he
Did climb the tree
His Lord to see.

The first *New England Primer* engauded its pages with pictures, from Adam and Eve and the historic apple tree to a full-page etching of Britain's reigning sovereign—treats in those days for the famished eyes of youth, the first time, indeed, that there had been pictures in a schoolbook since 1658 when the European Comenius spiced his Latin text, the *Orbis Pictus*, with pictorial seduction. Later, as the Revolution drew in view, the portrait of America's last king was elbowed out by that of George Washington—a minor note, no doubt, and one sordidly political. High above it towered the *Primer*'s effort to implant the seed of true religion. New England's Little Bible, moral scientists found, "taught millions to read and not one to sin." Exactly the same discovery was made some years later in Noah Webster's readers, and after that, once more, in those of the immortal McGuffey.

6

Though the Law of 1647 laid the foundation for compulsory education in much of New England, its life was sorely troubled. The fact that the law was disesteemed, and sometimes even flouted, led the Commonwealth to lengthen its fangs, but even after its fines had grown to an alarming £20, the feeling and friction persisted.

Some, as usual, laid the whole thing to Satan. But there were some other factors. The generation which witnessed the Law's adoption was also spectator to the tremendous tug of war between Parliament and England's first Charles Stuart. As the fates conspired more and more against the King, his Puritan opponents obviously had good reason to stay in England. By the same token, some in America began to head for the motherland for a short time, in fact, their exits surpassed their arrivals. Even more menacing to the Bible State, however, was the falling off in its supply of first-rank ministers. During the century's second half, discord stalked the yards of Harvard, and in the calamity the number of its graduates dwindled. From the first the Colony's holy clerks had been the mainstay of its learning and its most active promoters, but now, as their number diminished, the cause of education darkened.

Meanwhile, other forces were at work, strong, alluring, insinuating, which even the men of God, for all their power and sagacity, could not stay. The fierce piety which had filled the hearts of the first settlers glowed less strongly in their descendants, and as it eased, rearing the young in rigid and impeccable Calvinism became less urgent. Draw aside the curtain, and you will see not martyrs in flight from the threats of a king and the Established Church, but men swathed in religious security. Nor were they anesthetic to the blandishments of a more sumptuous material life—in truth, as the years moved on, many a New Englander was yielding more and more to the charms of moneymaking than to the commands and counsels of his clergyman. The Puritan, in short, was evolving into the Yankee. By the century's third quarter merchants were booming in trade and commerce. They made shoes and hardware, fashioned ships, caught the cod and herring, and distilled rum. Their barks plowed the seas, up and down the coastal waters, to the Indies, and of course, to Europe. As their money piled higher and higher, so did their prestige, and so, as usual, their political potency, until at length they displaced their theocratic rulers, and therewith the ecclesiastical grip on education. "It is a matter of sorrowful and sad resentment with me," mourned Urian Oakes, a president of Harvard and a divine, "that the nurseries of piety and learning should languish and die away, as they do in my apprehension of this account."

What overpowered the town school in the end was something more immediate. A community which in infancy had huddled its homes around the meeting house, and which found practically everything within footstep range, raised no problem in getting their young to trudge the short space to school. But time saw the populace fan out far beyond the township's original village, and as families settled more remotely, journeying to its school, especially in a region where the winter's land lay deep in snow and ice, became more and more onerous, and sometimes not a little grueling. In consequence, fathers soon found good excuse for keeping their children home—a liberty which was, of course, not displeasing to their little psyches. Yet if it was hard for the young to brave their way to class, then on the other hand, it was simple for their fathers to stiffen in their tracks at the mere mention of paying taxes in contribution to the school's support.

Out of these circumstances arose the moving school. It was in actuality no more than a schoolmaster who, instead of conducting his daily sessions in the town school, would translate himself from settlement to settlement, sitting for a spell in one, then packing himself off to the next, thence to the next, and so on, until at last he had canvassed his entire diocese—a tour which sometimes ran to three or four semesters. Need it be added that in a culture where thrift was pleasing to Omnipotence, and where men, hence, disliked to squander a single penny, the time such a perambulating virtuoso served in a community was in direct proportion to the funds the community had yielded to the township's treasurer?

The moving school was a visible compromise with geographic fact. Resorted to with reluctance, it was soon regarded with a somewhat fishy eye. Some instruction, of course, it dispensed; but its benefits at best were insufficient, and always their distribution was unequal. For under its regime the largest settlement, which by reason of its size, contributed the largest levy, obtained the longest service, while the smallest, which paid the least, got the barrel's bottom. The howls and catcalls which rose against this gypsy enterprise—fertilized also, no doubt, with local pride—presently caused settlements to cry out for the right to run a school of their own. Thus was hatched the district school. Under its flag every township divided itself into districts, each with its own school, manned by its own master, and each maintained from the money it put into the township's cashbox. Legalized in Massachusetts after the Revolution, it established itself not only in the fallen theocracy, but south of its border in the Middle States, and even in some of the new lands beyond the Alleghenies.

It has become the vogue to hail the early district school as the offspring of democracy, for its affairs were managed by a board chosen by the people's voice. That it endured so long, however, was due not so much to any equalitarian illusion as to its cheese-paring economy. The plain fact is that the cost of keeping the district school was paltry, and though what it offered at the most was little and even threadbare, with the taxpayer the appeal of its cheapness was overpowering. Later, in the mid-nineteenth century, when Horace Mann and Henry Barnard undertook to battle for decent schools, adequately financed and efficiently run and surveyed, it was the district school, now mildewed with age and hopelessly inadequate to its business, that received the brunt of their assault.

7

Taking them in the mass, the men and women who left England to make their home along the Chesapeake Bay, and in the region down below, bore no antagonism toward the motherland. Apart from the Catholics in Maryland, they were not, like the Puritans and Quakers, seeking to shake off the Anglican shackle. They were for the most part a conservative folk, and the run of them found England's ways agreeable. What brought them here, hence, was no hankering for reform, but the hope for better grazing, the desire, in sum, to enlarge their personal pocket.

Like the New Englanders, the Southerners were a cog in the national colonial enterprise. Theirs, at bottom, was the task of supplying the mother country with the raw materials she so badly needed, especially timber and its offspring pitch and potash, besides tar and petroleum—even iron, glass, and copper.

The business was given its start early in Jamestown's annals, in 1610, when John Rolfe, immortal to every schoolboy as the spouse of Pocahontas, discovered a new way of processing tobacco. The result was a leaf greatly superior to its Indian ancestor, smoother to the European palate, and infinitely more savory. In consequence, the demand for tobacco zoomed to a dizzy height, and presently its cultivation became Virginia's foremost occupation. To engage in it with the utmost profit, growers resorted to vast acreages, planting their fields for a few years until these were tuckered out, and then starting afresh with others. Though tobacco grows with ease, it needs constant care and grooming to attain its highest excellence. In those days such labor required many hands, which in the New World were in extreme scarcity. To increase their supply of workers, planters relied on the device of indenture, in which they financed an immigrant's passage, and the latter, for his part, agreed to pay off his indebtedness over several years, not in coin but in labor. Once the indentured servant, as the phrase then went, had sweated off his obligation, he could take wing, free as the proverbial bird. In a country blessed with abounding land and good wages the road of opportunity stretched ahead, smooth and full of pleasant possibility— not a few such fellows, in fact, acquired land themselves, and some were destined to die wealthy.

It is not necessary here to rehearse the numerous details of the Southern tobacco trade. Suffice it to observe that from its prospering issued the social and economic life of Virginia, Maryland, and in smaller measure, North Carolina. An agrarian world, it was run to suit the needs and likes of its landed gentry, its men of money and great estate, and by this token its rulers. There were merchants too, of course, but they were fewer than in New England, and not infrequently, once they had laid up a sufficient bank account, they forswore the rewards of commerce to take their chances as growers of the miraculous weed. In addition, there were the usual lesser people, the small landowners, and the yeomen, all free and full of hope. Finally, there were the indentured servants and, as time ran on, the slaves.

8

Out of these conditions emerged the main design of Southern education. Its resemblance to that of the motherland is at once perceptible. Here, as there, it grounded itself on the theory that the schooling of the young is the concern not of the state, but of the parents. Here as there, its finest variety was reserved for the paying trade, the upper few, that is, of wealth and family. Here, again, as there, the enlightenment of the heirs of privilege fell to the care of tutors and private schools, while that of the lesser orders drifted according to the varying winds of fortune. And since the state turned thumbs down on assuming more than a tepid responsibility for the education of its children, the task was discharged by the church, well enough in its way, but never adequately and never as resolutely as in Massachusetts.

Although Southern education was orchestrated on familiar English strings,

American conditions soon forced some variations upon it. In a country where settlers were scattered far from one another in an ocean of space, running a school in a town, or even in a parish, was next to impossible. In a place, moreover, whose servants and laborers counted as they did in Virginia, for the population's greater part, and where—even more horrible—the offspring of the meaner folk were swarming so copiously as to arouse and alarm their betters, it gradually dawned on the ruling class that the government, for all its prideful assumptions, could scarcely afford the luxury of shedding wishful tears into its beer. In consequence, as the years rode by, one Southern Colony after another ordered some sort of training for the multitude of its lower nobodies, the children of servants—to make an instance—and of paupers, the orphaned and illegitimate, and the mulatto issue of white mothers.

The first step in this direction was ventured in 1642 when Virginia put upon the guardians and overseers of orphans to instruct their wards in the "rudiments of learning." Four years later the Colony ordained "releife of such parents whose poverty extends not to give them [i.e., their children] breeding." In accordance with the "laudable custom of the Kingdom of England" the measure authorized the establishment of a workhouse school at James City to which each county was to apportion two of its children, male or female, of an age no less than seven, "to be imployed in the public flax houses. . . . " A plain echo of the English Poor Laws, the statute aspired to "the better education of youth in honest and profitable trades and manufactures, as also to avoid sloath and idlenesse wherewith such children are easily corrupted." Amended more than a dozen times, the law appeared not only in the sub-Potomac Commonwealth, but in other Southern Colonies as well. Subsequently, catching up with the Massachusetts Law of 1642, the Virginians gave their assent to the removal of "poor children from indigent homes to place them to work. . . . " By the early eighteenth century the Colony reached the point where it was willing to order its boy apprentices to learn how to read and write. About half a century later, in 1751, its girls were put under the same mandate.

If Southerners were averse to putting the state into the general educational enterprise, then on the other hand they were not lacking men of public spirit. As early as 1619 the Virginia Company set aside several thousand acres and £1,500 toward a university at Henrico, with a corps of missionaries "for the conversion of infidels," which is to say the Indians. Unhappily, the project came to naught. But philanthropy was not daunted, and pretty soon another of its flares ascended when Patrick Copeland, a preacher in practice aboard an East Indian ship, collected funds to found a free school in Virginia to instruct the young in the "principles of religion, civility, and humane feeling." Alas, this too was dashed on the rocks, and what happened to the money has fled from human memory.

The first visible success of which we have any news is dated 1634 when a planter, Benjamin Symes by name, left a parcel of land, and even better, a herd of eight cows, to endow a free school for the children of Elizabeth City and

Kiquotan. A quarter of a century following, Thomas Eaton, from the same parts, surpassed the generosity of his predecessor with a gift of several hundred acres, a number of buildings, a couple of Negroes, twenty head of hogs, two bulls, and a dozen cows.

Precisely what kind of schools these legacies propagated is not clear. There is good ground, however, to believe that they were not unlike the grammar schools of England, the lineal offspring, in other words, of St. Paul's and similar shrines for boys of the upper classes. In any case their prospering seems to have been fair enough—in fact, by 1649 Symes prided itself not only with "a fine house," but with a registration of horned cattle which now numbered no less than forty. Both Symes and Eaton remained in service till 1805 when they joined hands to become the famous Hampton Academy. Almost a hundred years after, in 1902, a portion of the endowment was syphoned into the Symes-Eaton Academy which did its work as part of the public school system.

Virginians, of course, had no corner on public benefaction. Indeed, in South Carolina, where altruism often sprouted cash donations as well as real estate, the art of good works was raised to a high power. Nor did they confine themselves to the efforts of the landed patricians—not uncommonly, in fact, the rich man's gift would be increased with smaller offerings from the lesser settlers. In those days as in these, constructive idealism was given organization, as witness such bodies as the Bethesda Orphan Home in Georgia, the oldest of its kind in the republic, the Winyaw Indigo Society, the South Carolina Society, and several others, all consecrated in one way or another to the advancement of education and "sound principles of religion."

The largest of them, and the most far-flung, was the Society for the Propagation of the Gospel in Foreign Parts, the SPG for short. Chartered in the home country in 1701, the society trained specialists for its foreign vineyards "for the purpose of . . . bringing the surrounding heathen to the knowledge of the truth," which is another way of saying, to instruct Indians and Negroes "in the tenets and worship of the Church." Its pedagogues waged their war against sin and ignorance wherever the Anglican Church held sway, not only in the Colonies, but in Canada and the Indies, and they maintained their campaign until the Revolution when their Anglicanism made them suspect to American patriots. In some Colonies—notably New York—their success was striking, but in the Southern wilderness, where their toil was under heavy handicap, they had more on their hands than they had bargained for, and for all their zeal and daring, their activity was comparatively slight. Though their first task was to vaccinate the young, whether heathen or otherwise, against false thinking and moral error, let it not be forgotten that in so doing they also flashed some light on reading and writing, and thereby rescued at least a few from the curse of illiteracy.

Despite the scattering of the populace, now and then planters managed to get together to put up a schoolhouse. Set usually in some worn out tobacco field, such shanties came to be known as "old-field" schools. To them youngsters made their way, usually on foot or by boat, but occasionally atop some friendly nag. What they learned was scarcely more than the stark essentials, namely, the catechism and the ABCs. When parents could afford it, they sought the service of a full-time and, if possible, competent, master. But such splurging was rare—and even rarer such a teacher. Consequently, the old-field school is not renowned for the wonders of its pedagogy. But let us be gentle. Let us bear in mind that the mere existence of such schools, together with the endowed establishments, constituted at least an attempt to forward knowledge, and though it flaunts a long record of assiduous futility, it was, nevertheless, an attempt.

9

Where education is a commodity to be bought like stocks and bonds, there the old chestnut that it pays to be rich makes sense. At all times under such conditions the children of money have been the beneficiaries of better service. But in the South, where government deliberately eschewed education as one of its concerns, the chasm between the schooling of those in funds and the numerous horde of others was much wider than, say, in Calvin's Massachusetts, where the zeal for literacy as a sword against Beelzebub pressed a knowledge of reading on everyone regardless of rank or purse. There schooling was not simply offered; it was ordained. In plain contrast, left to their own resources the Southern masses maintained the campaign against ignorance in a minor key, at times grimly, often indifferently, and not unusually in hapless renunciation.

Meanwhile, the well-fixed somebodies plied their offspring with earfuls of instruction from hired tutors, and after a while, in some first-rate private schools. House pedagogues, it is true, were not easy to obtain, and for a gentleman to spangle his mansion with such a prize was a cause for envy. On occasion a planter's neighbors or maybe his kinfolk would submit their children to the tutorial custody. In such case the visiting scholars were usually lodged and victualed in the planter's home. Sometimes, as such charges increased in number, their instruction was transacted in a house especially erected for such purpose. Thus arose and developed the small private boarding school.

Time saw such schools augment and prosper—by the early eighteenth century, in fact, about half of Virginia's parishes boasted of one or more. Fashioned in the genteel English tradition, the best of them put their confidence in the ancient classics, and needless to say, in mannerly deportment, piety, and rectitude. But already some were seized by the virus of the newer disciplines, for example, the living languages, mathematics, and the sciences. In the harbor town of Charleston one house of learning even advertised courses in navigation, surveying, astronomy, and fortification. Nor were young ladies of quality forgotten in the general shuffle. Like their brothers, they addressed themselves to the axioms of the catechism and the theory and exercise of decorum. Occasionally some bold miss traded blows with Cicero and Virgil, but never with navigation and fortification. On the other hand, girls released their ego lavishly in needle-craft, watercoloring, dancing, music, and as one of their seminaries let it be heard, "other embellishments necessary for the amusement of persons of fortune who have taste."

For those aperch the highest peaks of opulence even such delicacies did not always quite suffice. To obtain the finest schooling money could muster some fathers dispatched their boys and—in extraordinary cases—their girls to the motherland. But the hazards were so great that most parents, tempted though they may have been, preferred to raise their young in the lesser culture of England's American outpost. With respect to the higher learning, the story ran somewhat differently, for a collegiate student, having shed the green cast of childhood, presented a smaller risk. Weighing on the situation too was the absence, until the shank of the seventeenth century, of any higher learning. Yet, for all that, few Southerners proceeded to Oxford or Cambridge, or to study law in London at Inns of Court or the Inner Temple, or (did they chance to be Marylanders of the Roman rite) to the Jesuit colleges in France.

After the collapse of the Virginia Company's proposal for a college at Henrico, the idea of putting the higher learning into the South was laid upon the shelf. But it was not allowed to waste away. Dusted off from time to time, it continued to arrest attention until the early nineties when, revised and reorganized, it was embodied in a petition. Addressed to the mother country, the writ begged her Lords of the Treasury to give assent and assistance to the establish-ment of a college. To drive home their point, the Virginians dispatched the Reverend James Blair, their most potent Anglican cleric, to take the field in London, but for all his pleas and prayers, he was turned down. But the mills continued their inexorable grinding, and two years later, in 1693, the patient Blair was able to thank Providence for its benign intercession. When he returned to the Virginia shores, he had with him not only the royal assent of William and Mary, but an order for £2,000 besides a design for a building from the hand, it is thought, of the talented Christopher Wren.

The college—the second to rise in the Colonies—was befittingly named for its royal patrons. Like Harvard—now a young lady of fifty-seven—William and Mary started its career pianissimo, full of friendly hopes, but beset on every side by staggering obstacles. Scarcely more than a grammar school, it was manned by the Reverend James Blair, now in the toga of its president, and also serving as its professorial faculty. For years the school ran into hurricanes and tornadoes, but somehow it managed to survive. Founded, like Harvard, as a nursery for holy clerks—Anglican, to be sure, and not Puritan—the college, nevertheless, was far from despising the mundane arts and sciences. It was at William and Mary that George Wythe, a signer of the Declaration and the teacher of Jefferson, sat as America's first professor of law. And it was at William and Mary that the social graces, so vital to American learning, were given their inauguration. They sneaked in, it is true, like a Trojan horse, in 1716 when the college granted the use of one of its chambers to Master Levingstone "for teaching the scholars and others to dance until his own dancing school at Williamsburg be finished." The effects must have been generally excellent, for pretty soon the Reverend Hugh Jones, a man of great parts, was urging upon the college authorities that music, dancing, and fencing might well be taught "by such as the president and masters shall appoint. . . . "

William and Mary's chronicle glistens with numerous other academic scoops. As early as 1776 it established the eminent Phi Beta Kappa, the first intercollegiate fraternity in America. It was the first American house of higher knowledge to reward merit and industry with medals of gold; the first to embrace the elective and honor systems; the first colonial college to transmute itself into a university; the first to light its lamp in political economy; the first with a school of modern languages; and—to haul up—the first with a school of modern history.

The college's primary mission—indeed, the very reason for its being—was to prepare its youth for the Anglican pulpit, and in this domain there is no doubt about its triumphs—its clerical alumni, taking them as they come, were often men of a distinguished order. But as the political weather became more infernal, and Americans began to sass their king, the students turned more and more of their energy to the pursuit of the college's secular studies, and particularly its offerings in politics. In consequence, as time bore on, the college's nontheological alumni outdazzled even its gentlemen of God. Stars of the first brilliance, they include Thomas Jefferson, James Monroe, James Tyler, Edmond Randolph, and several others, less glittering, perhaps, than the aforesaid, but no less grand.

10

Strung out between New England and the South were the Middle Colonies, a stretch of earth and water which today contains New York, New Jersey, Delaware, and Pennsylvania. Unlike the settlements which framed them to the north and south, the Middle Colonies were not solidly English. For several decades of the seventeenth century the valley land between the Hudson and the Delaware was eyed by both the English and the Dutch, the one by virtue of the explorations of the Cabots, the other because of those of Hudson. But the Dutch were the first to plant their flag, and by 1610 New Netherland was displaying the first frail signs of being.

It was not easy for the Dutch to people this new domain. For the pressures which drove so many Europeans to America were for the most part missing in the Dutch Republic. Theirs was a small country, to be sure, but full of substance. Industrious and prosperous, it was caressed not only by plenty, but by freedom, political and religious, which, though held within bound, was for its time so rare as to be almost singular. Predominantly of a commercial bent, Dutch America, for all the enticements drummed up by its sponsors, never grew to great proportion. By 1664, the year the province yielded to the English, when

Massachusetts polled some 25,000 head, and Virginia some 5,000 more, New Netherland could scarcely scrape together a rough 9,000.

What fetches attention at once in the American Holland is its immense and extraordinary diversity. Here was a rubbing of international shoulders, predominantly Dutch, to be sure, but with Englishmen, besides Scotch and Irish, even Frenchmen, Scandinavians, and Germans. In the realm of creed and conscience the show was even gaudier. Officially, the way to Heaven lay over the route laid out by the established church, the Dutch Reformed, to which all paid a modest levy. But beyond such required tribute, side roads were open, and they flourished, each with its own powerful enchantment, here for Huguenots, there for Baptists, and so on for Quakers, Lutherans, and Presbyterians—in truth, there were even lanes to accommodate a trickle of Catholics and Jews. Save for a rare and momentary lapse, religious traffic in Dutch America flowed freely and unmolested.

Even so, despite its protean national and religious coloration, the Colony's deep and salient tone was Dutch. Though the air might be flogged by a babel of tongues, it was the Dutchman's gabble which overbore it. Though God might be glorified in a dozen ways, it was the Church of Holland, the Dutch Reformed, which alone had legal status. The Dutchman's mark was everywhere. One captures it in the sprawled and gabled houses, the narrow, twisting streets, the canals and windmills, the bustling wharves and their huddled ships, a small forest of bare, straight masts. Industry, such as it was, was carried on in the style and custom of the motherland, and so was farming. And so too, in essence, was education.

The nature of the Colony, so variegated and yet so utterly Dutch, colored and conditioned its education. But its start was slow, and its pace had neither bounce nor power. Disposed against it were serious encumbrances—the infrequence, for example, of towns, the sparseness of the population, the disparate tongues and creeds, and not the least by any odds, the lack of decent self-government. On the other hand, there were some agreeable assets. For one, there was the spur of the Protestant tradition, with its sharp insistence on a knowledge of reading. That the Colony's official church chanced to have a Calvinistic tinge was also something to be reckoned with. Not only were the Calvinists unflagging in their war on Hell's murky hopes, but whenever they got the chance, they allied themselves with the state for reinforcement. Thus things were in Holland, and thus they were to a large degree in the Colony.

In Dutch America, as in the parent country, religion exerted a vigorous influence on education. Here as over there, the tie between school and church was close, and here as there the church counted on the state for help. In New Netherland the task fell largely on the Dutch West India Company which, taking one thing with another, did not disdain its obligation. As early as 1629 it enjoined the settlers "to endeavor to devise some means whereby they will be able to support . . . a schoolmaster." Not only did the company provide schools;

it also helped to keep them in funds. Gnawed, however, by a lust for profit, the directors inclined to penny-pinching, and the schools they propagated were pockmarked with their avarice.

Nine villages sprouted in New Netherland, and at one time or another each ran a school—but never a grand affair. Sometimes there was a schoolhouse; more commonly pupils communed in the master's home. Once, for a flittering period, the pedagogic business was done in the village tavern. Though schools were nursed out of the civil purse, admission to their seances was not free, save only to the poor and needy who, the burghers told themselves, "ask to be taught for God's sake." As the church's liegeman, the school was expected to carry on in its behalf. To this end it gave its chief attention to Protestantism's trusted old reliables, reading and religion, with expeditions now and then into writing and arithmetic. It rehearsed its auditors again and again in the questions and answers of their catechism and in their common prayers until they could recite them quickly and correctly. As was only meet, prayer started every school day, and prayer brought its burdens to a thankful close. Beyond these elements there was little else, save on a parent's rare request, and for such accommodation the schoolmaster was allowed to lay on an extra levy.

In learning's secondary and higher spheres, unlike its neighbors to the north and south, Dutch America was bogged in almost complete sterility. Some of the colonists were sensitive to such ignobility, and in the Grand Remonstrance which they addressed in 1649 to the homeland, they uttered some mournful words. But a decade passed before their wail was given notice, and when the colonists were gladdened at length by the arrival of a Latin master, he came too late, for the grammar school which now appeared was scarcely under way when the Colony fell to the English.

Collegiately, the situation was no more benign. Some of the more illuminated settlers, it is true, dreamed of a tomorrow when the land could pride itself with a college all its own, the training station of its aspiring dominies, and a glory, hence, to God and country. But it was a delusive dream. Not until 1766, more than a century after Dutch America was laid into its crypt, did the Dutch Reformed come close to its fulfillment. Even so, the college they brought forth, designated then as Queen's but now as Rutgers, was hardly the seminary their remote predecessors had envisioned, for the world which they had adorned was gone—no doubt forever. Though the college's capital concern was to forward the interests of the Dutch Reformed Church, it was already charged with a newer spirit. It aspired—so its founders let it be known—"to promote learning for the benefit of the community and the advancement of all the Protestant denominations."

The chummy relationship between church and state showed itself in the teacher's chores and duties. Hired not only to teach and police his recruits, he was also under the burden of serving as the pastor's aid and orderly, and in the moments of his meager leisure, as a sort of ecclesiastical busboy. On the Sabbath in church he rendered recitals from Holy Writ, bolstered by the Ten

Commandments and the Twelve Articles of Faith. He led the flock in psalmody, and when the parson fell captive to the croups and pains that flay us all, the schoolmaster harangued the congregation in his place. In addition, he was put upon to swab and sweep the church, to clang its bell, and of snowy days to shovel a passage to its door. At life's one end he rejoiced the faithful with baptismal tidings; at the other he dug graves for their departed. Yet for all the high importance of his office, laic and spiritual, the Dutch schoolmaster was rarely of a respectable professional mark. The truth is it was not easy to attract first-grade men to a wilderness which offered them little more than hardship and peril, and whose directors, their lofty moralizing notwithstanding, were given to squeezing the last penny from their investment.

When, in 1664, the Colony changed from Dutch to English hands, its new owners, true to their English way, let the schools pretty much alone. The situation altered somewhat a decade later when, after a flutter of insurrection, Dutch hopes in America curled up forever. As the years plowed on, the English grew more numerous, and though the older Dutch clung desperately to their culture, the odds weighed too heavily against them, and for all their extraordinary resistance, in the end it was done in.

11

When New Netherland became New York, the Colony's educational policy became that of its rulers, which is to say they were content to do as little as possible. Apart from its insistence on the right to license schoolmasters, and to keep the training of apprentices and paupers under watch, the colonial government—as in the South—gave education little thought. Dutch schools were allowed to carry on, but shorn of their official support, they worked their art and mystery parochially, as did the schools of the other sects.

Although the official attitude toward education was to let it lie, the government was not unpleasant about it. In fact, in certain cases it inclined even to extend a cordial hand, light, to be sure, but helpful for all that. The Society for the Propagation of the Gospel in Foreign Parts—the same guild of Anglican evangelists that braved the forlorn marches of the South—was accorded the governor's special sanction. In New York, whose folk fretted even then under error and corruption, the SPG found a challenge precisely to its taste. Setting up shop in 1703, just two years after their order's founding, its professors soon were working on a large scale, and with a much greater success than in the region below the Potomac. In fact, on the eve of the Revolution, when their Anglicanism had come to be regarded as something of a major malefaction, they were running some ten schools in divers parts of the Colony, besides a few more on the Hudson's western bank in New Jersey.

The society applied its pedagogy not only to the infidel; it sought also to illuminate the lower rank of Anglicans. Under the circumstances, its first stress fell, naturally, on religion, the tenets and ordinances, that is to say, of the Church of England. To such purpose it introduced its children to their prayer book, the psalter, and in time, the Bible. In addition, they were taught to read and write, and to count and figure, and always, of course, they were fortified in moral jurisprudence. To teach its catechumens their rudiments and, more important, to condition them to be honest, modest, and polite, to abstain at all times from sin, to honor the King, his bishops, and his church, and to respect their betters—in short, to submit docilely to things as God hath ordained them—such was the substance of the gospel propagators' program. As for its quality, it was less than fair, though at its worst it was not appreciably worse than what was then commonly conceded the lower classes.

Although grammar schools were common enough in seventeenth-century England, in this respect New Yorkers evinced no desire to ape the motherland. Nor did the zeal for learning which fired the dreams of the Massachusetts godly, lay and divine, ignite the envy of their neighbors along the lower Hudson. The truth is that but for the volunteering of a number of private vendors of instruction in Latin and Greek, access to an understanding of those grizzly disciplines would have been decidedly confined. Actually New York had picked up not quite forty years of history before its government saw fit to dispatch a summons to the mother country for a scholar, steadfast in the Anglican faith and able to impart instruction "in language and other learning. . . . " Such luminaries were then readily available, a dime a dozen, as the saying goes, and in 1703, unballyhooed by press agents, one of them honored New York with his coming. Unhappily, his enterprise was handicapped from the start—so low, in fact, had New York's interest in the ancient classics sunk, that after a few months of huffing and puffing, the harried master threw in his hand and quit.

Convinced by this circumstance that New Yorkers constituted, as it were, a great Unclassical Association, their rulers granted themselves a stay of not quite thirty years before they risked once more, as they intimated, to encourage the teaching of Latin, Greek, and mathematics to New York's budding manhood. Their incitement bore fruit in 1732, but to give the business a more insidious lure than its hapless precursor, the school which now came forth sweetened its stock of offerings with bookkeeping, geography, navigation, and the like, a gross sullying, of course, of the ivied tradition, but in harmony, nevertheless, with the mounting insistence of the philosophers of the market place, and calculated to prepare tomorrow's Morgans and Rockefellers for a life of go-getterism, money-making, and success. Yet despite the glitter of this new enticement, the school could not make a go of it, and after a half-dozen years of trial and trouble New York's second attempt to spur the advancement of culture, sublimated though it was with material and practical considerations, succumbed.

Twice nullified thus by the general apathy, the hope of affording New Yorkers a chance to uplift and ennoble themselves in Latin and Greek slipped quietly from the scene. But—though no one seemed to care—the spark of life still glimmered within it, and by the mid-fifties, with the founding of King's College,

now Columbia University, it flared into flame once more. A training station for
the college's future freshmen, the school made a specialty of tutoring youngsters
who needed a bit of doing over, instructing and drilling them particularly in
Latin and Greek, so that when the time came, they could face the hazards for
admission to King's with hope and equanimity, a noble purpose no doubt, but
one far removed from the Renaissance ideal. Sustained by tuition levies upon its
clients, and succored in addition by moneys it tapped from a foundation set up
especially in its behalf in 1763, the school enjoyed an agreeable flourishing, and
remained in service for the rest of the century.

True to the English custom, high-toned New Yorkers educated their children
privately. Sometimes the business was performed under the family roof by a
hired specialist; sometimes it was transacted in school; and occasionally, where a
father's taste was finicky, he would ship his son to England. In any case the
chance to be instructed and improved was not lacking—in fact, by the mid-
eighteenth century the private master had become a fairly common figure. The
gazettes of the time swarmed with pedagogic offerings which ran from the usual
classics to almost any lore for which a customer could be had. For the liberal
arts—to cite a single illustration—there was Watson's house where "any Young
Gentleman . . . might have opportunity of Learning the same things which are
commonly taught in Colleges." For those fevering to make themselves men of
action as well as thought, there was the institute of Byerly and Day which
advertised instruction not only in all the elementals, useful or ornamental, or
both, but also in such sciences as bookkeeping, surveying, cosmography—even,
indeed, gunnery and fortification. Nor did New York neglect its girls. Now and
then they hazarded the enigmas of Latin, but mostly they confined themselves
to the three Rs and the fine points of the domestic art, besides dancing, music,
and drawing.

Yet for all this opportunity to shine in polite and practical learning, the New
Yorker who craved to sign himself B.A. continued to be stymied. To make an
end of such ignominy, a project to establish a college was announced in 1747,
with a public lottery to round up the required money. Within five years some
£3,500 had been bagged, and in 1754 King's College, now Columbia University,
was awaiting its first clients. Avowedly nonsectarian, the new grove announced
that none was to be denied access to its benefits because of religious belief.
Nevertheless, getting into its chambers was not easy; in fact, few of the horde
which currently bulges the Columbia register—in all probability not even its
faculty—would have been allowed to grace its classes. To be accepted, the
incipient *Artium Baccalaureus* had to know Cicero familiarly and enough Greek
to get the drift of the Gospel of St. John. In addition, he was called upon to
manipulate successfully "the first five Rules of Arithmetic, *i.e.*, as far as Division
and Reduction." Did the hopeful survive this stress and strain? Then he still
confronted the hurdle of being able to write "a good and legible hand."

Even more foreboding to the guardians of academic tradition than the
college's nonsectarianism must have been the intellectual views of King's first

president, Samuel Johnson. A friend of Benjamin Franklin, Johnson shared some of the doctor's advanced thinking. True, in his conviction that a college's first purpose was "to teach Jesus Christ and to serve him in Sobriety, Godliness, and Righteousness of Life," the Reverend Mr. President yielded to no one. At the same time he was all for a curriculum stocked with commerce, geography, history, government, navigation, and the full facts of nature, whether on land or sea or in the air. Unluckily, New York's intellectual tide was still running the other way, and the curriculum which King's College adopted was safely traditional, which is to say classical and literary.

What held for education in New York held also in New Jersey, though its projection fell on a smaller screen, and there were differences, of course, in detail. But the variations were mainly minor, and for more than a generation they were not thought about, for during this period the political fortunes of the two colonies were intertwined under the single executive command of the Governor of New York. Not until 1738 did the higher powers grant Jerseyites the right and dignity of obeying a governor all their own. Like the protean paradise across the Hudson, New Jersey flowered a lush assortment of creed and nationality, and like the English governance of the one, so also the other kept itself as aloof as possible from the educational endeavor. In consequence, New Jersey flaunted the familiar cleavage between the schooling of the high and the low, the former relying on tutors and private schools, and the latter on the mercies of the parish school, the SPG, or apprenticeship.

Seen at a distance, New Jersey's attainments in the lower learning were pretty slim, though their slimness probably was no greater than at any other place where England's high and mighty sat in power. Higher up in the academic stratosphere the record was better—even, in truth, memorable. As usual in that grave world, its prime intellectual propagator was religion. The passing years had witnessed a ponderable cooling-off in the old-time religious ardor, and per contra, a decided heating-up to the joys and rewards which entertain us here below. The new spirit stoked its fire with an energetic skepticism, not only the disciplined and calculated sort of an occasional thinking man, but also the much more common and rougher kind encountered among sailors along the seaboard, the inland merchants and artisans, and the frontiersmen tracking out their first lanes toward the West. Nor were the pungent challenges of the Enlightenment without effect. Blowing in from Europe, and projected by such thinkers as Locke and Newton, and even the mercurial Francis Bacon, they added fresh and powerful fuel, and presently the rising secularism was singeing even a few of the reverend clergy, as witness, especially, the aforementioned Samuel Johnson, a theologian of high capacity, and a gentleman of surpassing excellence.

Still, custom dies hard, and in 1732 at Northampton, Massachusetts, when the elder Jonathan Edwards unloaded a broadside of philippics in supporting of unbending and undefiled Puritanism, he struck at the new worldliness with a staggering counterblast. Although, despite his bedazzling spell, Edwards failed to overcome the threatening hosts of Hell, he managed nevertheless, to confine their fire. From the roll of his sonorous and terrifying admonitions sprang America's first massive revival, which presently swept over all New England and then over the rest of the land. As more and more penitents resumed their pews and gave up sin, the need to accommodate and hold them with trained and expert men of God began once more to flourish. Out of it ascended four new colleges, all consecrated to the making of divines, Brown and Dartmouth in New England, and Rutgers and Princeton in New Jersey.

Princeton made its advent in 1746 as the College of New Jersey. The child of Scotch-Irish Presbyterians, it started life in the image of its parents, full of lofty purpose, but with a pocket that was all but empty. Ten years wearied by before it possessed even a building. But then, as it began to steam and puff, it toiled to wind-swept peaks, the theological Sorbonne of Scotch-Irish America, training its emissaries of God, and sending them forth, once its job was done, to preach and teach in the far-flung Presbyterian fastnesses to the north and south, and even in the vast, outstretched plains beyond the Alleghenies.

The college was only thirteen when the Reverend Samuel Davies became its fourth president. It did not take right-thinkers long to notice that Princeton's latest master had fallen prey to the changing times. Like King's Samuel Johnson and other cocky thinkers, Davies put a great confidence in the secular subjects. He lined the library shelves with books on science and mathematics; he stood up for English prose as against the poesy of the ancients; and more startling, in chapel service, hitherto so strict and sober as to be almost Trappist, he ravished the student spirit with dulcet organ strains, a dereliction which President Stiles of Yale predicted would surely be of "ill consequence." When he bade his students his last good-bye, he laid before them his point of view in one terse and final apothegm. "Be the servants of the church," he urged them, "the servants of the country, the servants of all."

12

The largest of the Middle Colonies—as large as the motherland with Wales thrown in—was Pennsylvania. Established in 1681, this princely plot was granted by the Crown to William Penn to square a debt it owed his departed father. The province was to be a Quaker commonwealth, a holy land of virtue and good works, where gambling, swearing, and guzzling were outlawed, and where for years dancing, music, and play acting were under prohibition. It is only fair to state that such renunciation was more than balanced by moral progress in other directions. Under Penn, the Quakers treated the Indian considerately, even entering into contracts with him, and, better yet, holding themselves to their word. Jailing for debt, in those days of an almost unanimous usage, went out the window, and so did capital punishment, save only in cases of convicted assassins. Scarcely less remarkable was the Quaker practice of complete religious freedom. No one in the commonwealth—so the law read—was to suffer for his "religious persuasion or practice in matters of faith or worship." As a result, the land burgeoned with creeds of every kind, as it still does, of course, today.

Did Pennsylvanians breathe the fresh air of toleration? Then they also enjoyed the richness of their earth, seemingly unbounded and to be had almost for the asking. Nor were they unaware of the value of the water flow, the deep and navigable streams, nature's easiest highway to the inland and to the sea. For hard-pressed Europeans, land-hungry and forever under the pall of war, such wonders were hard to resist, and since the Colony inclined to be hospitable it had no trouble in attracting settlers. They issued from all directions, not only from England, but from Ireland, Scotland, and Wales, and from the mainland, Germans especially, but Dutchmen too, and even Swiss and Swedes and Finns.

The Quakers were not, like the Puritans, impressed by great learning. In truth, one might well ask why should they be? For, communing directly with God, without the usual professional aid of one of his ordained middlemen, the Quakers needed neither to train nor to sustain a clergy. The higher learning, in consequence, left them cold. What was needed, said Penn, was to sow "the Kingdom of God in the hearts of men." This, with some reading, a legible hand, and the useful parts of arithmetic should suffice. Toward such a simple purpose the province took its first step in 1682 when the governor and his council were put upon "to erect and order all public schools . . . in the said province." There the young were to make acquaintance with "the sensible and practical truths," capped, when they reached the age of twelve, with training in a "useful trade or skill to the end that none may be idle. . . . "

But between this ordinance and its execution there lay an enormous chasm. To promote "the simple and practical truths" was all very well until it came to the business of deciding precisely what they were—and then there was trouble aplenty. For in Pennsylvania with its immensely disparate creeds there were many truths, often divergent, and sometimes also in stout contention. The presence of so many sects, all panting to advance their truths, and all clamoring for a free hand in the schooling of their children, moved the Quakers, after no little soul-searching, to change the rules. Thus, where they had started by making the commonwealth the trustee of its youth and responsible for the establishment of schools, in 1701 they turned face to permit "religious bodies or assemblies and congregations of Protestants . . . to purchase any land or tenements for . . . houses of worship, schools, and hospitals," all a recognized and integral part in those days of the ordinary pious endeavor.

Thus enabled to work out their educational arrangements as they saw fit, Pennsylvanians proceeded more or less like their neighbors in New York and New Jersey. The chronicle runs fairly similarly, and apart from some instructive sidelights it need not long detain us. Thus, besides Quaker schools, one runs into the usual parochial motley, in addition to the charitable blandishments of the Society for the Propagation of the Gospel, and a number of private institutions, some of them of a high order, and mostly in Philadelphia.

As might be expected, the zeal for knowledge varied from creed to creed. The

Scotch-Irish Presbyterians, which is to say Calvinists, were, as always, eager for it, and in spite of poverty and hardship, they spared no pains to make their children literate and, of course, virtuous and godly. Convinced, like their comrade Calvinists in Massachusetts, that time might rob them of their learned pastors, they turned very early to the business of giving their youth the necessary grounding in the ancient classics. Out of this striving there presently emerged a full-blown secondary learning, in illustration, the Presbyterian Grammar School, conducted at New London by the Reverend Francis Allison, and the so-called Log College, which worked its students at Neshaminy under the tutelage of William Tennent.

Among the Germans, unhappily, the record is less laudable, and except for the Moravians, most of them were content to dodge and temporize. Some, like the Quakers, regarded learning with suspicion, a hemlock, as it were, to the soul, and they did little to risk its peril. Not a few Germans were still vassals to their peasant background, and they were more engrossed in growing crops than in trading in ideas. All the same, from the Germans came two of the province's most talked-about schoolmasters, Francis Daniel Pastorius and Christopher Dock. The former, a retired lawyer, and a gaudy and stalwart fellow, given to strong and rhetorical talk, served in the Free Friends' School, at Philadelphia, where he made himself known for his virtuosity in the classics and, even more, for the bite of his rattan. Less erudite, but also more tranquilizing, was Dock, a warm and tender Mennonite. He inhabits our memory today not for his classroom craftsmanship, of which we know almost nothing, but for his concoction in 1770 of the first educational treatise, the *Schulordnung,* to be printed in the Colonies, the first, indeed, of what has since turned into an ever-lengthening procession.

The least numerous among Pennsylvania's Germans were the Moravians; but they were also their most cultivated representatives, and the most inspired pedagogues then celebrating the land. In the Colonies they were the first to run an infant school. In 1749 they enriched Lititz with a boarding school for girls and a seminary for their older sisters. Also let it not be forgotten that these people lifted church music to the level of a glorious art—indeed, as early as 1742 in their *Singakademie* they sang Johann Sebastian Bach to the awestruck hills of Bethelehem. Finally, despite the gloom and grumbling of apprehensive Quakers, they persisted in teaching the magic of tone to their young at school.

Although a good part of Pennsylvania's pursuit of knowledge smacked of a sectarian flavor, there was no lack of laic effort. It showed itself especially in Philadelphia, which over the years had begun to pulse with the boom of business—in fact, by 1740, it had grown into an up-and-coming city, the largest in the land, and one of the greatest in Christendom. The new burgherdom soon reflected its values in a robust and flourishing private schooling. As in New York, it carpentered its offerings to all demands, whether cultural or vocational, from Arabic and watercoloring to spoken French and Portuguese, account keeping, and coastal sailing. For those who worked by day, but whose ambitions remained in flame at night, private schools were available even after hours.

Nor did learning limit its caress to paid professionals. Philadelphia was not yet fifty when Benjamin Franklin and a few kindred spirits joined in the Junto to further, as they remarked, "their mutual improvement." Every Friday of an evening they assembled in their stalls in a member's home or in some friendly tavern to engage their minds with the nature of sound or vapors or even fiat money, entertaining their stomachs meanwhile with the felicity of food and beer. Presently the Junto succumbed and some of its members, led by Franklin, founded the American Philosophical Society, the first scientific brotherhood in the Colonies, one of the most significant of its kind, and still in active practice.

It was Franklin who gave America its first really native school, the Academy. A plain response to the notion that education is not merely education, the new school proposed to teach "those things that are likely to be most useful and ornamental." Had Franklin had his own way, then, very likely, the Academy would have devoted its main energies to the modern and practical subjects. But the school's trustees, far more timorous than the idol-smashing doctor, were unwilling to join him in such heresy. As a result, in 1751, when the Academy's pupils eased themselves into their benches, they could—if the inclination seized them—apply their powers to the study of Greek and Latin. Such, of course, was an old and familiar operation, and one which was the hallmark of every grammar school in the land and over the sea. What set the Academy apart from its classical predecessor was its readiness to give instruction in the modern languages, besides—as it let out the news in Franklin's *Pennsylvania Gazette*—in "History, Geography, Chronology, Logic, and Rhetoric; also Writing, Arithmetic, Merchants Accounts, Geometry, Algebra, Surveying, Gauging, Navigation, Astronomy, Drawing in Perspective, and other Mathematical Sciences; with natural and Mechanic Philosophy, etc. . . . "

The Academy pranced in success almost from the start. In fact, by 1755 it had outgrown its first mission and was chartered anew as the College, Academy and Charitable School of Philadelphia. Under the new arrangement the classical and philosophical subjects became the business of the college. The sixth college to make its appearance in Colonial America, the College of Philadelphia later became the University of Pennsylvania, which is, of course, still in service and in the glow of health. The college's first president, the Reverend Dr. Smith, like the Reverend Dr. Johnson of King's, had a tender spot in his heart for Franklin's "useful learning," but the college trustees regarded it somewhat sniffishly, and they gave their support to the classics. But time applied its corrective hand, and as worldliness increased the pressure of its challenge, the older learning was compelled to make concessions. When this occurred, the college leaped forward. It was the first shrine of higher wisdom in America to honor botany with a professorial chair and the first to impart systematic instruction in medicine.

CHAPTER 14

THE RISE OF SCIENCE

For all the power of its attack on medievalism, its curiosity and ingenuity, and the magnificence of its creative expression, the Renaissance could produce no new explanation of the physical world. The valuations it put upon life were chiefly those of a glamorous classical paganism. It succeeded in making some of the established authorities suspect, but it could not drive them out entirely, nor could it replace their propositions with anything save conjecture, audacious at times to be sure, but conjecture nevertheless. What was needed to make the promise of the Renaissance something more than a promise was a stock of accurate and ponderable knowledge explaining nature and man's place therein—something more solid and sophisticated than the contentions of Aristotle and Christian theology.

The search for such a body of knowledge reaches into the abyss of the faraway past when the Orient braved its first expeditions into mathematics, astronomy, and medicine. The Greeks, with their flair for borrowing, minted this knowledge into coin of their own, and presently they were enhancing it in various directions. Their most sparkling performances are to be found in mathematics, especially its geometric and trigonometric sectors, and in astronomy, physics, and medicine. But they ranged in other realms as well, in illustration, geography, botany, anatomy, and physiology. It is not necessary to call the roll of Grecian scientists. Its names are too many, and they are not made for easy utterance. But several of them cut a figure even in the common folklore. There is Archimedes, the physicist, who, chancing to discover a natural law, leaped from his bath water and, clad without even a blush, tore down the street yelling "Eureka!"; there is Euclid, the father of plane geometry, once a required subject in every American high school; there is Hipprocrates, medicine's father, who is recalled in the oath which currently celebrates his name; and, finally, there is Aristotle, one of the greatest intellects to flash in civilization, and the master organizer and cataloguer of them all.

The Romans built upon the Grecian base. An immensely practical people, they were not, like the Greeks, greatly given to the chase of recondite theory. What concerned them, at bottom, was putting theory into practice to the end of satisfying their everyday needs. Hence, barring a handful of names, the list of Roman contributors to the advancement of pure science is comparatively brief.

The rise of Christendom, it is scarcely necessary to state, was no boon for the prospering of science. To a people bent on lodging themselves some day in Heaven, faith was paramount, and the pursuit of exact knowledge, like the apple tree, its Biblical mother, was a danger and a threat. Early in her history Holy Church issued her warning against "all the heathen books," and in the year 401, as has already been mentioned, the Council of Carthage snapped them shut even to the reverend clergy. Thus under prohibition, the ancient scientific legacy, though pallid at best, ran upon baleful times. Save for the bootleggings of an errant skeptic, the pondering of nature's secrets now fell into the hands of alchemists, astrologers, magicians, and similar experts in delusion.

2

So things sat, more or less, for most of the Middle Ages. Yet even before the Renaissance burst its first buds, signs of a change were visible, and by the twelfth of our Christian centuries the church was showing a disposition toward greater leniency. As a consequence, the ancient pagan writings were ready to be reexamined. The flutter of scientific interest reached near and far. It extended not only to professionals in the plants of higher learning, but to an even greater degree to free-lancers who worked privily—indeed, it invaded even the imperial fastness of Frederick II who, besides stocking his court with infinitely industrious scholars, himself ventured into scientific exploration.

Yet, for all this bubbling on the surface, the revival was no more than a revival. What it brought forth, in the main, was a vanished and half-forgotten knowledge, the novelty of an ancient yesterday. Despite its bold resourcefulness, its freedom, and its secularity, ancient scientific enterprise falls short of the simplest current canon. A stranger to the laboratory, it was a stranger also to the scientific method. Essentially an exercise in speculation, it bottomed itself on reason and imagination, and—not uncommonly—even on fantasy. Lacking the necessary tools of precision, it was obliged to contain its observation within the bond of human capacity. And wanting the fundamental mathematics, it sheared its findings of the necessary exactitude.

This does not mean that antiquity's scientific endeavor, with all its deficiencies, served no useful purpose, and that its great echo in the twelfth century was only an echo. The Greeks made the explanation of the physical world one of their major concerns. The first to exert themselves to free the human mind, they asked new questions, and they sought new answers. The twelfth-century revival, though cloaked in mystery and shackled securely to Christian orthodoxy, nevertheless let loose some of the ancient curiosity. It made possible, in a later day, the rise of a concerted attempt to penetrate the basic cosmic phenomena, which is to say, it gave impetus to the rise of modern scientific inquiry.

3

It was in the sixteenth century, as the Renaissance cascaded into the Reformation, that the movement had its start. Unluckily, the period was in no mood for free inquiry. The delicate tolerance Mother Church had allowed herself in an earlier day had been shattered by her conflict with the new religion. Though Protestant theologians were at odds with those of Rome, when it came to making concessions to the progress of the natural sciences, there was no difference between them. Both the new and the old Church denounced the natural sciences, and reserved their most sizzling anathemas for those who gave them countenance. Nevertheless, in spite of such ecclesiastical unfriendliness, as the centuries unrolled, a handful of bold and brilliant men ventured to push back the frontiers of exact knowledge. Their ranks, to be sure, were spare, but they spun their feats on a vast and extensive scale, from astronomy, botany, and chemistry to geology, mathematics, medicine, and yet more. Scan their puny roster, and again and again your eyes will fall upon some memorable name, to wit, Andreas Vesalius, the first in modern annals to carve and explore a human carcass and to report luminously thereon; Gerhard Kramer—or as the world more often speaks of him, Mercator—the Adam of modern cartography; Valerius Cordus, the reputed father in the West of presentday chemistry; William Turner, the remote ancestor of ornithology; and William Gilbert, the coiner of the word *electricity* and the author of the world's first treatise on its powers and properties.

The list runs much longer, but far and away its most dazzling representative, not so much for his discovery alone as for its vast and devastating effect on Christendom, was Nicholas Copernicus, a Roman Catholic cleric, a medico, and a student of the stars. In his work, *The Revolution of the Heavenly Bodies,* issued in 1543, the year of his death, and which he reverently inscribed to the Pope, the third Paul, Copernicus blew up the cardboard cosmos of the Middle Ages by the simple device of declaring the sun and not the earth to be the center of our universe. At one stroke the earth became, so to speak, a suburb of the sun, and man, though still the Heavenly Father's noblest handiwork, became just another of its creatures. Quick to grasp the menacing implications of the Copernican revelation, right-thinkers everywhere, whether Catholic or Protestant, made themselves rather unpleasant about it. When Giordano Bruno upheld it and undertook to explain it to the layman, he was conveyed to the flames for his trouble. And when, later on, Galileo corroborated its incontrovertible reasoning with telescope and equations, he was set upon by the Inquisition to recant. Yet, for all its bruises, Copernicus's theory remained impervious to threats, whether sacred or profane, and in 1822 the doctrine, once excoriated by the Holy See as "false and altogether opposed to Holy Scriptures," was accorded the nod of official sanction.

Copernicus arrived at his conclusion over the highroad of induction, a route not unfamiliar to the ancient Aristotle, but which, leading to unknown and perhaps even heretical ends, had been allowed by medieval schoolmen to fall into disuse. Dissatisfied with the conventional thinking, which is to say orthodox thinking, on the relationship of earth and sun, Copernicus put a searching eye on all the known writings for a clue to a better explanation. Then, reaching a tentative view, he established a hypothesis. Now, flashing the searchlight of truth up to the cosmos, he observed and tested his findings with unsparing care until—to make an end—he had convinced himself of the correctness of his assumption, and the truth, hence, of his new explanation. Such, in its stark essence, is the inductive process.

4

The method, as is not unusual with an intellectual novelty, was slow in getting forward. Individual and independent savants were alert to its possibilities, of course, for it alone held the key with which they could unlock the universe and bare its hidden secrets. But university professors, enwrapt in the comfort of their cherished traditions, were disinclined to accept it. It remained, indeed, for a layman to make its great merit known, and to take the field aggressively in its behalf. Francis Bacon by name and a Londoner by birth, he was the son of a prominent jurist, the Lord Keeper at one time of Elizabeth's England. The son himself was even more a man of parts. Lawyer, courtier, writer, a self-interested realist, yet a weaver of diaphanous Utopias, half statesman, half self-serving politican, he made his way up the precarious political ladder, becoming Lord Chancellor and enriching himself on the way with a couple of peerages. But ambition led him beyond the bounds of decorous corruption, and presently he was plummeted out of favor. Prosecuted and convicted, he was lodged in jail, from which he emerged after but an ephemeral stay to spend his remaining five years on earth in contemplation and writing.

Lord Bacon's claim to literary renown rests on his *Essays* which, despite the weight of time, are still read and enjoyed today. Intellectually, his eminence derives, in part, from the *New Atlantis* and the *Advancement of Learning,* but more especially from the *Novum Organum*. The first depicts a Utopia. Like all such baroque fantasies, it is full of ingratiating thoughts about life in the happiest of all possible worlds. But the millennium which it pictures is to be obtained not by prayer and good works, but by a mature and diligent probing of nature's laws to the end of applying them to the needs and comforts of man. The great men in Bacon's imaginary new world are scientists. Of greater worth and importance than politicians, and even priests, they work hand in hand in a superuniversity, the House of Solomon, where they apply their full energy to the pursuit of New Learning.

Bacon's confidence that the steady increase in our knowledge would surely enhance the collective welfare was surpassed only by his certainty that the key indispensable to such knowledge was the inductive method. It is to the formulation and explanation of this method that Bacon addressed himself in the *Novum Organum*. Published in 1620, the work was composed in the scholar's Latin, the last important philosophical discourse to be thus preserved in England. In it Bacon not only brandished his banner in behalf of induction; he also essayed to clear the arena of its main enemies—the half-baked learning, for example, of alchemists; the worm-eaten beliefs in the mysterious, and hence the irrational; the pettifogging wind music of academicians; the delicate but socially sterile learning of Humanists; and so on and on, down to the superstitions and old wives' tales that prey upon man's credulities.

Bacon's assault on the Old Learning and his powerful promotion of the New reaped and abundant and varied criticism. Some have hailed him as the father of the modern scientific method. Others, putting his method under a meticulous glass, have found it to be neither novel nor adequate—a proposal, in short, of a scientific pretender, and one no first-rate scientist could consider seriously. Still others, unable or unwilling to separate Bacon's work from his rectitude, and finding the latter somewhat damaged, have on this ground rejected the former. It has been pointed out not infrequently that Bacon himself fell short of the lofty intellectual standards he proclaimed so grandiloquently for others, and that he failed to purge himself of his own numerous prejudices. An ignoramus in mathematics, he shrugged off the subject as of no consequence—on the eve, in a manner of speaking, of Newton's monumental *Principia.* Gilbert's important pioneering in electricity and magnetism Bacon damned out of hand. And the Copernican theory he flayed as brashly as the most cocksure theologian of his era, though at the same time he put great stock in astrology, and resorted to its wonders regularly. Yet, for all his shortcomings, in intellectual history Sir Francis is not to be shouldered curtly aside. His influence on science itself was doubtless negligible, but as a propagandist for the advancement of knowledge, and the awakening of a larger public interest in its significance in our everyday living, no one, save possibly Voltaire, surpassed him.

5

Despite the restraints and disabilities put upon scientists, their stirrings would not still. On the contrary, as year fell after year, the ax and spade work of their explorations waxed in strength and significance to obtain such magnitude as to cause latterday recorders of intellectual history to display it prominently in their showcase as the Scientific Movement of the seventeenth century. There is not much to be gained by summoning its *prominenti* one after another to take a curtain call from an applauding posterity. Let it be noted simply that in the penetration of their arcana not a few were giants—some, indeed, were mastodons, such as Galileo, Harvey, Boyle, Leibnitz, and Newton, whose feats in physics served to make his name synonymous with the era. The knowledge of the observable universe which the seventeenth century unveiled, the eighteenth augmented and expanded. Thus the experimental hunt for the precise facts about nature, whether on land or sea or in the air, has been carried on century upon century until in the present day it bids fair to strain even our most extravagant fancy.

As more and more of nature's mysterious workings yielded their secrets to the searchings of the men of science, the monopoly which metaphysicians and theologians had heretofore exercised in such affairs was not only challenged, but as the years streaked on, it was broken. In fact, as generation followed generation, the authority of revealed religion, once all-embracing and almost incontestable, became more and more confined to the promotion and maintenance of piety and virtue. As the old certainties gave way one by one, there was a visible growth of skepticism, at least on the upper intellectual level. Did the medieval exemplars of divine science and their Reformation analogues seek to fathom the cosmic riddle by presuming a universe centered in Almighty God? Then some of the new intellectuals flashed their searchlight on a universe wherein man was at the core. And did the former rely heavily on revelation and other ghostly data to uphold their syllogisms? Then the latter leaned not on faith but on reason, and they turned their backs on supernatural evidence, relying instead on the objective and impartial findings of the natural sciences and mathematics. Not only did a handful of thinking men apply their talents to the search for a new explication of the cosmic riddle but, loosened from the fetters of the past, they were also free to alter their attitudes toward custom and tradition. After long years, in fact, they were even able to introduce objective methods of study into what we now call the field of social science.

On education the advent of science made no immediate impression. On the whole the latter's leading practitioners performed their prodigies beyond academic walls, and until the eighteenth century their efforts were stimulated and advanced not by the higher learning in the universities, but by enlightened altruists and a variety of associations, such as the Royal Society of London, the Accademia del Cimento of Florence, the French Academy of Sciences, the Berlin Academy, and several more. In the secondary schools conservatism was even more solidly settled. There the cleft between the old classical learning and the new scientific variety was not bridged until the mid-nineteenth century—not, in other words, until the appearance of the Darwinian teaching.

If the generality of practicing schoolmen kept themselves immured to the challenge of science, this does not mean that it could be ignored, or that the cultural climate wherein it thrived was without effect. Actually, a number of thinkers, impressed by the growing reliance on observation and experience in the pursuit of new knowledge, began to call for an application, or at all events, an adaptation of this practice to education. They vary in detail and stress, it is true, but in the support they gave to the study of things and ideas rather than words and definitions, they were on common ground. Although they never worked in concert, they have been bracketed by educational historians under the common denomination of Realists, a title they never heard of, and which doubtless must give some of them a postmortem chuckle. It is to these men, or at any rate, to a number of their leading representatives, that we shall now direct our attention.

Michel de Montaigne

In France the foremost spokesman for the revolt against mere book learning was
Michel Eyquem, generally known as Montaigne. Never a teacher, or even a
reformer, Montaigne was essentially a man who enjoyed playing with ideas. His
interests were numerous and of an extraordinary range, and among them was
education. He was born in 1533, the third son of a country lord, residenced at
Perigord, in the environs of Bordeaux, and he died on the family lands not quite
threescore years later. Time has obscured his parents, but his father—the dearest
of all fathers, his son called him—must have been an unusual, an almost singular
man. Living in Catholic France, and himself a believer, he nevertheless married a
Jewess who had turned Protestant. To his son's rearing he gave a great deal of
careful attention, and when Michel was yet an infant, he was put in the hands of
a German who knew scarcely a word of French and who was under orders to
talk with the child solely in Latin. Consequently, as the boy increased in years
and volume, he hobnobbed with the language as familiarly as a Roman, though
of French he knew not a whit until he was six. His father hoped he would
acquire an affable manner and an easy disposition, as befits a man of high estate.
Hence, though the times were brutish, young Montaigne suffered no indignities.
On the contrary, his youth was one of pleasant grazing, and it was happily free
from tears.

At six these carefree days came to an end. Designed for a classical education,
the hallmark in those days of a man of quality, the boy was consigned to the
Collège de Guyenne. At one time it had been the purveyor of a liberal Humanism, but now its work was being polluted by the pedantry of formalists and
wordmongers. Save for a couple of his teachers, Montaigne's mentors had empty
minds, and he held them in low regard. It was a sentiment which later on was to
work itself into his writing, and which he bore within him to the grave.

When he was fifteen, the boy left Guyenne to study law at Toulouse, and two
years later he took his degree. Four years following—he was now twenty-one—he
established himself in practice as a councilor with the Parliament of Bordeaux.
Subsequently his gifts were given an even greater acknowledgment when he was
made mayor of Bordeaux, an elevation, he said, he did not really want, but to
which, after he had served his term, he permitted himself to be renamed. He was
in his middle thirties when his father died, and he inherited the paternal title and
estate.

2

Montaigne has told us that he was not much at reading, but the assertion is wide
of the mark. His library was inhabited by over a thousand volumes, a monument-

al assemblage in those days, even in the mansion of a lord. Not only did Montaigne crowd his walls with books; he apparently also savored their contents, and in his compositions he embellishes page after page with classical quotations. His duties as a landed lord were not too onerous, and when he was not occupied with the management of his domain, he would frequently steal off into his study to loll in the company of his books.

He was not yet forty when the writing urge seized him. It was, at first, merely a dalliance in pleasant self-communion, a diversion from the dreariness that is begotten by too much leisure. Unlike the professional men of learning, he expressed his views not in Latin, but in French, and he wrote as the spirit rode him. His themes run to an almost incredible variety, from cannibalism, drunkenness, and liars—to instance a few—to idleness, inequality, and fortunetelling. He has often been likened to Erasmus, and in several respects the similarity is plain. Both stood for moderation and forbearance; both were exemplars of a suave urbanity and tolerance; both made a mock of obscurantists; and both were living arsenals of doubt. In the realm of letters each could turn a pretty phase, and each had a jaunty hand for satire. Yet, except in his lighter moments, Erasmus performed in the scholar's frock, while Montaigne worked, so to speak, in a dress suit. As the years swept on, his literary zeal completely overran him, and though he had promised himself not to reveal his thoughts in print, in 1580, after almost a decade of assiduous scrivening, he changed his mind, and the first edition of his works was put between covers. Their appearance marks the birth of the modern essay.

The times which Montaigne adorned were, like our own, frenzied and full of hatreds. The bright new day which the Renaissance had promised had turned out to be a false dawn. The land ran red with the blood of war and fanaticism, while Huguenots and Catholics engaged in reciprocal butchery, and Guise and Valois and Navarre conspired and jockeyed for the Crown. Meanwhile, France oscillated in uncertainty between Spain's Philip and England's Elizabeth, each in turn now a threat, now a hope, and sometimes both. Yet in the darkest moment of this strife, Montaigne managed to maintain himself aloof from partisanship. His castle, it is recorded, was never fortified, and its gates were open at all times to Protestants and Catholics alike. Those who speculate that philosophy, art, and letters are inexorably the products of the social forces which envelop their makers will have to do some hard stretching to fit Montaigne to their doctrine. He was, it is true, enormously taken by the New World, and particularly the vast diversity in human customs and beliefs that it presented. On the other hand, the grim struggles that blazed and roared all about him found but slight utterance from him. "I persuade you," he said, "in your opinions and in your discourses, as much as in your custom, and in everything else, to use moderation and temperance." Put together in this vein, his essays escape the academician's heavy hand. They may sink now and then into the inconsequential, and even the banal, but they are never dull. Turn their pages and you will find no sure cures to save us from our woes, nor even a hint of absolute and incontrovertible truth. "My profession of truth," he tells us, "is not to know the truth, nor to attain it. I rather open than discover things. . . . "

3

Montaigne dealt with education in two essays, *On Pedantry* and *On the Education of Children.* In another, *On the Affection of Fathers to Their Children,* a recurrent pedagogy is threaded into its theme. Like all Montaigne's literary concoctions, these discourses may be described as an expression of a personal point of view. Again, like nearly all his work, they are quarried largely from the sphere of his intimate experience, but refined and given glamor as his years mounted by calm contemplation and a deft and penetrating skepticism.

The decrepit formalism into which the classical Renaissance had sunk, and which had clamped its grip upon the schools, left Montaigne cold. "They stuff the memory," he protested, "and leave the understanding void." Does the learned textbook assert, for example, that sea serpents swim the Narrow Seas? That a poultice of chicken feathers will cure a cold? And that, barring Heaven, ours is the best of all possible worlds? And does the master submit to such authority and order it filed forever in the memory? Then let the pupil be on guard. Let him allow nothing to be lodged in his head on mere authority and trust, "for he who follows another follows nothing." The flesh and blood of learning is not memory but thought; not the content of books, but self-realization. "A mere bookish learning is a paltry learning," and he who possesses nothing more, for all his cramping years in the schoolboy's bench, is at best a rubber stamp.

As a noble, Montaigne addressed his educational views to the upper orders. Even so, studying under the counsel of a tutor, however meritorious his knack and skill, is not enough. What is needed in addition was some direct adventuring with the world, a steady and lively interplay with common folk, supplemented and fortified with trips abroad. Such contacts with the concerns of everyday, Montaigne believed, serve not only to put an edge on the learner's faculties; they will apprise him of other people's humors, manners, and customs, their politics, theology, and jurisprudence, their social system, and their public works. And nine times out of ten they will do it better than all the flyblown erudition stuffed into the heads of schoolboys from books.

It was Montaigne's belief that the generality of teachers, lacking the artist's sensitive touch, do not know when to make an end. They schoolmaster the young too much, he lamented, and their pupils' term of bondage stretches far too long. "Most subjects now taught," he declared, "are of no use to us; and even in those that are useful, there are many points it were better to leave alone. . . . "—a sentiment endorsed by schoolboys universally and unanimously.

Once the quest for wisdom and virtue is on the way, some concessions may be made to the study of that ancient trinity, logic, rhetoric, and geometry, in addition to what then passed for physics. But they are to be purged of their formalism, and they are to be carpentered in accordance with the needs of daily living. Of greater use and merit in this respect is some acquaintance with human experience, as displayed, for example, in history and, more attractively, in biography, and especially in the celebrated *Lives* of Plutarch. The capstone of all learning is philosophy, not the vague and gaseous stuff, however, which was then generally emitted by the practitioners of the higher learning, but rather the kind "which instructs us to live." Thus pursued, "there is nothing more airy, more gay, more frolic."

A large part of his sixty years Montaigne devoted to the husbanding of his property and, as the years moved on, to the mild and amiable reflections of a contented man. The usual show and luxury which festoon nobility he disdained. By the same token, he confessed a great admiration for the Spartans, and especially their simplicity and frugality. Neither a brawny nor a spacious man himself, he cast envious looks on their strength and sturdiness, and in his essays he commends the virtues of hardiness and self-reliance. "A child," he observes— taking a bold leap—"should not be brought up in his mother's lap," for "mothers are too tender."

Though Montaigne shed a warm glow for Sparta's austere wonders, this is by no means saying that he cried down the delights which charmed the courtly class of his own day. Common sense, as usual, bade him bear in mind that such graces are, as it were, the tools of the noble's trade, and to be at ease with life, it behooves the aristocrat to be their familiar. Hence it is no more than proper that the nascent noble be brought to their acquaintance while he is still young and flexible. The list of activities in this department is long, but for the current American surely not too long. On it one finds recommendations for leaping, fencing, running, and hurling. The incipient lord grapples in wrestling. He hunts and he rides horses. He applies himself to the art of music making, and he learns to swing a graceful leg in dance.

True to his usual forbearance, Montaigne regarded with some suspicion the severity and compulsion which were then the rule in the seminaries of know- ledge. " 'Tis a real house of correction," he expostulated. Reminiscent, one may guess, of his own good luck when he was very young, he put thumbs down on the school's grisly discipline, for "nothing more degenerates a well-descended nature"—a noble sentiment, to be sure, but one which made precisely no impression on the reigning birchmasters until several centuries anon.

By preference Montaigne disported himself as a Roman Catholic—in fact, he repeatedly professed himself to be a true and faithful son of Holy Church. At the same time he invested himself with the luxury of doubt. In his private credo he probably had very few articles of faith. He scoffed at miracles, and even though the Good Book tells us that witches exist and commands us to destroy them, he held the entire business in contempt. The Christian contention that we are in this vale to make ready for an endless and incorruptible bliss in Heaven he regarded dimly, preferring instead to woo the fleeting charms and satisfaction of here and now. He had his doubts about the possibility of absolute truth, and he was skeptical about the surety of what is right and wrong. His pedagogy of religion, under the circumstances, is simple: religious instruction is purely a matter of parental solicitude, and there are no general rules one can lay down, and certainly there should be no compulsion from without. Religion, in short, is a matter of the heart and not of the mind, and in learning these two must needs be kept apart. "My reason," he wrote, "is not framed to bend and stoop—that is for my knee."

Montaigne was not a great thinker; nor was he a great artist; he was in all likelihood not great at all. His influence, such as it was, was neither immediate nor direct. Some of his views, there is reason to believe, filtered into Locke, and in a later age into Rousseau, and out of the latter several have come down the long lane of time into the present. Examine Montaigne's main principles, and you will find a number which flourish prodigiously in our midst today, and particularly among progressives. Do contemporary schoolmen put their stress on the child's individuality, on learning by doing, and on social understanding? Then so did Montaigne. Do they give their support and confidence to a humane and civilized discipline, to individual differences, to the cultivation of the body as well as the mind? Then so, again, did Montaigne. And so one might go on and on—but there is no need to belabor the point. The fact is, the resemblance is there, and though the moderns are not Montaigne's immediate assigns and successors, they are nevertheless of the same line. Indeed, if certain French patriots are to be believed, he is the archfather of them all.

Richard Mulcaster

In England the new educational outlook is best represented by Richard Mulcaster, John Milton, and John Locke. The former, who was born in 1531, lived for eighty years, of which the best and happiest fell into the reign of the first Elizabeth. A professional educator and a man of notable talent, he rose to the top of his craft, serving for a quarter of a century as headmaster of Merchant Taylors', and almost as long at St. Paul's, two famous houses of the English secondary learning, both still in robust health. It is not for his endurance, however, that we remember Mulcaster. If we recall him at all, it is for his iconoclastic thinking which his own generation, sad to say, found wanting, and which, until the nineteenth century, civilization ignored.

Mulcaster published two books, one, the *Positions,* in 1581, the other, the *Elementarie,* in the year following. Both were agreeably small, but they were written in a drab and graceless English. Their ideas, on the other hand, were singularly fresh, and some were even daring—a trait which weighed against them almost as much as their deadly style. Yet, despite his shortcomings as a maker of good prose, Mulcaster made no secret of his admiration for the English tongue. It is, he intimated, the most glorious of them all. In a land which was feeling its national oats such a sentiment found a ready patriotic acclaim. But when Mulcaster proceeded to urge that all English young, male and female, should be made to learn to read and write the speech of their daily life, and that their instruction should be grounded on a sufficiency of support, then love of country suddenly yielded to love of pocket, and his proposal died in embryo.

Mulcaster's pedagogical views are of the common stock of Realism. Sometimes they lean close to those of Montaigne; at other times they approach those of Ratke and Comenius, both of a slightly later world. Like pretty nearly all the Realists, Mulcaster held for an education which furthered the free functioning of body and spirit as well as the mind; and he was sniffish of a schooling which kept itself apart from the realities of everyday living. He held a skeptical opinion of any education which restricted its bounties to the gentry and nobility and similar folk of high pretension. All the young, he urged, should have access to education regardless of where it has pleased Omnipotence to deposit them. In this stand he was seconded, as we shall see, by Ratke and Comenius, but in the England of Elizabeth public taste ran powerfully against it, and it was not until the Victorian heyday that it began to change.

Although Mulcaster practiced his art in the Latin grammar school, it was the lower learning which got his major consideration. Not only did he insist that it should muster all the English young to get them to know reading and writing familiarly; it should also introduce them to music and drawing, and to religion and rectitude. Classes were to be kept small, and they were to be taught by the ablest masters in the land who, Mulcaster let it be understood, "should in good truth be most liberally compensated." It was his belief that teachers, like doctors, jurists, and divines, need training to function at their best, and to work this magic special colleges should be established—a notion then so palpably absurd as to cause its owner to be treated with jocosity.

A man so full of bright ideas would naturally be expected to reserve a few for the subject of good teaching. Here Mulcaster sang the Realists' favorite tunes. He held, for example, that in education our first concern must be the child, and that whatever he undertakes to learn should be brought into harmony with his capacities. He felt that in the process of learning, the use of the senses can be of enormous help. Finally, he supported the view that learning can and ought to be a high delight, and that even though Johnny sometimes comports himself like a knave, more can be achieved in the long run with sweetness and light than with blood and iron.

In his daily practice Mulcaster sometimes fell off his lofty perch of theory, a failing which the historians of good intentions declare to be fairly common—indeed, some say it is the rule. Thus, he launched every lesson not with an effort to make it smooth and agreeable, but with a long and winding chalk talk on its grammatical and rhetorical flora and fauna, their potential griefs and burdens, and whatever else captured his fancy. Then he left his charges to sweat out their lesson by their own devices; whereupon he entertained them with merriment by sitting atop his desk to rehearse an hour's snoring. When he revived and found some indecorum, minor criminals got off with a reprimand; but the major practitioners of horseplay, for all his metaphysics about a kindly discipline, he would vigorously club. Fathers and mothers sometimes besought him to cease blacking and bluing their sons' posteriors. Unhappily, toward them he conceived a vast aversion. Despite his anticipation of a better day in pedagogy and some of its enduring charms and ameliorations, it cannot be said that he foresaw the advent of a cordial relationship between home and school, and certainly not the desirability of bringing teachers and parents into a fraternal organization.

Yet in his time Mulcaster stood in the forefront of his profession. Though he was overshadowed presently by Comenius, he was also the breeder of some of that man's most famous ideas—a fact which has been pretty well forgotten. Seen through the haze of centuries, he is not easily focused; but there can be no doubt that he must have been a most extraordinary fellow.

John Milton

Even more extraordinary than the headmaster of St. Paul's, not as an educator, but as a man of many parts, is John Milton, who lived and died in the seventeenth century. He has come down the road of history as Shakespeare's lyrical heir, the creator of *Paradise Lost* and *Paradise Regained,* but today his poesy is probably more praised than read. The call to make himself a profession-al bard came while he was still in youth when he composed some lines on *A Fair Infant Dying of a Cough.* Pretty soon, however, he was rhyming more merrily on "spicy nut-brown ale" and "ladies whose bright eyes rain influence." The Civil War of 1642 stilled his warbling for the time being, and led him, on the side of Cromwell, into the bullring of political pamphleteering, wherein his industry brought him the post of Latin secretary to the government. Twenty years of his life he lavished on political writing, yet save for the *Areopagitica: A Speech for the Liberty of Unlicensed Printing* and the *Doctrine and Discipline of Divorce,* the mass of his polemic output is now little more than a cobwebbed memory.

When Milton was still in his nonage, he found, as young blades usually do, that his allowance was too small. And so as other youths are wont to cut grass or wait on table to improve the status of their purse, he undertook to give instruction to the young. We know very little of his practice—indeed, apart from the fact that he performed for some seven years, and that his scholars were of a rich and altitudinous order, the record is blanketed in fog. Even so, his round of schoolmastering sufficed apparently to qualify him as a spokesman for educa-tional reform. He volunteered his views in a series of letters to a friend, and in 1644 he admired them well enough to publish them as the *Tractate of Educa-tion.*

As Calvin's disciple, Milton believed in all earnestness in a Bible state wherein religious and civil authority coalesce, and wherein education, reflecting the theocratic setting, is funneled into religious and civic ends. "The end ... of learning," he declared, "is to repair the ruin of our first parents by regaining to know God aright. ... " At the same time it is to fit a man "to perform justly, skillfully, and magnanimously all the offices, private and public, of peace and war." To attain to such a height, the schools in those days were obviously in need of some serious overhauling. They were bound, of course, to be corrupted by the Stuart hangover of an anti-Puritan culture; but, almost as bad, they dallied so long in "grammar and sophistry," and "in scraping together so much miserable Latin and Greek," as to waste seven or eight years on a task which, Milton assures us, might well have been dispatched in one.

Though he passed a harsh censure on the many years devoured by the study of Latin and Greek, this is not saying that Cromwell's Latin secretary put his foot down on the learning of these ancient tongues. On the contrary, he demanded enlightenment not only in these grizzly standbys, but also in Hebrew, Chaldean, Syriac, and for a chaser, Italian. Once the student was able to negotiate these languages freely and without mishap, he was to soak up the wisdom of the ancients by studying their confections in arithmetic, geometry, physics, astronomy, and geography, from which, after catching his second wind, he proceeded through surveying, architecture, navigation, and fortification, with organized forays into anatomy, physiology, logic, rhetoric, ethics, politics, and law—not forgetting theology and the diligent thumbing of the Good Book.

It is only fair to state that Milton did not intend a student to engorge this stupendous bill of fare to its last and smallest crumb. What he should attain rather was a "general insight into things," or ideas, so that he might deal with any subject easily and familiarly at any time and anywhere. Nor is Milton's weight put exclusively on the intellect. Like Plato, whose excellence as a wrestler is said to have startled onlookers almost as much as his feats of reason, Milton set a great store by physical culture. Thus, to train and develop himself corporally, the student is put upon to wrestle and to ride on horse. He roves on land and sea "with prudent and staid guides." He learns to fence and to spear game and fowl in times of peace, and men in times of war. His diet, Milton adds, with a brevity only seldom his, "should be plain, healthful, and moderate." And, finally, between his exercising and his feeding he should be tranquilized with organ music.

It has been said of Milton, as it has of several other diviners in pedagogy, that he laid down dogmas aplenty on what should be demanded of the young, but that on the means of doing it, he was comparatively silent—a contention which in the main holds water. There is, it is true, his observation that knowledge comes to the learner through the senses, and that periodically he had better reexamine and reorganize his stock of knowledge to give it solidity and coherence—two ideas which in the seventeenth century were scarcely novel. Aside from these, and the view that play might make the study of arithmetic and geometry something less than a schoolboy's curse—a pedagogical belief harbored as long ago as Egyptian antiquity—Milton offers no further light.

But if reticence invests him here, he is less chary in his portrayal of the scene of learning. An "institution of breeding" is to be established "in every city throughout the land." It is to be "at once both school and university," and it is to be called an academy, a name which the comparers of history tell us was a borrowing from Plato, as in truth, were several other Miltonian views. The academy is to be capacious in house and grounds—large enough to afford lodgment to at least 150 persons whereof a score or so "may be attendants."

Milton's "better education," as he called it, was not for the lower part of the social order, or even for the middle. Proffered solely "to our noble and gentle youth," running in years from twelve to twenty-one, it falls below the lofty proposals put forth by Mulcaster and Comenius. Milton wasted no time on elementary education. The fact is, he did not care very much for little children, and Comenius's effort to give them light and leading he dismissed with a sneer. Nor did Milton trouble himself—again unlike Mulcaster and Comenius—to make recommendations for the education of girls. In truth, of Eve's daughters the author of *Paradise Lost* took a dour view. "Nothing lovelier can be found in a woman," he sermonized, "than to study household good."

3

Thus the man and his doctrine. It is not of the first caliber, and very likely not even of the second. Even for its own time, its essence was not new, and in it there were also some yawning cavities. The direct study of nature, for example, as urged by Lord Bacon, it deftly sidestepped, as it did the suggestion by Hobbes and Descartes that the scientific method can thrive only when it is solidly grounded in mathematics. It is not wise to expect too much from anyone—and certainly not from the young at school. Perhaps in the austerity of Cromwell's Commonwealth this was less true than later, or perhaps Milton, eyeing his subject speculatively. chose to ignore it; in any case the curriculum he laid before the learner is one of the most staggering man has ever seen. It is at once solemn and absurd, a sign to all the world of what happens when a poet is swallowed by a pedant. Of Milton's own prowess as a teacher we know almost nothing. He charged himself with the education of his youngest nephew, but what part the uncle actually played has escaped us, and except for the fact that later on the youth became the writer of a book which the authorities denounced as "lascivious and profane," there is no record. Milton's daughters, having the misfortune to be female, got scant pedagogic attention from their father. As they grew older they were taught to read six languages aloud to help their father in his work—but when they expressed a hankering to understand what they were reading, Milton emphatically turned his thumbs down.

After Milton's translation to eternity his stock as an educational leader began to drop. Its appeal had been chiefly to his fellow Puritans. Certainly his views, even when they were of the general cast of Realism, did not reach beyond his tomb to make their way into the great stream of educational reform which washed over nineteenth-century Europe. It is true his academy came into being, but it was an altered academy, and its life, as time is measured in history, was that of a one-day fly.

With the return of the Stuart monarchy in 1660 the Puritans fell on hard times. Two years later by the Act of Conformity some two thousand nonconforming pastors lost their pulpits. Presently even the children of nonconformists felt the ire of the state and the Established Church by being refused access to the secondary and higher learning. Under the circumstances, many a jobless dissenting cleric took to schoolmastering, and some even to running schools of their own. Known as academies, these new establishments bore a certain resemblance to some of Milton's proposals. Their great yearning, of course, was to instill the faith into their offspring, and to aid the more dowered ones among them to lay the groundwork for the ministry. At the same time they undertook, as Milton had urged, to fit their youth for life's many offices. To these ends they plumed themselves with a curriculum which was partly classical and partly practical. As the years ran by and the exigencies of secular living started to mount, the stress on learning for useful purposes grew correspondingly heavier, with the result that the academies began to broach all sorts of new subjects. Aside from a very few, the academies were not the plush seats of learning Milton had envisioned— often, indeed, their students were housed in the stale quarters of the master's home; and they were not, as Milton had recommended, of the gentry and noblesse, but mainly of the middle class.

In 1689 the tide turned, and by the Act of Toleration dissenters gained a measure of religious right. The schools they had so laboriously nurtured for more than a generation were now authorized, if so they chose, to incorporate. Some, taking advantage of their new freedom, continued in service; others, abandoning their recent innovations, effaced themselves as academies to join hands with the conventional Latin grammar schools; while still others, too weary and too poor to maintain the struggle for existence, hauled down their flag and shut their doors forever.

John Locke

The spokesman for the New Education who attracted a large and sympathetic attention, not only in his native England, but in her Colonies as well, and to some degree on the Continent, was John Locke. He was born in 1632 in the reign of the first Charles, and during his lifetime he saw the sovereign beheaded and the monarchy uprooted by Cromwell and his Ironside Redcoats, who were themselves overcome in the course of time by the Stuart Restoration. When

Locke passed from these scenes at seventy-two, the Bloodless Revolution of 1688, to which he had given his support, was history, and the Bill of Rights of which he was in part the intellectual propagator was embedded in England's constitutional life.

Locke was the son of a lawyer, a man of high Puritan principles. While he was still young and full of wonder, the son hoped some day to wear the sacred collar, but Oxford dispirited him, and he abandoned his hieratic aspiration. Instead, he read Descartes and studied chemistry and medicine. He never took an M.D.—in fact, he was in his forties, his student days long since behind him, when Oxford at length converted him into a bachelor of medicine. Succoring the aches and pains of the human race was apparently to his taste, and there is good reason to believe that had he pinned his full concentration on medical science, he would have been outstanding. Meanwhile, however, his engrossment in politics had begun to press upon him, and when the chance had beckoned, he had attached himself to the Earl of Shaftesbury, a political hopeful on the rise, whom he attended as secretary and doctor, and whose offspring he serviced as tutor. Through the Earl's connections he was hoisted into public office, a common practice in those days as in these. But a politician's luck, as everybody knows, is fickle, and when the Earl found it prudent to become a sojourner in Holland, Locke honored his patron with his loyalty and joined him in his leave of absence.

When he returned to the motherland in 1689, Locke carried with him the manuscript of his first important philosophical work, the *Essay Concerning Human Understanding,* which went into print the year following. Meanwhile, he hammered out a couple of *Treatises on Government,* wherein he upheld the recent insurrection against James II, and did annihilation on the theory of divine right. His reasoning was well regarded, if not by the martyred James, then at least by the sovereign's foes, and it brought its author not only money and renown, but in due time a royal appointment as commissioner of trade. The man's industry knew no bounds, and as year succeeded year, he poured out one work after another. His *Letters on Toleration* came out in 1672. Therein he says in substance that, Catholicism and atheism excepted, all beliefs should be tolerated. Right on the heels of the *Letters* came *Some Thoughts on Education.* It went into five editions during its author's lifetime, and a whole horde of them thereafter, and it was translated into one language after another. His last output, the *Conduct of the Understanding,* appeared after his death in the infancy of the eighteenth century.

Most of his educational opinions Locke set down in *Some Thoughts on Education.* Like Milton's educational views, when they were first composed they were minted in epistolary form, and they were not intended for the public eye. Hence, they addressed themselves in the main to the cultivation of a particular boy, the eight-year-old Edward Clarke, a gentleman's son, and though they roved over a spacious territory, they made no effort to traverse the entire subject, or even to do it systematically. Locke's more general pedagogy, particularly its philosophical and psychological ramifications, he reserved for treatment in his graver works, the one in his *Essay Concerning Human Understanding,* the other in his *Conduct of the Understanding.* The latter, as was mentioned some lines back, was issued after his death, and hence it suffers a bit from incompleteness. Now and then, in addition, a few of its salient ideas are at variance with views he had expressed earlier in his *Thoughts.* Even so, the *Conduct's* essence was compounded during the man's good years when his mind was still nimble and full of power. Consequently, despite the book's insufficiencies it must be regarded no less soberly.

In his philosophy Locke started out by throwing overboard some of its most hallowed relics. It was his contention that, the human mind being what it is, which is to say subject to all sorts of infirmities, limitations, and aberrations, philosophy ought to confine its grappling to problems it can safely encompass. The real world, and the only one man can deal with with some surety of knowledge, is not an extraterrestrial one of spirit, but the world of objects and living things, human and otherwise. Fundamentally, Locke declared, like the ancient Sophists, Homo sapiens is a sensing and reflecting creature; hence philosophers would do well to maintain their quest for light and knowledge within the sphere of direct experience. At one thrust he thus swept away a multitude of problems over which theologians and metaphysicians have been ruminating with more or less futility ever since time's early dawn.

Locke's psychology came out of his philosophy. With Thomas Hobbes, a fellow thinker, he put psychology on an empirical footing, thereby beginning the process of blowing away the occult vapors which had obscured it since the remotest reaches of man's conscious memory. He directed the full power of his attack at the doctrine of innate ideas. A favorite since Plato and—thanks to Descartes—still on solid legs in the age of Locke, it held that when a man is born, ideas are already resident in his mind. Nothing of the sort, controverted Locke. When a man is born, his mind is vacant, a sheet of white paper, so to say, "void of all characters, without any ideas. . . . " On it sense impressions inscribe what we call ideas. Simple at first, they advance in complexity and sophistication by means of reflection. Hence, in the rearing of the human young their setting and instruction and the company they keep are of the utmost concern. Because Locke had urged experience as the source of psychological data, he is sometimes nominated as the father of modern psychology, a paternity which, as usual in such instances, is currently under some contention.

2

"A sound mind in a sound body is a short but full description of a happy state in the world." Thus run the first words of the *Thoughts.* It is a simple statement, perhaps the simplest ever recorded in the history of ideas. The work's introduction, it is also its quintessence. What follows is for the most part a filling-in and building-up of the major theme.

Locke wastes no time on rhetoric, but runs into his subject full tilt. What, he asked—at a time when death was forever tapping at the nursery door—what is necessary to keep a young boy of quality in abounding strength and health? What he needs first, declared Locke, are such things as fresh air, exercise and recreation, and sleep aplenty. His food should be light and plain, with less meat and more bread, washed down not with strong spirits, or even with a gentle wine—as was then an everyday practice—but with plain well water. His couch should be hard and his covering sparse. And his hygiene should be regular, and so should his toilet habits. Besides these primary concerns, which were generally regarded as something of a crackpot oddity, the rising gentleman needs to be physically hardened. To attain this end, let him brave the baleful elements, in heat and cold, thinly clad, his shoes full of holes, "made so as to hold water." Thus brought up, the lad will be steeled against nature's ravages—unless, as Spencer warned in a later day, the treatment had not hardened him out of life itself.

Like the body robust, the mind needs to be exercised and disciplined. The process should start early, the sooner the better, for, says Locke, it will influence the boy's life forever after. The great blunder parents make, he goes on, is that "the mind has not been made obedient to discipline and pliable to reason when first it was most tender." As to what every young gentleman should know, Locke puts God and virtue first, manners next, and learning last. A gentleman's function, he reminds us, is to render service to his country. Most of his hours he will pass not in the cells of learning, but on his land, or in the realm of government, or perhaps even in the executive arm of trade or commerce. Hence, though in education "Latin and learning make all the noise," the main stress should be on things useful to his calling. He ought to be securely grounded in the mother tongue. Not only should he be able to read and write it with the skill of, say, at least a parish clerk; he should also be able to swathe his discourse with a neat and caressing charm. In arithmetic let him widen the field of its application to the keeping of accounts so that in the years ahead, when he has come of age, it will serve him in the maintenance of his estate. Though Locke had laid down a caution of doubt against the piling up of a vast store of knowledge, it would be a mistake to assume that he let the learner get off softly. In fact, before the boy has stacked his books on the shelf for good, he will have taken aboard not only the three elementary Rs, but also history, geography, ethics, law, natural philosophy, astronomy, and chronology, besides French and Latin. Contrary to the practice which then generally obtained, he is to make his way into the languages not through the devious route of grammar and syntax but, like a native, over the broad concourse of conversation.

When the world was still richly supplied with cheap and first-rate servants, a gentleman, even of minor degree, seldom, if ever, attended himself. His daily needs, from barbering and victualing him to putting him properly into his clothes, fell to the care of hired hands. Fate thus forced upon him the handicap of a superabundant leisure. Some of this he deployed in reading and reflection, and some in social diversion and recreation. To ease the burden of excess leisure, Locke proposed, as we do now in a far more massive way, to offer appropriate instruction. To such a purpose he recommended a mastering of the dance. For its handmaiden, music, however, he conceived only a tepid sympathy. Not only was instruction therein not worth the suffering it entailed, but more important, "men of parts and business do not commend it." As for dalliance in the poetic art, Locke scouted the idea flatly. " 'Tis a pleasant air," he observed, "but a barren soil." Fencing, esteemed by Continental men of quality as all but indispensable, Locke rejected for the bourgeois science of wrestling. The playing field, which nineteenth-century fabulists cried up as one of the prime factors in Anglo-Saxon superiority, he dismissed as rather a waste of time. Instead of frittering himself away in sports, let the youth seek surcease in gardening and woodwork, two "fit and healthy recreations" for gentlefolk—and useful besides.

Like so many other sages, whether full or part time, Locke had his theories about the art and labor of education. They are best stimulated, he felt, not in school, but under the parental roof, and in the care and keeping of a tutor. Judiciously selected, he acts as mentor and exemplar, and over the years it is his function to help his ward make acquaintance, not only with knowledge, but also with wisdom, virtue, and good manners.

3

For many years it used to be the vogue among historians of pedagogy to pigeonhole Locke as a disciplinarian—an upholder, that is, of the formal training of the mental faculties, and an avant-gardist of what in after years psychologists designated as the doctrine of transfer of training. To a degree the historical brethren were right—but only to a degree. As was observed before, Locke gave his support to the process of physical hardening. He also put his confidence in the disciplining of the will. A gentleman, he contended, should be so molded as to be able "to deny his own desires, cross his own inclinations, and purely follow what reason directs as best." It was his belief that to reason with ease and correctness, the mind needs to be assiduously exercised, and that the earlier the business is undertaken, the better the prospect of success. But the schoolman's favorite mind trainers, namely, grammar, rhetoric, and logic, Locke brushed aside as passing for naught. Instead, he recommended instruction in mathematics, not, however, to make gentlemen into mathematicians, but "to make them reasonable creatures."

It was the common practice in Locke's time to set the schoolboy to cramming his memory with page after page of Latin. Such industry, it was believed, would develop within him not only the capacity to retain his schoolbook learning, but as manhood settled upon him, his memory would serve him powerfully in a general way, and he would have no trouble at all in remembering whatever he put his mind to. The notion that training in something specific, such as memorizing long stretches of Latin, would develop a potent memory became dignified, as time ran on, as the theory of transfer of training. It lived a very hardy life, and in the schoolman's articles of belief it grew to a hoary age—indeed, it was not until the present century that the theory finally curled up and died. Though Locke had expressed himself for a rigorous discipline of the mind as well as the body and the will, he was neither a remote inventor nor even a supporter of the transfer theory. The fact is, he detected therein an infirmity in logic, and he would have no dealings with it. "Learning pages of Latin by heart," he insisted—as do nearly all contemporary experts on the subject—"no more fits the memory for retention of anything else, than the graving of one sentence in lead makes it more capable of retaining firmly any other characters." And by the same token, "we see men frequently dexterous and sharp in making a bargain who, if you reason with them about matters of religion, appear perfectly stupid." It is a mistake, he added, to conclude "that he who is found reasonable in one thing is . . . so in all."

In the capital matters which bear upon learning, Locke's theories, generally speaking, were progressive. In fact, could he, by a miracle, return to earth, he would find a number of them not only in good standing, but even flourishing in active use. In an age, for example, when the science of personality was rudimentary, he believed that children are people, and that they are rational creatures. Their elders, hence, should accord them not only the deference which is their just and seemly due, but they should give them encouragement to develop their budding intellect. Locke's stress on the environment as a conditioner for good and evil in the upbringing of the young must certainly evoke a ripple of approval from today's scientific behaviorists, faint perhaps, but approval just the same. At the same time he was aware that none of us can transcend the limitations imposed upon us by nature, and that even though our minds may be blank when we make our entrance upon this globe, our capacity to fill them with ideas varies no end. With the advanced thinkers of his time, Locke concurred that the business of learning should be made as exhilarating as human sagacity and ingenuity can make it. He had no taste for the view, then almost universal, that education can be of little benefit, unless in its pursuit the learner is heavily trussed and belabored—a notion which was suspect as long ago as the Renaissance, but which, for all the penetrating criticism against it, is still clung to by a small but resolute group, both in this happiest of republics and beyond. "Masters and teachers," declared Locke, "should raise no difficulties to their scholars, but on the contrary should smooth the way."

Although the author of the *Thoughts* has been hailed as the father of the vocabulary of democracy, the inspirer of Jefferson and the intellectual ghost-writer, as it were, of the Declaration of Independence, it must not be taken for granted that the gospel he expounded so beguilingly on paper applied to all alike. The fact is that, for all his gifts, he was molded and conditioned by his time and class, which is to say an age and condition of privilege, of which he was a fortunate beneficiary. Hence, when he descended from his deliberations on the education of a gentleman to laying plans for the schooling of the common folk, Locke put the brakes upon his liberalism. "The knowledge of the Bible," he said, "and the business of his calling is enough for the ordinary man."

Locke's views on what ought to be done for those who issue from the shanty streets are explicit enough. Stated in a proposal set forth in 1697, while he was engaged as commissioner of trades, they called for the conscription of the pauper young at the age of three and their consignment to public workhouses, of which one was to be established in every parish. There, until they attained the ripeness of fourteen, when they were to be apprenticed, they were to be trained to be "sober and industrious" forever after, their health under watch and care, and their daily commons "with a bellyful of . . . bread," and if necessary, "a little watergruel" during the winter's clammy chill. Every day—forgetting Sunday—they were to be instructed in spinning and weaving and similar useful knacks, the money thus obtained by their labor to be applied to their board and keep. The Lord's Day was reserved for religion and virtue when the children were "obliged to come constantly to church along with their schoolmasters or dames." Not only were the young thus to be put under the reign of discipline and "from infancy to be inured to work," but by the same stroke their mothers were to be set free to go to work.

Locke's interest in education was neither primary nor professional. Even so, his views gathered a high regard and a large and widely scattered audience. Of his intellectual spadework in psychology and philosophy, and its impact on the world of thought, there can be no doubt. Nor can there be any doubt about his pedagogic Realism. It flaunts itself in his *Thoughts* on almost every page, persistent and pervasive. But when his *Thoughts* appeared, Realism as a general theory was already old. Its essence had been set down somewhat drearily, it is true, by Mulcaster long before Locke was even here. Read Montaigne, another forerunner, and you will find it again, and with a rakish charm to boot. And in Comenius, finally, it glistened in a manner so rare in pedagogy as to be almost unique.

Locke has been acclaimed for the questions he ignited. Is it the concern of education, for example, to prepare men in learning? Or is it to make them at home with everyday life? Should it lay its principal stress on the building up of good character? Or should it serve to cultivate the intellect? Should it condition the young for freedom? Or should it train them in discipline and obedience?

Such questions are, no doubt, of consequence—indeed, they still rage, unsettled and unsatisfied, in our midst today. But more important than Locke's queries are his answers, and these, even when gauged by their intentions rather than by their recommendations, are sometimes wanting.

Let it not be forgotten that Locke was, after all, a seventeenth-century Anglo-Saxon, and that despite his sinuous mind, his good humor, and his kindliness, he bore the burden of an inveterate class prejudice. He was, like Comenius, a believing Christian, but unlike this great Czech, he could not bring himself to soar beyond the world wherein he dwelt. That world he perceived with a prodigality of vision and imagination, but with the false perspective of a man of privilege. Hence, where Comenius sought to forward the common fellowship of all men, Locke was careful to keep them partitioned in classes, sects, and even factions. The gulf which separates the two men shows itself in their pedagogy. Thus, where Comenius advocated one school system for all, Locke, arranging his world into one of masters and servants, reserved his finest education for the former, with a meager and vitiated variety for the rest. Comenius, a practitioner of democracy and not merely its advocate, opened his elementary school to every child, whether boy or girl, and whether at the top of the human heap or at the bottom. Locke, though a lauder of democracy, permitted no such rubbing of shoulders. For those he knew, he was of a tender heart, but not for the indefinable mass of common people. They left him cold, and when he turned his thoughts to their education, it was not, as with Comenius, with a warm compassion for humanity, but with a sense of balance sheets and stark utility.

Locke has often been mentioned with praise as typically English. On this score there is, indeed, much to be said. His plan for the education of the poor failed of realization, but it was turned down not for its palpable inadequacies, but for what at the time was regarded as a somewhat unseemly radicalism. Nevertheless, as time flowed on, the education which emerged in England bore the distinctive mark of Locke, with very fine schools for those born to wealth and quality, and only the barest educational opportunity for the lowly multitude. It was, in truth, not until on in the nineteenth century, when social justice ceased to be something less than a meretricious theory, that the English took steps to remedy their educational insufficiencies.

Wolfgang Ratke

The first schoolman to hear the call of Bacon's ideas was a German, Wolfgang Raticius (born Ratke), who lived and labored from 1571 to 1635. A fanatical Lutheran, he had sought to advance himself into the pulpit, but a speech impairment sidetracked him, and led him in the end into a somewhat lower estate of schoolmastering. Even so, his theological training left its stamp; not only was he an implacable, crossgrained Lutheran, but he also took a dim and even bilious view of most non-Lutherans. Ratke had come upon the *Advancement of Learning* while he was in England, and so well did he regard it that he nominated himself to work its major propositions into a new method of teaching. Apparently his admiration for this was equally exalted, for he shrouded his work with an elaborate secrecy, and when at length it was ready to be revealed, he let it be known that he would entrust it to no one save some meritorious patron of ample and flowing purse and of the Lutheran persuasion. To find such a candidate Ratke made tracks from one German state to another, but with no success. Finally, in 1612, when a congress of German dignitaries happened to be gathered at Frankfurt for the election of a Holy Roman Emperor, Ratke seized the occasion to press his views upon them in what he called *An Address to the German Princes.*

His method, which he confessed to be the finest ever devised within the limits of civilization, was designed "for the service and welfare of all Christendom," but more especially, candor compels one to state, for its Germanic and Lutheran branches. Put into application in the schools, it would, he said, not only illuminate the young in the usual learning, but it would also assure the wrangling horde of German states "one and the same speech, one and the same government, and finally one and the same religion," and thereby visit upon them a peace and prosperity unheard of since Adam's time.

The princes showed a perfect willingness to grant Ratke their attention—some of them were even sufficiently inspired to engage a couple of professors from Giessen to take the measure of the man and his pedagogy. The savants raked Ratke with their doubts and questions, but so persuasively did he maintain his syllogisms that presently they themselves believed in his wonders, and they issued a favorable report. Unluckily for Ratke, by the time of its appearance the princes had other fish to fry, and apart from their demonstration of the fickleness of man, they did nothing.

But Ratke was not daunted, and in 1617 he distilled a summary of his views in his *Methodus Novus,* a work which has long since passed into undeserved oblivion. Meanwhile, he made connection with a number of the German high and mighty. The Duchess Dorothea Maria of Weimar, for one, hired him to instruct and edify not only her sons, but herself and her sister as well. More useful to Ratke than the confidence of these ducal ladies was the aid of Prince Ludwig of Anhalt Köthen. The Prince, who was given to hope and optimism, was possessed by a passion to spread progress and refinement among his subjects, and especially among those of low degree. For Ratke the Prince became the archangel he had sought so desperately. Ludwig lubricated him not merely with money; he also furnished him abundantly with buildings, equipment, textbooks, a corps of assistants, and to make certain Ratke also had pupils, the Prince ordered parents to commit their young to his school.

As a result some five hundred boys and girls became Ratke's first clients. The novices, as usual, were put to learning how to read and write and to mastering numbers. In addition, they rehearsed themselves in religion and music. In the fourth year, when they were somewhat hardier, they confronted Latin, and in the sixth and last year, they took on Greek. All this, Ratke promised, would be done effectively and without disrelish "by a better method . . . than had hitherto been used." The old torturing of the memory with a mountain chain of facts to be learned by heart was outlawed; instead, there was to be discussion and understanding. Whenever possible, the child was to cull his learning from experience; he was, in current pedagogic parlance, to study things rather than words. Everything in Ratke's seminary was to be dipped delicately in rose water. Thus, there was to be no forced studying, no scourgings, and no scoldings—in fact, the maintenance of order and discipline was to be left to the children.

Despite the furious trumpet blasts which had heralded its coming, Ratke's school soon ran into a sea of trouble, and after a little more than a year it sank from sight forever. And as if the collapse of Ratke's plans had not been calamity enough, to add to his woe he was tossed into the lockup. There the bewildered man languished for almost a year, until the Prince, overcoming his ire at last, turned him loose.

Some of Ratke's views, doubtless, were disingenuous and even nonsensical, but most of them were intrinsically sound—some, indeed, are still in contemporary favor. Nor can there be any mistake about the man's sincerity. How does it happen then, some will ask, that he failed so ignominiously? The cause of Ratke's ruin is to be found not so much in his ideas as in the man himself. Vain, quarrelsome, a cocksure Lutheran, beset by grandiose pretensions, he was lacking, on almost every count, in the most elementary prerequisites for successful leadership. Fortune, no doubt, treated him shabbily, but time has mellowed our memory of him. His pedagogy was fresh for its time; and though it fell short of its high ambitions, in the hands of another—a far better man—some of it was to attain an unforgettable dignity and distinction. That man was Jan Amos Comenius.

Jan Amos Comenius

Jan Amos Comenius (born Komensky) arrived in this world in 1592 in Nivnice, Bohemia, now in Czechoslovakia, and he died in Amsterdam seventy-eight years later. Joy was a stranger to his life—much of it, indeed, was beclouded by sorrow. A soft and amiable man, Comenius lived in a brutal, bloody age, full of aches and agonies, and recalled in the annals of civilization for its Thirty Years' War. His home was twice marauded, his wife and children slaughtered, and his books and writings put to flame. Often a wanderer, more often a refugee, he was driven from home and country to die in exile, a sad and disenchanted man.

Comenius was fervently devout. In spite of some gaping holes in his early schooling, he managed to prepare for holy orders, becoming a parson to the Moravian Brethren, and in the passing years their head bishop. The Moravians, whom he pastored, were a small flock of godly folk. Dedicated to the teachings of the martyred Huss, a forerunner of Luther, they sought to regulate their lives by Holy Writ, and they asked nothing more than to be let alone. Unluckily, fate snared them in the trammels of bigotry and war. Hated by Catholics, and suspect to Protestants, they led a sort of undercover existence, finding sanctum for a spell in Poland, only to have fortune dash them in the ruin of their hopes.

Except for his experience as a boy at school, Comenius was innocent of pedagogy until he reached twenty, when Ratke's *Address* came to his hands. For all its controverted nature, most of its ideas he regarded approvingly, and some of them even enthusiastically. In fact, in later years, when he himself was trying to bring some light to education, he worked a number of Ratke's principles into his own practice.

Even more powerful than the pull of Ratke was that of Francis Bacon. Although Comenius was a working man of God, he was not, like the run of his fellow holy men, a sworn and implacable enemy of the rising natural sciences. On the contrary, he regarded them with a hopeful eye, and he was even the possessor of a copy of *The Revolution of the Heavenly Bodies,* that ghastly Copernican horror. He got his teeth into Bacon's *Novum Organum* while he was still enjoying his twenties, and presently he gave his attention to the rest of Bacon's writings. To this plain and unpretentious Moravian the lordly Anglo-Saxon must, at times, have appeared remote; even so, to many of Bacon's ideas Comenius gave a large measure of approval, and some of them, for example, the stress on observation and induction and the proposal for a superuniversity, manned by the world's most powerful brains, he not only endorsed, but tried to put into being.

It was mere chance that brought Comenius into the teaching fraternity. He was twenty-two when he came out of Heidelberg, and though he had immersed himself in everything then known to theological science, the brethren, nevertheless, judged him too young to squire them as an ordained minister. Instead, they put him to schoolmastering in their village school at Prerov. Somehow the charms of teaching bore in on him, for when, a few years later, he was hoisted into the holy cloth, he insisted on combining his sacerdotal labors with his academic ones—a common double role in those days, and one which was to occupy him in one way or another for the rest of his life.

2

Comenius laid down the cardinal articles of his pedagogy in the *Great Didactic.* Composed in Czech during the 1630s while he was a refugee in Poland, it was later rendered into the scholar's Latin in which it came out in 1657. It is, for its time, a remarkable work, thrusting itself into educational themes of the widest range and sort. The first full-fledged pedagogical work to come from the hands of a Christian gentleman, it reveals, as it says, "the whole art of teaching all things to all men," and how to transact the business "quickly, pleasantly, and thoroughly," whether in science, virtue, or piety, to the end of giving preparation "for the present and for the future life."

Is it the business of education, as Comenius says, to achieve happiness here on earth and later on in Heaven? Then its benefits must escape no one, whether peer or peasant, rich or poor, in britches or in skirts. Hence, for six years at least, the young must be put to school. But their labors must be made agreeable, if possible, by setting them in a pleasant place—not, of course, in such splendiferous mansions of learning as now bedizen our republic, but in any case, in a schoolhouse bright and shiny, its rooms enlivened with pictures, a space reserved outdoors to let off juvenile steam, and a garden to rejoice the eyes. By the same token, what children learn should be attractive and useful, which is saying, it should serve them in their everyday encounters with life, and make them ready, late or soon, for bliss eternal. Nor should they be put to mere memorizing and book knowledge; rather let them contemplate "the living book of the world instead of dead papers." And since observation is the mother of learning, let the children see and hear—indeed, let them exercise all their senses, whether solitarily or in concert.

Although Comenius lacked acquaintance with the current psychological science, he displayed an instinct for some of its simpler propositions. "Children," he observed, "detest pedantry and severity"; hence, humor and lightness should be planted into every lesson. "The acquisition of knowledge," he went on, "cannot be forced"; nevertheless, a skillful master can make a child eager to savor knowledge. Nor is it possible, he added, to learn anything save by practice or doing. "Artisans learn to forge by forging, to carve by carving, to paint by painting. . . . " And so let it be with learning—"let children learn to write by writing, to sing by singing, and to reason by reasoning." In education, he contended, we should follow nature, by which he meant that the young should be treated in accordance with their years, their tasks adjusted to their capacities and powers, and their texts tailored to their understanding. In an age when it was a routine practice for teachers to go after their pupils with a stick, Comenius raised his voice in behalf of a respect for the dignity of every child. "Rods and blows, those weapons of slavery," he wrote, "are quite unsuitable for free men, and should never be used in schools"—an admonition which was not much esteemed until the present century.

3

To teach "all things to all men," Comenius proposed an educational system in four connected stages, each running for six years, and each designed to attain some special end. The first, the Mother School, confined its operations to the home. Speaking strictly, it was not actually a school, but a mother giving her child enlightened care and training. The Mother School attended its freshman as soon as he could safely toddle, and it continued to work on him until he was six.

Comenius's recommendation is the first of its kind in Christendom, and though it addressed itself among other things to laying the groundwork for knowledge, in its main aspects it is akin to the kindergarten, in which, indeed, certain genealogists detect a descendant.

On the heels of the Mother School followed the Vernacular School, so designated because its instruction was in the mother tongue, today the rule, of course, but then still something of a rarity. The Vernacular School was elementary, and attendance at its sessions, or in some acceptable equivalent, was mandatory for all, whether male or female, until their twelfth birthday formally emancipated them from any further academic service. True to its primary function, the school introduced its boys and girls to their letters and to the nature and behavior of numbers, with brief glimpses into geography, history, astronomy, and the elements of the common trades and occupations of the time. The world then being more pious than its present materialistic sucessor, the school naturally concentrated heavily on safeguarding the young from heathenry. In this respect Comenius's institute followed the general practice, drawing its main strength from Bible lessons, the catechism, tales about good and evil, and frequent excursions into prayer and psalmody.

Once out of the Vernacular School, the overwhelming number of its alumni ceased their pursuit of knowledge. The few who ventured on were boys, for in those cautious times the generality of girls was marked as too restricted in mental and physical potency to stand the strain of learning anything beyond the elementals. The seminary which now awaited an ambitious boy was the Latin School. Its chief purpose was not only to make him a top-notch Latinist, but also to ground him solidly in the intellectual discipline then deemed absolutely necessary for a successful assault on the higher learning. For this purpose the boy exerted his mentality not only in the Roman tongue in all its odds and ends from grammar to rhetoric, in prose and verse; he also wrestled with Greek, Hebrew, and the mother tongue, besides physics, mathematics, astronomy, logic, geography, history, chronology, and—lest he be bored with too much time on his hands—theology. Bolstering this broadside there was the usual instruction in virtue and religion, and fittingly enough, in music.

At the end of his sixth year in the Latin School, the youth, now a palmy eighteen, was wrung through a rigorous examination. If he survived, he was granted admission to the university. But if his luck played him false, his academic aspirations were done for, and he had to settle for one of the better vocations, or if possible, a job in the public service or even as a minor church official. If, on the other hand, he was given access to the higher learning, he was expected during the ensuing six years to apply "his undivided energies to that subject for which he is evidently suited by nature," in illustration, law, medicine, theology, teaching, or even oratory, music, or poetry. To save himself from degenerating into a mere bookworm, he was to relax his concentration during the last two years by seeking breadth and enrichment in travel. Should his mental cast be truly incandescent, then Comenius recommended that he "be urged to pursue all the branches of study so that there may always be some men whose knowledge is encyclopedic."

Once out of the university grove, ninety-nine of every hundred students, doubtless, put away their books, hung their diplomas, and set out to make their way in life. For the rest, that infinitesimal remainder of cerebral and studious chaps, Comenius proposed the establishment of yet another house of learning, the Universal College, higher in its reach than the common university, and the place where the world's foremost scholars put their heads together for the advancement of the arts and sciences. Another version of Bacon's House of Solomon, it was to promote research and the interchange of ideas so as "to spread the light of wisdom throughout the human race . . . and benefit humanity by new and useful inventions."

What was singularly fresh in Comenius's proposed school organization at the time it was put forth is that it provided for structural coherence–an "educational ladder," as Americans put it–by which every school, from the lowest to the highest, is joined into a single, unified system. By contrast, Europe's schools– primary, secondary, and higher–having come into being in different historical periods, and directing themselves to different purposes and social groups, lacked such an organizational integration. Comenius's scheme was, of course, only a blueprint, and so it was to subsist for long years to come. In truth, it was not until the twentieth century that various European lands, seeking to free themselves from the yoke of their organizational heirloom, took steps to link their schools in a more unified system. But the transformation was snail-like, and apart from the Bolshevik Russians, among the larger nations, an educational ladder, in its fullest reach from top to bottom, still has to see the light of day. Meanwhile, beyond the Atlantic's western shore, and before the middle years of the nineteenth century, the United States, partly by luck and partly by design, was evolving an articulated school system which in the passing years was destined to extend from the kindergarten through the university. Often taken for granted, it is, nonetheless, one of the glories of the republic, for by it the mechanism–if nothing more–has been wrought within which it is possible for every youngster to work his way up to education's dizziest height.

4

The stress Comenius laid on the gathering of knowledge infuses all his pedagogy –in fact, with him, to be in possession of exact knowledge amounted to something of a passion. It showed itself in his schools, where children bagged knowledge through the senses, and sometimes indirectly, through pictures and the printed word. And it worked its way into his writings, whether schoolbooks or dissertations on education. While residing in Poland, Comenius declared for a plan to enlist a corps of the world's outstanding savants to bring together the sum total of our knowledge, physical, metaphysical, and otherwise, in a work to be called *Pansophia.*

For all its excellent points, the project bristled with difficulties. To bring it to fruit demanded not only talents of the first order, but also an ever-flowing purse. Even so, Comenius's ardor blazed high, and in 1641 he took ship for England to snag a sponsor. He was persuaded to lay his idea at the feet of Parliament, but the lawgivers, absorbed in troubles with Charles I, revealed a disposition to hedge. Worse yet, at this moment the unruly Irish took it into their heads to harass and terrify the English, and when the rumor was presently tossed about that some 200,000 Englishmen had been butchered in a single night, Comenius packed his grips and hastened across the Channel.

This does not mean that he turned his back upon his plan; on the contrary, he held manfully to it, and during the years following he even concocted numerous essays for the proposed *Pansophia.* But the work, as it turned out, was doomed. As the shadows of age crept upon him, Comenius had still failed to enlist a publisher. What proved to be a crushing blow fell in 1656 when a mob, fevered by the imprudent politics of the Moravian Brethren, then fugitives in the Polish town of Nissa, stormed the place and put it to the torch. Comenius, luckily, escaped, but not without the loss of his books and manuscripts, and the many thousands of notes he had so laboriously assembled for *Pansophia.* With their destruction, his projected storehouse of universal knowledge perished.

It cannot be reported of Comenius, as candor compels one to say of some other forwarders of pedagogy, that he was mostly a theorist. His descents into everyday practice were frequent and numerous. He schoolmastered in his native Bohemia, and in Hungary and Poland. He devoted almost a decade to overhauling and improving the schools of Sweden. And he wrote a series of Latin schoolbooks which put the breath of life into a subject which had fallen on bad times. True, the gloomy grammars which had beclouded the schoolboy's life in the Middle Ages had been elbowed into the background by the newer texts of Lily and Melanchthon. But even these inclined to the hawking of words and definitions, and not uncommonly they were over the learner's head. Soon after he had set himself up as a teacher, Comenius undertook to rectify these faults by improvising a reader for his pupils. The result of his experience he put into print in 1631 as the *Janua Linguarum Reserata,* or *The Gate of Tongues Unlocked.*

Intended to introduce the novice to the Latin language, the *Janua* was, so to speak, a bureau of information, compounded of some eight thousand different words embodied in several hundred sentences. The general idea of such a handbook was not new, a closely similar one having put together by an Irish Jesuit, Batty by name and a teacher in Spain by calling. Nevertheless, the *Janua* was pounced on joyously, and before long it had become a smashing success. Hailed by its admirers as "the golden book," it boasted of an audience that circled the world. It was translated into almost a score of languages, including Arabic and Mongolian, and had its author been born to the protection of our current laws of copyright, he would certainly have piled up immense riches. Yet for all its marvels, the book had its imperfections. For beginners it aimed at far too much, and as Comenius soon discerned, it put a burden even on the smartest of them. Hence, he applied the corrective scalpel, and in 1633, two years after its advent, the *Janua,* its verbal prodigality vastly pruned, gave way to the *Vestibulum,* or *Vestibule,* which, like its parent, presently acquired a large and far-flung custom.

Comenius produced several other Latin books, including a grammar and an anthology. But the most memorable, by long odds, was a picture book, the *Orbis Sensualium Pictus,* or in English, *The World in Pictures.* Off the presses in 1658, it comprised some 150 illustrated subjects, ranging over a wide and diverse territory, from birds, flowers, and fish, to instance a few, to the parts of man, deformities, temperance, and a burial. Underneath each picture stands a two-column description, the one in Latin, the other in the vernacular. The book, its author let it be known, was "a pleasant introduction to the Latin language," besides giving aid "in the learning of the mother tongue." As the canny Czech had foreseen, children were surprised and delighted by the pictures. In fact, many a parent, yielding to the incessant badgering of his heir, invested in the purchase of the *Orbis Pictus,* not for its pedagogical merit, real or alleged, but simply to preserve the domestic tranquility.

Like the *Janua,* the *Orbis Pictus* was well received. It went into use in land after land, and as it appeared in its various editions, it was put into one tongue after another. In the Old World it flourished for almost two hundred years. In the United States, where the study of Latin fell into a low state much sooner than in Europe, the *Orbis Pictus,* nevertheless, was still awing New Yorkers as late as 1810. Pigeonholers of antiquity have been at pains to remind us that Comenius's handiwork was not the first illustrated book for the young, that, indeed, it had been anticipated by several writers, including a Chinese metaphysician. All this may be so; yet it is also beside the point. The ineffaceable fact is that Comenius's little volume was the first pictured schoolbook to be put to long and successful employment in the chambers of learning. In the annals of book writing, after all these years, it remains alive and unforgettable, whereas its forerunners have long since gone to the graveyard of shattered wonders. Rather curiously, despite the magnificence of its triumph, the *Orbis Pictus* bred no imitators. Perhaps it sufficed unto its trade; perhaps it was deemed beyond the power of imitation; or perhaps the tradition for the old-style text, dull, verbose, and revolting, was all too formidable. Whatever the reason, at least five generations came and went before another pedagogue, a Hamburger by the name of Basedow, made a serious attempt to instruct and edify the European young by means of pictures.

5

The shadowy wings of the spirit hovered over Comenius throughout his life, and for most of it he pined for peace and the brotherhood of man. Maybe he found them, as he was sure he would, in the eternity beyond the skies. Unhappily, they did not obtain in the vale he left behind. A world-minded man, he lived in a factious age, an age ravaged by the devilry of war. The peace following the Thirty Years' War was at best a fretful one, with little ground for optimism that the future boded better. A partisan of the natural sciences, Comenius was also a mystic—a believer, even, in the bemused predictions of seers and soothsayers. Most of his long life he dedicated to the enlightenment of his fellow men and to the end of easing and improving their lot. But in a world of greed and privilege his dream of freedom and equality was cried down as so much nonsense. Already before his death ill-favored critics were denouncing him, and even laughing at him. A seeker through most of his years, somehow he did not find, and though he was a prodigy of the first order, he went to his grave on the brink of obscurity.

Even in education where his vision swept over almost the whole panorama of a latter-day pedagogy, Comenius exercised but little influence. True, the school-books he had wrought continued to maintain themselves in favor long after he had left the earth. But the body of his educational thinking fell into almost complete oblivion, and it was not until the nineteenth century that it began to be even faintly comprehended. Meanwhile, some of the views for which he is today hailed and celebrated had found substance in the work and thought of others. Did Comenius, for example, urge upon us that education should adjust itself to the nature of the child, and that he should learn, in a manner of speaking, with his hands and feet before he learns to use his head? Then so, later on, did Rousseau. Did Comenius stress learning through observation and by the senses? Then so did Pestalozzi in the nineteenth century with his doctrine of sense perception. Did Comenius commend education for the very young, and did he give accommodation in the schoolroom to play and frolic? Then so, of course, did Froebel in his kindergarten. Even Herbart, as we shall see, for all his glacial intellect, thawed momentarily to agree with Comenius that nothing can be learned without interest to give it spark and practice in action to make it understandable. Seen through the veil of history, the image of the man some-times eludes and baffles us, but surely not his pedagogy. It may have been discredited, and even made a mock of, in the springtime of its youth. But since then its spirit has found its way into our own schools where in new and current form it enriches and irradiates the educational process.

August Hermann Francke

Moved by as deep a concern and pity for his fellow men as Comenius, as pious as the Czech and about as learned, was another divine, a German by the name of August Hermann Francke. He was born in 1663 at Lübeck, and he died sixty-four years later in the university town of Halle. Francke had a good head, and knowledge came to him with ease. He was just past his middle teens when he made for the intellectual yards of Erfurt, and later for those of Kiel, and finally Leipzig. When, at the age of twenty-one, he tricked himself out in his doctoral robe and hat, he was a specialist in sacred science and on easy terms with Latin, Greek, and Hebrew, besides French, English, and of course, his native Germanic guttural. He was familiar with the labors of Ratke and Comenius, and though he was a conscientious man of God, he bore no malice toward the up-and-coming natural sciences.

It had been his intention to become a distinguished and learned man—even, he has told us, "rich and living in comfort." But when doubts and misgivings presently nagged his spirit, his personal, material ambitions crumbled in collapse. At the same time he became a partisan of Pietism, a movement of religious revival then flowing over Germany and directed in large measure against the hollow formalism into which the teachings of Luther had degenerated. What the Pietists wanted, at bottom, was less cant and more sincerity, a Lutheranism, in short, grounded on faith and feeling and put to work in everyday living.

Francke's zeal was of the most relentless sort, and at Leipzig where he professed the ancient languages, it soon spilled into his instruction. His utterance evidently offered food for thought. Not only did students surge to his sessions in a tremendous flock, but as the months went on more and more of them were making their way into Pietist ranks. Needless to say, Francke's great success brought no joy to his conservative colleagues of the sacred faculty. Outraged and appalled, they badgered him mercilessly, and though Francke gave back as good as he got, time saw him transfer his activities to the University of Halle, then in the vigorous effervescence of its youth, a resolute supporter of academic freedom and an infinitely more agreeable place to propagate novel ideas. Before long, indeed, Halle was destined to become the intellectual headquarters of Pietism.

Francke's yearning to lift up humanity led him willy-nilly into pedagogy. His daily rounds had brought him face to face with the innumerable poor. He had seen their progeny staggering in their dreadful mire, ignorant and ignoble, a prey to every vice and marked unmistakenly for an early death. To succor them Francke invited some of them to share his bread, and in 1695 he undertook to give them instruction, at first in his lodgings, and later, as his venture prospered, in a regular school. The first of his so-called institutions, it was followed during the years by many others. In fact, his school for the down-and-out was scarcely on its legs, when, at the instance of well-fixed and titled parents, he opened a private boarding school to illuminate their young with classical instruction. There followed an orphan home for the poor, a classical secondary school for boys, another for girls, a modern school dispensing the sciences, pure and applied, and a seminary to train and counsel his teachers. The years saw the addition of a drugstore for the poor where they obtained medicine at cut-rate prices, besides a printing house which provided them with cheap Bibles, New Testaments, sermons, tracts, and other works of an uplifting nature. Francke worked at a dogged and furious pace, hatching his institutions in the same steady, free-and-easy manner that Comenius produced his books. When, in 1727, Francke went to his everlasting sleep, his schools confronted an audience of some two to three thousand boys and girls who were taught and attended by a crew of three hundred masters, pastors, and sundry workers.

Like Comenius, Francke believed passionately in piety. "Only the pious man," he wrote, "is a good member of society." The paramount business of the school, hence, is instruction "in the vital knowledge of God and Christ . . . and the principles of true religion." At the same time Francke held his eyes open to the demands of the world about. Always, he urged, "we must keep the pupil's station and future calling in mind."

The two purposes commingle in all his academic endeavor, but they show themselves most vividly in the elementary school. To lead a sober, upright, and godly life, its fledglings allotted four of their seven daily hours to religious study. They started and ended every class with a prayer, and at five o'clock, when the day was done, they gave praise and thanks to the Lord for an hour or so in the neighboring church. For at least sixty minutes every day they operated on their catechism, repeating its questions again and again, until, imperishable and inescapable, they were impaled forever in their memory. In the same unsparing way they ingested their Bible, devoting as much as an hour at a single sitting to learning vast patches of it by heart. And, to make an end, they engaged in hymnody.

Of the three daily hours reserved for the pursuit of secular knowledge, the bulk, of course, was deposited in the three Rs, with two hours a week allowed for musical practice. To attain an essential and useful knowledge of the vale we inhabit here below, the pupils sampled a variety of odds and ends—not systematically, to be sure, but merely casually—from geography and history, physics and astronomy, to the life, habits, institutions, and social practices of the birds and beasts, and if a pupil was lucky enough to be a girl, the household art and science. These things they conned not from books, but, as per Realist formula, from personal observation and experience.

In all Francke's secondary schools, whether for those of high and gentle estate or those lower down the social scale, religion continued to dominate the field. Their students, it is true, did battle with the ancient tongues, not only with Latin and Greek, but also with Hebrew. But the study of grammar fell into a minor key, and what they read and wrote concerned itself not with the scented rhetoric of ancient masters, but with the truths of Holy Writ. In addition, the heirs of the rich and noble carried on with French, in those times the language of courtly and elegant folk, and thus a trade tool, as it were, for members of their caste. But once again they drank in its idiom not from the bubbling fountain of Montaigne and Rabelais, or even the troubadours, but from a French rendition of the New Testament. Rather curiously, all classes were run in German—not in Latin, as per immemorial academic custom. A great weight, in fact, was put on the mastery of the mother tongue in both its written and its spoken incarnations—even in the art of effective public speaking, whether plain or fancy.

For all their cobwebbed stress on the conquest of the ancient languages, Francke's secondary schools made room for the newer learning. True, it was not of a large proportion, and nearly always its pursuit was after hours. Just the same it was there. Scan the inventory of its content and you will observe the presence of history and geography, besides mathematics, and a horde of natural sciences, to wit, botany, physics, astronomy, mineralogy, even anatomy, with a dash of materia medica thrown in and some discreet pointers on the maintenance of human hygiene. A few students challenged their ego with painting, and all of them let loose in sacred singing. For the future landed gentry there was opportunity aplenty to become familiar with such useful matters as the management of an estate, the planning and planting of a garden, and the cultivation of a vintage grape. Or, if the mood was on them, they could dally in wood carving, copper engraving, or glassblowing. For their use and instruction there was also a natural history collection, a herbal cabinet, a dissecting room, besides labs for amateur physicists and chemists.

To provide his institutions with high-minded masters, well filled with knowledge and practiced in the knacks and skills of their craft, Francke, in 1697, opened a teachers' seminary, the first of its line in Germany, and the model in the ensuing century for Prussia's first official teacher-training institute. Like all Francke's pedagogical undertakings, his seminary was overladen with piety and rectitude. Only the cream of Pietist youth was given access to its training. They were to be of a surpassing character, so surpassing, in fact, as to have no dealings with tobacco and alcohol, they should manifest an earnest desire to teach; they should like children; and like Francke himself, they should thirst for good works.

Francke's pedagogy was simple. To bring up the young, all of them, girls as well as boys, whether in velvet or in burlap, to an upstanding Christian life and to prepare them to live effectively in the station it had pleased God to place them in, was its overriding purpose. To this end his pupils immersed themselves in religious and useful knowledge. Though Francke disparaged mere memorizing and insisted that no child was to be put upon "prattling words without understanding them," his practice fell short of his theory, and the memory consequently was heavily burdened. At the same time the youngster was given acquaintance with the world of everyday. He not only saw and heard and sniffed its salient manifestations, but in his writing and reckoning he dealt with such actualities as business arithmetic, bills, receipts, contracts, and similar works of commercial belles lettres.

A grave and mirthless man, Francke lacked the Erasmian waggish charm. He laid great stress on the importance of feeling in religion, but in other spheres the stirrings of man's emotion, particularly when the effects promised to be pleasurable, were under his suspicion. In consequence, Francke had no taste for the arts and letters, and save when it served to glorify Omnipotence, the tonal art left him unmoved. Though he bore an affection toward children, and was sensitive to their wellbeing, he was, nevertheless, a stranger to their nature. Thus, where Comenius endorsed the educational value of play, and the Humanist Vittorino even pranced and danced with his charges, Francke, in contrast, forbade all gaiety and amusement—even "comedies, jokes, romances, novels . . . and other foolishness." Yet, for all that, he was at heart a kindly man, and in his schools he went to great lengths to see that children suffered no rough handling. His masters were ordered to eschew all name-calling. Never was a child to be cried down as a fool or knave, or even a pig, a dog, or an ass. Francke laid down his caveat against hair pulling and arm yanking. More children, he counseled, can be won with friendly words than with blows. But when milder measures went for nothing, then a master might resort to the rattan, prudently applied and on nature's appointed place.

The world which forgot the teachings of Comenius was far more hospitable to his successor. Francke, in truth, attained a high celebrity. The first Frederick William of Prussia honored him with his patronage and with a membership in the Scientific Society of Berlin. When the King of Denmark laid plans to save souls in East India, he summoned Francke's help and advice. Even the Church of England gave him an ear. Its Society for the Propagation of the Gospel in Foreign Parts, the SPG, which worked its moral and educational endeavor in the Colonies, appointed Francke a corresponding member. Meanwhile, his students and admirers bore his torch in all directions. Some appeared in Georgia, but a great many more came to the holy land of William Penn, where, much in the manner of Francke, they busied themselves with education and a variety of pious and social service.

Francke's most distinguished disciple, and by all odds his most successful one, was Johann Julius Hecker. A parson-pedagogue, he stood in the confidence of Frederick the Great, a sort of unofficial educational councilor, who, despite his lack of the dignity of high-sounding office, drew up the blueprint by which the monarch modernized the Prussian school system, putting it, from top to bottom, under the sovereignty of the state, the first of its kind the world had ever seen.

It becomes the fate oftentimes of insurgents to lose the reformer's zeal which brought them to the fore, or even to fall prey to the very evils they once decried. In any case time saw the Pietist movement become as stiff and dogmatic as the Lutheranism it had sought to inspirit with the breath of life. But its schools outlived their Pietist beginnings, and long after Francke had sprouted angelic wings, his institutions were still in active service. Indeed, attuned to the current world's more insistent secularity, not a few of them are still in daily practice.

François de Salignac
de La Mothe - Fénelon

While Milton and Locke were offering their views on the proper education of England's "nobler and gentler youths," on the other side of the Channel a Frenchman was directing his thoughts to the question of how to enlighten their Gallic sisters. In him ran the blood of the *noblesse,* and his name, hence, was befittingly long: François de Salignac de La Mothe-Fénelon. For all the rank and dignity of the familial line, François's parents were of a meager purse, a handicap which, however, they more than offset by the glitter of the family's service to Church and state. Young Fénelon declared for the former, and to prepare himself for the sacerdotal calling he listened to lectures at the University of Paris and the Seminary of Saint Sulpice. Put into practice for a while as a priest, he woke up one morning to find himself in charge of the New Catholics, a sisterhood in Paris which specialized in the religious and moral reconstruction of converted Huguenot girls. For his assignment Fénelon was well equipped. Not only was he fired by an enormous religious zeal, but doubtless his charm, good looks, and velvet bearing helped him not a little. He worked with a wise and patient hand, and presently his reputation was large—large enough at all events to gain him the notice of the Duchess of Beauvilliers, who, having acquired nine daughters, doubtless knew what she was about when she prayed the sagacious priest to grant her the benefit of his light and counsel in the education of her numerous bevy. The result was a number of reflective papers, which, in 1687—the abbé was then thirty-six—appeared between covers as *De l'éducation des filles,* or as we say it, *The Education of Girls.*

Some years after the publication of this volume, in 1695, its author was commissioned by Louis XIV to undertake the instruction of his grandson and heir apparent, the Duke of Burgundy, and his brothers. It is conceivable, as some maintain, that Fénelon's elevation was due to the influence of one of his admirers at the court, Madame de Maintenon, the monarch's friend, and after the death of the queen, in the course of time, his royal wife. The ducal heir has come down to us as a lad of dark and stormy moods, full of the grandpaternal oats, and the occasion of not a little dread and trembling amongst those summoned to attend him. To his task Fénelon brought not only the sapience and skill he had applied so deftly as dean of the New Catholics in teaching the salvaged Huguenot girls; he possessed as well, it seems, a natural knowledge of boy psychology. The upshot was that Father François not only tamed the duke, but he also broke him to his books. For the edification of his pupil, the abbé composed three more works: the *Fables,* a batch of the usual moral fabrications; the *Dialogues of the Dead,* which, despite its macabre title, relates history through the fancied colloquies of those who made it; and *Télémaque,* a novel, which propounds the opinion that sovereigns exist to serve their subjects and not the other way round, a proposition which Fénelon hoped his pupil would take to heart when he became king—but the lad, unluckily, died too soon. The story, sandwiched between the editor's introduction at one end and his explanatory notes at the other, still makes the rounds in college French. For his reclamation of the fractious dukeling—abetted also by some palace politicking—Fénelon was elevated into the archbishopric of Cambrai, with all the rights, privileges, and emoluments thereunto pertaining. At the same time he was glossed as Preceptor of the Children of France. Alas, the theme of *Télémaque* proved too heady for the fourteenth Louis, an upholder of divine right and a practitioner of utter and absolute power. In consequence, the holy man fell from royal favor, and where once Maintenon had admired his ideas, she now abjured them. His laurel halo was removed, and though he was allowed to continue his archepiscopal duties, for the rest of his life his presence at the court was under interdict.

2

All of Fénelon's books in one way or another bear upon education, but it is for *The Education of Girls* that pedagogues have stored him in their hall of fame. Its main ideas were scarcely novel—indeed, uttered in the high day of the Renaissance, not a few of them would have rung a familiar chime. But the years had seen them fall into neglect, so that when Fénelon expressed them in his work, they carried an air of extraordinary freshness.

What is the gist of Fénelon's historic effusion? It is overborne, as one might expect, with the assumption that the education of girls is important. Indeed, His Grace suggested—if one may resort to paraphrase—that even in the female ignorance is not bliss, and that, in point of fact, an ignorant woman can be dangerous. Like his older contemporary and fellow bishop, the masterful Comenius, Fénelon urged wasting no time in launching a child's education. Let it begin in the home at the mother's knee while her daughter is still a crawler. Not only will she be innocent of the wicked world, but at a time of life when Homo sapiens is supremely impressionable and pliable, she can readily be molded by her mother's benign example. Eve's daughters, as every man knows, are not angels—at least not here below. They are addicted, says the experienced Father François, to diffidence, fraudulent modesty, and above all to vanity. Let the mother forestall such vile corruptions by teaching her child to love truth and abhor pretense, for without these virtues a woman's life is doomed to futility. Nor, should piety be forgotten. In fact, when the child begins to venture her first frail steps into the realm of reason, her mother should take care to route them toward the Heavenly Father, the revelation of Christian truth through Christ the Savior, and the Ten Commandments.

It was not the good Lord's purpose, Fénelon reminds us, to make woman the peer of man. On her, indeed, he has placed some palpable limitations. Wars she cannot fight; statecraft is beyond her; and the holy priesthood she may not enter. To her the great professions are shut, and so are the mechanical arts.

Accordingly, it would be futile for her to freight her brainpan with the knowledge that is essential to the ambitious male. The fair ones should be educated, to be sure—but erudition ill becomes them. "It is enough," the archbishop declared, "if one day they know how to rule their households and obey their husbands without arguing about it," a sentiment which was stoutly supported three-quarters of a century later by the incomparable Rousseau.

Did Omnipotence tip the balance to favor men when he meted out the powers of body and mind? Then he redressed it somewhat by providing the frail sex more generously with capacities for industry, tidiness, thrift, and the like. Put together and allowed to function freely, they constitute the essence of God's appointed role for women, the career, namely, of wife and mother, and it is to that end that the education of girls should be directed.

3

Just what does a young miss have to learn to fit her for the part of accomplished domesticity? First and foremost she must needs be firmly fixed in virtue and piety, for the soul of every happy hearth, Fénelon has discerned, resides in a religious woman. In addition, she should be at home in the rudimentary Rs. To enhance her understanding of the cultural legacy, she should make acquaintance with the historical high points not only of Greece and Rome, but of her native land as well. To afford her and her family and friends diversion and pleasure during her moments of leisure, she should be sufficiently adept at music and painting. At all times the young, whether male or female, should be under safeguard against the beguilements of a wicked world. Hence, whatever reading they engage in, whether sacred or profane, should serve to teach them that only the good life can be beautiful. It should scarcely be necessary to mention that what holds for the perusal of books, holds even more for such perils to the passions as art and music. Needless to say, the nascent housewife must become thoroughly versed in the established principles and practices of the domestic art and science, from cleaning, cooking, and laundering to furnishing her home with whatever it requires, whether carrots or crockery, and hiring and managing honest and religious domestics. In all this, though her burdens may at times be irksome, let her learn to accept her place and not be tantalized by unfulfilled dreams of seeking to surpass her social standing. Say, however, that fate has chosen her to be the helpmeet of a man of great estate. Then it would be a good thing for her to have a knowledge of account-keeping and the simpler principles of law. For like the utilitarian Dr. Benjamin Franklin several generations following, the Reverend François de La Mothe-Fénelon had convinced himself that such knowledge would be useful to an efficient homemaker in the higher circles, and a superb preparation as well, should days of heartache ever befall her, for the lorn and lonely state of widowhood, when she may be called upon to manage her estate. As for a knowledge of the ancient languages—the hallmark in those days of a cultivated man—for girls such distinction is unnecessary, nor is it worth the pain of having to learn them. But if for all that, a girl should be put upon the study of an outland tongue, then let it be Latin, the language of Mother Church.

4

Despite the inclination for conservatism which oftentimes one associates with the run of professional men of God, in his pedagogical outlook Fénelon was a liberal—even, maybe, as not a few of his contemporaries decried, a radical. Scan his dossier, and more often than not you will find his fundamental principles bucking the current of the schoolmasters' prevalent opinion. He played with the notion, for example, that we never get over the way we are brought up, a contention which, even though he failed to grasp its significance, was so advanced that it was not until Dr. Freud and other probers of the hidden inner consciousness were upon us, that its meaning began to be understood. Contrary to the convention of his time, the abbé insisted that the best education is the kind that brings no tears. Such an education, he asserted—as did its most glowing advocate, Rousseau, later on—must be predicated on the nature of the child. Teachers, he wrote, "must content themselves to follow and help nature." The most efficacious instruction, the prelate let it be known, is informal and indirect, neither forced nor hurried. It is aided and forwarded by the child's natural attributes, his catlike curiosity, for example, his insatiable urge to play, and his proclivity to imitate whatever he sees and hears. Skilfully put to use, and coaxed by amiable palaver, they are nature's appointments to render the child's learning agreeable and even enjoyable. "I have seen various children learning to read at play," the archbishop confided. All that was necessary, it appears, was to enthrall them with some bewitching *conte,* a fable perhaps, or a fairy tale, taken from a book in their presence, and thereupon to induce them, without their knowing it, to try to master their letters—and presto, they are on their way to learning how to read! "Writing," Fénelon added, "can be taught in much the same manner."

Like the founder of the kindergarten, the nineteenth-century Froebel, this archepiscopal predecessor put a tremendous stock in storytelling to whet the child's appetite for learning. "Children," he declaimed, "are passionately fond of silly stories." Every day, he went on, your eyes will catch them "transported with joy or shedding tears, as they hearken to the stories that are told them." "Do not fail," he pleaded, "to profit by this propensity." But whatever tales you choose to tell, make sure that besides being entertaining they are instructive and elevating as well, and that in no case will they fever the imagination.

To call *The Education of Girls* a great book would be folly—possibly it may not even have been a good book. Diffuse and repetitious, it drifts much too often into the nebulous realm of generality, sprinkling its course, as it proceeds, with pious platitudes and lofty nothings. The path to happiness its author lays out for girls of gentle birth is sturdy enough, if not especially inviting. Nor, after making the necessary allowances for the values of his era, can there be any bickering over its moral and religious foundation with its stress on modesty, resignation, and the like, although in candor it must be said that, save for his intransigent love of God, the archbishop was himself sorely deficient in most of the virtues he so highly recommended. Yet, once these and other objections have been filed, the fact remains that Fénelon's book was important. The first discourse of any consequence on the education of girls, it spoke with authority, not only in Catholic France, but beyond its borders—even, in truth, in infidel Britain. Its audience is, of course, immeasurable, though, stretched over more than a century, it must have been considerable. Its ideas, such as they were, continued to exercise their influence long after their pleader was in the grave. In fact, when in 1762 Rousseau put forth his unforgettable *Emile,* his views on the education of women were attuned pretty much to the key of Fénelon, though more conservatively. Indeed, speaking comparatively, in this respect the Genevan may well have been a reactionary. The notion that the human female is the male's intellectual inferior, or to state it in Fénelon's phrase, that women's minds are weaker, was not seriously challenged, as we shall see in later pages, until the mid-nineteenth century.

EARLY MODERN TIMES

As Colonial America's traffic in secular learning picked up pace, across the ocean another land was taking its first gingerly steps toward putting its schools under the power and authority of the state. In the eighteenth century such an idea was, of course, no longer novel. Plato had entertained it in his *Republic,* as had several other metaphysicians, and the Spartans had even translated it into a rather lusty practice. Centuries later the idea sprouted anew when Reformation leaders summoned Protestant sovereigns to support and subsidize the education of the youth, this being necessary, as Luther explained, not only for their bliss beyond the grave, but also "for the sake of affairs here below." Out of these urgings there presently arose a number of school systems, in Saxony, for example, in Calvin's Geneva, and of course, in the Massachusetts theocracy. But all this activity, aided though it was by the civil government, was for predominantly religious ends. It was not until the eighteenth century, when the stream of nationalism began to flow more vigorously, that a modern state undertook to forge its schools into an instrument for the furtherance of its special interests and ambitions. That state was the Kingdom of Prussia.

Although the new policy did not acquire currency until well on in the eighteenth century, its first foreshadowing fell upon the land as early as 1694 with the establishment of the University of Halle. Saluted in educational chronicles as the world's first modern university (there are the usual doubts), Halle appeared in a great blaze of lights, for its professors, chased from the halls of Leipzig for the devilry of their sharply critical thinking, had attracted the approval of no less a worthy than Frederick III, Elector of Brandenburg, but destined pretty soon to expand into the first King of Prussia. From the start Frederick was intent on making Halle as up-to-date as possible, and for this purpose he combed the field for the finest brains, filling its chambers with men of great learning who were also bold and venturesome, and eager to break through the trammels of academic tradition. They began by lecturing not, as per ancient custom, in Latin, but in the student's familiar German. Under their light and leading Aristotle was hauled from his pedestal to give lodgment to the newer and more exact thinking of Francis Bacon and René Cartesius (born Descartes), while mathematics, disdained so long by the academic faculty, suddenly found a lively favor. Carried away by the rush, the law professors brought their propositions into consonance with the secular theories on which rests the modern state, while the professors of medicine, wiping their hands of the ghostly Galen and Hippocrates, turned their instruction, somewhat haltingly, it is true, to observation and experimentation. Even the university's praying brethren, the theologians, felt the impact—presently, indeed, they were discarding the Lutheran dogmatism for the softer Pietism of Francke.

To Halle chiefly we owe the doctrine of academic freedom, the right to teach, that is, without any outside meddling, whether political, religious, moral, or otherwise. To Halle too we owe the correlative doctrine of the freedom of learning by which students, having come to the right intellectual ripeness, may pursue truth to the inmost recesses of its lair without deference to any preconceived theories they might thereby shake or even shatter. It was a sign to all the scholarly world that facile answers no longer sufficed, that knowledge was no mere hand-me-down, that truth, indeed, had to be discovered and forever tested, and that such business was, at bottom, the scholar's free and unassailable right. Denounced by dogmatists and obscurantists when it first came upon the scene, the doctrine of academic freedom has lived precariously. Dictators, whether deceased or still in practice, have conceived a vast dislike for it, and even in our own land of liberty there have been not a few attempts to put the brake upon it. Even so, the doctrine, for all the assaults upon it, has grown, like its far-off cousin, the Bill of Rights, to something more than a mere emblem of pride and glory.

2

William's successor, the first Frederick William of Prussia, cared but scantily for the higher learning, and he did little to further its propagation. Lower down, however, his interest fevered, and there he applied himself with the utmost industry. Early in his reign, in 1717, he ordered parents to send their children to school. To keep everyone on the track there was to be "vigorous punishment" of all defiers, and lest—because of economic hardship—the poor might be tempted to keep their children from their books, they were to be helped from the local poor box. From time to time the monarch added fresh and newer touches. With a subtle hint of things to come, he turned to the kingdom's rural schools, urging the erection of more and better ones, and bolstering his proposal with a subsidy from the Prussian treasury. In a day when schoolmastering was, so to say, a free-for-all, when not uncommonly it was a minor sideline to some other occupation, Frederick William undertook to let in a measure of rule and order. Henceforth, he decreed in 1722, no one may engage in part-time pedagogic practice save only tailors, woodworkers, blacksmiths, weavers, and wheelwrights. Finally, the king gave his blessing to the establishment of Prussia's first teacher-training school at Stettin.

Far on in his reign Frederick unloaded his reformer's zeal upon the province of East Prussia. To arrest its widespread educational blight, he put upon its people to build schools, and to give them some help toward such an end, he reserved spacious plots of land, and better yet, he fortified the communal effort generously with grants from the royal strongbox. Lest there be any finagling— such being man's immemorial way even in Prussia—in 1737 the King formulated a code of Regulative Principles which put the whole East Prussian educational enterprise under law. The measure dealt with such necessary elements as the construction and maintenance of schoolhouses, governmental aid, and of course, the teacher's wages and his other usufructs, such as his lodging and provisioning, the tilling of his land, and the housing and victualing of his livestock. From their fourth birthday to their twelfth, children were expected to apply themselves to study. Their involuntary servitude, however, was not without the payment of a fee. For one child at school a father paid as high as a few cents a year; in cases where the stork's visitations had been more numerous, the state undertook to pay the tuition of every additional offspring.

As resolute and relentless as Hohenzollerns have so often shown themselves to be, Prussia's first Frederick William kept at his duties until 1740. When he departed, his kingdom was the better for his rule. He had routed the state debt, raised its wealth, strengthened the army, and forwarded its trade and industry. As dear to his heart as any of these deeds, however, were his accomplishments in the schooling of his people. For his time his program was far in advance; hence it ran head on into popular resentment. Even so, before he died, he could enjoy the agreeable feeling that during his reign his subjects had opened some 1,800 new schools, and even more important, he had laid down the ground rules for a national system of education.

3

Frederick William's heir was his son, the great Frederick, ruler of the Prussians from 1740 to 1786. The friend of poets and philosophers, of musicians and men of learning, Frederick was a man of great native shrewdness and ability, the most intelligent, doubtless, of the Hohenzollern clan, but also the most cynical and brazen of the lot. He was, like Franklin and Voltaire, a partisan of Europe's eighteenth-century Enlightenment, and he exhibited many of its higher virtues. Science and learning he pursued as unsparingly as he grappled with his foes in battle. In his years of evanescent peace he devoted his whole energies to promoting the arts and letters, wooing Europe's foremost luminaries to his Potsdam castle, and bedding and boarding them out of the royal purse. He graced his capital with fresh and exultant beauty, draining its marshlands, laying out new and grander streets, and adorning them with gardens and public buildings. Nor did he neglect the commonplace affairs of trade and industry—indeed, to many of the German handicrafts, then still in the frailty of their infancy, he offered the first solid governmental sustenance.

The state was Frederick's only love, and the advancement of its interests his overmastering passion. To this purpose he directed a ruthlessness as astounding as it was useful; a guile and sagacity which were a match for the most devious diplomat of his time; and an insight into military strategy which came close at times to being wizardry.

Like his father, Frederick held that a state could be no better than its schools, and like him, he made their increase and improvement a paramount concern of government. As the years ran through his reign there issued from his hand rule upon rule and decree upon decree, all to the end of liquidating the "stupidity and ignorance," as he said, of Prussian youth. In the very middle of his reign there appeared the Code of 1763. From boys and girls it evoked no mirth, but only sadness, for by its ordinance, those aged from five to thirteen were condemned to spend a good deal of their time at their desks in school. In addition, the measure clamped its regulation on such matters as curricula, textbooks, programs, tuition fees, scholarships, discipline, the licensing of schoolmasters, and so on. So that none might fall prey to the soft beckoning of truancy, a counting of all heads from five to thirteen years old was ordered, their names enrolled in the official ledger, and the constabulary duly apprised and put on watch. For recalcitrant parents there were fines.

Two years following, in 1765, came another code. It covered practically the same ground as its forerunner, but with special provisions for Frederick's Catholic subjects in Silesia, a province but recently burgled by the Prussians from the Austrians.

Although Frederick ruled his people with a rod of iron, the codes aroused a voluble dissent, and even opposition. Parents had no fancy for them because they wanted their children to go to work. The clergy dreaded and decried the steady penetration of state control. The upper classes, who had no desire to advance the enlightenment among the common folks, looked upon the whole business with ill grace. Even schoolmasters shed tears over a measure so harsh it required them to be licensed before they could establish themselves in regular practice. Despite the royal will and muscle there thus developed a wide chasm between the codes' high standards and their application in the everyday reality, and several generations were to come and go before Prussia at length brought its schools under the reign of state control. When this came to pass, the principles which obtained were essentially the ones inscribed in the Codes of 1763 and 1765. Indeed, modified though they have been in their details, they still display themselves to a greater or less degree, not only in Germany, whether East or West, but in every up-and-doing state which currently occupies this panting globe.

Frederick the Great departed for Valhalla in 1786. For a transient moment his policy of nationalizing education lingered, and in the year following it culminated in the formation of a national school board, the so-called *Oberschulkollegium.* Brought into being to replace the numerous Lutheran school boards, the body was to be predominantly secular. But the new king, Frederick William II, was not, like his father, dowered with a capacity for great vision; instead there was about him a palpable aroma of the second-rate. Afraid to risk the harsh frowns of his gentlemen of God, the monarch undertook to soothe them at every turn with an almost sheeplike willingness. In consequence, he staffed the *Oberschulkollegium* not with lay experts, but with consecrated men, thereby nullifying its chief reason for being.

Near the end of Frederick William's reign appeared the Prussian Civil Code of 1794. Its concoction had started many years ago, when Frederick the Great, pained by the disorderly state of Prussian law, with its endless duplication and overlapping, ordered a committee of the kingdom's jurists to recast the whole jumble into a single, coherent formulation. Its twelfth chapter, dwelling upon Prussia's educational statutes, sets down the theory which grounds them. "All schools and universities," it asserts, "are state institutions, charged with the instruction of youth in useful information and scientific knowledge." All public schools and educational institutions, it goes on, "are under the supervision of the state, and are subject at all times to its examination and inspection." To serve in the trenches of learning, teachers must have the approval and consent of the state. In fact, when they are engaged as its agents in the secondary school, they are to enjoy the rank and dignity of state officials.

Thus the manifesto for secular authority. In the years ahead one will see it adverted to again and again, not only in Prussia, but in other lands as well. On it, in truth, rests the doctrine of pretty nearly every present-day state, which is to say that in the educational enterprise, government, in one form or another, is the sovereign boss.

4

Meanwhile the tide of Prussian progress had begun to roll out. The enlightened despotism of Frederick the Great had not been emulated by his son, the second Frederick William, who had neither the resolution nor the natural talent of his forebear for the art and mystery of good government. As a result, the state, once so virile and robust, fretted more and more in weakness, and even knavery and corruption. The overriding effect of this downhill slide fell upon the reign of Frederick William III, who assumed his father's crown in 1797. A man who thought with his wishbone rather than with his brain, the new monarch confined his early statecraft to pious sugar pills rather than the acrid facts of political reality. The fates found him out in less than a decade when Napoleon shattered the Prussian army at Jena and heaved its pathetic remnant far back to the Russian border. By the Treaty of Tilsit, which followed a year later in 1807, the Prussian cup of bitterness poured over. What had taken them almost a century to piece together with such thought and toil and carnage was now within a bare few months slashed into a shredded memory.

Yet even the terrible sword of Napoleon was not enough to do the Prussians in. The colossal devastation at Jena and Tilsit had stunned them, but in the end it was not without its lesson. Their humiliation speeded their national heartbeat —in truth, in the stewpan of disaster even the King began to bubble with a fervor he had never shown before. "We will gain," he let it be known, "in intrinsic power and splendor." It was no merely wishful delirium. His ministers and his queen gave him brave support, and under their collective hand there presently followed a great outpouring of reform. Serfdom was swept away for all time, and so was most of feudalism; cities obtained greater rights of self-rule; the civil service was repaired and reinforced, and so was the army, its decaying generals dismissed, and universal conscription made the rule. "We will proceed," observed Stein, the King's first minister, "from the fundamental principle to elevate the moral, religious, and patriotic spirit in the nation, to instill into it again courage, self-reliance, and readiness to sacrifice everything for national honor and for independence from foreigners." To this end, Stein went on to say, "we must rely on the education and instruction of the young."

To put these words into deeds, the minister, a very dogged fellow, proceeded to reorganize and reform the entire system of Prussian education. He began in 1807 by knocking out the clerically saddled *Oberschulkollegium,* and replacing it with a Department of Public Instruction, an arm of the State Department of the Interior, and utterly secular in its membership. Ten years later the department's affairs had grown sufficiently to bring about its translation into a ministry in its own right and glory.

From the start the new office was directed by men who revealed more than an ordinary familiarity with their work. Its first head was Wilhelm von Humboldt, a man of moment in intellectual history, but also deft and able in the execution of public affairs. Though he graced his educational office all too briefly, he managed, for all that, to bring a number of reforms upon his country. At his instance the University of Berlin was founded in 1809. Designed to aid and solace the Prussians for their loss at Tilsit of Halle and Göttingen, and several of their other springs of higher knowledge, Berlin broke through the darkness of the clouds to shine like the moon at full tide upon the German learning. Its faculty counted some of the country's finest intellects, powerful, persistent, and sometimes even a little daredevil. Time saw Berlin scintillate more and more, with such capital stars as Hegel and Schopenhauer in philosophy, Wundt in psychology, Liebig in chemistry, Helmholtz in physics, and a galaxy of others too numerous to mention here. Even more than Halle, Berlin fixed a friendly eye on the advancement of knowledge through the scientific examination of its every aspect, however esoteric or specialized, from Egyptology to paleontology to earthworms and onionskins. It was a role exactly to its taste and one which, though sometimes obscured by the gray gloom of reactionary politics, it has continued at bottom to cherish. Transferred by the caprices of war into the hands of the East Germans, it was given a new incarnation in 1948 in West Berlin where it now functions as the Free University of Berlin.

As the eyes of Germany rested on the University of Berlin, some of its other halls of wisdom fell to the spell of the newcomer's unconventional but prophylactic industry. Senile ones, like Erfurt, Mainz, and Wittenberg, turned over and died, while new ones, modeled upon Berlin, sprang up to take their place. Thus came the University of Bonn in the birth town of Beethoven, and the University of Munich in the city of beer and *Bratwurst.* A delight to the connoisseurs of earnest learning, both places are still engaged in the full pursuit of knowledge.

Berlin did the higher learning a laudable service. As the nineteenth century gained in years, German universities stood at the peak of their class throughout the academic world. Their labs and libraries were unexcelled, their methods and standards the finest known to civilization, and their scholars of the highest bearable diligence. Their unquestionable superiority, as might be expected, brought them clients from all over the earth. Indeed, in a day when graduate research in our own land was still, so to speak, at nurse, it became almost imperative for Americans who flamed with a passion for graduate research to seek fulfillment in their specialty at firsthand under the counsel of one of its professors at some German university. Returning later to their homeland laden with enlightenment, and a Ph.D. to prove it, but even more, with a bold and fervid interest in the promotion of exact knowledge, not a few of these men donned professorial robes to serve in the American higher learning where presently some of them were giving it a bright, new edge. Thus, on the foundation of our college, which was of English origin, was erected the American graduate school which was full of German overtones. Dig beneath the surface of the present-day Johns Hopkins, which opened its doors in 1876 at Baltimore as the first research university in the United States, and you will surely unearth perceptible traces of the German model—indeed, dig a little deeper and you will even come upon its archinspirer, the extraordinary Wilhelm von Humboldt.

The University of Berlin was scarcely on the scene when, in 1810, the reform wave broke upon the Prussian secondary learning. What was envisioned was a school devoted to the most stringent standards, the training ground, as it were, of young Prussia's brains, and manned for this reason by tried and competent experts able to bring their students to the intellectual maturity required by the new-type university. To this end all secondary school instructors were made to possess a full and intimate knowledge of their subject besides being on familiar terms with pedagogy in all its divisions and subdivisions, its philosophic foundations, for example, its sociological meaning, and finally, the subtle and intricate operation of the human psyche as it played its part in the learning and teaching process. To rid the teaching ranks of their perennial quacks and dunderheads, it was ordained that all prospective aspirants for the teacher's long-tailed frock were to submit to a uniform state examination. Composed and conducted by Prussia's well-filled professorial heads, the examinations put an effective end to the easygoing local tests, which were often enough not tests at all but mere dalliance. The state examination, by contrast, was arduous, so arduous, in truth, that only the superior could hope to survive. Its relentless hand not only sifted the grain from the chaff; it also daunted those who regarded teaching as a convenient interlude to maintain themselves in pocket while they prepared themselves to graze on some tomorrow in greener pastures, say, the ministry or the law. At one stroke the new requirement lifted the Prussian schoolmaster from a mere hawker of knowledge, often a dullpate and transparently unfit for office, to a professional teacher of the first order.

As year chased after year the requirements were altered, but always for the purpose of rendering them more vigorous and, it was hoped, more effective.

Finally, lest applicants for the teacher's license, for all their sapience, might yet be strangers to the give and take of the schoolroom's everyday labor, candidates were made to surmount not only the rigors of the state examination, but before they could stretch their legs under a permanent desk, they had to put in a probationary year in actual practice, and always, of course, under supervisory watch and advice.

To bring the work of the secondary school into greater unity and coherence throughout the realm, in the year 1812 a final, comprehensive examination, both written and oral, was imposed by the state on all candidates for graduation. Known as the *Maturitätsprüfung*—the German's way of saying "test for intellectual maturity"—it had been ventured as long ago as 1788, but the massed aversion of the clergy soon brought it to naught. Now, back on the scene, it was destined to endure into the very present. To advance the desired academic uniformity, all secondary schools obtained a nine-year course of study, and all of them, whatever their former designation, received the name of *Gymnasium*. Finally, all students were made to drink from the same curricular jug, fixed, unvarying, and mandatory from one end of Prussia to the other, with nine years of Latin, besides Greek, German, mathematics, history, geography, religion, and science. Thus, well heeled with knowledge and a certificate testifying to his demonstrated intellectual powers, the *Gymnasium*'s graduate had access without further ado to any house of the German higher learning; or if the inclination was upon him, he could bespeak a place of promise as a junior executive in some citadel of affairs, or even in the civil service.

At education's other end, in the elementary school, the reform took on a similar intensity. Here too the government pressed for better and more efficient teaching. It opened its campaign in 1808 by dispatching seventeen of Prussia's most talented schoolmasters to Switzerland and squaring their bills for three years, while they warmed themselves in the ideals of Pestalozzi, then the head and forefront of the world's progressive pedagogues. "You will have reached perfection," the state let them know, "when you clearly see that education is an art . . . and what its relationship is to the great art of education of the nations." These words the seventeen gravely heeded, and when they returned to Prussia, they received preferment as provincial superintendents or heads of training schools, or other positions of no less importance.

Meanwhile, the Prussians scouted in all directions for men of Pestalozzian experience. Thus they commissioned Karl August Zeller to leave his beloved Württemberg to come to Prussia to lay the foundation of an up-and-doing program of teacher training. Under Zeller's lead there emerged in 1809 a new teachers' seminary. Founded to initiate its nascent masters in Pestalozzi's methods, which is to say the most up-to-date then known on this planet, the Zeller school was destined in the years to come to produce numerous lively descendants. In Prussia pedagogical seminaries rose to an almost imperial splendor—so well regarded, in fact, was their performance that pretty soon they were being imitated in the rest of Germany, the Netherlands, and Sweden, and even in some of the more advanced states of our own republic—even, indeed, in France, not known in those days for a love of anything made in Prussia.

Although the heart of Pestalozzianism was humanitarian, the necessity of Prussian politics was intensely national. As the two squared off in the classroom, the latter invariably held domination over the former. In consequence, on the one hand the *Volksschule* entertained the essence of Pestalozzi's method, its underlying psychology, its confidence in the learner's eyes and ears as aids in his quest for knowledge, and even its certainty that through education there can be social progress to the very end of time. Meanwhile, patriotism breathed and pulsed in every lesson. Not only was Napoleon made to look like an abhorrent fiend; but every German became a paragon of the highest manly qualities. So ran the story in every subject, especially, of course, in such social ones as history and geography. In speech the pupils were set upon reciting patriotic cantos; in music they intoned the national glorias; and in their gymnastics they stretched their arms and bent their knees for king and fatherland. Not even religion was spared the patriotic tinge. Compulsory in every school and imposed on every child, it concerned itself, as usual, with God's thou-shalts and thou-shalt-nots as laid down in catechism and prayer book, and of course, in Holy Writ. At the same time it was given a vigorous and generous supplement with homilies on civic rectitude, obedience to authority, and the joys to be obtained, surely and incontrovertibly, from humility and self-sacrifice, not only for Omnipotence in the seat of heavenly grace, but for his secular plenipotentiary on the throne of Prussia.

Thus arose the Prussian school system. Purged of its ecclesiastical control, it became an instrument to serve the state, the first of its kind to be visited on us in modern times. It was not, as in the United States in later years, a single, unified mechanism which in theory, if not always in fact, enables every child to ascend class by class and year by year from a freshman in the lowest learning to the doctorate's dizzy height. Instead, it was a double system with the *Volksschule* to service the multitudinous common folk, and the *Gymnasium,* separate and distinct, for the so-called elite, whether intellectual or something else. It was, of course, a plain reflection of the Prussian social order with its handful of leaders and its vast mass of schooled and decorous followers. Before long it rooted itself in nearly all the German states, and in 1871, when they were consolidated into the German Empire, the dual system became the national fashion. Since then, of course, there have been numerous alterations in both the lower and the secondary learning, but until the advent of the Weimar Republic in 1919, the two-track school system, with stray exceptions, remained the rule.

5

With Napoleon unhorsed in 1815, the liberal ideas which had flowered at the outburst of the French Revolution wilted, and presently they fell away. Lest some errant seed might somewhere nonetheless come to life, the victors at Waterloo kept themselves ready always and everywhere to snuff it out. Headed by the Austrian Metternich, a crafty and crusty man, and braced by his far-flung international constabulary, whether in uniform or false whiskers, they undertook, as they informed the world, "to promote religion, peace, and order." But it was a sinister peace, and one fretted with deeply pressing yearnings. For, having savored the wine of liberty, free-minded folk were parched for a deeper and more effective draught from the same bottle. Especially suspect in those baleful days were the German universities. There the ideals of freedom which had blazed so fiercely during the wars of liberation against Napoleon had never quite died out. Consequently, their men of learning found themselves under constant and almost microscopic watch. Muzzling the intellectuals came to a head in 1819 in Metternich's Karlsbad decrees. With grave finality they put the brake on students and professors, their fraternities and secret orders, on gentlemen of the cloth and of the press—in short on every holder of challenging ideas, however slight.

Even so, for all their ferocity, in the end Metternich's manifestoes failed. The clock of history could not be stopped, and though sovereigns bade their subjects to renounce the promises of the French Revolution, the redoubtable hand of a wishful memory was far too powerful. As the years ticked on, Europe flared in riot after riot. Again and again the high hopes of the men and women who had blown up the Old Regime in France in 1789 resounded. As one upheaval followed another, liberalism made slow but ponderable headway—though, unhappily, not in the same degree and by no means in every land.

In Prussia the Revolution of 1848 ended in colossal and devastating failure. Not only were the liberals crushed; for generations they scarcely breathed. A hard and contemptuous reaction seized the land. Its shadow fell on all men, and particularly on the kingdom's schoolmen. The pride and hope, not so long ago, of a fallen but resurgent Prussia, they now found themselves hounded on every side. "You," railed Frederick William IV, as he poured out his bile, "and you alone are to blame for all the misery that the last year [1848] brought upon the kingdom." Theirs, he told them, was a "pseudo education," and an affront to the honor and dignity of the Crown. As for their Pestalozzian methods, they were a "sham." He had hated them, he said, even before he came to the throne, and since his accession he had done everything to suppress them. "I mean to proceed on this path," avowed the King, "without taking heed of anyone, and, indeed, no power on earth shall divert me from it."

Foreboding words, indeed, and unfortunately also true. During the next few years most of the pedagogical enlightenment which had been so laboriously cultivated by Stein, Humboldt, Zeller, and others was uprooted. Pestalozzianism, such as it was, was plowed under. The teachers' seminaries, denuded of all instruction in educational theory, were transformed into mere knowledge factories. Even the kindergarten, then still something of a novelty in the world, succumbed to the reactionary frenzy. It was, observed the mandate which closed its sessions, "socialistic ... and calculated to train the youth of the land in atheism."

6

The tempest gradually blew itself out, as all tempests eventually must—still it was not until the autumn of the century, after the coming of the Empire, that Germany's educational reformers crept out of their gloomy cellars to venture their pedagogic aid and counsel once more. Asked by the government to apply their wisdom to the elementary school, they tailored it in 1872 with a new course of study. It revealed no startling innovations, for its makers, their psyche, doubtless, still somewhat shaken, kept themselves on a very cautious path. To the nation's ecclesiastics and the great majority of their clients they proffered balm by putting religious instruction, as they said, "in the center of the teacher's work." At the same time, with a bow to the sainted Frederick the Great, they reaffirmed his doctrine that in education the state is at all times the sole and sovereign authority.

The secondary schools were somewhat less arthritic. As long ago as 1859 the *Realschule,* a nine-year institution with compulsory Latin, but sweetened with modern languages instead of Greek, was accorded the standing of a recognized secondary school. But it continued to be hoofed by skeptical scholars who put their stock in the *Gymnasium,* somewhat shopworn by this time, but still on all counts the weighing station of young Germany's brains. But in 1890 the last of the German emperors, Wilhelm II, exhaled some primary and capital doubts about the classical *Gymnasium.* "We must," he let it be heard, "take the German as the foundation for the *Gymnasium;* we ought to educate national young Germans, and not young Greeks and Romans." This, the Kaiser went on in Latin, and most un-Germanically, was the *"punctum saliens"* of the whole business. The emperor's observation was, of course, not without weight, and pretty soon Germany's guardians of intellectual propriety confirmed that His Majesty had made an important point. By 1901 they had even convinced themselves that all graduates of the secondary schools, whether of modern or ancient cast, should be granted an equal chance in their drive for a rendezvous with the higher learning.

7

In 1914, just before the guns of August opened the First World War, Germany's education had solidified in form and substance. It was still, as it had always been, a double system, with an eight-year *Volksschule* for the general run of people, and a variety of nine-year secondary schools for the more fortunate. The one, in sum, addressed its wares to the masses, the other to the so-called classes.

The *Volksschule* was free, compulsory, and universal. At its fullest functioning, its sessions ran for some ten months a year, from twenty weekly hours for
the young and tender to thirty or thereabouts for the hardened ones in the
upper grades. The program, executed with an implacable diligence, made the
Germans almost completely literate. Religion continued to be taught, and so did
gymnastics, and so also the lore of nature, drawing, and music. In the more
enlightened schools—usually in the municipalities—boys were introduced to
shopwork, while their sisters practiced with needle and thread, and in the
preparation of tasty and nutritious food. Ordinarily, when the state of the public
purse allowed it, the sexes received instruction in separate chambers. The
teaching was carried on mainly by men, soberly attired for their rite in long-
tailed coats, and always rigorously rehearsed in knowledge and pedagogy.

Not all children sat in the public *Volksschule.* Some betook themselves
instead to a *Vorschule,* which accepted its fledglings at the age of six, and which
specialized in getting them ready, three years later, for admission to the secondary school. For a modest fee it instructed them in the elementals, besides giving
them a foretaste of foreign language and mathematics. Because of its tuition
charge, the *Vorschule* reserved its attractions chiefly for those whose material
estate and status rose above the ordinary.

Unable to scale the wall which surrounded the secondary school, the mass of
common children, whether bourgeois or proletarian, found themselves shut out
of the university, which is to say the road to the higher professions. Instead,
they had to console themselves with eight years of elementary knowledge,
overtopped not uncommonly by three years of graduate work in a continuation
school. Thus, instead of making ready to shine on some tomorrow as doctors,
lawyers, or divines, they equipped themselves for success in industry, trade, or
commerce.

At the age of nine those designed by fortune for the boons of secondary
learning confronted three choices. There was, for one, the venerable *Gymnasium.* The offspring of the Renaissance, it was still the citadel of the classics,
with nine years of required Latin and seven of Greek, besides the usual courses
in the mother tongue, religion, history, geography, a bit of science and mathematics, and a modern language. Did a boy—or at all events his parents—take a
dim view of the classical cargo? Then, perhaps, he might prefer the *Oberrealschule.* The youngest of the German secondary schools, it devoted its nine years
of instruction chiefly to mathematics, the natural sciences, and the modern
languages. Between the two seminaries stood the *Realgymnasium* which, though
exacting nine years of Latin from its recruits, turned its back on Greek and
tolerated instead the study of some living tongue. But whether classical, scientific, or half and half, all these groves agreed that to be fully cultured a German
must be practiced in drawing, music, gymnastics, and religion. All of them were,
of course, under the vigilance and control of the state, and all commanded fees,
slight, to be sure, by American standards, for their instruction.

The German secondary schoolboy had little time for skylarking. Not only was he heavily burdened at school; when the day was done, he was beset with gigantic commissions of homework. Not even his summers were without travail, for nearly always his masters had befriended him with generous assignments to keep him busy during his vacation. With so much to occupy his mind. he had no leisure for the hordes of activities which crowd the American high school. Organized athletics existed not; nor did clubs, service squads, brass bands, drum majorettes and cheer directors, and the numerous other extracurricular phenomena which endear our high school to its clients. Schools, the Germans gravely contended, were houses of learning, not amusement parks. One privilege, however, secondary education did bestow: it entitled its beneficiary to one year of military conscription instead of the usual two for those of the lesser learning. And of course, once disgorged by the secondary school, and the certificate of his intellectual maturity triumphantly bagged, the successful graduate was free to enter any university he desired.

Given the necessary capacity and diligence, German girls confronted no special difficulty in getting a secondary education. Their seminaries, it is true, were not so numerous, and the patina of antiquity did not caress them as it did the boys' *Gymnasium.* By the same token, they found themselves unburdened by its tradition, and much freer, therefore, to attune themselves to the spirit of their time. As in other enlightened cultures, the nineteenth century was upon the Germans before they granted their daughters a chance to invade learning's higher reaches. The fair ones savored their first success when, in 1872, the Prussians created a ten-year secondary school especially for them. Overhauled and enriched from time to time, it not only anchored itself in the kingdom's educational system; it also, as usual, became the model for similar institutions in other parts of Germany. The school, which came to be known as a *Lyzeum,* received its girls when they were still in pigtails, grounding them in the elementary essentials for three years, and continuing with the secondary subjects during the next seven, or until they were sixteen years old or thereabout.

For girls who wanted to advance themselves further there was abundant opportunity. They could, for one, enroll for a couple of years in the so-called women's school—the *Frauenschule*—where they engaged in the study of language, civics, art, and music, besides such feminine specialties as needlework, homemaking, and kindergartening. If they were gnawed by a hankering to teach, then for four years they attended the sessions of the *Lehrerinnenseminar,* which prepared them for service in the elementary school.

For those young women who made so bold as to aspire some day to grace a hall of higher learning, none of these academies provided the necessary preparation, which is to say a schooling equal to that obtained by the boys. For such light they usually studied at the *Lyzeum* until they turned thirteen, whereupon they moved into a higher grove, the *Studienanstalt.* Here the gentle sex came into its own. Like their hardier brothers in the *Gymnasium,* they could concentrate their intellectual appetite on Latin and Greek. Or, if the mood lay upon them, they could indulge themselves in the specialties of the *Oberrealschule,* namely, mathematics, the natural sciences, and the modern languages. Or if they preferred, they could steer the middle course of the *Realgymnasium* with its compulsory Latin and the living tongues, but without Greek.

Although Germany's secondary school had been altered and ameliorated on various occasions, the clutch of criticism remained upon it. There was, for one thing, its unapologetic stress on things cerebral. Like all secondary schooling, Germany's was suspect at all times and everywhere to the generality of men, which is to say the nonintellectual—nevertheless, some of its most insistent belaborers on this score were men of learning themselves. Nor was its lingering support of the classic tradition calculated to win it friends. What was needed—so the contention ran—was not a knowledge of a world that used to be, but of the world that actually is, its everyday affairs, its trade and industry, its politics, economics, science, technology, and all the other elements that make it function for good or ill. What was needed even more, patriots insisted, was to put the secondary school on a truly national basis, with lessons aplenty on the virtues and values of German life and culture. Finally, there were doubts about a school beyond the reach of the numerous middle and nether folk, however intelligent and dowered God had made them. To make an end of such discrimination, let there be, it was urged, "one people and one school," an *Einheitsschule,* which is saying: a single coherent organization, not unlike our own, with a basic elementary school for all and a secondary superstructure so diversified in its offerings that it should satisfy the needs and talents of every German, male and female.

Though the young people in the secondary school were select and their number, hence, confined, this does not mean that for the multitude of Germans formal learning came to an end with their exit from the lower school. The fact is a good many of them continued in one way or another to obtain instruction. It was for such ambitious ones that what we now call the continuation school set up shop. Reaching back into the seventeen hundreds, its first representatives showed themselves, not unlike those of the American high school, as a sort of postgraduate extension of the required lower learning. Its classes convened an hour or so of a Sunday, and the students, occupied on weekdays with making their living, came of their own volition, though under the influence, no doubt, of some paternal prompting. Such ventures were, of course, few, and in a day when book learning for the common people was still regarded with disfavor, they made slow headway. Nevertheless, they persisted, and as the antagonism toward the public enlightenment of the masses relaxed, the idea of giving them a chance to advance themselves beyond the confines of the ordinary schooling picked up power and momentum. By the middle years of the nineteenth century such enterprise was no longer the exception, but the rule. Indeed, so highly were its benefits adjudged that in Germany's more forward-looking states and municipalities, attendance at the sessions of a continuation school, or some meet equivalent, was ordained.

The earliest juridic words of any note in this connection are recorded in a statute designed to put the industry of certain trades and crafts under regulation. Framed in 1869, it summoned employers to grant those of their workers who were subject "to attendance at a local or state continuation school" sufficient free time to enable them to do their duty. In addition, the measure gave notice the boys and girls "engaged in commercial pursuits" and of an age less than eighteen could be compelled to study in a continuation school, whether communal, guild, or otherwise. Such instruction, however, was to be dispensed "only at such hours on Sunday as will not interfere with the main church services. . . . " With a change here and a modification there, the ordinance of 1869 made its way later on into the laws of the Empire. In fact, as the years rolled on and German industry grew to a formidable proportion, the compulsory continuation school came to be regarded, like the army and Wagnerian opera, as an indispensable organ of the national life.

In 1914, on the eve of the First World War, Germany's continuation schools were enjoying a robust vitality. Though they were the national style, they revealed themselves, nevertheless, in a variety of forms. They differed not only in the subjects they taught; they differed even in the number of years they exacted from their learners. Bavaria, for example, demanded no less than four, but Württemberg, ever easygoing, contented itself with two. It was in the city of Munich, the cultured Bavarian capital, that the continuation school fetched its greatest renown. The work, for the most part, of Georg Kerschensteiner, a man of parts in German pedagogy, particularly in the territory of administration, the Munich program called for an amalgamation of vocation and general studies. Did a youth, for example, earn his keep as an apprentice tailor? Then during his hours at school his teachers rehearsed him in the knacks and knowledge of his trade. He worked with needle and thread; he cut cloth, made buttonholes, and he took fittings. At the same time he studied materials, styles, and technical drawing. On the other hand, was the student an aspiring barber? Then for three hours every week he performed his operations under the expert eye of his instructor, himself a master chirotonsor. He snipped and shampooed his patients' locks; he lathered and shaved their beards. If, in the process, he chanced to nick them, then he learned how to stay the hemorrhage, apply a sanitary balm, and apologize politely. But whether he was a barber or a tailor, or of any other calling, he was made at all times to familiarize himself with arithmetic, bookkeeping, composition, religion, and gymnastics. Munich's continuation schools were of three kinds, namely, industrial, commercial, and general. The industrial specialists catered to machinists, woodworkers, printers, and the like. Those dealing in commercial endeavor fell into a number of divisions, in illustration, food, and provisions; draperies and textiles; banking and insurance; and porcelain, cutlery, and hardware. The general continuation schools, needless to say, paid no heed to such prosaic matters. Instead they devoted their instruction to the humanities, the arts, and the social and natural sciences.

8

Although by the prevailing standards of pedagogical weights and measures education in the First Reich ranked high, one need hardly say that its merits were not without its countervailing faults. Indeed, even amongst the Germans there was no lack of criticism, lay no less than professional. Unhappily, the bulk of it confined itself to words, and only a small portion, by contrast, found its way into actual application in practice.

The first reformer of any significant consequence to challenge the existing German educational order was Hermann Lietz. The son of an East Prussian landowner, he had been reared and educated in a most un-Prussian fashion, somewhat, in truth, in the easygoing manner of young Montaigne, under the guidance of an understanding tutor, and with plenty of leeway to enjoy the ever-present wonders of his father's spacious acres. Again as in the case of the illustrious Frenchman, when the advancing years removed Lietz from his rapturous adventuring at home to the strict and intransigent order of a distant secondary school, he found himself full of disconsonance and apprehension. A typical drill-house of the intellect, the school failed dismally to reach the boy with his deep yearning for active self-expression. The upshot was that he failed to respond to the familiar teaching ritual, a deficiency his instructors laid to his stupidity rather than to any shortcomings of their own.

Delivered by graduation from his bondage, Lietz installed himself at the University of Halle, where academic life was sweeter, and where, concentrating on philosophy and divine science, he made preparation to enter the holy calling. But the fates had other things in store for him, and in 1896 we see him, now *philosophiae doctor,* wielding his chalk and pointer at Abbotsholme, a pioneering progressive school in England. Two years following he retraced his tracks to the fatherland to establish a country boarding school or—to put it in its German collocation—a *Landerziehungsheim.* Like Abbotsholme, it was to be of the progressive order, in practice no less than principle. Sprung, on the one side, from his happy boyhood days on his father's farm, it glorified the countryside as an educational force; and derived, on the other side, from the anxiety and anguish he had endured at school, it put its taboo on the stiff and relentless intellectualism, so typical in those times, of the German secondary learning. In consequence, Lietz settled his school in the peace and tranquility of the country, in the heart of nature's eternal and mysterious promptings, far away from the rush and clutter of the city. And, in consequence, with attention to the learner's natural interests, Lietz, like Rousseau, took care to set before him a varied fare, judiciously balanced, and calculated to nourish and enhance him in body and spirit no less than mind. There was no want of cerebral industry, some of it of a rather high merit, but it was copiously supplemented with manual and practical work. There was physical and aesthetic activity, and there was individual and social work. What the father of the *Landerziehungsheim* hoped to attain, to put it in a figurative nutshell, was not merely the knower, but the seeker and doer as well.

Three years after he opened his first school, Lietz propagated a second, and three years after that, in 1904, he followed with a third. Presently his creations were breeding imitators not only in the Reich, but beyond its frontiers in Switzerland and Austria and elsewhere. For all their patent success, however, the new schools were but an atom in the endless pedagogic space, and their immediate effect on Germany's existing education was little more than nothing. But as the years edged on, the principles which fed their torch began to enjoy a benigner atmosphere. Still, it was not until after the birth of the Weimar Republic in 1919 when, young and full of newborn hopes, the regime undertook not only to give an ear to the doctrines invoked by Lietz and other free-spirited reformers, but even to encourage putting some of them to work in the nation's public schools.

In order to put his ideas into successful practice, Lietz sought teachers of the finest cut, creative and sophisticated men, dedicated wholeheartedly to the new education, and privy to the pulls and tugs which so often can play hob with the psyche of a growing boy. Among the several such men, two tower above the others, Gustav Wyneken and Paul Geheeb. Both held advanced pedagogical views, too advanced in certain particulars even for the liberal-minded Lietz, and in 1906, to allow themselves a freer hand, they disengaged themselves from his enterprise to found a country home school at Wickersdorf in the spruce-frocked slopes of Thuringia. Designated a Free School Community—a *Freie Schulge-meinde*—the new grove, though grounded on much of the Lietzian assumptions, was to be less conservative not only in education, but in its general political and social outlook as well. The school, as we discern it through the mist of many bygone years, became the work preeminently of Wyneken—indeed, after four years of collaborative effort Geheeb inaugurated a progressive seminary of his own.

An implacable antagonist of imposition, whether overt or subtle, Wyneken took the stand that Wickersdorf must be free, which is to say autonomous, in actuality and not merely in name. The Free School Community, he let it be understood, must be subordinate to no one, neither to church nor state nor society—not even, in truth, to the home. The family, he declared, somewhat reminiscent of Rousseau, "has obliged its young to ape their parents," and to the values of the elders Wyneken was openly contumacious. "Youth," he affirmed, with forge-hammer blows, "hitherto only an appendage of the older generation . . . is beginning to think for itself." It strives, he went on, to shape its own life by itself in order to be rid of "the indolent habits of its elders and the dictates of an ugly convention."

Like its Lietzian parent, only much more so, Wickersdorf was designed as a living society whose members enjoyed the right to make the rules under which they lived. To such an end they could speak their piece openly and freely, and even voice dissent, not just among themselves, but in the presence of their teachers. From such liberty of expression issued the "school community," a form of self-government which involved the entire school, faculty as well as students. When gathered in plenary congress, the school community enacted ordinances not merely on such common concerns as, say, gambling, drinking, smoking, and the like, but even on such questions as how many minutes a class ought to be kept in session, and whether the school should declare for an impromptu vacation.

In 1910, as has already been alluded to, Paul Geheeb seceded from Wickersdorf to come to grips with educational reform in a school of his own, the Odenwald Schule. Much less iconoclastic than the pyrotechnical Wyneken, Geheeb was the more philosophical of the two, a moderate, mellow man, who had drunk deeply from the wisdom of the ages, particularly from Goethe and Kant. Like its progressive forerunners, whether inspired by Lietz or Wyneken, Odenwald radiated the values and inclinations of its founder. Its broad purpose, like theirs, was to cultivate the human personality, to nurture and ripen the young into well-balanced, social-minded beings able to understand life and to live it well. To bring this about, the school put its stock in the progressive theorems, but with a number of amendments and inventions of its own. There was, for one thing, the familiar program of study, work, and play, but with a much deeper immersion in artistic experience, actual no less than vicarious. Like Wickersdorf, Odenwald cherished a high regard for the rights of youth, and like the former, the latter entertained a system of self-government wherein, in point of fact, the students had the last say not only in running their affairs, but also in coming to grips with those who broke the rules. So confident was Geheeb in the common sense of his youngsters that he reserved no veto power for himself.

What set Odenwald apart from its predecessors, however, besides the manifestation of an extraordinary esprit de corps, was its adoption of coeducation. At a time when the integration of the sexes with full and equal rights and responsibilities for girls was belabored with antagonisms not only in the Reich, but in other enlightened European cultures as well, Geheeb introduced it boldly and unblushingly at Odenwald. There ensued the usual moral alarms and tititlating whispers, but in the end coeducation held its ground, and for this triumphant achievement Germany's educational memoirists still honor the name of Paul Geheeb.

The years saw Odenwald attain renown throughout the world, and children came to it from all directions, from the Americas in the West to India and China in the East. In the First Reich its influence in remaking and improving the public learning was only meager—such is the usual way of the cultural lag. But Odenwald outlived the Empire, and in a chastened successor, the Weimar Republic, some of its revelation found a sympathetic echo in the renovation of the nation's public education. Unhappily, like the Republic itself, Odenwald, was suffocated by the Nazi supermen.

At this point it may well be asked, how comes it that imperial Germany, known everywhere for the exactions and restraints it placed upon the young, was yet tolerant of so much free-and-easy progressivism, while at the same time France, the mother of liberty, fraternity, and equality, permitted very little tinkering with the established pedagogical mechanism? The bald truth is that the rigid national centralization of the French was too formidable a yoke to allow much deviation, however desirable. In the fatherland, by contrast, there was no national centralization to speak of and, within limits of sense and decorum, each province—Prussia, Baden, Bavaria, and the others—was free to deal with education as it saw fit, though all too often Prussia, like the Kaiser's moustache, set the national style. In any case, had a schoolmaster been mad enough to make himself a menace to the national weal, the authorities lacked no means to calm him. Finally, there remains the matter of standards and examinations. Despite the freedom and gratifications they enjoyed in their schooling, in the end the students at the new schools were made to submit to the same state examinations as their comrades in the public nurseries of knowledge. As in France, these examinations granted no amnesty to incompetence.

CHAPTER 17

ENGLAND

While the Prussians were laying down the proposition that schools were state institutions, subject to state direction and control, the English in contrast entertained the notion that schooling the young was a strictly personal matter and not at all a seemly concern of government. Consequently, where the former went on to quarry a national school system, novel for its time and enormously efficient, the latter hung back until well into the nineteenth century before it braved its first steps in the national direction.

The reasons for England's dawdling are not hard to come upon. The first among Western nations to rise from the embers of imperial Rome, England was also the first to acquire a measure of self-government and, by the same token, a horror of bureaucracy and centralized authority. While French and Prussian sovereigns of the eighteenth century were immuring themselves in their absolute monarchies, the English were putting their confidence in their cabinet and Parliament. Nowhere had personal freedom attained a greater prospering. "The English," observed Voltaire, are "a nation fond of liberty," a land whose "people think freely and nobly, unrestricted by servile fear." It was a liberty, he might have added, which was enjoyed not only in high and mighty places, but which reached into every county and borough, even, indeed, into the meanest one-road hamlet.

Did the English cherish a high regard for personal freedom? Then they also cherished a deep aversion toward national regulation. Let Frederick fling out his fiats, his endless codes and regulations, to bind the waking and sleeping hours of every Prussian. As such things go, they had their place, no doubt—but not in England. There reigned a policy of let-it-alone, which is to say, a minimum of governmental control and interference not only in the affairs of trade and commerce, but in every human enterprise.

Where Frederick held that the state was all, and that its people existed solely for the execution of its purpose, whether in peace or war, as late even as the current century the English were being palsied lest "the Juggernaut of bureaucracy might roll over the liberties of local authorities." Where Frederick made all education subservient to the state and proclaimed that the essence of its function was to mold citizens to serve its needs and interests, the English dreaded that state action in education would effect precisely this result. "A general State education," asseverated John Stuart Mill in 1859, "is a mere contrivance for molding people to be exactly like one another; and as the mold in which it casts them is that which pleases the predominant power of government . . . it establishes a despotism over the mind leading . . . to one over the body."

The government's easygoing policy of exerting as little pressure as possible reaped an abundant harvest. Not a little because of it the English enjoyed gratifications beyond those of any other folk in Christendom. Their political freedom, for all its imperfections, was without parallel. Their trade boomed both at home and abroad. The breeder of wealth and power, "it made the difference," as Defoe remarked, "between one nation and another." Their textile industry underwent one revolution after another from the introduction of Arkwright's water frame in 1769 to Hargreaves's jenny in the year following, and Compton's mule a decade later. And what went for textiles went also for engineering, metallurgy, and mining. During the eighteenth century the English became Europe's foremost producers of iron and its most prodigious users. They spanned the Severn with the world's first iron bridge; they floated the first iron ship; and they built roads of rail to haul their iron from the mines. Meanwhile, James Watt perfected the steam engine, which, harnessing its power to industry, presently conjured up the factory, and thereby wrought still another revolution.

By 1714 the first creative surge of English science was spent. Boyle had left the earth, and Cavendish was not yet on it. Sir Isaac Newton, its most glorious representative, had done his work, though he continued to preside over the Royal Society until death took him off in 1727. Yet, even if, for the time being, the light of science was of a minor candlepower, it was nevertheless not without significance. An improved midwifery, to single out a homely example, introduced more infants safely into the world, while lying-in hospitals helped them to surmount life's first fatal hazards. The general effect, taking one thing with another, was a slight but ponderable gain in population.

In the meantime, the old religious frictions were slowly yielding to the emollient of a greater tolerance. The English Church remained, of course, the realm's one legal and established church, and for anyone aspiring to a place of even modest preferment, acceptance of her rites and dogmas was still prerequisite. But the disposition to ram the church's tenets down men's throats had lost much of its old-time heat. In fact, apart from Holland and Prussia, no other European power countenanced so much religious freedom. Once stoned and spat upon, and even jailed for their stubborn nonconformity, Quakers now assembled freely in their meeting chambers to commune in their silent way with God, while Baptists and Unitarians betook themselves to tabernacles of their own to worship Him as they saw fit. Even Deists, who renounced a personal Heavenly Father, and hence saw no use in buttonholing a divinity with prayer, were vouchsafed the pleasure of their convictions and the right to voice them without hindrance.

The unfolding religious forbearance was more than matched by the growth of a vigorous press. The way was paved as far back as 1695 when Commons had the good sense to reject the renewal of the Licensing Act which, adopted some thirty years earlier, had sought to throttle the publication of seditious and heretical opinions. A few years after, in 1702, appeared the first English daily. Tiny, and printed on only one side of its few sheets, it merchanted the local tidings, portentous to its readers but now forgotten, from their weddings, births, and departures, their increase in goods and livestock, to the woes and scourges of this one and the joys and triumphs of that one, and as per immemorial journalistic custom, the antics of the weather. Presently political views were ventured. In 1705 the first political pamphlet hove into view; and within five years the more enterprising gazettes had become not only the purveyors of news, but the ventilators of political controversy as well. Step by step the press progressed: in 1771 the right to print Parliamentary debates was won; another five years and the first Sunday paper was upon us; and five years following, the London *Times* put its first number into type.

From newspapers and pamphlets to books was just another stride. In those days as in these, discourses on faith and piety entertained a capital audience. Works of philosophical pretension, however, and especially those of a skeptical flavoring, say, Hume's *Treatise on Human Nature*, got scarcely any notice. But as the country increased in space and wealth, and as its trade and commerce reached out farther and farther, a new interest in the world began to fever. Before long, in fact, the demand for travel books was challenging even the old standbys on goodness and godliness. Their readers were not usually of a literary taste, but rather men of affairs with a judicious eye for untapped markets, and sailors who found such works instructive as they pointed their vessels into the fringes of strange and uncharted waters. Some authors, it is true, essayed to furnish diversion and entertainment rather than information. Of these the bulk, whether literary or didactic, have long since strayed from the memory of man—all, that is, saving an extraordinary two, *Robinson Crusoe* and *Gulliver's Travels*, which despite the weight of their antiquity, continue to attract an admiring audience.

2

All these forces—science and invention, the revolutionized industry, its mills and workers, its progeny of social and economic bafflement, the slow but steady rise of religious tolerance, and especially the proliferation of the written word—bore soon or late on education. A fair proportion of the people could read and write, but to the overwhelming number, and especially those of low estate, literacy remained a closed art. To induce some light into this darkness, a greater leeway was extended to non-Anglican schoolmen. In 1700, for example, the courts declared against a bishop's power to license schoolmasters, and thereby in effect hold England's lower learning under Anglican domination. Fourteen years later the church suffered an even harder thrust when Parliament exempted elementary schools from the strictures of religious conformity. Thenceforward dissenters were free to open and operate their halls of lower learning to suit their creed and conscience. As a result, the land presently found itself experiencing a mild boom in primary education. The dame school, which enjoyed a pretty good following in some parts of Colonial America, succeeded even more gaudily in the mother-land—there, in fact, it was still offering its instruction to the young far on into the nineteenth century. More numerous, however, were the so-called "charity schools." They popped up all over England, like herds of toadstools after a summer shower. The first ones were the work mostly of dissenters; but soon there followed an outpouring of Anglican effort; and as more years took off there were even a number of joint undertakings.

The most formidable of such academic Salvation Armies was the Society for the Promotion of Christian Knowledge—the SPCK—a blood cousin of the Society for the Propagation of the Gospel which performed overseas and to whose constructive idealism reference has already been made. The work of the two was pretty much alike, namely, to teach the poor their letters and numbers, the catechism and prayer book, and the rewards to be plucked from a clean and upright life. Not uncommonly they clothed them, and sometimes they victualed them. Though the society was national, with its headquarters in London, not a little of its success issued from its talent to inflame a lusty local ardor. Not only did it prevail upon small shopkeepers and artisans to make donations to its funds, but by enlisting their services as organizers and directors—even, indeed, as superintendents—it gave them an honor and dignity to which they were not insensible. In consequence, they made its affairs a matter of personal concern, and they worked powerfully to bring them success.

Side by side with the propagators of Christian knowledge labored the Society for the Reformation of Manners. Like the first, the second carried on to promote an exemplary Christian living. In the main, however, it addressed its pedagogy to the attainment not of literacy, but morality, and it devoted itself not entirely to the care and edification of the young, but more often to the improvement of their elders. As its name suggests, it specialized in putting down untowardness of every sort, particularly such malefactions as drinking, gambling, swearing, and Sabbath breaking. To this purpose it broadcast many tons of tracts—"kind cautions" it called them—directing them to all, but especially to such overt offenders as chimney sweeps, teamsters, sailors, and those ignoring the Day of Rest. Just how many it squired permanently into rectitude has escaped the statistical scientists—the chances are, not many. But its industry, nonetheless, was colossal. In a single year in London, for example, its watchdogs effected the prosecution of not quite 100,000 persons, a record which—allowing for time and circumstance—remains unmatched in moral annals even by the massed accomplishment of Calvin in all his term of Genevan glory.

Another boost for the education of the lower orders was the Sunday school. First heard of about the middle of the eighteenth century, it never amounted to much until 1780 when Robert Raikes, a printer in the city of Gloucester and editor of its *Journal*, enlisted it for the cause of human improvement. Despite the skepticism usually credited to men of his calling, Raikes was evidently of a soft and sensitive heart. The intolerable condition of the Gloucester poor, and especially their children, appalled him. He had observed them wallowing in the muck of their hideous haunts, filthy and ragged and, he let it be known, abandoned to vice and corruption. Of a Sunday, when the mills were still, and parents sought release in booze and bawdiness, the situation was even more malodorous, for then, left to shift for themselves, their young had no brake put upon them at all. Set upon salvaging these "little heathens," Raikes hired a woman for a shilling every Sunday to oversee a small posse of them and to teach them the catechism and the ABC's.

Meanwhile, in the *Journal* Raikes started a powerful crusade for his project, arguing that Gloucester's conditions were a disgrace to all decent people and an affront to God. His original band steadily increased—pretty soon it grew to such proportion he had to seek more room to give it accommodation. To pump up interest in the movement as well as a flow of contributions, its partisans joined hands in the Society for the Establishment and Support of Sunday Schools. Their hopes fructified beyond their wildest dreams. By the century's last decade several thousand Sunday schools with at least half a million pupils were spreading their light not only in England, Wales, and Scotland, but in the Channel Islands of Guernsey and Jersey—even, believe it or not, in rebellious and rambunctious Ireland. Time was to see them cross the ocean to settle in the American Colonies. A Sunday school modeled on Raikesian lines was sighted as early as 1786 in Hanover County, Virginia, and another a year later in Charleston, South Carolina.

Thus the start and spread of the Sunday school. For all their success, Raikes's seminaries were harried by a hostile sentiment. Their religious endeavor, attempting to steer a neutral course, roused the ire of dogmatists on every side. The upper classes scoffed at them. To educate and repair the lowly, they contended, would blow up the social order—in fact, it might set off a revolution far more sinister than the one then raging in France. Even the poor, the Sunday school's chief beneficiaries, were nagged by worries and misgivings. For why would their betters bestow such gifts without harboring some dark and ulterior purpose? Why, indeed, but to dose them with just another sugar pill?

Yet, for all that, Sunday schools continued to roll on. The years saw them change, of course. By the latter nineteenth century nearly all of them had stripped off their educational trappings to become an out-and-out church enterprise. In consequence, implanting the fundamentals of creed became their paramount occupation. Instruction in writing virtually vanished, and so did that in spelling. Reading lingered, but its content, considerably watered, confined itself principally to Bible lessons. Even so, despite such diluents, until 1870, when the English at length braved the plunge into public, tax-supported, elementary education, the Sunday school remained one of the main sources of the poor man's learning.

3

Somewhat later than the altruism of Raikes was that of Robert Owen, the creator of the so-called infant school. A successful industrialist on the one hand, he was on the other a utopian messiah. He held a considerable stake in a lucrative cotton mill; yet he also panted for the coming of a socialist millennium.

Certain chroniclers have even set him down as the father of British socialism, an ancestry which, as usual with such designations, has provoked some skeptical coughs behind the hand. Like other advanced thinkers of his time, Owen had persuaded himself that our social croups and cancers could be alleviated and even routed by education. It was his belief that when an infant is launched into the universe, he is fundamentally good; unluckily, his environment soon slides him down the slippery road to sin and ruin. To forestall this, the thing to do was to start the child's education while he was still in pristine innocence. Convinced that pedagogy could tailor the man, Owen was even sure that "infants of one class could easily be formed into men of another class"—a proposition which bears some slight resemblance to the current one of psychological conditioning. By this route Owen hoped some day to stamp out that prodigy of evil by which orphanages and foundling homes, and even parents, farmed out their tender young to manufacturers. Not only did they consume themselves in sweatshops from twelve to thirteen hours a day for a term which generally ran for nine years, but—even worse—when their servitude was done, they had learned practically nothing, which is saying that in the years ahead they could anticipate only poverty and an early grave.

Owen took charge of his mill in 1800, and almost at once he laid plans to dispense his social therapy. What he dreamed of was an organization which would instruct and ameliorate not only the offspring of his workers, but even the workers themselves. But his partners had no hankering for such idealism, and they put down a formidable foot against it. At length, in 1809, Owen managed to open a school, not, it is true, for infants, but for the more elderly boys and girls, ranging in years from six to twelve. Seven years later, after he had bought out his partners, Owen established the world's first infant school. Intended, as its name implies, for tots—its beginners generally had celebrated their third birthday—the school declared that within its walls no child was to be "annoyed with books." Instead, he was to be edified by a variety of objects discreetly displayed around him, from pictures and models to maps and the safer and more sanitary fauna and flora. His morals and habits were, of course, under constant watch, but under no circumstances was he ever to be rattanned. All of Owen's scholars, regardless of their vintage, were made to engage in dancing and singing—even in military drill which, mindful of the Napoleonic scourge then on the loose across the Channel, Owen fancied would aid "in the country's defense."

Owen took a rather high pride in his infant school, and he applied himself with a lavish diligence to making its services as good as possible. The years saw him evolve into an ardent connoisseur of pedagogy. Granted, he never formulated any of its important theorems; on the other hand, he was a judicious borrower, notably from Pestalozzi and his great disciple Fellenberg, then the two most impressive schoolmen on earth. Searching them out in their native Switzerland, Owen put their views and practice under scrutiny, admiring the vast kindliness of the one, but even more, the administrative competence of the other, and in the end trooping back to England, convinced more than ever of the power of education to lift us all to a better human society.

Far from despising the spotlight of publicity, particularly when it came to showing off his favorite beliefs, Owen labored indefatigably, both in speech and in print, to expose their merit. As a result, his notion of conditioning the very young at school gradually obtained a following, and in 1818 an infant school, conducted by one of his own experts, was opened at Westminster. But Owen's socialism, his free thought, and his many other nostrums to save the human race, won him no friends. Indeed, when he insisted not merely on airing his views, but on putting them into practice, even his supporters in education took alarm. Presently, in fact, he had affrighted a sufficient number of them to cause his ousting from the school he had founded.

Meanwhile, Samuel Wilderspin had turned his mind toward the infant school. He was a man of murky mood, far less beguiled by dulcet thoughts than the optimistic Owen, and he cherished little confidence in the power of good works. Instead, he had long since persuaded himself that man was inherently depraved, an evil fellow full of the Old Adam, and doomed nine times out of ten to spend eternity in a Hell which was deep and hot. It was in this spirit that he confronted his pupils. Where Owen had spared his infants from the annoyance of books, Wilderspin overwhelmed them with the printed word. He not only taught them how to read and write and cipher; he also weighed upon them with a vast cargo of information, from the table of weights, measures, and money to the manners of the birds and beasts, social and otherwise, the rudiments of science, and the salient declarations of the New Testament. Although he was not disdainful of employing actual objects to promote the piling up of knowledge, Wilderspin was at bottom a pedant, displaying all the familiar marks which signalize that dismal clan. Facts, facts, facts and words, words, words—such was the essence of his pedagogic stock. His schools, as a result, were little more than drill sheds.

Like Owen, Wilderspin had a pretty hand for public exudation. To advertise his doctrines he spoke and wrote at almost endless length. Mr. Owen's institution, he let it be heard again and again, was merely an asylum, whereas he alone possessed "the merit of inventing what is known . . . as the Infant System." His extravagant claims, as usual, attracted believers in droves, and his enterprise, hence, was a great success. In 1824 he founded the Infant School Society. With Lord Lansdowne as its president, it carried on, immensely admired and effectively successful. Wilderspin's version of infant education propagated with a lush abandon not only in its land of origin, but even in the bogs of Scotland—even, indeed, in the American republic, where it is still celebrated as one of the forerunners of the present-day public school.

4

In 1797 Andrew Bell, an Anglican holy clerk, put forth a monograph on the use of boys as teachers, or "monitors." He had essayed such a method while in charge of an orphanage in India, and he had come to regard it well, so well, in truth, that he was sure it could be put into useful service in England. A year later, or thereabout, Joseph Lancaster, a schoolmaster of Quaker persuasion, and the son of a redcoat in America's war with the motherland, opened a school for the London poor wherein he worked out a procedure very similar to the one reported on by the Reverend Dr. Bell. Lancaster's establishment was an instantaneous hit, and soon pretty nearly everybody was talking about it. To advertise its wonders even more, and particularly to propagate similar seminaries elsewhere, Lancaster toured the land, discharging speech after speech in its behalf. Dowered in the use of a convincing rhetoric, Lancaster exercised not a little influence, and it was not long before his pleas were generating monitorial schools all over the realm. Though he declared for order and system, Lancaster was fired by a powerful, altruistic zeal, and in 1808, when it overcame him completely, he landed in the debtor's dungeon. But he did not stay there long. Wealthy admirers got him free, and with their help and money, he set up the Royal Lancasterian Institution which was designed, one can guess, to promote the monitorial revelation.

Meanwhile, Dr. Bell was not disposed to retreat into obscurity. Lancaster, he charged, was an imposter, and his method a mere parroting of his own. Both men attracted supporters in droves, and although it is clear today that each had come upon his system single-handedly—that, as a matter of fact, even in those days the use of monitorial instruction was of a hoary vintage—their adherents showed no inclination to such belief. Instead, they belayed one another fiercely, and for years they flayed the air with uproar, not only over who had hatched the idea in the first place, but also over the faults and merits of the views entertained respectively by Bell and Lancaster. The fact that these worthies worshiped in different temples, that the one followed the established Anglican rite, and was even an ordained Anglican representative of God, while the other was a Quaker, bore inevitably on the controversy, turning it in the course of time into a war of sects as well as pedagogues. Both sides were organized, the Lancastrians as the British and Foreign Society, and the Bellists as the National Society for Promoting the Education of the Poor in the Principles of the Established Church, with the Archbishop of Canterbury as its first president. As usual in such contests for the minds of men, the fray produced a vast flood of propaganda, much of it in afterlight more comic than grave, and nearly all of it today pretty well forgotten. None of it did any serious damage to either side—on the contrary, because it served to give the method a robust and picturesque publicity, it actually aided in the long run in forwarding the schooling of the masses.

Pedagogically, the two men differ only slightly. Both introduced their scholars to writing by putting upon them to design their ABCs in sand—a device older than Christendom itself. Later, when their fingers were more powerful, the children undertook to engrave their communiqués on slates. Bell's boys used books, but not Lancaster's; instead, they learned how to read and spell from a huge chart hung high on the wall and within eye range of every pupil. Lancaster was vastly awed by quantity. Does a boy learn to spell a hundred words a day? Then in two hundred days he will have bagged a horde of twenty thousand, and in ten years at least a couple of hundred thousand. Similarly in arithmetic and reading. By the same score, the superior schoolmaster is the one confronting the largest flock, which is to say not Socrates with his handful, but Lancaster with his infinite divisions. Both Lancaster and Bell were, of course, concerned with moral and religious considerations, but where the one dwelt upon such matters in a bland, nonsectarian way, the other descended upon them dogmatically with catechism and prayer book, with promises of harps and halos for the good and brimstone for the wicked.

Of the two men, Lancaster seems to have possessed the greater inventiveness. He had, like his coworshiper William Penn, an abhorrence of physical violence. Upon evil pupils he applied no corrective birch; instead, he badgered their psyche with public ridicule. He would discommode them with a heavy wooden slab draped around their neck; or he would shackle their legs and make them hobble about until exhaustion felled them. But let us be charitable, for at bottom the man was more benign than punitive. Meritorious boys he rewarded handsomely with cards of eulogy, gauds of merit, tickets worth cash at the school exchange, and—in exemplary cases—the honor of holding some school or classroom office. Such lures the graver Bell discountenanced, and when his followers resorted to them at all, they were wrapped in doubt and reservation. Finally, there lurked in Lancaster something of a seer. Like the illustrious Owen, he put a tremendous stock in the power of education to hoist the masses above their lowly plane. Not so, however, the Bell men. Learning, like malt liquor, they warned, had to be taken cautiously. "There is a risk," they announced, "of elevating those who are doomed to the drudgery of daily labor above their station, and rendering them unhappy and discontented with their lot."

The monitorial business, as has been hinted, was so called because of its use of monitors. Under its technique a master would ground a number of older and—if possible—brighter lads in knowledge, each of whom would then seek to implant it in a small gang of his subordinates. Monitors discharged their duties not only as junior Aristotles, but as academic choremen whose duties were of a protean sort. There was a monitor to run the roll, a monitor to line paper, a monitor in charge of inkpots, and a monitor to stand sentinel over books and slates. A monitor policed the wardrobe, and a monitor queried and promoted the rank and file. There was even, so to speak, an archbishop of the diocese, a monitor over monitors. Because of the monitorial organization, a single school-master sufficed to give instruction to hundreds of pupils—even a thousand, it has been reported. The monitorial system, declared the poet Samuel Taylor Coleridge, was an "incomparable machine," a "vast moral steam engine." Conducted thus on a staggering wholesale scale, the monitorial system was also astonishingly cheap. Lancaster prided himself for having taught his wards for $1.06 per head per annum, though Bell, in 1814, managed to shave his competitor's figure to an even dollar, all of which, of course, helped to make the system powerfully attractive.

From the vantage point of our current pedagogic enlightenment, the monitorial schools, it must be plain, were transparently defective. Carried on in the manner of an assembly line, they were compelled, for weal or woe, to stress system and standardization. Their squads of children goose-stepped to their stations, and they returned to their benches in the same measured manner. Singly or in concert they rose on command, and they sat down on command. They looked, listened, and spoke on order; they removed their caps and showed their slates on order—one might readily imagine they scratched their heads on order. Compared with the light of Pestalozzi, then beckoning to the heights in Switzerland, the monitorial scheme was of a lower order, a technique freighted with repetition, drill, and rote, a hocus pocus whereby teaching and learning were reduced to a hollow formula.

But the system bore some good things too. Dealing with their amazingly numerous flock, the monitorians were obliged to give some earnest attention to the nature of their setting—the classroom, its appurtenances and equipment. Lighting, ventilation, seating arrangement, noise reduction, sanitation, and similar concerns, hitherto scarcely ever thought about, now became subjects for serious consideration. To the monitorians history has credited the invention of new and better equipment, such as slates, blackboards, and writing desks. They put subject matter under a regime of order, and they classified their pupils. Their use of the organized recitation, though overborne with commands and controls, was nevertheless much more efficient than the flyblown and laborious method of individual instruction whereby a schoolmaster operated on his patients one by one, flagging each one on when he was successful, and not unusually, fanning him when he failed. And to make an end, because of their need for masters able to employ their methods, the monitorians brought to public notice some of the advantages to be had from the training of teachers.

The monitorial system was enormously successful. From Britain it overran the Continent, from the lands that rim the Mediterranean to the Scandinavian north, the Netherlands, and various parts of Germany. When it showed itself in France, not only was it granted aid from the royal purse; presently its virtues were lauded even in verse, to become in 1818 the French Academy's prize-winning poetic masterpiece of the year.

Nowhere was the monitorial idea given a grander welcome than in the United States. Brought into New York in 1806, the system, which happened to be that of Lancaster, spread like pollen before the wind, and within a generation it had made its way into several of the larger cities from Massachusetts to Indiana to Georgia. In 1818 Lancaster, then in the fullness of his pedagogic grandeur, appeared in America himself. Received in an expansive manner, like a prophet of a new religion, he addressed himself to the promotion of his system, writing and lecturing about its miracles, and even haranguing the people's surrogates in Congress, little dreaming at the time that he was fated to finish his days in debt and disillusion. His end came in 1838 in the streets of New York when a horse and carriage ran him down.

The monitorial system's most telling trait, and the most appealing to its partisans, whether Bellist or Lancastrian, was its cheapness. Because of it, the boon of learning, however tawdry, was put within reach of almost every boy and girl. Brotherhoods in educational philanthropy, whatever their special mission, were the system's natural beneficiaries, for by the magic of its almost infinitesimal cost, they were able to stretch their charity beyond their fondest hopes. Thus they found themselves in a position to bring their instruction within the range of audiences so large they seem in the blur of faraway time to have been fantastic and almost unearthly. Nor was the fact that the lower classes were willing to put their young to school without its lesson. Once and for all it scotched the assertion then commonly noised about that the poor would do nothing to school their offspring, and that these, in truth, were congenitally incapable of profiting thereby. Finally, let it not be overlooked that by accustoming thousands of people to paying something for education, if only a pittance, the monitorial schools helped to pave the way eventually for taxation.

The spectacle of the nether multitude articling their progeny to their books was not lost on the more liberal politicos. Before long not a few of them were joining the heralds of human progress to give Bell and Lancaster their highest endorsement. Some, in fact, completely bowled over by the phenomenon, laid the whole thing to God. Whether divine or not, the monitorial enlightenment set off a voluble discussion of the whole question of public education in both the republic and the motherland, and presently as the conviction grew that the cost of educating the masses need not be out of reach, the notion that government should help to square at least a part of the bill became less repugnant.

The English braved their first step in this direction in 1833 when Parliament disbursed £20,000, allowing slightly more than half of it to the National Society (since it was Anglican) and the rest to the rival British and Foreign Society, to give a hand in the erection of schoolhouses for the poor. A mere molecule, of course, in the measureless sea, the grant nevertheless represents the historic beginning of national aid to England's lower learning, a financial affair which today burgeons with vast millions of pounds sterling. Other acts soon followed. Some spawned committees, some statistics, and some yielded money. In time Parliament broached the national purse less timidly and more frequently. In 1838 it augmented its yearly grant to £30,000; three years following it voted an annual subvention to establish schools of design in a number of manufacturing centers; another five years and it found itself applying its yearly contribution not only to the building of schools, but also to their maintenance. Meanwhile the lawgivers had begun to broaden the field of operation. In the early 1840s, for example, Her Majesty's Inspectors of Schools came into being. In 1845 Parliament gave its countenance to the so-called pupil-teacher system. Modeled upon the monitorial practice, it was at bottom an apprentice method of reinforcing the nascent birchman with at least a rudimentary knowledge of his craft. Soon after, in 1847, to the resounding hoots and catcalls of the opposition, Parliament declared for the nationalizing of education. But the proposal to make education free and compulsory got precisely nowhere, and before it fructified another generation had departed. Soon after midcentury a Department of Science and Art made its appearance, and in 1856, hard upon its heels, came a State Department of Education. It was not of an impressive power, and for a time it confined its energies chiefly to lesser transactions.

Meanwhile, with more and more sterling flowing from the government's vault, some of the lawgivers, assailed by doubts and incredulities, began to wonder just what their money was obtaining. As a result, a commission headed by the Duke of Newcastle was appointed in 1858 to put the country's lower learning under search and study. From its report, issued three years later, came the so-called "payment by results" system, a device by which schools got their grants not in accordance with their actual needs, but on the basis of the results fetched by their scholars in their yearly examinations. An object of challenge and dissent even before it came into being, the scheme did a base disservice to the advancement of the teaching art. For by the law's demands the task which now burdened a master was not to ignite the torch of learning, but to cram facts into his pupils and to drive them home unsparingly so that on a fateful tomorrow his recruits could muster them in profusion to the gratification of the state's examiners and, consequently, the school's hopeful bursar.

For all the Parliamentary searching and speechifying, and for all the grants in aid, with or without strings, the lower learning was insufficient to the nation's need. Next to that of Prussia, or even Massachusetts and New York, it was discernibly second-rate. In older days, when ruling the land was the business of the few, this made little difference. But those times of easy assurance were gone. The right to vote had been extended in 1832 and again in 1867—indeed, around the corner there even lurked the day when manhood suffrage would be free and universal, when, in fact, even coal diggers and garbage men could aspire to public office. Thus confronted, the gentlemen of Parliament, spurred by the judicious and the farseers, undertook to instruct and enlighten their "future masters." To this end they voted the Elementary Education Act of 1870.

The measure, taking one thing with another, laid the foundation for England's elementary education. To propagate schools more generally, and especially in the numerous spots where so far none had prevailed, or where they had fallen into a low state, the law provided for the election of school boards. Empowered to make regular levies on the local taxpayers, they were charged with the business of providing the young with an adequate elementary schooling. The centers of learning which the boards maintained came to be known as "board schools," a term which in American usage corresponds roughly to "public schools." Of a secular tone, the new schools were allowed, nevertheless, to conduct lessons in religion, but such traffic was to be nondenominational. Moreover, did a parent object to exposing his heir to even such a mild nonsectarian piety? Then the lad was to be excused to let him give consideration to matters more agreeable to his mundane-minded elder.

To the hordes of denominational schools—"voluntary schools" in the words of the English—for so long the almost single purveyors of the country's elementary learning, the state continued to show an amicable deference. Like the board schools, they shared in national aid, but from the local pocket they got not a farthing.

The framers of the Act of 1870 had aspired, so they remarked, to make England's primary education "universal, gratuitous, and compulsory." But they fell short of the mark, and the schools were not free, though their fees, to be sure, were slight. Only the very poor were exempt from its levy, their tuition being charged to the school board. The century was eighty years old before attendance at the sessions of the elementary school, or some seemly equivalent, was made mandatory; and it was ninety-one before it was made free.

The combination of board and voluntary enterprise, the one secular, the other sectarian, but both nourished out of the national till, gave the English the so-called dual system. Though the state regarded these institutions as equals, the times were still sufficiently pious to give the religious school an investiture of respectability. Indeed, in a day when the faithful were battening down the hatches in the face of the roaring hurricane of science, and in particular the blasts of the dreadful Darwin, the voluntary schools appeared, at first blush, to have something of an advantage. But it soon became evident that the board schools had an advantage all their own. Kept on their legs not only by national grants, but also by taxes laid locally, they mined their resources to good effect by offering their clients a superior schooling. Consequently, it soon became the fashion for parents to place their children under the care and tutelage of the board schools—in fact, as the century neared its end the secular schools were serving some seven out of every ten of the nation's eligible young.

Needless to say, the Established Church found it hard to suffer such a cheerless spectacle, and to make an end of it, its men of God bespoke the assistance of their perennial friend, the Conservative party. The century was almost over when the Conservatives came to power, and presently, in 1897, they increased the capital of the voluntary establishments by a special governmental subsidy. But the religious schools were too far gone to benefit sufficiently from this transfusion, and so, in 1902, the government gave them a supplementary shot by allowing them an equal share of the local school taxes. At the same time, save in the larger municipalities, the administration of all schools, whether board or otherwise, was put under the eye of the county council. By these strokes the chasm between public and church schools was narrowed, and in the process the dual system was shaped into a comprehensive arrangement, publicly supported and controlled, which in its essence is still at hand.

5

Higher up in the realm of the secondary learning the taste for change was more finicky. Come into being in the Renaissance, the so-called grammar schools had increased over the centuries to several hundred. Nine of them, the Great Public Schools, as witness, Eton, Rugby, Harrow—to illustrate only a trinity— stood above the general run, an emblem of national pride and glory. Privately operated, the grammar school sustained itself with tuition fees, and not uncommonly with the friendly help of an endowment. For all their plentiful number, there was something sequestered about these schools. As in their springtime, so centuries later they entertained no passion to advance the enlightenment of the masses; instead, they reserved their cultivation mainly for those of high estate. Nor had they ever made any visible compromise with the demands of the modern world, especially its science and industry, its workrooms and its shops, a phenomenon whose educational aspirations they cried down almost unanimously as against the honor and dignity of their ancient classical tradition.

Against this staid convention there presently resounded the attack of two eminent laymen, Thomas Henry Huxley and Herbert Spencer, both stalwart Darwinians, the one a biologist, the other a philosopher, and both masters of a robust and resonant prose. The two men trained their guns, as one might suppose, on the imperious classics, and they called upon Britain's laggard schoolmen to open their eyes to the surging natural sciences, and to pay them due and proper heed in their teaching of the young. Although Huxley was doubtless the more tough-minded of the two, yet it was Spencer's powerful plea for instruction in the sciences which in the long, slow run of time ignited the public sentiment. His *Education*, put between covers in 1859, has since attained the stature of a classic, and it is for this reason that a place for a fuller exploration of its content has been set aside in later pages.

Time saw the pressure of the new culture grow more formidable, and by the middle years of the nineteenth century it had become insistent enough for Parliament to give it notice. The lawmakers took the field, warily enough, with the usual searching parties, in illustration, the Clarendon Commission which deliberated from 1861 to 1864 and the Taunton Commission which sat till some three years later. They investigated the houses of secondary learning very elaborately, the one concentrating its talents on the Great Public Schools, the other roving the whole broad dominion of more than nine hundred secondary schools. Their findings, which they spread in their usual official recitals, were far from exhilarating. An insufficiency of secondary schools laced the land, in cities as in country towns. The generality of grammar schools inclined toward snootiness, giving preference to the rich and high-toned over lesser folk. Draped in the spurious satin of a learning which once had been civilization's glory, but which was long since frayed, they bemused themselves, half-tranced, with the false values of a curriculum now shopworn and inadequate. Worse yet, their teaching masters, by and large, were not of notable gifts—all too often, indeed, they were of the shoddiest order. Even materially, things stood badly: buildings in decrepitude, mess halls and lodgings foul and full of smells, food too grisly to consume, and furniture that had done its effective service so long ago that not even the most grasping memory could recall precisely when.

The commissioners' words brewed a flood of controverted response, but aside from the Public School Act of 1868, which put endowments under rule and order, and the Endowed School Act of 1869, which placed the funded institutions under governmental vigilance, for a time no further lawmaking was hazarded. Plainly, what was needed to bring about a sweeping and satisfying improvement was not investigations, reports, and recommendations—not debate but revolution.

When it presently showed itself, it issued not from the ponderings of the Justinians on the Thames, but from the good sense of the men who ran the local school boards. It was in the hives of commerce and manufacturing, bustling municipalities like Birmingham, Manchester, and Sheffield, that the demand for a more spacious education, of a useful and practical sort, was most articulate. To give it heed and recognition a number of board schools began to enhance their offerings with instruction in advanced knowledge. It was, as it were, a postgraduate elementary education, and it represented, for the nonce, a triumphant invasion of a province hitherto reserved for the secondary learning. As the years rolled on, the endeavor increased, though never to any vast proportion—nor did it leap across the land into the smaller enclaves where farming still was, as it had been since time forgotten, the mainstay of everyday living.

The guardians of England's vaunted grammar school tossed the newcomer no kisses, but only frowns. It was, they protested, an upstart, an intruder into Academe's sacred vestibule—worse yet, it boded no good, for by the grace of its helpings from the public purse, local and national, it brought harassment to every private secondary fount in Britain. Even the laity was gnawed by misgivings. Tax-supported learning beyond the rudiments, as many of them saw it, was a luxury, and an ever-hungry one which could be sated only by more and more taxes. The controversy flared into full fire in 1901 when one Cockerton, an auditor for the local government, disallowed expenditures incurred by the London School Board in providing free science and art courses, on the ground that these were not elementary and hence not chargeable to the tax fund. When the case came to an airing in the court room, the bench declared against the school board.

The new secondary learning thus was shouldered out of the public fold—but only for a transient year. For in 1902 Parliament put upon the local government the duty to support instruction not, let it be noted, in secondary education, but "in subjects beyond the elementary work." Whatever the designation, whether secondary or higher elementary, there was no disinclination to sample its wares—in fact, within less than a decade more than three hundred such schools came upon the scene. The bulk of them, of course, performed their operations in the cities and the larger towns. Given to practical idealism, they frittered away no time on the ancient classics, but put their weight instead on a learning calculated in the years ahead to improve the chances of their alumni for money-making and success. As such studies took on shape and substance, the time an average child needed to bring them to terms was fixed at three years. Given the desire and a bit of luck, an English youngster, hence, could carry on academically in a tax-run local school until at least his eighteenth birthday.

Meanwhile, the older and more exclusive secondary schools were not forgotten. To them the Act of 1902 offered the balm of national aid. Did they accept the government's jingling comfort? Then they also accepted its right to lay down the terms and to pass judgment on their work. Such inspection was generally benign—nor was there any such purpose behind it as, say, that in Prussia to unify the schools. Instead, they were allowed to enjoy the gratification of their singularity, such being the English way. Then as now the boon of national aid exercised a powerful enchantment. As the years passed on, school after school yielded to the practice of supplementing its genteel traditions with the substance of good, hard English sterling. Before long, indeed, the practice became the rule.

6

In spite of Spencer's exhortation in the late fifties to snip the classical tie and tails from Britain's secondary learning, and to frock it instead in the sciences, in the main its Harrows and Rugbys, and similar elderly seminaries of learning, continued, as they had for the many generations preceding, to put the bulk of their intellectual investment in the ancient tongues and letters. Although it is no more than fair to remind ourselves that the masters urged their pupils to give a sportive vent to their animal spirits on the playing field, and that they struggled resolutely to impress the importance of good manners upon them, still, when all was said and done, what counted most was the drilling of the mind with the classical calisthenic.

It was in challenge to this narrow and outworn pedagogy that in 1889 Cecil Reddie founded Abbotsholme, a private school set in the serene and expansive comeliness of England's Derbyshire. The new grove was in several ways a reflection of its maker. A man of great inner harmony, respectful of the spirit as well as the brain, aggressive in a quiet sort of way, but capable of a self-chuckle every now and then, Reddie possessed the power to rouse and inspire. What he sought to bring forth at Abbotsholme—to lean a bit on his own words—was a youth "superior and fully developed in every respect," a lad capable of leadership not because of the accidents of birth and wealth, or the caprice of politics, but simply because of his competence.

Abbotsholme, designated in the phrase book of pedagogy as a country home school, which is to say, a boarding school situated in the country, confined its services to males ranging in years from five to sixteen. Its primary purpose, as it took care to make known, was not to weigh them down with knowledge. Rather, like the Athenians in their finest days, it sought to cultivate a well-balanced person, his body, mind, and emotions cooing in amicable concordance —in short, a well-adjusted, free-functioning individual, able and willing to reason and judge, whether by himself or with others. Unlike the Greeks of antiquity,

however, Abbotsholme harbored no disdain for practical work. Indeed, participation therein in some form or other, in the shop or on the land, was required.
Other differences set off Reddie's school from the English grammar school
tradition. Textbooks, for one, though they were resorted to, were subordinated,
nevertheless, to the realization which comes from intimate and firsthand investigation, and the recitation, then everywhere the reigning fashion, bowed to the
exchange of light through group discussion. Finally, the pursuit of sports, so
highly prized by the older schools in their effort to make men of character, was
reduced to a position of smaller consequence, much of their place being given
instead to self-expression in some form of productive activity.

For all the weight Reddie put on nurturing a boy's individuality, he was not
unmindful of education's social and civic purpose. Conceived as an active
organism full of vital sap, rather than as a mere disburser of intellectual
hand-me-downs, Abbotsholme undertook to involve not only its students in
common enterprises and responsibilities, but with them its director and faculty
and sundry personnel—a familiar enough idea in advanced democracies nowadays, but in the 1890s still highly uncanonical. Though Reddie labored at a
time when the rattan and dunce cap were indispensable to the promotion of
sound knowledge, the founder of Abbotsholme discountenanced such incite-
ments to human betterment. In place of duress he relied on understanding, and
instead of schoolmasters, he wanted his teachers to be educators. To put this
aspiration on something more than a utopian footing, Abbotsholme had recourse
to a form of self-government, sallow, to be sure, in the glare of present-day
lights, but sufficient unto its needs and, more important still, effective in its
operation.

For many years Abbotsholme enjoyed an agreeable prospering. Its pioneering
was watched far beyond the British shoreland, and the example of its success
gave heart to hopeful educators everywhere. Time saw the advent of schools
with the mark of Abbotsholme plain upon them, not only in the motherland but
across the Channel, in the Low Countries, in Denmark, Switzerland, Austria, and
especially in Germany where Hermann Lietz—who, as was noted in the chapter
preceding, had taught at Abbotsholme and drunk from its exhilarating taps—
initiated his famous country home schools, the *Landerziehungsheime*. In just
recognition, the Germans have saluted Reddie as the *Grossvater* of their country-
home-school movement, while the world at large has set him down in its
memory book as the father of the so-called new education, or as the phrase is in
America, progressive education. In England, however, the mills of reform ground
slowly. Though Abbotsholme and other schools of a more or less similar
persuasion made headway, their appeal at the most was limited. On the older,
established strongholds of the secondary learning, the impact of their example
made scarcely a dent—indeed the twentieth century was well on its course before
some of them undertook to relax the ivied bonds of their tradition to make
some better-late-than-never concessions to the newer ways.

7

Higher up on the university plane too there was progress. It was kindled, as in the lower learning, by an interested Parliament. Heads were laid together there, first in the 1830s and again in the 1850s, to put Oxford and Cambridge under study. The two schools, the most venerable in the English-speaking world, glowed with the pleasant patina of age, but they also showed blemishes which in the realm of learning did them serious damage, and which in nineteenth-century England were sometimes jarringly out of key. It was upon these that a handful of liberals applied their prophylactic pressure. Taking a cue from the Germans, they began by reanimating the curriculum, injecting into it the red blood of the natural sciences, first at Cambridge in 1851, and then at Oxford in 1853. The years saw more infusions, and before the century was in its grave, the two old schools were giving instruction not only in the newer sciences, but also in medieval and modern history, besides, of course, mathematics and the humanities. In 1856 there followed another stride in the secular direction with the abolition of the theological requirements for a degree. In consequence, the two universities were frequented more and more by youths whose cast of mind was far from clerical. And what went for students went also for their teaching dons—presently, in truth, the laymen amongst them outnumbered the divines.

The final and culminating thrust came in 1871 when Parliament put the ax on the regulation which prohibited Nonconformists from taking their degree—the so-called "religious-test requirement." The taboo, laid down in the reign of Elizabeth, had nestled in the lawbooks for more than three hundred years running. With its repeal Oxford and Cambridge shook themselves free from the last shackle of what once had been a powerful church monopoly. Their liberation, which at bottom had resulted from a combat of politics, brought these ancient groves much closer to the national life. As the years plowed on, and the practice of civil service replaced that of patronage, they became, so to speak, the nation's training station to fit young men of talent and capacity to carry on some day in the country's highest public service.

It is only fair to add that they were no longer England's sole dispensers of higher knowledge. The University of London was chartered in 1836, and on in the century others came upon the scene. Disdainful of a tradition which was denied them, they attuned themselves to the culture from which they sprang, which is to say the world of industry, science, and technology, and all the problems, human and material, which increasingly these begot. One finds them not in the remote and cloistered countryside, but in the very citadel of the new order, the lusty urban centers of trade and manufacturing. Thus universities came to Bristol and Birmingham, to Sheffield and Manchester, and to Leeds and Liverpool. Some arose mainly from philanthropy, some from communal enterprise, some from a combination of the two, and all of them, as time ran on, became beneficiaries of Parliamentary assistance.

The progress which lit up eighteenth-century England had no counterpart in France. There the century started in the reign of Louis XIV. He was a short man, but a regal one, and one of high pretension. Unlike his fellow king across the Channel, he ruled his subjects with an absolute hand, industrious to be sure, but often reckless, and only seldom benevolent. And what went for the fourteenth Louis went pretty much for his successor, the fifteenth. As a consequence, while England surged ahead, the tide of its liberty, religious and secular, steadily rising, its commerce and industry bubbling, its people set on self- and national improvement, France, in contrast, dragged its feet, its masses steeped in prejudice and ignorance, staggering under the yoke of bigotry, barbarous laws, an inept and scandalous administration, and a treasury that was not only bare, but mortgaged almost beyond help. "I have seen," Voltaire wrote in 1717, "the Bastille and a thousand other prisons filled with brave citizens and loyal subjects ... soldiers perishing with hunger ... the altar polluted ... the prelacy sold. ..." All these evils, and more and worse, he went on, he had witnessed when he was not yet twenty.

Indifferent to the populace, its Bourbon overlords were insensible to its schooling. In the main the business of education was executed pretty much as it had been during the two centuries preceding, which is to say it was regarded as a privilege and not a right, the concern not of the state, but of the church. The Jesuits were still upon the scene, dispensing their formidable discipline, their curriculum and their methods scarcely altered, and their aim, as in their beginning, the enhancement of the glory of God. For a handful of lesser folk—given a little ambition—there remained the charity of the teaching orders of which the head and forefront were still the Christian Brothers. But the zeal for knowledge was feeble, and the struggle for meat and money far outweighed it. Sometimes the children of the multitude were taught, but more often they were not. The result was a massive illiteracy.

To wage war on the Old Regime there rose a band of bold and intrepid intellectuals, the so-called philosophes. Strictly speaking, they were not philosophers, at least not of the usual professional order. D'Alembert, for example, practiced mainly as a mathematician, and so did Condorcet. Condillac occupied himself as a psychologist; Turgot as a statesman; Buffon as a naturalist. Diderot, coeditor of the *Encyclopedia*, and the one chiefly responsible for squiring that suspected work into print, was a man of letters, and so were Montesquieu, Rousseau, and Voltaire. Though they varied in their specialties, all of them were iconoclasts. Their great purpose was to rouse the public mind, to bring about such a stupendous transformation of the national spirit that the ancient order would be swept forever into the trash can. Their ammunition was not gunpowder but reason; and their weapons were not shotguns and sabers but pen and ink.

Nearly all the philosophes volunteered their counsel on education, some tersely and often tartly, and some, as witness, Rousseau, at lavish length. It is not necessary here to rehearse them all, for in their views there is a considerable overlapping, and some of them were little more than vapor. Not a few expressed the confidence that men, even those adorning life's lowest rathole, possessed the capacity for self-improvement, and that taken collectively and powered by reason, the human race could soar to the heights of infinite progress. Did nature bestow her gifts on the infant with no eye at all on whether he was swathed in satins or in rags? Then all of us, whether highborn or lowborn, of fat purse or lean, have a right to develop our natural dowering. For this purpose, they contended, government must in one way or other take a hand in the schooling of the young. Only thus may the state expect on some tomorrow to gather the harvest of their good citizenship. "Education," Condorcet let it be known, "is for the government an obligation of justice."

Of a somewhat similar tone, but much closer to the reality of everyday living, were the theorems of Louis-René de Caradeuc de la Chalotais. A successful politician, and hence not averse to speechmaking, he was also of a notable talent in the more exacting art of making sense on paper. His *Essays on National Education*, which was issued in 1763, a year after Rousseau's *Emile*, laid down the ground assumptions for educational reform. It was Chalotais's belief—then still a novelty among the French—that in the struggle for survival the best-educated nation will always have an edge. Hence the need for a system of national education. In such endeavor the state can brook no subversion: in consequence, it must be run to suit the secular need and taste. Chalotais entertained a vast disrelish for ecclesiastics, especially the Jesuits and the Christian Brothers who, he was convinced, "have just appeared to complete the general ruin." Is education an instrument to serve the state? Then, he argued, it should be in the hands of seculars, "and preferably layman," though this is not to say that an occasional man of God, of proper civic rectitude and pedagogic competence, and "free from the prejudice of Scholasticism and the cloister," should be deprived of a chance to instruct and rattan the young. Let him exercise his art and mystery. But let him always bear in mind that the real end of education is, and must be, to make efficient citizens.

Much bethumbed, the *Essays* were well regarded. Diderot cologned them in eulogy, and so did Turgot—indeed, even Voltaire gave them a grinning nod. Afterward, when the Revolution made a bonfire of the Old Regime, and the victorious insurrectionists addressed themselves to the task of getting the new order safely on its legs, it was Chalotais's thinking that made its way into nearly every legislative proposal for school reform.

With so much ado about education for the national welfare, it is easy to forget that Chalotais had no hankering to school the masses. The idea of literate blacksmiths, goat keepers, or even snake charmers, roiled him, and he would have none of it. The lower classes, he declared, should learn a trade anything beyond that is a waste.

It was another practitioner of politics, a Parisian by the name of Bathelemy-Gabriel Rolland d'Erceville, president of the local parliament, who ventured in 1768 to recommend a scheme of universal education. Under the supervisory eye of a national authority, its elementary schools would reach from the nation's end to end, from the meanest country mudhole to the proudest cobbled municipality. Above them, and less numerous, would range, not only the usual secondary and higher learning, but also an advanced seminary to train and illuminate fledgling masters for the secondary schools, and finally, atop it all, a national university—all securely riveted to the state with the iron band of centralized control.

2

In 1789, in the reign of Louis XVI, the gathering storm broke loose, and the Old Regime collapsed, a casualty of its own deficiency. Events now moved at a dizzy pace: the government had to be overhauled, a constitution made, new laws enacted, and the ever-lurking menace of counterrevolution uprooted. To convert France into the fair and civilized land the Revolution had envisioned, its idealists met in congress in three successive waves, starting on summer's eve, in 1789, as the Constituent Assembly, and hauling up in the fall six years later as the National Convention. True to their immemorial fashion, they were talking men, and they consumed much of their energy in endless parley. But among them were also some men of spacious ideas, full of alluring charm, and so, for all their vocal rumble, they succeeded, before adjournment stilled them, in concocting a number of astonishing reforms.

From their collective brain they minted the Declaration of the Rights of Man and the Civil Constitution of the Clergy. They pronounced their taboo on titles; they confiscated the lands and castles of the nobility and of the Church; and by another stroke they made it possible for peasants to translate themselves into landlords. To advance the arts and trades, the sciences, whether theoretic or applied, and even the Oriental languages, they generated a variety of museums, conservatories, and institutions of specialized learning, some of which are still in active and useful practice. Finally, they adopted the metric system, and they revised the calendar.

From the start they dallied in plans for educational reform. Led by Mirabeau, a reconstructed noble, and Talleyrand, once a bishop and a Royalist, but now all for liberty, equality, and fraternity, they attended soberly to those of their colleagues who, presumably, were versed in such matters. Yet what they actually accomplished beyond the robust exercise of their arms and larynx was very little. Six years brought forth harangues, debates, bills, reports even reports on reports—but only three laws, a Niagara, so to say, strained into a tub.

In 1793, with the suppression of the schools of the Christian Brothers, Chalotais's secular chickens came home to roost -but not his notion of excluding literacy from the lower orders. To fit France's youth for life in the First Republic, all children were to be schooled, and for such a purpose the establishment of state elementary schools was ordained. In their benches they were to apply themselves to the study of French—"to speak, read, and write [it] correctly." In addition they were to come to terms with arithmetic, not only the ways and byways of numbers, but also "the compass, the level, the system of weights and measures, the mechanical powers, and the measurement of time." They were to be familiar with their country, at firsthand whenever possible, and not merely its land and water, its shape and length and breadth, but also its offices, its workshops, and its farms. And, finally, they were always to love France, to know its constitution, and to be practiced in "republican manners."

The following year saw another statute, the Lakanal Law. Aside from the addition of "lessons on heroic actions and songs of triumph," and the changing of a jot here and a tittle there, its instruction covered practically the same ground as its forerunner. The measure was supplemented in 1795 with an order establishing central schools, a new fountain of secondary learning, to replace the old *collèges*, now nearly all deceased and buried, and their property, which not infrequently had been considerable, seized by the state. The new schools did not shut the door on the ancient classics, but their preference was modern, with instruction in the living tongues, mathematics, science, grammar, literature, drawing, and the main laws of the First Republic.

The final act of jurisprudence was Daunou's Law of late 1795. Signalizing the triumph of the conservative middle class over the leftist republicans, it kept pretty close to bourgeois prejudices. What it had to say for the lower learning was slight. Instead its main weight fell on the secondary and higher learning.

Thus the essence of the Revolution's school reform. Meager though it was, it was planted with a high hope, but that hope never fructified. In fact, even the Republic itself was doomed. Short of funds, rent by schisms, menaced from without, it presently succumbed to a five-man Directory, while just around the corner lurked Napoleon.

3

Napoleon took the bridge in 1799 when he became the nation's First Consul. Five years later he mounted the imperial throne. Until 1815, when he came to grief, he had France and much of Europe in his pocket. He was abundantly gifted. Of tremendous vitality and intelligence, he inclined toward the practical and the pragmatic. Theory-makers gave him a pain—"idealogues," he called them, "a mere rabble." To his office he brought an immense capacity for work, and a lust for glory that was unquenchable. It gratified his vanity to make France "the mother of all other sovereignties" and Paris "the one and only city . . . the capital of capitals."

His genius flamed, of course, in war, but in the work of peace its light was by no means pale—in truth, not a little of it was more enduring. Pushful and restive of restraint, he was a tyrant and a troublemaker, and those who crossed him—even the great ones—he knocked about. He ruled, as he confessed, at his "good pleasure." What that pleasure yielded was often calamitous, but not always. The laws, for example, which he begot and the old ones he chose to retain, he consolidated into a coherent entity, the Napoleonic Code. Its essence still lingers, not only in France, but in faraway places, even, in fact, in Louisiana. He succored a variety of industries, from wool and silk and cotton to the sugar beet and iron. He executed a program of public works which, for its day, was calculated to astound. He improved the harbors of Brest and Cherbourg; he conjured up canals, one joining Nantes with Brest, and another the Rhone with the Rhine. But it was Paris that got his most lavish attention. He enhanced it with spacious boulevards; he crossed its ageless Seine with bridges; he brought forth the Bourse and what now stands as the Church of the Madeleine. And, finally, he bestowed upon the city the Arch of Triumph, which for all the battering of man and time, still stands, a monument of stone and beauty, and a meet memento to his genius and his mad and terrible ambition.

Of all political questions which agitated the Empire, Napoleon considered education a primary concern, perhaps, he confessed, "the most significant." To safeguard and perpetuate the government, it was essential to secure the young, and to this end it befell the state to mold their minds. The process was launched while Pierre and Marie were still in life's vernal greenery. As soon as they could mouth the words of their catechism, they were introduced to their duties not only to God, but also to the Emperor. To the Lord's terrestrial appointee in France they were bidden, at all times and everywhere, to give "their love, obedience, military service, and the taxes levied for the preservation and defence of the Empire." Should they ever be tempted to ignore their obligation? Then let them ponder the caveat of St. Paul that by so doing they were resisting "the order of God himself," and thereby rendering themselves subject to eternal incineration.

Wasting no time, Napoleon started his labor of educational reform in the days of his first grandeur when, in 1808, he diverted the endowment of the Collège Louis le Grand (founded by the Jesuits in 1567) toward the establishment of four seminaries of military science. The year following he came to an evanescent understanding with the Holy Father. By it priests returned to their abandoned altars, with a state solatium toward their wages, while the Christian Brothers, but yesterday under prohibition, were permitted once more to proffer their charity of piety and pedagogy to the multitude. Their budget too was augmented with a subsidy, but at best it was a measly sum—never, indeed, more than $800 or so a year. Beyond this pittance the state contributed not a penny toward the nation's elementary schooling. All other primary schools, whether in municipal or private hands, had to fend for themselves. Thus neglected, France's lower learning, unlike its counterpart across the Rhine, languished in sad decrepitude.

Higher up, the situation was spiced with a new and pungent flavor. Whether plowhands and vinedressers knew their ABCs made little difference to Napoleon. What he needed first and above all was scientists and technicians besides an elite of brains to man the professions and the higher civil offices. For this purpose he reorganized the secondary schools, throwing overboard the central higher school, which had never found prosperity, and replacing it with the *lycée* and the *collège*, the one national, the other local. Both lodged and fed their clients; both exacted payment for their services, whether culinary or instructional; both were under the vigilance of the state; and both, although considerably altered, still adorn the current Gallic landscape.

Of the two, however, it was the *lycée* that enjoyed the imperial pleasure, and before long it became the standard secondary school. Though it harbored the classics, it played up mathematics and physical science, logic, ethics, a bit of modern language, and a dash of drawing. But it carefully abstained from instruction in philosophy, history, and similar subjects of potential seduction, which, by stimulating the student's critical acumen, might some day beguile him into false steps.

The spirit of the barracks ran through the school. Both professors and pupils were under military discipline. All learners were arrayed similarly, and all were under strict and uniform regulation. Drums roused them in the morning, and drums bedded them at night. Drums summoned them to their meals. Drums rolled them to class, and finally, drums rolled them out.

Needless to say, the Emperor's omnivorous eye did not spare the higher learning. Building on what the Revolution had wrought, the state, which is to say Napoleon, put the business into the hands of special faculties, or schools, of law, medicine, letters, and science. In 1804, after the Emperor and the Pontiff had puffed their pipe of peace, the theological faculty was vouchsafed a return to practice. In addition a number of technical higher schools were pressed into service, one—to confine examples—for mathematics, another for the social sciences, and another for the arts and trades. To prepare *lycée* graduates for teaching, the Higher Normal School was established in 1808. Dreamed up even before the Revolution by the far-visioned Rolland, the school made its advent with less than forty students. In the years following, as one government succumbed to another, the school had its ups and downs. Somehow it survived the precarious currents of politics, and though kings and emperors are now but a memory in France, its Higher Normal School is still in active service.

In 1808, on the seventeenth of March, Napoleon laid the block of granite on which he resolved to erect "the strata of the new society." Hailed as the Imperial University, it was not a university at all—at least not in the usual sense—but a mechanism to regulate and administer all public education, whether high or low. Specifically, as witness the decree from which it sprang, it was "to assure uniformity of instruction, and to mold for the state citizens devoted to their religion, their prince, their country, and their families." Suffusing all instruction was the theme of "fidelity to the Emperor and the imperial monarchy, the guardian of the people's welfare," with side themes in "the precepts of the

Catholic religion," it being Napoleon's observation that "a society without religion is like a vase without a bottom." His aim in establishing the university, he let it be known, was "to have the means of directing political and moral opinions."

The Imperial University was headed by a Grand Master, a magnifico of considerable power and standing. To ease his burden was the function of a council, an entourage of twenty-six head, all appointed by the Emperor. Going down the scale, one confronts a swarm of functionaries, of rectors, councilors, inspectors and subinspectors, examiners and subexaminers, all panting to uphold the Napoleonic dynasty, the unity of France, and the constitution. To keep this colossus safely on its course, the nation was divided into a network of twenty-seven "academies," or administrative districts, thence downward, diminishing in size, into departments and communes.

Napoleon built better than he realized. After the fates had taken him off, the Bourbons returned, and with them they brought back their royal crown. Imperial was now a dirty word, and so it was stricken from the university's shingle, and it became instead the University of France. The Grand Master too was stripped of his title and the trappings of his office, but not of his power and responsibility. He now addressed himself as Minister of Public Instruction. So he remained until Hitler began to lather over the Treaty of Versailles, whereupon, also given to patriotic foaming, the French converted their man into a Minister of National Education, a title he currently continues to enjoy. As for the system itself, save for a deletion here and an addition there, it stands pretty much as when it first took form, which is to say the most centralized system of national education the world has ever seen.

4

Napoleon was succeeded by Louis XVIII whose reign stretched from 1815 to 1824. On Louis's heels came Charles X who ruled till 1830 when, incautiously, he ventured to set aside the constitution, and in the ensuing hubbub found himself dethroned for his pains.

The era did not glow with grand attainments. Bourbon that he was, Louis could scarcely be expected to admire the Revolution, though, it must be confessed, he took it with good grace, and he never gave any visible signs of desiring to do it in. All in all, it was a period of chaste placidity, in which the Revolution's salient social gains managed to survive.

In education the winds of fortune were equally moderate, and when they stirred at all they blew in the same conservative direction. The first change—a curious proof in point—came in 1815, during Louis's maiden year in the king business, when the *lycées* were renamed royal collèges. As the years drifted on, the number of academies lessened, and so did the higher intellectual centers. The lower schools which Napoleon had resigned to the keeping of the Christian

Brothers fared a bit better. The $800 which he had deigned to grant them—a mere crumb, of course, for so large an enterprise—was multiplied more than ten times over, and though this was still a scanty ration, it was nonetheless useful and agreeable. In 1818 the brethren were gratified by yet another boon when the state allowed them to teach without the formality of an examination. To be admitted to classroom practice all that such consecrated men needed in testimony of their competence was a letter of obedience from the head of their order.

After chasing out Charles, the French soured on the Bourbons, and resorted instead to Louis-Philippe in whom ran the familial blood of the Duke of Orleans. History recalls Louis-Philippe as the Bourgeois King, an apt characterization, and one in which he often displayed himself. He was a man of simple habit, a Truman, as it were, lifted to the purple, who set great store on his daily walk and on singing the Marseillaise from the palace balcony to the cheering throng below. His one dissipation, if so it can be called, was his great affection for his family. Disdainful of the courtly show, he preferred to rove the shops, hatted in his gray chapeau, his green umbrella tucked underneath his arm, and with an ever-friendly bow for those who greeted him. He was, he remarked, "a citizen king ruling citizen kings."

Though he declared for the Revolution, and was sworn to uphold the constitution, there was hidden in his soul a haunting reminder of his past, the Revolution's ghastly bloodbath, his long and arduous exile and a poverty he had known face to face. From the start he inclined to take no risks. His governance, he announced, would seek the golden mean. Alas, fancy never kissed him, and he ruled the land with an avarice and greed worthy of the most prehensile pawnbroker. The years saw him grow more and more reactionary until, forgetting his vows, he caused criticism of the established order to be made a crime. But arresting enemies does not make friends—on the contrary, the opposition, whether from the Bourbon right or the liberal left, steadily increased. Soon, indeed, the streets of Paris, barricaded once more, teemed in riot and insurrection. The sovereign promised to execute a vast program of reform, but it was too late, and his adversaries would give him no ear. Late in February, 1848, the Bourgeois King gave up, and the Second Republic was hatched.

Louis-Philippe had adorned his throne for almost twenty years, yet most of the important educational reform was crammed into the springtime of his reign. The one who gave the enterprise its light and leading was François Pierre Guillaume Guizot, a literary man and a professional historian, but now sitting as Minister Secretary of State and Public Instruction. The monarch had scarcely eased himself into his throne when an annual allowance of a million francs was heaped upon the lower learning. In 1831, the year following, the religious brethren lost their prerogative of teaching without a license. Meanwhile, the state ordered the establishment of thirty new normal schools.

Next, the government dispatched Victor Cousin, the headmaster, or dean, of the revitalized Higher Normal School, across the Rhine to survey education in

Germany, and especially in Prussia. Cousin put the business under his glass, examining it minutely for weary nights and days and, in 1831, rendering a report on his observations. Notwithstanding his Gallic predilection, he was tremendously impressed. What amazed him in particular was the colossal efficiency of Prussian education, the spectacle of a resolute national authority over education, its centralized, secular control, its trained and educated professional schoolmasters, its up-to-date teaching methods, its planning, financing, and supervising, and—to come to an end—its bold and effective employment of the schools, from the bottom to the top, as an instrument for national ends. German education, Cousin declared, was immensely superior "even [in] the most insignificant duchy, over any and every Department of France in all that concerned ... primary and secondary education"—an extraordinary effusion, if there ever was one, from a 100 percent Frenchman.

From Cousin's *Report* issued the Law of 1833. By its writ, the commune—the township in the American parlance—either solitarily or in concert with its neighbors, was put upon to run a primary school. Not only was it to provide the schoolhouse; it was also to muster sufficient funds to keep its schoolmaster in good health and spirit, and of course, at a reasonable professional efficiency. For this purpose it was allowed to levy fees upon the pupils, save in the case of the poor, who got their learning with the kind compliments of the community. The school's nonpedagogic affairs—economic, social, and the like—were under the executive arm of a communal trinity composed of the mayor, the priest, and a meritorious layman with an itch for public service. Though primary education was a local responsibility, it was by no means without national strings. The state kept a watchful eye over the educational practice, and to insure a national uniformity, it provided every schoolmaster with an official *Manual of Primary Instruction* which told him precisely what to do. The curriculum, which was exactly the same throughout the land, carried the familiar stock: the three Rs, with special stress on the French language, besides morality and the Catholic religion. Rather curiously, though Guizot, the author of the Law of 1833, was a Protestant, he entertained no disposition to tamper with the Catholic religious monopoly in France's lower learning. In this respect he was, as the French say, *tout propre*. Karl Marx, on the other hand, scorned Guizot as a typical reformer of his day.

The law was not always accorded its due deference, especially among the peasantry and the hard-pressed lower classes to whom the advantages to be had from literacy seemed remote and even futile. "It is vinedressers we want, not readers," growled a grower of the Bordeaux grape. Since, unlike the Prussians, the French had failed to make their lower learning compulsory, the statute was only defectively observed, and numerous youngsters continued to leap through its loopholes. Even so, for all its limitations, Guizot's law gave the education of the masses its first surety and strength. Although some fathers might be hostile to its purpose, and even berate it with public raillery, the communes, taking one with another, took the business gravely. Five years after the law's enactment a round fifteen thousand primary schools, all the property of the communes, covered the land; not quite a decade later their number had increased almost an additional ten thousand.

Upon the base of the rudimentary learning was built the so-called higher elementary instruction. Not unlike the first American high schools, it aimed its erudition at the progeny of the middle class, and especially those who had no ardor for foreign languages, whether living or dead, and who did not crave on some tomorrow to enlist in a shrine of the higher learning. Those of such restrained ambition the higher school accommodated with instruction in geometry, linear drawing, surveying, natural science, geography, and history—the two latter with a fortissimo stress on the glories of France—and finally, with counsel and practice in the art of warbling the nation's favorite tunes.

There was no great rush for the higher elementary schools—in fact, their effectiveness at best was dubious. They languished not so much from any want of merit, but rather for their lack of social tone. In those days as in these, finicky fathers were sensitive to their communal standing, and whenever they could manage, they dispatched their sons to the more exclusive, and more costly, *collèges* and *lycées*. When the boys emerged, usually at the age of seventeen or eighteen, the classics still ringing in their ears, they were pronounced fit to carry on in the benches of the university to equip themselves, if so they willed, as medicos, jurists, holy clerks, or maybe, university professors. Did such callings leave them cold? Then they could always anticipate a place of promise in the world of affairs, in commerce or in government. At all events, as *collège* and *lycée* graduates, they entertained the pleasant feeling of being esteemed as persons of high potentialities, the nation's cerebral elite, whether real or illusionary, but in any case towering above the common stock of men.

There were other reforms, but they were afterclaps, and of no ponderable, immediate significance. In 1836 classes for adults, launched in Paris not quite twenty years preceding, were authorized for all of France, but the public was not yet ready to submit to them, and almost half a century ran by before they came into their own, an integral part of the national learning. For life's beginners, infant schools were commissioned in 1837, and three years later they were granted assistance from the national purse. Finally, in 1845, the state found it possible to do a like favor for the *lycées* and *collèges*.

5

The Second Republic, born in 1848, passed into its tomb four years later. It was done to death by Louis Napoleon Bonaparte, its first president and a nephew of the Corsican. Like his uncle, he had himself empurpled, and he ruled as Emperor Napoleon III. But Louis was no more than a wan shadow of his ancestor. The years, it is true, saw his country prosper. The national wealth piled higher and higher; industry and agriculture picked up power and momentum; new and ambitious public works sprouted everywhere; and with more railways and larger and speedier seacraft there was a palpable improvement in the means of transport and travel. Yet for all this gleam and glistening, doubt and apprehension gnawed the country. Scratch beneath the surface, and you will see tyranny. Search a little closer and you will find not only the well of liberty polluted, but also corruption and inefficiency, and a hell-bent diplomatic and military adventuring. It reached its melancholy end in 1870 in France's swift and appalling rout by Prussia.

The Second Coming of Napoleon brought the land no educational progress. In the upheaval of 1848 and the travail which followed, not a few of France's schoolmen had savored of liberal notions—an indecorum to which the Emperor turned out to be allergic. To purge these men of their wrong ideas, Napoleon caged their leaders in jail or banished them, while the rank and file, whatever their political libido, he put under relentless watch. All practitioners of the teaching art, whether they ministered to novice infants or savants of doctoral aspiration, had to swear the oath of loyalty. They were allowed to read but one gazette, the state-kept *Monitor*. Their whiskers, once the symbol of virility, and more recently of revolution, they were put upon to disperse, to cleanse their faces besides their minds of all unseemliness. Finally, should they ever show signs of wobbling, they could be fired on the spot "in the interest of the public peace." Victor Hugo, whose antipathy for the Emperor knew no bounds, caricatured him as Napoleon le Petit. The novelist prudently went into exile.

The clerical pedagogues, by contrast, suffered no such indignities, for unlike their once bewhiskered comrades, they were disposed to hobnob with the new regime. In consequence—like his uncle before him—Napoleon regarded them not as public menaces, but as "the sacred gendarmerie of the state." Thus esteemed and respected, the black-robed brethren worked gratefully and to good effect—in fact, in less than a decade they were running more schools and instructing more children than ever before.

Meanwhile, the public schools fell into a low state. Not only did they yield more and more of their pupils to the religious and private groves, but at every turn their instruction was badly crippled. Wages of primary teachers, which were never more than thin, were pared still thinner. By the same token, their training in the normal school, cried down by the government as a luxury, was reduced to an almost Trappist restraint. But not so the classroom burden. Despite the odds against them, teachers were expected to provide their youngsters with instruction that covered more ground than ever. Not only were they to reveal all the elementals, from the three Rs to history, geography, and science; they were also to flash their torch on religion and morality, on trade, agriculture, and hygiene, on surveying and leveling, and once they got their second wind, on singing and gymnastics. In the evening hours of the Empire the government attempted an amelioration of some of its more unpleasant tactics. But the patient, like the throne of France itself, was too far gone for pills. What was needed was a knife and a saw—and maybe even whiskers. The end came in 1870 in the fatal war with Prussia. It not only unhorsed the Emperor, but in the revolution which followed it brought forth the Third Republic.

The largest of the European states, both in the extent of its domain and in the number of its people, is Russia. About three times the size of the United States, Russia's territory currently takes in one-sixth of the surface of our planet. The beginnings of this stupendous realm reach into the dark backward of time when tribes of Slavs, emerging from their bleak Carpathian haunts, roamed and rampaged toward the east and the north. Time saw them trek into central Russia, putting the ax on the forest, settling now here, now there, and growing, as the years ran by, into villages and later into towns. Before Christianity was even a name a sort of commercial intertraffic was struggling between the Black Sea and the Baltic. By the ninth century, bands of Swedes with a ready eye for self-improvement appeared on the scene, mixing trade with robbery and assassination as they worked their way to the Dnieper, the most important waterway in western Russia. Kiev became their foremost stronghold, and it is to them in all likelihood that we owe the word Russia, from *Rous*, an appellation hung on them by the neighboring Finns.

It is not necessary to dwell upon their fortunes save to say that what they had built up with so much labor was at bottom an artificiality, and by the eleventh century the country fell apart, crushed under the load of its feuding princes and the mounting onslaughts of Asiatics, a marauding people of forbidding force and ferocity. The fates now swung their spotlight upon the region to the north, and especially upon Novgorod, a town of substance and powerfully attractive for its brisk and prospering commerce. Russian growth and unification now shifted to these parts.

But it was not given to Novgorod's burghers to become the molders of later Russia. That role fell, instead, to the princes of Moscow. The struggle for control raged for long and bitter years until one day, unexpectedly confronted by Genghis Khan and his pugnacious Mongols, burghers and princes hastily joined arms to do violence on their common enemy. Unhappily, they were in for some rough handling themselves, and in 1224, utterly dashed, they lowered their flags and submitted. Thirteen years later the Mongols broke loose again, and this time they not only conquered, but they stayed, setting up their main quarters on the lower Volga within nose range of the Caspian's salty breezes. Here they remained, practicing a primitive husbandry, and except for occasional flights from the boredom of peace, they contented themselves with a diligent plucking of the Russian princes.

For their part, the Muscovites displayed a high talent for dealing with their extortioners. For all the menace of the sword upon their throat, they not only contained the Mongols—they outlasted them. Time saw the horde devoured by schisms, and as faction fell upon faction, the Mongols, but yesterday so colossal and devastating, dropped from the peak of their indecent might to a level of minor consequence.

The way was now open for the Moscow lords to extend and consolidate their sway. To this end they toiled indefatigably, at the very time, oddly enough, when Henry VIII was exerting himself likewise in England, and Louis XI in France. But what a difference in the courses these nations ran! Long after constitutional government had gained currency, first in England, then in France, the Russian czars still held their subjects in their fist, ruling them with no checkrein on their power—save only their own weaknesses—and with a club handy at all times to snuff out dissenters.

The Russians came under the cross late in the tenth century when their chief executive Vladimir the Great consented to be baptized. Vladimir's Christianity was not of the Roman Catholic brand, but of the variety favored by his wife, which is to say the Eastern Orthodox Greek. As the years increased, the Russian church took on a national tinge, with its own pope, or patriarch, seated in his sacred chair at Moscow. Needless to say, his powers, though grand and glorious to the eye, were carefully fettered, and for all his connections with Heaven, he was at all times under the government's surveillance.

2

During the centuries of its youth Russia turned its back on Europe. The Renaissance lit no lamps in Muscovy, and the wild red fire of the Reformation gave it no concern. So things passed until 1689 when Peter the Great ascended the throne. He has gone into the human chronicle in a riot of guises, half human, half monster, a mortal who, while he sojourned on earth, transcended all familiar limits. His gustos were gigantic. Gorging and guzzling enchanted him, and so did carnality. A lover of gaiety, he had an inspired hand for humor, but when he was crossed, his rage was wild and stormy, roaring like a tempest that knew no end. Yet, despite his delight in revelry, he never allowed it to interfere with business, and despite his disdain for the ordinary conventions, he seldom permitted himself to forget to count his beads and say his prayers.

Peter's one master, if so it may be called, was the state. To advance its interest was with him, like love, an absorbing passion. The staid conservatism which befogged his country, and especially its aloofness toward the West, invaded his composure even while he was a prince. Europe's unmistakable attribute, he told himself, was its willingness to venture upon untried paths. This was the glory of its greatness, and this, when his imperial moment struck, he had resolved to aid and encourage in Russia.

Toward such an achievement Czar Peter worked with infinite industry and not a little shrewdness. His aids he selected with calculated care—even his wife, his second one, who was destined to succeed him, was a German he had encountered extracurricularly. To school his people in Europe's ways and methods, he dispatched a herd of bright young men to its workshops, and even to its labs and classrooms. Indeed, for a spell he himself was at large in England,

Germany, and Holland, prying with an alert and penetrating eye into their latest methods of manufacturing anything and everything, from a haircomb to a battleship. There he rounded up a troupe of artisans and scientists, besides sea captains, drill sergeants, and experts in military science, packing them off for Russia with the promise of handsome wages and sundry fringe rewards, including the right to worship as they chose.

Meanwhile, on the home front the Czar commanded his subjects to shed their long and flapping vestments and cover themselves instead with short coats and pantaloons. They were to shave their Oriental whiskers, or by the Eternal he would uproot them! His fiat, needless to say, bred horror and objection—in truth, among the nobility and the high ambassadors of God it even hatched revolt. When it spread to the palace guard, its partisans were beheaded for their pains, and the imperial edict was given at least an overt obedience.

Though Peter could barely read or write, he put a great store on learning. "I belong to those," his royal seal announced, "who seek knowledge and are willing to learn." The words are no mere catchphrase. They were imprinted in his mind and implanted in his heart. Oxford beckoned to him as one of its honorary doctors, and for a time the French Academy perfumed him with gallant compliments. Early in his reign he commissioned a Dutch printer to publish Russian books, though these were then a novelty in the land, and apart from the holy clergy scarcely anybody undertook to look at one. This grieved the Czar considerably, and to remedy matters, in 1719 literacy was ordained for the children of priests and nobles. To forestall any dodging, state examinations were ordered. Finally, before a gentleman was allowed to kneel at God's holy altar to translate himself into the state of wedlock, a prerequisite was put on him to produce visible proof of his literacy. The measure got no handclapping except, possibly, from an occasional bachelor—though it is no more than fair to add that it was only imperfectly enforced.

Among Peter's numerous gauds and honorifics one finds reference to him as the father of Russian education. It is an accolade not unmerited, for it was during his regime that elementary and secondary schools showed their first signs of taking hold. When Peter left this earth in 1725, slightly more than a hundred elementary schools, of a secular persuasion, were reported in common service—not a staggering flotilla, to be sure, for a land of thirteen million folk. But let it not be forgotten that this showing was not appreciably worse than in France, and had it revealed itself in Spain, it would have been trumpeted as a miracle of God.

In the main, however, the imperial appetite inclined more to specialized learning than to the general—hence Peter's promotion of the so-called "cipher school," a fountain of practical knowledge, designed to supply the government with semiskilled technicians with a fair grounding in arithmetic, geometry, and geodesy. Like England's Henry VIII, Peter cherished an affection for the navy, whether for peace or war, and to man his vessels with trained and able men, he not only decreed the establishment of a naval academy at St. Petersburg; he also concocted the articles for its operation. To Peter, finally, must be credited the Academy of Sciences, a higher cerebral center which was to exert itself in the pursuit of new knowledge and to give instruction and training to Russian scientists and men of higher learning. The idea for such an institution generated, no doubt, in the brain of the erudite Gottfried Wilhelm Leibnitz, whom the Czar met while making his rounds in Europe in 1716. But almost a decade had passed into history before the academy made its advent, and by that time Peter was already enjoying his first postmortem year.

3

During the hundred years following Peter's passing only two of his successors entertained an itch to amend and extend the public enlightenment: the one, Catherine the Great, and the other, Alexander I. The former, who was of German origin, eased herself onto the throne in 1762 when her spouse, the third Russian Peter and a first-grade nonentity, was dispatched from this vale to the ghostly world beyond.

From the start Catherine displayed herself as a woman of extraordinary vigor and capacity who knew her trade, whether in politics or in the boudoir, in its every shading. Under her ministrations Russia increased in power and circumstance, and in the concert of Europe's squabbling nations, it attained to something akin almost to deference. An admirer of brains, like her fellow autocrat in Potsdam, the great Frederick, she exchanged letters with Europe's foremost intellectual and literary worthies, in illustration, Diderot, Rousseau, and Voltaire, and she did her utmost to induce them to settle, if only transiently, at her side in Russia.

Catherine worked much in the vein and manner of Peter, though she painted her canvas on a larger scale, and in education she favored it with a distinctly feminine stroke. It pleased her to profess a belief in the education of the many, hoping thereby, as she remarked, to produce "a new breed of fathers and mothers"; but it pleased her even more to lay special weight on a new education for girls. Before Catherine's time girls were seldom the object of instruction; those who nonetheless were educated were generally of a high social tone, and the tutorial operation was performed in the home or in a nunnery. The mood to ameliorate the girls' hard lot was on Catherine even before she ornamented the imperial purple, and in 1764, her second year in office, she gave her support to the establishment of the Educational Society of Noble Girls. A seminary of learning and refinement, Noble Girls was of the secondary school variety, and though the state had a hand in its making, the attainment of its service was strictly c.o.d.

Its students, who ranged in years from six to eighteen, were ranked and organized in two groups, the daughters of the well born, for one, and those of the respectable bourgeoisie, for another. Both orders, whether of a higher or lower altitude, were booked for arithmetic, geometry, history, Russian, and foreign languages. Girls whose blood was blue as well as red were schooled besides in the art of courtly manners; their lesser sisters were indoctrinated in the postulates of household science. Until 1783, when Catherine was greatly taken with purifying and improving the Russian tongue, all instruction was executed in French, then generally esteemed as the most elegant language in civilization. Not unlike the so-called "finishing schools" which still practice their mystery in our own fair democracy, their Russian forerunner devoted a great deal of time to the cultivation of a proper ladylike deportment. There was a right way to place oneself in a chair, and a right way to confront a dinner table. There was only one meet and judicious way to spoon one's soup, one only to haul it to the lips, and one alone to discharge its content.

As florescent ladies of quality, the girls were expected to develop a correct and mellifluous speech. To this end they were scrupulously rehearsed, not only during their everyday sessions in the classroom, but also while they were grazing at the dining board—even, indeed, during the ebb and flow of their carefree chatter when, presumably, they were at ease and leisure. Needless to remark, their manners and morals were carefully and constantly policed.

The high support Catherine gave to the education of the gentle sex, she matched with the confidence she put in the pedagogic powers and properties of the woman teacher. Catherine not only hired women for service at Noble Girls; she also manned the classes of the St. Petersburg cadet corps with a squadron of schoolma'ams and a headmistress in command. They were to instruct and counsel their boy recruits, treating them at all times "with patience, tenderness, and love," and they were never to let them out of sight, "either by day or by night." Their endeavor, it should be added, was reserved for junior cadets whose ages ran from five to nine. The more aged and sophisticated ones of ten to fifteen came under the jurisdiction of men.

Like Peter, the Empress cherished a vast respect for Western ideas, and like him, she set her snares to bring their foremost votaries to her land. For a time she wooed Rousseau, but the author of the *Social Contract* and *Emile* had fallen low in body and spirit, and aside from drawing up a plan for the education of Catherine's Polish subjects, he was content to stay at home and lick his wounds. When Catherine rolled her eyes at Voltaire, she got in return his finest blandishment and some beauteous gifts besides, but unhappily, no Voltaire. With the philosophical Denis Diderot her luck lit up. He not only accepted her bid to install himself in Russia; presently he also confected what she so much desired—a plan, that is, for the organization of the Russian schools. Pumped from the artesian depths of the latest French liberalism, Diderot's scheme showed no lack of constructive idealism. It called—to cite an example or so—for the free and compulsory schooling of every Russian child, whether in skirts or britches, and it urged a secondary learning concerned not only with the shadowy Greeks and Romans, but with current knowledge as well. But when the Frenchman went on to declare that a knowledge of the human body, its various parts and their functions, was something every boy and girl should have, he brought blushes even to Catherine's cheek, and she would have none of his ideas, Western or not.

With the exit of the shameless Diderot, Catherine turned over to herself the business of educational reform. She took a stand for more schools in the towns and larger villages; unluckily, she was in no mood to lubricate the enterprise with the necessary funds, and so, handicapped from the start, it never attained to any great proportion. At bottom, moreover, Catherine's ardor for the advanced thinking of the West had never been completely quashed. For a while she cast sugary glances at Friedrich von Grimm, a German writer and a baron, but he would not let himself be tempted. The man who accepted the nomination to overhaul Russian education was Jankovitch de Mirievo, a Serbian pedagogue of distinction, fresh from his labor of repairing the school system of the Hungarians.

De Mirievo discharged his new duties adroitly and effectively. At his instance the best schoolbooks then circulating in Europe's leading chambers of knowledge, which is to say mostly German ones, were translated into Russian and published in large supply. But the bulk of Russia's teachers were of a primitive order, and for most of them the new books, for all their magical marvels, were a burden on the understanding. The sanitary knife was not long delayed, and in 1783, at St. Petersburg, with de Mirievo as head surgeon, the first Russian training school for teachers came into its own.

Meanwhile de Mirievo and the Commission for the Establishment of Schools, of which he was a member, put their heads together to lay plans for the organization of a national school system. As men of great learning, they were, of course, at incurable pains to explore and examine every detail and subdetail of their project, so that when at length they were ready to disgorge their proposals, they had grown four years older. Presented in print in 1786 as the *Statutes for Public Schools in the Russian Empire*, their writ extended to 113 articles. One finds in them, especially in their preamble, the familiar agreeable ointments, sweetly scented and beautifully vague. But there is much solid stuff as well. The statutes, for example, recommended the establishment of schools, from rudimentary to advanced, the one to adorn the meaner towns and one-road hamlets, the other the more sumptuous communities and municipalities. All schools, whether of the lower or higher candlepower, were free, and all were under the watch of the commission, which is to say the state, with appropriate aid and hints, however, from the local Boards of Public Assistance.

In the primary school, which required two years for the consummation of its business, children made acquaintance with the three Rs, a dash of grammar, some drawing, and a heaping portion of religion. In the studios of the more advanced knowledge, as usual, life became more onerous. Not only were their apprentices put upon grappling with the same subjects they had encountered in their younger, carefree days—in much harder and perplexing substance, of course—but they also had to reckon with foreign languages.

As for what the Empire expected from its schoolteachers, the statutes left neither doubt nor loophole. They were, of course, to be loyal subjects, flaming for good works, and on familiar terms with the immutable axioms of Russia's orthodox Christianity. They were to be privy to their subject, and versed in "the prescribed method of instruction." At all times they were to "teach exactly according to the rules," allowing themselves no such liberties as, say, wandering from the officially laid-out route of the daily lessons to nose around in uncharted side roads, however interesting and instructive. They were to maintain their roll book up-to-date and immaculate. They were to know their students familiarly, their psychology, sociology, biology, their ethics, esthetics, and metaphysics. And if they were not called upon, as are so many of their contemporary American successors, for service in bus loading, lunchroom patrolling, or coaching actors, weight throwers, or lady drum majors, then on the other hand they were to show their novices "how to sit decorously, to walk, to bow, to make requests courteously." Finally and fittingly, they were to crook their knees and chant their prayers with their flock several times a day, invoking Omnipotence to guide them all to virtue and right-thinking.

So much for the statutory blueprint. How did its mandate fare in the hard actuality of practice? Put into operation in 1786, it went off with an auspicious bang. The number of public schools augmented, and so did their candidates for light and leading, and so also their teachers. But, presently, what had started as a sprint became a waddle, and pretty soon the waddle settled into a halt. What knocked out the program was not any intrinsic deficiency, for, taking the statutes' articles one with another, and remembering their time and setting, one must rate them as actually meritorious. What beset and undid their effective execution from the very start was the lack of a large and flowing purse. Scarcely less damaging was the almost total absence of first-rank teachers. Their best exemplars went into private practice, where wages were higher and benefits more numerous, and so, despite the government's wishing and wooing, its efforts to improve the quality of the general teaching were baffled. The superiority of the private educational endeavor was not lost, of course, on the paying clients, and though the authorities strove to harness and arrest it, among well-heeled parents the preference for private schools continued to prevail. Nor should it be forgotten that of Russia's thirty-five millions almost nine of every ten engaged in farming. Did Ivan, milking in the cowbarn, know his letters? Then his patient, for all that, was unimpressed. Could he, furthermore, add and subtract, or even trace the migrations of the Dnieper and the Volga? Then his agriculture derived no benefit therefrom. For Russia's multitudinous millions, suffering the pains of book learning was scarcely worth the trouble. It brought them no surcease from their far greater misery, the pressing and endless struggle to stay alive. Consequently they turned their back on education, so obviously futile to their immediate purpose. In sum, for all the imperial dragooning of experts, the drawing up of lavish codes and statutes, and the official drumbeating for public schooling, Russians as a mass were not yet ready to crawl out of the dark woods of ignorance.

As middle age closed in on Catherine there were signs that her fire for liberal ideas was dying. Even in her young and palmy days, its flames had been carefully contained, and although she confessed a wish to advance learning throughout her land, its chief beneficiaries in the last resort were not the horde of hard-pressed lower folk, but a handful of the upper and the clerical orders. Doubts and misgivings had overcome her as early as the seventies when the peasantry erupted in rebellion. The French Revolution in the decade following shocked and dismayed her, and when, in 1793, the French brought their King, the sixteenth Louis, to book and the guillotine made an end of him, Catherine's eagerness for Western progress was decisively hushed. Henceforth there would be no more hobnobbing with the New Thought. The bearers of its torch were to be kept out of the land, and their writings were put under taboo. Lest their seductions might steal into print just the same, all private presses were ordered to shut up shop.

Catherine's heir and successor was her son, Paul I. A man of dark and sullen vapors, he not only despised the enlightened thinking of the West; he feared it to the inmost conduits of his soul. To protect his realm against its sinister pollutions became the overriding purpose of his reign. For this end, the importation of foreign writings was outlawed, while the publication of native ones was put on strict and compulsory rations. Russian students were to confine their pursuit of knowledge to the native groves, and those resident in foreign places were laid under summons to return at once because of the prevalence abroad of "a licentious and depraved philosophy which inflames immature minds." Meanwhile Paul's spies were all about.

Soon even the ironical fates seem to have had enough of Paul and his lugubrious mandates. At all events, in 1801 palace plotters butchered him to death. And so, after only five years in the imperial costume, the heir of Catherine passed on, one may charitably hope, to a world of infinite reactionary bliss.

4

Russia's first Paul was followed by its first Alexander. He began his reign by sweeping out the melancholy measures of his predecessor. Next, he turned his virtuosity upon an overhauling of the country's administration, integrating its diffuse and jumbled organs, and coordinating their various endeavors. In the process, in 1802 the Commission for the Establishment of Schools gave way to the Ministry of Public Education, with Peter Vasilevich Zavadovskii, a noble born and bred, and the last director of the deceased commission, in charge of its affairs.

The ministry was scarcely out of the shell when it proceeded to the business of reforming the Russian school system. As such things go, its collaborators worked with extraordinary dispatch, and despite their professional proclivity for talk and fatuous detail, they managed to complete the greater part of their assignment within a couple of years, a feat which in the academic world is surely rare. Their proposals ran to the usual many miles of print, and they were planned upon familiar lines. They ranged from the lowest learning to the highest, covering everything then known to educational science, from the way the schools were organized and run, the money that kept them going, the subjects dispensed, to the requirements, education, and training exacted from their teachers, and the precise manner of conducting their sessions. Under the new regulation learning was to be within reach of all the Russians, whether peer or peasant; but with the nation's class cleavage hobbling it at every turn, the stipulation turned out to be more illusory than real.

The reform gave Russia's school organization a unity and coherence it never enjoyed before—it was, indeed, a national educational system, which is to say a national network of schools, integrated from the shabbiest one-room country school to the most sumptuous palace of higher intellectuality. It was the nearest imperial Russia ever got to an educational ladder such as that of our own great land. But where the American system issued laboriously from its unfolding democracy, that of Alexander's Russia was an artificiality, contrived, as it were, on the drawing board, and predestined for an early grave.

Like Catherine's earlier reform, its successor began with a high flourish, but like the one, the other presently floundered. The fact is, circumstances, not only in Russia, but in the lands beyond, were against it. Alexander had come to his throne just as the dawn of Napoleon's sun was reddening, and willy-nilly he found himself forced into its orbit. It is not necessary here to recount the details—the library shelves harbor them by the ton. Let it be merely stated that by June of 1812, with more than a half a million men, the Corsican was heading for the heart of Russia. The fourteenth of September found him pitching camp in Moscow, and the next day, by hazard or Muscovite design, the ancient city was a mass of flame. Four days it burned while Napoleon stood by expecting Alexander to sue for peace. But the Czar was derisive, and he sued not. Meanwhile the winter's chill was giving notice—soon, indeed, it was speaking with sharp authority, and by mid-October Napoleon gave orders to retreat. The recession turned into a colossal rout. Napoleon, to be sure, got back to his beloved Paris, but between him and Moscow lay the festering remnants of 300,000 of his ablest men.

All these things bore heavily upon the Russians. In the West, grantedly, their stock had never been so high. Bathed in Europe's smiles, their sovereign was on all fours with its high and mighty, and in the remaking of its tattered shreds, he was honored with their attention. He presently rewarded them with the Holy Alliance, a union of Europe's foremost monarchs, pledged henceforth to ground their mutual relations "on the sublime truths of the eternal religion of God our savior." Nevertheless, behind the ecstasy there was the agony, the poignant and unshatterable memory of the horror and grief Napoleon had brought the Russians, and the French Revolution which had given him a start.

Once more the shadows of reaction closed down upon the land. It is possible that Alexander believed in the Holy Alliance as an instrument for virtue, good works among men, and brotherhood among nations. If so, he was made to be fooled. Despite its pious flummery, it soon showed itself for what it actually was, namely, an international constabulary bent on the arrest and slaughter of all expressions of liberal thought. To such things Russians were, of course, accustomed—perhaps one should better say, conditioned. They had run into them in the bilious days of Catherine, and more recently in the reign of Paul. Moscow's cremation was not calculated to make them love the foreigner—on the contrary, it projected his unpleasant image more sharply than ever. By the same token, their deliverance from his evil was accounted for, not simply as a powerful and heroic feat of arms against heavy odds, but as a miracle, divinely vouchsafed, in time of woe and trouble. The upshot was a revival of the old distrust and disrelish of aliens, and a vast and powerful upsurge of soul-searching—a phenomenon which is, of course, no novelty in human history.

It was not long before the new mood made its way into education. It is in plain view in 1816 in the appointment of Prince Alexander Nikolaevitch Golitsyn as Minister of Public Instruction. In the green innocence of youth the Prince had attained a reputation as a free thinker, but the years had seen him mend his error, to become the foreman of the Russian Bible Society and chief procurator of the Holy Synod. The new minister had scarcely stretched his legs under his desk when the sign on his office door was amended to Ministry of Spiritual Affairs and Public Education. The alteration in title was no mere window dressing. It was, in the words of the august Alexander I, an indication to all the world that "Christian piety should always be the foundation of true education." Soon after, in 1819, all schools were ordered to put the catechism and similar works of sacred inspiration in the forefront of all instruction.

Next the minister shook his stick at higher learning. Russian universities had long been suspect for their crimes against virtue. The whole baleful business, one of the minister's catchpoles had reported, was due "to the books and men we have borrowed from German universities," where, he went on, "the infection of unbelief and revolutionary principles, which began in England, and gained strength in prerevolutionary France, has been erected into a . . . system." So serious was the contamination at Kazan University that the ministry found it necessary to fire eleven of its infidel professors and to order the purging of all curricula to bring them into consonance with the propositions of Russian divine science. Whereupon it heaved the teachings of Copernicus, that mischiefmaker, into the garbage can, and followed them with those of Newton. No student, it was ordained, was to study philosophy or similar unsettling sciences before he had given unmistakable proof of "his devotion to the sacred evangelical subjects." Finally, a Dean of Morality was appointed to edify and police the students, and to punish the wicked.

The ax swished correspondingly in other centers of higher thinking. Here a professor was shouldered out for having lectured on the philosophy of Schelling; there another came to grief for having found fault with serfdom and the flood of

Russian paper money. Men of learning who had prepared themselves in the outlands were intellectually radioactive, and hence unfit for practice in a Russian grove.

And that is the end. What had started out so promisingly in Alexander's early days turned into no more than the briefest honeymoon. The inheritor of a public school system under state control, he had given it his approval and encouragement—for a time, in truth, he even gave it fortification and improvement. But as the years settled on him, fears, of a ghostly as well as an earthly nature, beset him, and the bold vision of his younger days deserted him. More and more he yielded his governance to celestial guidance and to the counsel of the higher holy clerks in the service of the Orthodox Church. When Alexander went to rest in 1825, he could say in honesty that he had left Russia with more schools and with more students than when he came. But if you pinned him down, he would also have had to admit that the number of sacred edifices, whether churches or monasteries, had increased, and that the holy houses outnumbered the schoolhouses four to one. All in all there were in Russia some fifty-six million people whose progeny, had the fever seized them by some miracle, could look to 1,000 schools to give them instruction—a mere dust grain, of couse, in so vast a land as Russia.

Not long before his death Alexander restored to Russia's chief educational office its former title of Ministry of Public Education, and thrust the execution of its affairs to the command of Admiral Alexander Semenovich Shishkov. The new minister was peculiarly equipped for the business. He brought to his office not only the administrative talents of an admiral, but a lifelong pondering of Holy Writ, besides a fanatical conviction that political autocracy was God's holy will. Knowledge, he let it be known, was a good thing, but, like salt, it is better to use too little than too much. "To instruct all the people in literacy," the pedagogic admiral explained, "would do more harm than good." On the other hand, "instruction in the rules and principles of Christian conduct is needed by everybody." So precisely was this sentiment to the taste of Nicholas I, Russia's new sovereign, that he made it one of his first official acts to keep Shishkov at his post. The minister for his part rewarded his master's show of confidence by putting the Russian press under a hard and rigorous censorship.

Meanwhile, Nicholas himself had things of moment to say. For one thing, his lamented predecessor had been much too liberal. Next, the ladder system which enabled peasants to raise themselves to a higher plane was a public menace. Nor was it meet to allow those of nether and higher estate to rub shoulders within a single school. Finally, schoolmasters should lay less stress on the chase for knowledge and, per corollary, a great deal more on the development in the young of a sound character, which is to say, their duties to God and those it hath pleased Him to put above them.

The Czar's effusion was scarcely on Shishkov's desk when the minister embodied its substance in 325 school regulations. The ladder, cardboard creation though it was, was trimmed of all its rungs. Henceforth the instruction of each social class was to be rigidly partitioned from that of all the others. For peasants the village school sufficed, while for the middle class the district school was quite enough. Only the upper class could reasonably expect the boons of secondary and higher learning. To seal all loopholes, nonpublic schools were put under the strictest governmental vigilance. The first prerequisite put upon a candidate to teach, even in a private home, was not his knowledge or professional capacity, but a certificate of rectitude and political reliability. In consequence, the Pedagogical Institute at St. Petersburg, the paramount training arena for teachers in Russia, was ordered shut, its services "being unnecessary."

Although schoolmasters now occupied themselves less with cramming knowledge into reluctant heads, their lot was no less burdened. For, as is well known, keeping the young on the trail that leads to a good and upright life requires unrelenting watch and effort. It did not take the authorities long to notice this and, to give the teacher some assistance, they ordered him not only to police his charges, but when occasion demanded, to rattan them with fervor and dispatch. Thus the teacher's immemorial right of which he had been disarmed by the rough-and-ready Peter the Great was restored to its old and respected authority. To render the schoolman yet more efficient, every school was reinforced with a posse of deputies, or monitors. It was their duty to stand sentinel over their charges at all times and everywhere, to help them with their homework; to repair "their mistakes in language, decorum, and taste"; to inform authority promptly of any untowardness, whether grand or petty; and finally, to make certain that there would be no bootlegging of forbidden writings.

Lest a birchman might himself fall victim to the seductions which, since Adam, have preyed upon us all, a governmental inspector was given sovereignty over every school. An official watchman, as it were, he kept a sharp and challenging eye, not only on its palpitating pedagogues, but on their principal as well. His duties and powers, needless to say, were tailored to the magnitude of his office. He surveyed his men during their daily classroom seances. Did their operations soothe and satisfy his pedagogical palate? Then he could reward them, say, with some extra benefit or, maybe, on some tomorrow even with a better job. On the other hand, did they fall short of his critical canon? Then he put them under reprimand and issued an ordinance for reform. The inspector alone promoted pupils, and he alone granted their diplomas. And befitting his rank and dignity, he led the chalk talk when the faculty convened in regular monthly meeting.

Shishkov carried on his work for public enlightenment for four years, until 1828, when he yielded the bridge to Count Uvarov. The change in command made no perceptible difference, for in his pedagogics the count was a carbon duplicate of the admiral. The platform on which he stood, and in which he took a fierce pride, he disposed of in one brief burst as "Orthodoxy, Autocracy, Nationalism." The purpose of his office, he took pains to make known, was to curb and circumscribe false thinking, "to hold up," as he explained, "the flow of new ideas in Russia, and thus prolong its youth." Toward this attainment he worked and warred with scarcely a halt, and to a triumphant end. When, in 1849, he walked out of his office for the last time, the count had succeeded even beyond his wildest dream. Not only had he held Russia's intellectual advance at bay; he had also prolonged its youth—indeed, he had even pushed it back cerebrally into early childhood.

5

Alexander II, the son of Nicholas, came to the throne in 1855. He was, for a Czar, a social-minded man, and with an understanding grip on the theory and practice of government. His reign opened, like that of his earlier namesake, with soft music. It was his hope, he declared, that the years ahead would see a vast improvement of the public weal, soothed and illuminated by justice and mercy, and an ever-burgeoning "desire for education and all manner of useful activity." The Czar was the first to strike out for this land of hope and glitter when, soon after his advent, he lifted some of the harsher taboos propagated by his father, including even—within limits—the prohibitions put upon the press.

But five years came and went before Alexander's ode to progress showed signs of being something more than the sough and sigh of rhetoric, when—to give an instance—in 1861 he ordered the emancipation of Russia's forty million serfs, a number almost ten million in excess of the total population of the United States. Other ventures into constructive public service presently followed, not always, it is true, in the actual deed, but at least in serious contemplation. To grant localities a greater say in their communal governance, elective county councils—the zemstvos—were created. To humanize the administration of the law in the halls of justice, the English jury system was adopted. To make the corruptible judges, if not incorruptible, then at least somewhat less corruptible, they were put on steady wages. In 1865 public journals were given a freer hand; but what they said in print had better be above suspicion—otherwise the jail gates beckoned. Reform spread its ripples even into the military when, in 1874, every able-bodied Russian, whether highborn or otherwise, was made subject to conscription.

Meanwhile, Alexander had nullified some of the measures which bore so repressively on education, particularly in its secondary and higher spheres, but the progress of learning to which he had proposed a toast in the infancy of his reign was deferred. The truth is, the Czar's enlightened thinking was not given a rousing applause by the ruling classes—not even, in fact, by his early ministers of education. When university students began fevering for a more spacious reform, and even advertised their convictions in public hullabaloo and riot, Count Putiatin, an admiral by occupation, was summoned to the ministerial post and commissioned to restore peace. He proceeded, as officers usually do, not with argument, but with orders. From now on students were to confine their ardor to the Muses. They were not to hold converse with one another over matters which concerned them not—in particular such an inflammatory subject as change, academic or otherwise. Under no circumstances were they to gather in public assembly. And they were to cease arraying themselves in the student's traditional uniform, a mark of merit since the dawn of the Russian higher learning, but now fallen suspect, and a cause for alarm.

The admiral might have saved his pains. The students did not submit; on the contrary, they increased their public clamor. The upheavals, indeed, grew so huge that authority, on the verge of apoplexy, resorted to the services of the police, with reinforcement from the military. The result, needless to say, was a serious damage, not only to property, but to health and spirit.

The scandal, of course, gave the Czar no cheer. But if he was displeased with its makers, he was even more put out by its immediate cause, the admiral, who presently, in point of fact, was returned to the consideration of matters more suitable to his professional experience. The minister who succeeded him late in 1861 was A. V. Golovnin, a man with a wide range of knowledge and, more important, a liberal inclination.

There issued in the course of time the usual detailed writ for a brand-new Russian education. Put into effect in 1863, it restored to the higher learning most of its vanished prerogatives, including the professors' immemorial right to select their university chief executive besides their deans, assistant deans, and similar academic figures. Chairs in constitutional law and philosophy, heaved overboard by Nicholas I as noxious to decency and good order, were reinstated, and several new ones were added. Finally, faculty salaries were given a gentle and salubrious boost. For students too there were boons. For one thing, getting admitted to a university was made less burdensome; for another, tuition charges were put on a reasonable basis—in fact, when a student found himself lean in purse, a not unusual situation, the bursar honored him with an exemption from his levy. But his beloved uniform, alas, was still denied him.

A notch down, in the secondary school, late in 1864 a special regulation, the Secondary School Code, was put into effect. For service and instruction, Russians could choose the conventional classical shrine with its familiar and weather-beaten Latin and Greek, and with either German or French for a booster. Or they might deal with Latin alone, but with a powerful injection, in that case, of both German and French. Finally, if Latin threatened to be a hazard or a nuisance, they might forswear it altogether. In such instance they were put to pondering the vagaries of German and French besides natural science, mathematics, penmanship, drawing, and design. All students, whether specialists in antiquity or in the more current knowledge, were bathed regularly, fourteen hours every week, in divine law.

With learning's humble pedestal, the elementary school, the projectors of reform were not disposed to do much fussing. True, the pursuit of knowledge, scorned and scourged by the late Nicholas, resumed its ancient stress, but religion, virtue, and hymnody remained, as previously, of paramount importance. In pretty nearly all concerns the lower school executed its industry under the rein of St. Petersburg. There were, to be sure, the newly constructed councils of local government. But these were still, so to speak, in babyhood, and their educational powers, whatever they were intended to be, were not to come to their full ripening until later in the century.

Since their heyday in the reign of the blessed Catherine, the girls of Russia, and particularly the daughters of the plain people, had to content themselves educationally with scanty rations. Like their brothers, of course, they ran into the hard barrier of a reactionary government. But when that wall was breached by the reforming Alexander, it was the boys who poured through, while the girls lagged behind, confronted by the additional obstacle of being female. Not long after his ascent Alexander did the fair sex a good service when he gave recognition to two new-type schools for girls, the one performing its feats in three years, the other requiring six. Though these seminaries offered their revelation to all, regardless of their social circumstances, pretty nearly always they were maintained by private hands, and so, inevitably, this high resolve ran aground in a world ruled by a stern determinism. It was 1871 before girls attained access to a secondary school modeled on that of the boys, though scarcely its equal.

As for the higher enlightenment, the statutes of 1863, which had performed so many wonders for the male, vouchsafed no such exaltation to the female. To women the university was closed—though in fairness it should be stated that its boons were not completely beyond the feminine reach. If women insisted, for example, they were allowed—like the fair ones of imperial Rome—to visit the lecture halls of the medical professors; in truth, like their faraway predecessors, if it lay within their gifts, they were even admitted to the practice of some of the more rudimentary phases of the anesthetic art and science. Only a handful of the ladies, however, were attacked by such desire. Those who counted in the Russian scheme of things, namely, those orbiting in the upper social circle, usually besought the more dulcet, nonprofessional edification of the liberal arts, preferably in some reputable establishment in the civilized outland. The situation, as might be expected, frenzied some of their lesser but ambitious sisters, and at length, in 1872, the authorities yielded women a halting welcome to courses given of a Sunday or holiday evening by professors in regular regalia at St. Petersburg University. The practice presently made its way to other centers of higher study, and by 1880 what had started so asthmatically had grown into a robust and healthy four-year program.

Thus the main line of Alexander's program for school reform. It shows a high degree of imagination—sometimes even ingenuity—and as one year followed another, it produced some tangible improvement in Russian education. Not since Catherine's days of flirting with the public enlightenment had there been so much moving ahead. Schoolhouses increased in number, and so did their attendants. Save in learning's lower reaches, there was a visible rise in the intellectual demands put upon students; indeed, in the halls of higher learning scholastic standards were said—by Russians—to be on a par with those of the most exacting

American college. The secondary school too was cutting a new and enterprising figure. To the eye, at any rate, the choice it proffered the learner between the classics and the modern subjects, such as the living languages and the sciences, brought it abreast of the most up-to-date curricular style then known to pedagogy. And what held for the secondary learning held also for the higher variety, where similar blasts of fresh air were blowing out the old stagnation. Finally—though unfailingly not the least—there was the laudable gain in the educational opportunities of women.

So much for the ledger's credit side. On the other side there were some entries too—old and familiar bogies that had not been scotched. There was, for one, the government's cheeseparing financing, especially in the support which it gave to the elementary school, which it scarcely financed at all. For another, there was the state's traditional fatuity in its relationship to the orthodox established church. Not only were its holy clerks granted vast concessions in the lower school; they were even encouraged to take command. There ensued, as a result, a curricular class system in which the predominant rights and privileges fell to the sacred subjects rather than to the ABCs. Finally, there was the utter lack of compulsory learning, or for that matter, even a desire to bring it about. Because of its absence, of the millions of Russia's boys and girls, at the very crest of the Alexandrian reform wave, only 800,000 were sighted at their books—not just in the elementary dens of knowledge, but in all the schools combined. All this weighed heavily on the national learning. By design or accident, the government's thumb tipped the educational balance. Overwhelmingly the ones who introduced themselves to knowledge were those whom fortune had caressed—that is, the upper middle class and the nobility. Consequently, in the schooling of its masses, where Russia's educational enterprise should have been the strongest, it was the weakest, and for the 800,000 who graced the academic bench, there were divisions—nay, armies incalculably large—of peasants and workers wallowing in the slough of illiteracy.

But Alexander was an understanding man, and in time these defects might have seen some alleviation. Unluckily, destiny was in a capricious mood. On a day in spring of 1866 a terrorist, his psyche heavily laden, took a shot at the Czar. The attempt failed, but Alexander, suffering the viper's bite, put a fast brake on his liberalism. The next day, Minister Golovnin, the benign architect of Russia's school reform, was elbowed out of office to make room for Dimitri Tolstoi, a despot of ruthless ingenuity.

There followed a full retreat into futility. Almost at once the ax fell on the natural sciences. Hip deep in sin, they had but recently hatched Darwin, an English monster, whose teachings stood in plain derision of the Good Book. Worse yet, they had stimulated the young to wrong thinking, even to radicalism and revolution. In the secondary school, hence, they were excommunicated at once and completely, while in the houses of advanced thought, their sharp teeth pulled, they were put under the vigilance of a twenty-four hour guard. With its labs deserted, the secondary school returned to the contemplation of the standby classics. But even these, stripped of all seduction, were reduced to a laborious boiling of the grammatical pot. Thus the mind was safely crammed and drilled, and by this route alone could one expect on some dubious tomorrow to win admission to a university.

Needless to say, academic freedom, so hard won, became purely imaginary, like a perfect circle or a platonic beer. To hold professors to the straight and narrow line, spies lurked all about—even students were put upon to snoop on one another, not only in academic chambers, but outside beyond their walls. Their uniform, which only yesterday they had been made to shed, they now were ordered to put on. But where in happier days it had been a garment of distinction, it was notice now, like a WANTED sign in any American post office, to the police to be on special watch. To purge the schools still more, all textbooks were minutely sifted for traces of subversion, and only the safe ones were admitted to classroom use. Newspapers that forgot to watch their step were not simply warned; they were shut down. In sum, what was wanted from the youth of Russia was not thinking, but submitting.

In the trenches of the lower learning the pall was no less dismal. Instruction of the ABC recruits, which had never really glistened, was reduced to the dullest mechanism. The frail financial support that even the benevolent Golovnin could barely scratch together was obliterated entirely. Did parents pine, nevertheless to make their little Peter literate? Then let them put up their own rubles. Did local boards mumble protestingly about communal rights? Then they'd better hush up, for in their midst the minister had packed his placemen.

Thus the pursuit of knowledge after that fateful day in spring. Its central aim was to make good citizens, which is to say, a mass of dummies indoctrinated and conditioned with the government's official axioms, and hence able, automatically and at all times, to think *right*.

In 1881, while cruising through the streets of his capital, Alexander became the target of a bomb. This time he fell and did not rise.

The third Alexander, who now brandished the scepter, had no weakness for liberalism. It was, he had persuaded himself long ago, an insidious and sinister poison compounded by Beelzebub against decency and good order. The Czar's thought was no mere speculation. His father's sudden exit had given him ocular proof of its validity—indeed, it even carried the confirmation of his entourage, and especially of his most intimate advisor, the procurator of the Holy Synod, who was able to prove its points by the Bible. Under the circumstances, the Czar's first duty was to smoke out this maker of evil, and to batter it down wherever it showed itself, however faintly. Just as important was to vaccinate the mass of Russians against knowledge, to keep them, so to say, on the level of a herd of puddingheads, and hence immune to false ideas. Thus safeguarded against the liberal notions then enflaming the West, Russia might conceivably retain its normalcy. We need not occupy ourselves at length with the details— they fall into the familiar pattern. Once again orthodoxy, autocracy, and nationalism pawed and pressured the populace with the usual heavy hand and the usual rampaging in the academic house, whether in its basement or in its highest tower. The lamp which here and there still braved a feeble flame when Alexander ascended to his mission was soon snuffed out, and everywhere darkness descended.

6

Such, generally speaking, was the state of learning in 1894, when the nation fell heir to its second Nicholas. He was a man unblessed by any talent for his craft, stupid and unimaginative, doomed to wander in a maze, until forces far beyond his ken blew him up at last to make an end, not only of him and his line, but of an era as well. Dedicated, like all the reigning Romanovs, to the messianic delusion, Nicholas despised liberal ideas no less than Alexander. There would be none of their nefarious traffic during his regime—on this point, he declared, there could be no argument. As for those who talked hopefully of change, let them cease their deceptive prattle; such hopes, the Czar made plain, are but "senseless dreams."

Nevertheless, change forced its way through his guard, not, it is true, in the realm of liberal thinking, but in the more material world of industry and economics. Far on in the nineteenth century, when the overwhelming mass of Russians still wrung their living from the soil, the government undertook to lay the foundation stones of industry. Aid from France and Britain animated the enterprise with the necessary capital. Pretty soon the miner's pick was making noise in the Donets coal basin, while from the fields of Baku issued the pleasant sound of bubbling oil. Presently the blast furnaces of steel added their raucous note to the emerging industrial cacaphony.

Meanwhile there had come to the Ministry of Finance a man named Witte. A wizard of remarkable gifts, he not only put Russia on the gold standard; he even succeeded in what has since become a dying and derided art, namely, putting the national budget into balance. But Witte's heart—if such a prodigy may be said, even metaphorically, to give an ear to its subtle promptings—was reserved for the conjuring up of railroads. He had worked himself into the business when it was still a novelty, and with an immense success—indeed, living in America today, he would bathe in the national dazzle as a self-made man. Starting out in 1892, Witte applied his go-getting talents during the dozen years following to the multiplication of Russia's railroads, doubling them in mileage, and extending their network in all directions, even into the distant and forlorn fastnesses of Siberia.

By Western standards Russia's industrial march moved slowly—nevertheless, it moved. Its inevitable manifestation, as everywhere else, was the factory, and as the years proceeded, an ever-lengthening line of workers. They had come, for a large part, from the farm, turning their back on its hard and endless struggle for the promise of something ponderably better. But it was a bemusing hope, and the mill, it soon turned out, was no promotion. Sweat as they would, they got nowhere. Those above them paid them no heed—even when the workers became insistent and resorted to strikes, their efforts were always baffled. For a moment, in 1897, their sun seemed about to rise when the state ordered some small amelioration of their joyless lot, and at the same time reduced their working day to eleven hours. Unhappily, it proved to be a false dawn. Thus balked at every turn, proletarian Russia turned its mind more and more to redressing its trouble by violence—even, if need be, by a vast upheaval of revolution.

Meanwhile, a small band of intellectuals, their Marx clutched to their breast, joined force in the formation of the Socialist party. It was in human annals a tremendous phenomenon, not only for the earth-shaking triumph reserved for it on some far-off day, but more immediately, for the sheer audacity of its venture. For in Russia the road to reform was a grueling one. No Bill of Rights gave comfort to its traveler—instead, everywhere lurked the imperial secret police, devoted at all times to the ferreting out of liberals and radicals.

Even so, agitators conspired just the same. Chased underground, they worked by stealth, communing behind bolted doors, and forging their arsenal of revolutionary broadsides on presses unbeholden to the law's inquisitive eye. When, for all their artful guile, some of them were snared, they were rewarded, if they were lucky, with incarceration; not uncommonly their fate was death or, scarcely better, a long sojourn in the vast and creepy vault of bleak Siberia. Such a man was Lev Davidovitch Bronstein, more familiarly known as Trotsky, who, while still in his teens, suffered exile for having organized a party of Odessa workers. Another was Vladimir Ilytch Ulianov. Inscribed in his niche of immortality as Lenin, he was dosed in 1896 with three years of Siberia. Joseph Djugashvilli—his stable name was Stalin—was penned at least a dozen times for his radical and revolutionary enterprise; but since his talents for breaking out of jail were even greater than his gifts for getting in, he was at length immured in the mephitic waste of eastern Siberia.

As Russia stretched its railway farther and farther across Siberia, its interests, particularly in China, ran head on into those of Japan. There ensued between the two rivals the familiar piling up of strife until, at length, in 1904 the pot ran over, and they squared off in war. The advantage, it did not take long to notice, was with the Japanese—in fact, the conflict was scarcely a year old when the Russians were done for.

What ailed Russia's effectiveness was not only the superiority of Japan, but the weaknesses that rotted the state from within. To the generality of Russians the conflict in the East was vague and remote, brought about by cynical and mainly disreputable men, an economic and political adventure of which they wanted no part. The judicious were antagonistic to the whole business, while the radicals voiced their hope for a Russian defeat.

Already before the final collapse in the field, on the home front the fires of dissent were flickering. Insurrection presently flared up in various places. In far-flung rural grasslands, peasants wreaked their fury on landlords, forcing themselves into their mansions, frisking them for their treasures, and destroying what they did not bag or pocket. Strikes fell on the country like the Biblical locusts. In St. Petersburg strikers launched a council of workers, and elected Trotsky, now suddenly risen from obscurity, to be its president. Moscow, paralyzed by a general strike, succumbed to the workers. But these uprisings, though impressive and even frightening, were diffuse, and in the end they went for naught. Pretty soon, the Czar's troops, back from their rout in Manchuria, were set upon the insurrectionists, and this time the soldiers worked swiftly and efficiently.

In the first flush of the rebels' success, the Czar and his fellow masterminds, scared green by what was happening, and greener yet by the prospect of even worse things to come, pledged a number of reforms, including full civil rights and a legislature, or duma, to be elected by universal suffrage. Though these promised boons were given being, in one way or another their free functioning was impaired. Consequently, as the approaching world war threw out its advancing shadows, the mass of Russians, still bereft of man's essential rights and dignities, continued to be the doormat of orthodoxy, autocracy, and nationalism.

7

Thus the essence of the Russian culture during the reign of the last of the Romanovs. Its reflection, as per the almost invariable rule, revealed itself in education. Perceived in the uncertain light of statistics, Russian education during this period shows signs of what has come to be regarded as progress. There was, for one, a tremendous surge in academic enrollment, and by this token, a proliferation of the groves of learning, from the lowest to the highest. For another, the enterprise was more generously supported out of the national treasury than at any previous time in Russia's history—though its gleanings, let it not be forgotten, were the lowest in the state's entire budget. So much for what reaches the eye. Put the business under an X ray, however, and you will see at once the old and familiar malignancies. For all the hearty boom in the number of its pupils, the elementary school was still hagridden by clericalism and nationalism. The secondary school was still the mansion of privilege, inaccessible to the numerous lower folk. The same, of course, may be said, though to a lesser degree, of France and Germany. But in Russia the chasm between the primary and secondary learning ran infinitely wider. For in the former lands the rudiments were at least effectively implanted, while in the latter the operation was only deficiently performed. As a result, when Russia tallied heads, it found that for eight of every ten of its vast population, reading was a closed art. In the higher learning too the number of students had augmented, and so also the number of universities. But the academic spirit, of students and professors alike, was in full collapse, while the standards of scholarship had sunk so low, one needed a spyglass to give them scrutiny.

Though in pretty nearly every vital concern, Russia's educational endeavor sagged very badly, in keeping a watchful eye on teachers and students it had no peer. Privy to every turn in the bureaucratic maze, and versed in every trick of snooping and spying, the hordes of governmental inspectors executed their catchpole art with unremitting thoroughness. The run of them were men with nitric acid in their veins, and though they served the ruling class with an agreeable effectiveness, from teachers they got little more than hatred and contempt. When the Communists blew up the old regime, the Czar's inspectors were made to drink from the same jug with their former employers. They were among the first to go—not a few, in fact, were not only cashiered from office; they were promoted to their eternal, ghostly rest.

8

In 1914 Russian elementary schools were under the jurisdiction of the state, but this is not saying that they were state-maintained. Only a handful were so honored—the rest had to scratch for themselves. Not uncommonly the church undertook to give instruction to the young, in which case the state granted it a subvention. When the business was left to the secular arm, it was attended to by the boards of local government, the zemstvos. Considering the heavy handicaps they carried, they rendered a capital service—in truth, but for them the Russians would have found themselves almost devoid of public schools. The teeth of compulsory education, bared long since in every energetic and self-respecting state, had scarcely sprouted in Russia. In consequence, for not a few, school bells never rang. In any case, the time a youngster occupied the academic pew was indefinite. If he happened, like so many others, to be resident in one of Russia's myriad country specks, then his chances for more than four, or even three, years of instruction ran against heavy odds. If, on the other hand, fortune had settled him in one of the larger and more affluent communities, he might—if his father was so disposed—find the trail of elementary learning stretching over as many as eight or nine years. For the service and instruction of the public school there was no charge, and they were available to girls as well as boys. But to make such big-heartedness possible, it was necessary to bulge a classroom to the limit. Legally, the number of occupants per room was set at half a hundred; actually, it ran much higher.

Once a child was enrolled for schooling, his teacher undertook to ground him in the four conventional elements of reading, arithmetic, writing, and penmanship. Some time was also reserved for cramming him with the cardinal articles of Russian history and geography. Where it could be done conveniently, once a week or so children were given a stay from their book learning to gladden themselves, if they were boys, with spade and hoe, or if girls, with needle and thread. But all this transaction, whether academic or otherwise, was subordinate to religion. Compulsory in all schools, sacred study required more time and energy than the pondering of arithmetic and writing. Generally, religious lessons were conducted by the local man of God, who performed his operations when he was not occupied with his regular pastoring. With so vast a store laid on religious study, it necessarily obtained a considerable substance, including mighty gulps of the Old and New Testaments, the Creed, the common and special prayers and psalms, and the church's rites and rituals, besides its immutable ordinances.

Though much was on their hands, Russia's young enjoyed at least one salient concession—they were not rocked now and again, as were their fellow creatures in other lands, with tests and examinations. One solemn inquest into their mind and spirit sufficed. Held at the very end of their several years of labor, it was rarely more than casual, and it was always oral. To boys, for whom three years of struggle in the lower academic bench bore no terror, the state granted a very special reward: their term of conscript servitude under arms was reduced from six years to a mere three.

A peasant child exposed to anything more than the scantiest fundamentals was, like one with three eyes or half a dozen legs, so rare as to be scarcely imaginable. The more advanced learning was merchanted privately, or if its dissemination was public, it was to be obtained only in the larger towns. Even then, its patrons were for the most part boys. Their ruminations began with a rewarming of all their old knowledge—in truth, for two years their scholastic victuals consisted of little else. Everything was strictly table d'hôte, with no substitutes whatsoever, whether sacred or secular. Once the leftovers were out of the way, they were followed with elementary geometry, some physics and natural history, a more substantial geography and history, besides Slavonic, drawing, the more delicate points of handwriting, and more religion. To give a friendly hand to those aspiring some day for desk work in an office, some schools offered instruction in the primary principles of the business science.

Could the great Catherine have taken some time off from her postmortem session to examine Russia's repositories of elementary learning, some of their doings, doubtless, would have been disturbing to her spectral quietude. But the presence of girls on an equal footing with boys would have dispelled this momentary upset. And as she flitted from school to school, she would have confronted a spectacle which during her days on earth she had entertained only as a vague and wishful thought, namely, the coming into her own of the woman teacher. For every male practitioner there were now at least two females. Their pay was never princely—less, in fact, than a dollar a day with their lodging thrown in. As might be expected under the circumstances, their pedagogy was of the meanest sort—indeed, in the more advanced lands not a few would have been barred from practice. Nevertheless, they performed their ancient rite with a commendable diligence, and considering the heavy burden put upon them by a stupid and unsparing bureaucracy, one must needs offer them an admiring salute.

9

Moving upward into the secondary learning, one runs into the old and established European practice of keeping it within the bound of a selected few. Its
favorite purveyor, like its German ancestor from whom it had taken its name,
was the *Gymnasium*. Of a lesser luster, and by no means an equal, was the "real
school," the offshoot of the scientific subjects on which Alexander II had done
execution before he himself was fetched by an assassin's bomb. Both schools
were under the flag of the Ministry of Public Instruction, and subject, of course,
to its authority. Operated sometimes privately and sometimes publicly, in either
case they insisted on payment for their instruction. Save as visitors, hence, the
poor rarely roved within their premises. Yet for all their cautious screening,
these schools had no attraction for the aristocracy who, sniffing at them for
their bourgeois tinge, consigned their children to the care of expensive and
exclusive academies abroad.

Generally, candidates for a secondary diploma got under way at the age of
ten, and, if they were serving their time at a *Gymnasium*, and if everything went
well for them, they emerged eight years later, wearied, perhaps, but exultant.
Like its Germanic namesake, the *Gymnasium* was, first and foremost, a language
mill, which specialized in grinding its apprentices in Latin and Greek, besides
Russian, Slavonic, and either French or German, but with an additional belaboring in mathematics, physics, history, geography, and the inevitable drawing and
penmanship. As in the lower school, so also in the upper one, religion was
mandatory from the first session to the last. Meanwhile, every boy was given
acquaintance with the formal laws of logic, not, however, to the end of helping
him to think new thoughts, and to think them straight, but rather to enable him
to corroborate and uphold the accepted ones.

The real school had no dealings with antiquity. As a consequence, the whip it
cracked was not Latin and Greek, but the modern languages, mathematics, and
natural science, and occasionally for a certain few the business subjects. Taking
one thing with another, its students got off more easily than their colleagues in
the *Gymnasium*—in fact, given a normal dowering and diligence, the former
could harvest their diplomas in seven years, while the latter were hard pressed to
get them in eight. By the same token, however, graduates from the *Gymnasium*
attained a greater distinction, and they alone had access to the higher learning.

Though the subject of religion saw hard service in the regular secondary
groves, for those given strongly to considerations of faith and morals, the church
operated special schools. Supported by funds drummed up locally, such seminaries were open without cost to the progeny of the clergy—all others, though, were
levied upon. Their course of studies bore a close resemblance to that of the
Gymnasium, with a much heavier pedal, however, on the divine studies. For not
a few, four years of its mentoring usually proved to be quite enough, whereupon, the fact of their achievement duly noted, they were free. The rest, with an

eye to working some day in the field of Christian endeavor, and preferably as holy clerks, continued for six years more. Those who showed themselves of a higher potentiality were generally persuaded to enlist at one of the church's advanced colleges where they might train for some transcendental spot in the ecclesiastical hierarchy.

There remains the cadet school. It had come upon the scene in St. Petersburg in 1731 as the Noble Cadet Corps. As might be gathered from the tone of its title, it was of a finicky taste, and it accepted none save those of a noble pedigree, receiving them when they were thirteen, and putting them through their paces for four years or so, to pack them off for a career in soldiering or for some civilian office of comparable dignity. For this purpose it worked them briskly in modern languages, not only in the conventional standbys of French and German, but in Italian and Polish as well. To enable them on some tomorrow to fathom the complexities of military strategy, siege gunnery, fortification, and similar applied sciences, it grounded them securely in mathematics and physics. Finally, it rehearsed them in the accomplishments so necessary for living in the gala world, and without which a nobleman, whether of the military or civilian order, could not possibly be expected to make a success. Thus they were put upon to dance, to make music, and to discharge their lovelier thoughts in flights of rhyme. They learned how to grace the saddle, and they worked industriously toward perfecting themselves at swordplay.

So things sat more or less as the years trailed on. The school grew larger, of course, and the number of its connoisseurs increased, and so did the patina of its old tradition. The incomparable Catherine, it may be recalled, had given the world something of a start when she placed the younger cadets under the tutelage and command of women. But presently the practice was out the window, and the boys resigned themselves to the custody of men.

When, in 1914, the Cadet Corps honored its 183d birthday, it was pretty much what it had been at its advent, namely, a military academy addressing its training to a patronage which issued almost entirely from the Russian *haut monde*. As in the case of the real school, the Cadet Corps engaged its incipient troopers for seven years, and the studies of the latter were for the most part those of the former, but with a powerful military overtone—in fact, its instruction was executed not, as in other schools, by secular Pestalozzis, but by military professionals. Once graduated from the Cadet Corps, a young man had easy access to a career in arms, or if ambition had him in its grip, he might enter one of the advanced military colleges to fit himself some day for a higher officer's regalia.

If the reservoirs of secondary learning flowed only moderately for the mass of Russia's boys, then for girls they barely trickled. Schools there were, of course, and a girl was free to attend any one of them according to her lights and—naturally and inevitably—the state of the family checkbook. For those soaring in society's higher altitude there were the usual de luxe private schools. Lower down several miles, where the middle class bedizened its own little world, the girls' *Gymnasium* ruled as favorite. Finally, there were the diocesan schools which confined their shepherding to the daughters of the clergy. A diploma from any of these shrines conferred upon its owner the right to give instruction in the elementary grades. To practice the pedagogic art in a secondary school, the aspiring schoolma'am, befittingly enough, was made to take more courses. Apart from Latin and Greek, which were regarded as too formidable for the ordinary feminine puissance, girls occupied themselves with the same subjects as boys. If, for all the warnings about the hazards of the classical pursuit, a young miss craved to brave it nonetheless, then she had to resort to private accommodation. Generally speaking, the secondary schooling available to girls was on a par with that of their brothers, though the boys' *Gymnasium*, with its eight years of forced learning in Latin and Greek, was commonly taken to be vastly more difficult, and by this token, superior.

10

For lads having no palate for the general culture featured by the regular dispensaries of secondary learning, happily, there were other possibilities. If, for example, they were given to making things—as boys not uncommonly are—they could seek instruction and training for three or four years in a school for artisans. Or if they lathered for the combat of the marketplace, they might make a start by hearkening to the experts in its fundamentals in a school of business. The most distinguished academies in this specialty required seven years for the attainment of such an end. Less demanding were the so-called "business classes." Designed for office workers, they carried on nocturnally, and they concerned themselves largely with a brushing-up of the common elementals, say, spelling or penmanship, the putting together of a simple letter, or even the adding in the wink of an eye of a gigantic column of figures.

For admission to the higher learning of business, the aspirant needed to possess no less than a secondary school diploma. Thus fortified, he was at liberty to pursue knowledge at one of the advanced seminaries of commerce. By the American yardstick—even of that primitive time—much of their learning would doubtless have fallen short. Run through their pronouncements, and you will look in vain for courses in window display, direct selling by mail, or hosiery and underwear—indeed, you will not even unearth a seminar in business research. Instead, you will observe a steady and relentless prying into the nature and operation of the business cosmos, from its banking and bookkeeping, its buying and selling and insuring, to its ethics and jurisprudence.

Actually, not many youths outfitted themselves with the higher business lore. Hence, for one so equipped, there was usually no long waiting in line for a job. In fact, if he preferred, he might even teach commercial subjects at one of the regularly appointed business schools.

CHAPTER 20

JEAN-JACQUES ROUSSEAU

L ike dreaming up better worlds, reflecting on education—what it is and what it ought to be—is an ancient and venerable practice. Plato and Aristotle exercised their fancy on it, and so did Cicero, Tacitus, Suetonius, and Quintilian, the first professor to grace a public payroll. The list runs to length, and now and then it flashes with unforgettable names—Erasmus, Vives, Milton, Montaigne, Locke, Comenius, and Fénelon, to point to just a few. Yet, rather curiously, though reformers rose again and again to cry down education's stale and senseless ways, on the generality of birchmasters their challenge had but slight effect. Inspect almost any of their operating rooms of the eighteenth century, and you will observe their practice to be pretty much what it was in the recesses of remote and faded time. Their primary objective was still what it had ever been, namely, to stuff the memory with a mass of facts, and to reinforce the business, in difficult cases, with bluster and a large and powerful stick.

Even so, the eighteenth century saw the coming of a man whose ideas, though too wild and visionary for the general run of his contemporaries, were destined to leave a deep and ineffaceable mark on our educational practice. His name was Jean-Jacques Rousseau, and he was born in 1712 in Geneva, then a free municipality. Though Calvin had long since taken off for his predestinate duties in the ghostly world, his melancholy shadow still haunted his ancient fastness, a fact Rousseau was to learn from sad experience. Some compensation, perhaps, for the city's moralistic gloom lay in the natural finery of its setting. Nestled hard by the Alps at the mouth of Lake Léman, on fine days a sheet of liquid sapphire, Rousseau's hometown was ever a feast for his eyes and a prod to his romantic heart. If, as year succeeded year, he became the eloquent advocate of nature, and if he held certain moralists and theologians in low regard, then in all likelihood the earliest fashioner of his mood had its inception in the surroundings of his childhood.

When Rousseau wrote of his birth as his first misfortune, he may, as some experts assert, have been engaging in the stratagem of attention getting. Nevertheless, at the bottom of his announcement there lies a sliver of truth, for a few days after Rousseau's introduction to this earth his mother died. With her passing the burden of rearing the infant fell upon the father, who neither understood nor enjoyed its mystery. To give him aid and advice, he summoned an aunt, but she too was far from competent. As a result, the boy grew up unbridled, devoid of the simplest self-command, and with more vices to his credit than virtues. It was during his early nonage, however, by being made to keep his ears open into the morning's infant hours to hearken to his father recite from books, mostly of a trashy sentimentality, that the boy obtained an introduction to the written word.

As the years brought him to his beard Rousseau undertook to learn a trade, and after several false starts he became an engraver's apprentice. But he had no heart in what he was doing, and save for a trim and lovely hand and copious floggings, he got practically nothing. In fact, at sixteen, when the chance suddenly beckoned, he took flight from his trade and master, and turned his back on his native town.

It is not necessary to embroider the details of the boy's next few years. Let it be enough to note that in their course he drifted to the villa of Madame de Warens, a lady less renowned for her morals than for her pulchritude. She lodged Rousseau in her home as her protégé and later as her lover. This is not to suggest, however, that in the shaping of his life the madame was of slight significance. On the contrary, she saw to it that his meager learning was extended and enlarged with tutoring in music, philosophy, Latin, and what then passed for natural science. Through her he abjured his Protestantism for Roman Catholicism, which later on he traded in for Deism. As the years flowed on, his relationship with Madame de Warens wore itself out, and in 1741 the couple, somewhat dewy-eyed, agreed to call it quits.

Rousseau now headed for Paris where he hacked for a while for a publisher. He then went to Venice as secretary to a minor French diplomat. His sojourn was short but not without consequence, for in his courtly enclave he found himself in a world of cant and guile, a Babylon, Italian style, whose pretense and fraudulence maddened him, and the like of which, in later years, as the protagonist of a let-nature-save-us scheme of things, he was at pains to castigate unsparingly.

Back to Paris in 1744—Rousseau was now thirty-two—he began to frequent the company of Diderot and the philosophes, that tinderbox of intellectuals whose subversions were presently to make a bonfire of the Old Regime. It was during these years that he succumbed to Thérèse Levasseur, a creature of the lower orders and of no discernible luster. They set up housekeeping together on an experimental basis, and there issued five offspring, each of whom their incomparable father presented to a foundling home. After his bond with Thérèse had run more than a score of years, Rousseau decided to make it official and, until death, indissoluble. And so, in 1768, in a simple civil rite consummated in a tavern, he conferred upon his consort the rank and dignity of Madame Rousseau.

Though he had tried his hand at writing at various times, it was not until 1750 that Rousseau snared success. In that year he compounded an essay in reply to the question of the Academy of Dijon whether our advance in the arts and sciences had helped to advance us morally. His answer, diverging from the conventional, was a flat and gorgeous "No!" and it fetched the academy's prize. Much more important, however, was the fact that at thirty-eight, after a life of utter undistinction, Rousseau at one stroke had brought himself into notice not only at Dijon, but throughout the whole civilized occidental world.

Fancying himself appointed by fate for a career in letters, Rousseau now fixed his mind on writing. Saving only when he got himself into a low spirit or when his health ran down, he was at the business without letup. From his pen there gushed a torrent of letters, verses, plays, operas, essays, an interminable novel, besides no end of pamphlets and philippics. Three years after taking the Dijon laurel, he nominated himself to win another, this time on the origins of inequality. It brought him some flattering cheers, but no prize. In 1760 he completed *The New Heloïse.* A novel which runs for a thousand pages and which was then regarded as somewhat lascivious, it was a romantic acclamation of the natural man, the so-called Noble Savage. Two years later *The Social Contract* and *Emile* followed, two meditations in prose which, more than anything else, have reserved for Rousseau his niche in immortality. The one, a treatise on the ideal government, need not detain us here; the other, which considers education, requires some particular attention.

2

Cast into four parts which delineate the course of education from the first mists of infancy to the dawn of manhood, *Emile* leads off with a preamble on Rousseau's views of nature. "Everything," he says, "is good as it comes from the hands of the Author of Nature; but everything degenerates in the hands of man." Though on this score theologians held differently, Rousseau permitted himself no compromise with them. In fact, his insistence that man at birth is good and that our so-called progress is the great pox of human happiness is the one recurrent and consistent note not only in *Emile*, but in all his major writings. If the newborn babe is naturally good, then, Rousseau believed, his education must be in consonance with nature. Converging on this task, he sights three kinds of educations or "teachers." One is just growing up or letting our body and capacities develop. Next, there is the education derived from things about us, things which teach us for good or ill that fire burns, that ice is cold and slippery, and that skunks can be unfriendly. Finally, there is the education imparted by man. Over the first kind we have no control; over the second scarcely any; but over the third a great deal. "The cooperation of the three," Rousseau goes on, "is necessary for their perfection"; and as long as this is so, "it is to the one over which we have no control that we must direct the other two." Thus the theme which underlies *Emile.*

The book's first part traces Emile's education from his arrival at the domestic fireside to his sixth birthday. There is in it a palpable echo of Comenius and Locke, and a soft murmur now and then from Montaigne. The main task during this period is to give heed to nature's requirements. Does little Emile bawl for food? Then let his mother put him to nurse. Does he seek to squirm and wiggle? Then away with the hindrance of long and cleaving wraps. Let the babe be a healthy primate. Let him exercise his muscles and his senses. Above all, keep him away from the medicos and their arsenal of medicines, salves, and bleedings— save only when the child has one foot in the grave. Then, says Rousseau, brushing away a tear, "the doctors can do no worse than kill him." Like the medical brethren, habits too are to be avoided, the only permissible habit being "to contract no habit whatever." Play, which comes unbidden to the young, should be courted freely, but Emile's playthings should not be the costly gear whose seductions are mainly to bemuse and flatter the ego of the adult who buys them. Rather, let them be the simple gimcracks of nature, such as "branches with their fruits and flowers, or a poppy-head wherein the seeds are heard to rattle." In all this early education nature obviously holds the prompt-book, and the most seemly place to let the script unfold is in the field and woodland amid the daily wonders of the countryside.

The second part, which conducts Emile to his twelfth anniversary, runs along in much the same tenor. "Develop the body, and keep the mind fallow," is the recurrent phrase. To such an end Emile learns to swim. He makes long treks over hill and dale. Thus his muscles are given tone and hardness, and an edge is put upon his senses. For reinforcement he grapples with weights, and he measures distances. To train his hand and eye he sketches. To attune his ears he warbles.

During these years all recourse to formal learning is under strict taboo. There are to be no bouts with history or geography—not even, indeed, with the featherweight, fundamental Rs. Reading, in fact, fills Rousseau with bile. "It is," he cries, "the scourge of childhood," and "at the age of twelve Emile will scarcely know what a book is." The formal learning, it appears, puts a demand on reason, and in childhood such capacity is absent. By the same token, fables, though admired and recommended by Locke and Fénelon, are dismissed as mere jabber. The child, Rousseau explains, may negotiate them with a certain deft-ness—even, perhaps, with a sneaking pleasure. But at bottom he is impervious to their meaning, and so they are outlawed.

"We are always looking for the man in the child," comments Rousseau, "without thinking what he is before he becomes a man." To safeguard him from error, Emile must be taught only what he can understand. Not only must booklearning be held at bay, but until Emile reaches the age of reason, "he can form no idea of moral beings and social relations." Hence, sermonizing him about the meaning of right and wrong is futile. Does he comport himself like a budding Machiavelli? It is sad, of course—but put away that rod. Let there be no cloutings or to-bed-without-suppers. Instead, apprehend the wretch by means of "natural consequences." If, for example, he smashes a window, then let him sit in the draft, and, maybe, even catch a cold. Does he trespass on the neighbor's melon patch and plant himself a crop of beans? Then let the neighbor return the compliment by uprooting Emile's sprouting beanlings. Thus Emile will be taught "the sanctity of private property."

On his twelfth birthday Emile stands on the doorstep of what Rousseau designates as "the time for labor, instruction, and study." Although he is still expanding in height and width, the reserve of his strength now exceeds his physical needs. Hence, there appears a lull in his corporal and sensory training to yield more time to the pursuit of knowledge. But the chase is for "useful knowledge," and it is prompted by Emile's natural desires. The main stress falls on science, but its phenomena are to be tracked down not from the well-stocked tomes of knowledge, but from firsthand experience. Emile "is not to learn science, but to discover it." Geography is borne in on him not with globes, atlases, and similar academic contraptions, but first by setting him to exploring his environs, and then by moving him in an ever-widening circle to scenes farther and farther away. To translate his experience into meaning he is made to draw maps. The study of astronomy is broached by exposing Emile to the flaming magic of the rising sun. Electricity is smuggled into his consciousness through the mystifications of a juggler who, by the sly use of a magnet, snatches metal ducks out of the air. In all this exploration Emile is to be furnished no working equipment. Should he need a funnel or a strainer, he is to make it himself. Crude and impromptu though such devices may be, Rousseau believed that they make more sense than the finest specimens to be had in the shops. Although Emile's life is now centered in learning, books are still suspect. "I hate books," seethes Rousseau, "they merely teach us to talk about what we do not know." But his aversion is mellowed a bit by a concession to *Robinson Crusoe*, since therein "all the natural needs of man are exhibited in a manner obvious to the mind of a child."

Up to his twelfth year Emile has passed his day mostly by himself or with his tutor. Bereft of a chance for ordinary human congress, he is not privy to the art of social dealing. To remedy this deficiency, he now goes into society. Launched by being made to observe working people in practice, he is to discover how interdependent all of us really are. Not only is he made familiar with the fundamental human relationships; he is also put upon to master a trade—the carpenter's august craft which somehow Rousseau regards as being "nearest the state of nature." Thus armed vocationally, Emile will be ready for his rainy days and thereby he ought to spare the rest of us from having to support him.

In his middle teens Emile comes to adolescence, and for the next few years he will feel the suction of strange and powerful forces. "Here," says Rousseau, "is the second birth ... when a man really begins to live." The lad's social enlightenment, so far scarcely touched, now goes into high gear. "We have formed his body, his senses, his intelligence," declares Rousseau, "it remains to give him a heart." As usual, he strikes out for his goal over the route of personal experience. But his introduction to the human race is not to begin at the top with admirals, bankers, bishops, and similar spangled worthies. Such contacts, Rousseau fears, have their hazards—in time, indeed, they may rack his protégé with a lust for power and glory. To be rendered compassionate of the common folk, Emile must move in meaner circles, even among the shanty wretches at the bottom of the human pile. And so, like a social worker, he goes aprowl in hospitals and orphan homes—even in murky jailhouses.

This is also the time set aside for taking stock of human values. For this purpose Emile gives his attention to the nature of inequality and the powerful hand of prejudice in the making and breaking of human careers. It was a subject on which Rousseau, having written an essay, esteemed himself as something of an expert. Lest the youth be bowled over by man's folly and fraudulence, he is to salvage his confidence by pondering the great historical past. Like Carlyle in a later day, Rousseau believed the historical cream to be biographic, and of all the writers of lives he had ever heard of he picked Plutarch as the most meritorious.

If Rousseau once entertained doubts on the study of fables, he is now free of his misgivings. Come to the right ripeness, Emile is safe from the snares of illusion, and fables, once ruled out, are now apt, meet, and essential for Emile's progress, for "by censuring the wrongdoer under an unknown mask . . ." they "instruct without offending him." The time for fables is also the time for art and letters and the development therein of some serious discernment. It is the time also for social science, and in this province what could be better for Emile than to absorb *The Social Contract*? Finally, this is also the period for ethics, metaphysics, and religion. "In his fifteenth year," observes Rousseau, "Emile does not yet know that he has a soul; perhaps he will find it out too early in his eighteenth." It was Rousseau's belief that in this matter Emile's education must proceed warily. "A child, it is said, must be brought up in the religion of his father; and he must be taught that it alone is true, and that all others are absurd. But if the power of this instruction . . . depends only on authority, for which Emile has been taught to have no regard, what then? In what religion shall we educate him?" The answer is "in none." The end to be sought is simply "to put him in a condition to choose for himself that to which the best of his own reason may bring him."

The last part of *Emile* is gratuitous, and aside from the light it sheds on its maker, it might just as well have been left unhatched. Unlike the rest of the book what it has to say is mainly trite. It lays down an educational program for Sophie, contrived by Rousseau to be Emile's mate—more particularly, though, it puts forth Rousseau's main theorems on the education of women. Our sister in skirts, he takes note, is naturally subservient to the male, and so her education "ought to be relative to men." Her elemental function is "to be useful to them, to educate them when young, to care for them when grown, to counsel them, to console them"—in a phrase, to service and comfort them. Whatever learning may be granted to such a creature must be within this premise. Commence by making her obedient and industrious. Develop her figure. Array her with grace and charm. Fortify her with health and strength so that she may breed a flock of robust young. Initiate her in the knacks of sewing and embroidery, and for good measure, make her adept with brush and easel, and in song and dance, for thus illuminated, she will be "agreeable and sweet" to her man. By the same token, lest she alarm and harass him, let her not unsettle herself with philosophy and science—let her major instead in the study of men. She should "learn how to penetrate their feelings through their conversation, their action, their looks, their gestures. . . ." As for dealings with the Heavenly Father, if she be wed, then she is to kneel in the temple of her mate. If she has not yet stalked a man at the altar of God, then let her worship in the religion of her mother. Needless to say, under such prerequisites her religious training is different from that of Emile. Instead of lying in wait for her fifteenth birthday for her soul to announce its presence, she is to take no such risks, and at a tender age she is impressed into a respectable and established rite.

3

Historians have chronicled that Rousseau died in 1778 and practically out of his mind—a detail, perhaps, but not without its sardonic overtones. For, as in the case of Henrik Ibsen and Friedrich Nietzsche, Rousseau's detractors wasted no time in trying to turn his tragedy to their advantage. If the man passed from these scenes in a shaky state of mind, then, they contended, traces of his infirmity must have lurked within the caverns of his mind even before the end. Hence, his views generally ought to be eyed suspiciously. In several ways they were able to give their argument some plausible support, for inconsistencies and puerilities from Rousseau radiate like heat from the summer sun, and even his most fevered fans are sometimes hard put to explain his strange and transcendental lapses.

The fact, however, seems to be pretty well forgotten that Rousseau was neither a man of science nor one of logic, but something of a mixture of evangelist and poet; and true to the license of their ancient office, he allowed himself a frequent holiday from plain sense. His ideas welled from his heart to his head, but his brain was not always able to coax them into lucid meaning. Given to emotional enchantment, he seldom put down his facts, like an outline, in clear and shapely form. His books, in truth, traffic not chiefly in facts, but in ideas, and his importance lies not in the answers he formulated, but in the questions he raised. His century, like our own, was one of enlightenment, but that enlightenment, he felt, maintained itself apart from human happiness— often, indeed, it collided with it. Life as we live it, he held, is tragic because it is unreal, and it is unreal because it is unnatural. Of what worth, he asked—posing the question of questions—is such a bogus and tormented civilization? What was needed was a change of values, a vast transvaluation of the true, the good, and the beautiful. The transformation Rousseau was seeking, whether in *Emile* or *The Social Contract* or his numerous essays, placed humanity above reason, and feeling above meaning. As such his rebellion was profoundly spiritual, a fact which can be baffling to those who would take his measure with tape and slide rule.

If Rousseau was right when he lamented that *Emile* did not fetch the attention it deserved, then the fault, as has been hinted, was in part his own. But was the man even remotely right? The book had no sooner appeared on the shelves than praise and censure beat down upon it like sheets of rain. Intellectuals like Diderot, Duclos, and d'Alembert pomaded it with critical hosannas. The great men of the Sorbonne, appalled by Rousseau's religious apostasy, excoriated him as the Devil's advocate. The English for their part welcomed the book with a festive air and twice rendered it into their own language, an honor they had never accorded a Frenchman. At the same time the Archbishop of Paris damned the whole business, and recommended its author for faggot and flame. When Rousseau sought asylum in Protestant Geneva, he found the city battened down, its gates bolted, and his book commandeered for burning by the common executioner. Outlawed in most right-thinking Continental lands, but vastly bootlegged, it attracted readers in swarms, as usual. Though Rousseau felt confusedly, nevertheless, he felt powerfully. Surely it is not altogether astounding to witness the common folk of France hailing Rousseau as their savior when the guns of the Revolution belched out their doom of the old order. Nor is it astounding to behold them reposing his bones in the monumented sanctuary of the Pantheon. Nor is it astounding to see him feted even today in some of the very places he once lashed to fury.

No other pedagogic treatise has ever caused the sensation of *Emile*, and none has ever been more controverted. "Rousseau," said Madame de Staël, "invented nothing. He set everything on fire." Voltaire, that incurable scoffer, shrugged off *Emile* as "a hodge podge of silly wet nurse in four parts." The sagacious Immanuel Kant, on the other hand, confessed it to be one of the rare things he had ever allowed to intrude upon his daily walk. Even the ranking critics damned and hymned Rousseau, as their successors still do today. Lasserre, to cite one, dismissed *Emile* as "not worth a shrug of the shoulders," while Lanson scented it with asphodel as "the most beautiful, the most thorough, and the most suggestive treatise ever written." The truth, as often, ranges somewhere in between. Recorded on *Emile*'s debit side are numerous entries, the most glaring being that it is negative, impracticable, individualistic, and even at times a mushy pishposh. On the credit side there is a stress on reason and a respect for the dignity of the child. "Begin," Rousseau urged, "by studying your pupils more thoroughly, for it is certain that you do not know them," a bit of counsel which is as fresh and valid as when it was first volunteered. Rousseau contended that nothing should be taught a child until he is ready to understand it, a proposition which, though somewhat suspect to the common run of teachers, has enjoyed a hearty support from the latter-day progressives, both pedagogical and psychological. Against an almost solid front of practicing schoolmasters Rousseau insisted that physical activity and health are of paramount concern; that a child's natural interests, such as curiosity and play, should be put to use in learning; that education should depend less on books and more on observation and experience. "Our first teachers," he let it be known, "are our feet, our hands, and our eyes. To substitute books for all these is to use the reason of others." Like the Humanists and Realists before him, Rousseau declaimed against the overtaxing burden put on the child's memory, and, finally, it was his belief that to be worthwhile, education must be broad and manifold so as to assure the full flower of all the child's powers and capacities. "I demurred a long time over publishing the book," Rousseau avowed, "but after vain efforts to make it better I believe I ought to print it as it is . . . and though my own notions may be erroneous, I shall not have lost my time if I inspire better ones in others." And such precisely was his effect.

CHAPTER 21

JOHANN BERNHARDT BASEDOW

Even before Rousseau had delivered himself of his naturalistic evangel in *Emile*, someone else was working out a more or less similar doctrine. He was a German, Johann Behrend Bassedau, or as he later addressed himself, Johann Bernhardt Basedow. He was born and baptized in 1724 in Hamburg. His childhood, like that of Rousseau, was full of disquiet and distress. His mother, there is reason to believe, died in a fit of madness. His father was inconsequential, an earnest, wooden man, full of dark humors, and given to assiduous drinking. But Basedow, for his part, was no angel, and his father must have suffered aplenty from his bizarre and devilish capers. Even so, the man entertained high and gaudy hopes for his heir, and actually succeeded in teaching him to read and write Latin before he was eight. Yet for all the paternal effort, young Basedow could not restrain his monkeyshines, and presently he ran off. After a brief spell, however, he consented to return to the family fireside and to apply himself at school.

Basedow had a good head and an easy way with books. He was slightly over twenty when, as per his father's ordinance, he repaired to the University of Leipzig to prepare himself in divinity. His work was diligent and, to a degree, commendable, but he inclined to eccentricity. Worse, his thinking, overladen with unbounded self-confidence, found itself frequently in open disagreement with that of his professors, a trait which the men of learning failed to appreciate. Indeed, before long, they began to cherish some serious doubts about his fitness for the pastoral gown, and Basedow's decision to forego holy orders was probably prudent.

Instead, in 1749 he went into service as a tutor in Holstein, where, during the three years following, he contracted his ardor for teaching, a desire which amounted to almost a passion, and which was to fever him to the end. Even then he enjoyed a vast disdain for mere schoolbook learning. Like the Realists before him, he put his confidence in learning by observation and experience. Geography, for example, he approached through a searching of the local environs. Latin he dispensed conversationally by parleying with his pupil naturally and freely like a Roman. His results, making due allowances, were good—at all events they revealed beyond any doubt that he had something of a flair for teaching.

From tutoring he went to a full-scale job as a schoolmaster in a Danish academy, an inheritor of the better days of the Renaissance, but now a finishing school for the sons of high-class Danes. Basedow worked indefatigably with his charges, seeking to impress upon their souls the necessity of virtue and the loveliness of the literary art. Meanwhile, he made several expeditions into writing, breaking into print with *A Practical Philosophy for All Classes*. He was apparently versed in the many tricks of teaching, and his pupils regarded him well. His colleagues, on the other hand, disliked him, not only for his success, but for his iconoclasm. He was, it was given out, an "enemy and abominable seducer of Christianity," a role which, of course, disqualified him as a molder of the Danish carriage trade.

In 1761 Basedow brought his operations to a classical secondary school at Altona, close by his native town of Hamburg. But his unsavory reputation shadowed him, and from the start he was under apprehensive eye. To make matters worse, he proceeded to toss off a number of broadsides wherein he put his grip on morality and religion in a highly rationalistic fashion. As a consequence, he and his family were barred from holy communion and, to safeguard the public well-being, the Basedows were clapped under an ecclesiastic ban. To make assurance extra sure, his writings were drummed out of circulation, and anyone resorting to them was threatened with exile. One such experience is usually enough to bring a man to his senses, but Basedow, who took delight in public uproar, continued in his acid expostulation, letting loose one tirade after another, and stoking his fire, meanwhile, with generous draughts of spiritous fluids.

2

Amidst all this scandal he succumbed to *Emile*. So powerful was its impact that he decided hereafter to work out his energy in educational reform. Thus concerned, he issued a tract in 1768 wherein he combined his favorite pedagogical dogmas with an appeal for funds. He called it "An Address to Philanthropists and Men of Property on Schools and Studies and Their Influence on the Public Weal." Three main ideas run through it. For one thing, schools should be nonsectarian. For another, the clergy should keep their nose out of the public learning. For a third, education should be reformed in the vein, more or less, of the recommendations of the Messrs. Comenius, Locke, and Rousseau. Not the least important part of the address was its drive for funds to allow its author to furlough himself from his everyday work in order to compose new and improved books for the lower learning. The appeal, persuasively phrased and sentimentally perfumed, turned out to be an enormous success. Money was thrust upon Basedow from all directions, from Catholics, Jews, and Protestants, and from idealistic Freemasons. The poor, as often, outdid themselves. Even reigning princes stumbled over one another to give him a hand. When Basedow finished counting, he had amassed several thousand dollars, a sufficient bounty, surely, in those days to tide him and his family over for quite a while.

Two years later, in 1770, Basedow put forth his promised books. The first, again heavily titled, was the *Book of Methods for Fathers and Mothers of Families and Nations*. Compounded of familiar ingredients, it included such staples as "follow nature," "nonsectarian religious instruction," "direct method in language teaching," "sense training," and the like. His second work, *The Elementary Book*, soon followed. In it Basedow was at pains to gratify his more liberal benefactors, singling out each worthy for eulogy, each on a separate page, in fat, black Gothic type an inch at least in height. Four years after, in 1774, the two books were merged as *The Elementary Work*. Printed in four volumes, it was engauded with a hundred engraved illustrations, the first earnest attempt to make pedagogic use of pictures in the halls of learning since Comenius's *Orbis Pictus*, which had startled the school world more than a century earlier in 1658. Like its famous predecessor, Basedow's book represented a prodigy of knowledge covering almost everything then known to Christendom, from virtue and elegant manners, commerce and science, to insubordinate servants and death-room scenes. All in all, the book's good points outweighed its bad ones, and it scored a palpable hit. Characteristically, its author did not blush at his achievement. It presented, he admitted, "an incomparable method, founded on experience, of teaching children to read without weariness or loss of time."

3

Meanwhile Prince Leopold of Dessau, having got word of Basedow and his marvels, persuaded him to settle in his domain to open a school. For his enterprise he was to be remunerated with an annual $800, and he was to be given a free hand in the application of the principles he had so often and so flamboyantly hawked. The school, known as the Philanthropinum, opened in 1774. Its pupils, Basedow announced, would be treated as children, and not as mere carbon duplicates of their elders. Powdered tresses and rouged cheeks, then the established fashion in chic juvenile circles, in both the male and female sectors, were under strict prohibition. On the other hand, play and gymnastics were allotted a generous favor. Foreign languages, of which there were French and Latin, were pursued conversationally. Almost the whole day was arranged into a routine. Five hours, for example, were reserved for study; three went for swordplay, physical exercise, the dance, and the tonal art; six were set aside for manual work, play, and the consumption of victuals; and one hour was given to the ordering of one's lodging. Needless to say, Basedow's academy was nonsectarian. In it, he gravely let it be known, there was to be the air of religion, but positively no slicing of theological hairs.

Though great things were promised by the Philanthropinum, most parents, daunted by its novelty, were reluctant to submit their young to its experimentalizing. In truth, the school had a hard time, and not counting Basedow's own two youngsters, it never had more than half a hundred pupils. This handful, however, was taught by Basedow and three assistants.

In 1776, with his usual faculty for public drumbeating, Basedow advertised an examination of his scholars. "The results," he said, "that can already be perceived show that what we promise is true." It might be a good thing, he added, for the various governments to dispatch some of their experts to the scene, "where so much of importance will be seen, heard, investigated, and discussed." Taking one thing with another, Basedow's pupils gave a creditable account of themselves. His own daughter, Emilie, something of a wonder child, attracted particularly favorable notice. The sage Immanuel Kant gave the school his approval, and in a couple of newspaper essays he ventured to demand a subsidy for its founder. The more bilious Herder, however, in a letter to one of his friends, declared the whole business to have been horrible, "like a hot house or a table full of human geese."

As things turned out, the latter's critical judgment was intrinsically sound. Even before the year's passing, portents of doom were shadowing Basedow's seminary of learning. The first blow landed squarely on Basedow when he was cashiered as the school's headmaster. Soon after, he quit altogether, and betook himself elsewhere. He continued in practice for a time, though in a modest and private manner. Finally, in 1790, a hemorrhage felled him. His last thoughts were considerate no less than characteristic. "I wish," he murmured, "my body to be dissected for the good of my fellow men." But even here, ironically enough, Basedow's hopes were not fulfilled.

Three years after Basedow's death the school he had founded in such radiant hope came to its end, a dismal and depressing smudge. Its ignominious finish was in no small part the fault of Basedow himself. Egotistical, full of upheaval, contentious, excessively romantic, a man who was acutely aware of his merits, whether real or imaginary, Basedow had never quite recovered from the wounds to his childhood psyche. There was in his secret spirit a yearning to instruct and improve his fellows, yet all too often what he succeeded in doing was only to enrage and estrange them. There is no lack of sense in some of his proposals. Yet sound though they may have been, the bombastic clamor in which he draped them grated on the public nerves. Nor could the plain people forgive him his assaults on their Christian idealism, and especially the libels and indecencies he had flung at their pastors.

Basedow's pedagogy, as has been said, grounded itself on Comenius, Locke, and of course, Rousseau. Like the latter he played up the child's naturalness, and like the first, he based his teaching on sense appeal. Again like Comenius, he wrote a picture textbook which turned out to be a great success. Like the ancient Socrates, he instructed his wards through conversation, and he undertook to develop their reason rather than their memory. Finally, like Quintilian in ancient Rome and Froebel, the inventor of the kindergarten in a later day, Basedow recognized the pedagogic worth of play and gaiety, and in his program he gave them admirable encouragement. His school, the Philanthropinum, was the first to push forth from the seedbed of *Emile*, and in the sense that it was a testing place for new and untried ideas, it was also an experimental school. It was, indeed, the archfather of them all.

Basedow was no mere jobber of other men's ideas. In fact, some of his innovations so far transcended the conventional, which is to say the old and approved, that they affronted the common mind. He believed, for one thing, in ¡education, a practice which in many places on the Atlantic's other side is still ¡ighted with doubts and misgivings. For a second thing, there were Basedow's views on religion, which, if it was taught at all, he insisted must be in the form of an unfettered nonsectarianism. His views on sex pedagogy, however, were far from neutral. He not only contended that the facts of sex should be imparted to the young; he also insisted that the business should be executed in a forthright manner, with plain names and anatomical charts, and with no allusions to daisies, June bugs, and similar folklore. His notions, needless to say, ran so far ahead of those of his time that they were marked not only as singular, but as offensive to the common pruderies. The aim of Basedow's whole pedagogic industry, as he estimated it, was the simple but optimistic one of preparing the young to become "citizens of the world."

Even more than Rousseau, Basedow has suffered from his critics. Unable to draw the line between Basedow the man and Basedow the pedagogue, they almost succeeded in doing him in. In fact, it was not until the present century of enlightenment that his work and thought were given the sober and impartial examination they deserved. The Philanthropinum, on the other hand, fared somewhat better. It may have been laid in its coffin when it was still in the flush of early youth, but the power of its example was certainly more than transient. Soon after its collapse one of its masters, Christian Salzmann, founded a similar institute at Schnepfenthal in Saxe-Coburg. It began its work in 1784, and though the era was still happily pious, Salzmann's school, like its prototype, was overwhelmingly secular. Unlike the Philanthropinum, however, it reserved its charms for those of courtly blood, or at least of an abundant pocket. Even so, Salzmann put his charges through a regime which bordered on the Spartan. Made to rise at cockcrow, they set themselves up with several hours of labor in their gardens or on the farm, whereupon they assembled to take flight, like the lark, in song. Finally, after the last note had melted in the air, they adjourned to the breakfast table to appease their vacant stomachs. For eight daily hours they had their noses in their books; one hour was granted to gymnastics; and several were conceded to play and recreation.

Salzmann was a first-rate master, and among the ranking members of his craft, he stands out for his elementary common sense. His school prospered, and after his passing, its direction fell into the hands of able successors. In 1884, the centenary of its advent, it was still doing a flourishing business.

Besides Salzmann several others took up Basedow's principle of combining study with practical work and play, and put them to use in seminaries run more or less along the lines of the Philanthropinum—men, for example, like Wolke, Behrdt, Campe, Trappe, and several more. In the procession of the years such endeavors gained more and more adherents, and by the end of the nineteenth century they were to be sighted not only in Germany, but in Switzerland, Austria, Holland, Scandinavian parts, and England. They were in certain respects the heralds of the country home schools in England and similar groves, the *Landerziehungsheime* in Teutonic lands. Through them and others like them their principles and practices worked their way here and there into the public educational practice of Europe's more advanced and progressive countries.

CHAPTER 22

JOHANN HEINRICH PESTALOZZI

Though Basedow had been the first to attempt to give some of Rousseau's speculations a classroom application, the task of doing it wisely and with insight fell upon another, Pestalozzi by name and a Swiss by birth. Born in Zurich in 1746, Johann Heinrich Pestalozzi was grafted from sturdy burgher stock. Apart from the early loss of his father the days of his youth ran well for him. Certainly they were not beset by the wild travail which tormented the adolescent life of his two predecessors. Like them, however, he harbored longings to salvage the human race, and especially its representatives of low estate. The dew of youth was still upon him when he undertook to prepare himself for the pulpit, but the miscarriage of a trial sermon made him change his mind. Still full of wistful hopes, he turned to the study of law, but again the tide of fortune ran against him. Later at Neuhof he ventured into farming, hoping thereby to demonstrate to the hard-pressed peasantry the value of employing the most advanced methods then known to agricultural science. But his large and confiding soul attracted bilks and charlatans in packs, and in 1774, after five years of struggle, he saw his project succumb to his illusions.

Meanwhile, a copy of *Emile* had fallen into his hands, and after working his way through its eight hundred pages he emerged, like so many others, afire with pedagogic ambitions. He began to fulfill them on a small scale by keeping Jakob, his first-born, under careful watch, jotting down his observations and storing them in his diary, a practice which years later was to be regarded highly by the first more or less scientific students of early childhood.

Pestalozzi's next step came with the collapse of his Neuhof farm. As it faded into the past, he converted part of his home into a school where he undertook to shepherd a score or so of down-and-out peasant children. He aspired not only to make them literate and virtuous, but also to introduce them to housekeeping, spinning, weaving, and similar arts and crafts of country people. By making the project pay for itself, with the aid of benefactions from friendly humanitarians, Pestalozzi was able to pluck a fair success. But almost at once he took it into his head to increase the number of his wards to almost a hundred, a load which was far too staggering for his meager resources. For two years he struggled doggedly to stay afloat, living, as he later explained, "in the midst of fifty little beggars, sharing in my poverty my bread with them, living like a beggar myself in order to teach beggars to live like men." When the two years were almost gone, failure descended on Neuhof.

With its ruin Pestalozzi put aside his altruism to occupy himself with book writing. Presently, in 1780, he published his *Evening Hours of a Hermit*, a concoction of aphorisms, very heavily sugared but containing, some believe, the germ of his pedagogic credo. Even so, when they appeared, they got scarcely any notice. The year following, when his novel *Leonard and Gertrude* came out, his luck agreeably improved. In consonance with the period's romantic mood, it related how Gertrude, a plain but gracious homebody, by sheer moral amperage not only transformed Leonard, her jug-loving spouse, into a man of rectitude, but with the aid of the village schoolmaster, raised her debauched community of Bonnal from the slough of its corruption. The narrative soothed the feelings with moral balms, and in a short time it became something of a best-seller.

More important in the long run was that it offered some earnest recommendations for political, social, and educational reforms. Though these were wasted on the general mind, they did not elude some of the advanced thinkers of the time. Indeed, as a consequence of *Leonard and Gertrude*, its author came in contact with some of the most enlightened and reflective figures of his time. From Austria, Germany, and Italy they trailed to Neuhof to witness the shaggy-maned creator of *Leonard and Gertrude*, and even to invite his help and counsel on all sorts of social enigmas. With so many bravos buzzing in his ears, Pestalozzi sought to repeat his literary triumph, as writers not uncommonly do, by turning out some sequels. But they were a mere rewarming of the pot, and they brought him very little. And so, instead of lolling in blissful plenty, Pestalozzi had to content himself with honors. The mighty metaphysician Fichte clasped his hand, and France made him an honorary citizen. Yet, for all these laurels, at fifty Pestalozzi was a disappointed man, baffled in the fulfillment of his main and higher aspirations and vanquished in nearly every major undertaking.

Ever since his days at Neuhof Pestalozzi had itched to become a schoolteacher. He had bespoken the help of friends in the government, but save for some feathery phrases, he got nothing. Then, in 1798, his luck changed. That was the time, it may be recalled, when the French were pining to plant their flag of revolution in other lands. Switzerland, ever a haven for evangel, responded by tailoring some of its governance in the French fashion. Not all the Swiss, however, were disposed to give it their support. In fact, some of the Catholic cantons were at violent odds with the new deal from France, especially its warfare on Holy Church, and in the canton of Unterwalden, inflamed by Capucian monks, the dissent presently flared in riot. The French, having in a way conjured up the new regime, were bent on keeping it on its legs. To this effect they sent a squad of soldiery who worked with alacrity. The hamlet of Stanz they put to the torch; many of its inhabitants they butchered; and when at length they filed away they left behind a swarm of orphans. These, after some temporizing, the Swiss government vouchsafed to the care and instruction of Pestalozzi who, hastening to Stanz, let it be known how delighted he was to be able "to offer these innocent, little ones some compensation for the loss they have sustained."

Little did he suspect what gratuitous trouble he was making for himself. Not only was he marked by the town's surviving adults as a partisan of the infamous French; he was also suspect to the children. On the loose several months before Pestalozzi's coming, they had flowered into journeyman hoodlums, derisive of ordinary rule and order, and a menace to the public peace. Their health, habits, and morals had gone so badly to pieces that any effort to repair them seemed doomed. In addition Pestalozzi faced an almost unbelievable scarcity of materials. The French had provided the orphans, and the Swiss a roof to give them cover. But beyond these there was little else.

Yet this deficiency Pestalozzi presently turned to good account. In the absence of books, he conceived what he called the "object lesson," whereby the child studied things rather than books about things, and what his senses caught he communicated in the spoken rather than the written word. There lingered at Stanz a residue of Neuhof, for here as there Pestalozzi was eager to connect learning with the manual arts.

Pestalozzi's stiffest test, however, was not pedagogical, but psychological. How to enmesh himself in the confidence of his distrustful renegades—this was his primary problem. Discipline, he had come to believe, was not a matter of clubbing the young into submission. It was rather "a thinking love," by which he meant that the business called for the teacher's tolerance and understanding, but that at the same time it must be sensible—there are occasions, indeed, when the therapeutic birch becomes necessary. Viewed pragmatically, his method was effective. Granted a sympathy they had never enjoyed before, the children began to flourish, and Pestalozzi was apparently a success. But the fates had other things in store. The French troops, themselves now on the run from the pursuing Austrians, suddenly reappeared at Stanz, where they commandeered the building which housed the orphans. For Pestalozzi the abrupt termination of his task was doubtless a good thing. He had worked himself far too hard, and his health had fallen into a low state. He was no sooner out of earshot than critical tongues began to flap. At fifty-two, it was generally agreed, the old dunderhead had failed again. What nobody discerned, even vaguely, was that the modern elementary school was cradled in the tiny town of Stanz.

Soon after Stanz Pestalozzi taught for a while at Burgdorf. It was a twilight intermission between his main works and it helped at least to tide him over until the century's final year when the government offered him lodgment in an old castle to enable him to open a school of his own. He was joined by a few collaborators who helped him to work out his theories, the essence of which he distilled in 1802 between the covers of *How Gertrude Teaches Her Children*. Burgdorf prospered. Money streamed to it from all directions. People journeyed to it from afar—even from across the broad Atlantic—to con its wonder. But as sometimes happens, the vagaries of politics presently collided with the ideals of pedagogy, and in 1803 the authorities requisitioned the Burgdorf castle, and Pestalozzi had to move. He betook himself to Hofwyl to work with Phillip Emmanuel von Fellenberg, one of his admirers. Unluckily, the two men, though in pedagogical accord, were of altogether different temperaments, and their joint venture soon blew up.

In 1805 Pestalozzi established himself at Yverdon. He was to remain there during the next twenty years, carrying on what he had begun at Burgdorf, but on a larger and grander scale. As at Burgdorf, part of his work was devoted to giving preparation to prospective teachers. So novel was such practice in those days that pretty soon a number of alert and progressive nations began to grant scholarships to their most promising schoolmen to attend the sessions at Yverdon. Like Burgdorf before it, Yverdon was soon transmuted into an educational showplace, attracting laymen and professionals from over land and sea to observe its work and to cast admiring eyes at its director. At Yverdon Pestalozzi climbed to the peak of his fame, especially during the first five or six years of his activity. After that, doubts and dissensions rent his staff, and the flame of his torch began to sputter. In 1825 the curtain dropped on the last scene of his long labor. Now, at the brink of eighty, he retired to his old Neuhof haunt, where so long ago he had first dreamed of the great purpose in his heart. Two years later he died.

2

Thus the man and his work. What were his outstanding teachings, and what was their significance? Like Rousseau and Basedow, he rejected the religious motive in education, a motive which had overborne the primary school to the end of the eighteenth century. For Pestalozzi, as for Rousseau, education was a living, organic process—"the natural, progressive, and harmonious development of all the child's powers and faculties." As such, he insisted, it must be regarded not as the privilege of a favored handful but, like breathing in and breathing out, as the natural right of every child. Nor was its concern merely the amelioration of the individual, but rather of all individuals, and hence of society. Thus applied on a full scale, education was to serve to rectify our social ills.

Like other reformers before him and after, Pestalozzi decried the schoolman's universal belaboring of the memory. Learning by rote, he remarked, was no more than "empty chattering." Our first learning, he declared, comes to us not through words and books, but through our eyes and ears and hands, and even the nose and tongue. "When I look back," he once mused, "and ask myself what have I done for the very being of education, I find I have fixed the highest . . . principles of instruction in the recognition of sense perception as the absolute foundation of all knowledge." Unlike Comenius, the archpropagator of the notion of studying things rather than words about things, Pestalozzi saw in it not merely a means to build up a supply of knowledge, but also a way to exercise the mental faculties. But his unshakable confidence that the senses are the reservoir of all our knowledge benumbed him to the realization that for those of the human race who resort to it, the intellect can also be an important source of knowledge.

Observation, as mentioned a few pages back, became the basis of Pestalozzian instruction. Guided by the questions of his teacher, the child, observing an object, proceeded step by step from what was perceptible to his senses to the generalizations which lay beyond. In Pestalozzi's deft hand the procedure became a creative act. Fashioned from the thing before the eye, and illuminated by a fine fancy, the lesson began to glow with a freshness it had not known before. It was in this respect a work of art—and one in which the old man outshone many of his imitators who, though vastly more systematic and learned, lacked his bouyancy and, even more, his inner warmth, and thus reduced the object lesson to a perfunctory cant. In sad truth, as the years ran on, the object lesson, like the old-style recitation, became just another way of stuffing the child with a mass of facts.

Pestalozzi wanted, as he said somewhat cryptically, "to psychologize education," by which he meant that the pupil should begin his learning with simple things, and as he became their master, move to the more and more complex. Unluckily, in the half-light of a primitive psychology, Pestalozzi's sparing acquaintance with the workings of the mind often played him false. What tripped him was his delusion that what was simple to him was also simple to the child. In consequence, as Pestalozzi undertook to simplify what the youngster was to learn, he sometimes unwittingly did just the opposite. Take reading, for example. To strip the business to its simplest terms, he sawed words down to their barest combination, which is to say a vowel and a consonant, as witness, *ab, eb, ib*, and so on through the entire alphabet. These pairs, which he marshaled into a collection known as "syllabaries," and which ran to a large number, the pupil was made to learn before he was allowed to introduce himself to actual words, and in due time, sentences and paragraphs, and on some remote tomorrow, books.

Although Pestalozzi generated great heat on behalf of observation, he did not, like Rousseau, let the learner draw freely from what he saw. Like reading, drawing was first rolled into the dissecting room where Pestalozzi anatomized it into its barest elements. Consequently, before the child was put to sketching, say, a house or a cowshed, or even the flaming sun over an Alp, he was made day in and day out to practice on curves, angles, and lines, vertical, slanting, and horizontal. In the same manner handwriting became a subdivision of drawing. Letters, separated into their component parts, were found to contain elements which were bent, sloped, or straight, some running up and some down. These the budding penman was set upon in long and arduous rehearsal before he was trusted to try his hand on actual letters, followed in the course of time and practice by words, sentences, paragraphs, and cantos.

It is no secret that much of Pestalozzi's thinking was mere intellectual wandering. His basic psychology, the so-called faculty psychology, has been found to be spurious—it was, in fact, cried down critically during his own lifetime. Yet, despite his limitations, Pestalozzi, like Basedow, insisted on giving his pedagogy the test of classroom practice. Unfortunately, at the time he toiled he had practically no help from the sciences, since neither the exact ones nor the social ones had got into their full stride. Hence he had no way of putting an impartial yardstick to his labor; nor did he have any way of knowing whether what worked for him would work in general.

Although Pestalozzi floated in a sea of unverified assumptions, common sense sometimes came to his rescue and steered him safely to sound practice. He held, for example, that a teaching method is no better than a teacher's ability to use it, and that there is a difference between teaching and ramming knowledge into bewildered heads. In current educational science these are, of course, settled principles, but when Pestalozzi volunteered them, they were still a novelty. Not uncommonly in those days instructing the young was a sort of minor vocational sideline, carried on by its executants in their home or shop, and even, on occasion, in a tavern. Such practitioners were usually ignorant and unimaginative men who relied heavily on the switch to perform their ancient mystery. By contrast, when Pestalozzi began to operate upon his charges, he dazzled them with enthusiasm and even with gentle affection. He was stirred not only by his art, but by the child as well. "Let the child be a human being," he counseled the aspirant masters under his training, and he added, "let the teacher be his trusted friend." To this purpose he devoted his energies at both Burgdorf and Yverdon.

3

As a scholar Pestalozzi lit no flares. He was innocent of arithmetic, disorderly in grammar, and a stranger to good penmanship. He had a striking incapacity for even the most elementary practicality, and except for the help of partisans and coworkers, he would have had to resign himself to failure, or at best a mixed success. They bore in upon him from everywhere, and through their work and writing his influence radiated over two continents. Several achieved fame in their own right, and one of them, Phillip Emmanual von Fellenberg, even wove a spell for a time in the United States. While still a youth he chanced to read *Leonard and Gertrude*. So strong was the pull of its ideas that he vowed to his mother, a very hallowed and friendly lady, that he would dedicate the rest of his earthly life to education, and in particular to the service of the children of the poor. And since he also happened to have a well-filled pocket, he had no trouble, when the time came, in keeping his promise.

To carry out his purpose Fellenberg founded a school—the Institute—on his country estate at Hofwyl. It specialized in supplying instruction to the lower classes, offering them the common elementals besides a simple farm and industrial training. To advance what experts nowadays designate as "human relations," Fellenberg also gave accommodation to the progeny of the well-to-do. They too were made to swing a hoe and pitchfork, but unlike their less genteel comrades, they were spared from cart making, leather tanning, blacksmithing, and similar utilitarian arts and crafts. Instead, they were fitted out with the ornamentation of a classical culture.

Fellenberg ran his Institute from 1804 to 1844, and under his expert hand it thrived. A quarter century after its advent, it had spread over some six hundred acres of rolling countryside. It boasted an agricultural school to train tomorrow's farmhands; a seminary for teachers, especially those designed for service in rural parts; and a school to give training in the manual arts and some of the more attractive burgher callings. In addition it enriched its practice with a printing plant, a shop to make tools, another to tailor garments, and several more of diverse variety.

All in all, Fellenberg's work enjoyed a hearty respect, and before long, its director found himself garlanded from head to toe with public approbation. People made for his estate from all over the earth to inspect its doings and to report thereon in a staggering pile of documents. Pretty soon the Institute was being aped not only in the Old World, but in the New as well. For a time it drove a very lively trade in the republic, but with the rise of the mill and the machine, and the opening of the stupendous acreages beyond the Mississippi, its strength was soon dissipated, and its popularity leeched away. Later it recaptured some of its old appeal. With the manual-labor feature deleted, it underlay the demand for advanced instruction in the agricultural and mechanical arts which flowered in the passing years in the so-called A & M colleges, which, of course, are still in practice.

4

As the glory of Pestalozzi soared ever higher, his ideas gained more and more adherents—save in Switzerland where, but for the efforts of a few chronic enthusiasts, he was given the treatment said to be in store for native prophets. The truth is, to the generality of Swiss Pestalozzi's notions seemed disconcertingly sinister, foreboding catastrophe to both church and state. Consequently, it was not until the Revolution of 1830 had ventilated this stultifying atmosphere that the Swiss began to draw upon the legacy their son had left them. Since then his name has been enshrined in the national heart, and for the Swiss to call a teacher a Pestalozzi is to confer upon him the highest pedagogical accolade at their command.

While Pestalozzi's contribution was allowed to lie fallow in the conservatism of his native land, beyond its borders, and especially in Germany, it sprouted a luxuriant boskiness. Both Herbart and Froebel—two giants in the annals of education—called at Yverdon, and the latter even worked in its classrooms. It was in Prussia that the new ideas exerted their first large influence. When, early in the century, Napoleon knocked the once-mighty kingdom from its pedestal, its leaders looked to education, among other things, to restore its lost grandeur. For this purpose they overhauled their school system from top to bottom, and to stock it with the finest teachers to be found anywhere, they sent a small band of handpicked schoolmasters to Yverdon for special training in the new methods. In addition, they summoned the Rev. Karl August Zeller, a Württemberger and a professed Pestalozzian, to establish a school to give training to the land's future teachers. By this route the New Education made rapid headway in Prussia, and as has happened more than once in German history, from Prussia its influence soon or late made itself felt in other German states.

What Zeller accomplished for the Germans another parson, the Rev. Dr. Charles Mayo, did for the English, although with outstanding differences. Mayo appeared at Yverdon in 1819 and stayed three years, conducting sacred services and instructing in religion, with occasional side jaunts into choir leading. During his sojourn he made himself familiar with Pestalozzian propositions, and following his return to the motherland he opened a private school not far from London where he made the new pedagogy a special feature. Unlike Pestalozzi's academies, it offered its services mainly to the carriage trade. The reverend doctor was given a helpful hand by his sister Elizabeth, a sort of subdeacon for the enterprise, who was also responsible for a number of schoolbooks, one of which, *Lessons and Objects*, attained a decorous popularity. Both Mayos were grimly staid. Intrinsically, they were pedants, and so their adaptation of the old master was never tuned on the sensitive strings of his art. In consequence, the Pestalozzianism they brought the English, for all its to-do over objects and observation, was deadened by a leadlike formalism—at best a pale apparition of the original and living form.

In our own republic, Pestalozzian pedagogics got their first public airing as early as 1805 when William McLure composed a piece on some of their manifold aspects. The year following Joseph Neef, one of Napoleon's innumerable veterans and a former don at Burgdorf, was persuaded to come to America to demonstrate the Pestalozzian principles. For a time he gave instruction in Philadelphia and in the Midwest, but excepting a couple of treatises on the subject, he did very little to advance the cause. Almost a score of years after Neef's landing in the New World, the historian George Bancroft opened a small school in Massachusetts. Its objectives, admittedly, were confined by its special catering to the upper orders; even so, its procedures extracted a good deal of their inspiration from Pestalozzi—in fact, the school even pleasantly troubled itself with the mission of social progress. Meanwhile, in 1821, when Warren Colburn came out with his *Lessons in Arithmetic on the Plan of Pestalozzi*, some of the new principles filtered into the field of textbook writing. So superior was Colburn's work that for a while it was able to maintain a safe and profitable monopoly, an attribute which soon brought the book a host of imitators. Still another impetus for the new ideas emanated from the drive for the American common school, and especially from the vastly discussed writings of its leading spokesmen. All these efforts, however, were just so many loose threads, and they were never embroidered into a coherent design. Saving the advertisement they gave Pestalozzi and his movement, their general effect was slight.

It was not until after Appomattox that the new education came into fashion in America, but when it finally arrived it made a tremendous hit and enjoyed a run for at least a generation. In great measure it was the work of Edward Austin Sheldon, who, like Pestalozzi, had donned his first teaching robes by taking the ragged and the homeless under his wing and who, like Papa Johann again, believed that education was the sure cure for all our social woes, and the indispensable key to human progress. He was far better versed than the Swiss, however, in the prosaic affairs of everyday schoolhouse practice—in fact, he had just crossed the frontier of thirty when Oswego, New York, converted him into its first school superintendent. In 1859, while summering in Canada, he caught his first glimpse of Pestalozzian object materials. They were of English origin and hence standardized along the Mayo line. On Sheldon, nevertheless, they had such an overwhelming effect that then and there he made up his mind to give them a trial at Oswego. To this end the necessary books and equipment were brought from England; a training class for teachers was got under way; and a specialist was imported from the Mayo school, by now England's leading purveyor of Pestalozzianism. At the same time Oswego's course of study was revamped with a switch from the conventional stress on the piling up of knowledge to the observation of things.

After a couple of years of trial and suffering, the scheme was given countenance by the dignitaries in assembly in Oswego's city hall, when they ordained the establishment of a city normal school to perfect its future Pestalozzis in the new procedures. There were, of course, the usual vendettas. Sheldon, one faction contended, was a mere glory hunter; another, even more discourteous, dismissed him as a visionary. Whatever the man may have been, there remains the fact that his plan was successful. In 1862—three years after its inception—it was being frescoed with public eulogy by the country's foremost educators. Another three years, and the National Teachers' Association—currently the august NEA—after some sober pondering, gave object teaching its collective benediction. In the meanwhile, the State of New York had taken an interest in the normal school, even rejoicing it from time to time with a tender subsidy. Finally, in 1866, the state clasped Oswego Normal to its bosom by transforming it into the state's second normal school.

All this, naturally, gave Pestalozzianism a powerful boost, not merely within the frontiers of New York, but throughout the whole republic. Visitors from faraway places—even alien civilizations—swarmed to Oswego Normal. The demand for its graduates knew no limits, and presently they found themselves ensconced in some of the best jobs in the land as teachers, principals, and presidents of normal schools. Appearing just at the moment when the American normal school was poised to leap into a great expansion, the Oswego movement, which is to say the Pestalozzian movement in America, started a fashion in the country's teacher training, and thereby in its public schools, which was a living influence for at least a generation.

CHAPTER 23

JOHANN FRIEDRICH HERBART

In the American republic Pestalozzianism reached its heyday in the late sixties and early seventies; in Europe, overlooking stray exceptions, it began to run down a bit earlier. What was sound and significant in the movement has, of course, been with us in various incarnations ever since. But there was also much which was not durable, to wit, its fallacious psychologic underpinning, its misconceptions about the simplification of learning, its overrating of the value of sensory experience, and its lack of any coherent systematizing of its chief ideas.

The man who put pedagogy on a surer footing was a German, Johann Friedrich Herbart. He was born into a family of the higher middle classes of Oldenburg in the year of political upheaval, 1776, and he died at Göttingen in 1841 on the threshold, so to say, of the Marxian and Darwinian explosions. Though the span of his years on earth was rocked by one social and political blast after another, his own days were spent in the calm hermitage of university study, and only seldom was he made to suffer from the pressures and anxieties of the everyday world.

Unlike his illustrious forerunners, Herbart was bred from a dazzling intellectual pedigree. His paternal grandfather was in service for almost forty years as executive-in-chief of a classical secondary school, a post whose first requirement in those days was brains. His father, though a cold compress of a man, did a brisk business in law—he was, as a matter of fact, something of a public servant with the pay and dignity of *Justizrat* and *Regierungsrat*. The boy's mother must be rated even higher. A correct and zealous Lutheran, she trained him to house discipline at a tender age. She assumed full command over his education, even reviewing her knowledge of Greek and penetrating the depths of mathematics in order to work with him. When the time came, she squired him about the University of Jena and shielded him from the seductions of beer and dueling swords, and similar sorts of indecorum. Later, when the youth reached his quarter century, she effected a separation from her spouse and went to live in infidel Paris.

Herbart himself was obviously of a superior cut. His memory teemed with rare and amazing information from which he could fish out almost anything at will, from the whereabouts of the weasand to the population of Yezo, and similar astounding specimens. He could even, it is said, repeat word for word a lengthy homily by his pastor.

If skeptics have treated Herbart's possession of such talents with some snickering, they have never permitted themselves to dispute his enormous capacity of mind. He was by all odds a magnificent negotiator of ideas. Even as an apprentice learner in the Oldenburg *Gymnasium* he showed unmistakable leanings in this direction. He was on a familiar footing with Latin and Greek, and mathematics, physics, and philosophy he put down as easily as a glass of water. At thirteen he hazarded an essay "on the proof of the existence of an eternal

God," which he followed in the next year with a treatise on the *Doctrine of Human Freedom*. A little later, still a teenager, a speculated on the *Commonest Causes That Affect the Growth and Decay of Morality in the Various States*. And on the celebration of his commencement he excited the wonder of assembled friends, relatives, and teachers with a recital in Latin on the ideas of Cicero and Kant. Though cerebral affairs were obviously Herbart's first concern, the musical art also had some attractions for him. He played the violin, the cello, the harp, and the piano, and he composed a sonata—in fact, he even delivered himself of a treatise on harmony.

Herbart arrived at Jena in 1794, and at the instance of his father he enrolled in law. But he took no pleasure in it, and presently he found himself stealing into the lecture halls of the philosophers. Pretty soon he renounced the study of law outright and put himself under the tutelage of Jena's metaphysicians. His favorite was Johann Gottlieb Fichte, a salient idealist of the day and one of the most powerful speechmakers his order has ever produced. Yet for all the veneration heaped upon his learned professor, Herbart was not long in detecting some flaws in his principal propositions—soon, indeed, he threw their essence overboard. "Fichte," he confided afterwards, "taught me mainly by his errors."

After a couple of years, more or less, Herbart was ready to take a holiday. He made his base in Switzerland where, in 1797, the Governor of Interlaken hired him to instruct and inspire his three sons. A very meticulous employer, the Governor exacted the submission, at regular intervals, of an annotated audit of the conduct and progress of his heirs, a prescription which did not daunt their system-doting tutor. For two years Herbart practiced under the Governor's roof, warily grappling with the mysterious processes of learning and teaching; and though in after years he was to urge upon us the necessity of giving a thorough training to every apprentice teacher, his two tutorial years at Interlaken constitute the only basic exercise he himself ever experienced in the art of giving enlightenment to the young.

While Herbart was in residence in Switzerland he seized the chance to go to Burgdorf to visit Pestalozzi. The man impressed him greatly, and he accorded him all the deference due a master. Some of his broader views met with Herbart's approval, but with Pestalozzi's psychological assumptions he expressed severe dissent. As usual, he presently delivered himself of a monograph on the subject.

After he returned to the fatherland, Herbart set himself down for a while at the University of Halle. Thence he headed northward to Bremen where he put the finishing touches on his doctoral studies. Upon his ascension to doctorhood at Göttingen in 1802 his migrations ceased, and he became one of the university's lecturers. For the next seven years he tended his job, performing Academe's well-known chores, from discoursing on philosophy and pedagogy to attending the seances of the faculty and writing erudite books. In 1808, in meet reward for his numerous talents, the university translated him into a professor. But the year following saw him hoisted even higher when the University of Königsberg summoned him to fill the chair once warmed by the celebrated Immanuel Kant. His promotion was succeeded by a long term of glittering accomplishment. His industry, in truth, was stupendous. He not only expounded his subject, directed seminars, gave counsel to candidates in philosophy, and supervised a practice teaching school; he also put together the bulk of his more important books. His output during this time, weighing several pounds, included, among other things, a *Manual of Psychology* (1810), a *Psychology as Science, Founded according to a New Method on Experience, Metaphysics, and Mathematics* (1824), and *General Metaphysics* (1828). Thus his labors and lessons flowed on until 1833, when the Prussian government, seized by one of its recurrent fits of reaction, eyed him suspiciously. When it threatened to hamper him in his work he turned his back on Königsberg and returned to Göttingen. There he continued to work and shine until 1841 when a stroke laid him low. He entered eternity, so to say, in cap and gown a day or so after having committed his last lecture.

2

Herbart had no yearning, like Pestalozzi, to edify and elevate the lowly. Nor did he sigh, like Rousseau, for the best of all possible worlds. Instead, steering clear of poetic impulse, he took God's perplexed world pretty much as it was, and in his rational way he sought to make it understandable and, maybe, tolerable. Unlike either of his predecessors, he was barren of sentimentality, and though he put emotion under the glass to examine its nature, he himself was emotionally frostbitten. He was, first and last, an intellectual, a disciplined man of learning with an agile mind who spent the preponderant portion of his sedate and respectable life within the academic cloister. In his approach to education he lacked the warmth of the simple-hearted Pestalozzi and the insight of Rousseau, that anointed knave. By contrast, he brought to his business the assurance which comes from the possession of great knowledge and a virtuosity of the intellect. As a result, Herbart probed far deeper and much more keenly than anyone before him.

Like nearly all pedagogical thinkers since ancient times, Herbart cherished the notion that education's foremost mission is moral. But the principles which underlie right and wrong, he held, were formulated by the society which they are intended to maintain in peace and happiness. Education's primary mission, consequently, is to mold the child in the morality of the enveloping social order. Not knowledge mainly, nor nature, nor even the development of the mind should be education's goal, but character and social morality. "The term *virtue*," Herbart declared, "expresses the whole purpose of education"—a laconic classic, if there ever was one, in pedagogic utterance, but one which, it must be said in candor, he proceeded to distend with several hundred additional words.

To understand what underlies good and evil, Herbart took a sharp look at man's interests and activities. The former, which he found to be numerous and diverse, had their origin in man himself, his surroundings, and his relations to others. The latter were derived largely from the demands put upon him by the society in which he lived and roved. Through the use of objects Pestalozzi had introduced the child to his setting; and through the spoken word he had hoped to provide for the child's dealings with others. Next to these Herbart put a third, namely, the establishment of at least a nodding acquaintance with the cultural heritage, and particularly history and literature. The purpose to be served, however, was not to set the learner aglow for the loveliness of letters or the charm and monitory message of certain bygone events, but rather to fan the fire of righteousness—the delusion, in short, that literature is primarily a moral document.

On the matter of grounding pedagogy on psychology Herbart stood arm in arm with Pestalozzi. But he discarded the latter's premise of mental faculties, holding instead to the maturer and current view that under normal conditions mental behavior is a fairly coordinated and unified process. This is not saying, of course, that Herbart was a modern psychologist. A stranger to the lab and the couch, he came to the study of the psyche in the manner of a philosopher, conducting his searchings a priori, and sifting them through the finely woven screen of logic. In spite of these serious limitations, he was able to frame a number of important theories regarding the then-obscure processes of learning and teaching, for example, his doctrines of interest and apperception, both of which he later wove into a method of teaching, the so-called Formal Steps.

The view put forth time and again by various educational reformers that a child's learning is launched most effectively when it is sparked by his interest got Herbart's full endorsement. After some careful attention to the matter he concluded that interest shows itself in two major varieties, to illustrate, the natural, self-generated kind, which a child gives freely and without any external stimulation; and the fabricated kind which is conjured up by his teacher to make him want to learn. The notion then in common favor that in order to be worth anything the business of learning must be onerous, and even distasteful, did not sit very well with Herbart. Not only did he consider interest a necessary prerequisite to all effort in learning, but he thought that, in the event of its absence, the duty of the master was to employ all the tricks of teaching to lure it forth—a belief which nowadays, of course, enjoys a large support.

Pestalozzi, it will be recalled, made a considerable bustle about going from the known to the unknown, as had Rousseau before him, and Comenius before Rousseau. Herbart embraced the same conviction. As usual, he subjected the principle to the full voltage of his sophistication. Thus, he not only modified and enlarged its meaning; he also tinged it with a new psychological shading. Called "apperception," this doctrine, stripped to its skeleton, holds that all new ideas are interpreted through those already resident in the consciousness.

Interest and apperception became the bedrock on which Herbart built his method of teaching. Known as the Formal Steps, it originally comprised four parts, namely, clearness, association, system, and method. As the years ran on, the four were reconstructed and overhauled, and in the process they took aboard a fifth, thus:

1. Preparation   An application of the doctrine of interest and apperception, this undertook to put the learner into a receptive mood and mind. The lesson's purpose was explained, and such previous knowledge as might throw light upon the new was mustered into service.

2. Presentation   The new material was set forth and explained.

3. Association   The new material was compared with the old and familiar, and pertinent likenesses and differences were noted.

4. Generalization   The several facts developed in the foregoing were framed into a general statement or principle or rule.

5. Application   True to the ancient dictum that nothing is ever learned until it can be readily employed, the learner's understanding of the generalization was put to practice with appropriate problems and exercises.

Like Pestalozzi's object lesson, the Formal Steps were well regarded, not only in their land of origin, but beyond its boundaries as well. They reached their summit in the nineteenth century's last quarter; thereafter, under the challenge of a sounder and more penetrating psychology, it became their fate to be outmoded.

Beside the theories aforesaid, Herbart favored us with several others. He was the first among educators to suggest that subjects should not be dealt with as isolated entities—as independent islands, so to say, separated from one another in the broad sea of knowledge. Instead, whenever feasible, their matter should be brought together over the bridge of intelligible association. It was the professor's contention, for example, that "mathematical studies, from elementary arithmetic to higher mathematics, are to be linked to the student's knowledge, and so to his experience." He went on to say that "when the ideas generated form an isolated group ... they contribute little to personal worth." The business of association Herbart called "correlation," which is still its designation in these later days. Although the Göttingen professor merely hinted at the broad idea, his followers, true to the immemorial wont of disciples to compound and complicate their master's simplest thoughts, laid heavy hands upon it. They not only altered the doctrine's name to "concentration," but against the sage counsel of its propagator they sought to apply it in all directions and in staggering doses. By virtue of the concentration scheme, instruction presently found itself wrapped around a "core of study" to the end of revealing the "moral universe" to the child. The denizens of the second grade, for instance, were put upon to "concentrate" on *Robinson Crusoe*. The narrative served not only as an exercise in reading; it became as well the base for expeditions into ciphering and composition—even, indeed, into virtue. In a similar vein the more elderly pupils in the third grade and upward were made to engross themselves in some central and engulfing theme.

Herbart's last years, as was observed a few pages ago, brought him to the approaching dawn of the Darwinian theory of organic evolution. That a man of his muscular mind should take an interest in the advanced thinking of the men of science, and even derive some pedagogical hints therefrom, is surely no cause for wonder. From it issued the Herbartian "culture epochs theory," which held that inasmuch as man, the individual, in his unfoldment from embryo to adult, apparently repeats the developmental stages of the species as it emerged from its primordial tar pits to its present exalted state, therefore a similar evolutionary phenomenon might conceivably apply to his cultural evolution. It is only fair to add that, once again, Herbart merely let drop a few vague and dulcet suggestions about the possibility of such a parallelism. Nevertheless his successors, who entertained no such self-restraint, lost no time in pouncing on the suggestion and welding it into the canons of their pedagogy.

By virtue of the culture epochs theory, Herbart proposed that it might be a good thing to initiate the beginner into the elemental epics of the race, in illustration, the *Iliad* and the *Odyssey*, and then over the years, let him gradually toil his way to our more recent and recondite expressions of the literary art. But Herbart's devotees swept on to far greater lengths. For some of them, in truth, it was not uncommon to give the novice an intimate contact with a year or so of savage culture, followed by a couple more of the barbarian variety, and hauling up by commencement day with specimens from the modern, ranging from the early to the middle, and, if lucky, to the late. Despite the rickety underlying logic, the culture epochs theory attracted an eager following, and it even enlisted the support of such sagacious men as Herbert Spencer and G. Stanley Hall. Today, like the horse car and the celluloid collar, it is a museum relic.

The bulk of his threescore years and five Herbart invested in study and reflection. Even though he was a severely closeted man, it was Herbart who first let it be known that a science of education is possible. In a day when the study of the human psyche was largely speculative, the enterprise mainly of metaphysicians and theologians, Herbart undertook to give the subject a measure of exactitude by grounding it on mathematics. It was Herbart who succeeded in getting pedagogy admitted into the university sanctum as a field of study essential to the advancement of learning. And to conclude, it was Herbart who, in conjunction with his pursuit of educational theory, employed a model and demonstration school where he and his aides applied and tested their doctrines and where they observed and guided the teaching of their students.

3

For all the magnitude of his work and vision, when Herbart died, the Germans scarcely knew him. Perhaps his ideas were premature, or perhaps they were too coldly intellectual. Whatever they were, another generation had ripened before Herbart came into his own. Then, as if to redeem themselves for their previous indifference, schoolmen everywhere leaped up to cheer and handclap the forgotten man from Göttingen, and where only the other day his ideas had fallen into an apparition-like neglect, of a sudden they became alive and everything redounded to their glory.

The Herbartian vogue began modestly enough, with the appearance in 1865 of Tuiskon Ziller's *The Basis of the Doctrine of Educative Instruction*, a work which withdrew the veil from Herbart's views on education as a moral force. The study not only blew up the ignorance about the man, but served to work up so much pressure for his teachings that before long his admirers found it desirable to join forces in the Association for the Scientific Study of Education. Under Ziller's deft and talented hand its ranks grew to vast proportions, and in the years following, its membership swarmed not only with Germans, but with aliens as well. Although the Herbartians were propelled at first by a desire to study and promote their master's views, time soon saw their zeal drive them beyond the limit of such simple purpose. It was they who adulterated and altered many of their idol's teachings. It was they who subordinated the scientific studies to the literary and historical ones in a world which actually was projecting itself more and more toward science. And it was they who elaborated the Formal Steps. From them, finally, emanated the extravagant belaboring of the doctrines of concentration and culture epochs, both of which in historical afterlight appear to be not a little absurd.

Less transitory in influence, at least in its major aspects, was the work of Karl Volkmar Stoy. Though he gave his assent to many of the new adaptations imposed on Herbart, he was more intent on reaffirming the departed professor's original gospel. Treading in Herbart's footsteps, Stoy founded a pedagogical seminary and a practice school at the University of Jena. There his accomplishments attained such a striking success that Jena soon became for Herbart the shrine that Yverdon had been for Pestalozzi. There Herbart's teachings were sedulously inspected; lesson plans were assembled and put to work; and under the watch and counsel of their professors young men made ready for teaching service. They came from every quarter, even from places scarcely ever heard of, and when, eventually, they departed, they took the new revelation with them.

As the years increased Herbartianism made its way to the New World. It was borne in by Americans who had witnessed it abroad and returned to the homeland bursting with ardor for its wonders. Through their unflagging evangelism, and especially through the labors of the Brothers McMurry, Charles and Frank, and those of Charles De Garmo, the Herbartian propositions captured an ever-growing adherence. By 1882 it had grown numerous enough to bring into being the National Herbart Society. Founded to advertise and advance the new pedagogy, the association carried on with a fine success for something like a decade. Then, as usually happens after a protracted period of anything, the style began to pall, and in 1902 the organization rid itself of the Herbartian label and became the National Society for the Scientific Study of Education.

Once under full draft, Herbartianism made rapid progress. Like Pestalozzianism a generation earlier, it transformed the work of the American normal school and with it the practice of the American school itself. Where, only yesterday, the teachers of teachers had orchestrated their work in harmony with the principles of sense perception, oral language, and the object lesson, they now rendered it on the strings of interest, apperception, concentration, and the Formal Steps.

It was the fate of Herbart's teachings to be exhumed by time and to be given a second chance. Alas, their maker could not defend himself against the false interpretations and exaggerations imposed upon them by his overzealous successors. Thus, suffering from the high fervor of those who followed in his footsteps, Herbart is often raked for their excesses and damned for faults which were never actually his. Nevertheless, when his doctrine, whether pure or mongrel, came to our shores, it was for Americans new and full of promise. Arriving in the republic when the spell of Pestalozzi had wearied and, indeed, was almost spent, Herbartianism gave American education a lift it sorely needed.

4

Now the Herbartians are all in the shadows, and their revelation seems remote. But not all of it surely. Since when has goodness of character ceased to be an end in education? Who but numskulls and dullards would venture to teach the young without the powerful enchantment of interest? And what is a lesson plan but a current version of the Formal Steps, whether they are bunched in fives or fours, or fewer or more? Even correlation remains, as does the general idea of putting our grasp of education on as scientific a basis as is humanly possible. This is not saying that, even in faint degree, the contemporary practitioners of the pedagogic art are Herbartians. It is merely suggesting that a good portion of Herbart's doctrine was of an intrinsic soundness, and that some of its essence, refined and modified, has found its way into modern form.

For the sake of the full record, however, it must be said that Herbartianism was not without its unseemly spots. Its partisans, for example, essayed to maintain the cultural legacy, a worthy motive, no doubt, and one shared by its connoisseurs everywhere. But in the pursuit of their lofty mission they addressed themselves largely to the gathering of knowledge and information. They thus gave scant nourishment to the feelings. The beautiful and majestic chords which resound through great literary art they underestimated completely. In their hands the pondering of lovely letters became an intensive ritual for bagging names and dates, for the analysis of rhetorical flora, and for moral uplift. Did the Herbartians magnify the education of the mind? Then, by the same stroke, they minified the training of the hand. Unlike Pestalozzi and, even more, his magnificent disciple Fellenberg, they were strangers to some of the urgent needs of the vast multitude of people and to the elementary dictates of their surrounding culture. And though they preached eloquently about man's many-sided interests, they were blind to his many-sided personality. Certainly they did not, like Rousseau, catch a glimpse of the inner man and the complex, nonintellectual urges which operate, sometimes almost overmasteringly, within us all.

CHAPTER 24

FRIEDRICH WILHELM AUGUST FROEBEL

It befell another German to deal with the varied nonintellectual manifestations of human life and to offer them a rich and abundant accommodation in his school. He was Friedrich Wilhelm August Froebel, and he was born in 1782 in the green-walled hills of Thuringia. He was still in infancy when his mother died, and his father took himself a new wife. The elder Froebel was a country parson, a solemn and astringent man, full of certainty and moral self-ascendancy. Neither he nor his spouse found much relish in young Froebel. They deemed him headstrong and stupid, and when their efforts to mold him into conformity failed, they gave him up as hopeless and consigned him to a girls' school.

Actually the pastor's son was neither nincompoop nor renegade, but rather a highly dowered and fanciful child. When, for example, he was bundled off to a country uncle, also a man of God, but a rare and kindly one, the spirit that dwelt within young Froebel quickly soared. Unluckily, after five years of free and easy functioning, when the lad returned to his domestic quarters the old rancors rekindled. To still his brooding anguish, he sought surcease in the peace of the lovely countryside, roving its meads and woodlands, and pondering the magic of their impalpable poesy. He had all the seriousness of a sensitive youth, and ere long he found himself speculating on the meaning of vale and hillock, the everpresent forest, the endless sky—indeed, the universe itself, and his own infinitesimal relation to it all. He was, in sum, wrestling with the riddle of existence—beguiling from time out of mind even to the sages, and certainly far beyond his own frail adolescent capacity, but something, nevertheless, which was to haunt him until he was well on in his more mature and perspicacious years.

Soon after his homecoming, without being consulted, Froebel was apprenticed to a forester. Save for its high-handed manner, the decision was doubtless a good one. Its promise, vocationally at any rate, was excellent; at the same time it afforded him the chance to disport himself outdoors in the nature he cherished so warmly. On the other hand, the business had its drawback. His life was still inordinately isolated, and though time had accustomed him to solitude, what he needed now, and above all, was the comfort and strength which emanate from the flow of normal communion with one's fellows. He found this comfort and strength in small and insufficient degree in a friendly doctor who lent him books which served to spark his zeal and promote his interest in nature's underlying science.

After a couple of years his apprenticeship came to an unexpected and disappointing close. At length, after considerable disputation with his father, he was allowed to make for the groves of Jena. Under the personal watch of Goethe, the university was in those days the most brilliant jewel of academic Germany. The fame of its philosophers radiated in all directions, and so did that of its men of letters, and to a lesser extent, its scientists. Jena's enlightened air delighted Froebel—but not for long. He ran into debt, and for a while he was jugged in the university jail. His father reluctantly fetched him out, wringing from him the concession that he would go to work. He tried his hand at various jobs. He clerked, he surveyed, he kept accounts, he even ventured to manage a country estate. But he disliked them all, and all he got from them was an immeasurable dose of boredom.

In 1805, still without vocational mooring, Froebel journeyed to Frankfurt to study architecture. But again his plans went astray, and presently we see him in the long-tailed coat of the German schoolmaster, at work in a small Pestalozzian school. Here his groping came to an end, and his unrest and anxiety bowed to peace and serenity. "From the first," he confided later, "I had found something I had always longed for, but always missed; as if my life had at last discovered my native element." For three years Froebel applied himself to his practice with all the skill at his command. Then, realizing that for all his natural capacity for the teaching art, he still could benefit from the counsel of an expert, he went to Yverdon. For two years he attended its sessions, working and studying under Pestalozzi, and becoming in the process a convert to the New Education.

But his was not the awe of a little man for a great one. Papa Pestalozzi thrilled him, needless to say. At the same time Froebel sensed certain imperfections in the old man's work. He not only disputed parts of Pestalozzi's pedagogy, but even then his mind's eye was catching flashes of a strange, uncharted land in the continent of learning. It was inhabited by little children—a place where they might unfold naturally and without grief, amidst affection and understanding, without the bedevilment of drill and duress, but in the gayety of song and play. Such was Froebel's first vision of the kindergarten.

It is not necessary to reenact Froebel's next few years in detail. On his return to the homeland he resumed his affiliation with the higher learning, first at Göttingen, and then, in 1812, at Berlin, where he came to grips with mineralogy. There, at last he put an end to the bafflement which had dogged him since his youth. Through his rocks and crystals he became, as he said, "convinced of the demonstrable connection in all cosmic development." His quest for a "law of unity" had reached its successful fulfillment not in the winding alleys of philosophy, but in the laboratories of natural science. Then, in its uncanny way, fortune thrust him into the soldier's uniform to fight and bleed for the fatherland in its war against Napoleon. Peace brought him to Keilhau, a crossroads village in Thuringia, where, in 1816, he opened a school. He called it—of all things—the Universal German Institute of Education, and he ran it somewhat in the Pestalozzian manner, but graced it also with play and music.

Despite its grandiose title, it was a precarious enterprise from the start, with little more than an idea to uphold it and with a roster of five small boys—all of them Froebel's nephews. Uncle Fritz was joined presently by a couple of friends, but the institute continued to be roweled by trouble. There was strife among its backers; there was no money in the till; there were even rumors that it was against God and *Vaterland*. For much of this Froebel had himself to blame. He had no head for the practical, and like so many seers, he was not only full of surety, but contumacious to those who ventured to question him. Yet, though Keilhau's hopes proved delusive, in the furtherance of Froebel's pedagogy the school offered nourishment aplenty. From it came his *Education of Man (Die Menschenerziehung)*, which he published in 1826. It is a heavy and forbidding book drenched in symbolism; yet it is also a substantial book, the sole, systematic exposition of his views that Froebel ever projected.

When the inevitable ax struck down at last on Keilhau, Froebel transplanted himself to Switzerland. He worked for a while at Wartensee, then at Willisau, and finally, in 1837, at Burgdorf in the selfsame castle once enlivened by Pestalozzi and his flock. In Switzerland Froebel's pedagogic beliefs gradually came to a crystal. There he became convinced that "all education was yet without proper initial foundation," and—more important—that "until the education of the nursery was reformed, nothing solid and worthy could be obtained." To advance these ideas into practice he urged the special training of "gifted and competent mothers"—a wild idea, as anybody can see, in an era when Germany's chambers of learning, from the meanest to the noblest, were in the hands almost exclusively of the superior sex.

In 1837 Froebel came back to his native Thuringia to settle in Blankenburg where he started a school for the very young. He gave it the appalling name of *Kleinkinderbeschäftingungsanstalt*, but after some second thinking he amended it to kindergarten, a word which currently enriches many tongues, and which promises to endure to the end of time. The kindergarten was conceived as the child's own world. Here he was to "develop in harmony, peace, and joy within himself, and with those around him." It was to be a world wherein he could pulse and breathe and function freely in concert with his fellows—a rich and joyous wonderland of action, of song and story, of clay and sandpiles, of color, paste, and scissors. To such an end Froebel and his staff invented games and songs for little children, besides a variety of activities to satisfy their craving to be up and doing. For all his romantic bubbling, Froebel could not escape the academician's predilection to classify and pigeonhole his wares. He sorted his activities into "gifts" and "occupations." The former, he was at pains to explain, were unalterable in form, say, cubes, spheres, and cylinders, and they all harbored a symbolic meaning. The latter were materials which underwent change as they were put to use, such homely and familiar things, for instance, as clay, sand, cardboard, and the like. Betweenwhiles, Froebel busied himself with songwriting, putting together one of his most ingratiating works, his *Mutter- und Koselieder*, which came out in 1843, and which some years later was published in English as *Mother and Play Songs*.

But again Froebel fell prey to his innocence in practical affairs, and before long his school, gnawed away by debt, put out its lights and drew its shutters. He now mounted the lecture platform to summon support for his mission. Though public talking did not come easily to this shy and reticent man, he kept at it for almost half a dozen years, addressing himself principally to women, and astounding even himself with a measure of success. By 1849 he was able to start afresh, this time at Bad Liebenstein, a watering place where the rich and fashionable gathered to wash away their aches and ailments, whether real or imaginary. Here Froebel launched another kindergarten as well as a seminary for aspiring teachers. To ensure himself a sufficiency of clients, he assembled the neighboring peasant young, leaping and cavorting with them like an itching kangaroo, a practice which aroused no end of public snickers, not to say misgivings and suspicions. No doubt Froebel's second venture would have washed down the drain in failure like the others, but for the aid and devotion of active friends and coworkers, in particular Baroness Bertha von Bülow-Wendhausen, who—so the story goes—had contrived to meet him because he had been described to her as an "old fool named Froebel." Confident that what Froebel was seeking was fundamentally right, and that his rumored idiocy had much more sense to it at bottom than much of our so-called reason, she volunteered to make the work of this strange and bewildering genius known to a world bent, apparently, on ignoring him.

The baroness was amply equipped for such a task. She had money and connections, besides an almost fanatical ardor, and she had all the exuberant vitality of an auctioneer. To the end of her days this spritely amazon labored for the kindergarten, lecturing and writing in its behalf, defending it from its detractors, and prowling all over Europe to disseminate and propagate its doctrines. When death took her off at last, she had enjoyed the felicity at least of having savored victory, for the kindergarten had won the hearts of people the world around.

2

A man of deep religious feeling, Froebel sensed the mysterious whisperings of God in all growing things. Education's great purpose, hence, was not to bind, but to loose the personality which nestles in every child. Thus conceived, education puts its stress on the unfoldment of the native personality, and the kindergarten, true to its name, becomes the place where it is encouraged to grow and fructify. Such education, contended Froebel, must be self-development, carefully and tenderly cultivated by adults, it is true, but self-development just the same. By the same token, the kindergarten, holding the mirror up to nature, takes the young child as he is, which is to say a creature bursting with urges to be physically expressive. "To learn a thing in life and through doing," asserted Froebel, "is much more developing, cultivating, and strengthening than through the verbal communication of ideas." Hence the kindergarten's sumptuous provision for self-activity. In this respect Froebel sprang several notches higher than his predecessors, and indeed, many of his successors, for among educators he was the first to capture the vast educational significance of the child's own world. Though there is in Froebel a recurrent echo of Rousseau, particularly in his devotion to nature and the development of a free personality, in his attempt to give the individual a social balance he differs radically from the mercurial Genevan. Man, said Froebel, should live not only in inner harmony, but with others as well—and this, he went on, should continue "in all the various circumstances of life, in the family and school, in domestic and public life." The kindergarten, hence, was conducive not only to self-expression; it was also a hive for social interaction. It was, remarked the ever-ready Baroness Bertha, "a miniature state for children, wherein the young citizen can learn to move freely, but with consideration for his little fellows."

Much of Froebel's thinking sojourned in the lotus land of mysticism. In consequence, his writing, and even some of his kindergarten practices, are frequently blanketed in a fog of halftones, symbols, and allusions. Today Froebel's mysticism carries no more weight than fortune telling, and if the kindergarten continues to be well regarded, it is because in the main it is rooted in psychological and sociological verity.

Froebel's life came to an end pretty much as it had begun, wrapped in the shadows of frustration. The kindergarten had won friends, to be sure, but those who bore it malice were much more numerous. Even worse, Froebel's liberalism made him suspect to the Prussian bureaucracy—then in one of its moods of bleak reaction—and in 1852, unable and unwilling to differentiate between Froebel and an anti-Hohenzollern nephew, the authorities, deferring to its experts in morals, outlawed the kindergarten on the ground that it was socialistic and "calculated to train the youth of the country to atheism." Despite vigorous efforts to undo it, the ban remained in effect for almost a decade, by which time Froebel had taken flight for eternity.

3

Had he been able to hold on just a bit longer, he would have witnessed the kindergarten attracting audiences far beyond his native soil. Nowhere, however, was it given a heartier encouragement than in the United States. Its first partisans in the republic were Germans who, despairing of living in the fatherland after the collapse of the Revolution of 1848, pulled up their stakes and made the long journey to the Middle West. There, in 1855, in Watertown, Wisconsin, Mrs. Carl Schurz, a former student of Froebel, established what may have been the first kindergarten in the United States. It was a modest affair, in private hands, and conducted in German. Five years later the first English-speaking kindergarten, owned and managed by Elizabeth Peabody, made its appearance in Boston. Finally, in 1873, Froebel's creation was welcomed to the public service when St. Louis opened the first tax-supported kindergarten in America. Rather curiously, in this hemisphere it was not the United States, but Ontario, Canada, which in 1885 was the first to make the kindergarten an integral part of the public school system. Since then, though altered with the changing times and the coming of fresher and surer knowledge, the kindergarten has been clasped to the national bosom, and forgetting momentary lapses, it has multiplied steadily, so that at the moment about half the country's five-year-olds exult in its numerous benefits.

In the course of time the kindergarten became food for thought and inspiration for some of America's foremost schoolmen, as witness, Colonel Parker, the suspected father of progressive education, and John Dewey, the nation's foremost pedagogical thinker. As the kindergarten worked its way into the national system, many of the ideas on which it rested ascended into the higher sphere of the elementary school. The belief, for example, that the child is an active animal is surely no longer the monopoly of the kindergarten. So too the notion that play has educational worth. And so also with creative education, self-expression, learning by doing, and many similar objects of esteem in progressive education, whether public or private. Time saw them favored even in the secondary learning—until, that is, of late when because of their apparent overstress on the nonintellectual aspects of behavior they became subject to a mounting censure.

The kindergarten's traffic in needlecraft, weaving, and paper folding, together with its use of sand, clay, glue, and paint, eventually aroused an interest in a more pretentious training of the hand, and led, in the flow of time, to a development which Froebel, even in his maddest fancy, had not reckoned with. The first people to invest their schools with manual training were the Finns, who, in 1866, under the guidance of Uno Cygnaeus, an admirer of Froebel and one of their outstanding educators, succeeded in getting courses in basketmaking, woodcarving, and metalwork into the schools. Not long after, a sympathetic echo was heard from neighboring Sweden with the introduction of woodworking as an integral part of that country's public schooling. Doubtless the program's economic promise had something to do with its popularity. More specifically, though, its furtherance was the work of Otto Salomon, a man of moment among the Swedes and a protagonist of the new development. Some of his views appear sound enough even in the glare of critical afterthought, as witness, his insistence that the things which pupils make should be useful, and that they should do their own work from start to finish. But like so many other prophets, Salomon was also the concocter of nonsense. It was his contention, to cite a few examples, that the schoolboy's fabrication of penholders, soup ladles, and bucket handles would not only inspire him with awe and affection for the dignity of labor, but that somehow it would also contribute to his virtue. Salomon believed that the confection of such goods would develop not only the specific skills involved in the process itself, but that these would transfer to general situations so that the precision and tidiness a pupil developed in carving a coat hanger would serve him in the years ahead in the general circumstances of everyday life from, say, his maintenance of personal hygiene to his selection of his agents and spokesmen in the Congress on the Potomac. Though psychological science has since routed such claims, in Salomon's time, and indeed for some time after, the belief in such transfer of training was given a stout support, and—whether true or not—it helped to put the movement on its legs and to hold it there.

From Scandinavia the manual revelation fanned out to other lands. It showed itself in England by midcentury, and in France soon after that, and in Russia and the United States some years following. What gave it powerful notice in our republic was an exhibit by the Russians in 1876 at the Centennial Exposition in Philadelphia where they showed samples of work in metal and wood done by their boys in the Imperial Technical School at Moscow. The handiwork caught the eye of President John Runkle of the Massachusetts Institute of Technology, who soon after allowed himself to extend it a rapturous justification. His authoritative appreciation infected others so that presently manual training was being quarried in various municipalities throughout the republic. The honor of being first on the scene goes to St. Louis where, in 1880, a manual training high school, a private one connected with Washington University, made its advent. The first manual training high school of the public variety was established in the nineties in Baltimore. Meanwhile, the movement had broken into the halls of the lower learning. In fact, by 1890 some half a hundred schools, mostly along the Atlantic littoral, were practicing the new art in one guise or another. As the movement gained in power and celerity, it spread in an ever-expanding circle until, in due course, here and there even girls were allowed to endanger themselves with saws and hatchets, and not merely with needles and flatirons. Today, whatever one may say in favor of the movement, the tides of fashion are ebbing from it. Not only have psychologists stripped it of the deceptive charms which once were its great strength, but even the tools themselves have changed from the simple manual ones of yesterday to the mechanical dinosaurs which currently roar and shake in every mill and farm. Even so, though manual training scarcely exists—at any rate in its own pedagogic autonomy—the promise which it bore has blown afield into industrial education and into the arts and crafts where, it is scarcely necessary to add, today it flourishes abundantly.

CHAPTER 25

HERBERT SPENCER

While the great minds of pedagogy were applying themselves to transforming our educational theory and practice, on other fronts developments of a vast and widespread consequence were taking shape. They were dominated, for one, by the growing power and multiplication of the factory and the machine and, for another, by the new and insistent challenge of the natural sciences. Under way in England and the United States and in some of the German lands by the 1850s, the two movements made rapid progress, picking up steam and setting their gauge cocks to whistling as they proceeded into the twentieth century, to bring forth the civilization we now enjoy and extol.

If, as some authorities hold, education reflects the culture of which it is a part, then obviously these forces should have put their grip upon the schools. Science and industry, in sum, had a right to expect some serious consideration from the schoolmasters. But their overwhelming number were conservative, disinclined to traffic in novelties, and convinced beyond all doubt that what was important in learning lay not in the subject matter under study, but in the mental discipline to be wrung therefrom. To such right-wing academicians the training that schoolboys derived from their daily combat with the old-time classics was not only sufficient to its purpose, but well-nigh perfect, and second, hence, to none.

To loosen schoolmasters from their ancient moorings and to waken them to the culture burgeoning all about became the work not of an educator, but of a layman. Herbert Spencer by name, he was born in 1820 at Derby, in England, the issue of Methodist parents, and he died eighty-three years later, a bald and bewhiskered evolutionist and agnostic. He was cremated at Golders Green without any religious solemnities.

From his father young Spencer acquired a streak of individualism which was to break into flame now and again, and which was to smolder within him to the end. His favorite occupation when he was a boy was laziness, an inclination his easygoing father was far from discouraging. But when the lad passed thirteen, a new leaf was suddenly turned, and he found himself packed off to study under an uncle, the Reverend Thomas Spencer, an uplifter and teetotaler, who taught at Hinton Charterhouse, near Bath, and who was famous for miles around for the sting of his rattan. Even then, apparently, young Spencer gave no heed to reputations, however high, and he promptly made off. Three days following he was back at the family fireside, having walked, as he carefully reported, over a hundred miles and refueled along the way with bread and beer. But this time the father brooked no nonsense, and the boy was returned to his books to serve his time for the next three years. They were, according to Spencer, a total and utter loss—a fact in which he took some pride, and which later he was at pains to tell the world. "That neither in boyhood or youth," he wrote, "did I receive a single lesson in English, and that I have remained entirely without formal knowledge of syntax to the present hour are facts which should be known," especially, he added, "since their implications are at variance with assumptions universally accepted."

By some of his biographers Spencer has been portrayed as an insatiable devourer of print, but the facts point the other way. He lumbered through six books of the *Iliad*, and then tossed it aside, saying that he "would rather grant a large sum of money than read it to the end." At thirty he tackled Kant, but he soon concluded that the German philosopher was an ass, and not worth bothering about. On the word of his secretary we have it that he never read an entire volume on science, and that when he composed his first book on *Social Statistics*, he had read only one other discourse on the subject. If Spencer was educated and informed, it was plainly not by the route of books. The enormous herd of facts he drove into his writings he lassoed in the main by observation and experience. Hawk-eyed for every fact, he was, at bottom, a self-educated man who seized a great deal of his knowledge as he encountered it in his daily living.

Professionally, he made his start as a railroad engineer, but tracks and trestles proved irksome, and presently he transferred his activities to journalism. It was in his writing den that he did his most impressive work, a work which reached its consummation in his treatise on a synthetic philosophy. He was a stranger to emotion, and he had all the humor of a dishrag. On the other hand, he was logical, and his effort to be precise was akin almost to a phobia. "It has been remarked," he observed in his mature and reflective years, "that I have an unusual faculty of exposition—set forth my data and reasoning and conclusions with a clearness not common." The contemporary and supporter of Darwin, Spencer made evolution his god. He became its ready and relentless advocate, and its most eloquent mouthpiece, working himself unsparingly in its behalf, and against obstacles which not infrequently were scarcely bearable.

2

A man of Spencer's cast of mind, with his devotion to the Darwinian cause, his intense participation in modern life, and his scorn for formal learning would scarcely be expected to put much stock in the classical tradition. He made public assault on it in 1859 in the *Westminster Review* in an essay on education, the first of a series of four. "What education," he archly asked therein, "is of most worth?" It is, he replied, science. Science, he went on, it is on every count—for self-preservation, for gaining a livelihood, for rearing and disciplining the young, for the maintenance of proper political and social relationships—even, indeed, "for the most perfect production and enjoyment of art in all its forms." For all purposes of discipline—intellectual, moral, religious—he concluded, "the most efficient study, once more, is Science."

A presumptuous proposition? Without a doubt. But it was also novel, and it was graced in a luminous and vivacious prose. Under the Spencerian onslaught, the conservators of Latin and Greek found themselves for the first time in an unaccustomed and uncomfortable strait. Not only had Spencer put their vaunted values on the defensive; in the process his magnificent defiance had brought him a vast and far-flung audience. Look at it how you will, his contention was bound to ring the academic rafters.

Those who declared for the teaching of science grounded their case on two main points. What mattered in education, they let it be known, was not method and drill, as the classicists so stoutly maintained, but the actual substance of what was learned. The ancient tongues, they insisted, despite their long and useful service in the chambers of learning, were hopelessly insufficient to the needs of contemporary life. The sciences, in contrast, were not only attuned to the current culture, but to be ignorant of them was to be unprepared to cope with modern living. The Spencerians' second argument revolved around the business of mental training. In a word, it did assassination not on the doctrine, but on the notion, cherished for centuries, that in this department the classics had no rival. Are subjects taught to exercise the mind? Then the sciences are eager and ready to fill the bill, and they promise to do it not merely as well as the senile classics, but even better. Today, of course, that argument no longer carries any weight. For through the probings of scientific psychology, the theory of mind training has been reduced to nothingness, and no educator of any standing would grant it countenance.

In his remaining three essays Spencer aired his pedagogic beliefs. Two stick out above the others: first, that the Latin grammar school, which had been in service, scarcely altered, since the sixteenth century, needed to be scrubbed of its mold and mildew and brought in line with the times; and second, that to be prepared for everyday life all the people—not just the few—should be given access to general instruction in science.

As for the rest of Spencer's views, they were little more than a warming-over of the ideas of others, some sound, some spurious, and save for the spell of their animated utterance, they add little to his stature. Thus, with the seventeenth-century Comenius, he held that in learning one should proceed inductively from the known to the unknown, the near to the remote, and so on down the rest of that clichéd lane to its terminus, which is to say, from the specific to the general and the concrete to the abstract. With the Herbartians Spencer agreed, quite correctly, that interest is the necessary tinderbox for learning, and that without it no blaze can be ignited. The Herbartian culture epochs theory, that as a child grows to manhood he retraces the successive cultural stages of the race from low to high, Spencer swallowed 100 percent; in fact, like its original partisans, he was all for building a curriculum based thereon. Since his time, of course, the doctrine has becomes scarcely more than a curio, and except for its singularity, it no longer fetches notice. The son of an indulgent father, Spencer might be expected to stand up against the blood-and-iron discipline which in the mid-nineteenth century was still the domestic and academic rule. Instead, he embraced Rousseau's notion of punishment by natural consequences, a penology which today's moral scientists generally pronounce wanting. In the Spencerian pedagogic garden, room aplenty was set aside for the cultivation of the body, and here Spencer took most of his ideas from John Locke—apart, that is, from the immortal John's "hardening process," which he rejected out of hand. It was Spencer's conviction that, by and large, grownups bear much too heavily upon their young; that these, as a result, are under an onerous and even perilous strain; and that later on, all too frequently they are unfit to fight the battle for existence. Finally, as already mentioned, Spencer upheld the doctrine of mental training, a doctrine which is today sealed in its vault. In his own time, however, this was not the case, for the belief in mind training, like that in man's inability to fly through the air, was then robust and universal.

Time saw Spencer's four monographs preserved between book covers. Under the title *Education*, the volume attained a high celebrity, to become something of an intellectual best-seller and an instrument of light and instruction in the foremost seminaries of teacher training not only in Britain but also in the United States.

Like Francis Bacon, so long ago, Herbert Spencer was not only a booming enthusiast for science and its place in human life; he was also an adroit and effective propagandist in its behalf. His argument for teaching science may have rested on a shaky psychological assumption, but to a utilitarian-minded populace the view that in our everyday living a knowledge of science is of more worth than Latin and Greek made plain sense. The years were to bear him out. We see his hand in the inauguration of a "modern side" in England's tradition-ridden classical grammar school; and we see it, of course, in the recognition of science as a meet and necessary subject for general instruction.

Like Herbart and Pestalozzi and other European educators, Spencer was gravely hearkened to on this side of the Atlantic. In the school of mid-nineteenth-century America, science was, of course, no stranger. Franklin and Jefferson had given it their justification, and so had President Johnson of King's College and President Smith of the College of Philadelphia, as well as several others. Even in the colonial era a variety of science was being taught in numerous academies and private schools, and subsequently in a few of our more daring and enterprising colleges. In the sixties when the vogue of Pestalozzi invaded America, his stress on observation and the object lesson gave science study a modest and scattered entry into the elementary school. Early in the decade following, at the instance of William Torrey Harris, the superintendent of the St. Louis schools, the subject was given a gentle and formal introduction in the city's lower learning. For all that, however, when Spencer let down his tornado, the status of science in the American school was of low degree.

The most prominent and by a long shot the most effective supporter of the Spencerian proposition was Charles William Eliot. A professor of chemistry at Harvard, he ascended to its presidency in 1869, whereupon during the next forty years he proceeded to transform the oldest of American colleges into an institution of the highest quality, respected and admired the world around.

Needless to say, his insistence that the sciences be given a place of rank and dignity in the American learning carried a considerable authority, and though it aroused hubbub and opposition, as the century unfolded, the idea prevailed not only amidst the elms of Cambridge, but in an ever-growing number of other higher groves as well. Not only did the sciences make themselves at home in the college curriculum, but presently they were being accepted as part of the requirement for college admission.

Though Spencer evoked applause, he also evoked derision. In either case it served his cause, for the catcalls like the cheers gave a lively advertisement to his argument, namely, that a vast breach runs between the school, merchanting its age-worn stock, and the world outside, pulsing with new and staggering happenings. In this respect Spencer may well have been the first in the annals of modern education to put his finger on what students of the science of society currently call the "cultural lag." Spencer's plea for the study of science, as has been said, came to an abundant harvest, and in this education, and hence society, was the gainer. But if the result was meritorious, some of the reasoning behind it was not without flaw. Thus, to put down the classicists, the Spencerians belabored them with their own favorite argument. Like the classicists, the Spencerians contended that the mind can be trained, and that the powers of discernment and exactitude that are developed when it exercises itself with such specific objects of study as, say, electrolysis, osmosis, or even the lowly dog flea (*Ctenocephalis canis*), will in the long run translate themselves into life's general situations whether political, social, economic, ethical, or religious. This doctrine is known as the transfer of training or learning, and as stated some pages back, modern psychologists have effectively laid it low. The training, moreover, which Spencer advocated was overwhelmingly cerebral. The magic enchantment of art and music and literature which rejoices and exalts the human spirit left him almost unmoved. What the Spencerians did, in short, was to substitute a one-sided scientific training for a one-sided classical training.

CHAPTER 26

THE MAKING OF THE AMERICAN SYSTEM

A s the eighteenth century headed Americans toward the Revolution, their interests immersed themselves more and more in subjects of a lively political and economic hue. Even before, there had been signs of some relaxing in the religious partisanship which had burned so fiercely in so many first-generation colonists. As early as 1647, for example, Rhode Islanders had taken a strong stand for religious liberty when, the first among English-speaking folk, they wrote a bill for freedom of worship into their law. Marylanders followed two years later with a similar measure, and though time later saw it blown away, it was, even so, a foreshadowing of things to come. The old religious intransigence yielded not so much to doubts and anxieties assailing it from within as to forces from without, subtle at times, it is true, but of a power, nevertheless, which moved them inexorably forward to their ends. They revealed themselves in various shapes and guises: in the frontiersman's resolution as he fought nature's harsh defiances; in the lure of money to be made in trade and industry; in the growing vigor of the secular political arm; and not the least by any count, in the breakdown of usages and traditions, often venerable, and the rise in their place of younger ways, bold, virile, and American.

By the middle years of the eighteenth century the way the wind was pointing was plain to see. Most of the Colonies, to be sure, continued to give some support to the established Anglicanism, but the church lacked the august power of its transoceanic mother, and as Bunker Hill and Lexington drew closer, it was even being viewed with something of a bilious eye. Gone too was Calvin's theocratic stronghold in Massachusetts, and gone the potency of its prophets of damnation. Henceforward there were to be no more such ecclesiastical monopolies—time, indeed, was to behold not only the government's written assurance of religious freedom, but the divorce of state and church as well.

As religion was gradually edged from its place of dominance, its reign as the primary subject of colonial thought and utterance fell under the challenge of rivals. More and more, men of urbane habit refused to have their lives hedged in. One finds them adverting to matters of a highly worldly consideration, things they found interesting and enjoyed doing immensely. The expanding secularity functioned most frankly, of course, in the cities, not only in Boston and New York, but also in Charleston, Annapolis, and Williamsburg, and most gorgeously, as we have seen, in Philadelphia. It poured forth in various devices, in news gazettes, in secular books, and in circulating libraries. It splurged in the building of elegant mansions. It generated an interest in the arts and sciences, concerts and plays, games and sports, and the numerous other pastimes men engage in to give charm and enjoyment to their living.

The secular mood presently impressed itself upon education, bearing upon both the nature of its support and the character of its learning. Without religion to fan the fire, the desire to teach the common child even the elements of reading lost much of its ardor. In consequence, collecting fees to support such instruction, whether from the individual or the communal pocket, became vastly more difficult. In New England the town school, envisioned by the vanished theocracy as the nursery of its faith, had descended into the district school, and with no resolute leadership to flag it on, its industry ebbed rapidly. Elsewhere, one by one, parochial schools closed their doors, while those remaining in operation suffered a general decline. In the South, where the sentiment to illuminate the people had never obtained more than a listless support, the need for a general lower education all but faded away.

There were other shifts and alterations, some of a minor sort and now pretty well forgotten, but others of a considerable reach and consequence. To squeeze their last penny's worth out of their scanty capital, for example, some places conceived the practice of combining the work of the reading school and that of the writing school. By this route the three Rs took shape, to become in the parade of years the basic intellectual stock of the American elementary school.

The worldly concerns which exercised an influence on the lower learning left their mark also on the secondary species. The Latin grammar school, so long the undisputed champion in the domain of secondary education, continued to offer its ancient knowledge. But the belief in the potency of its wisdom was on the wane, and its best days were done. The newly risen nabobs of the marketplace inclined to show it no awe—nor can one blame them. For in their world of practical affairs what a chap needed to know was tinged deeply with utilitarian considerations—hence the popping up of a flourishing private teaching. Uncapped and ungowned, for the most part, but of a powerful allurement, most of its practitioners were ready to merchant their wares in almost anything for which they could cadge a fee, from, say, the confection of a business letter, a bill of sale, or a promissory note, to the arithmetic of the counting room, geography, modern languages, surveying, and navigation. Time, as has already been made evident, brought such enterprise form and substance, first in 1751 in the incarnation of the Philadelphia Academy, and later in numerous similar shrines in various parts of the land.

Academies were of diverse kinds. Privately maintained, they demanded payment from their customers—though this is not to say that they turned up their nose at outside benefactions. Indeed, after the Revolution extramural assistance of one sort or another became fairly common—here and there academies even succeeded in getting financial largess from the state.

Like the grammar schools, the first academies addressed their offerings only to boys; a few more turns of the hands of the clock, however, and some were braving the establishment of a "female department." But in those wholesome days such an integration of the sexes offended the public pruderies, and it evoked no little talk—hence, after a while, the appearance of the "female academy." The exclusive precinct of the fair sex, it hawked all the regular academic staples besides such delicacies as needlecraft, watercoloring, wax modeling, and music, both vocal and instrumental. Such houses of knowledge and refinement, whether for boys or girls, sprouted nearly always from denominational enterprise, but as more and more years crowded into the past, and the secular note increased in strength and stridency, not a few of them laid aside their sectarian stresses to yield their learning to anyone of goodwill and virtue, and of course, of the prerequisite pocket. Whatever their special nature, the academies, taking them one with another, remained true to the purpose which originally brought them forth, which was to relate education more intimately to the needs of everyday living. For this purpose they put their weight on a learning which they esteemed as useful and salubrious to man, in illustration, the living languages, the natural sciences, and the knacks and instruments of commerce—"the great end and the real business of living," as Phillips Academy of Andover, Massachusetts, so neatly summed it up when, in 1778, it declared itself ready to train and instruct its first recruits.

The secularity which displayed itself so robustly in the academy winked an eye also at the college. There, true enough, the zeal for the old and trusted values lingered tenaciously, and the higher learning continued, as in its childhood, to concern itself chiefly with the preparation of young men for the holy calling. But strange notions were being bandied about. As alluded to earlier, Dr. Samuel Johnson, in New York at King's College, gave them expression when he proposed a curriculum freighted not only with the conventional classical and religious cargo, but in addition spruced up with courses in commerce and the natural and social sciences. At Philadelphia the Rev. William Smith, the head of the college, was reciting a similar heresy. Unluckily, neither Johnson's nor Smith's counsel got into actual practice. In Virginia, on the other hand, the reception was somewhat better. There, in 1779, the College of William and Mary dismantled its chair in divinity as "incompatible with freedom in a Republic"; at the same time it seated George Wythe as America's first professor of law. Meanwhile, at Harvard, which was now more than a centenarian, Professor John Winthrop was setting forth the Newtonian theory besides putting his students to work in a classroom full of odd and unearthly gadgets—a room where belief in the unknown was discountenanced and where everything was subject to impartial observation and verification. Meanwhile, across the corridor, the brilliant Edward Wigglesworth was reminding his students that Almighty God had vouchsafed man more than one way to knowledge. "Faith," he told them, "responds to prayer, rather than investigation."

2

As the years rolled by, the new ideas gradually made their way into the schoolbooks. *The New England Primer*, it is true, continued to provide its advice and instruction, but its cheerless meditations, as indispensable in the Puritan heyday as castor oil, were losing favor, and its days of lush grazing were coming to an end. But it was not until 1740, when Thomas Dilworth put out his *A New*

Guide to the English Tongue, that the *Primer* began to feel a competitor's hot breath upon its collar. Dilworth, who was an experienced birchman in the motherland, was at great pains to fill his volume with linguistic erudition. He dealt, as he said, with words "both common and proper and from one to six syllables," including their spelling and their "sound and signification." For good measure he entertained his readers with a brief discourse on English grammar "in the most familiar and instructive Method of *Question* and *Answer*." Though in all this his stress was clearly laic, the author was not averse to engauding his volume with pieces of a moral and pious tone, followed and fortified, befittingly, with "forms of prayer for children."

The book drew high praise from ecclesiastics and pedagogues alike. Bards wreathed its creator in verse—he was, said one, "the man by gracious Heaven sent, a friend, a father to the human kind." As a result, the *Guide* drove an affluent trade, not only in its native England, but in the Colonies too. Appearing, moreover, at a time when the study of English grammar was still a subject of lofty derision among the reigning gentry of the academic faculty, the work served magnificently to give that discipline a measurable lift in status.

But not even Dilworth could cope with the shifting American culture, and by the time the Revolution was upon us, he and his British learning had fallen suspect. The man who finally did him in was Noah Webster, a country schoolmaster in New York, and the author of the *American Spelling Book*. Issued in 1783, it quickly chased the older favorites from the yards of learning to become the schoolboy's basic textbook—oftentimes, indeed, his only one—and as important to his traffic in human affairs as his marbles and his fishhooks. Like the *Primer* before it and the *Readers* of McGuffey in a later age of light, the *Spelling Book* swept through edition after edition, aggregating by the latest estimate at least 100 million copies, bethumbed and explored by over a billion readers—a record surpassed in this land only by that of the Holy Bible.

Webster, who was a flaming patriot, proposed to give the American people a spelling which matched their pronunciation, then somewhat free and easy. For this purpose he not only put American spelling under regulation but also succeeded in emancipating it from the older English precedent. Without a doubt Noah was a pedant, and in his later years often a very irascible one. For all that, he was also America's first professional scholar, a man of vast pertinacity, and pragmatic rather than merely theoretical. His *American Dictionary of the English Language*, which he published in two large volumes in 1828, and which is the ancestor of all the Websters of today, bears testimony not only to his learning, but to his endurance. His pedagogy, which blistered as intensely with patriotism as even some of his most frenzied outcries against the motherland, called for the Americanization of our native schooling. Cleanse the schools of their British corruptions, boost America, expound and extol its history and geography, its hopes and visions, and root them in the child "as soon as he is able to lisp the praise of liberty"—in this mood Webster assembled his readers and even his grammars. One catches traces of it even in his spelling book. A combination primer, reader, and speller, it traverses the literary high road from *ab, eb,* and *ib* to berylline, mesentery, mucilaginous, and parachronism, and from "The sloth is a lazy animal" to a dissertation on "precepts concerning the social relationships." Webster not only fixed the fashion for American spelling; he also made it the most well-regarded subject in the chambers of learning. Indeed, because of him, spelling games became as popular at the American fireside as bridge and pinochle in a later and more sophisticated era.

Although Webster's blue-backed spellers have become something of a treasure in the national memory book, this is not saying they were the only textbook wonders of their time. There was, to begin, the *American Universal Geography*, published in 1784, and the *Elements of Geography*, which was set in type some ten years following. They were the work of Jedidiah Morse, a practicing pastor prepared for his science at Yale. The acknowledged father of American geography, he was the father also of Samuel, the inventor of the telegraph. Like Webster, Morse was possessed by the patriotic frenzy, and he refused to hold his geographic disquisitions to their usual limits. In fact, in 1789, when the scholars of Yale adopted the *American Universal Geography*, at least a third of it dealt with the American past, some of it real and some imaginary.

The first schoolbook to address itself solely to American history appeared in 1787, the year the Fathers convened in Philadelphia to put together the Constitution. Entitled *An Introduction to the History of America*, the book was compounded by John McCullough, a printer but not even in the remotest degree an historian. What the man lacked in historical sense, however, was no handicap —at all events he easily compensated himself for its absence by pilfering generously from the readers of Noah Webster, a practice which was then sanctioned both in ethics and in jurisprudence.

Arithmetic got its first American textbook in 1729 when Isaac Greenwood, a Harvard professor of the subject, ventured his *Arithmetic, Vulgar and Decimal*. But the book was precariously rudimentary, and it acquired no great custom. Far more corpulent and complicated was Nicholaus Pike's treatment of the subject. Put into the bookshops in 1788, it was introduced by its composer as a "new and complete arithmetic for the use of the citizens of the United States." With a rule for nearly every one of its five hundred pages, it endeavored to give light to its readers on such matters as conjoined proportion, alligation medial, tate and tret, how to gauge a mash tub, and the proportion and tonnage of Noah's ark. Tables and statistics swamped its pages, often of repulsive length, but sometimes more than a little useful, as witness, its calculation of the number of cubic inches of beer one has a right to expect in a pint or even a puncheon or a butt. The work carried accolades from several men of mark, as, for example, President Ezra Stiles of Yale, Governor James Bowdoin of Massachusetts, and even George Washington. Unhappily, for the run of Americans, whether in schoolboy britches or in the master's frock, the book's demands were too colossal for the understanding. In the studios of elementary learning, consequently, the third R remained largely a mystery.

In fact, it was not till 1821, when Warren Colburn turned out his *First Lessons in Arithmetic on the Plan of Pestalozzi* that the novice in numbers obtained a satisfactory schoolbook. Despite its thousand-legger title, Colburn's text succeeded in making the study of arithmetic, if not a stark delight, then something which was at least humanly bearable. Not only did it strip the subject of much of its extravagant pedantry, but in seeking to reduce it to Junior's level, Colburn also put it into greater concordance with the computations encountered in everyday living—a practice which is, of course, still highly thought of by experts in such matters.

3

The nation which ran up its flag at Yorktown came out of the Revolution badly damaged. Its land and goods had been racked and its trade and commerce all but strangled, while a debt of $75 million hung like a noose around its neck. Worse, and the cause of no little doubt and soul-searching, was the impotence of the national government. Denied even a fundamental authority, it ruled with a weak and ignominious hand, its laws disdained and even defied, the target abroad of a sardonic mirth and the main reason for the widespread belief that some day soon the young republic would surely wash down the drain.

In education the outlook was no less dour, but in the agony and upset of the times this scarcely mattered. What was needed above all was to get the country on its feet, to forge the squabbling states into a people of a single piece, to make them, in short, a nation under the reign of law and order, and able at all times to fend for itself. To this practical end the Fathers bent their utmost industry. Their paramount stirring, hence, revealed itself in the political and economic rather than in the educational domain.

Though learning was, so to say, a martyr to the national emergency, this does not mean that the business was of no conceivable concern. True, the national government still entertained a reluctance to take a vigorous part in the schooling of its young; nevertheless, the doctrine that such a course was seemly and even patriotic was no longer without support. Numerous prominenti broke into ardent outbursts in its behalf, and some of them—for instance, Benjamin Rush, Du Pont de Nemours, and the irrepressible Mr. Webster—even called for the creation of a national system of education. Under the Articles of Confederation the government went so far as to express its interest in the forwarding of knowledge in some of its law, as witness, especially the Ordinance of 1785, which set aside a certain square of land, six miles by six, in every township in that massive trans-Allegheny province, the National Domain, for the support and promotion of public enlightenment. By this token the national government not only stated the case for Federal aid to education—the first intimation of what has since become a familiar practice; it also gave a helpful boost to public schooling in those states which in later years were staked out of the public lands.

The Constitution's failure to apply any of its writ to education was taken to mean that authority in this sphere had been conceded to the states. Thus the ground was prepared for the development later on of the state system of education. It is, of course, still on hand, flourishing and full of vim, and a stand-out characteristic of the current American educational way. Although the Federal Constitution washed its hands of education, some of the early state constitutions on the other hand entertained no such inclination. In fact, as the eighteenth century descended to its end, of the sixteen states then under the Stars and Stripes, seven had permitted themselves some remarks on the subject. North Carolina and Pennsylvania went on record—warily to be sure—as early as 1776. The most garrulous statement on the educational theme was written into the Massachusetts constitution some four years later. The composition in the main of John Adams, it asserted among other things that a people's rights and liberties depend "on spreading the opportunities and advantages of education in the various parts of the country and among the different orders of the people." For this purpose it called for a "school in every town," besides bidding the lawmakers, their assigns, and their successors "in all future periods of the Commonwealth to cherish the interests of literature and the sciences, and all the seminaries of them."

As democratic ideas began to speak with more authority, it was only natural that to some extent they should be echoed in education. In 1820 a number of states had ventured to flavor their constitutions—somewhat delicately—with declarations for a greater and more generous schooling of their people. The most arresting, and by all odds the most promising, was achieved by Indiana when, in 1816, it gave notice to its lawgivers to take steps toward the establishment of a system of education reaching from the meanest one-room school to the halls of the state university "free and open to all." It is no more than right, however, to add that for all the high wishes behind its utterance, the state took pains to remind its legislators to put off such action "until circumstances will permit" –a loophole they did not disdain to use.

Meanwhile, there were some other works of noble aspiration. As early as 1750, for example, Connecticut's lawmakers, bursting through the trammels of their everyday sagacity, made provision to succor their struggling schools with a permanent endowment. The fund was admirably administered, and for long years it performed its monetary miracle. But the demands put upon it steadily grew heavier, and in the long run, insufficient to its ends, it collapsed, a casualty of its good intentions. On the other side of the Connecticut Valley, New Yorkers, in 1784, irradiated their educational history when they brought forth their University of the State of New York. The title, despite its simplicity, is deceptive, for the university is not a house of higher wisdom, but a state board of education, the first of its line in the republic, and after all these numerous years, still in robust and salutary practice.

Below the Potomac, meanwhile, in Virginia, Jefferson had delivered himself of a legislative proposal by which girls and boys were to obtain their first three years of schooling at public expense, whereupon in the years following the "best geniuses" were to be raked from the "rubbish" to be sent to the College of William and Mary, there to be "educated, boarded, and clothed," with the compliments, once more, of the taxpayers. Jefferson's plan attracted a great deal of attention—even some eulogy—but when it came to converting it into law, the Commonwealth's elected burgesses shied away, and they voted it down.

Yet all this, gratifying though it may have seemed, was no more than slight, a pallid candlelight, at best, of a progress that was still tucked away in the faraway future. As the nineteenth century got under way, only a few states had hazarded the first steps in the direction of free and universal schooling. The task was not light, of course, and the obstacles confronting it were enormous. A few men of vision had come to its support, but the ruling classes stood overwhelmingly against it. Some states had begun to regard education as their sovereign right and responsibility, and a handful had even attempted a cautious assertion thereof. At the same time it would be hard to find any unwillingness to let the job be done, as traditionally, by the churches or by private hands, or, as in New England, by local effort. The surpassing difficulty, of course, was the harsh and transparent fact that general public education meant higher taxes.

4

The custom of larding the poor man's educational opportunity with philanthropy, so agreeably viewed in colonial America, rolled on well into the nineteenth century—its exercise, if anything, increased. For Britain's Society of the Propagation of the Gospel there was, of course, no fancy in the states, and with the outbreak of the Revolution it extinguished its lights and stole away. But other orders, more attuned to the republican credo, quickly leaped into the breach. They transacted their good works especially in the cities, where under various impressive names and dignities, they flung their challenge in the face of ignorance by offering free instruction to the poor.

Of these guilds the one that sticks out above all others was the Free School Society of the City of New York. Chartered in 1805 and headed by the estimable De Witt Clinton, the society undertook to provide knowledge for such children as might be "proper objects of gratuitous education." The society got off to a fine start, with a flow of contributions from big-hearted burghers, besides a small subvention from the city fathers, and even an allowance from the state's school fund. From this capital, which was never princely, the association managed, nevertheless, to give New Yorkers their first earfuls of general, free, nonsectarian instruction. In 1826, when the organization was rechartered, it was also rechristened as the Public School Society and was allowed to lay a small fee on its clients. Almost at once attendance at its classes swooshed down the chute, and the Public Schoolers, somewhat wiser after the fact, abandoned the practice.

At length, in 1828, the state sanctioned a tax to permit the society to continue its idealistic endeavor.

Despite its meritorious services to humanity, the Public School Society engendered sneers as well as smiles. The fact that its bursar could make music in his cashbox with coin out of the public purse was not lost on rival well-doers, and especially on those of the consecrated cloth. Unluckily, whenever ecclesiastics bespoke their lawmakers to grant them a share in the state fund, they were greeted by an almost unanimous silence—a situation which caused them to suffer deeply, and which was not calculated to make them admire the Public School Society. Even more disturbing was the question of religious neutrality. Though the society had pledged to carry on its work in an utterly nonsectarian manner, again and again it was bestormed with the charge that it had violated its promise. The objurgations kept resounding year in and year out, and even penetrated into the legislative corridors at Albany. Finally, in 1842, the lawmakers, having their crop stuffed once too often, created a board of education for the city of New York and passed to it the responsibility of running its public schools. The Public School Society continued to execute its industry for another half-score years when, its windows boarded and its doors shut tight, it resigned itself to history, happy in the confidence that it had given instruction to at least a half a million boys and girls who, but for its grace, would have been condemned to the hulks of ignorance.

Although much of the country's educational charity bubbled from the native heart, some of its good works were based on importations from abroad. A Sunday school, modeled on the English variety, showed itself in Hanover County, Virginia, as early as 1786. A year later another, reserved exclusively for African children, was heard from in Charleston, South Carolina. Others followed, slowly but steadily, and by 1826 they were dispensing their lessons in knowledge and godliness to an ever-proliferating audience, mostly of the submerged classes, in various parts of the land.

From the Atlantic's other side Americans also obtained the infant school. Strictly speaking, it was not always a venture in pure philanthropy since on occasion its sponsors found it necessary to pollute their altruism with a tuition charge. But such demands, whenever they were put forth, were small, so small as to be infinitesimal. The infant groves achieved their first prestige and popularity in the Eastern cities where, as was then a common practice, a child was not allowed to honor the first grade of the elementary school with his presence until he enjoyed at least a nodding acquaintance with reading. To introduce him to this art and mystery presently became the infant school's chief excuse for being. In fact, in 1818, Boston, having become aware of its charms and possibilities, appropriated $5,000 to incorporate the infant school into the city's school system. Designated a "primary school," it accepted its freshmen at the age of four, preparing them in a couple of years or so to be disgorged to the regular lower school which now assumed the name of "grammar school." The way was thus made ready for the full-fledged elementary school with its primary and grammar grades. The new-style infant school kept open from one end of the year to the other, and it was manned entirely by schoolma'ams. Boston's example was soon followed elsewhere—in fact, within a generation the infant, or primary, school had become a striking success.

The prodigious achievement of the Public School Society and similar purveyors of popular enlightenment would surely have been harder to bring about without the aid of the monitorial system. Reference to its magic has already been made, and it is not necessary for us to give it another rehearsal. Suffice it to recount merely that the Free School Society employed it in New York in 1806, and that before very long the system had become as sensational as a front-page hanging, and had pressed into one city after another. Its singular charm lay, of course, not in its pedagogy, which was preposterous, but in its cheapness, which made it possible for the multitudinous common children to obtain at least an introduction to their ABCs.

5

For the republic the second quarter of the nineteenth century was in many ways remarkable. The irresolution which had palsied it during its cradle days had all but shriveled away, and what lingered of the old dreads and doubts was no longer a major peril. During this stretch of time America increased enormously in latitude and longitude as the number of its people more than doubled. By midcentury Old Glory was floating over Texas, and far off in the West it was catching the Pacific's breezes. Many new cities had heaved into view while the older ones were getting bigger and bulkier. No less than thirty accommodated some thirty thousand inhabitants each, and a few ran a roll so long one must needs be amazed. Philadelphia, for example, gloated over its 340,000 head, but with more than half a million on its roster, New York remained unfailingly the kingpin of the nation.

Meanwhile a hundred things were happening. Canals were being trenched, harbors dredged and widened, and fast express roads built. Steam met its master and was put to work. With iron it conjured up the steamboat, the locomotive, and dozens of other astonishing contrivances. But there was also the surge of a new industrial system, swift, turbulent, and not a little awesome, with its capitalism, its factories, and its workers, the hatchery, as the years swept on, of infinite enigmas and complexities, social, political, and economic.

The epoch's salient social phenomenon was the rise of the common man. Henceforth, every John Doe, as long as he was white, twenty-one, and a citizen, could vote and run for public office. All in all, it was an era of airy hopes, moral and humanitarian causes, uplift zeal, and visions of progress certain and neverending. And to bring the curtain down, it was a period of national exuberance, enlivened by the wild cockiness of a nation in its youth, but more significantly,

by the strength and assurance which derive from liberty and a sense of fulfillment.

Thus the culture which gave birth to the common school. Publicly financed
and under the governance of the state, it was to be free and accessible to all. It
was, in short, the far-off harbinger of the present American public school.

To transform the common school from dream to fact was not easy. On every
side antagonisms frowned upon it. There loomed, for one, the age-old dogma
that a child's education must be for a predominantly religious purpose, and that
any schooling which divorced itself from religious tutoring—which the tax-
supported school was bound by law to do—was base and, even worse, contumacious to the Lord. Nor had the contention that education was not a proper
business of government been hushed. A few liberals, it is true, had cried it down,
but their reasoning, however puissant, had passed for naught. Far more numerous and effective were those who insisted that the pursuit of knowledge was a
purely personal prerogative, molded and conditioned by a man's purse and taste,
and that, in consequence, for a state to seek to teach the generality of its
children was against all fact and reason. No less baleful—in particular for
gentlemen of property—was the prospect that public education would result in a
ponderable bulge in taxes. Though the poor did not indulge themselves in the
luxury of such speculation, not a few of them conceived doubts about an
education that was free. They could not forget that, in the popular phrase, free
schools were "pauper schools," doling out their paltry learning to those who
were too poor to pay for something better. Nor could they forget that all too
often instruction that was free was designed, not so much to elevate those of low
degree as to keep them in subservience. Hence, at first glance, the common
school appeared to many to be just another promise, lovely but delusive.

The tax-supported school gathered its main strength neither from the high
nor the low, but from the middle. Its partisans were generally of a broadly
liberal mark. They represented a variety of endeavors, from public office to the
pulpit and the schoolroom. Some manned the editorial desk, and a few were
leaders of labor. Finally, there were those without portfolio, the rare and
scattered remnant of reflective citizens.

It was in the city that the reformers made their first successful forays. No
other citadel was better suited to their challenge. The city was at once the glory
of the republic and the very sewer of its civilization. Here sojourned the rich and
mighty, but here also teemed the numerous poor and meek. Here dazzled an
enlightened culture, but here also wallowed ignorance with all its dark and brutal
degradations. The city not only flaunted the problem, but with its vast and
powerful resources it was marvelously equipped to lay and resolve it.

6

The campaign for better schools sent up its first flares in Massachusetts. In the
Boston Transcript in 1824, James G. Carter, a farmer's boy with a Harvard

education, and by his mid-twenties a pedagogue of consequence, took a long and sober look at the Commonwealth's schools. Through it tolled the mournful knell of New England's learning, in the Puritan's high day without a peer, but now in decrepitude, its schools done in, its teachers a ghastly joke, its administration incompetent, and its financing so starved that it scarcely financed at all. Two years following, Carter burst into a second expostulation. Designed to raise the schools out of their mephitic bog, it laid its stress on the making of high-class teachers, knowing in their lore and skilled in their craft. To this end it urged the establishment of special training seminaries. Of such tremendous power was Carter's suggestion that presently it came to the notice of the legislature. The lawmakers gave it grave attention and no little parley, and then, by a single vote, they decided to turn it down. The next year (1827) Carter evened the score by opening his own training school at Lancaster. The first normal school to bedeck the state, it has made Carter memorable as the father of teacher education in the Commonwealth.

If the givers of law said no to Carter's proposal, then a bit later they made more agreeable history when they created a town board to keep an eye on the district school, then in decay and making heavy weather. Very stoutly resisted by the districts—it was, its princelings let it be heard, an invasion of their historic rights—the statute signalized the state's first stalwart stride toward the assumption of its authority over the schools. At length, in 1837, under the relentless advocacy of Carter, now himself a lawmaker, the legislature established a state board of education.

If, during the next few years, education in the Bay State took a new tack, the reason was, beyond a doubt, the board's first secretary, Horace Mann. One senses in him almost at once a humane and powerful personality. If he was an inveterate romantic, he was also a realistic and successful politician. In the Massachusetts upper house, which his presence enriched and enlivened for a decade, Mann showed a capacity not only to imagine better worlds, but more important, to campaign ruggedly, and at times very convincingly, to bring them into being. In the legislature he battled for religious freedom, for a decent treatment of the insane, for jails that corrected and improved their clients rather than merely penalizing them. He stood up for temperance, for the liquidation of poverty, and for the right of handicapped Negro children to receive instruction together with the whites in special schools. And he gave himself unremittingly to the cause for better schools. For twelve years the secretary executed the duties of his office, toiling into the wearied watches of the night, with no surcease even to let him catch his wind, and for wages which at their very pinnacle reached no higher than thirty cents an hour.

Mann's first task was to examine the sickened school system and to prescribe some powerful remedy for its cure. For this purpose he projected himself into school after school, up and down the state from Boston, Lexington, and Concord to its swarming Hayvilles and Pipsqueaks. To rouse the public conscience, he unloaded speech after speech. To fortify his crusade yet more, he resorted to the printed word. In his *Common School Journal* and his dozen *Annual Reports*, he laid bare the conditions he had witnessed: schools crippled in the freedom of their functioning by the vested interests of sect; teachers of a fourth-rate competence; supervision in the hands of bogus experts; equipment and buildings broken down and going to pieces; and so on to scholastic standards so disabled they were almost fabulous.

The secretary's bold reporting brought him woe aplenty. Cocksure clerics saw on him Satan's hellish mark. Politicians hoofed him as an enemy of the people. Not a few of the laity dismissed him as a mere spinner of grandiose plans. But many more denounced him as a gross materialist.

But Mann had a natural talent for strong rejoinder. Despite the efforts to rub him in the mud, he was able in the end to break down nearly all the barriers. When, after a dozen years, his combat was done, he could point to a triumph so colossal it was amazing. During his regime, school appropriations in the Commonwealth almost doubled. Two million dollars—a hair-raising sum in those simple times—went into the construction of new and up-to-date schoolhouses. Teachers were shocked with bigger paychecks—but in return they were told to improve their practice. To urge them on, the state founded three public normal schools—the first of their myriad flora to spring from American soil. The school year was lengthened. Supervision, invigorated with an investiture of professional dignity, was made more effective. The number of public high schools was slightly augmented. School libraries were increased, their stock and service enhanced. Meanwhile, textbooks, stripped of any lingering shadows of Calvinism, were brought into harmony with the spirit of the new America. Gone too was the old indifference to pedagogy. Once regarded by the generality of schoolmasters as of no ponderable value, it was now engrafted on the thinking of its leading experts, who were flowering in various parts of Europe. The general effect in Massachusetts was a slow but discernible improvement in the quality of teaching.

Mann's virtuosity found its counterpart in Henry Barnard. Less the battler than was the free-swinging Mann—temperamentally, indeed, inclined to reserve and restraint—Barnard has come down the hallway of time as the scholar of America's educational awakening. Like Mann, he drank from utopian springs, and as a framer of Connecticut law, he worked unsparingly to bring about a fairer world. But of the two, Barnard was much more cautious—even, one might say, fastidious—and as the middle years ran over him his ardor for humanitarian causes burned out in all save education. There it continued to glow until the last year of the century when he himself expired, a landed and bearded octogenarian.

Barnard's career as an educational reformer began in 1838 when, as a member of the Connecticut legislature, he successfully promoted the passage of a law to create a state board similar to the one across the line in Massachusetts. Like Mann, Barnard became the board's first secretary and worked his way from the state's end to end to arouse public opinion in support of better schools. But the tide still pulled powerfully the other way, and in 1842 the Connecticut states-men made an end of the board.

Barnard was not long among the unemployed. His services were promptly bespoken by Rhode Island, which commissioned him to apply his vision to the remaking of its schools. From his counsel to the legislature issued a measure similar to the one kicked to death in Connecticut, and in 1845 Barnard was made Rhode Island's first Commissioner of Education. By and large his work falls into the general form of Mann's, and there is thus no need to repeat the details here. Suffice it to observe that when, after four years, it came to an end, he had succeeded in giving Rhode Islanders a school system of thoroughgoing excellence.

The outpouring of Barnard's many wonders was not lost on Connecticut. In 1851, after a considerable amount of debate, it induced its migrant son to return for the honor and glory of the state to carry on as chief executive of a new normal school, and to exert his powers once more as secretary of the board, now reestablished. The reforms he had brought forth in Rhode Island Barnard now proceeded to conjure up in Connecticut. He worked, as ever, at full and furious blast until, in 1855, almost slaughtered by exhaustion, he was compelled to quit.

The same year Barnard shut up shop, he helped to launch the American Association for the Advancement of Education. He sat as its first president and, more important, he squired its *Journal of American Education*. Looked at over the bridge of many years, it is as the *Journal's* editor and publisher that the man's actual stature reveals itself today. Here he plowed his ground and planted his seed. In its thirty spacious volumes is spread for all time the account of virtually every pedagogical idea and practice known to the nineteenth century, whether here or abroad. In its pages reside a criticism and a doctrine which, as such things go, even now come close to sense. To the *Journal*, finally, must be credited the active and persuasive support of pretty nearly every important educational reform undertaken in the republic before the ascent into the White House of Grover Cleveland.

Barnard's herculean capacity for work soon brought him back to academic duty. For a time he directed the fortunes of the University of Wisconsin, whereupon he migrated to Annapolis to head St. John's College, even then an old purveyor of the liberal arts, and like so many others of its kind, awed by its own antiquity. The new president swept out its self-infatuation, and though he gave his full support to the ancient arts, he at least managed before he was through to rid them of their cobwebs. In 1867—he was then nearing the frontier of sixty—Barnard forsook the grove of Academe for the bureau political to become the first United States Commissioner of Education. The office still exists, though neither politically nor intellectually is it of a very powerful enticement.

Although New England was the first to make education a dominant state concern, candor compels one to add that concerted drives toward a similar end presently showed themselves in the rest of the nation. In their general run they covered pretty much the same ground, though in their detail they varied not a little. Here, as in Pennsylvania, the heavy fighting was over the pauper school; there, as in New York, for a time the grappling was over the elimination of sectarianism. This is by no means saying, however, that there were no other contentions. The same issues and the same contestants appeared on every side. Now the controversy fevered over the educational powers of the state authority, now over the government's right to levy taxes. Some devotees raised their pressure for better teachers, better methods, better schoolbooks; others bawled for more and better buildings.

If, at bottom, the struggle was similar, then so were the sentiment and enterprise which propelled it, the social feeling which engendered it, the publicity and propaganda which brought it notice, the pressure on the lawmaker, and of course, the industry of its idealists, so vast in scope and so powerful in effect. America's eduational coming out glitters with famous names. There is New England, of course, with its Carter, Mann, and Barnard. But there is also Ohio with Samuel Galloway, Calvin Stowe, and Samuel Lewis; Illinois with Ninian Edwards and Jonathan Turner; Kentucky with Robert Breckenridge; Michigan with Isaac Crary and John Pierce; North Carolina with Joseph Caldwell and Calvin Wiley. And so the parade goes on and on, here soon and there late, in state after state, from seaboard to seaboard. But wherever and whenever it passed, always leaders bobbed up able and eager—nay, determined—to direct it to its goal.

7

Near the end of the century, the principles of compulsory education were secure and favorably regarded in every state in the Union. The number of years a child spent at school varied, of course, as it still does today. Tax-supported schools had become the rule, and though their secularity was still lamented by the pious, attempts to obliterate it fell on sterile ground. The principle of the state's authority over education, though still a cause for controversy among scattered American moralists, had become, nevertheless, a settled question in law. State authority over education, once a spur to hubbub and even insurrection, was no longer a matter for serious challenge—indeed, everywhere state control had become the vogue. Yet, despite their redoubtable power, the states were content to rule with a benign and liberal hand, so that taking one thing with another, localities enjoyed a considerable autonomy in the running of their educational affairs.

Thus America's educational system attained its dominant traits. It is not, speaking exactly, a national system of education like that, say, of France, with a national, unified body of schools, under the eye and thumb of a national command, with uniform methods, textbooks, curricula, examinations, and all the other odds and ends which currently grace every up-and-doing French school. By contrast, American education splurges in lively diversity. Consequently, what holds for Stock Yards, Nebraska, may be suspect in Alligator, Mississippi, and not even heard of in Sleepy Eye, Minnesota. Nevertheless, for all this differentiation, there has developed a system which is distinctively American, with characteristics common to all the states, and bottomed on principles which are generally much esteemed.

The reigning theme of America's educational reform was the common school, or as the phrase is at the moment, the public school. Free, tax-supported, and open without strings to everyone, it was a novelty not easily lodged in the communal heart. The first common schools, as might be expected, were often primitive—not infrequently they were no more than one-room shacks. Their scholars, instructed and held in line by a solitary master, male or female, varied in their years, as they did in height and width, while scholastically they ran from the seedling beginner to the horny veteran beyond his middle teens.

In the years which have come and gone since then the common school—or public school—has grown powerfully attractive. Like the flag, it has become an emblem of the national pride and glory. From its tenuous inception it has evolved to immense proportions, into a mansion whose tenants are carefully sorted and sifted into classes, each class accommodated in a chamber all its own, ministered by its own teacher, with instruction addressed to all the children rather than to each separately as was once the everyday wont. The dispenser, when it started out, of the simple three Rs, the school proceeded, as the years increased, to augment its academic stock, necessitating thereby more and more school days to bring them to terms, and by the same token more and more years to bag a diploma. Needless to say, these things did not happen overnight. They bridged the thirty years or so before the sixties—except in the South, where a variety of causes, and particularly the decay after Appomattox, combined to postpone a better day in that region for a long time to come. As has already been said, the Awakening distilled its pungent essences most effectively in the cities and in some of the more thriving settlements close by. But out in the nation's vast and outstretched solitude whose vales and hillocks had not yet fallen to progress, and where the bulk of Americans still lived and carried on, there the Little Red Schoolhouse continued to bear the torch—as, in truth, it still does even now in several thousand small and scattered enclaves, a frail and flickering reminder of a vanished past.

8

The world in which America's lower school took root became the planting ground pretty soon of yet another school. Some of its elements were visible as early as the eighteenth century, though somewhat vaguely, when the academy came upon the scene. Sympathetic to the aspirations of the middle orders, the academy assumed to instruct and counsel their progeny for the successes and contentments of bourgeois life, luminous—so it was hoped—with the radiance of its virtues and refinements. The academy came to its full florescence in the middle years of the nineteenth century, or just about the time when the free, tax-supported common school was entertaining its first triumphs. These, of course, did not impinge directly upon the academy. Even so, the academy's transparent class appeal, so freely flaunted, collided with the new ideal of equality, as did the galling fact that though the academy insisted on a large and freehand way in the running of its affairs, it was not above crying for largess from the public pocket.

Once the common school was safely beyond the shadowy incertitude of infancy, the restricted opportunity it offered to the ordinary mortal to raise himself above the general run came under an ever-sharper critical eye. Was it right to compel the young to make acquaintance with the elemental Rs, and to furnish them for this purpose with free, tax-supported schooling? Then—so the contention ran—it was just as right to give similar aid to those pining for higher knowledge.

The idea, then still a stranger to the world, was given the reception so often reserved for novel ideas—particularly when they threaten to cost us money. It ran into a fire-raking resistance, more blistering than even that once enjoyed by the common school. But for all its horror, the idea would not down. Presently, it was even winning a polite deference, when a number of common schools, yielding to parental pressure, began to offer courses beyond the elementary diploma. A graduate extension, so to say, of the lower school, it constituted, unwittingly, the larval beginning of what later on, much enhanced and refined, was to become America's free public high school.

The first public secondary school of which we have any news appeared in Boston in 1821, when the English Classical School opened for business. Not long after, it rubbed the word "classical" from its signboard to become the English High School. Kept by public moneys, the school offered free instruction to the sons of the "mercantile and mechanic classes." To be admitted to its sessions, a boy had to be no less than a dozen years old, and he had to be at home in the three Rs. To go through the whole mill, he had to serve his time for three years, coming to grips, as he progressed, with composition, grammar, and declamation, besides mathematics, navigation, and surveying, followed by history, geography, and logic, and to cap it off, a broadside of moral political philosophy. With no frills to lighten his burden, the boy was at least spared the anguish caused by the study of foreign languages. The year which is honored by the coming of America's first public high school saw the advent of a similar communal undertaking at Worcester, Massachusetts. Four years after, in 1825, New Yorkers, never disposed to play second fiddle to anybody, massaged their civic pride with what is very likely the first venture into free secondary education outside New England.

The year following, Boston, advertised the inauguration of a high school for girls. But its offerings were diligently diluted, perhaps because, as was then common knowledge, the frail ones could not be expected to have the capacity of the merchant and mechanic sons in attendance at English High, or perhaps simply because the girls' master himself was no monument to knowledge. Even so, when to everybody's amazement, the fair ones' demand for instruction ran way ahead of expectations, the city's masterminds, scared half to death, abandoned the whole business.

What really gave the nascent high school power and momentum was not these isolated undertakings in public service, but a law adopted in Massachusetts in 1827. Fought for by the Hon. James G. Carter, it put upon every town of five hundred families to supply free, tax-supported instruction in American history, algebra, geometry, surveying, bookkeeping, besides the usual elementary learning. Besides all this, towns of four thousand head were to give instruction in general history, rhetoric, logic, Latin, and Greek. But like the Old Deluder Satan Law of sacred memory, Carter's law was booed on every side, and within a couple of years it was done for. Despite its ignoble fate, the law was of deep and vital importance. It not only mandated the public maintenance of free secondary education; it also became the model on which other states patterned themselves when the desire seized them to stake their children to something more than the usual lower learning. In the Commonwealth that inclination, though throttled by the sheer weight of its foes, was never really dead. In fact, as the years accumulated, the measure managed to survive its critics, and in 1857 it attained a glorious resurrection. Returned to the statute books, it was now accepted, its boons and usufructs ready to be enjoyed. By the sixties some three hundred public high schools were being sighted in various latitudes and longitudes throughout the land.

Yet, though the high school was clearly gaining the respect and confidence of more and more Americans, just as clearly a great many others still scouted the notion that government had a right to lay taxes to provide free secondary schooling for everybody's children. In fact, it was not until well on in the century, in 1874, that the scorning and resisting finally wilted, when the Michigan Supreme Court, declaring for the city of Kalamazoo in litigation brought against it by one of its citizens, held its high school to be a legal and proper part of the state's public school endeavor. There had been similar cases and similar decisions in several Eastern courts before 1874. Nevertheless, even though the Kalamazoo verdict said nothing new, it spoke with grave finality. Its overriding effect was to make an end of a very controverted question. All things considered, the Kalamazoo pronouncement, together with the Massachusetts law of some fifty years prior, did more to get the high school squarely on its feet than any other bit of jurisprudence conceived in the nineteenth century.

The high school, unlike its transatlantic forerunner, the Latin grammar school, is native to the United States. The one is the natural and inevitable manifestation of democracy; the other, born and bred in a world of privilege, leaned toward exclusiveness. A projection of the lower learning, the high school escorted its youth over an extended and more difficult route to the end of its formal education. The grammar school, in contrast, specialized in getting its boys into college freshmanhood or—to descend a notch or so—at least into some meritorious occupation of agreeable reward. The modern high school still retains its original purpose, but like the grammar school of old, it now offers also to prepare its boys and girls for admission to the higher groves. As an extension of the elementary school, the high school gave the American populace what they sometimes call their educational ladder, by which a child is enabled to ascend rung by rung from his first beads of sweat over the ABCs to his academic apotheosis as a high school graduate. For the attainment of such a goal, the high school mustered its beginners when they could attest to at least a dozen birthdays or, presumably, when they were in command of the common elements. The grammar school, on the other hand, started its nurslings when they were nine—again a hoary and alien practice, but one which is still cherished and defended in many civilized places.

Needless to say, the coming of the high school proved momentous. From its shaggy and resented beginning, it has become an institution as familiarly American as TV and the coffee break, and it doubtless is no less essential to the pursuit of a good and useful American life than the Bill of Rights. The high school gave coherence and unity to the native public education, and in the ebb and flow of time it furnished the mechanism which—disregarding for a moment all hazards, whether human or divine—enable every child to toil his way up the slippery slope to learning's highest peak. Meanwhile, as has already been observed, Europe, holding fast for the most part to its effete traditions, committed itself to a double educational system, with one set of schools for the masses, and another, separate and unrelated, for their so-called "betters," whether intellectual or otherwise.

9

The drive to give the state a larger and more powerful hand in education gave no quarter to the higher learning. One catches a glimpse of it in various places in the land as early as the republic's infancy in Virginia's College of William and Mary, for example, in Pennsylvania's College of Philadelphia, and in New York's Columbia—even, indeed, in the sedate and musty halls of venerable Harvard. But it was in the heart of New Hampshire's green-clad hills that the struggle obtained its fullest vehemence. There, in 1816, the state ventured to convert Dartmouth into a state school. The college, however, had no taste for such a role, and when the state showed no signs of changing its mind, Dartmouth besought the aid and reassurance of the courts. Defended ultimately by Daniel Webster, one of its own sons, the college emerged triumphantly from the fray in 1819, when Chief Justice Marshall let it be understood that although Dartmouth's charter had been conferred by George III, it was—for all its unpleasant origin—a contract, and hence under the Constitution inviolable.

Marshall's judgment not only spared Dartmouth; by the same stroke it dispelled the cloud of fear and uncertainty which blanketed other private colleges. Safe from the trespasses of the state, the American college began to breed with an almost shadlike fecundity. Most of these seminaries of the higher arts and sciences were modest undertakings, one-building shrines, given usually to the promotion of sectarian learning, Methodist, Congregational, and Presbyterian predominantly, but also Episcopalian and Roman Catholic. A great many have long since been removed above worldly cares, but some, like Amherst, Haverford, and several dozen more, emancipated from the confinement of their orthodox beginnings, continue to ply their industry to this moment, and not infrequently in a distinguished and penetrating manner.

If Marshall's ruling was a spur to private collegiate endeavor, then on the other hand it put no brake on the public higher learning. Deprived of the magic wand by which they had planned to transform the private groves into public ones, some states now took the more laborious route of building and organizing a university of their own. They confronted, of course, the usual derision and deliriums, and the usual prophesies of catastrophes lurking just around the corner. In consequence, their advance was heavily hampered. Actually, the idea of a state university, even then, was no novelty, North Carolina and Georgia—to cite cases—having ventured into this domain sometime earlier, the one in 1795, the other six years later. But admission to their lectures was restricted, and it was not free, and their work was overborne with religious and moral considerations.

The first frankly secular state university raised its flag in 1825 when the University of Virginia introduced itself to its students. The materialization of Jefferson's dream, the university bore witness to its founder's rationality as well as to his vast and audacious creative fancy, from the classic line of the buildings he designed to the faculty he personally picked. The learning they professed was as up-to-date as the times then knew, with courses not only in the age-old classics, but the newer languages as well, besides the natural sciences and even the social ones. Excoriated on every side by the custodians of academic rectitude, Mr. Jefferson's university was able, nonetheless, to ride out the storm, throwing out, as the world grew older, its own ripples of light in an ever-enlarging circle, and especially in the South.

By a strange twist it was not the states but the national government that offered the state university one of its most effective tonics. And what a tonic it was! Known as the Morrill Act of 1862, it volunteered to give every state 30,000 acres of public land for each of its men in Congress "to promote the liberal and practical professions of life." It was a stroke of foresight rarely encountered among lawgivers, and it was destined to fructify amazingly. From it arose the so-called land-grant colleges, of which some seventy now adorn the country. Because of it a number of sick and run-down state universities were saved from a certain grave, while at the same time several new ones were brought into being. All the states, including Alaska and Hawaii, have availed themselves of its bounty. All told, they have gathered almost twelve million acres of public land. With their cultivation, moreover, of the practical and liberal learning or—to use

Franklin's phrase—the useful and the ornamental arts, their foremost practition-ers have long since taken a respectable place in the forefront of the American higher learning.

10

The common school, as has been mentioned, granted its benefits to girls as well as boys. But above the elementary plane, equality between the sexes ceased. There were, it is true, some female academies which found it profitable to shed their light on the rising ladies, but they confined their efforts to the paying trade, and they were never in great number. Aloft in the college we enter a world of men, and if, for all that, a young miss harbored dreams of stowing herself within its sanctum, her motives certainly would have aroused some grave and anxious wondering. Under the circumstances, to quench her thirst for higher knowledge, the best she could do was to resort to other means. For in America, as in the rest of the world, it was then a settled principle of legal and ethical science that woman's place was at the domestic hearth. As late as the century's middle age, when the meanest common man could entertain the hope of hoisting himself into the elegance of a coroner or county judge, or even—who can tell?—into the White House, his sisters, whether in satin or in calico, were beset by taboos on every side, from a denial of the suffrage to restricted property rights, one-sided divorce laws, and a double moral standard, both general and connubial.

When the republic was in its springtime such inequities preyed on no one. But as it went galloping into its industrial transformation toward the utopia we now enjoy, the yearning of women for a freer and fuller life began to catch fire, and with it, with sound reason, the desire for a better education. As in the war for the common school various champions arose to lead them—Emma Willard, Catharine Beecher, and Mary Lyon, to single out their salient trinity. Like the Manns and Barnards, and the various other male reformers, they made their assault at full arms, allying themselves with friendly writers, cajoling pastors, educators, and lawmakers, and raising the wind in all directions with tornadoes of words, both in speech and in print. All founded schools where they were teachers, deans, and presidents: Willard in the Female Academy at Troy, New York; Beecher in a similar fount at Hartford, Connecticut; and Lyon in the Female Seminary at Mount Holyoke, Massachusetts.

What makes these women memorable in educational chronicles is not the lustihood of their zeal, which, after all, is not a stranger in the history of the human female. Nor is it their pedagogic science, most of which is today deservedly forgotten. What makes them singular is the demonstration through their schools that girls have brains, and that, given a chance, the best ones can conquer the highest and steepest mountain of the intellect—a proposition which was then so obviously nonsensical that it shook the land with gales of laughter. From their gallant efforts came the woman's college, not immediately, of course, nor numerously, for the clatter against it kept going for a long time. By midcentury, however, a number of colleges for women had come upon the scene in the South and in the West. But nearly all were rudimentary, with only the slimmest means and professors of the dimmest candlepower. As lighthouses of the mind, hence, they set off no great glare. For their Yales and Harvards girls had to wait a while longer—at least, at any rate, till 1861, when Vassar set out to offer them a higher education, as lofty in its intellectual reach as that of the finest men's colleges in the republic.

Meanwhile, in Ohio, when Oberlin began its practice in 1833, it admitted four young women to its classes on equal terms with men. Thus collegiate coeducation came to being in America. But the idea ran into a powerful antagonism, especially in the wary and fastidious East, where coeducation was recognized as a threat to virtue and displeasing to God. To the west of the Mississippi, where knowledge of such matters was less certain, every state university, save Missouri, sweetened its learning from the start with the presence in its classrooms of feminine charm and beauty.

In the East the first man's college to brave such peril was Cornell. Led by its president, the audacious Andrew Dickson White, it took the plunge in 1872, thereby joining the company, not only of Oberlin and its imitators, but even of Plato who, although a practitioner of single blessedness to the last, had accommodation in his Academy for women as well as men. Today, of course, coeducation is part of the national way, as American as foreign aid and the United States Marines.

11

As long as education directed its benefits and benignities to the few rather than the many, the need to prepare schoolmasters for their calling was of minor concern; and until the state assumed sovereignty over the schooling of its children, the training of teachers, such as it was, had to be entrusted to private hands. The honor of being the first in Western civilization to engage in such endeavor—as far as our frail records have been able to unearth—falls to a Catholic priest, Father Demia by name, in pastoral service at Lyons, where in 1672 he undertook to coach a small group of teachers of reading and the catechism. More ambitious and better planned was the effort of Jean-Baptiste de la Salle who, in 1685, established a Seminary for Schoolmasters, the first of three, to prepare his Christian Brothers for duty in their numerous schools in France.

The practice showed itself on the Rhine's other side later in the century when, at Halle, the Pietist Francke, referred to in earlier pages, opened a school to give special aid and instruction to youths aspiring to install themselves some day in pedagogic office. From Halle the idea blew to Berlin, and in 1738 Julius Hecker, also of the Pietistic persuasion, opened a similar grove. By the century's end such enterprise was no longer news, especially in German lands, where some thirty institutions were giving their energies in one way or another to making tomorrow's teachers.

However, it was not until 1809, when, as recounted earlier, the Prussians, suffering severely from Napoleon's *coup de pied*, reconstructed their entire school system, and in the process brought forth the first state-operated teacher-training school. Modeled upon the advanced views of Pestalozzi, it was as up-to-date as the Prussians could make it, and as the years went on, it became the object of admiration and even imitation in several other lands. Somewhat earlier, in 1794, when revolution had put its clutch upon the French, the new regime established a higher normal school under the authority and control, needless to say, of the state. But like so many of the Revolution's gaudy hopes, the seminary presently sickened, and it was not until 1808, when Napoleon applied his magic hand, that the Ecole Normale Supérieure took firm root—so firm in truth, that it has remained in efflorescence to this moment.

In America the belief that teachers, like practitioners of any other art and mystery, could perform their operations more effectively by undergoing some special training was being aired as early as the eighteenth century. The enlightened Franklin was one of the first to discern its potentialities, and he even ventured to recommend the practice as one of the public services to be rendered by his Academy. All in all, though, the notion of training prospective teachers caused no buzz of conversation. The truth is, the land was submerged in far more momentous matters, and until long after Yorktown—until, in fact, the business of schooling the American young had been set on a hard and solid foundation—the training of schoolmasters remained mostly a subject for the consideration of seers and rhetoricians.

The first plea to be heard in the republic for a seminary devoting its whole energies to the preparation of candidates for future teaching berths was sounded in 1816 in the halls of Yale by one of its professors, Dennison Olmstead. Others presently followed, all to the same end, and all more or less alike. In 1825 a new note rang out when Thomas Gallaudet of Massachusetts urged the creation of a state normal school, a proposal to which James G. Carter gave full support, and which some years later he helped to translate into law.

Meanwhile, on another front the Lancastrians were pursuing the matter in their own direct and realistic way. Their system—in case your memory has mislaid the facts—was one wherein a master imparted knowledge to a corps of monitors, each of whom thereupon undertaking to implant it in a small squad of his fellows from the ranks. Because of this deputizing of teachers, and also because of the great weight laid on system and order in the management of their inordinately huge classes, it did not take the Lancastrians long to notice that their juvenile pedagogues needed some special rehearsing for the effective performance of their duties. To such purpose they conceived the "model school" which turned out to be precisely what was needed—in fact, by the 1820s, when the monitorians went into high gear, they were running some twenty of such training stations.

The monitorial system was pedagogically inferior; nevertheless, it was cherished. One of its heartiest admirers was Governor De Witt Clinton of New York, who perceived in it nothing less than the grace of God. In 1818 the governor recommended Lancaster and his methods to the New York lawmakers, but they were frosty to their charms and paid them no heed. Eight years later, in 1826, Clinton tried again, counseling the legislature "to make provision for a seminary for the education of teachers in the monitorial system." He tried again the year following, and again the year after that, but to no avail. Meanwhile, in 1827, the givers of law took another tack by subsidizing the privately operated academies "to promote the education of teachers." Reinforced thus with public moneys, which in the passing years were amplified with special grants, the academy—for a while at any rate—became the training ground and chief source of the state's better-qualified teachers.

In New England the advent of teacher training is bracketed with the Educational Revival. Its earliest manifestation was in Concord, Vermont, where, in 1823, the Rev. Dr. Samuel Read Hall opened the first normal school in America. A private venture, it supplemented the doctor's labors in divinity. Besides reviewing learning's lower branches, its apprentices were put upon to ponder its higher ones, especially mathematics and some sciences, besides ethics, logic, and the "evidences of Christianity." On in the third and final year they were introduced to the knacks of teaching, the essence of which Hall had impounded in 1829 in his *Lectures on Schoolkeeping,* the first handbook of its kind in the English language to be published in the republic.

America's second normal school was also private. It was the work of James G. Carter, and it came to being in 1827 at Lancaster, Massachusetts. A lean and scraggy thing, it went downhill almost from the start, and when Carter's call to the legislature for help went for nothing, it expired. Its owner, it may be recalled, was the same Carter who, later a lawmaker himself, was in a large measure responsible for the law of 1837 which gave the people of Massachusetts their State Board of Education. Two years afterward in historic Lexington, the Commonwealth opened its first public normal school, the first, in truth, in the country. It was followed some months after by another at Barre, and a year later by still another at Bridgewater.

Despite their swift multiplication, the first public normal schools were anything but impressive. Lexington, for example, began its history with a faculty of one and a study body of three girls. Though boys were eligible to seek its boons, they found no relish in them, and even after the normal school had established itself in the public confidence, its custom remained predominantly female.

The new schools accepted girls at sixteen and boys at seventeen, and their work was planned to occupy them for a year. However this may be, not a few students found it beyond their capacity, whether intellectual or otherwise, and they gave up long before the appointed end. This is not to say, however, that scholastic requirements were more than modest. Actually, in its infancy the normal school was scarcely more than an advanced elementary school. Like Dr. Hall's seminary in Vermont, it drilled its hopefuls heavily in the elemental Rs besides raising the curtain on some of the studies usually encountered in academies of the better sort, in illustration, algebra, geometry, bookkeeping, surveying, the Constitution and the history of the United States and Massachusetts, human physiology (with side trips into hygiene), philosophy, and the settled principles of Christian piety and rectitude. Finally, they were broken in "in the art and science of teaching." An adjunct of the normal school, and one of its features, was its model and practice school. Here in an exemplary lesson the professor demonstrated the principles the student had absorbed in his book and classroom work. And here also he was expected to emulate his master.

In all this the main stress fell on the academic subjects, pedagogy being reduced to a somewhat subsidiary position. Its chief standby, even after thirty years, was still Hall's dissertation on schoolkeeping, supplemented in the advancing years by such newer treatises as David Page's *Theory and Practice of Teaching* (1847) and Jacob Abbott's *The Teacher: Or Moral Influences Employed in the Instruction and Government of the Young* (1833). Neither had anything to say that had not been said before, and in the case of such masters as Comenius, Locke, and Pestalozzi it had been said infinitely better. Nevertheless, they represented the cream of America's pedagogic thinking, and in a land caressing its national ego more and more they were highly prized.

For years the normal school was the butt of public animosity and derision, the same malevolence which had bedeviled the growth of the common school. Not only were taxpayers aligned against it, but vested interests, such as academies and private schools, taking alarm over its menace to their cashbox, resisted it very stoutly. Among some of its most acrid critics, rather curiously, were the teachers themselves who, because of their own lack of professional training, sensed an aspersion on their competence, and thus cried down the normal school as so much nonsense, a waste of time and money.

Throughout the land the state normal school ran into the same squalls. As a result, its progress was gravely damaged—in fact, by the end of the fifties only a dozen such pedagogical seminaries existed, and of these half were settled in New England. The rest reached from New Jersey and Pennsylvania in the East to Illinois, Michigan and Minnesota in the West. New York, with considerable misgiving and not a little legislative debate, took the leap in 1844 when it graced its capital with the state's first normal school.

Besides these few, diffuse ventures, in one form or another normal schools appeared in a number of cities. Boston hazarded one in 1852, and four years later New York saluted the birth of its Daily Normal School for Females. As the sixties got under way, municipal normal schools had sprouted here and there from coast to coast. Philadelphia harbored one, and so did Trenton and Baltimore. There was one in St. Louis, and one even in faraway San Francisco.

But all this enterprise, whether state or city, lit no conflagration. Not only was it insufficient in its volume; it was inadequate also in its pedagogic grounding. The truth is tha- for all its grand pretension about "the art and science of teaching," pedagogy in mid-nineteenth-century America remained starkly rudimentary. Then, as since time out of mind, what the successful teacher needed to know—aside from subduing the young into silence and submission—was how to stuff them full of facts. To this end running a recitation and keeping order were his primary—nay, his indispensable—tools. So things were to sit, scarcely changed, until after the Civil War, when the more benign and somewhat sounder doctrines of Pestalozzi, and after him, those of Herbart and Froebel, took root in American soil. With their rise, pedagogy in America embarked on its long and toilsome journey toward its present state. In its course the everyday business of teaching, once so obvious and simple, burgeoned with complexities and complications it had never known before. Where once it had confined its operation to hearkening to recitations and maintaining law and order within the academic precinct, it now demanded an understanding of education's very nature, the philosophy which underlay it, its aims and principles, its social meaning and implications, and—not the least by any count—the problems inherent in the learning and teaching act.

In the world of teacher training the new ideas had a deep and widespread effect. It was still essential, of course, for a teacher to be at home in what he taught. But it now befell him also, as the perceptive Rousseau had recommended so long ago, to penetrate that complex and often baffling bundle of human growth, the child confided to his care and teaching. To help him unlock the gates of understanding became the task, as the years flowed on, not of preachers and philosophers, however sage, but of a brand-new breed of probers, the scientific students of the psyche. In the normal school, in consequence, psychology became the pedagogic master key. It gave access, even in its young and uncertain stage, to at least a better understanding of what hitherto had been inscrutable, namely, the learning and teaching process, and per corollary, the most effective methods of giving instruction in the various subjects.

The newer pedagogical thinking, as has already been alluded to, attained its first prominence at Oswego, New York, where Edward Sheldon, proposing toasts to Pestalozzi and his methods, undertook to train the city's teachers in their classroom application. From his industry, there emerged in 1861 the Oswego Normal School, the most advanced and influential of its time, and destined five years following to become the state's second normal school. When the vogue of Pestalozzi succumbed to progress a score of years later, or thereabouts, there appeared the more luminous and more certain pedagogy of Herbart, and where only a while ago Johann Heinrich Pestalozzi had been the guiding star of the national teacher training, it was now Professor Johann Friedrich Herbart.

With the development of a more sophisticated educational theory, the need to prepare teachers for their craft became appreciably more discernible. Thus the American normal school came to ripeness. Its days of uneasy faltering behind, it began to pick up power and momentum and in the process its increase and proliferation carried it to great lengths. By the end of the fifties, as has been said, the state normal school could count a dozen representatives. In addition, there was a scattered sprinkling of municipal endeavor. A decennium later the number of normal schools all told stood at sixty odd; another decade, and it had climbed to eighty; and so on, increasingly, to the end of the century.

Meanwhile, the subject of pedagogy had begun to make advances into the higher learning, but nearly always its savants were chock-full of aversion toward it and spared no pains to exclude it from the academic cloister. Following Appomattox, one finds the mood beginning to relax, and here and there a college ventured to advertise lectures on pedagogy, being careful, however, to gloss the term as "the art of teaching." But at best such progress was by slow stages, and it was not till 1879—almost twoscore years since Herbart's translation to the ghostly world—that the University of Michigan hazarded the creation of a full-time chair in education. Shortly after, the University of the City of New York—now New York University—gave the subject lodgment in its curriculum with a number of graduate courses which in 1890 expanded into a full-blown graduate school of pedagogy. A couple of years earlier the New York College for Teachers had come into being. With Nicholas Murray Butler on the bridge, it entertained a lively traffic—in fact, after but half a dozen years, its name shortened to Teachers College, it was brought under the house flag of Columbia University, in which capacity of course, it has never ceased to function.

Today the normal school is done for. It reached its peak just before the First World War. Thereupon, after almost a century of service, it bowed to the demands of a newer culture. As it faded from these scenes its place was taken by the four-year, degree-granting teachers college. By the end of the twenties some half a hundred were in practice; by the forties they numbered a couple of hundred; today, though the liberal arts colleges have not ceased to sniff at them, they are nonetheless the national vogue.

UP TO RECENT TIMES

When the First World War made an end of the German Empire, the onerous business of reconstruction passed into the hands of the Second Reich, the so-called Weimar Republic. It was born in 1919 into the sorry haunt of a trampled glory, and it went to rest fourteen years later, dashed under the load a cruel and cynical fate had hung upon it. Though its sorrows were many and its errors legion, not all its labors went for naught. During its brief day it succeeded in bringing about some alleviation of the harsher penalties imposed upon it by the peacemakers of Versailles. It managed to get the Reich's palsied trade and industry moving ahead once more. It was even able, after a period of prodigious sweating and panting, to put the bridle on the nation's runaway inflation. And despite the Reich's stupendous collapse in 1918, it made progress toward restoring the country to a position of acceptance among the European powers.

Unluckily, its defeats were of a greater magnitude than its victories, and in the end the former devoured the latter. As if by a miracle the Republic had stemmed the fantastic flood of paper money, but when presently a gigantic depression poured over the land, the government's capacity for wonder-making failed. As a result, trade and industry, which only yesterday had staggered from the sickbed, relapsed alarmingly, and as the number of jobless soared higher and higher, a vast misery gripped the land.

Meanwhile, the new government had not been able to make democracy palatable to the run of ordinary Germans. From the Republic's infancy derisive attacks had been made upon it, not on speculative grounds alone, but by enemies openly gunning for its destruction. Instead of grabbing such fellows by the ear, it suffered them not only to hawk their hostile views, but even to organize and arm, and to engage in public roughhouse. As Germany's economic troubles piled up, the onslaughts on its democracy increased in frequency and ferocity. Alas, its statesmen, wandering in the maze of their idealistic world, could not cope with the shrewd and ruthless Hitler. When the end came in 1933, the Republic passed away under a cloud, rejected and unwept, the victim of its visions and its gross and pathetic ineptitude.

The framework of the Weimar democracy rested on a constitution. A document of 181 articles, it made provision among other things for universal suffrage, a president to head the land for a term of seven years, and a bicameral parliament to make its laws. Unlike the Constitution of the United States, the Weimar writ had things to say about education. The arts and sciences, it stated, and the teaching thereof, must be allowed to function freely. Public school teachers were employees of the state, with all their usual rights and privileges. As in their imperial incarnation, so in their republican one, the schools were the wards of the state, subject at all times to its governance and inspection. But that surveillance was to be executed by none save secular, professional experts. Schooling the young was, of course, compulsory. For at least eight years they were to study their books, after which a continuation school of one sort or another awaited them. For their first four years in the seat of learning all children, regardless of the family pocket or position, were to attend a public common school, the so-called *Grundschule*. For these years the private hives of learning, whatever their special pretensions, could expect no clients, and so their labors ceased. By this stroke the *Vorschule*, the traditionally exclusive preparatory school for the *Gymnasium*, was abolished.

Aside from these few ground rules, the constitution contented itself with recommendations of a more or less airy amiability. All schools, it counseled, should instruct and improve their pupils with "a moral education, a sense of responsibility to the state, individual and vocational efficiency in the spirit of German nationality and of international conciliation." For such a purpose the subjects of civics and manual training were given lodgment in every school, and also religion. But whereas in the Kaiser's day the pursuit of piety had been compulsory, it now became a matter of free choice. In fact, even communities were granted a say in the matter, for the constitution guaranteed them the right to base their religious lessons on the creeds predominant among the pupils.

2

In the *Grundschule* the child made acquaintance with the lower learning's common stock—the three Rs, drawing, singing, some handiwork, and physical exercise. During the first year his subjects were not rigidly roped off from one another, as per timeworn practice, with so many minutes, say, every Tuesday for this, and so many every Friday for that. Instead there was an easy intermingling of subject matter, like friendly guests, so to say, at a party. The new school put a great store on relating the classroom learning to the world which breathed and throbbed and spoke outside. Was little Fritz a Berliner? Or a Hamburger? Or maybe a Frankfurter? Then, with his mates and master he explored the city vicinage, its highways and byways, its shops and marketplaces and mills. He prowled in parks and gardens. He nosed about in zoos. Was he, on the other hand, resident in some bucolic enclave—perhaps in the Black Forest? Then he got to know its spruce-clad slopes, its tilled and tended acres, its city hall, its ancient church and graveyard. He had speech with the local artisans, the weavers and embroiderers, the makers of wine and cuckoo clocks. He introduced himself to the communal lore, its truths, its legends, and its myths. But whether he was a city boy or a rustic, in the end his classroom practice acquired a pattern which was pretty much the same. What his senses captured in the world about him, he invested in his learning. It became the substance of his reading and writing and even his reckoning. It worked its way into what he sketched and painted. And it accounted for his first steps in geography and history and nature study.

Though at first glance such learning seems akin to some of the pleasant meandering of the latter-day progressives, it was never permitted to be haphazard. Planned and directed by the teacher, it was given fortification with systematic instruction, with required book reading, and with classroom discourse and recitation. In fact, the child was even belabored with homework.

Once the required period of service in the *Grundschule* was done, the pupil faced a number of options. For one thing, he might ruminate in the elementary bench for another four years or so, applying his powers more or less as in his younger days in the lower grades. If so he chose, then his hand-to-hand encounters with the three Rs and their various confederates continued, though, naturally, now in ponderably stronger force. In addition, they were given reinforcement with German history, civics, and geometry. Religion remained, as before, on a take-it-or-leave-it basis. For a furlough from their bookwork, boys had the joy of exercising their dexterity with saws and hammers, while girls dueled with pots and pans and the various other articles of the household arsenal. The stress on bringing the school into consonance with the surrounding world remained, and so did the foraging in the local culture.

Those who pinned their ambition on higher things usually brought their primary schooling to an end with their exit from the *Grundschule*. For their accommodation the old academic trinity was still on hand: the *Gymnasium* of cobwebbed vintage, with its mandatory study of Latin and Greek; its younger sister, the *Realgymnasium* with its required Latin and modern languages; and the youngest of the three, the *Oberrealschule* with its concentration on the natural sciences and mathematics. Time and circumstance had brought these schools only the slightest change. They still exacted payment for their instruction, though in deference to the needs of the new democracy they reduced their fees and made a more generous provision for scholarships. Their enterprise still savored strongly of the intellectual. Their masters were still men of great knowledge, and until the Republic fell on baleful times, they continued to uphold their standards and lead their students a fearful dance.

Challenging the monopoly of the older groves was a newcomer, the *Deutsche Oberschule*. Like them, it required nine years to perform its mission, and like them, it pressed for a knowledge of foreign language—in this instance two living ones, usually French and English. Unlike its forerunners, however, the *Deutsche Oberschule* laid a powerful accent on German culture, its language and literature, its art and music, and needless to say, its history and geography.

For girls the door of opportunity was wide open. If, for example, any of them longed some day to be addressed as doctor, whether medical, philosophical, or otherwise, then, like their brothers, they could make preparation for the higher learning in one of the three conventional schools or in some equivalent counterpart, established and set aside for their exclusive profit and enjoyment. In addition, as in the days of late imperial memory, they were favored with a number of seminaries which devoted themselves to considerations of special interest and value to girls.

3

Although Germany's new education brought forth a generous applause from enlightened educators the world around, from the native masters it got only a qualified allegiance. The reason is not hard to find. Consider for a moment the schoolmaster of the Kaiser's Reich. You behold a practitioner of a high-grade calling, a man of some authority among his fellow men, well regarded and well rewarded, and with a pension to gladden his falling days when senility began to creep upon him. Look at him later in the Republic. His savings, so hard won, have floated down the inflationary drain. His pension has shriveled into insignificance. Gone is the class-divided world he adorned and admired, and which had set him apart from the multitude as a better man. The new regime, with a saddlemaker sitting as its first president, had brought him mostly tears, and though the Republic needed him desperately for the forwarding of its democracy, its aspirations generally left him cold. In consequence, he not infrequently hobbled them, within the classroom and without, and when Hitler began to play upon him with his talk of hair-raising miracles, all too often the teacher was ready to embrace him.

Nor was the secondary school calculated to promote the general welfare. Totally unreconstructed, it continued as of old to be the training ground for the university and for the nation's better jobs. On the middle classes the prestige which it bestowed had always exerted a powerful attraction, and although not a few parents put little stock in its intellectuality, for economic and social reasons they nevertheless went to great lengths to expose their offspring to it. The troubled times had not dimmed its luster—on the contrary, they had enhanced it. Indeed, as the struggle for vocational preferment fevered hotter and hotter, the rosters of the secondary schools showed an enormously increasing clientele. Though its concerns were oftentimes much more economic than cultural, the secondary schools remained anesthetic to their existence. Thus, instead of bringing freshness and life to their curriculum, they continued to ply their young with the old and familiar nostrums. The upshot was that many a youth with no capacity for cerebration dropped by the wayside, and of the ones who succeeded, more and more were managing to survive by a mere hairline.

In the old days most of such near-misses would have bidden the Muses a last good-bye and gone to work; but with new jobs so scarce as to be almost obsolete, a substantial number now betook themselves to the centers of higher thinking. The result was an enormous burgeoning of their enrollment—so enormous that the university's vaunted scholarship, the pride for so many years of the Reich and the envy of many a people abroad, fell into decrepitude. Their students, protested the professors of the University of Berlin, were ill prepared; they were intellectual dabblers; worse yet, they entertained an aversion for "the discipline which is characteristic of scientific work." So powerfully, however, was the current running against the old ideals of thoroughness and excellence that soon they were all but washed away. Classes got bigger; standards sank deeper; and the ascensions into the doctoral degree became so frequent as to be almost routine.

Sadder than even this decline was the craven abnegation of academic freedom. Once free of mind and utterance, and judged almost entirely by their scholarly competence, Germany's men of learning found themselves beset and defamed at every turn. The chains were clamped upon them, rather curiously, not by a cautious and self-protective state, but by rebellious students. Did a professor's pronouncement, whether in the lecture chamber or in the world at large, give them disrelish? Then they vented their ire in public uproar—even in strikes and riots. Four times at least they bellowed for a professorial head, and even though their victims were scholars of a high celebrity, their merit availed them nothing, and they were fired. Meanwhile, behind the screen, Nazi leaders, alert to the possibilities of such chicanery, did their utmost to feed its flame. The peace disturbers they forged into trained and practiced Nazi blocs. Charged with cleansing the higher learning of its un-Germanic contamination, they proceeded to make it increasingly Nazi, which is to say, nationalistic, reactionary, and anti-Semitic. The years saw their numbers rise, and when, in 1933, the National Socialists overran the Republic, they became the party's hatchet men in every German university.

4

When Hitler took the helm, he promised the Germans all the marvels they had wanted so long to see. There would be food and jobs for all, and the country, enfeebled by discord and despair, would be united and its vanished might restored. The pledge soon became the deed. By a staggering program of public works, by rearmament, by the enforced "cooperation" of capital and labor, and by a variety of economic sleight of hand, the Third Reich reduced the number of its jobless to practically a vanishing point. But the Germans also got a powerful dose of totalitarianism, a rule by fiat and force in which a man's inalienable rights and dignities were under anathema, and jailers and executioners were always busy.

Hitler's doctrine made its way into his book *Mein Kampf*. Put together for the most part in 1924, while its author was lodged in jail, it was destined to enjoy a triumphant progress. As the years passed, it became a sort of Nazi Holy Writ, and it was made mandatory reading in every German school. Time saw it rise as the Reich's foremost best-seller, appearing in numerous guises, from newsprint snatches to voluptuous volumes, morocco-bound and gold-encrusted, and aggregating during its prolific lifetime an issue of several million copies.

From its pages flowed the cardinal articles of the Nazi faith. It is not necessary to wrestle with them all—prying into those of educational consequence will suffice. There is, to begin, its primary and all-embracing doctrine of Race and Soil. Nature's grandest achievement, Hitler tells us, is the Aryan race. It alone has brought civilization to its present high estate. The most dowered of all human kind, whether in the pursuits of peace or in those of war, the Aryan has shown himself the most fit to rule. All other races—by nature's inexorable working—are bound either to decay and disappear or, at best, to settle into subservience. The capital task of the Reich hence is, first, to rally all Germans around a single flag; next, to obtain an abundant space to accommodate their master race as it propagates and expands; and, finally, to attain the position nature has reserved for it, namely, the head and forefront of civilization.

Is the Aryan the paragon of all the manly virtues? Then the Jew is his abominable counterpart. Groveling, unprincipled, vicious, he is an object of contempt and objurgation. Naturally devious and subversive, he is a menace to the German people, and until he and his horror are suppressed, they can enjoy no prospering.

For all their obvious numskullery, Hitler's racial doctrines obtained a large and cooperative audience. From them sprang the most brutal and exigent anti-Semitism the world has ever known, and one which civilized men cannot but remember grimly.

Correlative to the Führer's anthropological dogma was his insistence that Germans must fructify numerously. To fulfill her duty to the master race, the German woman must return to the domestic hearth. Let her mate at an early age and people her home with a plentiful progeny. For such a patriotic end the Third Reich granted a loan to its matrimonial beginners. Once a couple had succeeded in producing four children, sound in health and spirit, the indebtedness was wiped off the books. In addition, parents of a considerable flock enjoyed other rewards and usufructs, including rental allowances, tax remissions, priority in public employment, and discounts on amusement tickets. To celebrate and decorate mothers whose fecundity ran to an exceptionally high proportion, the Führer struck a special medallion, the Cross of Honor of German Motherhood, with an appropriate ribbon to help them hang it around their necks.

5

No sooner had the Nazis swept out the Republic than they began to undo its educational reforms. No concessions were to be made henceforth to the promotion of international understanding, for this was "a poison threatening to destroy the German soul." Instead, the schools were to direct their instruction to wholly nationalistic ends. German culture, from its first stirrings in the prehistoric bog and woodland to its most recent burst of Nazi light, was "to be treated thoroughly." Riveted into all instruction was the revelation of Aryan supremacy. Straight from the cantos of *Mein Kampf*, it was to ram home the message that "the history of Europe is the work of the Aryan peoples." The glory of Greece, the builders of its Parthenon, the writers who composed its masterpieces, its poets, sculptors, and philosophers—all, let it be drummed into the student's head forevermore, were Aryan. And so were the Hindus in their salad days, and so also the Medes, Hittites, and Persians. A large portion of what used to be taught as biology now fell under the caption of "racial science." Its basic postulates were simple, as witness, "Jewish traits are wholly opposed to the most valued German traits"; another, "The mixture of Germans and Jews is disastrous"; and another, "No poem of Heinrich Heine [the author of the *Lorelei* and a Jew] can be read without perceiving this too clearly."

Not to be outdone by the biologists, the historians tuned up their science on the bull fiddle of propaganda. "Propaganda and education," the teacher was told, "today operate together." For this purpose the government assigned a formidable part to instruction in Germany's recent history, especially such matters as—to paraphrase its official writ—the Reich's heroic struggle in the First World War against a world of foes, the odious Treaty of Versailles, the treacherous Jews and Marxists who put their names to it and who later hatched the unsavory Weimar Republic, the advent of Adolf Hitler, the organization of the Nazi party, and the restoration of liberty to the German people. Dates, that eternal curse of schoolboy life, were to be used sparingly. Far better to tenant the rooms of memory with catchy verbal formulas, such as "We need colonies!" and "Führer command and we will follow!" Upon the history teacher fell the duty of conditioning his listeners for right-thinking. He must, the official mandate told him, "lead his pupils to take definite positions which . . . will clearly contrast friend and foe."

Second only to history as an instrument in furthering young Germany's national and political edification stood geography, or as the word became later, geopolitics. German children, the authorities lamented, were better informed about the outlands than about their own fatherland—even worse, all too often they inclined to laud the former at the cost of the latter. To exterminate such false thinking, the young were put upon to make a firsthand observation of the national scene—in the company of experts, of course, to give them counsel and thereby "open their eyes to the truth." Only those youths who were on a close and friendly footing with the Reich's geography, and who, in addition, were of the right maturity and sharpness "to consider foreign peoples critically" were granted permission to rove abroad. The end of all such geographic fieldwork, whether at home or abroad, was "an increased national consciousness."

Though it was important to ground young Germans in Nazi truth and virtue, it was equally important to rear them in health and strength, so that in the years to come they would be fit to carry on powerfully for the fatherland. The Republic, of course, was far from overlooking the value of physical training. But as of old in Athens, it had regarded physical training not as an end, but as an element in the cultivation of a harmonious integration of body, mind, and spirit, or, as the phrase currently is, "a well-rounded individual." The Third Reich, however, had no fancy for such a person. Taking its cue not from the many-sided and versatile Athenian, but from his archantagonist, the stone-headed and muscle-conscious Spartan, Nazi pedagogy ranked body training first, character next, and the mind last. "I will have no intellectual training," expostulated the Führer; "it is a disease of life."

Even before Hitler's Germany returned to conscript arms, its youth was being hammered and hardened in military elementals. Glossed officially as a "sport," such rehearsing was made a compulsory part of physical education. As sports go, it called for a colossal expenditure of energy and effort. Even so, its participants enjoyed it greatly, for it gave them a holiday from the schoolroom. Instead of stooping over books, they marched over ever-lengthening roads. They ran, they leaped, they crawled. They sprang over chasms, scaled walls, swam rivers. And they learned how to shoot straight. The ideal behind it, as indeed behind all Nazi education, was the soldier. "A youth," exulted the Führer, "will grow up before whom the world will shrink."

As might be expected, Nazi pedagogy soon made its way into the secondary school. The springs of its being were pretty much the same as lower down in the elementary schools, to wit: The world is the Aryan's oyster, and more especially that of his current Nordic exemplar. Propaganda is the necessary and reinforcing handmaid of instruction. To fashion young Germans into active and politically reliable citizens, which is to say Nazis, is the great end of education. Under the circumstances, the *Gymnasium*, with its devotion to the ancient humanities, lost much of the little favor it still enjoyed. Though it was not sent apacking, its enrollments dwindled rapidly into insignificance. Its classical discipline, it is true, was granted a stay of execution, but the ideal which for centuries had exalted it came to an end. Henceforward, it was announced, instruction in the ancient languages was to give a dominant place to the physical and spiritual powers of the old Greeks and Romans in whom Nazi blood analysts discovered the same Aryan corpuscles as in the Nordic Germans. Nor should the learner ever be allowed to forget that it was the loss of their racial purity that plunged these ancient Aryans into the abyss—a fate which, unless the Jews were rigorously curbed and proscribed, would surely overtake the fatherland.

If the *Gymnasium* fell into disfavor then, on the other hand, the *Deutsche Oberschule* with its concentration on German history and literature was precisely to the Nazi taste. Purified of all Jewish and Marxist taints, it presently unfolded as the Reich's favorite secondary shrine.

The anti-intellectual refrain which ran through the elementary school had its echo in learning's secondary house. The nine years it used to take a pre-Nazi lad of even the highest diligence to bring its requirements to terms were reduced to eight. At the same time his extracurricular hours were increasingly bespoken. "The youth of Germany," he was given to understand, "belongs to the Führer." Lest there might be some doubt about it, all Germans, male and female, of an age from 10 to 18, were enlisted in the ranks of the Hitler Youth. Snappily arrayed in a uniform all their own, they were given a great deal of information about duty, obedience, discipline, and sacrifice for the fatherland, with supplementary earfuls about Race and Soil. However, expected above all to be men and women of action, they were also mustered to drum up funds for Nazi good works. To advance the cause of a bigger and better Germany, they drove against waste, salvaging countless tons of rags and paper, besides old bones and metal scrap, all useful, of course, in the Reich's rearmament. When they reached their fifteenth birthday, they were rewarded with a sojourn in the country where, between sunrise and sunset, they were put to work as assistant farmers. After hours they attended classes in the theory and practice of National Socialism. On special days they paraded.

A novelty in German secondary education was a six-month turn of duty in the ranks of the Labor Service. Required of all nineteen-year-olds, it took its toll from the secondary school graduates before they entered the higher learning or before they plucked a job. Lodged in barracks, they lived under military discipline, delighted, as Germans nearly always are, by being able to show themselves in a uniform. The labors they performed were usually of some public benefit, such as draining marshes, reforesting the countryside, or laying concrete for a stretch of superhighway. To inject iron in their muscles they were put on a heavy diet of "exercises of all kinds and shooting weapons of small calibre."

Not only was schoolwork made subordinate to a horde of nonacademic doings, but in 1933 curbs were placed on all school enrollments. Purportedly, this was a device to arrest the overcrowding of certain professions. Actually, it effectively quarantined the Reich's schools against the presence of undesirables— especially non-Aryans.

To staff its classrooms with masters bursting with Nazi ideals and able to impart these successfully to their pupils, the Third Reich needed, of course, to overhaul its training of teachers. This task it assigned to the care of a higher school for teacher training, the *Hochschule für Lehrerbildung*. The school had existed in the republican era under the name of *Pädagogische Akademie*, but this term was of Greco-Roman origin, and hence unpleasant to the Nazi's sensitive ears. More significant than the Germanization of the school's title was the alteration of its purpose. No longer, its sponsors gave notice, was the teacher to receive preparation, as in the Republic, "to educate youth for the international ideas of humanity." From now on the Reich would see to it that its schoolroom Führer would be "a genuine teacher who will lead youth to a real national consciousness." Inasmuch as it was to be his frequent business to rate his pupils according to race, it was important for him to get a strong grip on the science of race. Instead of dallying, as formerly, with "social and industrial sciences and novelties," the Reich's minister of education explained, "our teachers will learn something about our boundaries, study races, and military geography." At all times their endeavor was to be executed "in the spirit of our great . . . army." Teachers, he concluded, were "the Storm Troop leaders of German national education."

The minister's words had scarcely faded into the air when the province of Hesse, often in the forefront of Nazi progress, announced that it would suffer only veteran storm troopers to practice in its schools. Pretty soon the Reich added its own touch when it put upon all candidates for schoolmastering to have rendered active service as National Socialists. Their teaching art, needless to say, fell on infertile ground. They were to stay away from "cultural forms ... rejected by the Reich as unsuitable." They were to be "politically reliable." And they were to pay their dues to the National Socialist Association of Teachers, a totalitarian bund ruled from on high with an ax.

Thus education in the Third Reich. Its essential characteristics were implicit, as usual, in the social order which gave it birth. Foreshadowed in the demogogic rhetoric of *Mein Kampf*, it was violently nationalistic, centralized, militaristic, and anti-Semitic. The best of Germany's educational legacy, the constructive work of Stein and Humboldt, its Pestalozzis and its Froebels, and now and then an exceptional and enlightened Hohenzollern—all this the Nazis conveyed to the flames. The freedom of learning and teaching, gained at Halle and given fresh vigor later on at Berlin, slid into fatuity. Individual tastes and talents, whether of the child or his teacher, scarcely counted. To flog the Nazi hand-me-downs into his pupils became the teacher's paramount function. In the process he was being pushed about no less than his wards, like pawns in a game.

6

When, in 1945, the last curtain came booming down on the Nazi Reich, its vanquishers partitioned Germany into four zones, manned and governed respectively by the United States, Russia, France, and Great Britain. Until a unified administration of all Germany could be worked out, each of the powers was to exercise jurisdiction and authority over the affairs of its own sector, including the overhauling of education. To the latter end the Potsdam Agreement had laid down two general specifications, namely, (1) all traces of Nazi and militaristic doctrine were to be ferreted out and eliminated, and (2) a democratic school system was to be developed. Aside from these stipulations which applied to the entire land, each of the Allies was free to plant its ground as it saw fit.

Giving German education a new form and substance was, of course, not easy. The war's ghastly mark lay all about—schoolhouses in ruin, materials and teachers scarcely to be found, records lost, schoolbooks insufficient to the need, families split and dispersed from their native moorings, to say nothing of a youth shattered in mind and body.

Yet, for all that, by autumn of 1945 education was showing palpable signs of life. Most elementary schools were open once more, and so were some of the secondary ones. As might be expected, the means which gave them sustenance was never ample. To stretch them to their utmost, not infrequently classes had to be jammed, sixty and seventy children in a room, often some of them without seats, working in shifts, two and three a day, in quarters which, though good enough in their way, were often little more than tolerable.

Time saw the pall gradually lift. New school buildings appeared; old ones were spruced up and put in order, if possible. One by one, universities, some old, some new, took up their age-old quest. Textbooks, purged of their Nazi corruptions, leaped from the presses by the millions. The Hitler Youth, needless to say, was unfrocked. In the American sector it yielded its place to clubs and teams, bands and orchestras, and centers reserved for the pursuit of gladsome diversions, from games and dances to athletics. The Russians, not to be outdone, remodeled the Nazi young on the Communist pattern. Meanwhile—save among the French who cherished their own ideas on the subject—former Nazi schoolmasters were prohibited from practice, and they had to provide themselves with other means of earning their wages.

Thus, with millions in allied aid and a copious expert counsel, the new German education got under way. Like the country itself, it is at present sharply divided, with one system for the West and another for the East. The former reared itself on the foundation stones of the martyred Weimar Republic, while the latter poll-parroted the Russians.

Apart from a handful of safeguards inscribed in the seventh article of its constitution, the German Federal Republic (West Germany) has left the educational enterprise to the care and sovereignty of its various states. There is, thus, as in our own republic, a considerable diversity, and what strikes the eye, say, in Hamburg may not reveal itself again as one rolls southward into the latitudes of Baden and Bavaria. Yet tradition dies hard, and where it has been of a national sweep and puissance, it often reflects itself in a measure of educational uniformity. Such, for example, is the case of religious instruction. A child of the Reformation, it has maintained its position in the public school through the many centuries, fiercely controverted, it is true, in the Weimar Republic, and almost—though not quite—asphyxiated by the Nazis. Today the old battles are over, and save by historians, half forgotten. Currently, instruction in piety and morality, whether Catholic or Lutheran, flourishes as not since the memory of living man—its well-being is even assured by the constitution which has acknowledged it as a proper and meritorious practice, and one which is essential to the national prospering. This is not saying by any means, however, that infidels must give the subject of religion an ear—nor even that a master, warned against it by his conscience, may be compelled to teach it. Not uncommonly, in fact, such instruction is left to the specialized hands of a professional man of God, of either the Lutheran or the Roman rite, as the situation may require.

The *Grundschule*, which was invented by the First Republic as a cradle for its infant democracy, and subverted afterwards by the Nazis for fascist ends, is still in active and useful service. The Weimar *Grundschule* summoned its fledglings when they were six, and it held them to their books until they were ten—except, that is, those who at the age of nine took wing for freshmanhood in the secondary school. In most of the German states the four-year *Grundschule* is still the favorite, though in a few advanced places, in illustration, Bremen, Hamburg, and West Berlin, its industry has expanded into a six-year operation.

Until his fourteenth birthday—or in a few places his fifteenth—a German may not cease his grapples with learning. After he has mastered the fundamentals in the *Grundschule*, the boy—or rather his father—with the help and advice of his teachers and an expert counselor, must determine whether the pursuit of knowledge will be continued in the upper grades of the elementary school, or whether it is to be shifted to an arena of the secondary learning. Should he find neither one nor the other satisfactory to his purpose, then he may steer between the two into the so-called "middle school." It will occupy him with subjects of a more or less practical concern—including a foreign language—until he is about eighteen.

If he migrates into the secondary school, he will encounter the familiar standbys. Their designation, it is true, has been altered, and they now all answer to the name of *Gymnasium*. But their specialties remain the same. There is, for one, the original *Gymnasium*, the senior member of the secondary clan, with its compulsory study of Latin and Greek; another, formerly the *Realgymnasium*, with required Latin and modern languages; and a third, in the old days the *Oberrealschule*, which demands its toll in mathematics and the natural sciences. All basic subjects are required—there are also electives, but they are few and of a minor consequence. The high intellectual standards which plunged to the depths in the grisly gloom of Weimar, and which were snickered at by the Nazis, have been restored to their former wind-swept altitude. In consequence, Germany's secondary school students find themselves heavily belabored. To do their work effectively they must sweat over their lessons for nine years at least, whereupon. as per the old convention, they confront a series of searching, comprehensive tests, both written and oral, which, if passed, open the door to the higher learning. Plainly, the road is long and arduous, and of those who hazard it, less than half traverse it successfully. Although democracy is now the national fashion, in nearly all the states the secondary school continues to lay a tuition levy on its learners. Inevitably, thus, its main custom derives not from the ranks of the numerous commoners, but from those of the middle and upper classes.

The subjects which engage the attention of Germany's present generation of school children, whether in the elementary grades or higher, are pretty much what they were during the Weimar epoch—except for one enrichment, the social studies. Introduced to the Germans soon after the war by the American Commission on the Reorganization of Secondary Education, they made their first appearance in the classroom in 1947. Since then they have put a tight clutch on the curriculum, and in one form or another they show themselves in all the schools, high and low, from one end of the Republic to the other. There is, as in the United States, not a little variety in their stress and content—even, indeed, in their nomenclature. Look for them, for example, in Hamburg, and you will find reference to them as *Gemeinschaftskunde*; Bavaria teaches them as *Sozialkunde*; and West Berlin flaunts them gravely as *Politische Bildung und Erziehung*. And so on and on. But whatever their title, the general motive behind them is the same, namely, to put the young in consonance with the complex and enigmatic world in which they live, not only to the end of knowing it familiarly, but more important, to the end of being able to cope with it effectively.

There was a time, not so long ago, when German schoolbooks showed a disinclination to waste words on the Hitler Horror. Today the facts run the other way. Not only have the newer books put the Nazi regime under the glare of powerful lights, but in the workrooms of the social studies the Third Reich is being exposed to a candid autopsy. On the theory that this chapter of the national life, however sordid and ignoble, needs to be imprinted forever in the German mind and conscience, the government has rendered reinforcement to the schoolmen with the publication of a long line of bulletins, pamphlets, handbooks, and sundry state papers, besides a gallery of photographs and films depicting the Nazis in the practice of their gruesome art. Finally, it has put together a number of frank and unsparing documentary films, such as "Hitler," "Eichmann and the Third Reich," and several others, which it has disseminated and shown all over the nation.

7

What holds for education in West Germany obviously does not hold for the estranged East Germany. Inspect the one, and you behold the cultural reflection of a free society; look at the other, and you see that of a totalitarian Communist state. It takes no racking of the imagination to detect the resemblance of East German education to that of its Russian propagator. Like Russian education, it is a state monopoly. Dispensed in a single coordinated system of schools, it is uniform throughout the land. Its requirements are everywhere alike, and so are its curricula, and even the teaching methods of its masters.

From its lowest to its highest plane, education is free, and it is available to male and female on equal terms. Completely secular, it has put religious instruction under interdict; at the same time it has made the study of Russian obligatory. As in Russia, education's overriding purpose in the East German satellite is to forge and hammer the young into active and efficient Communists. To this purpose every boy and girl is put to school for at least a dozen years. What they undertake thereafter depends not on the voltage of their individual ardor and ambition, but on their more or less demonstrated capacity and even more, of course, on the decision of the state. The road to the secondary learning is bestrewn with infinite obstacles, and only a small proportion of the populace manage to negotiate it from end to end. As for learning's upper house, the university, only those of surpassing qualification, political no less than intellectual, are admitted to its sessions.

Communist education, whether distilled in Russia or in any of the other Marxist Utopias, makes no pretense of liberating the mind; on the contrary, much in the manner of the Nazis, it seeks to hold domination over it—even, indeed, to incarcerate it. As a result, its every aspect has been placed under relentless watch and control. Not even the schoolbooks escape. The millions of texts used in East Germany, from the three Rs to the humanities and the sciences, issue from the state-owned publishing house in East Berlin, the largest textbook mill in Europe. Written to specification and heavily freighted with Communist propaganda, they are inspected and reinspected for their political doctrine until, finally approved and ordered into print, they roll like so many Fords from the assembly line into the schoolrooms of East Germany. With teachers the story is much the same. Chosen on the basis of their pedagogical promise and their political impeccability, and trained for their practice in special schools, they are not expected to become bearers of the torch of light, but the executants of the Party leadership.

CHAPTER 28

English education, as observed some pages back, evolved over the centuries as the nation passed through the ebb and flow of its unfolding culture. It was not, as in the Prussia of Stein and Humboldt, the result of some grandiose master plan. Fashioned slowly—one might even say haltingly—in piecemeal stages, the English system seems in contrast to have been almost haphazardly conceived. Rest your eyes on it, and you will see an amalgam whose elements are often incongruous and sometimes not a little paradoxical. Within it you will find public schools that are private; private schools that tap the public till; tax-supported sectarian and nonsectarian schools; secondary schools with elementary subjects; and primary schools with secondary subjects. You will discern local authorities confined in their activities to little more than the lower learning, and others splurging far and wide with scarcely any limit put upon their doings. Though the scheme is national, with its chief command sitting in London, that command has no say, as does, for example, the national authority in France, over curricula, methods of teaching, or texts. In the same manner the local educational authorities display a generally loose and easygoing relationship to the schools under their jurisdiction.

Like their fellow creatures living under other flags, the English young are expected to become fluent in the three Rs. Just before the First World War they usually introduced themselves to learning at the age of five, and they continued their intellectual labors until some seven years later when they were liberated and, one hopes, happily literate. It was possible, if a local authority so ordained, to hold children at their books until they were fourteen, but such practice was so rare as to be almost singular. Actually, the English were not disposed, as were the Germans, to the strict enforcement of compulsory attendance. Country children, for example, helping their elders in the hayfield and the cow barn, were allowed to cut the time of their academic obligation in half as soon as they were eleven. Those aspiring to toil in industry were not so lucky—they had to wait another twelvemonth, whereupon they were excused from being educated. Nor were the English—at least in their general run—of an inclination to keep their children at school beyond the elementary plane. The ones who did stay in school were the exception rather than the rule, and they dwelt in the larger towns and cities where, since Parliament's memorable Balfour Act of 1902, provision for a "higher elementary" education, usually with vocational overtones, had shown a great multiplication.

This is by no means suggesting that Englishmen, taking one with another, contented themselves with their schools as they were. Riffle through the pages of their gazettes, whether lay or professional, and you will find contention, and even dissatisfaction and disparagement, aplenty. From such critical give-and-take was bred the Education Act of 1918, also known as the Fisher Act, for the Hon. H. A. L. Fisher, then President of the nation's Board of Education, and the one chiefly responsible for enactment of the measure. It undertook a thoroughgoing reorganization of English education, settling it more securely on a national base and, more important, seeking to open the door of learning to all classes of people right up to the university. It is not necessary here to embroider the details, for most of the law's provisions came to grief, a casualty of the hard times which descended upon the English on the heels of the First World War. Yet for all the ferocious slaughtering of school budgets up and down the land, some gains prevailed. All children, for example, were now made to go to school until they were fourteen. At no time was any one of them to be granted a dispensation to stack away his books, even transiently, so that he might work on the farm or in a mill. With part-time schooling thus outlawed, child labor, though still in furtive practice, suffered a serious crippling. To bring the secondary school within reach of a more numerous public, particularly among those of a scanty purse, the number of scholarships was increased. And to keep the young in the glow of health, medical facilities were ameliorated and extended.

Meanwhile, until the economic winds blew more favorably, the nation's public servants busied themselves, as they had already done time and again, with putting England's education under scrutiny. From their observations swarmed a host of plans and recommendations, often wordy and sometimes platitudinous, but at bottom of sense and meaning. The first of such studies is the report of Sir Henry Hadow and a committee of collaborators. Printed in 1926 as *The Education of the Adolescent*, it was followed in 1931 with *The Primary Schools*, and two years later with *Infant and Nursery Schools*. The last emission of any consequence, the Spens report on *Secondary Education*, came out a year or so before the outbreak of the Second World War, after which for a time the English addressed their thoughts to more pressing concerns.

It is only fair to say that for all the intrusions of war, the findings of Hadow and Spens and their fellow experts fell on a soil that had long been preparing for them. We see them sprout in the speculations of Parliament as it turned its dreams toward better days ahead, and presently we see them bear fruit in the Education Act of 1944, the so-called Butler Act. Like the Fisher Act of a quarter century earlier, the new law reached over the whole range of English education—"from womb to tomb," as the phrase then went. There is in it too an echo of the wistful idealism of the earlier statute. But there is also within it a better understanding of the hard and inescapable facts of postwar reconstruction. Very alert to its realities, its framers planned their program of reform to take effect not in a handful of imminent tomorrows, but over a stretch of numerous years—even, indeed, a generation.

What were the main stipulations of the act of 1944? To begin, the law did execution on a number of old and established linguistic usages. The elementary school, for example, was to be spoken of hereafter as the primary school. Council schools became county schools. Day continuation schools, hatched by the Fisher Act in 1918, but long since done in by rigor mortis, were to be given reincarnation as county colleges. Finally, the national Board of Education, its powers and dignities enhanced, became the Ministry of Education.

In the matter of holding the young to their studies the law was not disposed to go easy. It raised the age of required school attendance to fifteen and prepared the way to hoist it to sixteen some day in the future. By mid-century, moreover, girls and boys not yet over the line of eighteen, and not engaged full tilt in the pursuit of knowledge, were to have part of their time articled for study at a continuation school, or in the new parlance, a county college. As for the tender young, not yet sufficiently sturdy for the rigors of book learning, local authorities were called upon, where a demand was voiced, to give them care and accommodation in an up-to-date nursery school.

It was in the realm of secondary education that the Butler Act quarried most deeply. For one thing, up to the age of fifteen it made access to its benefits free to all. For another, to render them more palatable to individual preference, they were to be dispensed in three distinct flavors, each available in a house devoted especially to its confection, to wit, the grammar school, the secondary modern school, and the secondary technical school. Of these the first is, of course, our old and ivied friend, the inheritor of the ancient, classical tradition, and the conveyor of a general culture fitting its possessor for the university, and by this route, the professions and the higher public service. The modern school is a comparatively late comer. It too bestows a general culture, not, to be sure, of a Greco-Roman sheen, but cultural nevertheless. What makes it modern besides its name is its earnest endeavor to attune its offerings to the pupils' interests and practical needs. To this end it usually reserves some of its instruction for those arts and sciences which might help to ease one's way in business or industry, o· in the case of girls, in compounding a decent meal or running a household with efficacy and enchantment. The technical school, despite its name, is also a purveyor of a general education, though its rendering is in a minor key, and it relates itself in one way or another to some salient branch of industry, agriculture, or commerce. As envisioned by the framers of the Butler Act, the school was designed not to further any capacity for ratiocination, but rather for the accommodation of boys and girls "with a practical turn of mind."

There remain the many hundreds of private groves. Not a few have adorned the English landscape for numerous centuries. Time, of course, and circumstance have brought them inevitable alterations and adjustments. But from the fountain of their heart there still flows an old and honored tradition. They charge fees for their services, of course, and in the case of their foremost exemplars such levies by English standards run to a dizzy height. In consequence, they still are, as they have ever been, the favored grazing ground of the high-toned and well-to-do, the prep schools for the advanced learning, but even more, perhaps, the finishing schools for cultivated ladies and gentlemen. Democracy, though properly respectful of their excellence, has not looked kindly on their exclusiveness, and in various ways, especially through scholarships and other grants in aid, it has sought to spread their boons to the lesser folk. They were under sharp sniping during the First World War, but like that War to End War, the attacks failed. But the onslaught went on, and during the Second World War they found themselves once more under full assault—and this time with some promise of success. At all events, when the Butler Act was put together, the government put upon the local school authorities to make these ancient cradles of culture accessible to young people of competence, regardless of their parents' place or pocket.

2

Historically, the roots of the English primary school reach deep down into a religious soil. Coming to practice in an age which made religion the chief of all the human values, the first lower schools instructed their attendants not only in their letters, but also in the tenets and worship of their church. The business was voluntary, and it was conducted by the clergy with the aid, in the process of time, of organized Christian endeavor eager to instill piety and virtue as well as knowledge in the young. Parliament, as has already been said, eyed these undertakings approvingly, and early in the nineteenth century it began the practice of assisting them with grants from the national treasury. The schools, for their part, performed the laudable service of educating the multitudinous offspring of the lower folk, who, but for their help, were doomed to everlasting ignorance.

Such, in sum, was the situation in 1870 when Parliament paved the way for the coming of the public primary school. Supported by taxes laid locally as well as by national grants, the newcomers were no less opposed to irreverence and sin than their forerunners, but their assaults on that old bamboozler, Satan, were limited at all times to a nonsectarian godliness. Meanwhile, the older groves not only continued to draw their parliamentary gratuity but, as the years proceeded, they were conceded the right to share in the local taxes without, however, yielding the right to wage their war on Beelzebub with a full denominational armament.

This double system of sectarian and nonsectarian tax-supported schooling has served the English in one form or another to the very present, though not without strife and wrangling and even opposition. The system, some insisted, ought to be put on the shelf. Let the church schools, they urged, be taken over by the secular arm; let public money be disbursed for their general improvement, and let all religious instruction be nondenominational.

The act of 1944 shut the door against such extremism. Taking the church schools into the state system as equal partners, it offered to pay half the cost of their relocation in new quarters, comparable in equipment and facilities to those of the state schools. The other half of the bill was to be footed by the schools. In return they were to retain a free hand in picking their teachers, and they were to continue to teach religion according to their sectarian lights. Schools too pinched financially to pay their share were to be supported out of public funds. But unlike their better-heeled brethren, their right to appoint their masters freely was put under restriction. As for their lessons in divinity, they were to devote two weekly sessions to denominational instruction.

Rather curiously, all schools, whether sacred or profane, currently engage in a daily "act of corporate worship," and even the tax-supported state school requires the study of religion. It would be unfair not to note that in this instance the subject has been stripped of all denominational content, and that any pupil having no desire for such revelation may, on grounds of conscience, be allowed to abstain therefrom.

3

The Butler Act has resided in the tomes of law for more than a generation. Not all its ordinance has been put into effect—the chances are that some of it will never see the light of day. But its most important mandates are at work, and signs of them are everywhere at hand. There is, for once, the new Ministry of Education. Its direction and control of the nation's schools, though too bland and insufficient in the eyes of the centralized French, and puerile in those of the Russians, is for all that, of a greater potency than ever before, and it is at least pragmatically effective. Although the Ministry exercises its authority with a soft pedal and grants the local school boards a tremendous leeway, its power to maintain minimum standards throughout the realm is sure and inescapable.

From the ages of five to fifteen an Englishman is subject to compulsory education. If his father possesses a brimming purse, his heir can perform his civic duty in a private hall of learning, or as a friendly concession to his station in life, he may submit to the learning process under the family roof. The vast flock of children, of course, enjoy no such luck, and they do their pondering in the free public school. They enter academic service in the infant school where, somewhat like the young in that faraway and ineffable dreamland of Robert Owen, they play and learn until they are seven, when they are expected to do simple sums, make sense out of not too difficult books, and write a tidy and legible hand.

They now ascend to the so-called junior school where they carry on as before in study, play, and exercise, though, naturally, under a heavier draught. The standards generally are of a decent respectability, and the Johnnys who cannot read remain in scarce supply. At eleven the children reach the end of the elementary trail, but before they venture the next step they are given a diligent inspection. The probing varies from locality to locality, but usually it takes stock of their intelligence, their special talents and capacities, their ability to compose clear and coherent prose, and finally, their record, scholastic and otherwise, during their several years at school. From their study of these excavations the local school officials direct the next step. Children of an intellectual promise are routed into the grammar school; those of a mechanical proclivity are steered into the secondary technical school; and the overwhelming rest—some two of every three—are assigned to the so-called secondary modern school. All these schools are free, and in rank they are purportedly equal.

Until the mid-fifties, the "eleven-plus" examination, as this weighing and sorting process has come to be called, was granted popular approval on the ground that it was a fair and accurate device. Since then, however, frowns have furrowed the public brow, and the examination has fallen under challenge and charges, particularly because of the great store it has placed in the results of the intelligence test, whose infallibility just about this time was becoming not a little suspect. As a result, some local boards have heaved the test over the rail, while others, though continuing to resort to it, incline, nevertheless, to play down its importance. Some boards, taking their cue from a number of pertinent surveys, have even found that teachers' judgments, though they are the product of weak and faltering mortals, when assembled together as a whole, are nonetheless accurate enough to offer examiners valuable and useful data.

English parents, taking them as they come, love their children no less dearly than other civilized folk love theirs. Hence, when English youngsters suffer unduly, their elders suffer likewise. There is no doubt that the eleven-plus, like all examinations of momentous importance, presses heavily upon the young, taxing their tender psyche all too often with anxiety and anguish. In consequence, outraged fathers and mothers have at times risen to cry out and dissent. To such frayed and upset nerves local boards, happily, have not been insensitive. Some, for example, have revised their system, and instead of subjecting their eleven-year-olds to a massive and long drawn-out examination, they now conduct their searching in a more dulcet and even surreptitious manner through a series of tests scattered without fuss or fanfare throughout the pupil's last year in school. It is a procedure which is doubtless more humane; but it is also one which academic diehards regard with sobs and dire predictions.

The secondary modern school, which is now denominated a high school, is sprung, as reference has been made, from the Butler Act of 1944, and it has enjoyed the countenance and support of the Conservative Party. Labor, for its part, has pinned its idealism on the "comprehensive school." This accepts all primary school graduates and services them for two years with a common course, whereupon it determines their strengths and weaknesses, and sifts them accordingly. But, whatever specialty they are then set upon, whether academic, commercial, or technical, the comprehensive school is at pains to maintain them together, teaching them either under a single roof, or somewhat in the style of an American college, sprawled as a complex of edifices over a common plot of ground. There currently exist a few hundred comprehensive schools, and they may be seen not only in such overflowing municipalities as London, Liverpool, Manchester, and Bristol, but in lesser places, as witness, Stoke-on-Trent, Southend-on-Sea, and several others.

The Tory Party is divided in its estimate of the comprehensive plan, but the Labor Party, as has been said, is dedicated to it. To make it more generally attractive to a nation of class-minded people, Labor has gone to great lengths to garland the new school in the social glamor enjoyed by the venerable grammar school, a stratagem which in the main fooled scarcely anyone. Despite the Labor Party's loyalty to the comprehensive principle, and for all its hard striving to put it into successful operation, the harsh reality of economics, especially the problem of providing the wherewithal for new and sufficient buildings and equipment, has compelled it to move slowly. Though Labor insists, as its spokesmen say, "on the comprehensive principle," yet it has also come to the realization, as the vulgar saying goes, that there is more than one way to skin a cat, that, indeed, "there may be more than one way of putting comprehensive education into practice." Unluckily, since those memorable words were conceived, the reins of government have slipped from the grip of the Labor Party.

The bellwether of the academic flock, the grammar school leads to the higher learning, and to openings with a future in the world of affairs. Though they are free and orchestrated on democratic chords, they are also selective, only two of every ten of the secondary school populace being admitted to their sanctum. Despite the recency of their advent, they are not unmindful of their ancient name, and here and there one catches tangible traces of the respect in which they hold it. Save in rare and exceptional cases, for example, they are not given to the charms of coeducation, as are the lower and the other free secondary groves; instead, like the private grammar schools, they favor the monastic way with separate establishments for boys and girls. Like their patriarchal forerunners, they put a great stock in rigging their clients in a common, though not undistinguished, attire. Visit any of their haunts, and nearly always you will see the boys similarly bedecked in jacket, shirt, waistcoat, and pantaloons, and, of course, the one and only school tie. And like the boys in the grammar schools of old, their current namesakes are at pains to give themselves an air of primacy.

The uniformity which marks the pupils' vestment is characteristic also of their studies—at least in their early stage before they become specialists. Examine their first-year program, and you behold algebra and geometry, language both foreign and domestic, general science, or maybe a beginner's biology, besides history and geography. In addition, consideration must be given to music, physical culture, and as has been said, an examination of the Christian religion, discreetly drained of all sectarian juices. A second language is taken on during the next year; and those to whom linguistic study is not a curse may elect a third in the year following. By this time the natural sciences bear down more formidably, and so does mathematics. Not unusually, boys exercise their manual skill in a variety of workshops, while their sisters give consideration to household science, including, sometimes, the theorems of "mother craft."

It is not an easy route, though its harassments are not so frequent nor so menacing as those in France. Where French schoolboys have scarcely any time to divert themselves in jinks and jollity, their Anglo-Saxon brethren roll and frolic like a herd of cats in a field of catnip. In England, as in America, though less intensely, recreation illuminates the schoolboy's life. He enjoys the gratifications of all the familiar clubs and pastimes, from hoarding stamps to snaring bugs and butterflies. Does he like to flog the air with argument? Then a debating club awaits him. Does he fiddle? Or drum? Or toot a horn? Then an orchestra would like to share his art. And so on and on, from actors, hikers, and camera clickers to all the others that comprise the partisans of extracurricular action. The English, of course, go in for sports, and for a self-respecting school to be without them is almost unthinkable. But they are kept within modest bounds, and they proffer their benefits to all the students instead of a few of surpassing powers. They are, in a word, games rather than events.

Fifteen is the age when compulsory education comes to an end, and more than half the boys and girls celebrate their emancipation by quitting school. The vast bulk of them go to work, though some will tarry to seek quick reinforcement in some school of trade or business where they arm themselves with shorthand and typing, or some equally useful instrument, not usually available in the regular schools.

Those who continue their secondary studies now concentrate on the onerous business of getting ready, a year later, for a tussle with the government examiners. The various examining boards are under university operation, but about half their members are of the teaching craft, and all of them, or at any rate nearly all of them, are persons of great knowledge. Taken together, the questions they ask traverse the whole territory of the secondary learning, and to give them all a commendable treatment would call for the knowledge of an Aristotle. Happily, a candidate may choose to suffer only in his specialties, in illustration, the natural sciences, mathematics, history, a foreign tongue, and English, which is compulsory. Or if he happens to be a language virtuoso, he may face his inquisitors with German, Latin, and Greek, the required English, and say, the social sciences. If he manages to survive the inquest, he is honored with the Ordinary Level of the General Certificate of Education, the GCE, a meet reward for his endurance and industry. He is now sixteen and in most instances school bells will summon him no more. But there are strings to his liberty, for until he is eighteen the Butler Act bids him patronize a continuation school, the so-called county college. So far, however, only a relatively few of these have come to being, and to all intents and purposes he is free to go his way.

There remain the few of a resolute will who will pant for an even greater learning. They will continue their pursuit until they reach their eighteenth anniversary when the examiners greet them once more. Their questions, needless to say, are searching, and put to the generality of American eighteen-year-olds, they would wreak a dreadful havoc. They are, in truth, demanding enough to gnarl the brow of the average college senior. In fact, even the English have found them arduous, and there has been some talk of mellowing them, or even abandoning them, but so far to no avail. Those who come through them with their flag still on the staff are granted the Advanced Level of the General Certificate of Education. Among England's teenagers they are, so to say, the intellectual cream. Yet, for all their prodigies, should they hanker for admission to a university, they have no assurance that they will pass muster. The truth is, England's higher learning is a heavily specialized enterprise which confines itself to a narrow and circumscribed field of academic concern and to preparation for the loftiest plane in a few professions. To be accepted for university work the candidate must be not only highly qualified, but also well grounded in his specialty, besides mathematics and the sciences.

The secondary modern school is a descendant of England's first attempts to furnish free, tax-supported instruction "in subjects beyond the elementary knowledge." Given legal sanction in 1902, the practice showed itself at first in the larger municipalities, and like sin, it was an entirely voluntary undertaking. Time saw it grow and spread, and as the years of compulsory education gradually increased, more and more boys and girls became involved in its transactions. Currently, of course, they have no escape since the act of 1944 has caught them in its dragnet by ordaining their presence in a secondary school. As has already been mentioned, two of every three of England's youth frequent the secondary modern school. Even so, it is not hymned in the national esteem as is the grammar school, and despite its large enrollment, it is less generously financed. In some respects it bears resemblance to the present American high school. True, its buildings are not the palatial flaunts which have recently risen to gild the American scene; nor are its appurtenances and equipment nearly so sumptuous. But like its sister across the ocean, it has declared against the yardstick of caste and condition. Its standards are not those of the grammar school, but this is not saying that it holds the intellect in low regard. In fact, there have been occasions when some of its aspirants have confronted the same examinations for the General Certificate as the clients of the grammar school— and with excellent results. The modern school's main concern, however, lies in another direction, namely, to guide its youngsters toward happy and responsible, and hence well-adjusted, living in the world in which, for good or ill, we find ourselves.

CHAPTER 29

FRANCE

The exit of the third Napoleon in 1870 marked the end of the Second Empire. Once again the French put their hope in a republic. But it was a dim prospect—a rushlight that scarcely glimmered. The guns of war had stilled, but the agonies of peace remained. Alsace and Lorraine were lost, and an enormous war debt pressed upon the land. The German forces had not withdrawn, nor would they until the last pfennig had been handed over. Meanwhile, as so often in their hectic history, the French were fighting among themselves. Though dethroning kings and emperors had become something of a national habit, royalists were still roving the grounds, and so were their archfoes, the messiahs from the left. Between these shoals the Third Republic groped precariously. That it did not dash to pieces was due in part to luck, but much more to the uncommon sense and powerful spirit of its leaders. To the world's amazement, including that of the French themselves, in less than three years the Republic disposed of its German debt, and soon the last enemy regiments were heeling their way beyond the border. In betweentimes the new rulers swept away the shabby remnants of their oppressive past to replace them with a new and lively liberalism. Henceforth all men were to possess the right to vote, and the joys and perquisites that go therewith. The reins of government were entrusted to a parliament and a cabinet, tailored in the English fashion, but with a president as its foremost adornment instead of a king. People were guaranteed the right to assemble freely, and no brake was to be put on their liberty of expression, whether in speech or in print. For these boons the French were not ungrateful. In fact, when they got their chance in the election of 1878, a majority of them swept the Third Republic triumphantly into its own.

2

Thus powerfully fortified with the public's confidence and support, the government promptly turned its mind to educational reform. It began, under the direction of Jules Ferry, with a vast outpouring of public money, a practice which, of course, has long since ceased to be either singular or startling. A flock of new schoolhouses presently speckled the land. New normal schools were ordered, with a special one to accommodate the fair sex in each of the Republic's eighty-odd departments. In 1881 the government made elementary education free and accessible to all. In the next year it ordered all the young between the ages of six and thirteen to submit themselves for instruction either in the chambers of the public school or in some other seemly place, subject, however, at all times to state inspection and regulation.

The state's gigantic effort to make itself the unchallengeable sovereign over public instruction was orchestrated on the strings of secularity, a tune which had been composed so many years past by Chalotais, but which was now boldly rearranged and reinforced to suit a far more mundane temper. Instruction in religion, the historic germ cell of the modern elementary school, was read out of the curriculum to make room for training in civics and morality which, though granting the Deity a decorous deference, sought to maintain itself on a predominantly secular ground. To be admitted to public school practice, every teacher, whatever his obvious virtuosity, was required henceforth to be licensed by the state. In 1886 the state did the clergy yet more damage when it ordered their gradual replacement by secular masters. Another blow—and a formidable one—fell in 1904 when the government mandated the dissolution of all teaching congregations. A year later the enterprise of state and church was made completely separate, not only in education, but in all other affairs as well.

The rise of the public school, free, laic, tax-supported, and subject at all times to state authority and control, did not bring ruin to the private halls of learning. Their pride and glory, of course, was damaged, and the monopoly they had enjoyed so long was done for. But the state had no inclination to shut them down—in truth, it even allowed them the solace of preserving their wonted stock in trade, the teaching, that is, of religion. At the same time it forced them into a number of renunciations. Their bursar, for example, could expect no help from the public pocket. Their teachers were made to meet the same standard as their brothers in secular cloth. Their course of study was required to have the state's approval. And so were the textbooks—so even their works in divinity and moral science, indeed, even their catechism. There was, of course, not a little yelping, but as the years trekked on, the din died down, and the private schools, notwithstanding their burdens, drove a modest but steady trade.

Thus the main reform. Its first concern was to secure for the Republic the loyalty of its young. To this end, it concentrated on the lower learning. But time saw it break through its trammels to ascend into the *collège* and the *lycée*, and in the old age of the century even into the university. It did not take long, however, to notice that the secondary schools, being elderly, enjoyed a sort of sentimental esteem, and that they were reluctant to yield themselves to a major operation. As a consequence, the reforms which they suffered were swathed in a cautious delicacy. Their course of study now reached over seven years, and it was to be uniform throughout the country, though its patrons were to be allowed a choice between languages, ancient and contemporary, on the one hand, and science and the modern languages on the other. The secondary schools continued to exact a slight payment for their instruction, and despite the democracy which soothed the Third Republic, they reserved their benefits for a highly restricted clientele. As in the beginning, and as in the present, their stress remained overwhelmingly intellectual.

One important change there was, not, it is true, in the sphere of the privileged male, but in that of his shackled sisters. As figures in civilized society, the women of France, like most of their sex in other places, had come into the nineteenth century with scarcely any rights. As the years swept on, however, and the world pointed more and more toward science and industry, women began to press for a fuller and freer life, and so that they could deal with it more meetly and effectively, a far more spacious educational opportunity. The movement varied in pace and power, and from land to land. But it was hard sledding—indeed, in our own sweet land of progress, midcentury was over before any substantial advance was made. And it was not until the current century that most of the old taboos against women were uprooted.

In France, for all its hospitality to revolution and for all the bruited gallantry of its men, the movement to emancipate women precipitated no great rush. Thus—to confine ourselves to education—whereas America braved the perils of collegiate coeducation as early as 1833 with the founding of Oberlin, and followed a little less than thirty years after with Vassar, which was the first full-fledged college for women to rise in the American republic, France held back until 1880 when its lawgivers, led by Camille Sée, ordered the establishment of special *lycées* and *collèges* for girls. But these cerebral springs were not the powerful intellectual tonics that braced the boys. Overborne by the notion that the frail sex—at least in its general run—lacked the essential intellectual sap to flourish beyond the lower learning, the French lawmakers permitted the girls no unnecessary risks. Where boys were put upon with seven years of service in the trenches of secondary learning, girls confronted only five. As though such balm were not enough, their course of study was considerably watered. Latin and Greek they escaped entirely, and their math and science were kept in a minor key. On the other hand, hygiene and homemaking they got to know familiarly, and they dallied copiously in music and drawing.

The higher learning in France, as was recounted earlier, reaches back into the gray remoteness of the twelfth century when the University of Paris came upon the scene. Paris was destined to become Christendom's foremost dispenser of divine science, and in the late Middle Ages her renown rose to alpine heights—even, some said, to the Throne of Grace itself. Presently, as the world grew older, the university was joined by other founts of sapience, and as they came to their fullest flow they were attracting notice, not only by their power to translate young men into doctorhood in theology, but in law, medicine, and letters as well.

So things quietly ran without much change until the storms of the Revolution had washed away the Old Regime. Thereupon, as the country teetered uncertainly, now toward republicanism, now toward monarchy, its cloisters of higher thought fell upon baleful times. Finally, when Napoleon propagated the Imperial University, that prodigy of centralization which clamped the nation's learning under a rigid national control, the higher education, drained of its autonomy, subsided into a condition of sorrowful sterility.

Thus matters hung more or less until 1885, when the Republic accorded its universities the right to own property as corporate bodies and, better yet, to run their own affairs under a board of governors. A decade or so later a more thorough overhauling was undertaken. Out of it arose fifteen universities, eight of them full-bodied and ready to advance their hopefuls in medicine, jurispru-dence, science, or letters. Theology, once the cock of the academic walk, still had audiences, but in a state where government eyed the church with more and more ill favor, the business of preparing men for holy orders confined itself perforce to private hands.

French universities are state institutions. Hence their men of learning carry on as public functionaries, and their wages issue from the public treasury. Although the universities are public, their instruction is not free. But to the undergrads who currently swarm in American collegiate halls, what the Frenchman lays on the bursar's counter must seem a paltry levy—so trifling it puts the green of envy in their eye.

By the American yardstick the universities of France count as graduate schools, paving the way to advanced degrees, and by this route to a professional estate. To be admitted to the university's sessions, the candidate, whether male or female, must possess the baccalaureate, or in the jargon of everyday French, the *bachot*. It is a sign to all the world that its holder has been fished out of the ocean of teenagers and that he is of surpassing intellectual powers. He has survived seven difficult years in one of the enclaves of secondary learning. He has passed a physical examination. Finally, he has emerged, tired but triumphant, from the national written and oral tests, as one of the few who did successful execution on such questions as whether the feeling of guilt has moral value, whether there is room for finality in science, and whether by saying a man is free we mean that he escapes all determinism.

One catches in the educational endeavor of the Third Republic a discernible echo of the Revolution. Its secularity would have brought exultant gloats from its departed partisans, and so would its nationalization and its centralization. That in addition it was free and compulsory would, no doubt, have made a high appeal to the Revolution's advanced thinkers.

3

Time, as usual, brought criticism, and criticism begot change. As in Germany—as, in fact, pretty nearly everywhere else—the first onslaughts fell on the secondary learning. In a world where science and technology were galloping ahead briskly, and were even promising on some tomorrow to make themselves a prime mover in the shaping of our everyday living, the training bestowed by Latin and Greek began to be viewed with more and more disrelish. The knowledge every enlight-ened Frenchman needed—so ran the gathering contention—lay not in the ancient Muses, but in the physical sciences and the living languages. Such dissent came not, of course, from the professors of the gray-haired classics, but from the laity, and especially from its representatives in the middle classes. But the old classics turned out to be of a formidable stuff, and the war against them took long years of hard grappling. Six times the Third Republic essayed reform, and six times its labors produced no more than a puny belch. In fact, the Republic itself was gone when the chasm between the ancients and the moderns was finally bridged. The latter, however, snared an important gain as early as 1902 when the secondary curriculum was quartered into four options, to wit, (1) Latin and Greek, (2) Latin and modern foreign languages, (3) Latin and natural science, and (4) modern languages and the sciences. Thus made sophisticate, the learner was expected in his last year, his seventh, to bear down on either philosophy or mathematics.

So the business stood for some twenty years when the moderns, bursting with a new cockiness, demanded that the secondary groves grant a place of dignity to vocational and technical training. But this time they ran their heads into a wall of stone, and instead of the consideration they had besought they got another and more powerful dose from the classical bottle. Henceforth, decreed the government, the study of Latin and Greek was to be mandatory for every student. The order had scarcely been inscribed in the statute books when the fates, compassionate, for once, to France's belabored young, elbowed the reigning cabinet out of office, and replaced it with one more friendly to the modern disciplines. The new one not only made a swift end of compulsory Latin and Greek, but also restored the modern language option.

Meanwhile, the mills kept grinding, and in 1925 they disgorged another innovation. This time it based itself on the theory that specialization should be stayed as long as possible, and that instead there should be an identical course of study for all. To this end all students were conscripted for six years to a common course in general subjects. In addition, during their first four years they were to get on close terms with Latin or a modern language. Greek remained, but now it could become a student's second language, and he could take it or refuse, as he chose. Besides building themselves up with alien tongues, the scholars flexed their minds assiduously with history, geography, science, and of course, French, both in speech and in writing, and from its grammar to its rhetoric and letters. The last, or senior, year continued to be of either a philosophical or a mathematical and scientific stress.

In the meantime, things had begun to stir on another front. Girls, it will be remembered, had secondary schools all their own. But their offerings at best were spindly—spare, as it were, in cerebral proteins—and altogether inferior to the robust fare set before the boys. Consuming them, a girl could aspire to a diploma, a joy to the eyes, no doubt, when she beheld it hanging on her boudoir wall, but one, nevertheless, that opened no university door. Did mademoiselle long some day to be another Portia? Or perhaps a lady Galen or Hippocrates? Or maybe a technician or researcher toiling for science in some shining and sanitary lab? Then she needed to prepare herself in some hall of higher learning, and for this, of course, a baccalaureate was prerequisite. To such an end the soft stuff of the girls' secondary school availed her naught—her only recourse, hence, was to confide herself and her ambitions to the instruction of some first-rate private enterprise.

As long as the fair ones kept their professional yearning within modest bounds, the practice aforesaid worked sufficiently well. But time saw more and more of them deserting their mops and dishpans to seek their fortune in the world beyond the hearth. Some headed for offices, some for mills or shops, and increasingly some laid plans to find themselves a place in the professions. To give the latter a helping hand, some of the more venturesome secondary seminaries gradually extended themselves by offering instruction in subjects which would arm the girls, if not totally, then at least partially, in their combat for the baccalaureate.

For all the odds against them, the girls held themselves well—so well, in fact, that in 1924 their secondary school lengthened its period of attendance another year. Girls pining for higher preferment could now make acquaintance with more foreign languages, even Latin, if they chose, and a more substantial science and mathematics, besides history, geography, and French—all, of course, essential for the harsh and grueling operations demanded in the national test for the coveted *bachot*. If, after having drunk from these springs, a girl thirsted for yet more, she was given accommodation with an extra year in which she concentrated her gifts upon either philosophy or science. For the more numerous girls who wanted merely a secondary diploma the requirements remained less onerous, and hence in academic esteem somewhat subordinate and even inferior.

The new program was scarcely under way when, in 1925, the government, no longer underestimating the power of woman, granted young ladies equal rights with their brothers by permitting girls' secondary schools to offer the same course of study as that of the boys. Five years more and the feminine world was gladdened by the dawn of an even better day when girls were allowed to grace the sessions of the boys' *lycées* and *collèges*.

Though the victory carried the lovely ones to heights their grandmas had never dreamed of, the winning of another boon, more expansive in its embrace, and to the state certainly more costly, must be regarded as of no less consequence. Once the caterer to the mind and to those of money and position, the secondary school had started out by offering its edification to a group which was, to say the least, exclusive. To pay its way, the *collège* had relied partly on gifts but even more on tuition. It was a well-regarded practice, and in a day when education was not a right but a privilege, it was sanctioned on grounds both sacred and profane. That day, of course, ran aground in the Revolution. Even before the venting of its fury some of its more sagacious heralds, it may be recalled, had hazarded some radical doubts on the subject of educational privilege. Brains, they insisted, were the monopoly of no class, and hence education, at least on its lower rungs, ought to be freely available to all. The proposition was picked up by liberals, both politicians and moralists. But to translate it from rhetoric into practice required a great deal of labor, and it was not until the flowering of the Third Republic that it came into being with the creation of the free state-supported and state-operated elementary school.

Higher up, the watchmen of tradition were in greater force and power.

Though the *collèges* and *lycées* had been put under the eye and hand of the state, this is not saying that they were made easily accessible or that they were made free. This grieved the connoisseurs of democracy no little, but until the tide shifted there was little that they could do. Signs that it was turning showed themselves late in the nineteenth century and in the infancy of the twentieth when, in response to an augmenting parental pressure, the state resorted to granting more and more scholarships. But the pressure did not abate—on the contrary, it augmented in power and persistence. At length, in 1925, it won its reward when the entering classes of the *collège* and *lycée* were to receive their learning gratis. The new practice was to be extended until finally, seven years later, secondary education was to be completely free to all who could survive its high and devastating standards.

Thus the Republic's most notable educational deeds. During the years of ferment which followed the peacemaking at Versailles, several others were urged, but none of any moment materialized. Whatever chance any might have had was dashed by the outbreak of the Second World War. There is no need here to belabor the details. Its general effect on education was the usual one, which is to say a massive deterioration and decay.

4

Unlike the English, the Germans, the Swiss, the Danes, and the Dutch—to restrict our examples to a mere handful—until recently, the French have not been notable for their achievements in educational progressivism. Confront a Frenchman with this observation, and he will riposte, if he is worth his Gallic salt, that France, after all, is the mother of the sixteenth century Montaigne, an educational avant-gardist of the first magnitude, and the avatar of all progressives, whether they are still on Earth or in the spectral realm beyond. The fact is that France has not lacked progressive-minded pedagogues, not as adventurous, perhaps, as a Reddie or a Lietz, to say nothing of such daredevils as Wyneken and Geheeb. Unluckily for the advancement of pedagogic liberalism, the country's stiff centralization, forged by the Revolution, fortified and perfected by the first Napoleon, and conserved by the Third Republic in the interest of national solidarity, put a firm brake on any educational innovation. As a result, the bulk of educational reform, as it evolved during the passage of the Third Republic, was directed at the public learning, high as well as low, in the form and substance of laws and decrees hereinbefore described.

The first pedagogic venture of an unmistakable liberal stamp, and for years the most talked about in France, was the work of Edmond Demolins. It began andante in 1897, when in an essay Demolins volunteered his countrymen the opinion that the English were their betters. "Wherein," he asked, "lies the superiority of the Anglo-Saxons?" It is imbedded, a little pondering told him, in their better education with its "broader goals and more natural methods."

"What must we do," he went on, "to give our children an education which will ensure individual and national supremacy?" His response took a double form, a book, *L'Education Nouvelle*, wherein he bared his appreciation of progressive education and, in 1899, the Ecole des Roches, a school where he essayed to put them to work. When, some eight years later, Demolins died, his earthly labors were assumed and successfully carried on by Paul de Roussiers and Georges Bertier, both able and industrious disciples.

Cradled amidst the peaceful Norman landscape, a couple of hours or so from the charms and abominations of Paris, des Roches, like Abbotsholme, its Anglo-Saxon model, began its being as a country home school. Again like Abbotsholme, des Roches reserved its boons for boys, though the passing years saw it attempt to redress this slight to the fair ones by admitting a few of them to its circle. Finally, and again like the Reddie school, des Roches was dedicated to the evangel of the new pedagogic messiah. What was striking about the Demolins school, however, was not its devotion to progressive idealism and the liberal practices it engaged in, for these had ceased to be front-page news. What was significant—even amazing—was that such pedagogic freewheeling should have shown itself in a land whose educational authorities were not only unremittingly conservative, but who possessed high and abundant powers to implement their point of view. If, for all that, they raised no fuss over des Roches's deviation from the established tradition, then let it be remembered that behind the whiskers of such benevolence there always lurked the face of a vigilant state. Did it vouchsafe des Roches the privilege to pick its own tunes? Then it also insisted that it pay the piper. For all the ease and freedom the clients of des Roches enjoyed, in the end they confronted the same examinations as their brethren in attendance at the conventional seats of learning. Under the control and surveillance of the state, this final reckoning of intellectual accounts, never easy and always exigent, made no concession to ignorance.

If the schoolmen of France, working within learning's private emprise, found the search for a new and better education somewhat bureaucratically bedeviled, then their comrades, panting in the public schools, found the quest infinitely harder, if not forbidding. The truth is that the state viewed pedagogic innovation in a wary mood, and any attempt to bring it about in the public shrines of knowledge needed its official sanction, a concession usually not easy to come by. Consequently, until after the First World War the roster of those smarting to alter and ameliorate the public educational practice remained sparsely peopled. Nearly all its few inhabitants, of course, have long since taken to their eternal rest, and of them only one is still less than half-forgotten. His name is Roger Cousinet, in his best days an elementary school inspector, or in plain American, a superintendent. A prime mover in the establishment of La Nouvelle Education, a society of forward-looking teachers and parents, with chapters dispersed throughout the longitude and latitude of France, Cousinet, and his associates, worked for the propagation of the progressive cause. A man of such obvious talent could not easily be denied his chance, and so when he made application to try out some new ideas, his superiors granted their consent. Working experimentally in several public schools under a watchful governmental eye, Cousinet succeeded in showing that the humaner procedures extolled by the world's foremost progressives of his time were not only workable in France, but that of and by themselves they were not detrimental to the exacting academic standards demanded by the national authorities. For his performance Cousinet won the plaudits of progressives everywhere. In the summer of 1921 he explained his program's special qualities to admirers sitting in congress at Stratford-on-Avon. In the United States the Progressive Education Association conferred immortality upon him when it invited him to enshrine its essence in one of its special broadsides. His native land, alas, was somewhat less beholden. Eulogy, of course, there was, both for the man and for his work, yet on the run of France's public schools the impact of Cousinet's explorations at the most was slight. Another generation succumbed, and so, indeed, did the Third Republic itself, before France was ready to exert some earnest effort in the renovation of its educational theory and practice.

5

Soon after France's liberation from the Nazis a commission was assembled to make plans for a vast and thoroughgoing educational reform. Headed by Paul Langevin and Henri Wallon, both capital men, the one a physicist, the other a psychologist, the body, after long and patient pondering, issued its report in 1947. What it proposed was nothing less than a complete upheaval of the French school system which, for all its unmitigated centralization, was found to be "vaguely conceived with no clear and definite plan of operation." It was, so ran the indictment, insensible to the everyday world, in particular to its industry and technology, and even worse, to the needs of the French democracy. What was required—to make a start—was to put every boy and girl to school until at least his eighteenth year. Thus summoned, they were to have their learning without paying a single sou—in fact, once past their fifteenth birthday, they were even to be paid a modest wage.

To narrow the cleavage between the school and the vibrant world outside, especially in its industrial and business sectors, all curricula, whether vocational, technical, artistic, or intellectual, were placed on a footing of equal academic respectability. But before a fledgling could engage in such specialties, he had to serve a number of years to ground himself solidly in a general education. Meanwhile, his particular powers and qualities were to be put under the vigilant scrutiny of his masters, besides psychologists, sociologists, and the sundry scientific guides and counselors who conduct the current pedagogical enterprise. If, after all this, he was well regarded and still of a resolve to commune with the higher learning, the door was open. Not only was higher education reserved for those of a demonstrated competence, but since at bottom they were at work in the advancement of knowledge and—so it was predicted—thus serving to enhance the commonweal, let them, like any other men of honest toil, be gratified with a salary.

The report took the critical measure of a number of other matters. To cite only an outstanding few, the school was out of communal touch; consequently, the transactions executed in, say, the schoolrooms of Paris were pretty much like those in some vineyard village in Burgundy or in some herring-scented hamlet on the Atlantic littoral. As for the teachers' methods, issuing as they did from the assembly line of the national normal school, they were, like the legendary peas, all more or less alike. What was needed was a greater leeway for a master's fancy, a chance to experiment, and a learning by doing rather than by rote. Finally, less stress should be placed on academic tests and examinations, so often dreadful and inhuman, and more, per contra, on the student's achievement in school.

The Langevin proposal ran into powerful squalls, and it was not adopted. The reasons are plain enough. Run your eye over its recommendations, and you will find behind them not the realist, but the romantic. What ailed so many of its recommendations was their remoteness from an old though by no means impotent tradition. To put the secondary education of France's nascent plasterers and plumbers on all fours with its future Platos on grounds of democracy seemed to many not only bizarre, but a violation of the academic canon. The suggestion that students ought to be placed on the national payroll was enchanting, to be sure, not only to the young, but to their fathers, stripped financially by six years of war. But to a nation which was low in funds, and which was struggling to get on its economic feet, the proposition was little more than a sweet illusion. Even on the subject of reforming the prevalent teaching method, there was dissent, especially from the more elderly teachers. Their method, they granted, was old, and even perhaps a bit sclerotic; yet it was also tried and tested, while its younger rivals, notwithstanding the colossal support they got from enlightened pedagogues the world around, were dubious, and to the integrity of France's scholastic standards not a little dangerous.

6

But change there was nevertheless. Compare today's educational scene with that of a generation or so ago, and you will come upon some striking differences. For one thing, a measure was enacted which, by 1967, put every French child under the obligation to ponder and sweat over his books until he was sixteen. For another thing, a rift appeared in what was once a high and impregnable wall between state and church. The breech was effected in 1941, when the Vichy regime granted financial aid to the hard-pressed private schools. Fallen upon by the guardians of secular rectitude, the practice came under the collective assault and battery of Socialists, Communists, and various others of profane leanings.

To put an end to such unseemly dissidence, in 1950 the government resorted to the services of a special commission, a familiar practice in democracies when their statesmen confront hard and, possibly, unpopular decisions. However, through the commission's recommendations the following year saw the enactment of a statute sanctioning direct grants to private schools, whether secular or sacred. There the matter rests, somewhat precariously it is true, for the contention for and against it continues to fever.

There is for yet another thing, the advent of an educational ladder, not, to be sure, of the spectacular reach of the one which adorns and celebrates our own republic, but a ladder, nevertheless, and one which promises to enhance the learner's chance to toil from the lowest rung to those that range above.

To make the completion of a child's primary schooling less agonizing, the general final examination, which for generations had oppressed his forebears, was abolished. Instead, the decision to pass or fail a pupil has been entrusted to the judgment of his teachers, superintendents, and a board of advisers.

Gone too is the advanced elementary school, which had proffered its useful service for more than a century. Raised to the higher order of a secondary school—the so-called *collège moderne*—it takes its place side by side with the laureled *lycée* and *collège*. A similar rank and dignity has been conferred upon the out-and-out vocational school. While the christening party was glossing old schools with new names, it proceeded to elevate the secondary technical school to the status of a *lycée technique*.

To encourage more primary school graduates to continue their studies in the secondary learning, the French have devised a *cycle d'observation*—an observation group, in common American. This allows a child to try his hand in the basic secondary school subjects for a couple of years during which, needless to say, his efforts undergo a hawklike scrutiny and, true to the French academic way, a mountain chain of testing. Rather curiously, before the die is thrown to decide a youngster's educational future, that is, whether it is to be economic, technical, or general, parents are given a chance to express their hopes and predilections.

More astounding to the lovers of the old and cherished has been the appearance in the secondary school of a cautious dalliance in progressive education. Known as the *classes nouvelles*, the venture embraces progressivism's familiar looseness of gait and goal, with stress aplenty on the pupil's self-development, creative work, cooperative group spirit, study of the communal culture, an amicable rapport between hearth and school, and so on to small classes and special teachers, besides a miscellany of experts to render counsel. The *classes nouvelles*, so disdainful of French academic tradition, and hence esteemed by not a few as suspect, are in the nature of an experiment, seeking to let some light and fresh air into the secondary school's dust-beladen conservatism. The participants are volunteers, and they number only 20,000—a mere dewdrop, in other words in the enormous sea of French secondary learning, which, for all the wistful pining of liberal parents and pedagogues, continues to be heavily barnacled with intellectualism.

Changes have also been visited upon the examination for the baccalaureate, the *bachot*. To begin, the test now vouchsafes a place to the technical subjects as well as the old-time literary and scientific standbys. The herd of baccalaureate seekers has steadily become more numerous, rising from a mere 50,000 in 1930 to more than five times as many in 1962, and an anticipated 400,000 in just a few more turns of the years. In fact, the way the tide has been running, certain soothsayers have offered the opinion that by 1985, at least forty-five of every one hundred Frenchmen will possess the coveted bachelor's gaud. To cope with this burgeoning mass, the authorities have resorted to screening it through the fine mesh of a "probationary examination," administered locally, which, for the survivors, is followed by the customary written examinations. To make these somewhat more humane and bearable, they now confine their probing to two days instead of three or even four, as used to be the case. The oral examination—*the orale de contrôle*—remains, as heretofore, the last hurdle in youth's mad scramble for career, standing, and success.

Like some other advanced and enlightened folk, in recent years the French have felt powerful tremors of discontent in their shrines of higher learning. In May 1968, to cite the supreme example, Parisian students engaged in street rioting, roughhousing the public, battling the police, and seizing and occupying a part of the French capital. From Paris the disturbance mushroomed to other groves, thence to the factories, and when presently labor walked out on strike, the French government wobbled. The explanations of all this uproar and fracas have been numerous, some emanating out of Marx, some out of Freud, and not a few from the mouths of current moral and social sages. For the historian, it goes without saying, the event is too proximate to his presence to allow him to appraise it with ample elbow-room for a full historical perspective—nevertheless, some of its roots display themselves plainly enough. They reach back to the early 1950s, when France, groggy but triumphant, emerged from its nightmare with the Nazis, and enrollment in its universities began to rise and swell beyond all expectation. The upshot was a dreadful bulging of their classrooms, with not only a correlative lack in physical space but, worse yet, a depressing insufficiency of essential equipment, from chairs in the library and books in its stacks to thermometers, microscopes, radiometers, and suchlike paraphernalia of precision in the labs of natural science.

Of all this the generality of France's professional savants took scarcely any note—their greater number, indeed, maintained, as they always had, a statuesque detachment from their students. Similarly, they continued to enact their ancient preceptorial rite, as they had since time out of mind, which is to say, they filled their students' ears with an effluence of lectures, some of them not a little stale, and even fetid, from years and years of unaltered substance. For students, moreover, with more important things to do than to give such sodden talk an earnest ear, often enough their professor's harangues were readily obtainable in verbatim replica from a friendly booklegger, so to speak. A base and devious practice? Without a doubt. But for the student, nevertheless, a very helpful service, since most professors based their examinations on the content of their lecture-hall recitals.

That French students are examination-ridden is hardly a secret. They are harried by the ordeal of their baccalaureate tests, which for all their recent alleviation, continue to inflict heavy—one might well say massive—casualties. Once admitted to a center of the higher learning, the aspirant for advanced letters again runs head-on into the examination anthropophagus. So stupendous is its appetite, it devours more than half the students before they ever snare a degree. Organized and controlled by the state, which is saying, a centralized bureacracy with headquarters in Paris, the examining mill grinds with terrific and terrifying efficiency. Surely, it is no cause for wonder that during their short ascendency in 1968, when student insurgents occupied the universities, one of their first acts of jurisprudence was to do execution on the examination system.

There have been, of course, yet more complaints—the writ of charges, indeed, runs to an appreciable stretch, as witness just a few examples: the university offerings are too confined; the requirements are too corseted to facilitate individual thinking; professors are too wrapped in their own specialized microcosm, and they evince little or no concern for its relationship to other realms of knowledge; the bulk of students are drawn from the middle and upper bourgeoisie, namely, the social and economic haves, but hardly ever from the less lustrous have-nots; students, whatever their place in the world, have no say in making the rules under which the university expects them to live and work and even suffer; finally, so bogged is the higher learning in the quagmire of tradition, it ignores the needs which weigh so heavily on present-day society. Academe in France is, in truth, the world with the backward look.

It is only fair to remind ourselves that not all of France's men of higher learning are myopic. Again and again some of them have risen to bawl for reform. In 1958, to come to cases, France's director general of higher education urged the development of an independent and creative mind as a reasonable and proper aim of university education. Two years later a national commission put forth its Rueff-Armand Report which, among other things, declared for a greater attention on the part of the seminaries of higher thinking to the pressing needs of the everyday world. To these and other promptings there has been some response. There has been, in illustration, a modest augmentation in the number of universities—seven new ones having come into being since 1963. The curriculum, too, has been favored with a somewhat greater breadth, with courses of study, for example, leading to a new degree in the applied sciences. Finally, there is evidence, small but palpable, of an effort to grant greater support and sustenance to such traditional academic untouchables as technology, sociology, business science, journalism—even, in fact, such spanking younglings as demogra-phy and population study. Unhappily, the chasm between the government's promises and its deeds remains unbridged—such is the way of politics. Spurred, moreover, by radical activists of various political sects and dogmas, French students on the whole are convinced that the reforms, such as they are, are too little and—who knows?—they may well be too late.

The crushing blow dealt the Revolution of 1905 did not put an end to Russian dreams of better days. On the contrary, when the government reneged most of its pledges for reform and embarked instead on a policy of gross and obstinate reaction, the revolutionary gentry stole back to their murky recesses to hatch vaster and deadlier schemes than ever. These reflections took much of their hemlock from Karl Marx's *Das Kapital*. Put into circulation in 1867, less than a decade after Charles Darwin's *On the Origin of Species*, the Marxian lucubrations were destined to become an even greater disturber of the peace. The intellectual stream pumped into the cataract of *Das Kapital's* 2,500 pages springs partly from Hegel's philosophy of state evolution, partly from Darwin's theory of biological evolution, and partly from the speculations of the so-called "utilitarian economists." Into this blend Marx injected his own dogma of an inevitable and inexorable "must."

This argument, stripped of its verbal thicket, is simple enough. Did certain significant social and economic events mark the days of generations now gone to dust? Then, as surely as x leads to y, they are but the causes of events which must follow. Thus persuaded, the father of *Das Kapital* addressed himself to the task of putting into plausible and ingratiating form his picture of tomorrow's better world and—more important—of laying down the precise prescription to bring it about.

The picture, taken by itself, was scarcely novel. Other messiahs, mostly of a utopian socialist faith, had essayed its main lines before. What gave Marx's gospel a new and singular pungency was its formulation of strategy, tactics, and method necessary for the attainment of the world of his vision. In its essence, his formula called for the rise to power of a small party of Communists specially schooled and steeled for service of the most relentless sort. The revolution's shock troops, they were charged with overpowering a country's masters, and working their will on its entire population by seizing control of its means of transport and communication and of all its vital resources, which would presently be disposed of in accordance with the blueprint of the party leaders. The day would surely rise—so Marx gave the world to understand—when the class system, already sorely beset, would go to pieces; when social inequalities would vanish like the morning dew; and when the class system would "wither away," leaving behind it a classless and, presumably, happy human brotherhood. Preaching his gospel with a fervor and a certainty scarcely matched since the Apostles, Marx proclaimed the imminent collapse of Europe's capitalistic order. When at length its last bells began their knell, if the workers of the world were solidly and effectively organized, the keys to the millenium for which they had sweated and suffered would unfailingly be theirs. Spontaneous insurrections—as witness the spasms of 1905—were disingenuous and predestined for failure. The eventual revolution, Marx let it be known, would be executed by a trained and disciplined revolutionary party acting through the workers' own associations.

Thus the main Marxian contentions. From the day their author let them loose they have set men to clashing wherever they have adverted freely to a consideration of the nature of organized society. Marxism has been derided, denounced, and damned; at the same time it has been lauded as the fairest creed the human mind has ever conceived. From its assumptions communist parties have sprouted all over the earth; and on its premises Soviet Russia made its advent. On the other hand, countering the Marxian revelation are powerful arguments from modern psychology, sociology, and organized religion, from newer historical data and interpretations, and from economic, technological, and scientific developments about which Marx, for all his high gifts, knew no more than Socrates.

2

The First World War touched off the Russian Communist upheaval. On the heels of the imperial collapse in the field and a separate peace with Germany in 1918, there followed three years of the goriest carnage known in Russian annals. Embattled at home, and obliged in the midst of their revolution to fight off their foreign antagonists, at times on more than a dozen fronts, the Communists managed to come out of the ring battered and groggy, but nevertheless on their legs. The program they now proceeded to put into service called for the swift and thoroughgoing communization of every important phase of Russian life. Bottomed, as one might expect, on Marxian precepts, the ideology which inspired it fell under a dozen or so captions, all more or less hanging together.

There is, to begin, the principle of dictatorship. "We are not liberals," the Communists informed the world. "We put the interests of the Party above the interests of formal democracy."

Arm in arm with this tenet strolls the corollary of a single-party rule. Numerous parties, it is held, are but an artful camouflage, designed to beguile the unsuspecting masses and the moony liberals who would save them, while behind the screen the actual dictatorship of the vested interests operates.

The Communist must be militant everywhere, and ready at all times to fight for his principles. Until the class foe has been obliterated, peace remains a fiction, an ephemeral moment at the most, in the total and engulfing struggle of "worldwide revolution."

The virtuous Communist must be a man of action. The shroud of sloth, so disabling to Russia's prerevolutionary folk, must be shed once and for all. Henceforward, "all citizens must labor for the common weal as the dictatorship directs."

On some tomorrow, so ran the Communist prediction, Russia would become a classless society. Unluckily, until the capitalist and bourgeois classes have been totally liquidated, that day of days must be indefinitely postponed. Meanwhile, class prejudices must be kept in flame "to prepare the proletariat for the coming and inevitable struggle."

A high place, needless to say, was reserved for the worker. The common man, as it were, of the Communist scheme of things, he is the producer of the necessities of the national life and prosperity, and in this capacity he alone has a right to reach into the national breadbasket. By contrast those who do not produce, which in the Marxist lexicon of useless mortals includes the capitalist, the bourgeois, the merchant, the clergyman, and similar figures—all in former times men of more or less consequence—have fallen into contempt, for they are parasites who maintain themselves by the labor of others.

Ideologically, the first Communists broke with religion, organized or otherwise. Consequently, the church, for centuries the state's powerful and at times even dominant consort, was stripped of its secular powers and prerogatives. From now on the clerical emprise must confine itself strictly to the shadowy realm which lies beyond.

The Communist citizen must at all times be political. To such a purpose he must be rigorously drilled in the cardinal articles of the official political doctrine from his kindergarten freshmanhood to his last day at school. In addition he is to be constantly worked on by the press, the screen, the radio, and similar conditioners of human behavior.

Did Communist leaders put a great store on the principle of dictatorship? Then by the same token, they had no use for individualism. Wherever it has been allowed to function freely—thus the essence of their argument—it has degenerated into a scramble for selfish gain and, hence, into the exploitation of the weak by the strong. For individual enterprise the Communist has substituted collective enterprise.

The Marxist raised his glass not only to the coming of the classless world, but to one unfenced by national boundaries. But as in the case of the one, so in that of the other, its arrival would have to wait for the triumph of the worldwide revolution. Meanwhile, the principle of non-nationalism was to be given application within Russia itself. Despite the czars' long and pertinacious effort to Russianize their polyglot people, when the empire vanished, its stupendous domain was still what it had ever been, namely, a crazy quilt of nationalities, harboring cultures of immense diversity and flabbergasting the ear with a babble so vast and varied that it strains the imagination. Instead of clamping a common language on all, on ground of national interest, as has been the custom in pretty nearly all the national states, the Soviets allowed their heterogeneous nationalities not only to jabber in their native idiom, but to resort to it in their daily sessions at school.

Bracketed with the nonnational principle is that of the "international mind." Through its employment, communism, which envisions itself as international, undertook to forge the mind of the worker into a single and solid bar of iron to the end of promoting the class struggle in every land and thereby hastening the appearance of the classless and nationless workers' world.

In its infancy Communist Russia gave its support to the principle of the complete equality of the sexes. Akin somewhat to the Platonic practice in the imaginary Republic, the discriminations placed on woman on the mere ground of her sex were brushed into the discard. Put into service in the schools, this signified the end of male priority. Not only was the fair sex to entertain the same academic rights and privileges as the strong sex from the nursery to the highest possible learning; the two were even to be chambered together. Such progress was ordered for all Russians, save only those in Central and Southeastern Asia, who are preponderantly of the Moslem rite, where such public integration of the sexes was regarded as unseemly. There, in the name of decency and decorum, separate elementary schools were decreed. It is only fair to add that in the flow of time and after considerable second thought, the principle of sexual equality, like so many of the Communist ideological canons, was given some qualification and amendment.

For all the Marxian hope and confidence, as the Soviets took on years the state did not "wither away." On the contrary, it bulged with vital sap, and as the thirties gave way to the forties, it had increased to an almost incredible heft, requiring the labor and service of thousands of bureaus and a herd of governmental functionaries so vast that it put the older and experienced bureaucracies to shame. Communist Russia exhibits not only the familiar ministries known to political science, say, those trading in foreign affairs, finance, war, and so on; it has also thrown up many new and singular ones, such as—to skim only the surface—the Ministry of Grocery Supplies, the Ministry of Cinematography, the Ministry for the Fish Industry of the Eastern Areas, and the Ministry for the Fish Industry of the Western Areas.

Though Marxists talked with great heat of the coming dictatorship of the proletariat, in Communist Russia its materialization has been quietly deferred. Now, as in the beginning, the reins of authority are in the keeping of the Party. Even the preferment promised the worker has run into shallow water, the nation's choicest rewards going to the Party's high and mighty, the armed forces, and of late, the wonder workers in experimental science. Taking one with another, the current run of Russian workers, male and female, enjoy a more prosperous and respectable life than their forefathers of czarist memory. Stand them beside their comrades in the military, however, and their conditions at once begin to dim. The rewards they net are less numerous, the victuals they eat are in shorter supply, and their living generally is on a lower plane. The knaves of capitalism who once racked and rooked them have long since gone, but not their methods—at any rate not all of them. Indeed, some of their favorite devices, for example, production speedups and automation, are well regarded in high places and even put into daily service.

Although the rosy dreams of the sainted Karl have not come true—at least not yet—this is not to say that the U.S.S.R. has been neglectful of what the West designates as progress. It has hopped and skipped ahead, notably in the domain of the material, in medicine, science, technology, and public welfare, where with bold, sharp strokes it has cut through the tangled web of old and unrealistic traditions. In the nonmaterial realm it has attained no such virtuosity. The sempiternal, earthly dilemmas which moved Tolstoi and Dostoievski, and—to drop several flights—Gogol and Goncharov, remain scarcely plumbed. The men of letters who currently practice their art, brushed though some of them have been by the kiss of genius, cannot exercise their creative powers without restraint. If, for all that, they occasionally try, they run the risk of being professionally gagged, or even jailed, or sent on leave to Siberia. Their primary task is not to yield to the impulse of self-expression, however compelling, but to disseminate the Communist doctrine. As for the tonal art, there is no blinking the fact that their foremost masters, of whom Khachaturin, Prokofiev, and Shostakovich have risen to celebrity the world around, are graced by a tremendous gift, and that their finest works are in a class with the best of Russia's giants of the past. Yet even they, for all their power and renown, have had to hear unpleasantly from their commissars, not for deficiencies in their art, but for flaws in its Communistic rectitude. The truth is that under the hammer and sickle ideology swallows the creative artist.

But the sweep and direction of the Russian line has not always been straight ahead. At times, in truth, it has been as shifty as that of a parlor magician, and as baffling. Where the original Communists called for an absolute equality of the sexes, that proposition has since their time been discreetly watered with "ifs," "buts," and "whereases." Where once the comrades fevered for quick and easy marriages, and for divorces no less swift and simple, they now put on the brake. Where once abortion was as permissible as the plucking of a wart, it is now for the most part under interdict. Did the Soviet founding fathers blast the influence of religion and declare for the unfrocking of every priest? Then their successors permit houses of worship to be open and priests to have their moments. Did Lenin and Trotsky, and—for a spell—even Stalin exalt the virtues of a nonnational scheme of things? Then Russia has succumbed to the national pox, and is today as nationalistic as the lands its first statesmen reviled.

In one outstanding respect, however, there has been no change. Though the ebb and flow of the political tide has brought forth shifts and even about-faces in policy, communism still cherishes the idea of a worldwide revolution, and the rise thereafter of a single Communistic world society. When the revolution failed to fructify in 1918, as most of its partisans were sure it would, they undertook to render it some prodding. For this purpose they launched the Third International in 1919. Over the years it has changed its guises, and during periods when communism itself was in serious trouble, for example, in the Hitler heyday and the Second World War, it has even suspended its operations. But its purpose has never altered. Now, as in its youth, it still seeks to hasten the "inevitable" revolution by agitation, propaganda, infiltration, and similar troublemaking tactics.

3

Late in 1917, while the Communists were warring with their enemies both at home and abroad, their superiors gave notice of an imminent overhauling of Russian education. Framed against the Marxian ideology, the new schooling, whether low or high, was to be a state monopoly. Charged with making the young into correct and upstanding Communists, it was to be free, compulsory, and 100 percent secular. To put such a gigantic venture into successful operation, it was important, as its partisans were at pains to note, to train a new body of teachers who were at home not only in their subjects but in their craft as well and, perhaps more important, of a habit of mind which was resolutely and incontrovertibly Communistic. Finally, Russia's new education, unlike its czarist forerunners, was to enjoy a generous underwriting from the state treasury.

Needless to remark, difficulties of immense magnitude bore upon the carrying-out of the government's proposal. The fact is, during the four years following its public announcement, the Communists were too busy fighting off their foes to give much thought to some uncertain tomorrow, however marvelous the promise of its blessings. When at last the blood-letting stopped, the Soviets were beset by war's inevitable hangover, and especially by a shortage of essential materials, and even more by a lean and famished purse. School reform, consequently, did not leap merrily ahead. Nevertheless, as the years unfolded and things turned somewhat better, there were unmistaken signs of its presence. Not only were the young being marshaled into school from one end of the land to the other; even their elders, for the most part innocent of the written word, were being put upon to learn their ABCs. Scarcely less astonishing was the construction of an educational ladder, state operated, of course, and reaching from the nursery for three-year-olds to the lofty ridge of advanced research for men and women in their beginning twenties. Though toiling up the ladder involved the payment of no fees, general access to it was permissible only on the lower rungs; for any traffic higher up, students had to be specially appointed by the government.

Starting from scratch, Communist educators were eager to make the new education as up-to-date as their science allowed. Put into their own parlance, it called for a stress on socially useful labor, a close connection with everyday living, a study of nature, and the development of a materialistic outlook.

In its cradle days Communist schooling, for all its Marxist beat, was instrumented on the delicate strings of progressive education, much admired at that time even in capitalist schools, and notably in our own republic. All the well-known chords resounded, from learning by doing to the project method—even, in truth, student self-government and no final examinations.

It is only fair to state that not all Russian schoolmen were carried away by the rush for the new pedagogy—some, as a matter of fact, professed to dislike it powerfully. But in such combats of controversy, the government, which is to say the Party leadership, had the final say, and its inclination at the moment ran strongly toward the progressives. Even so, there was no unanimous leaping to its cue. Not only did the wailing and moaning persist; presently, misgivings on the subject were even fretting Party sessions.

Against the new ideas towered the ineffaceable fact that their main distillery was the United States, a land peopled by stockbrokers, hardware dealers, vegetable vendors, and other such profit-minded men, all devoted more or less to Rugged Individualism and America First. The new method, concluded Bubnov, an expert in pedagogics and a well-regarded Communist, was "designed to educate an individualist able to stay afloat in a society based on competition." Even graver was the discovery that in actual schoolroom practice, the progressive pedagogy made for intellectual shoddiness. In the Don region—to cite just one example—official searchers came upon a host of pupils to whom reading and writing remained a mystery—who, in fact, were at a loss to copy a simple sentence without making a mistake. When time and again similar unearthings were made in other haunts, the new methods fell more and more suspect, and when presently they began to corrugate even Stalin's august brow, their days were numbered.

The first blow fell in 1931 when the Central Committee of the Communist Party swung its ax. Pretty soon other blows fell. First, the steady use of standard textbooks was ordered. Next, geography and history were to be taught "systematically" with a plentiful stress on facts. Next the project method and similar darlings of progressivism were shouldered out. From now on—thus the official writ—"the accepted form of teaching in the elementary and secondary schools must be the classroom recitation." Over the railing too went the progressive premise that the teacher's role was essentially that of guide and counselor. Beginning forthwith, the authorities told him, his duty was to impart knowledge "in a systematic and sequential way." By the same token, pupils were to apply themselves industriously to their lessons, to do their homework regularly, and to hold themselves ready at all times for a test, whether scheduled or impromptu, and for a final examination bristling with difficulties. Gone too was their pleasant dalliance with self-government. The young, they were informed, were in school to do their work and to obey the rules. To this end, full constabulary powers were restored to their master. When, despite his art and science, his efforts failed, then as a last resort wicked pupils could be expelled.

Meanwhile, the wind came sweeping down on another front—the science of child study. Known to Russians as pedology, it occupied itself with scrutinizing "the child's . . . development under conditions of a definite social environment." The new science made very fine weather of it, and when the Soviet fathers undertook to remake their schools, they assigned a prominent place therein to its professors. Not only were they expected to apply all the yardsticks and plumb bobs familiar to psychologists everywhere; they were also put upon to prescribe special educational treatment of such children as, in the light of pedagogical science, were in need of it.

Although in enlightened progressive lands such practice has long since been granted approval, in the Soviets it set schoolmen to gnashing their teeth. What alarmed them was not so much the sudden upsurge of a new and untried science as the high deference given to it and, even worse, the making, all too often, of their own work subordinate to that of the pedologist. The years, nevertheless, brought the teachers no relief. Instead, they saw the pedologist briskly bounding ahead, expanding his operations, testing and charting the qualities and growth of his subjects on a more lavish scale than ever. Then, of a sudden, in the thirties his science, which only the other day had made him a man of national distinction, betrayed him, and his fall was even swifter than his rise. What undid him was not the teachers' collective bile, but his proposition, unchallenged for a decade but now suddenly pounced upon, that the quality of tomorrow's adult is determined, not by his childhood surroundings or even his education, but by his natural powers and capacities. Such a proposition, reported the discerning Professor Voskressensky, was plainly "a bourgeois philosophy," and even more unfortunate, it was "contradictory to Marxism." Other alarums brought the Party's Central Committee galloping into action. All pedologists, whether experts or mere bunglers, were put under taboo, their activities outlawed, their experiments, however promising, discontinued, and the use of intelligence tests strictly forbidden. At the same time the teacher was issued a reassuring reminder that "the educator can direct in any direction the consciousness and behavior of men," and that in the making of tomorrow's up-and-doing Russians, he plays an integral and capital part.

That molding and conditioning was begun soon after the child was housebroken. Articled at the age of three to the care and keeping of a nursery school, he was introduced to the simple elements of self-care, for example, cleansing his face and hands, transplanting himself into his garments, and consuming his victuals in a safe and civilized way. As he increased in years and size, he frequented the outdoors, at times alone, but more often in congress, investigating its flowers, its pebbles and its boulders, the familiar birds and beasts, and the more law-abiding subjects of the insect world. Later, as his wisdom grew, he transferred his attention to the human world, dropping in on cobblers, plumbers, machinists, and similar proletarians, and wherever possible, on the neighborhood collective, whether farm or factory. Betweentimes he sketched and warbled, and waved his arms and legs in dance. After his seventh birthday he was pressed into more arduous service. He now addressed himself to the three Rs, and even, in humane and scattered doses, to grammar. In addition, he was drafted for the lighter forms of useful labor. He helped to bring in the harvest; he toted lunches to workers; he assassinated potato bugs. At all times, of course even when he was a toddling freshman at the age of three his psyche was imprinted with the message of what it means to be a good Soviet Russian.

Training and indoctrinating the tender young is, of course, no novelty. It was on hand, doubtless, even in the remote backward of faded time. In civilized times the Spartans, it may be recalled, gave it a vigorous workout, and after them the Romans, and after them others too numerous to be recounted here. On psychological grounds, the business makes sense, and of this the first Communists were aware. But there were other reasons for declaring for a national nursery school. There was, for one, the fact that women, delivered from the caste and condition of domestic servitude, turned their back on the family kitchen and the laundry to join the ever-lengthening line of labor. By the thirties, the Russians tell us, more than a million of their women were in its ranks, and after that, when the land's industrialization began in earnest, they were joined by many more. Meanwhile, however, the eternal laws of biology were not repealed, and consequently the family did not wither away. And so, as mother followed mother into the mill or some other socially useful endeavor, tending and rearing their progeny became a concern of the state, and to this purpose the nursery school directed its major effort.

Behind the enterprise, however, there bulked still another reason for its being, no less powerful and, at bottom, grim and not a little foreboding. War had spawned its usual horde of orphans, and so had several famines. The free and easy mating and divorcing entertained and encouraged during the Soviets' younger years had lengthened the melancholy train of shattered children whom life had, so to say, mislaid. Their number ran into the thousands—precisely how many nobody knows. But that they needed succor and salvaging was plain, and for such service the nursery school was singularly and magnificently equipped.

The wall which commonly rises between what a youngster learns during his day of labor in the schoolhouse and what he takes in after hours beyond its precinct has been effectively leveled in the Soviet Republics. Not only is the learner so heavily laden with homework that his time is severely cut, but he is called upon to invest a substantial portion of what remains in some form of communal service. Thus the theory of public spirit which has been drummed into him in the classroom is given reinforcement in the test run of actual practice. But even here his doings are under the eye and hand of his teacher or various officially designated plenipotentiaries, among whom the youth organizations stand in the forefront. Somewhat like a school system, they are arranged on a lower, a middle, and a higher plane: the Octobrists for the six- to ten-year-olds, the Pioneers for those ranging up to fifteen, and the Young Communists, whose years reached into the mid-twenties. To be a cardholder in any of these associations is greatly prized. It not only bestows an investiture of distinction; it yields certain rights. A pioneer, for example—whether male or female—splashes his affiliation before the world with a scarf of flaming scarlet wreathed around the neck, thereby setting himself off from the not-so-lucky schoolboys and girls who are made to dress in the regular uniform of doughnut brown.

Benefits in plenty befall the organized young. Walk into any of their chapter houses, and you will see chess players, camera fanatics, music makers, book-worms, actors, gymnasts, and athletes. You will, in fact, behold most of the industry cherished by a representative American YMCA, saving, of course, its stress on Christian conduct. But aside from such agreeable and amicable exercise, there remains the overriding business of training the members for Communist discipline. They are expected to be activists, materialists, nonreligious, and productive workers. And they are at all times to maintain themselves physically and morally fit, ready and able to strike a blow for the Communist cause. On the lush and adventurous fancy of the young, such things, as everybody knows, exert a powerful enchantment. Hence it should be no cause for wonder that some nine of every ten of Russia's youths dream hopefully of that bright and blissful day when they will be inducted into the nation's youth corps. Not all, however, are granted admission to its ranks; and of the chosen ones not all are permitted to remain. The truth is that they are forever being tried and tested, and those found wanting are rigorously combed out. The general effect in the end, as in nature itself, is an inexorable movement toward the survival of the fittest—the potential members, in other words, of the Communist Party.

Thus the course of Soviet education as it moved from its nascency in the early twenties into the precarious thirties. Like the state from which it took its origin, it was designed in accordance with the Marxist ideological tenets, which is to say that its essential nature was social, economic, and political. With these fundamental specifications the Bolshevik fathers were in full accord, and they gave them a hearty and repeated endorsement. But the pedagogical and social sciences do not always see eye to eye—sometimes they are even at unseemly odds. Thus things stood as Communist education took on its early incarnation. Although the reigning theme of Soviet governance was dictatorship, the fore-most Communist pedagogical thinkers were far from disparaging the freedom of the child. The upshot was that when Russia's new school fared forth, it arrayed itself in the loose and glamorous vestment of progressive education.

There ensued a period of experimenting, not to say conflict and confusion, during which the Russian schoolmen strove to get their ideas and practice on a firm and steady footing. But their effort was doomed to fail. Even before the new pedagogy was officially adopted it had generated antagonism. But the booings and the beatings it got were flung upon it on strictly pedagogical grounds. Presently, however, the attack was turned into another key. For, as year followed year, what the Bolshevik sages had somehow overlooked became increasingly clear, namely, that progressivism's free and easy fluency and the doctrinaire certainties of Marxist ideology were impossible partners, and that the one seriously disabled the attainment of the other. As a result, progressivism was not only shown the door, but its place was filled by the older and stricter pedagogy, a more likely maker, it was felt, of an instructed and disciplined totalitarian citizenry. Under its new flag the Soviet school system acquired a national uniformity which, save for transitory and unavoidable lapses during the Second World War, it has maintained to the present.

4

The school system which currently enjoys official favor dispenses its knowledge over a span of ten years. Divided somewhat as in America into a lower, a middle, and an upper level, it fetches its boys and girls when they come to their seventh birthday, instructing and processing them thereafter for the next seven years. It then confronts them with a grueling and comprehensive state examination, so rigged that only those of a formidable caliber will pass. For the rest, which is to say the greater portion, school bells chime no more. Only those who break through the barrier of the government's test may leap onto the plane above, where for the next three years they traffic with additional learning, followed by another frontal assault from the examiners, a diploma if everything goes well for them, and—for a lucky few—a card of admission to a university.

Except in the higher learning, the Russian young are spared the trouble of making choices. From their first to their final day in school what they study is precisely prescribed, except for the foreign languages, where an option is granted. The schoolbooks they lug and ponder are everywhere the same, and so is the publishing house which gets them out, namely, the state itself. They are allotted their place on the classroom bench, and they must adorn none other. They are assigned their teacher, and though they find him to be a donkey, or even a gorilla, they must show him deference. When the master makes his entrance, they must rise, and so again when he departs, even if but for a moment. At all times, naturally, they must honor him with their attention. Does he pose a question and issue a summons to one of them to make an answer? Then the nominee must not only get to his feet, but while he discharges his reply, he must stand at strict attention. Thus the respondent must remain until ordered to resume sitting. But even then ease does not settle soothingly upon his frame, for his twenty Rules for Pupils, which he was made to learn by heart, warn him always to sit up straight, with never a slouch or a leaning on the elbow. Should the principal pop in, as principals are wont to do, then needless to say, the boys must promptly rise. The respect for his office reaches to the world outside where, should they encounter him at large, they are to bow politely and tip their cap. For all the rigors of decorum, however, they may not be physically punished. The corrective birch may not be applied, nor even the palm of a striking hand. Teachers are cautioned against the use of raillery, and they may not rant. Instead, let the wrongdoer be made to mend his way by the massed disapprobation of his comrades.

In spite of his eminence the teacher is allowed only the slightest leeway in the practice of his craft. The method he employs is put upon him by the state's highest authority. Impressed with the government's hallmark, it is the "correct" one, and he is forbidden to resort to any other. Even more, he may not ornament it with his art, however tender and alluring. Try as he will, his wings are clipped and he cannot soar like, say, a Huxley or an Osler, or even an Alcuin or an Abelard.

5

The Russian schoolchild begins his learning, as per the immemorial and universal custom, with an introduction to the academic Rs. For four years he concentrates on getting to know his mother tongue. Did an untoward fate place him on this planet in one of the several non-Russian republics, and thereby impose on him a non-Russian mode of speech? Then he is made to perfect himself in his native utterance, both vocally and on paper. But before he is ready to stack away his schoolbooks forever on the shelf, he is required to learn Russian.

Second only to language is arithmetic. Four years of six weekly hours are devoted to its pursuit. If, after that, its laws and operations are still a mystery, the pursuer wins no grace—he must carry on until he reveals at least a passing understanding. In the fourth year come history and geography, not, however, in their American blend of social studies, but each a straight brew in itself, and 100 proof. In addition, in the form of two hours of biology every week the natural sciences announce their presence.

Happily, not all the schoolchild's exercisings take place in the arena of the intellect. There are the usual noncerebral expeditions, but they are for the most part restrained. A couple of hours a week for physical culture, one for drawing, one for singing, and one for useful labor constitute their substance.

In the fifth year, after having been duly examined and officially approved, the schoolboy issues from his larval state to find himself in the middle school, or to use the vulgate of America, the junior high school. All his masters now are specialists, and during the three years allotted them, they will do their best to instruct and edify him in their particular lore. For another three years forced marches will continue in the domestic language, mathematics, history, geography, and biology. In addition, there will be a two-year grappling with physics and a one-year tug of war with chemistry. At the age of ten or thereabouts a European schoolboy is regarded as of sufficient power to brave the study of a foreign language, and though the cultural heritage here is of a bourgeois and even aristocratic origin, in this matter, for once, Communist Russia is not sniffish. And so for the next three years of his middle school existence the learner, whether girl or boy, is set upon mastering some outland tongue, say, English, French, or German. But if his native speech happens to be Georgian or Lithuanian, or any of the non-Russian parlance, then he must apply himself to the study of Russian. As in his primary days, he continues to work his prowess in two weekly seances of physical exercise. He keeps up his practice in the tonal and pictorial arts. And he is made—somewhat more insistently now—to contribute usefully in some form of labor.

If, at the end of his years in the middle school, he is able to placate his examiners, he is granted a three-year extension of scholastic life. He is now of an age which in the American republic would mark him as a patron of the senior high school. There is no letup in his industry. On the contrary, the going gets more and more onerous, and when in the final year a senior reads his program, he tallies no less than a dozen subjects. Three years are reserved as before for the consideration of the Russian language, its grammar, rhetoric, and the outstanding literary concoctions, judiciously selected and carefully edited by the application of the Communist measuring rod. Foreign language demands another three years, and so do history and mathematics. Geography is dispatched in two, and so also biology. But the toll in physics is now raised to three, and similarly in chemistry. During the final year in a weekly sitting of astronomy the student examines the behavior of the heavenly bodies, and in another in psychology he gives attention to the behavior of the human animal.

There remains the nonacademic enterprise. The drawing class continues to hold its session once a week, but now the pupil occupies himself not with what meets his eye and fancy, but with the technical science of the draftsman. He still engages twice a week in useful work. But his singing has ceased.

Thus the comprehensive ten-year school. Its requirements obviously are of the most exigent sort—in fact, to do them full and proper justice, the school performs its operations six days a week. From beginning to end it is free, though with some strings attached. Books and writing materials must be paid for, and so must the uniform which is the required habit of every schoolchild. The school expounds its learning to boys and girls alike, and it draws no line of race or color. Designed, among other things, to speed the dissolution of the class barriers, it has been touted by its partisans as a socially "classless" institution, but—its popularity notwithstanding—sinister whisperings have been floating about that its actual practice not uncommonly belies this claim—that, in sour truth, it bestows favors upon the offspring of Party high panjandrums.

Not all children—even in Soviet Russia—are wooers of knowledge; in fact, even among those of sufficient intellectual dowering, there will be some with a preference for the practical. For their accommodation there are a variety of vocational schools, the so-called technicums. Access to their boons and benisons is granted only upon the passing of a special examination, and only, of course, after the candidate has served his required seven years in the regular academic grove. Hence, the technicums are no mere dumping ground, as vocational schools sometimes are, for those of a second- or third-rate talent. In fact, a large proportion of their custom comes from those who have already plucked the prized diploma of the ten-year school, but who, for one reason or another, are of a mind to become an industrial engineer or a legal worker, or maybe a musician or an artist, or even a ballet dancer. Taken together, the technicums give preparation for some two thousand callings.

It is in the pedagogical technicum—now spoken of as the pedagogical secondary school—that Russia prepares its teachers for service in the kindergarten and in the lower grades. Since it will become their duty to teach all the subjects, they are put upon to rehearse and perfect themselves therein. In addition, they are given acquaintance with the necessary pedagogical lore, including psychology, educational history, and the officially sanctioned method of teaching. Needless to add, they are also given a thorough going-over in the cardinal tenets of Communism, including a two-year study of the history of the Party. To bring all this material to heel, they apply themselves for two years, six to seven hours a day, six days a week. There follow the usual penetrating tests and searching, and for the successful ones, a certificate to teach.

Though the ten-year school fulfilled its function effectively enough, in the mid-fifties that function was somewhat altered. To tone down the strong stress on book learning, the prescribed rations in all academic subjects were reduced, saving only in physics where an increase was prescribed. The time thus released was to be put to use in the labs and shops, and more particularly, in the consideration of the agricultural and mechanical arts and sciences. But even this triumph of handwork over headwork was not quite enough. Too many of the Russian young, it seems, were still disdainful of toiling with their hands—a grave offense in the Marxian lexicon of vice and virtue. To remedy matters, Khrushchev, in 1958, proposed that during his first seven years at school every Russian child should be made to yield more of his time and effort to manual work, and that thereafter only those of the highest brightness should be permitted access to the senior high school. As for the rest—the overwhelming majority—they are to be put in harness in the field or in the factory. Should any of them be gnawed by a desire for more than seven years of schooling, they may seek instruction nocturnally, or they may attain it easily enough by mail. It did not take the Supreme Soviet long to notice how right the Premier was. Pretty soon, in fact, its sages ordered the Khrushchev school reform to be put into effect. With one stroke, thus, the state was able not only to arrest the growing line of those hoping some day to advance into the higher learning, but it also made available a vastly enlarged labor force, a factor which in a labor-hungry land like Russia is not lightly to be dismissed.

Unless his natural gifts have marked him for the pursuit of advanced knowledge at either a university or some other repository of higher education, the Russian is through with his academic grappling when he is about seventeen—unless his examiners knocked him out three years earlier. But whatever his time in life, in one way or another he will continue to receive instruction. It is, in fact, inescapable. The radio, which is an arm of the state, will pump it into his ears; and the press and TV, which are also the liegemen of the state, will drive it to his eyes. Engaging his attention also is a vast planned enterprise, ranging from desk work in a night school to a large variety of mail-order courses. Awaiting him also is a fleet of special schools and classes, connected, say, with a factory or a farm collective, besides cooperatives and miscellaneous communal organizations. On duty, finally—as always and everywhere—stand the library and the museum.

6

Getting into a university involves trial and travail in abundance. Without a record of excellence in the learning down below, not only in scholarly achievement, but in numerous other matters as well, admission to a higher campus becomes unthinkable. In addition, in his various combats with the state examiners the would-be university man is required to perform somewhere in the neighborhood of *cum laude*. But even this is no positive assurance of his ascent into learning's highest heaven—he must suffer the further prying and probing of the university savants themselves. Only after they have stamped him with approval may he proceed into the ranks of the university novitiate.

Happily, there are compensations. For example, unlike nearly all his American comrades in learning, he is not annoyed by a bursar's perennial forays. Not only is his education free, but as he shows signs of progress, he is rewarded with an enrichment of his privy purse. In addition, he enjoys lodgment in comfortable and sanitary quarters. Finally, as long as he is committed officially to the pursuit of the higher knowledge he is exempt from shouldering arms in the Soviet military. Once enlisted on the university roster, the student devotes his energy to five or six years of lecture listening and seminar attending in one of the major departments of knowledge, whereupon, having withstood all assaults and batteries from his professors, he emerges, festooned and spangled, as a university alumnus. Academically, he is a man of surpassing merit, a member, so to say, of the Soviet intellectual honor guard. He is, in short, a man who in the Soviet world may look with a fair confidence to the years ahead. With so much to be gained the pressure for access to a university education has become enormous— so enormous that only the most promising candidates are chosen.

For the many others of a surpassing talent for whom the university gates did not open there remains, happily, an alternative—the institute. Some eight hundred are now in active practice, offering instruction to men and women in almost nine hundred specialties, mostly in the applied and technological sciences, predominantly in engineering of one sort or another, but also in physical culture, foreign languages, and the social sciences, with Marxist-Leninist overtones, of course. Though the institute stands below the university in rank and esteem, its demands are nonetheless exacting. Like their brethren in the more exclusive intellectual temple, the instituters are borne upon by their professors for five to six years before they are diplomaed. In standing and dignity they are next only to the university graduate, akin perhaps to holders of the American M.A., though only to those of the better quality. The bulk of Russia's vast army of engineers and scientists issue from the institute, and so do the specialists who teach their subject in the secondary schools, whether junior or senior.

Like these and the lower school before them, the disseminators of the higher learning open their sessions to women and men on equal terms. Raise the familiar American question, "Is there a doctor in the house?" and of every four who raise their hands three may be expected to be women. Women grace all the professions, even those which were once the exclusive dominion of the stronger sex. They are officers in the armed forces—even generals. They run heavy machines. They dig in subterranean depths. They fly through the air. And of late one has even orbited into outer space.

7

Soviet education, which is now past the half-centenary of its birth, is grounded pretty much on the propositions of the Bolshevik fathers. Unsparingly secular and a state monopoly, it has outlawed all private school endeavor, whether sacred or secular. Attendance at school is compulsory for everyone between the years of seven and fourteen. No charge is levied for instruction, whether in the lower or the higher learning, but only those of a formidable capacity may proceed aloft. The rest are shunted in one way or another into an occupation. To give them aid and training, the state has developed a vast assortment of vocational, technical, and special schools. In keeping with the Marxian teaching, the school is an instrument for political indoctrination, and in keeping with that of the physiologist Pavlov, it is also the conditioner of human behavior. Thus designed, the school shapes its young not for individual ends, but for social and political conformity.

To the credit of the Soviets stand a number of outstanding educational accomplishments. The pall of illiteracy which blanketed imperial Russia has been lifted. Down the chute have gone the educational privileges of birth and wealth which worked so powerfully against the multitude of Russian people. There have been gains too in the preparation of teachers. To practice their craft, school dames and masters must submit to governmental training. Far better rewarded than their imperial predecessors, they are socially well regarded, lower in standing than miners and engineers, it is true, but above the medicos. Their very best exemplars are garlanded publicly with the Supreme Soviet's "Teacher of Merit," a laurel which is prized at least as highly as the *Croix de guerre* in France and the grand cordon of the Paulownia in old Nippon.

The Russians have been extraordinarily successful in their output of scientists, engineers, and mathematicians, so much so that they have caused a stir, and even alarm, in our own republic. The consequence has been a grave reexamination and reappraisal of American education, and some tightening up and overhauling. Of late, as Russians rocketed into the outer void and left their mark on the moon, it has become something of a fashion to cry up the effectiveness of the Russian schools. There is no doubt of their stress on quality, but high standards in education are no historical novelty. They have existed before, and they exist in many places even now. Europeans have cherished them for generations, as they still do, not only in England, France, and Germany, but in all their civilized and enlightened nations, and they attain them, moreover, without clouting the freedom of the human mind and spirit into insensibility.

CHAPTER 31

NEW WAYS FOR OLD

It scarcely needs to be said that the effort to improve educational theory and practice did not draw to a stop with the passage of the nineteenth century. Great though the accomplishments of the Herren Pestalozzi, Froebel, Herbart, and others were, under the fresher and sharper light of later thinkers and searchers, what had served education effectively enough in an earlier day and culture, was found wanting in its unfolding successor. The springs of pedagogic progress bubbled, as usual, from a variety of sources, from philosophy and the natural sciences, besides psychology, sociology, and anthropology, and let it not be forgotten, the dreams and toil of schoolmen striving to perfect truer and, they hoped, wiser ways to educate the young. Let us sample the work and thought of some of these reformers, or at least a few of their eminent paladins, first those who made their mark in Europe, and later in pages farther on, those who stood out in America.

Maria Montessori

When, in the ebb of the nineteenth century, the University of Rome elevated Maria Montessori to its doctorate in medicine, she became the first woman to be thus invested by that seat of learning. Turning her back on the dignities and emoluments of a practice which might some day possibly be hers, she launched herself instead as a teacher of mentally retarded children, spoken of in the blunter vocabulary of her time, as feebleminded. Some years following, a group of these disabled young, subjected to her special methods, managed to pass a public examination in reading and writing with results on a level of those attained by normal children. It was an exhibition which flabbergasted not only her critics, but her most ardent advocates as well. But while Italy's deep thinkers were contemplating this intellectual wonder, its propagator turned her thoughts in another direction. As she saw it, "the boys from the asylums had been able to compete with the normal children because they had been taught in a different way." What would happen, she found herself thinking, if the methods she had used so effectively with "these idiot children" could be applied to normal children? In that event, she was pretty sure, the miracle her friends talked about would no longer be impossible.

Her chance came in 1906 when the directors of the Roman Association for Good Building commissioned Montessori to undertake the organization of infant schools in the society's model apartment houses. A project to regenerate the suffering lower orders—besides fetching its backers an attractive revenue from their investment—each of the society's several houses was to enliven its appeal with a *casa dei bambini*—a children's house—where youngsters betwixt the years of three and seven might gather for work and play under the watch and care of a trained teacher. Apart from requiring their wards to be "clean in person and clothing," and to show the utmost deference to the principal and all others connected with the house, the authorities abjured any further regulation.

2

From the welter of Montessori's pedagogy two ideas rise above the others, the one concerning itself with the growing child's need for freedom, the other with the training of his senses and muscles. Nobody, the doctor insisted, "is free unless he is independent," which is to say, unless he is able to fend for himself without aid or reinforcement from anyone else—a platitude, to be sure, but of pedagogic significance for all that. For if her premise holds water, then it should follow that the less a pupil needs to lean on others, the freer he actually is.

What, one may well ask, is the meaning of all this dither about freedom? Does it impinge, even remotely, on a teacher's daily practice? Dr. Montessori believed it did. "We must respect," she explained, "the first indications of individuality." Therefore, she went on, "it is important to avoid the imposition of arbitrary tasks." Traveling this highroad, a Montessori pupil selects his own educational activities. Once he has announced his choice, he is thereafter not to be summoned by the alert of gongs to lay aside his chosen task in order to attend to something else. In the Montessori scheme of things a youngster presumably learns in accordance with his need and taste. Does he pick his own activity? Then he also proceeds with it at his own pace. There is no instruction in the traditional sense. To be sure, a teacher strides the deck, but she is more the steward than the officer. Her task, says Montessori, is "to put the pupil on the right road to self-education."

Free activity is the keynote of the Montessori score. One discerns it in the absence of the conventional classroom decor. In place of the familiar files of desks and benches in those days unalterably essential to the progress of learning, Montessori's *casa dei bambini* was served by commonplace chairs and tables, dwarf-sized to accommodate their users, who if the mood assailed them, were free to haul them about to any spot that suited them. Every Montessori chamber was enriched by the presence of basins, soap, soap dishes, and similar aids to sanitary welfare, in order to promote what Montessori called "exercises in practical life." Based on the idea that freedom implies self-sufficiency, these exercises sought to train the growing young to master such essential knacks and know-hows as dressing, maintaining themselves clean and tidy, dusting and sweeping, table-setting, meal-serving and the like. Even the youngest in Montessori's infantry were put upon perfecting themselves in lacing and buttoning, whose mastery in days before the present zipper millenium, was prerequisite to a successful and happy life, but which, it is easy to forget, represented a formidable trial to young and unpracticed fingers.

3

The fact that a Montessori child is, as it were, his own chief executive, does not mean, as some critics have decried, that the doctor was disdainful of discipline. But, as usual, she entertained her own ideas on the subject. Discipline, she asseverated, comes through liberty, not by rendering a child "as artificially silent as a mute and as immovable as a paralytic." A person is disciplined "when he is master of himself and can, therefore, regulate his own conduct." In the Montessori seminaries the way to discipline starts not with decrees from above, supplemented, if necessary, by coercion, whether by moral suasion or by application on the caudal sector, but with a task "controlled and regulated by the pupil himself." When he becomes enwrapped therein, he is, Montessori asserted, on the path to discipline. Such interest, she held, is the surest route to concentration, which, exercised on the stage of unforced learning and unhampered action, may be expected to incite self-control, which, in turn, is the mother of independence. Once this is snared, then obviously there is no need for any superimposed discipline.

To attain this goal, Montessori's protégés were granted a generous leeway. Working with their numerous objects day in and day out, they gradually found out how to use them. Actually, it has been said, they learned how to translate their tables from one place to another without stirring up so much as even a pianissimo decibel. Rather curiously, though, in the matter of noninterference even the indulgent doctor found it necessary to draw a line. She would put a slow brake, for example, on "all things we must not do," and "little by little" she would arrest them altogether. Children "with their feet on the tables, or with their fingers in their noses," and suchlike indecencies were under positive prohibition.

4

Sense and muscle training, as has been said, play leading parts in the Montessori performance. Specifically, by "muscular education" the doctor had in mind a set of exercises "tending to aid the normal development of physiological movements, such as walking, breathing, speech . . . and to encourage those movements which are useful in the achievements of the most ordinary acts of life. . . ." To this end she contrived a series of exercises besides an assortment of "gymnastic apparatus," such as wire fences, wooden staircases, and rope ladders, all serving to stimulate physical activity, and helping in the long run to effect Junior's mastery of everyday acts.

In the Montessori lexicon sense, education has been denominated "auto-education," which is saying that, once the learner has come to terms with the general nature and purpose of his project, he is thereupon able to proceed under his own power. Should he, nevertheless, fall into error, he is bound—given ample time—to detect and repair it. But supposing, innocent of his error, he goes blithely on, only to come to grief? Or, realizing that something is amiss, try as he will, he cannot rectify it? Then, says Montessori, this simply goes to show that the child is not yet ready to cope with his chosen task, and so he had better occupy himself with something better suited to his capacity.

To bring about her sensory "auto-education," Montessori devised an array of special objects—"didactic materials," she called them. Addressed to the training of every sense, save taste and smell, they run from simple pink cubes to musical bells and chests of drawers. The freshmen of the group—the three-year-olds— usually began their adventure in sense by trying to fit wooden cylinders of diverse sizes into appropriate cavities in a block of wood—an exercise Montessori catalogued as visual. To develop the chromatic sense the child matched colors. The thermic sense he put to practice by sticking his fingers into bowls of water ranging from hot to cold. His sense of touch he trained by passing his fingertips over some unknown object. In all this sensory enterprise an attempt was made to render each sense autonomous of the others. So that the sense of touch, for example, would get no help from that of sight, the pupil was blindfolded. The sense of hearing was exercised not only in the midst of silence, but in the depth of darkness as well.

5

Dr. Montessori, as has already been alluded to, came into the educational limelight when a small contingent of her retarded pupils emerged in triumph from a public examination in reading and writing. From this and other exper- iences in teaching the slow-witted, she concluded that before a child—whatever the horsepower of his mentality—is introduced to the act of writing, his finger muscles needed to undergo a course of training. To serve this purpose, the rising penman was put upon a batch of geometric figures, tracing their varied shapes on paper, and thereupon giving them substance with colored crayons. True to the Montessori ground rules, his movements were at all times to be free and unforced. He could wield his stylus as he chose, with his left hand or his right, as the Lord God had seen fit to make him. Besides building her child's digital power, his mentor worked upon his senses. Thus, before he ever confronted pen and copybook, he made sensory acquaintance with the members of the alphabet, learning their shapes, like a blind man fingering his braille, from letters cut out in sandpaper and glued to cards. Rehearsing these overtures until he was privy to every detail even in the dark, he awaited—without knowing it—the day when, in Montessori's words, he would "explode into writing," which is to say, that without ever having been formally taught, he will have somehow learned how to write. No less amazing is the time required by a Montessori pupil to conjure up this miracle. From the first gentle massaging of his finger muscles to the final "explosion into writing," the Montessorians have let it be known, a four-year-old child, male or female, of ordinary capacity, can turn the trick in six weeks. Another six weeks or so, and they are generally expert.

As for the writing's time-honored mate, reading, Montessori, after some hard and patient deliberating, concluded that instruction in the first R had better be held at bay until the child had made himself master of the second one. Again, her method was of her own confection, and as in the case of writing, it has evoked some glittering tributes. The run of normal Montessori apprentices, for example, have been reported to be on close terms with reading as early as their fifth birthday. Interestingly enough, the English-speaking young, for all the dreadful phonetic obstacles put upon them by their native speech, have fared as well in learning how to read it as the Italians do their own, which is phonetically far less anarchistic than ours.

6

Needless to say Montessori's claims have been given frequent critical inspection. She herself, in fact, has thus performed. Despite the fact that her learners had demonstrated an ability to read with fluency, she, nevertheless, harbored some doubts. Did the words the youngster quarried from the printed page and minted into oral speech actually mean that he was master of the reading mystery? Did he, in truth, really fathom the message that spilled so freely from his lips? Or was his rendition a mere mechanical tour de force which made no more sense to him than the recital of so much syllabic mumbo-jumbo? Such and other questions the doctor never successfully answered. The one certainty she was able to muster was that in order to bring about proficiency in reading, the best assurance for success was an ' explosion" into composition. Let the novice burst into a piece of connected writing, however puerile, and he will, Montessori was convinced, invest his words with meaning and read what he has concocted with understanding. Meanwhile, however, the doctor had made up her mind that "it is unnatural for children under six, unless they are overstimulated, to read or write continuously."

On the debit side of Montessori's account the ledger displays a number of critical entries. Doubts, for example, have been recorded as to whether her methods, with their ponderable stress on sense and muscle training and their assorted didactic exercisers, lend themselves as suitably to the teaching of the normal young as they do to the retarded. It was the contention of William Stern, a celebrated child psychologist at the University of Hamburg in the pre-Nazi Reich, that the Montessori system was out of step with some of the basic tenets of modern psychology. The stress put upon learning in the *bambini* home, he found unsuited to the nature of children this age, since during this time of the child's life pretty nearly everything he handles or sees "is the object of involuntary learning." Consequently, the Hamburg professor insisted that not only is it a mistake to prepare the child's occupations in such fashion that in each something definite has to be practiced, but it is also wrong "to arrange the occupations in a systematic sequence." Finally, Stern expressed a skeptical opinion of Montessori's insistence on "pupil freedom." The absence of any direct compulsion upon the child, he volunteered, has by itself no pedagogical justification.

7

Scarcely more than a year after Montessori opened her first *casa dei bambini*, her praises were being sung up and down the civilized world. Through Teresa Bontempi, a disciple, her revelation made its way into Switzerland, ever a paradise for good things for the little ones. Presently it was bobbing up in other Continental countries, notably in the Netherlands, and before long it had traversed the waters into the Argentine. In the United States it began to attract attention about 1910. But its progress was sluggish—indeed, some twenty years later the Montessori movement was pronounced to be nearing its last rites. More recently, however, with Montessori schools springing up in various parts of the land, what pedagogic embalmers had once eyed as a likely prospect has suddenly become surprisingly alive. France accorded the system a welcome in 1911 when it established its first children's house in the national capital. England, as usual, approached the new system with diffidence. Its first important gesture, however, bore an official cachet when the government sent Edmund Holmes to Rome to study the schools and to report thereon. Finally, in 1913, there was founded the Montessori Society for the United Kingdom, a guild which, through its prodigious propaganda, labored successfully to advance the Montessori gospel amongst the Anglo-Saxons. Like the kindergarten, the Montessori schools have flourished at their best in lands that cherish human liberty. Conversely, they do not readily take root in authoritarian soil. The Nazis, for one, suppressed and proscribed them. In their Italian motherland the fascist climate proved no friendlier, and after some valiant striving to preserve them, their founder departed for more hospitable environs.

Whatever their faults, real or illusory, Montessori's doctrines left their mark. They gave comfort and reassurance, for one thing, to the augmenting suspicion that the recitation at bottom was little better than an educational treadmill which all too often hampered the development of the individual. Partly because of Montessori's stress on individual learning, thoughtful schoolmen here and abroad renewed their search for better methods of teaching fairly large groups without in the end converting their members into so many human Model Ts. The Dalton Plan and the Winnetka Plan, both of American origin and highly touted in their palmy days, were outcomes of this quest.

The main notes in the Montessori theme, whether old or new, have been echoed not only by her partisans, but by numerous others. Thus one beholds high and respected practitioners among the teaching brethren asserting that there must be no coercion to induce learning. One sees them trying to set ablaze an interest in what the child is to learn. One witnesses them encouraging the learner to be the maker and judge of his own pace. And one observes modern educational thinkers declaring themselves for the idea that the good teacher is first and foremost a leader who gives help and counsel, and even inspiration, to his charges, without finding it necessary to assault the air with orders in order to perform effectively.

Jan Ligthart

Beyond the European mainland the name of Jan Ligthart is scarcely known, yet on the scroll of their illustrious great the Dutch have accorded it an endearing immortality. Its owner was born to poverty—the year was 1859—and had it not been for the kindness and generosity of an understanding teacher, the chances are that his talents would have remained forever fallow, and he would have plodded through this vale shrouded in obscurity. As it was, he was able to prepare himself for teaching, for which he soon betrayed a deep and unrestrained affection. It was an attachment which lasted until his death, and which brought him not a little pleasure and satisfaction. Destiny installed him in the royal palace where for a time he taught Wilhelmina, the future Queen of the Netherlands. His monarchical connection reaped him some flattering notices, and even some estimable offers, but when his job was done, he turned aside from grandeur to serve instead in the public school in one of the poorest sections of the Dutch capital. There he performed his wonders as teacher and principal, and more important, as a tracker of new paths in Holland's worn and rutted public schooling.

Not an innovator like Herbart and Froebel, or even Pestalozzi, Ligthart was nevertheless a convert to some of their fundamental articles. Like the first, for example, he held that interest is the instigator and mover of the learning act, and that without the one the other cannot germinate. Unlike the meticulously methodic German, however, his lowland applauder looked askance at pedagogic science, and he approached its propositions with doubt and disrelish. Like Froebel, he endorsed and upheld the view that by nature the child is an active animal, and that he learns more readily from his own prowling and doing than from having facts riveted into his memory. Again like the father of the kindergarten, Ligthart believed that learning should be inspirited by joy, and that in order to work this miracle, nature uses play as her magic wand. Like Pestalozzi, Ligthart put a great store in learning by observation, but unlike all too many believers, he had the good sense to understand that in instruction words are indispensable. "How," he wanted to know, "can a teacher impart the facts of the past without using words?" But those words, Ligthart warned, had better be something more than a mere concatenation of letters. Does a teacher, for instance, undertake to discourse on Napoleon's adventure in Russia? Then let him begin by putting his imagination's eye upon the scene as it was in the long ago. Let him thereupon fire his utterance with all the art that he can muster, and willy-nilly he will set his pupils' hearts to thumping. So conceived and so executed, his recital becomes "an object lesson as beautiful as one can imagine."

2

Two problems engaged Ligthart's thinking. How, for one, could he unveil the big world within the confines of the classroom to reveal "not only how rich, but how lovely it is?" And how, for another, could he make the school a place where youngsters "learn what they live and live what they learn?" In short, how could he transform the common knowledge mill of his time into a place rife with activity where children learned by experience rather than by rote?

To bring the spacious world into the schoolroom Ligthart began, like Pesta-lozzi out of Rousseau, with the world close at hand, seeking to show his fledglings the parts played in their surroundings by work, industry, gardening, and farming. During the first year pupils were to become familiar with the school neighborhood and with the life of the nearby peasant children. To fortify their learning they dabbled in rudimentary husbandry, making acquaintance with the local flora and raising friendly fauna. The year following they confront-ed the theme of "food and shelter," and advanced themselves into growing grain and potatoes. The next year saw them address their talents to an examination of "building materials and simple geology," with side attentions to vegetables. During the fourth year they concentrated on "local vegetation, soils, and industries, and trade relations with the outside world," with special considera-tion to textiles and foodstuffs. In the fifth year they added starches to their list, besides grappling academically with geography, history, and science. In the last year they bore on elementary biology, physics, and chemistry. During all these many twelvemonths, whenever the weather was agreeable, they busied them-selves in dozens of ways in the school garden. In addition, they occupied themselves in the workshops, pottering and carpentering and even blowing glass. Whatever Homo sapiens was up to in mind and deed—within bounds of rectitude and decorum—became a meet and proper object of study.

Despite his excursions into the domain of the new education with its proposition that in the school living and learning must be interlaced, and its correlative stress on experience and doing, Ligthart insisted that whatever new trails his learners entered upon, they must never cease trying to perfect them-selves in the essentials, especially in the indispensable tools of intercourse of reading, writing, and speaking. Himself something of a virtuoso of the deft and graceful phrase—he was hailed by his colleagues as the "wizard of one syllable words"—he composed a series of juvenile readers which, fresh and sprightly, and full of useful and exhilarating information, were so different from anything then visible in the school-book world as to make them singular. It scarcely needs saying that as a literary artist Ligthart was disdainful of the schoolmaster's age-ridden reliance on rhetoric and formal grammar as the never-failing means to good writing. "We live from habit and not from logic," he chided the guardians of linguistic chastity. What counts in the teaching of writing, he went on, is not to get the young to write like a herd of so many others, but rather to lure them into self-expression. Joy in spontaneous composition, he declared, is the main-spring of a child's desire to write.

3

Ligthart's concern for pupil freedom constituted, so to speak, the bloodstream of his method. Disinterested in what dialectitians, metaphysicians, and even theologians had to say about it, he cared not whether freedom was a pupil's inalienable right, as some of pedagogy's latterday libertarians contended, or whether, as per the orthodoxy of his era, it was a privilege volunteered by schoolmasters to meritorious children, which is saying, tractable children. All he cared about was what his daily classroom rounds had taught him, to wit, that without a fair measure of freedom no child can effectively learn the meaning of human responsibility, whether personal or social. "The health of the child's mind," Ligthart insisted, "and the health of his body are at stake, for these can flourish only in an atmosphere of reasonable liberty." Unluckily, the science of child welfare was then not the hearty thing it is in this, our present, more perfect world, so that what Ligthart evoked from his contemporaries, apart from the applause of a handful of advanced thinkers, was mostly derision.

The warmth Ligthart radiated for children played inevitably on his views of discipline. An unmitigated romanticist, he was convinced that by nature a child is inherently good. Does he, nevertheless, sometimes lapse into roguery? Then the fault, Ligthart was certain, lies in the presence of some intruder. Perhaps the child is in the clutch of some arrant gland? Or maybe his stomach is harboring some subversive invader? Or could it be that his subconscious smarts from some adult slight, real or imaginary? Whatever the cause, the cure for his waylaid natural goodness lies not, as per convention, in a clouting of his gluteus maximus, but in sympathy and understanding. It was Ligthart's practice to woo malefactors with tenderness, a subtle and delicate strategy, to be sure, and one which his brother teachers were positive was calculated to undermine the maintenance of law and order. Rather curiously, though, for all its purported softness, and the occasion ever so often of some anguished inner doubts, in Ligthart's hands the method achieved a triumphant success. It was an exercise of authority, and not, as iron-handed schoolmasters maintained, an abrogation of it.

4

When Ligthart died in 1916, the school he had served so long and so devotedly had attained fame far beyond its walls. A grove which was at once public and progressive, a pedagogic paradox, if ever, in those far more rigid days than ours, Ligthart's school drew the curious in droves not only from the mother country, but from the outlands as well. What they found was the materialization of the progressive's dream, namely, a community of active and contented children at work and play and at their books, a place, in short, of good living where the young enjoyed rights and dignities no less than responsibilities, and where teachers were gentlemen even after the classroom had made them officers. In the educational memory book Ligthart is not mentioned as a breeder of ideas. The few he held, however, were generally of a liberal tone, and he entertained them not to show them off, but as instruments to be employed in educational practice. An artist rather than a scientist or, for that matter, a philosopher, he gave more heed to the whisperings in his heart than to the promptings in his head. There is no pigeonholing such a man, save only as an artist reaching out into the harsh and troubled world and striving to form it into something better. The Dutch remember Ligthart as their Pestalozzi, a veneration born from affection no less than respect. On the stone beside his grave they have inscribed his words, weathered now and worn, but unforgettable. "All education," they remind us, "is a matter of love, patience, and wisdom, and the latter two grow where the first prevails."

Ovide Decroly

Belgium's foremost representative in the ranks of Europe's modern educational reformers was Ovide Decroly. He originated in 1871 in the town of Renaix, and after suffering the customary dressing of the intellect in the secondary school, he made for the University of Ghent to equip himself for medical practice. A diligent student as well as intelligent, he took his doctoral letters to the accompaniment of high professorial commendation, whereupon, reinforced with a slight subvention, he repaired for Berlin to make acquaintance with the newest disclosures of the healer's art and science. Six months or so later Dr. Decroly was back in his homeland, where presently we see him in Brussels hungering for his first paying client.

During his early hospital service in the Belgian capital the fates mapped out the course of his career. His daily clinical inquests brought him in contact with things he had never seen or even dreamed, the never-ending procession, that is, of damaged young, the deaf, the dumb, and the mentally deficient. He saw them come and go—treated, sometimes solaced, and sometimes helped, but seldom mended for more than a passing spell. The sight of these unfortunates moved him and, as in the case of Montessori, a passion to help them presently gripped him, so firmly, in fact, that, in 1901, on the city's fringe, he opened a school for them. There he treated and taught them, ministering to their special needs, and applying the full armament of the most advanced psychological and pedagogical knowledge. Needless to say, the progress of his proteges was slow—still, it was progress. In fact, as the years accumulated, it became transparent that Decroly's undertaking was a success. So well regarded was his work that before very long admirers were beseeching him to apply his imaginative and talented hand to the education of normal children. For a while he paid no heed, but in 1907, with the opening of his Ecole de l'Hermitage, he finally bowed to what had become, if not a command, then doubtless a sore temptation. Henceforward, both the normal young and those not so lucky were to get his attention.

Like many another pioneering schoolman, Decroly founded his enterprise with great and gaudy hopes, but with only a spindly purse to give them form and substance. Yet by marshaling his aspirations with a judicious restraint and, better still, by prevailing upon friendly altruists to make an occasional monetary offering, Decroly succeeded in transforming the school's necessity into a virtue. Consequently, what he had started so inauspiciously in a modest city dwelling, frequented by only a handful of children, was gradually transmuted into a spacious edifice cradled in the picturesque landscape not far from Brussels, with a roster of not quite three hundred pupils reaching in their years from four to eighteen.

2

During most of his maturer years the founder of l'Hermitage disclaimed credit for any pedagogical originality. He was not, he was at pains to make clear, a begetter of educational theories, but rather a tester of such existing ones as fed his fancy, and these in the main carried the liberal's hallmark. His viewpoint was the familiar one of America's bearers of the progressive torch—his apothegm, in illustration, that "education is life through living" might have emanated from the headquarters of any one of them, including such mastodons of the native pedagogy as Drs. Dewey and Kilpatrick. Although Dr. Decroly had discarded the white habit of the medico for the pedagogue's more somber robes, his grounding in medical lore forced itself into his pedagogical assumptions, which he described as "biosocial" and "biophysical." Reduced to simple terms, they run somewhat as follows: (1) The child is a living organism which needs to be taught to live effectively and happily with others. (2) This living organism is a developing entity whose every moment, *ab infantia*, marks growth, however imperceptible it may be. At any given age, say 3, Junior is not exactly the same as at any other age, say 4-1/3 or even 3-7/8. (3) No child is ever a carbon duplicate of any other. (4) Every age of youngsterhood entertains its own interests, and these impinge upon the child's thinking. (5) The child's most prominent activity is sensory and muscular. Duly and properly cultivated, and directed and controlled by the mind, such activity is unfailingly related to all other activity.

3

On this foundation Decroly erected his "good school," visionary to a measure, but an inspiration none the less to all his effort. What are its essential features? Let it be situated, its author began, in the midst of what the child is studying, preferably beyond the city gates in a place where the countryside unfolds, where he can see and hear and feel the presence of nature's immortal spectacle. Such a seminary is of a gentle size; its clients run from four-year-old freshmen to elderly sophisticates in their upper teens; and despite the harsh opinion of Decroly's Europe against the mingling of the sexes in the house of learning, the good school offers its edification to the fair ones no less than to the strong.

As might be expected, Decroly had no liking for the formal recitation, with its morguelike stillness, broken only by the rumble of a talking teacher or a reciting pupil and, perhaps, an occasional stolen whisper. Instead, it placed its confidence in the newer gospel of learning by doing. To such a purpose it converted the old-style recitation chamber into a workroom. Here, with all the attendant din and bustle, activity was the rule, and to egg it on, the room was equipped with chairs and tables, a workbench or two, some closets for tools and sundry articles, shelves and counters, water on draught—even central heating, a convenience found in Europe in those remote and hoary days mostly in the mansions of the rich and in the tonier hotels.

Such a palace, for all its lures and amenities, can, of course, be no better than its teachers. Not only must its masters be thoroughly versed in what they undertake to impart to others, they must also be on familiar terms with the nature of the child, ever complex and often archly elusive. Yet, important though it is for them to know, it is equally important for them to feel—in short, Decroly expected his teachers to be artists.

The good school makes no bones about it: for the fulfillment of its purpose it regards parents no less important than its teachers. Not only must fathers and mothers be made privy to the problems, general and special, which prey upon the education of their offspring; they must also be pressed into service as active aids in forwarding the school's educational endeavor. Towards such a goal it befalls the school to take parents into its confidence.

There is about all this an air of free-and-easiness—but only at the first glimmer. For although the teaching of subjects was no longer on a regulated arrival and departure schedule, with bells a-ringing to announce their coming and going, yet the day's doings were carefully laid out. In the case of the younger children, for example, the mornings were given to rehearsals in the fundamental Rs, beginning *vivacissimo* with play and games and proceeding to a more earnest cerebral effort. Thereupon they were put through a variety of exercises to enable them "to improve their powers of observation." Once these had been improved, the youngsters were given a chance to let loose their built-up steam in bursts of warbling. Thus restored, they were ready to consider their stomachs, which by this time, no doubt, were advertising a growing vacancy. Afternoons were generally reserved for shopwork and foreign languages.

Betweenwhiles Decroly's pupils attended to various chores described in the official lingo as "practical work." Inaugurated during the school's leaner years when the number of its hired hands bordered on zero, the program was retained in later, flusher times on grounds of pedagogy if not economics. Of opportunity for such pedagogic enhancement there was no lack. A sanitary squad, for example, made it its duty to keep the school clean and salubrious. Brigades of junior horticulturists tended the gardens. Others waited on the school's numerous pets, feeding and bedding them, and selling or trading their progeny when they multiplied too freely. Some of the older children took care of the Decroly poultry, laying in grain to victual them, hawking their eggs and chicks, and keeping an accounting of their transactions. Still others, mostly girls, prepared meals, and when the season was right, they embalmed the surplus fruit and vegetables, to await their joyous resurrection on some future table. Even the youngest were set upon to better themselves by rendering some practical service. In truth, like the chanticleer at cockcrow, in a way of speaking, they ushered in the day by setting the breakfast board.

Thus ran the daily train of events. It is only fair to state that it was not rigorously enforced. There were times when a country hike was judged to be more desirable than deliberating on the state of equality of vertical angles, and an inspection of a noodle plant more enlightening than prying into the habits of a relative pronoun. Children, Decroly confided, need to go fishing, to snare beetles and butterflies for collections, and to inspect museums and suchlike depositories of culture.

If Decroly hammered another nail into the coffin of the old-style recitation, then how, one may wonder, did he proceed to teach? The basis of his method, he let it be known, was the so-called center of interest. Divested of its esoteric designation, this resembles what American schoolmen commonly celebrate as the project method, whose main features are dealt with in later pages. What Decroly wanted was a method based on the latest disclosures of psychological science and calculated to whip up the pupil's interest by relating what he was expected to learn to his basic needs. After long searching and even longer pondering, the doctor settled on four distinct types which he identified thus: the need, for one, to eat and drink; the need, for another, to safeguard ourselves against the inexorable elements, such as heat and cold, and study their bearing on the way we live; next, the need to protect ourselves against our enemies, whether human or otherwise; and finally, the need to work and act. Of the aforesaid, each provides a center of interest with substance sufficient, purportedly, for a year of study, the entire quartet occupying the learner for a quadrennium. Like the project method, the center of interest concerns itself with a large and expansive topic that, as the pupil applies himself to its study over the succeeding weeks and months, confronts him day in and day out with the necessity of increasing his specific knowledge and skill in arithmetic, history, geography, language in all its phases, and so on.

Although the liberties Decroly took with the prevalent practice were many, to the traditional curriculum, rather curiously, he offered neither challenge nor resistance. The simple truth is that in this domain the state held a guarded rein. Did the doctor need its sanction to open a school of his own? Then it behooved him, like any other private-school man in the land, to bow to its mandate that he offer instruction in the subjects taught in the nation's public schools. How he taught them—that, as the saying goes, was a horse of another color. In this respect he was free to work his will, so long as his pupils managed to make their way successfully through the examinations imposed by the state upon their colleague learners in the conventional groves of knowledge. In consequence, it was not for the subjects his schools dispensed, but rather for the manner in which they were taught, that Decroly won his pedagogic spurs.

Like Pestalozzi, Decroly was persuaded that all learning—or, in any case, the greater part of it—rests on observation. But he also believed that in order to make the business effective, the child's power to observe needed to undergo systematic training. Like Rousseau, Decroly declared against teaching the young child how to read, not, however, as the Genevan had insisted, because it was the "scourge of childhood," but simply on the ground that no child is ready to make sense of the written ideas of others before having acquired a sufficient supply of experiences of his own.

When at length the reading mystery is broached, the first words and phrases the learners confront relate to what they know familiarly, their toys and games, the school's dogs and cats and other animal personnel, the nearby pond, its carp and frogs and other dampish denizens, and so on. Later, when the pupils' initial bafflement has worn off, their reading material issues from things they have been up to, for example, some special undertaking or a project which may be under way or even a visit to a factory or a call on the burgomaster or the city zoo.

Writing is reading's handmaid. From the first, children learn to write what they read and, better still, to read what they write. Presently, they find themselves confecting simple reports and chronicles which, like their makers, have a way of increasing in heft and beam, until the day dawns when they inhabit entire volumes. As the young grow older, their teachers nudge their creative impulses, and presently we see them concocting tales for their younger mates. When time and industry have advanced Decroly's girls and boys to their last class, they undertake the publication of the school magazine.

The third R, a pest and a plague so often to schoolboys because of its occult abstractions, is approached like its comrade Rs, by referring it to the learner's personal experience, though the main reason for its being continues to be the familiar one of apprising the young "to make precise relationships." To put the pupils on a realistic footing with the subject, they are made to supplement their book learning, like the budding scientist exploring his mystery in the laboratory, with some concrete applications. For a start, they are asked to take their measurements, their altitude and their circumference, the length and width of their hands and feet, and so on, carefully storing their data in their notebooks for further consultation. Pretty soon they are applying their metric stick to whatever is about, ascertaining for example, the latitude and longitude of their classroom floor, the dimensions of its tables and chairs and closets, the schoolhouse itself, the neighboring sheds and dependencies—even, indeed, the schoolyard. From their delvings into measurement the pupils proceed to the consideration of weight. The method is pretty much the same. Every day, for example, the youngster steps on the scale, eyes its testimony, and records the reading in his memoranda. The same courtesy is extended to some of the school's quadrupedal inmates. Subsequently, when the children gather for colloquy, their gleanings, whether in measurement or in avoirdupois, become the subject for analysis and comparison, besides exercises and other enlightenment.

5

When Ovide Decroly came upon these scenes in 1871, the term New Education, or as we say in America, Progressive Education, was still in the womb of time. Some threescore years later when he died, the phrase had not only fixed itself in the pedagogue's professional lingo, but what it represented had taken on the proportion of a movement which at about that time had attained flood height. To its rise and spread the doctor had contributed more than a little, not, it is true, as a creator of any of its special canon, but as an advocate and promoter of its practice. Not only was his name hailed and celebrated throughout much of the Old World, but contrary to the common folklore, he was an honored prophet even amongst his countrymen—in fact, his native city alone had conjured up at least a dozen schools operated more or less in accordance with his doctrine.

The doctor was worthy of his honors. During the better part of his manhood he had driven himself unsparingly to make his dream of the "good school" come true. To such a purpose he had dedicated his Ecole de l'Hermitage. And to such purpose too he had crossed the land and waters, assisting at conventions of the learned and of the laity, disgorging speeches on his favorite pedagogical themes, and leaving a trail of writings which testify, in afterlight, not only to a colossal diligence, but to a sharp insight as well into the educational dilemmas of his era. Unhappily, for those who cannot fathom French, the doctor compounded his lucubrations solely in his vernacular, and except for outside help the light of his star might still be invisible in our great republic. Standing out among such self-appointed publicists was Amelie Hamaïde, a coworker in Decroly's vineyard and something of a crusader for his methods. More than anything else her book *The Decroly Method,* which was rendered from French into German and English, brought the Belgian schoolman to notice on this side of the Atlantic.

Because of it Decroly's work became known and appreciated, if not by the rank and file of American educators, then at least by their progressive wing.

Emile Jacques-Dalcroze

In the Old World, as in the younger one, the successors of the great master pedagogues of the nineteenth century laid a considerable weight on the development of what they were pleased to call a "well-rounded personality." What they sought, as previous pages have already alluded to, was the cultivation of a many-sided person, a small-scale da Vinci, or at least a Goethe, as it were, his body, mind, and spirit humming in perfect harmony—in sum, a well-balanced being, on a good footing with himself and others, and able to contend with life in all its aspects, bitter no less than sweet. Toward such a goal the newer pedagogues spread their light over a spacious realm, applying their thinking to the pupil's pursuit of the traditional subjects, but sublimating his quest with an array of progressive innovations. As is the rule in other lines of human endeavor, the enterprise of the general practitioner was presently amplified by that of the specialist who, though he subscribed to the liberal's confession to its every comma and period, was given, nevertheless, to lavishing his industry on one of its articles to the virtual exclusion of the others. Such fanciers of the particular—to limit our inspection to only two of their more eminent exemplars—were Emile Jacques-Dalcroze and Franz Cizek, the one practicing his art in Switzerland, the other in Austria.

By the keepers of the pedagogical record, Dalcroze, a music teacher in the city of Geneva, has been credited with having invited our attention to the important relationship existing between the tonal art and a person's rhythmic bodily development. The idea, at bottom, was not new. In point of fact, in their heyday the Athenians had prized it highly, and they had even put it into their educational practice, but in the succeeding centuries for one reason or another it had gone down the drain of popular fashion. It remained for the Genevan not only to restore it, but in the process to inspirit it with fresh and lively meanings, psychological as well as physiological.

2

In the course of his adventuring with the young, Dalcroze had observed that of every ten children embarking upon the study of a musical instrument, no less than nine "had no music within themselves." He had also noticed that whenever he was able to infuse them with a sense of tone and rhythm, their progress was appreciably enhanced. They had become—to borrow his own locution—"musically developed human beings." The more he deliberated on this phenomenon, the more he convinced himself that such a condition was the unqualified prerequisite to all musical education. Hence, he presently concluded that before the uninitiated elected to meet the challenge of a piano, a cello, or a tuba, or even to lift his voice in an arietta or two, it behooved his master to arouse and develop in him "his natural bodily rhythms," to enable him to feel music physically within himself.

How did Dalcroze undertake to transform his raw clay into "musically developed human beings?" He began, not as per venerable rite, by drilling their ears and fingers, for in the consummation of a creative tune-maker, he had found such training to be fruitless. Essential instead was "to set free his mental, physical, and emotional capacities." By such a liberation, the Geneva music master hoped to produce an integrated response, one wherein the pupil's muscles and senses, his nerves, will, and emotions functioned in smooth and harmonious concordance. To work this wonder with any degree of certainty, Dalcroze found it necessary to give some earnest thought to the education of the body. It was in major part an untilled field, and save for the aid he culled from the writings of psychologists and physiologists, he had to turn the soil himself. But when his labor was done, the harvest it yielded was something never heard of before, the art and science, namely, of "eurhythmics," a "rhythmic method of gymnastics," which seeks to "develop, by repeated exercises, the natural rhythms of the body."

3

What are the claims of Dalcroze and his eurhythmic tribe? There is, they assert, a palpable increase in muscular control which, in turn, engenders a feeling of physical mastery, and which, per consequence, soothes the writhings of the psyche. Muscles and nerves are made to perform their mystery in harmony, and so are body and mind, thus chasing tensions, and by the same stroke producing "an integration of personality." Rhythm, the Genevan contended, is attainable only in the integrated movement of the entire organism. By frequent exercising there is the possibility of attaining even such a boon as a "muscular memory," which, when it is brought to full flower, effects automatic muscular and mental coordination. A year of systematic eurhythmic training is usually sufficient to allow any pupil of everyday mental and physical dowering to respond to any rhythm ever heard of on this God's green footstool. The lord and master now over his body, mind, and emotions, he is ready, speaking in eurhythmic parlance, "to grow in an integrated way." What differentiates the Dalcroze system from any other form of physical culture is not only its liaison with music, but also its aesthetic pretension. Eurhythmics, its father allowed, bears directly on the development of an appreciation of the good, the true, and the beautiful.

Although Dalcroze conducted his pedagogical explorations within relatively narrow limits, still this put no brake on the spread of his renown. His ideas found support far beyond the Alpine front not only among professional musicians and educators, but among the thinking laity as well. In our own land, ever fertile for the propagation of a new evangel, whether pedagogical or otherwise, the Dalcroze Institute undertook to promote the eurhythmic cause. Besides venturing to improve the rhythmic responses of the general herd of *Homo sapiens americanus*, it also made a point of preparing teachers to give instruction in its specialty. It was not very long before some of the nation's leading teacher-training colleges began to make room for the new art and science. Today, the recognition of rhythmics in one form or another has become, if not the rule, then at least fairly common.

Dalcroze's brief on behalf of transforming music into motion to enable the prospective tonal artist to experience music actively in his inner being, though it has been well regarded the world around, has not escaped the critical barb. Indeed, even among the Genevan's own students—aye, even among his disciples, there has appeared an occasional deviationist. There are some, for example, who have rejected the master's calisthenic regime as too involved and baffling for a youngster's easy execution, and who have therefore modified it to suit their taste. Others—particularly in our free democracy—have held that rhythmic education ought to be less rigidly grounded. Finally, there are those—skeptics, no doubt, one and all—who dismiss the value of rhythmic education as so much buncombe. What they want first and above all is some convincing scientific proof. Meanwhile, however, the ardor of the rhythmists, whether of the Dalcroze orthodoxy or not, glows unabated.

Franz Cizek

While Dalcroze was carrying on in Geneva to ignite a sense of tone and rhythm in his flock of aspiring music-makers through their bodily self-expression, another devotee of the creative specialty was beating a fresh trail in the schools of old Vienna, a city then of gay and self-sufficient folk. Franz Cizek by name, he earned his living as a teacher of art. Fame nodded at him for the first time when his work in the art classes for gifted children was singled out for special praise. In later years, as he shone his lamp more vividly in the School of Arts and Crafts and, while he was about, rolled a log or two for his educational philosophy, the initial nod became a warm embrace. When the Hapsburg imperial hodgepodge fell apart on the heels of the First World War, and the Austrian Republic arose from the shambles, Cizek was summoned by the new authorities to give his help and advice in overhauling the nation's schools.

2

A fevered advocate of what the current pedagogic patois calls "creative education," Cizek toiled over a generation and a half to promote its cause, urging schoolmen to renounce their grizzly impositions and gratuitous regulations. "The lid," he insisted, "must be taken off." Only thus can the child's natural capacity for self-expression be released. Every young one, he announced, entertains an inborn proclivity to express himself through some form of creation. The urge lurks in all of us, and when we are young its spring lies in our surplus energy. Later, when the child's store of energy begins to lessen, his inspiration for creative expression issues from what Cizek called the "spiritual heritage of the ages." Finally, the child's creativeness is borne upon by the world in which he lives. Some youngsters, the Viennese artist observed, are "spontaneously creative," like Schubert, ever cocked to break into a novel melody. Others seem to be so fettered to time and circumstance as to be palsied in their capacity to create. Yet others fluctuate between the one and the other: now they are free-and-easy and now they are bridled. Nor does Cizek's "spiritual heritage" escape variation. It might, for instance, be dormant; or it might be absent altogether. Cases have been known in which it was confused. Is the legacy dormant? Then it needs to be awakened. Is it confused? Then it needs to be clarified. Is it absent altogether? Then, unhappily, until science finds the remedy, there is little that can be done.

3

Residenced in the *Vaterstadt* of Sigmund Freud, Cizek inhaled some of its psychoanalytical vapors, in moderate doses to be sure, but sufficiently heady, nevertheless, to attack his thinking. There are, he declared, two egos in every one of us, one of them conscious, the other unconscious. In the rise and growth of the junior artist, the latter ego is the more important, for it is the one which illuminates the child's creation with its own special qualities. Unfortunately, the conventional school knew nothing about the hidden self—indeed, had it suspected its presence, it would have eyed it with disrelish as an enemy to its purpose, which was, at bottom, to cast all pupils in the same mold. Yet, though it was oblivious of the seductive promptings of the child's subconscience, the truth is that in its insistence that Tom's drawing should look like Dick's and Harry's and the others', like so many blades of grass—all too often the school had successfully snuffed out the child's unconscious ego. Such being the sad case, Cizek appointed himself protector and preserver of the child's inner world, which is to say, his subconscious self. By discreet praise and soft suggestion he tried to help the child to give shape and substance to those ideas clamoring in the dungeons of his subconscience for release. Although the impulse to play freely with ideas and forms in the manner of an artist resides in every child, its presence, Cizek believed, is only transient. Properly cultivated, it might endure through childhood, only to disintegrate and disappear in early adolescence. This being nature's inexorable way, Cizek held it to be essential to grant the child's creative urge the utmost freedom, and to coax and conserve it as long as possible. Then, later, when childhood succumbs to adolescence, and the youngster's subconscious drive to express himself creatively responds to other urges, he will at least have laid the artistic foundation for work in the more formal crafts. Those rare spirits, the odd men dowered with more than ordinary talent, will continue to exercise their creative powers. The tedium and drudgery of endless practice will be their lot as they ache and sweat to strengthen their grip upon their craft. In the end, the road to their fulfillment lies wide open, and—who can tell?—maybe it will also lead to fame and fortune.

4

A man of Cizek's cast of mind could scarcely be expected to hold a flattering opinion of the conventional Austrian school. It was, he let it be heard, a mere assembly line "which manufactured children instead of letting them grow." For all the Viennese love of song and dance and their many connoisseurs of tone, and of the brush and color, the art education which prevailed in their public schools, Cizek insisted, "strangled the child's individuality" and, thereby, his creative impulse. The usual teacher—which is to say the acceptable teacher—tries to mold the pupil's work in the image of his own, and under such an imposition, art as self-expression unfailingly goes down the chute. For creative work, a teacher's influence, Cizek asserted, is bad. In fact, he went so far as to remark that even his own influence, however enlightened it might be, did his pupils harm. "Let children be children," he chimed with Froebel; in short, they do their best creative work—for ill, one might interject, as well as good—when they are left alone. "The teacher," Cizek summarized, "should be a cipher." It was his boast that he employed no special teaching method. "We must let children grow," he said; and in order to do this "there is no better method than the inner god." When this Viennese Pestalozzi went to work amidst his pupils, there was nothing about him to suggest a pedagogic purpose. He came to class, so to say, unprepared, sans system, sans lesson plan, but not, by the grace of God, sans inspiration. Taking his cue from his pupils, he worked impromptu, tapping the golden vessel of their youthful fancy, and enticing them to surrender their thoughts and feelings to the shimmering magic of self-expression.

Cizek's aversion for the old school's authoritarian ways allowed for no exceptions—not even in the matter of discipline. Order and routine were *verboten* in his school, and his pupils labored under no duress; often, indeed, they let loose their creative urge to the sound of a fortissimo racket. The only external aid to the promotion of something akin to order was a recourse to singing, not however, because certain explorers of the psyche had reported that music possessed the power to calm the most savage breast, but because, with Dalcroze, Cizek had found it, as well as rhythmics, to be a brew which was highly palatable to the "inner God."

Cizek's antagonism toward the schoolmaster's tried and cherished formulas was not, of course, the recommended way to win friends and influence people. Nevertheless, so extraordinary were his results that before long they were muffling the outcries of his most malevolent detractors. Progressives, needless to say, whether of the general species or of the specialized creative subvariety, were quick to press him to their bosom. Through their annual convocations in scattered parts of the world, and through their numerous parochial organs, which were printed in the principal languages of the Western world, the work and thought of Franz Cizek was presently being talked about in latitudes and longitudes far from the city on the Danube. As usual, the curious, whether skeptical or merely nosy, trekked to the ancient city to catch a glimpse of the master weaving his spell in his favorite setting. At the same time they had occasion to feast their spirit on the confections of his proteges, gorgeously chromatic, often lovely, and always honestly original. The individuality of his pupils, so precious to their teacher, was there for anyone with eyes to see. Meanwhile, some of Cizek's advanced students prepared to follow in his foot-steps and though—remembering they were individualists—they differed in this jot or that tittle from the precepts of their master, yet in their essential pdagogic beliefs and practice, they were plainly his disciples. Through them Cizek's gospel overflowed into the rest of Austria and, as the years increased, even across its borders. What the man's precise influence was, is hard to determine—nor does it greatly matter. As we glance back over a half-century or so, there is little doubt that what once passed for art education had undergone a radical overhauling. Where, at the beginning of the century, its capital concern was getting the learner to reproduce the model on paper, to which, with thirty or more others, he had been assigned without even having been consulted—"representation," the business was called—his present successor is allowed the freedom of his fancy. Where former generations were drilled in the rules of light and shadow, vanishing points, and similar recondite matters, to the end of drawing cups and saucers, books lazying on their sides at every conceivable angle, an occasional jug, and now and then, depending on the master, a chianti bottle, discreetly emptied, today's child not only copies, he also interprets and invents—in short, he creates. In communion with his "inner god," he lights a tall candle on the altar of self-expression, depicting not only what he perceives, but what he feels and fancies, be it a portrait of a vacuum or of the sound of a brass horn. Like faith, what he shapes and forms on paper represents—so spake Paul the Apostle in Hebrews XI, 1—"the substance of things hoped for; the evidence of things not seen." Thus conceived and pursued, art as it is taught in the current schools is much closer to what in his earthly days Franz Cizek had labored so diligently to promote.

CHAPTER 32

THE UNITED STATES

A s the nineteenth century ran through its last quarter the school system which currently obtains in America had acquired its basic features. It is not, as has already been made evident, a national system in the sense that it is under national watch and direction, uniform and unified in all its major aspects from one end of the land to the other. Yet, for all the variation, there is an American system with clear and identifiable traits, which are based on principles generally esteemed and respected, and wrung from a long, arduous, and at times tortuous experience.

There is in that design, for one thing, the absence of Federal control, though not of Federal concern and—better still—aid and benevolence from the national treasury. There is, for another thing, the so-called educational ladder, whereby our schools are joined rung by rung from the lowest to the highest. In the philosophy of our democracy and in its jurisprudence there is to be equality of educational opportunity; unhappily, in actual practice the deed thus far has dragged behind the precept. There is, for still another thing, the fact that our education is free, obligatory, and universal. Next there is the principle, now affirmed by the highest court of law, that though the state may compel parents to put their children upon their studies, it may not make them commit their children to the sessions of the public school. Finally, because the Constitution separates state and church, the public school may impart no religious instruction. Nor, by the same token, may the public purse be broached for sectarian ends, whether educational or otherwise. However, the right of parochial and private schools to exist may not be gainsaid, and as long as they abide by the laws which bear upon us all, they are free to do their work in accordance with their lights.

So much for the system's essence. Wrought from the social ferment of the nineteenth century, it was given its shape and substance first in New England, and then over an ever-spreading space from East to West. Its evolution bridges the three decades or so preceding the Civil War, though it required the rest of the century to consolidate its gains.

2

The South, too, entertained educational stirrings. Most of the Awakening's hallmarks were visible—the bands of dedicated reformers, the logic and rhetoric to shape the public mind, the shock troops to spur lawmakers into action. There were also the same resentments, the feeling against school taxes, the conviction that any schooling not grounded on religion is against God, and the troubled boding that free, universal education would surely upset the social order. In the South the notion that education is a personal and private affair was still full of potency, as was its handmaiden that a state's responsibility ceased once it had provided a measure of instruction, however meager, for those unable to afford it themselves. What bore even more heavily on the sub-Potomac region was its primitive rural culture, with its ruling plantation aristocracy, its hordes of submerged folk, sweating and impoverished whites and several million slaves. The Industrial Revolution had scarcely grazed the South. Its industry, hence, was kept within narrow bounds, and so were its business and its banking. Cities, which rose and flourished in other regions, grew less easily in the South. There was, in consequence, a lack of bold, imaginative, and ambitious urban striving, a lack, in short, of counterpoise to a flaccid provincialism.

Despite the heavy odds against it, the South made progress. Educational advance was slower than in the North, less galvanic, and more confined—still it was an advance. By 1860—to single out the most glittering instance—the people of North Carolina could take pride in their schools. Free, tax-supported, well attended, and manned in large measure by trained and licensed teachers, they were the fruit of the infinite industry of Calvin Henderson Wiley, the state's first school superintendent. So towering was this man's achievement that several other states, notably Virginia, South Carolina, and Georgia, presently were wooing him for his service. Unluckily, Sumter dashed such hope and promise, and the disaster which followed Appomattox crippled Southern education for generations to come.

Not till the end of the century did Southern education emerge from its long and cataleptic langor—indeed, the century was already a memory before what has since been cataloged as the South's Second Educational Revival was under way. With grants in aid from divers sources, but especially from the overflowing pocket of the General Education Board, the way was prepared for better times. During the course of the twentieth century's first ten years tax money to buoy up the public schools gradually became more plentiful. Some of it was marked for the erection of new and better schoolhouses, some for more and larger libraries, some for teacher-training schools, and some for higher salary checks for teachers. By the century's middle teens, all Dixie, saving Georgia and Mississippi, had adopted measures for compulsory schooling. The laws, it is true, had loopholes; even so, taking them one with another, they were fetching more children into the schoolroom than ever before. In fact, with a school year running an average 130 days, the Southern small fry were suffering their most sustained period of academic trial since the founding of Jamestown.

As more industry made its way into the South, and the state of the South's purse gradually improved, educational investment showed an appreciable increase. The value of its school property, real and other, has steadily risen. Libraries are no longer in short supply. Laboratories, practice kitchens, and the sundry workshops for exercising the arts and crafts no longer incite public amazement. Nor in the general advance have teachers been forgotten. As everywhere else, the demands put upon them to obtain a license have become more severe, and so have their training and education—and so, let it not be forgotten, have their professional duties in school and beyond. In just reward, their wages have been made more tolerable.

There is no doubt that the fog has lifted—but not altogether. The gap between the South and the rest of the republic has narrowed. But Dixie flaunts its own disparities, and the high standards that hold, say, for Florida and North Carolina, are far from holding in Alabama and Mississippi. The old prejudices and rancors, as we shall presently see, are by no means obliterated, nor is there a lack of demagogic politicians to fan them into flame. Even so, there is now at least a small but growing number of earnest and enlightened citizens ready to give them challenge.

3

Although the crusaders for the common school were far from disdaining the importance of pedagogical theory, the problems which confronted them were preeminently practical. What was needed, first and foremost, was to make the common school a going concern. For this purpose it was essential to rally a friendly public opinion, to get the school a sufficient tax support, to fortify it with the authority and power of the state, and when the time was ripe, to project the system of free, tax-supported schooling into the higher plane of secondary education. When at length Americans had occasion to give some sober thought to educational theory, they turned, as we have seen, to the Old World masters, first to the teachings of Pestalozzi, and then to those of Herbart.

Meanwhile, things were booming on other fronts. The cultural changes which had put their grip on the America of Horace Mann went on in full blast. The number of its populace continued to climb. The tide of immigration, swelling in the forties, flooded higher and higher until in the eighties it was bringing several million aliens to these shores every year. All over the country cities were enlarging in size and number, while farms, on the other hand, were lessening, though by the magic of a better husbandry the American farmer was producing more than ever. Following the Civil War the nation's industry plunged ahead with new and powerful force, and so did its trade and commerce, and so, in consequence, its wealth. Nor had there been any relaxing in the national exuberance—far on in the century, in fact, it broke loose in a war with Spain which not only drove that power out of this hemisphere, but brought the Stars and Stripes over the waters of the far Pacific.

In this America, and particularly out of its expanding democracy, public education came of age. Unluckily, its prospering propagated a host of unexpected problems—problems which the fathers of the common school, despite their sagacity, had never even dreamed of. So vast had become the patronage of the public school that the number of available teachers proved utterly inadequate, and their pedagogic capacity, hence, was seriously disabled.

To attend and instruct its gigantic flock, the emerging public school pinned its hopes on regimentation. Its offerings it arranged as graded subjects, teaching them by a rigorous timetable, and assigning certain years for coming to terms with certain facts and operations. The effect was that, for all the massed wisdom of the world's foremost pedagogical minds, teaching in the public shcool was reduced to drumming knowledge into pupils, belaboring them stiffly with homework and examinations, goading the slow, and exacting penalty from the loafers and skylarkers. What the learner did was translated into the record as marks, of which the most meritorious went not necessarily to the brightest, but more likely to the ones who could summon forth the most numerous facts from their files of memory. It was, of course, education of a dreary order, a hollow artificiality, but until someone came along to do it in, it was to be the rule.

A number of first-class men arose to its challenge, but the most spectacular, both for his achievement and the dexterous formulation he gave to his ideas, was a New Englander, Francis Wayland Parker. A many-sided man, he worked at odds and ends, farming for a spell and soldiering in the Civil War, before he finally settled himself in the teaching service. When the chance came, he made for Germany's higher groves to study philosophy. At the same time he made it a point to get acquainted with some of the newer pedagogical procedures which had issued largely from the advanced thinking of Pestalozzi, Herbart, and Froebel. Not a few apparently were to his taste. In any case, when Parker returned to practice in America, he ventured to give them a trial, first in the public schools of Quincy, Massachusetts, where he was superintendent, and later at Chicago, where he headed the Cook County Normal School.

A man of liberal lights, Parker kept his labor close to his principles. He scouted the school's "stiff and unnatural order," proclaiming instead for "work with all the whispering and noise compatible with good results"—not a novel idea, to be sure, in the late nineteenth century, but then still suspect to everyday teaching. Much of his fire Parker directed against the stuffing of the memory with multitudinous, meaningless facts. Geography—to confine examples—he approached à la Rousseau and Pestalozzi, whereby a firsthand study of the surrounding region carried more importance than an abstruse knowledge of Biisk or Lüderitz, or the ins and outs of the Son or the Sura. The same went for arithmetic and for language. Parker introduced Quincy to the arts and crafts, to a discipline that was decent and humane, and—most important—to "quality teaching," by which he had in mind a teaching caressed by the creative touch, the act, in other words, of artists rather than mechanicians.

Though he dipped generously into the rich pool of European pedagogy, Parker was not just a transcriber of other men's ideas. His New England individualism and, in particular, his confidence in the democratic process lifted him above the Continentals. When his experimentalizing at Chicago brought misgivings to his teachers, he met them in weekly congress to have them voice their views, and by general discussion to help to ease and, if possible, to arrest their fears. When parents were apprehensive of his novel and disconcerting doings, he invited them to parley in a fraternity of parents and teachers, the first of its kind in Chicago, one of the first in the republic, and an early ancestor of the current PTA.

There were, of course, the familiar distrusts and derisions from those of ar older habit of mind. At Quincy Parker was able to muffle them when, in 1879, his boys and girls, subjected to the state's examining eye, not only passed thei tests, but accomplished the feat with honorable supremacy over the rest of th Massachusetts young. At Chicago, where he carried on in the same progressive manner, he was not so lucky. There, assailed by right-thinkers, and especially the public functionaries of politics, he was hobbled at every turn. Consequently, in 1901, when opportunity nodded, he transferred himself to the University o Chicago. But his emancipation was destined to be brief, for in the year follow, ing, at sixty-five, he died.

Parker has been hailed as the pioneer of the American educational tradition and as the father of progressive education. To such titles let us not dispute his right. But in his thought and labor, in spite of his immense individuality, there is still a ponderable borrowing from beyond the ocean. The man who plowed America's pedagogical sprout land and planted the native seed was Parker's friend and colleague, his successor at Chicago, John Dewey.

4

Like Parker, Dewey sprang from New England. He was born in Burlington, Vermont, in 1859. He passed through its public schools with no sign that he had a mind beyond the general—in fact, his junior year in college was upon him when an interest in philosophy flared into flame and he began to flash with cerebral sparks. Time saw him booked at Johns Hopkins, then still in infancy, but already celebrated for the intellectual powers of some of its men of learning, as witness especially, Granville Stanley Hall and Charles Peirce. Dewey's favorite was George Sylvester Morris, a lesser light in intellectual annals, but a teacher of surpassing merit. Morris brought his student to grips with the propositions of Hegel. A philosophic descendant of the Idealist Plato, Hegel contended that mind is real and matter illusory; that the universe is founded in "spirit", and that life is man's eternal, upward struggle toward the perfect and changeless Universal Mind of God. It was a view that—for the time being—satisfied the young man's thirst for certainty.

When Dewey came to Chicago, he could look back to a decade of college teaching. In keeping with academic ground rules, he had contributed a fair share of his more spacious thoughts to the organs of learning. He had written a well-regarded book on psychology, then still a pastureland for ruminating philosophers. And he had remained steadfast in the persuasion that the ultimate reality is God.

But the harbor of Hegelian surety in which ten years ago he had taken refuge had lost its former smugness. Life in midwestern America was of a vast and gorgeous vitality, a hurly-burly of political, economic, and social change. It was a world full of prodigious possibility, of free and rugged enterprise, where a pushful and not too finicky man might lay up a quick and colossal fortune. But it was also a world which wreaked its toll, and for every well-heeled worthy which it spawned, there were myriads of losers in life's battle, the legion of worn and wretched poor. In such a world, and particularly in Chicago where things transformed at a dizzy pace, it was not easy for a social-minded man like Dewey to dwell in the blue empyrean of Hegel where reality was not matter, but spirit, absolute and unaltering. The upshot was that Dewey's concern absorbed itself more and more in the social problems which seethed all about. And so, as the years drew by, his thinking turned its power increasingly on social reconstruction, and especially on the conflicts which result when the forces of science, democracy, and industry meet head on.

In 1896, two years after his installation at Chicago, Dewey, his wife, and some neighbors established a school for their children. Intended to educate boys and girls between four and fourteen, it was to serve as a testing place of philosophical and educational principles. Officially, in fact, its designation was the Laboratory School of the University of Chicago, though today it is commonly spoken of as the Dewey School.

Even in those days the idea of a school experimenting with children was no novelty. As long ago as the eighteenth century Basedow had been its familiar, and so in the years ensuing had Herbart and several others. But the idea was still sufficiently disruptive of convention to stiffen conservatives in their chairs—and in this respect the Laboratory School was no exception.

Look at the Dewey seminary, and you will find none of the familiar academic spectacle. Gone are the neat and measured rows of desks and benches, gone the teacher's desk with its bell and ruler; gone the drill and recitation. Even the subjects, the mainstay in those days of every well-run school, and the reason for its being, are in absence. Instead, you will see a workplace of busy children, some working singly, others together. Some might be preoccupied with books, some with pen and paper. Others might be banging with a hammer, or daubing with brush and paint. Still others might be rapt in earnest conference. As for the teacher, she has left the chair which once enthroned her, to mingle with her charges, asking here, counseling there, and everywhere giving ear to question and comment. There is no cold and stony stillness here. Instead there is activity and talk, the insistent, eager jabber which cascades from the young when they are freely interested in what they are about.

The Laboratory School proposed "to train children in cooperative and mutually useful living." Like Rousseau and some of his successors, Dewey had convinced himself that the roots of educational activity lie deep "in the instinctive and impulsive attitudes of the child." Beyond the academic frontier he is forever learning. Does he long to make an airplane that flies through the air? To erect a residence in a tree? To stand on his hands for five minutes? Then he will exert himself with the utmost diligence to fathom and master the underlying mystery. As in life, urged Dewey, so let it be in school. To this end what the child learns should ground itself on his everyday domestic and communal living. The school, in a word, should reproduce in miniature "the typical conditions of social life."

Under the circumstances, the Herbartian formula with its imposition of subject matter "from above and from outside" got no countenance from Dewey and his coworkers. Instead they relied on what in the jargon of teaching has since become the "activity program," and which embraced every department of the child's individual and collective living, from play, construction, self-expression, to contact with flora and fauna and other things. All subjects—even the time-honored Rs—were to be learned not by a regime of planned and systematic instruction, but rather as they announced their presence in the child's activities. Thus transformed, said Dewey, the school is inspirited anew. Now the "child's habitat," where he learns by "directed living," it ceases to harry and hamper him with lessons "having an abstract and remote reference to some possible living to be done in the future." Education, as the phrase presently went, is not preparation for life; it is life itself.

On American education the immediate influence of Dewey's seeking and probing was almost nothing. For the rank and file of Americans what the Laboratory School was up to was too removed from the familiar practice to make sense. In truth, even among professional educators it attained only a slight esteem. Critics discerned in it the usual unseemliness. They said it coddled children; it failed to teach them the fundamentals; and it made them "contemptuous of authority." Even worse, suspicions were aired that Dewey was attempting to obliterate a belief in God. These impressions the professor undertook to correct in a book, *The School and Society*, which came out in 1899. Diffuse and freighted with a heavy and abstract wording, it was not read with eager interest. In fact, like the school itself, it persuaded scarcely anyone. In time, though, as Dewey's ideas focused into sharper clarity, the book received another printing and now it began to sell. The years saw its translation into pretty nearly every civilized tongue—currently it is even honored with paper covers.

The Laboratory School shut down in 1903, and the next year Dewey migrated to New York to teach philosophy at Columbia University. For ten years or so the professor did his main pondering in philosophy, venturing only a few minor sorties into education. Then, in 1916, with the publication of *Democracy and Education*, the long hiatus came to an end. Almost at once it placed Dewey in the forefront of American thinkers. Heavily burdened though it is by a tangled and difficult prose, *Democracy and Education* has been acclaimed as the most momentous book on education to issue from an American—in fact, some pundits, led by the wish rather than the fact, have even raised it above *Emile* and the *Republic*. However posterity will decide to rank it, for at least a generation and a half the work served as a prime mover in the remaking of America's educational theory, the indispensable Bible, as it were, of the overwhelming proportion of the native professional schoolmen.

In *Democracy and Education* Dewey reveals his major philosophic propositions and their educational corollaries. In education, he submits with Pestalozzi
and Froebel, two aspects stand before every eye, the psychological and the
social. The burden of education, he goes on, is to direct the one, which is to say
the child's natural and individual impulses, to the other, namely, as desirable
social behavior. Morally, Dewey contends, the child is trained when he is able to
fulfill the demands of living properly with his fellows. It thus befalls the teacher
not to sermonize him with saws on right and wrong, but rather to invent
situations from which the child will fashion concepts of right and wrong as they
bear on the common good. As in his younger years at Chicago, Dewey is at pains
to remind us that the school is above all a social institution, and that its doings,
hence, should be framed against the common activities of society at large. In
addition, the school should resort to the youngster's daily living at home and at
play, for they are the fountainhead of his primary experience. But this does not
mean that the school should not step outside the familiar social patterns. Its task
is not simply to keep things as they are; it is also to anticipate a better world.
Actually, insisted Dewey, in a free-functioning democratic society, education is
man's fundamental method of reform and progress. Toward such an end it
behooves the school to chart its course.

It was Dewey's contention that in education, as in life, our attitude should be
scientific. Nothing, he declared, should be regarded as fixed and immutable. All
truths, however hallowed and adored, must be subject to perpetual reexamination and testing. And what we believe should at all times be based on plausible
and impartial evidence. Thus approached, education becomes an unflagging and
endless quest, a "continuous reconstruction of accumulated experience."

The whole thing may be put very simply. Education is actual living, not just
making ready for eventual living. Education is a process of growth, and as long as
there is growth there is education. Education is the never-ending overhauling and
reassembling of previous experience. Finally, education, at its best, is a social
process, and to further it the school must be a democratic society.

Cheers from critics notwithstanding, *Democracy and Education*, like the
Chicago Laboratory School in the nineties, made no appreciable dent in the
general practice of the American school. The truth is Dewey's thicket of words
was too much for the mass of America's teachers. What was obviously needed
was someone to reduce them into understandable speech, and someone, in
addition, to bring them into actual practice. The passing years brought both. By
1918 William Heard Kilpatrick was disentangling Dewey's complex thinkings
before his colossal classes at Columbia's Teachers College, investing them, as if
by magic, with a brightness and clearness they had never known, and while he
was at it, bagging converts by the score. At Ohio State, in the meantime, Boyd
Bode was performing a similar wonder. From the classrooms of these professors,
and from others like them, proceeded an ever-lengthening line of teachers, rapt
in the Dewey principles and prepared to put them into practice, especially in the
elementary school.

It would be doing Kilpatrick a grave wrong to set him down as a mere mouthpiece, a ventriloquial dummy, so to say, for Dewey. The truth is that although Kilpatrick reaped fame as a magnificent translator of Dewey's belabored, and at times baffling, expression, and that, at bottom, he was an ardent apostle of the Dewey gospel, even so, he must be honored for a number of laudable achievements of his own. To him, for one, must be credited the rise and proliferation of the project method, which was inaugurated at the turn of the century by advanced sages in the domain of manual training, and which Kilpatrick adopted and developed, giving it a philosophical and psychological grounding, to bring it to its latter-day maturity. Taking the Dewey pronouncement that in order to be effective, education must be a living experience, Kilpatrick proposed the replacement of the old-style recitation with its stress on the mastering of subject matter by a method which called for the fusion of intellectual and aesthetic activities involving the learner's total organism. Such is the ideal that buoys up the project procedure, which, it scarcely requires saying, varies multitudinously in form and substance. There are projects which are preeminently creative, as, for example, constructing a machine that will fly through the air, or building a safe and comfortable lodging for Rover. Others are largely of a vicarious nature, such as lending one's ear and heart to a tale well told or a tune touchingly executed. Some projects may be essentially of a problematic sort, such as, say, trying to figure out the mysterious origin of a yawn. Finally, projects may be employed to implant knowledge or develop skills, a hoary practice to be sure, but, until some satisfactory alternative is found, necessary just the same.

From his cerebrations over the project method Kilpatrick derived his view of "simultaneous learnings." Reduced to simple parlance, this holds that we learn not just the specific material put before us, as, say, the mathematical identity of π, but also some related matters, namely that π is a Greek letter, that its mathematical formulation represents the ratio between the circumference of a circle and its diameter, and that this is not simply the curt, classroom 3.1416, but an interminable concatenation which, if carried on, would run 3.14159265 . . . , and so on and on, like eternity, forever without a stop. In all learning, furthermore, there are any number of side learnings—"concomitant" Kilpatrick christened them—which, for good or bad, bear upon our attitudes and ideals, and even our values and standards. These, Kilpatrick was convinced, weigh significantly on the making of human behavior, whether solitary or in concert, and which, in consequence, every project-planner must at all times anticipate. "I learn," the Columbia professor explained, "in the degree that I think it feels important to me, and how it fits in with what I have already learned and believed. What I thus learn I build into my character."

5

Slightly more than two years after the appearance of *Democracy and Education*, the Progressive Education Association came into being. It started in a modest but hopeful mood with a few hundred members. Ten years later its ranks had multiplied to about ten thousand, and it had become the most vigorous voice for educational progressivism in the nation. Its members were mostly teachers working in scattered private schools and subscribing in one way or another to the cause of better education. Dewey's case against the conventional school, needless to say, charmed them immensely—indeed, in testimony of their esteem they made him an honorary president. True, only a few of the first Progressives conceived of the new school as a social laboratory, the incubator of tomorrow's better world. The hope which filled their dreams was a school where the young learned from experience rather than rote, where they were allowed to be themselves, where individual talents were given notice and brought to flower, and where learning soared from interest, and at a pace that was never forced.

So things ran, more or less, through the twenties. But when depression came sweeping down upon the land, and people began to wash their hands of individualism, some Progressives, preaching warnings against the perils of individualism, took a strong line for social planning. "Education," wrote Dewey, "must share in social reconstruction." The school, added his colleague, Professor Counts, must "dare to build a new social order." Its function, Kilpatrich went on, is "to help youth think through a defensible social program."

With so many of its leading members disposed to repair and ameliorate our social order, the Progressive Education Association was not the brotherhood of the days of its youth when it pressed its suit for the child-centered school. It is only fair to remind ourselves, however, that not a few of the brethren put little stock in the new gospel, and continued, as formerly, to lay their primary stress on the individual. Nevertheless, the current was running strongly the other way, and by the thirties the association was navigating in a manner that would have mystified the founders. With committees, commissions, and workshops the PEA ventured into research. In 1935—to specify a couple of examples—its Commission on Educational Freedom turned its lamp on academic freedom, and in the year following, its Commission on Intercultural Education did the same for "the tensions and misunderstandings . . . among the various cultural groups that are parts of America."

In the forties, after grave self-examination and reappraisal, the organization volunteered to do some reconstruction of itself. Though it still held to its original credo, it frocked that credo now in the habiliments of social significance. "Growth," it gave notice, was still "the individual's richest reward," but that plum he could pluck only when he "in concert with others brings intelligence and good will to the shared task of creating the values for which the culture is to strive." What is the meaning of this weighty talk? It signifies, in translation, that when the young are disgorged from school, they should be able to face the problems which beset us; that they should stand ready and willing to solve them; and that they should be guided by an enlightened social conscience But in no case does it mean that the association gave its support to the engineers of social planning. On the contrary, with "those who begin with a social blueprint," it dissented very flatly.

Despite its interest in social reconstruction, the PEA's efforts to bring it about were mild. In 1944 it changed its name to the American Education Fellowship, thereby acquiring a slightly social tinge. At the same time it formulated a number of "special purposes," all directed to the dawn of a better day.

Following the end of the war, while the world was adjusting itself to the perils of peace, the fellowship spoke again. "Inasmuch," it announced, "as the forces that shape society are those that determine education as well, educators must understand what is taking place in the community, and must take stands as adult citizens on controversial issues of the day." In addition, the society volunteered to give active aid to "the reconstruction of the economic system in the direction of greater social justice and stability," and the "establishment of a genuine world order ... in which national sovereignty is subordinate to world authority in crucial interests affecting peace and security." Unhappily, the society's days on earth were nearing the end, and it never got a chance to realize its rosy hopes. In June, 1955, in its thirty-sixth year, what remained of the Progressive Education Association gasped its last.

Born from the zeal of dissent, Progressivism, whether of the Parker or the Dewey strain, or some other blend, has been frequently beset and knocked about. The variety of its adversaries ranges from philosophers, psychologists, journalists, and preachers to the DAR, the NAM, and the American Legion. But it has also creased the brow of numerous others, especially parents and teachers. The principal and most energetic professional belaborers of Progressivism were the Essentialists. Come upon the scene in the latter thirties, the Essentialists insisted that the school's first and all-important business is to ground its pupils effectively in fundamentals, to wit, "reading, writing, arithmetic, history, and English," besides training them in discipline and obedience.

The standard-bearer of Essentialism and its most spectacular pepper-and-salter was William Chandler Bagley. A professor at Columbia's seminary of teachers, and hence confronted by Progressives all about, Bagley preached his evangel with unflagging industry. There were, he conceded, some meritorious achievements by the new pedagogy, for instance, its "condemnation ... of ... parrot-like learning"; its "efforts to make school life a happy and profitable series of learning experiences"; besides its use of the activity program. But, declaimed Bagley, the bad in Progressivism outweighed the good -to cite cases, its veto of any enterprise suggesting imposition by the teacher, its denial of value in the sustained and systematic study of subject matter, its crying down of pupil effort, and its weak-as-water discipline. By such things, expostulated Bagley, Progressivism had done the American people a great disservice. Not only had it pushed the quality of our education down the hill; it had also contributed "to our appalling record of . . . serious crime."

To make an end of such untowardness the Essentialists proposed a return "to the exact and exacting studies." Progressivism's carefree and aimless manner they would fling into the trash can. They would resort but sparingly to projects. They would lay less stress on interest and more on effort. The standards of scholarship, which have been suffering from too much sugar-water, they would revive and fortify with powerful shots of algebra and geometry—even Latin. What the patient needed, commented Dr. Bagley, was "a strong tincture of iron."

Now most of the Essentialists are gone to the world beyond—but not their criticism. Barely smoldering during most of the forties, it suddenly flashed into flame when, to the national surprise, the Russians orbited the world's first satellite into the faraway blue. It was for Americans a day of disintegrating illusions, of deep uneasiness, followed by a great wave of criticism of which not a little rolled over education. Did the Russians beat us into interstellar space? Then the reason, some were certain, was their tougher schooling, their stress on science, for example, and mathematics and language, the unsparing demands they put upon their young, from homework and examinations to grades and promotions, their special programs for those of high capacity, and to make an end, their insistence on discipline and obedience.

There are some holes, of course, in this thinking; nevertheless, it served to good effect, for presently it directed a new and sharply critical eye on the American school. At Columbia's Teachers College, so long the country's foremost vineyard of Progressivism, President John Fisher, proclaiming doubts about the child-centered school, implored schoolmen "to give priority to intellectual competence." On the republic's western edge, as a consequence of a survey of the San Francisco schools, the aim of education, it was found, is "to inform the mind and develop intelligence." In the nation's capital the Council for Basic Education, the inheritors of the Essentialists, worked up its pressure against the "softness" of the American school, its "life adjustment" courses, such as driver training, and getting and holding a job, and especially the false thinking of the professors of education—all of which Vice-admiral Rickover stoutly seconded.

In a graver tone, and less inflammatory, was the New England voice of James Bryant Conant. Once American ambassador to the new Germany, and prior to that for twenty years president of Harvard, the man spoke presumably with some authority. In his report, *The American High School Today*, Conant revealed what his eyes had caught as he made his way from school to school from one end of America to the other. Of some he held an agreeable opinion, but numerous others he regarded with disfavor. Too many high schools—some seven of every ten—were so small that they seriously incommoded their operations. Hundreds entertained inferior programs, and equally as many a scholarship so low as to be almost out of sight. And finally, very few of them granted any special attention to pupils of notable talents.

As is usual in our free and enterprising democracy, the new mood soon brought forth an outpouring of counsel and recommendations, some sage and useful, but some merely noise. President Eisenhower's Commission on National Goals reported in 1960, and the Rockefeller Brothers Fund had its say the following year in its *Pursuit of Excellence*. Both studies were under the direction of John W. Gardner, president of the Carnegie Corporation, and later under President Johnson, Secretary of Health, Education, and Welfare. In educational circles his name has become something of a synonym for a stress on quality and competence. Excellence, however, he is at pains to explain, is something more. It implies "a striving for the highest standards of life," whether political, industrial, creative, or educational. In this vein we must seek to mold and equip the young for "the age-long struggle of man to realize the best that is in him"—a proposition which, though hoary in the memoirs of learning, was received, nonetheless, with alacrity.

Needless to say, the criticisms directed at American education have been disputed and discountenanced; but there is no gainsaying that their seed has fructified in a serious effort at improvement. Moribund for years in the secondary school, science and mathematics presently pulsed with an amazing vitality as school after school hastened to strengthen its program therein. As one might expect, the sudden deference paid to mathematics and science brought misgivings to the adherents of the humanities. What was needed, they let it be known, was not just scientists and mathematicians, but a cultivated youth, versed in all the sectors of life, which is to say history, language, and letters as well as the natural and mathematical sciences. It is, of course, an old and familiar view— even so, to the judicious it still made sense. In truth, so much sense did it make that in 1960 the Ford Foundation came to its support with a ten-year grant of not quite 6 million dollars to render assistance to scholars toiling in the nonscientific domain. Since then the people's attorneys in Congress have taken note. There is, declared the Hon. John E. Fogarty in 1962 in an address to the House, "a pressing need for Federal legislation that will build up nationwide support for the arts and humanities comparable to the support that is provided in other areas, such as science and technology."

With so much to-do over quality and competence, it was only natural to give some fresh and serious thought to the education of the child of high and special dowering. Needless to say, he was no newcomer in the grove of learning, but until not so long ago, his needs had been subordinated to those whom fortune had used badly, the blind, the deaf, the sick and crippled, and those of slow and feeble mind. By contrast, the gifted child seemed to present no problem, and so he was expected in the main to fend for himself. Plausible enough at first glance, such views were presently put under the glare of psychological and sociological searchlights, and as the years followed, they were seen to be short of the actual facts.

The number of such studies has remained strikingly small. Even so, some of them, as witness Lewis M. Terman's pioneering *Genetic Studies of Genius*, have not only done serious damage to many of our most cherished fables about the gifted; they have also revealed some new and sometimes astounding data about them. The notion, for example, that those of surpassing brightness range below their fellows in health and physical growth, Terman found to be devoid of substance. In their character they stand as high as is humanly bearable, as high, that is, as the best among the average, and sometimes a notch or so higher. They are not lacking in social adaptability, but at times they do need urging. Nor do they confine their interests to the world of books. Like their more common comrades, they make merry in games and sports—though again they may need some spurring to get started. Despite their extraordinary powers and capacities, their education offered them nothing special. Not uncommonly, in fact, they were not even granted a faster promotion than those of average wit.

So things stood more or less as the century passed through its middle age, all the probing of psychological science notwithstanding. Today with our current concern for excellence, they are patently out of key. To let in some light on the matter, the National Education Association, with a subvention from the Carnegie Corporation, undertook a study of "the academically talented student." From this effort, the last few years have witnessed the publication of a dozen monographs or thereabouts, all in the cause of providing the superior child with an education designed and tailored to his special needs. Meanwhile, through the length and breadth of the republic, city upon city has entered into arrangements to educate its nascent Darwins and da Vincis in a manner befitting their exceptional properties. In the high school the increase and proliferation of special classes for girls and boys with brains has been truly staggering. Thus, where a decade and a half or so ago they were so rare as to be almost unique, and where as recently as 1959 Conant announced such enterprise to be negligible, today in one way or another three of every four municipalities are engaged therein. Nor has the lower school been oblivious of the needs of the gifted—in fact, more than half the nation's city elementary schools are exercising themselves to some degree in their behalf.

6

The notion that some aspects of education might yield their secrets to the precise and impartial searchings of science stretches back to the days of Herbart. He gave it expression, vague to be sure and almost lost in the vast outflow of his writings. He even sought to give his psychology a measure of exactness by summoning reinforcement from mathematics in which he was something of an expert. Yet the project proved too much for even his tremendous mind, and in the end he abandoned it as hopeless. Not daunted, others followed in Herbart's tracks, mostly professors of natural science of one kind or another, and all eager to liberate the study of the psyche from the speculations of metaphysicians and theologians.

The accredited father of scientific psychology was a German, Professor

Wilhelm Max Wundt. A specialist in physiology, but also on excellent terms with physics, Wundt brought psychology into the laboratory. It was a work which occupied him for sixty years running, until 1920, when the angels took him off, an advanced and bewhiskered eighty-year-old. His most famous book, and for years the ruler of the field, was his *Principles of Physiological Psychology*. Put into print in 1874, it passed through various editions, the last one appearing shortly before the opening of the First World War. Through his pioneering in the lab and lecture hall and in his writing, the professor put his mark on a new generation of psychologists, not only in the Reich, but all over the earth, and notably in the United States, where it shows itself in the performance of such prodigies as William James, James McKeen Cattell, and Granville Stanley Hall.

Some time in the middle seventies—the precise date has gone astray—James requisitioned a forgotten hall room at Harvard, filled it with mysterious-looking apparatus, and proceeded, as he said, "to work at psychology." Although he had an acute aversion to the tedium of experimental labor, and engaged in it as little as possible, his reconstructed hall room marks the birthplace of American experimental psychology. Not long after, James augmented his prestige still more when he introduced Harvard to its first psychology course. His finest achievement, however, James reserved for the year 1890, when he published his *Principles of Psychology*. Freighted with almost half a million words, hundreds of footnotes thick with book titles, besides an assortment of recondite quotations, the book must needs amaze us. Yet, despite its palpable scholarship, it was also full of force and charm, a rare and savory dish, indeed, to set before a student. The years, of course, have staled much of its psychological doctrine, but not the ripple of its prose, nor the impress of its extraordinary composer. Some connoisseurs, in fact, now appraise the work as a classic.

What Wundt achieved for psychology in his elaborate and microscopic manner, James attained with his deft and delicate, though by no means superficial, touch. Both men served to place the subject on a scientific foundation; both provided it with a corps of trained and instructed scholars; and both caught a glimpse of psychology's potentialities for other domains of life, and especially for learning and teaching.

One of the first to explore this territory was Granville Stanley Hall. He had made acquaintance with the new science in the workrooms of Wundt, and when he got his chance, in 1883, he installed a psychological laboratory at the Johns Hopkins University, then just getting under sail. Soon after, he got out *The American Journal of Psychology*, the first of its kind in English, and for years without a rival in its class. Later at Clark University, where he stood sentinel as president, he launched and edited *The Pedagogical Seminary*, an advanced journal on educational theory and practice, with erudite and elevating pieces from contributors the world around. The harvest of Hall's most ravenous searching, however, is stored in his *Adolescence*, a huge and spacious work dwelling on the subject's every phase, from psychology, anthropology, and sociology to sex, crime, religion, and education. Time, as so often, has worn down and destroyed much of its revelation. Even so, it was Hall who raised the study of adolescence from the bog of quackery to a plane of serious educational research.

The name that sticks out above all others in the making of educational psychology is Edward Lee Thorndike. At Harvard he hearkened unto James, but after taking his master's degree he headed for the classrooms of James McKeen Cattell, once an assistant to Wundt, but now practicing in his own right at Columbia University. Thorndike's swift and incisive mind soon pushed him into the forefront of psychological science, bringing him to his doctorate in the field of animal psychology, and after a short time to a place on the faculty of Teachers College, where he remained to enhance its fame and luster until his time ran out.

Few have tilled their ground more diligently or on a scale so wide and long. From Cattell out of Wundt he was seized by a passion for exactitude which led him to make tracks into the unknown region of educational measurement. He came to grips with the mystery of learning and the so-called theory of the transfer of training, going after them with a measuring stick and disrupting some of education's most prized beliefs. He eyed the psychological nature of individual differences, of mental capacities, of skill and growth, documenting his findings and incarcerating them in statistical graphs and tables. His studies of adult learning were not only fresh and comprehensive; they altered the common view that only the young can learn easily and effectively, and that people on in years, like the proverbial old dogs, are through. He thus served to put the adult education movement in this country, or as some say nowadays, continued education, on a solid psychological base. Finally, it was Thorndike who formulated the stimulus-response psychology, and who in the long run made S-R as familiar in American education as the IQ and the NEA.

In the annals of educational psychology the name Thorndike must be written large. During his more than forty years at Teachers College he gave counsel and instruction to several thousand students, not only expounding to them the substance of his views, but quickening not a few of them with a high ardor for the scientific spirit, though his inclination, it must be said, was mainly toward the quantitative and statistical. For the bulk of his students, whether they became teachers, administrators, or psychologists, Thorndike set the fashion. Thus the man left his mark upon his times. He reached his apogee during the twenties. Since then not a few of his unearthings have fallen into disfavor. Even the essence of his viewpoint, the S-R psychology, has seen challenge. Once a cardinal article of faith in the credo of nearly every professional educator, its insistence that learning is a purely mechanical process is today under heavy criticism.

Thorndike's leaning toward the quantitative interpretation of his findings carried him into what eduational chroniclers commonly set down as the Measurement Movement. Its foreshadowing is faintly visible as early as 1890 when Cattell broke into print with his *Mental Tests and Measurements*. Fifteen years later two Frenchmen, Alfred Binet and Theodore Simon, succeeded in putting together a scale to measure what, for want of a better phrase, they called "general intelligence." Repaired and altered, the Binet-Simon measuring rod was given revision in 1908 and again three years later.

It did not take long for the new light from Paris to project its beam into the laboratories of American psychology. But to put the Binet-Simon tests into general and satisfactory operation over here, it was essential to bring them into consonance with the American culture, a labor which was completed in 1916 when Professor Lewis Terman issued his Stanford Revision. Spread over a dozen pages, its queries were calculated to track down the intelligence of any one ranging from the age of three to what was described as the "superior adult."

Rather curiously, another boost for mind measuring issued from the First World War. With assistance from some of America's foremost psychologists—now arrayed in military regalia—the Army constructed the so-called "alpha and beta intelligence tests." Administered on a scale so huge they flabbergast the imagination, the tests excavated massive data about the American's intelligence, sometimes astonishing and sometimes even alarming. However this may be, more important in the forward march of psychological science was their demonstration of the feasibility of testing in a wholesale manner.

Since those primordial days mental testing has become a national commonplace. Not only has it passed from the barracks to other walks of life, and especially education; it has also become increasingly refined and reliable, though this is not to suggest that its results speak with infallible authority.

Meanwhile the measurers had extended their operations beyond the bounds of the intelligence test. Was it possible to make a quantitative appraisal of the schoolboy's mental power and capacity? Then, they reasoned, it should be no less possible to put an objective yardstick on his various aptitudes and achievements. To such purpose Thorndike applied his great ingenuity and enterprise until, in 1908, he succeeded in devising a scale unit to measure educational achievements. The same year saw one of his students produce the world's first objective test for arithmetic reasoning. He was followed a year later by his professor with a scale to measure handwriting. The year of its publication, 1910, is honored in the annals of science as the birth year of the movement to measure the products of education mathematically.

In the Midwest, especially at the University of Chicago, the zeal for the quantitative magic fevered no less than at New York's Columbia. There its outstanding herald was Professor Charles Judd. During the years ensuing, things went ahead briskly, the general idea being, as Thorndike let it be known, that "everything that exists, exists in quantity, and is measurable," provided, he sagely added, the essential measuring rod is at hand. Judd and Thorndike not only confected their own tests and scales; they also had a hand in dozens propagated by their students and apprentices. Some stalked spelling; some language; some reading; some composition; and so on and on from handwriting movement and eye-voice in reading to mental fatigue.

The nursery days of educational measurement are long since gone. Its early deficiencies behind it, it has ripened into an integral part of American education. There are tests and scales not only for IQ, but for all the familiar subjects from algebra ano arithmetic to the languages, and the sciences whether social or natural. It is possible to take soundings of aptitudes, from the shallowest mechanical sort to the deep and complicated kind that lurk within an Aristotle or a Copernicus. Even character has become an object of the quantitative quest. There are tests to gauge your honesty, your power of will, and—rather fittingly— your psychic tensions. Appreciably more reliable than their forerunners, today's tests are resorted to more and more for educational diagnosis and guidance. Even the higher learning now makes use of them—in fact for screening candidates for collegiate freshmanhood such tests are no longer the exception, but the rule. But when it comes to putting the tapeline on the act of the total organism, say, the supreme performance of a great teacher, the measurers, for all their resourceful- ness, have found it next to impossible to remove the personal equation. As with the judges of letters or music or art, their dependence, for good or ill, is still on a method rooted in judgment rather than measurement.

What holds for the complex entity of the whole man holds for any other entity, from a school to a school system, whether city, state, or national. Known currently as a "survey," gathering and judging the facts about schools is not new to the twentieth century, nor is it even of American origin. There come to mind the reports of Horace Mann on the goings-on in the Massachusetts centers of learning—but there is also the earlier searching of Phillip Melanchthon in Saxony, of Wilhelm von Humboldt in Prussia, and somewhat later, that of Victor Cousin.

The first twentieth-century school survey of which we have any record was conducted at Boise, Idaho, by Calvin Kendall. A simple affair, it was transacted in a few days, and its findings were published in the local newspapers. By the twenties the survey was enjoying something of a run, and ever since it has been firmly lodged in American educational practice. No longer the creature of its nonage, today's full-scale survey has grown to a considerable proportion. Direct- ed by a high command, it is executed by an organized crew of experts, including not only professors of education, but sociologists and psychologists, besides statisticians, tax authorities, accountants, management and efficiency engineers, and various colorful fauna. As educational measurement gained currency, its standardized tests and scales became indispensable instruments in the surveyor's working kit. Surveys may still be small and simple, say, the study of a depart- ment in a one-building university. More commonly, though, they rove a more spacious territory, a school system, for example, or a state system, or even the schools of the nation as a whole.

The full-fledged survey lays its hand on pretty nearly everything which bears upon the educational enterprise, from the quality of instruction and learning to the way schools are managed, staffed, and operated. In addition, it may scrutin- ize the pupil's nonacademic life, his health and virtue, his spirit and demeanor, and his pursuit of everyday living. Not uncommonly it may take stock of the schoolhouse itself, its facilities and amenities, such as heat and lighting, the purity of its air, the decibels in its rooms and corridors, its state of sanitation, the efficiency of its janitorial and maintenance officers, and so on to the nature and condition of the victuals it serves its clients in its mess hall.

All things considered, though the survey is hampered by the limitations imposed upon its science, it has nevertheless been useful and salubrious in its public service. Not only has it unearthed flaws and inadequacies—and even a waste of the public money—but often enough its recommendations have led the way to better practice.

7

Among civilized peoples Americans were the first to make provision for free universal education from the elementary through the secondary schools—and, in a few scattered places, through the college. In the process of its development there appeared, as we have seen, our educational ladder, an arrangement by which every school, from the lowest to the highest, is fitted into a solitary coordinated system. It is a device which—forgetting other obstacles—enables every child to climb to the loftiest educational pinnacle. Though the ladder is simplicity itself, during the nineteenth century it stood unique—in fact, even after all the years that have come and gone since then, there are still not many like it.

In the springtime of the century that we currently grace with our presence, the lower public school—but for stray experimental deviations—ran for eight years and comprised three primary grades and three intermediate ones, followed by two which were distinguished as "grammar grades." For most Americans the eighth grade marked the end of their formal pursuit of knowledge—indeed, not a few had preceded them in its renunciation even earlier. For the small number who hazarded on, the four-year public high school stood ready to give its service and instruction.

Thus the system which taught our forebears—twelve years of learning in a free public grove, classified on its lower eight-year level in three categories of grades and coroneted with a four-year high school. Nowadays the primary grades are still with us, but their old intermediate and grammar associates have drifted from the scene. Even the arrangement of an eight-year lower school and a four-year higher one has felt the teeth of challenge, and though it still exists in considerable quantity, its ranks are getting thinner. The newer formation, which in the nomenclature of the trade is the "6-3-3 system"—as against the senescent 8-4 variety, instructs and advances its abecedarians in a six-year elementary school, followed by three years in a junior high school, and if all goes well, by three more in a senior high school.

The six-year lower shrine, like its eight-year ancestor, is still the workplace of a nascent democracy, and it still seeks to push aside the veil of ignorance by making its attendants literate. Its stock of subjects, needless to say, has increased. All the old standbys are on hand, though often in a newer and sometimes scarcely recognizable guise; in addition there are such latecomers as health, hygiene, safety, citizenship, and arts and crafts. Its methods are for the most part attuned to the newer teachings of pedagogical science, with supplemental aid from film and television, and of late in certain places the so-called and somewhat controverted "teaching machine." Taking one thing with another, today's elementary school, whether the six-year or the eight-year kind, is friendlier and more benign than its earlier forerunner, the living manifestation in more ways than one of the great dreams of reformers through the ages.

The junior high school welcomes its freshman from the six-year elementary school when they are about a dozen years old. As is typical in our republic, the school's purpose is not everywhere the same. Nearly always, though, one of its ends is "exploratory," by which is meant that it tries to help its pupils uncover their lurking potentialities, intellectual, scientific, artistic, mechanical, or whatever they may be, and if possible, to direct them by a prevocational sampling of life's many callings. At twelve, as nearly everybody knows, Junior finds himself on the doorstep of adolescence, and before long he will feel the surge of subtle and powerful forces. To guide him, an up-to-date junior high school is ready with trained experts to render him aid and counsel. At the same time it gives heed to the adolescent's natural social groupings, and to such purpose it offers him a considerable social program.

From the junior high school the pupil makes his way into the senior high school where, if the mood is on him, and he is at least of an ordinary capacity, he will capture his diploma three years later. From end to end, thus, his schooling spans a dozen years.

When, in 1821, the first public high school in America opened for business in Boston, it offered its nonclassical wares to the sons of the "mercantile and merchant classes." Today's high school flaunts no such labels, nor does it confine its boons to males. The school of all children, it is mindful of their differences. Hence the instruction it offers is as varied as the human appetite. Some it will seek to prepare for college; some for a vocation; and all for the practice of successful everyday living.

Not only has the educational ladder been modified at the bottom; it has also been altered higher up. Although the idea from which the junior college issued harks back more than a hundred years, the lusty favor it currently obtains is rather recent. It was in the thirties, when hard times were upon the land, that the movement for the junior college, with Federal support to give it fuel, picked up momentum. Since then, like the much-sung river, it has just kept rolling along. When the veterans, back from the Second World War, bestormed the colleges ever increasingly for admission, a number of states and cities conjured up junior colleges for them. Not a few of these, as things turned out, were scarcely more than impromptu contrivances and have long since vanished into the abyss of things deservedly forgotten. But others, especially in Illinois and

California and in Idaho and Texas, where the movement had a head start and was well under way, were of a superb quality and on a footing—give a little, take a little—with the best of the more elderly colleges.

In its general run, the junior college is a two-year school. Sometimes it is privately supported; sometimes it is kept by public money. Not uncommonly, when it is under a private flag, it is also of a sectarian persuasion. Anatomically, it functions at times as an organ of the higher learning, grooming its apprentices, if they are so inclined, for the status of college juniors. At other times, when it serves primarily to enhance and enrich a student's stock of high school education, it is in effect an advanced secondary school.

What can be said for the junior college? There is, for one thing, the fact that it offers the boon of two years of college training. When its support comes from the public treasury, there is the extra advantage that its tuition levy is pleasantly mild—in truth, in certain states, notably California, Illinois, and Mississippi, and in a number of enlightened communities, the junior college offers its edification without charge. There reign, of course, the usual biles and prejudices of the preservers and protectors of old and established ways. When, for example, the junior college burst into its first lush flower, there was a tendency on their part to snicker at it, to cry it down, as it were, as an Aristotelian woman, a creature incomplete and inadequate. Nor is there any blinking the fact that the public junior college has raised the cost of public education, which was already stratospheric. Like the high school in its youth, the junior college has had to stand up for its legal right to public moneys. But just as the courts sanctioned the laying of taxes in support of the public high school, so in 1930 at Asheville, North Carolina, the state's supreme judiciary found in favor of the junior college.

8

The educational ladder, as has been remarked, provides the mechanism by which the young can ascend from the kindergarten to the republic's highest learning. But this is by no means implying that the ladder is the magic equalizer of educational opportunity. Needless to state, there are all sorts of inequalities in education, some imposed by the stern determinism of nature and beyond repair, others man-made and correctable. Of the latter the supreme one, and by long odds the most fevered, bears upon the Negro.

The first legal assault on segregation in the public school occurred not in Dixie, but in Boston in 1849, when the city fathers closed the door of a white primary school to a five-year-old Negro girl. Though the jurists upheld the city, its victory was not for long, for six years afterward, Massachusetts honored itself as the first state to outlaw separate public schools for Negroes.

But there ensued no stampede in other places to emulate the Bay State's illustrious example. Indeed, after Appomattox compulsory segregation became the rule in all the Southern states, and permissible segregation in several others. Though Negroes protested that such business made a mock and scandal of their constitutional rights, and they employed lawyers to seek redress in the courts, their best efforts in the end went for naught. The earlier Boston verdict had taken on the power of a legal precedent. It not only swayed the state courts; it weighed even upon the thinking of the Supreme Court. Thus, in 1896, in the case of *Plessey v. Ferguson,* involving Louisiana's mandatory segregation in its public conveyances, all save one of the justices held such practice to be constitutional as long as the facilities, though separate, were equal. Thus the "separate but equal" principle. Settled in law, it presently put its grip on Southern education and also on that of the nation's capital

The age in which we live has seen the problem of race relationship given a great deal of reexamination. New ideas forced themselves into it, mostly, as one might guess, from the era's large events—its wars and depressions, its hounding of the racial nether folk—besides the newer revelations from the psychological and sociological sciences. The pressing need for manpower during the Second World War conducted the Negro increasingly into America's industry, putting an agreeable bulge thereby in his wallet and lifting him in his standard of living, and per consequence, in his social standing. Once having enjoyed such gratifications, he was not disposed to yield them—on the contrary he thirsted for more. At the same time, the possibility of his further ascent in power and status brought misgivings, and even fears, to his white competitors, whether below the Potomac or above. Across the ocean, meanwhile, the fascist terror was wreaking its fury. It not only brought a shudder to the national conscience; it also stirred up calls for effective steps against discrimination over here. The upshot was a report in 1947 from the Truman Committee on Civil Rights with recommendations to the lawmakers to put such steps into being.

In education the attack on discrimination led directly to segregation. The first small breach in its formidable wall is dated 1935 when the Maryland Court of Appeals ordered the state law school to admit a Negro to its sessions. Other breaks presently followed, now in Missouri, now in Texas, now in Oklahoma, all in the higher learning and all favorable to the Negro. Though the gains confined themselves to individuals, in the succeeding years they fell to others. In fact, by midcentury Negroes were making their way into the halls of higher learning not only in the states aforementioned, but also in Arkansas, Delaware, Kentucky, and Virginia. Their advance, it is true, was modest and groping, and it was hobbled with devious devices—nevertheless, it was an advance. In the lower learning, however, there was no such progress. There the full firepower of "separate but equal facilities" held the Negro at bay, and in seventeen states and the District of Columbia compulsory segregation remained the rule, while in four others it was a matter of local option.

But in May, 1954, the Supreme Court, declaring against such practice on the ground of the Fourteenth Amendment, put its unanimous taboo on racial segregation in the public school. "Separate educational facilities," the Court held, "are inherently unequal." In consequence, it ordered the integration of public schools with "all deliberate speed."

The Court's declaration changed no segregated heart—soon, in fact, it became plain that the end of legal segregation did not mean the end of actual segregation. Some states, seeking to hamper, or even thwart, integration, amended their constitutions—some even resorted to the artifice of abolishing their public schools and sending their white children to white schools maintained by private moneys. But the Federal courts, holding to the Fourteenth Amendment, struck down such legal sophistry, even though in the process they stepped upon the state's traditional right to organize and operate its schools according to its own lights. All in all, despite the stalling and resisting, the years since 1954 have seen some progress. Throughout the land, not only in the South, but in the North as well, countless communities have taken steps to bring their schools into conformance with the law's requirements. In the meantime, however, in the die-hard White Supremacy Belt, all too often the "deliberate speed" the Supreme Court had ordered has shown far more deliberation than speed. Thus the issue was volleyed back and forth over the years like a tennis ball, until in October 1969, the Supreme Court ruled unanimously that school districts must make an end of segregation "at once" and operate integrated schools "now and hereafter," replacing the Warren Court's optimistic but unworkable "all deliberate speed" policy with a much more stringent standard of immediate compliance.

9

If the courts have been summoned to put out the flames of racial inequality in our public schools, then they have been no less occupied with disputes involving religion. Our colonial schools were solidly grounded on religion. They not only taught denominational religion; in some places, say, in the Massachusetts Bible State, they were even supported out of the public till. But as the years drew on, and religious feelings succumbed more and more to materialistic lures, the school likewise yielded, and pretty soon it was sailing along with the racing secular current. Far on in the eighteenth century, signs of the changing times were plainly discernible—in fact, in 1792 New Hampshire put its constitutional ban on public sectarian instruction.

The American public school is the legatee of this tradition. A state institution, it must hold itself apart from any church; hence, it does not—nay, it may not—teach religion. However, Americans being what they are, there reigns among them no unanimity of opinion over what is and what is not religious teaching. In consequence, what some states permit others forbid.

As for actual religious instruction, the churches, as so often in their past, find themselves in disagreement. The Roman Catholic Church naturally favors religious instruction, for by its illumination religion is the very essence of education. Among Protestants, as among Jews, there is no solid front. Some, eyeing the republic's enormous conglomeration of religious persuasion, consider it better in the interest of the general good to hold state and church apart. But to certain Protestants such a cleavage is palpably against God, and a menace, hence, to civilization. To remedy it they have advocated some form of nonsectarian religious teaching in the public school. It has exhibited itself most commonly in states which are densely Protestant, and usually in the republic's more bucolic regions.

More satisfactory to most of the faithful is the compromise of furloughing the young from their secular scholastic duties and permitting them to devote such time to pondering the teachings of their religion. Known as "released time," it is imparted beyond the academic ambit, and is usually executed under the ecclesiastic hand and eye.

But this practice too has bred antagonism. A plain violation of the principle of separation of state and church, it discriminates, some contend, against the offspring of agnostics and atheists, wounding their psyche by compelling them to watch their colleagues escape from their studies, even if only for a spell, while they for their part must sit and suffer with their books. To deal with such contention religious leaders have given their countenance to "dismissed time." Under this scheme children are turned loose from school for, maybe, an hour once a week, presumably to edify themselves in piety, but with neither checkup nor penalty, should temptation steer them toward more worldly and even sinful pastimes.

There have been times when contention over religious instruction has eventuated in litigation. When, in illustration, the board of education of Champaign, Illinois, gave its support and cooperation to a program of religious instruction in its schools, Mrs. Vashti McCollum, a nonbeliever, brought suit. Though such study was to be voluntary, she argued that her son's abstention made him a public spectacle, the target of derision, thereby causing anguish and sorrow to both child and mother. Ruled against by the state court, Mrs. McCollum made appeal to the United States Supreme Court, which in March, 1948, by 8 to 1 reversed the lower court. Beyond all question, declared Mr. Justice Black, the spokesmen for the majority, Champaign had employed the tax-supported public school "to aid religious groups to spread their faith." Thus, he continued, "it falls squarely under the ban of the First Amendment."

For all its weight, the Court's opinion was not given a universal approval, and some places continued to release their pupils during school hours to attend religious classes conducted in a sacred edifice. With so much uncertainty on the subject, the issue inevitably made its way before the bench of justice. But even this brought no solution, for some courts, as in St. Louis in 1948, declared against the practice, while others, as in New York, in the same year gave it their support. At length, four years later, when the New York case came before the nation's highest tribunal, the New York plan for "released time" was upheld. Unlike its predecessor in Illinois, the New York practice did not effect a working partnership between government and religion, but merely enabled each to recognize the other's right. "Ours," remarked Mr. Justice Douglas, is "a religious people whose institutions presuppose a Supreme Being." And he went on, "we cannot read into the Bill of Rights . . . a philosophy of hostility to religion."

If the dispute over "released time" brought sleepless nights to many public educators, then the controversy over Bible reading and the recital of the Lord's Prayer fretted them even more. Is the mere reading of the Good Book an act of religious instruction and thereby in contravention of the secular principle? Some states said yes and put such practice under prohibition. Others, in contrast, said no and allowed it. Some states outlawed certain portions of the Bible, but sanctioned others. Finally, in a few states the reading of certain Biblical verses was made compulsory. What went for the reading of Holy Writ went also for the recitation of the Lord's Prayer—some states vetoing the practice, some permitting it, and a few requiring it. Eventually, in 1963, when the dispute was aired in the Supreme Court, the justices ruled that prescribed Bible reading and recitation of the Lord's Prayer in the nation's public schools are in violation of the First Amendment. Speaking for the Court, Mr. Justice Clark offered the partisans of Biblical reading at least a straw of hope. "It may well be said," declared the justice, "that one's education is not complete without a study of comparative religion or the history of religion and its relationship to the advancement of civilization." It certainly may be said, he went on, "that the Bible is worthy of study for its literary and historic qualities." And, finally, "Nothing we have said here indicates that such study of the Bible or religion, when presented objectively as part of a secular program of education, may not be effected consistent with the First Amendment."

Although nonpublic schools are under the state's watchful eye, and are subject to its authority, their right to merchant their views has the sanction of the courts. The notion that attendance at a private school, whether lay or religious, is somehow contrary to democracy, and that, per corollary, every child should be put upon to go to public school—that notion has been solemnly scotched. Put into law in the early twenties, when Oregon undertook to article every child between eight and sixteen to the public school, it was rejected by the Supreme Court in 1925. Not only was the statute held to be in violation of the constitutional provision for due process of law; it had also interfered "with the liberty of parents and guardians to direct the education and upbringing of children under their control." The state, the Court let it be known, may require children to be schooled; it may fix educational requirements; and to ensure that they are properly and effectively met, it may inspect all schools, whether public or private, religious or parochial. But in no case may it compel children "to accept instruction from public teachers only."

Another bone of contention to stir up the respective partisans of state and church is the use of public money in education. Already in the nineteenth century they were belaboring one another, and as the drive for universal public schooling gathered momentum, the caloric intensity of their controversy mounted. To keep state and church asunder in public education, most states enacted laws which prohibited or, at all events, severely impaired the use of public money for religious ends. Needless to say, few ecclesiastics have granted such jurisprudence a hearty approval, and to this moment they array themselves against it. You may separate church and state, some of them concede, but not religion and education. Since under present conditions the public school fails to meet the needs of those for whom religion remains a paramount concern, several million of the faithful are obligated to run their own schools, thereby freighting themselves with a double financial cargo. For not only must they maintain their church schools, but, like everyone else in this land of the free, directly or indirectly, they are levied upon to support the public variety. In effect, hence, they are doubly taxed.

To lighten their burden not a few have pressed for assistance from the public till. Their argument is not only that they suffer what amounts to a double exaction on their pocket, but that without some succor from the state, in these our present times of ballooning prices, the very existence of their schools is in jeopardy. Rather interestingly, in a number of test suits they have emerged victoriously. Courts, for example, have upheld their right to share the public money in order to safeguard the health of their pupils on the ground that such enterprise is an integral and necessary civil function of the school. In other instances they have been accorded the right to transport their young to their various parochial schools in conveyances which are publicly owned and operated and, hence, financed out of the people's purse.

The question of granting dollars to private and parochial schools has corded the brows of the Congressmen on the Potomac no less than their analogues in the state shrines of lawmaking. Indeed, until a few years back one attempt after another to extend Federal aid to the states came to grief over the church and state issue. So, more or less, the situation stood until 1965, when Congress enacted the Elementary and Secondary Education Act, under whose articles a portion of the $1.3 billion of the national grant was made available to private and parochial schools.

Since then the cost of according aid to American education for one thing or another has shown no signs of abatement. On the contrary, it has steadily soared. In 1967, in illustration, the government disbursed more than twelve billion dollars for the support and sustenance of education. Recently, in 1970, President Nixon put his signature on a bill calling for the expenditure over a three-year period of $26.4 billion in aid of elementary and secondary education, a colossal extension, needless to say, of its famous historic antecedent of 1965. The President let it be known that he was signing the bill "with considerable reluctance."

Nor has the problem of keeping American private schools, be they sacred or profane, on their legs shown any inkling of getting better. In truth, despite the sweat and sobs of their owners and operators, every day sees at least one center of private learning foosh down the dreadful chute of extinction. To offer some light and leading to stem this melancholy trend, President Nixon in 1970 named a panel, headed by the illustrious Dr. Clarence Walter of the Catholic University of America, to direct its collective intelligence to the crisis confronting America's nonpublic schools. The board has been vouchsafed two years to work its miracle.

Meanwhile, several states, braving the incertitude of possible constitutional litigation, have in one way or another provided subventions to lighten the burden of the hard-pressed parochial groves. Between 1968 and 1969, for example, Pennsylvania, Connecticut, and Rhode Island consented to grant direct assistance to their parochial schools. New York took the plunge in 1970, when its lawgivers made provision for an annual expenditure of $28 million in state aid. Of this lovely monetary bundle the first installment of $10.1 million was paid in February, 1971. Disbursed to 1,365 religious schools in the state, it is to be employed "for nonreligious activities." All these laws have enflamed a considerable amperage, and it is not unlikely that eventually they will have to be adjudicated by the nine sagacious jurists sitting in the nation's capital. In point of fact, the Pennsylvania statute, which grants direct aid to the state's parochial schools, is already under challenge in the republic's highest court. Enacted in 1968, the measure provides for the "state purchase of teacher services, in nonpublic schools," to be paid out of the public treasury. Is such payment within the intent and purpose of the Constitution, or is it not? Some say yes and some say no. Presently the Omnipotent Nine will say the word.

10

The hope of using education to make an end once and for all to the scourge of war—a hope more highly cherished today than ever—is actually of a grizzly age. One hears it voiced no less than six hundred years ago when Pierre Dubois proposed the establishment of international schools which, he was convinced, would pay their way from the money they saved us by the abolition of war—an Eden which, unfortunately, he was unable to bring about. Later, in the war-wracked seventeenth century, the monumental Comenius came forth with a plan for a Pansophic College where the world's foremost scholars would put their heads together to bring about peace and goodwill on earth, universal and everlasting. But like Dubois's proposal, the Pansophic College remained wholly imaginary. Two centuries following, Marc-Antoine Julien, a Frenchman, urged upon us the creation of a corps of savants to cull and spread information about European education, to the end, among other things, of promoting international amity and cooperation. As our globe spun on, other luminaries invented educational schemes to give us universal justice, tranquility, and welfare, but none of them fructified.

The first American to use education to make war on war was Fannie Fern Andrews. Though her fame in intellectual history has descended to a tenuous footnote, in her time she enjoyed a creditable standing. A doctor out of Harvard, she was a specialist in international law and an advocate of international understanding. Doubtless she also had the gift of tongue, for in 1912 she persuaded the State Department to negotiate for an international conference at The Hague. Unhappily, the drums of war were already beating, and before the assembly could be summoned to order, the First World War had begun.

Following Versailles, when the world was sick of war—at least transiently—a number of organizations, all dedicated in one manner or another to the further-ance of international goodwill, came upon the scene. The first of any note, the Commission of International Cooperation—CIC for short—arrived in 1926. Com-prised of some of the world's most dazzling intellects, and heir more or less to the thinking of Dr. Andrews, the commission set out (1) to hold international congresses among the world's custodians and promoters of learning, its universi-ties, libraries, museums, and the like; (2) to find out what schools were doing to enlighten the young about the League of Nations; (3) to examine schoolbooks with a view to purging them of any overnationalistic pollution; (4) to make effective use of mass communication in advancing international cooperation. But as the twenties flowed into the thirties, nationalism was once more frenzying civilization, and the dreams of the commission were dashed.

Meanwhile, another alliance, the International Bureau of Education, with headquarters at Geneva, made its advent. Transformed presently into an inter-governmental body, it fell under the control of its member nations, and in a moderate manner they squared its expense account. The bureau toiled with a fair success. It arranged international educational seances, printed monographs on comparative education, issued annual and monthly bulletins, and laid the foundation of an international library on education. Unluckily, its membership was never ample, neither the United States nor Great Britain being on its roster; and so in the main its efficacy fell far lower than its aspiration.

There followed several other attempts to propagate understanding and good works among the nations. In the thirties, for example, Great Britain, France, Germany, and the United States embarked on a "cultural relations program." An integral part of the Department of State, the representation of the United States proposed, besides the usual things, "to serve mankind." Unhappily, the world was too far gone to give an ear, and in 1939, the very year the United States launched its program, the Nazis launched the Second World War.

Smaller in scale, but more salubrious in its outcome, was the endeavor to effect better cultural relations between the United States and its Latin American neighbors. Brought into being in 1936 at Buenos Aires, it has directed a variety of interchanges, from students and teachers to works of art, films, books, radio programs, and similar enterprises to advance enlightenment.

Among the various private ventures in the domain of international education, the oldest and by long odds the most celebrated is the Institute of International Education. The work of Stephen Duggan, now departed from this earth, the institute began in 1919 with a grant from the Carnegie Endowment for Interna-tional Peace. During its long and eminent career the institute has aided the exchange of numerous thousands of students and professors; it has worked out an effective student advisory service; and it has supported and promoted the Junior Year Abroad, a plan whereby handpicked American collegians may spend their junior year in study—for American college credit—in some foreign center of the higher knowledge. In the dark and disreputable days of Fascism, with its wholesale dismissal of some of civilization's foremost scholars, the institute gave aid and comfort to not a few of these hapless men, translating them to freer lands—in many cases the United States—to light their torch afresh.

With so many organizations at work to forward international education, the efforts of individual colleges to such an end might easily escape notice. Their participation in programs of exchange professors and students is of course no novelty. Since the war, however, their industry, lubricated by foundation money, and especially the government's well-known Fulbright grants, has prospered enormously. Meanwhile, on the American campus the systematic study of foreign cultures has gone into high gear.

Finally, and perhaps most important, there is the United Nations Educational, Scientific and Cultural Organization, or in acronymic parlance, UNESCO. Come to life in London in 1945 as an organ of the United Nations, it embraced forty-three member nations, sans Russia at that time, but since then in the fold. The idea—or ideal—which flags it on is that education can be an effective weapon for international understanding and, hence, enduring peace. It is the hope which gladdened the dreams of so many bygone seers, from Dubois to Comenius to Fannie Andrews, but supported today with an infinitely greater knowledge, and certainly a desperate necessity. Wars, contends UNESCO, begin in the minds of men, and so "it is in the minds of men that the defenses of peace must be constructed." To such a goal there must be an open door at all times and everywhere "to the unrestricted pursuit of objective truth and the free exchange of ideas and knowledge"—a millenium into which the human race, so far at any rate, has not entered. For all that, however, UNESCO aspires and works some day to achieve it.

There is no doubt that during its quarter-century or so in practice—a mere speck of time in so vast a program—UNESCO has performed meritoriously, sometimes even miraculously. It has exchanged students from land to land on a far grander scale than ever. Through its reports, transmitted by the most up-to-date means of communication, it has kept the world abreast of educational, scientific, and cultural developments in nations the world around. With schools, laboratories, and libraries it played no small part in getting the war-ravaged lands of East and West back on their educational legs. Finally, it has brought the light of the written word to people who since time unknown have groped and stumbled in the dark night of illiteracy.

Unlike its forerunners, UNESCO enjoys the boon of monetary support from the governments that comprise it. Unlike them also, it enjoys a position of rank and respect—at least in the world's more enlightened quarters. Hence, both in its standing and in its power it is superior to its predecessor, the hobbled and hapless Commission on Intellectual Cooperation. Yet, despite these gains, UNESCO suffers from a number of flaws and deficiencies. Its statutes, to cite an example, prohibit it from grappling with "matters which are essentially within the jurisdiction" of its member nations—a provision which at present doubtless is necessary, but one which at the same time gags and ropes UNESCO's free and forthright functioning. The loophole here is a crater. For, given man's greed and guile, who can determine precisely what is a purely national concern, and hence subject solely to a nation's jurisdiction? Were the Frenchmen's anti-German latherings as they exhibited themselves in their schools before and after Versailles a strictly Gallic matter? And were the blood-curdling dogmas of the Führer and his yes-men for Germans alone? Or were they, and others like them, matters that concerned us all? Even did UNESCO know the answers, it is doomed by its ordinance to stillness. The most it can do is to refer the business to the Security Council. The greatest handicap UNESCO will have to surmount if its ideals are to bear their promised fruit is nationalism. Not even UNESCO's most voluble critics are likely to dispute the worth of its aspiration, save possibly on the ground of their messianic optimism. But between its bold and lofty assumptions and the actuality of national self-interest there stretches a hard and hazardous trail. Nationalism killed the hopeful CIC, and unless science presently figures out how to rid us of its curse it bodes to destroy UNESCO too.

Meanwhile, there is still hope.

11

In America's educational chronicles that 1960s may well go down as the decennium of student revolt. Preeminently, its blasts have shaken the ancient college elms, but to a lesser extent, though scarcely less tumultuous, it has driven its way into the halls of the secondary learning. The fact that collegians, being young and frisky, are full of animal spirits, and hence given to a certain amount of hell-raising, has tended to blanket the fact that from their very beginnings in this home of the brave they have resorted now and then to earnest protest and even riot. At colonial Harvard they balked at the degenerate food their commons besought them to consume, and when their loud lamentations availed them naught, the students went on strike. At rival Yale, though its scholars were no less concerned with their gastronomic well-being, they made news of their gross vilification of their tutors. Not content to ply them with public abuse, they stoned their windows, and when hazard brought one of them into their presence in the darkness of the night, they were not averse to bludgeoning him with massive sticks.

In Charlottesville, in Virginia, though the libertarian Jefferson was all for the exercise of free and open dissent, and even delegated all disciplinary powers at his university to a council of student "censors," the stillness of the Blue Ridge was dissolved, for all that, by student turmoil and even bloodshed.

Nor is student direct action on public questions a recent emanation in this country. One sights it as long ago as the Revolution—even, indeed, in the prior years of its gathering storm. On a night in May, in 1775—to recount just a single instance—uproarious King's College students, fortified by a posse of the public laity, vented their rage before the quarters of the college's Tory president, Myles Cooper. So upset was the poor man, he took off, clad in barely more than a nightshirt, leaping over a fence and racing at full speed for a British sloop, where he judiciously remained until it deposited him safely, and decently clothed, on the soil of his beloved motherland.

As the years bore on, and the issue of slavery fretted the land, students, both above and below the Mason-Dixon divide, engaged in public agitation. In fact, in Ohio at Oberlin College, where abolitionist blood pressure ran extremely high, students helped to run an underground railroad to transport refugee blacks to safety in nonslave territory.

Following Appomattox student concern in public affairs assumed the more decorous guise of promoting serious colloquy in associations expressly established for such a purpose, in illustration, the Yale Assembly, founded in 1887 to offer its members a chance to ventilate their social and political animadversions. The century through which we are presently groping witnessed the incursion onto the campus of lay idealists seeking to rally students to the reformer's flag. The first upon the scene was the International Socialist Society, organized in 1905 in the city of New York, under the direction of Upton Sinclair, with help and advice from Clarence Darrow and Jack London.

But socialism on the campus, like socialism in the republic, never roused more than a scant support. With the surge and spread of international communism, moreover, on the heels of the First World War, the ISS was done for: its members either embraced the new revelation from the left or they threw in their lot with the existing social order or they sought solace in the depths of metaphysical speculation. In the twenties, when times were flush and pockets full, the vast run of collegiate America was no more interested in social and economic change, not to say revolution, than their money-making elders. But when hard times began to wrack and ravage what only yesterday had been acclaimed as the fairest of all possible republics, tortured students, like their tortured parents, suffered a change of mind. Once more we behold some of them joining hands, spurred and abetted at times, it is true, by extramural clans, to agitate for social and economic reforms. In the springtime of 1934 we see them in colleges and high schools laying down their books and pencils in a nationwide strike against war. A year later they commemorated the anniversary of their act with another performance, and in 1936 they accorded it yet another rehearsal. Betweenwhiles, they busied themselves with other complaints, from loud protestations against child labor to outcries against the suppression of the Negro's civil rights and the harassment of the unions.

Whatever harvest these tactics of dissent may have reaped is, of course, impossible to ascertain. The hand of Mars the Student Peace Movement obviously did not stay. When, after 1945, the doves of peace once more fluttered across the land—even, if only for a sardonic interlude—the millions of retired GIs who trudged the college corridors turned out in the main to be an earnest lot, eager to get their degrees and, thereafter, a job and success. Needless to say, they had little taste for social upset and upheaval. In our national annals they have been denominated, a bit too patly, perhaps, as the Silent Generation. So things sat more or less until the 1960s.

What sets apart the present-day student insistence on reform, be it in the academic grove or in the world beyond its bounds, from any of its historic predecessors, is not only its complexity, its tremendous reach and magnitude, but also its determined activism—one might even say its well-nigh fanatical militance. What its partisans seek—which is to say, the well-meaners in their cohorts—is the fulfillment of man's perennial aspiration, the creation, in short, of a better world, not in some fictive remote utopia, but actual and alive, and without delay. Peace, poverty, housing, racism, the deterioration and decay of our cities, the befoulment of our air and land and water, the quality of our education—these are some of the malaises of our society that rouse them to a high heat, and, unhappily, all too often to an explosive combustion. No longer satisfied to work for change merely within the confines of strikes and parades, to realize their goals today's campus protestors, black and white, seize college buildings and facilities, sometimes at gun point; they interrupt and prevent classroom sessions; they hold faculty members—even, indeed, deans and presidents—in captivity; they destroy student records, research data, and other irreplaceable materials; they commit assault and battery; they engage in arson and set off bombs, causing loss of life and limb and many millions of dollars of property.

It is easy to forget in the welter of all this upset and agony, that the proportion of its active fomentors is small. And so also is the number of afflicted campuses—in truth, on the word of Attorney General John L. Mitchell, a ddclared defender of law and order, and in his outlook a high conservative, no more than nine of every hundred colleges have suffered serious disturbance. Active student dissent, in short, is in the hands of a minority, vociferous and bellicose, and sometimes, sad to say, utterly ruthless.

In the execution of their belligerence, college dissidents hae not been entirely solitary—some of them, in fact, are card-carriers in various radical guilds, some black, some white, some both. The most formidable amongst them has been the Students for a Democratic Society, the SDS, for short. The self-styled New Left, it laid the groundwork for the assault on Columbia University in 1968, where it directed the vandalizing of equipment, the burning of books and manuscripts, pillaging the president's personal files, and polluting the air with filth and obscenity. The avowed enemy of the established order, whether academic or otherwise, the leaders of the Students for a Democratic Society have given notice that they are out "to create more Columbias."

What outcomes will issue from all this conflict and terrorism is for the prophets to say, not the historians. There is no doubt, however, that in the academic world, if not in the world at large, some alterations have been wrought. Some colleges, for example, have granted students representation on their governing boards of trustees, thereby vouchsafing them a say, though frail and pianissimo, it is true, in the discussion and making of policy. Others have extended them the right to review and appraise the effectiveness of their instructors, and to air their views, for weal or woe, in public. Still others have abandoned their historic role of chaperoning their students' private lives; some have even assented to the integration of the sexes in their dormitories with male and female students living not only under the same roof, but door to door on the same floor. The greatest gainer in many colleges has been the Negro. Not only has the higher learning manned its teaching staffs with more and more blacks; it has also admitted them as students in an ever ascending number. Not a few of the houses of the higher sapience have gone to great lengths to minister to the Negro's special needs and interests—some, in fact, have instituted new departments and even centers specializing in Negro culture, past and present.

So much for the agreeable side of the legendary coin. There is the usual obverse. That the students' uproar has damaged the traditional academic quietude is, of course, transparent. Worse yet, it has thrown into jeopardy not only the freedom of teaching, but also the freedom of learning, without which honest scholarship needs must perish. The vehemence of the students' outburst has appalled and even frightened some of the more liberal professors who otherwise inclined to give the protestors a sympathetic ear. Finally, it has brought doubts and misgivings to men of wealth, whose gifts to the shrines of the upper learning in the past run to astronomic figures. Dashed and dismayed by the campus's train of unhappy events, current philanthropists have become chary about bestowing their largess to colleges in ferment. The upshot is that some of them already foresee a grimmer-than-ever financial future.

Education is one of civilization's oldest concerns. In consequence the literature of its history is vast—so vast, in truth, that no reader, however industrious, can hope to persevere through more than a minor portion of it. There are, happily, a number of aids and summaries to guide him through its mazes, and the one that suggests itself almost immediately is the five-volume *Cyclopedia of Education*, edited by Paul Monroe and originally published by the Macmillan Company in New York. Though it has given over half a century of service, for the student of educational history many of its treatises still speak with authority. A new and modernized edition, with an editorial word by Dr. William Wolfgang Brickman, "with the assistance of department editors and several hundred contributors," was published by Gale in 1968. Restricted to the more recent past is the *Encyclopedia of Modern Education*, edited by Harry Rivlin and Hubert Schueler, and published in 1943 at New York by the Philosophical Library, Inc. Within the limits of its time span, it offers itself as a satisfactory escort to the educational ideas and movements of only yesterday, or at all events the day before. Supplementing and fortifying these works is the *Encyclopedia of Educational Research*, issued for the fourth time in 1969. True to its title, it puts its eye chiefly on research. Taken together, its four editions provide a fine conspectus of the course of the scientific movement in education during the past three decades.

For the social and cultural context of education the most useful reference work is the *Encyclopedia of Social Science*, published in 1937 in fifteen volumes. It is well informed and—humanly speaking—fair, and it grapples with a variety of educational phenomena, both practical and theoretical.

Nearly all the standard encyclopedias make reference to the educational past, and especially to its salient workers and thinkers. The *Britannica*'s twenty-four volumes (revised edition, 1961 and a new edition about to appear) are the most up-to-date, and the student would do well to consult its articles.

For a bibliography of educational history the best at hand so far is William Wolfgang Brickman's *Guide to Research in Educational History*, put out in 1949 under the colophon of the New York University Bookstore. Though it bogs now and then in academic trivia, the judicious student need not be daunted. Expertly arranged, the book's annotated listing of the writings in educational history is the longest between book covers in the English language. There are in addition several other meritorious bibliographic storehouses, such as *Bibliographies and Summaries*, by Walter Monroe and Louis Shores (1936), and *World Bibliography of Bibliographies* in four volumes by Theodore Besterman, published in its third edition at Geneva during 1955 and 1956. For the meticulous searcher, finally there are Robert Collison's *Bibliographies: Subject and National* (1951) and his *Bibliographical Services throughout the World, 1950-1959* put out in 1961. To doctoral aspirants in the higher learning it offers leads not commonly available elsewhere.

For educational statistics there are several sources. Two important ones to confine cases—are the *Biennial Survey of Education in the United States*, published by the U.S. Office of Education from 1919 to the present, and the *World Survey of Education: Handbook of Educational Organization and Statistics*, published by UNESCO in 1955 and revised and reissued triennially thereafter.

The list of general texts on educational history runs to great length. Unfortunately, the bulk of them are not a little dull, and the student would do himself a favor to scout the library shelves, leafing through the pages of some of their holdings to come upon something satisfactory to his taste. Among the more recent ones he will find *A Cultural History of Western Education* by R. Freeman Butts, first published in 1947 and extensively revised in 1955 (New York: McGraw-Hill Book Company); *A History of Education*, by James Mulhern (New York: The Ronald Press Company, second edition, 1959); *A History of Western Education* by H. G. Good (New York: The Macmillan Company, second edition, 1960); and *The Foundations of Modern Education*, by Elmer H. Wilds and Kenneth Lottich (New York: Holt, Rinehart, and Winston, 1961).

Rather curiously, there are not many texts dealing with the American educational past. Among the newer ones, in order of their appearance, are *A History of Education in American Culture*, by R. Freeman Butts and Lawrence A. Cremin (New York: Holt, Rinehart and Winston, Inc., 1953); *The American School in Transition*, by William Drake (Englewood Cliffs, N.J.: Prentice-Hall, Inc., 1955); *A History of American Education*, by H. G. Good (New York: The Macmillan Company, 1956); and *An Educational History of the American People*, by Adolphe E. Meyer (New York: McGraw-Hill Book Company, 1957; second edition, 1968).

Historians, as everybody knows, are given to grubbing in original sources, and in this connection their specialists in education run true to type. To make their probings more conveniently accessible, some of them have assembled a repertory of representative source materials. The first to come out in America was Paul Monroe's *Source Book of the History of Education for the Greek and Roman Period* (New York: The Macmillan Company, 1901). More comprehensive is Cubberley's *Readings in the History of Education*. Published at Boston by Houghton Mifflin Company, in 1920 and again in 1948, it remains the standard work of reference in the field. For primary material on the American educational past there is Knight and Hall's *Readings in American Educational History*, published at New York by Appleton-Century-Crofts, Inc., in 1951. Another volume of interest and value is *Main Currents of Western Thought* by Franklin Le Van Baumer (New York: Alfred A. Knopf, Inc., 1952). Its selected readings in Western European intellectual history from the Middle Ages to the present offer a first-class supplement to the more conventional ones already singled out.

There are several texts on the history of educational thought. One of the best, considering its small scale, is *The Doctrines of the Great Educators*, by Robert Rusk (London: Macmilland & Co., Ltd., 1926; revised, 1955). An older standard bearer is *A History of Educational Thought*, by Percival Richard Cole (London:

Oxford University Press, 1931). It gives attention to the educational thinking of several outstanding nonprofessionals—Dante and Anatole France, to cite only two. The *History of Educational Thought*, by Robert Ulich (New York: American Book Company, 1945) runs from Plato to Dewey, with chapters on Benjamin Franklin, Thomas Jefferson, and Ralph Waldo Emerson. For those able to make their way through foreign languages there are many useful references to pertinent material in Latin, French, and German. For correlative reading the student should introduce himself to Ulich's *Three Thousand Years of Educational Wisdom* (Cambridge, Mass.: Harvard University Press, 1947; 2d edition, 1965), an anthology of human sagacity, some real and some pretty close to nonsense.

In the realm of intellectual and cultural history the number of studies in English, and especially by Americans, remains small. One of the first to address the collegiate audience was John Henry Randall, Jr.'s *The Making of the Modern Mind* (Bonston: Houghton Mifflin Company, 1926). Brought up to date in 1940, it is still widely read. *A History of Modern Culture* (New York: Holt, Rinehart and Winston, Inc. 1930-1934) in two volumes from the pen of Preserved Smith covers the ground from 1543 to 1776. Although the time it examines is shorter than that of Randall's work, it traverses a far greater territory, including not only education, but also art, letters, science, politics, religion, manners and morals, and superstition. The most encyclopedic, though not always the most dispassionate, treatise in the field is Harry Elmer Barnes's *An Intellectual and Cultural History of the Western World* (New York: Harcourt, Brace & World, Inc., second edition, 1941). The volume weighs 4½ pounds and runs for 1,278 pages. Much slimmer, yet full of knowledge, is Crane Brinton's *Ideas and Men* (Englewood Cliffs, N.J.: Prentice-Hall, Inc., 1950). It is agreeably written, and it contains an annotated bibliography. Useful as a collateral reference is *The History of Magic and Experimental Science*, by Lynn Thorndike (New York: Columbia University Press, six volumes, 1923-1940). For all its monumental scholarship, it is full of interesting and sometimes even amusing stuff. For an account of the long struggle between the scientific spirit and Christian theology one can do no better than ponder Andrew Dickson White's *History of the Warfare of Science with Theology in Christendom*. Put out at New York in 1896 by Appleton, the book has been stoutly denounced by Christian apologists ever since, but its main contentions have not been shaken. The work is now available as a one-volume paperback.

There is a large library of books concerned with special aspects of the educational past. Many are no longer in print and are extremely hard to come by. Those that follow are standard and well-known writings, and they can be found in most public or college libraries of any standing and self-respect. There is, to begin, Thomas Woody's *Life and Education in Early Times* (New York: The Macmillan Company, 1949). A rare combination of scholarship and comfortable prose, it stands as a fine memorial to its author, now departed. Its multilingual list of reference works is a singular achievement in American studies of this kind. On Greek education the most complete and authoritative treatment is to be found in the three-volume German work by Werner Jaeger, *Paiedia: The Ideals of Greek Culture*. Its translation was rendered by Gilbert Highet (Fair Lawn, N.J.: Oxford University Press, 1943-1945). There remains the briefer but informative study by K. J. Freeman (London: Macmillan & Co., Ltd., 1922). On Roman education there is no comparable literature—at all events in English. The best, perhaps, is the somewhat senescent *Roman Education*, by A. Wilkins (London: Cambridge University Press, 1905).

When we come to the Middle Ages our pickings become less lean. The basic and all-embracing study for this field is *The Medieval Mind*, by H. O. Taylor (Cambridge, Mass.: Harvard University Press, two volumes, revised edition, 1949). For special topics, from architecture and handwriting to the status of women, the most useful single volume is *The Legacy of the Middle Ages*, edited by C. G. Crump and E. F. Jacobs (Fair Lawn, N.J.: Oxford University Press, 1926). Harry Elmer Barnes's *An Intellectual and Cultural History of the Western World*, already mentioned, devotes some two hundred large and well-filled pages to the subject. In contrast to his aversion to certain aspects of medieval culture stands the devotion of J. J. Walsh, as shown in his *The Thirteenth, Greatest of Centuries* (New York: Fordham University Press, special memorial edition, 1943). Just as illuminating is Charles Homer Haskins's study, *The Renaissance of the Twelfth Century*. First put forth in 1927 by the Harvard University Press, the book has since been incarcerated between paper covers by Meridian Books, Inc., of New York (1957). Haskins, who was one of the most competent medievalists ever to grace this republic, is also the author of several other important writings, as witness, *Studies in the History of Medieval Science* (Cambridge, Mass.: Harvard University Press, 1927); *Studies in Medieval Culture* (Fair Lawn, N.J.: University Press, 1929); and *The Rise of the Universities* (New York: Holt, Rinehart and Winston, Inc., 1923). Haskins not only deals with his subject from a full and intimate knowledge; he also presents his exposition with charm and not a little wit. The work on the higher learning which rises above all others is the *Universities of Europe in the Middle Ages* by Hastings Rashdall, published at London by the Oxford University Press. Written as long ago as 1895, it was given revision in three volumes in 1936 by F. M. Powicke and A. B. Emden, both scholars of the first chop. For the gaudier side of the academic endeavor there is R. S. Rait's *Life in the Medieval University*, an entertaining little volume issued at Cambridge in 1912.

Though the literature on the Renaissance is vast, it offers very little on education. George Clarke Sellery's short essay "The Renaissance: Its Nature and Origins" (Madison, Wis.: The University of Wisconsin Press, 1950) throws light on some of the period's important cultural features. Interesting and valuable also are *Studies in the History of Educational Opinion from the Renaissance*, by S. S. Laurie (London: Cambridge University Press, 1903), and *Vittorino da Feltre and Other Humanist Educators*, by William Harrison Woodward, published by the same house in 1912.

Good critical studies of Protestant education are scarce. Two instructive volumes on this controverted subject are *Early Protestant Educators*, by Frederick Eby (New York: McGraw-Hill Book Company, 1931), and *The Reformation and English Education*, by N. Wood (London: Routledge & Kegan Paul, Ltd., 1931). For background briefing on the period, *The Reformation of the Sixteenth Century* by R. H. Bainton (Boston: Beacon Press, 1952) is helpful, and even better is Preserved Smith's *The Age of the Reformation* (New York: Holt, Rinehart and Winston, Inc., 1920), in which the author also treats the Catholic Reformation and its impact on education are to be found in *Saint Ignatius and the Ratio Studiorum*, by Edward A. Fitzpatrick (New York: McGraw-Hill Book Company, 1933); *La Salle, Patron of All Teachers*, by the same writer (Milwaukee: The Bruce Publishing Company, 1951), *Jesuit Education: Its History and Principles*, by Robert Schwickerath (St. Louis: B. Herder Book Co., 1904); and *The Jesuits and Education*, by William J. McGucken (Milwaukee: The Bruce Publishing Company, 1932).

The history of education as a national enterprise in France, Prussia, England, and the United States is explored in *Nationalism and Education since 1789*, by Edward Reisner (New York: The Macmillan Company, 1922). More recent and concerned primarily with the relationship of education and nationalism in our own republic is Gladys A. Wiggin's *Education and Nationalism* (New York: McGraw-Hill Book Company, 1963).

For the evolution of education in the outlands, save in the case of England, the most expert accounts, as one might expect, lie buried in the works of some alien parlance. But there are a few in English which offer some guidance, however modest. A good introduction to the early glimmering of the French liberal, secular viewpoint is set forth in *French Liberalism and Education in the Eighteenth Century*, which is to say the educational expressions of La Chalotais, Turgot, Diderot, and Condorcet, translated and edited by F. de la Fontainerie (New York: McGraw-Hill Book Company, 1933). Other books of more or less use are *The Primary School System in France*, by F. E. Farrington (New York: Columbia University, Teachers College, 1906); *French Secondary Schools*, by the same author (New York: Longmans, Green, & Co., Inc., 1910); *Recent Reforms in French Secondary Education*, by D. W. Miles (New York: Columbia University, Teachers College, 1952); and, finally, *Education in France* (Paris: Comité France Actuelle, 1956), a terse but illuminating exposition on the problems which currently bedevil the French in their pursuit of a better education. Valuable also is *Education in France*, which occasionally prints material of a historical nature. It is published four times a year by the Cultural Services of the French Embassy at New York and may be had on request.

For Germany's educational history the most satisfactory treatment is to be found in Friedrich Paulsen's *German Education, Past and Present*, translated from the German by T. Lorenz (New York: Charles Scribner's Sons, 1908). *German Higher Schools*, by James E. Russell (New York: Longmans, Green & Co., Inc., 1899), deals with the history, organization, and methods of the German secondary schools. Though it is badly bent by the weight of its years,

Russell's study is still worth examining. The story of education in the Weimar Republic is set down in *The New Education in the German Republic*, by Thomas Alexander and Beryl Parker (New York: The John Day Company, Inc., 1929). It indulges at times in a somewhat gaseous optimism; yet for all that, it is well informed and not badly written.

Of late, several monographs on education in the Bonn Republic have come into print. Of these, two stand out. One, written by two Germans. Erich J. Hylla and Friedrich O. Kegel, goes by the name *Education in Germany* (Frankfurt am Main: Hochschule für Internationale Pädagogische Forschung, 1958). The other, by Theodore Huebner, a New York schoolman but an old hand at German education, is *The Schools of West Germany* (New York: New York University Press, 1962). Of the two, Huebner's work is the more instructive. A bit more recent and somewhat more penetrating is R. F. Lawson's *Reform of the West German School System, 1945-1962*. A doctoral dissertation, it was published as #4 in the University of Michigan's Comparative Education Dissertations, 1965.

There is no shortage of material on Russian education, though the far greater portion directs its attention to the Soviets. For a glimpse at Russian education through the reigns of its various autocrats, male and female, there is the pioneer study of Nicholas Hans, *History of Russian Educational Policy, 1701-1917* (London: P. S. King & Staples, Ltd., 1931). More recent is *Russia's Educational Heritage*, by William H. E. Johnson (Pittsburgh, Pa.: Carnegie Press, Carnegie Institute of Technology, 1950). Very soberly written, it quotes judiciously from Russian primary sources. Its bibliography, which is in Russian and English, embraces the most useful works of reference.

The first study of early Soviet education to make a stir in our republic was Thomas Woody's *New Minds: New Men?* (New York: The Macmillan Company, 1932). It is scholarly and discerning, and though when it was written, its author's eye was on the contemporary scene, its main value to us lies in the fact that what was then young and fresh is now old and some of it even cold and dead. Another work of interest is *Soviet Education*, by James Bowen (Madison, Wis.: The University of Wisconsin Press, 1962). It deals largely with Anton Makarenko, a pedagogue of a high order whose theories inspired Soviet educational method in the Stalin heyday. The close tie between dictatorship and education is fetchingly set forth in *"I Want to Be Like Stalin,"* translated by George S. Counts and Nucia P. Lodge from the Russian *Pedagogica*, by B. P. Yesipov and N. K. Goncharov (New York: The John Day Company, Inc., 1947). Once a required textbook for every aspiring Soviet birchmaster, it is now under official frown. A work which has been much discussed by Americans is *The Challenge of Soviet Education* by George S. Counts (New York: McGraw-Hill Book Company, 1957). Two other useful compilations are *Soviet Education*, edited by G. L. Kline (New York: Columbia University Press, 1957), and *Education in the USSR*, a bulletin issued by the Office of Education, U.S. Department of Health, Education, and Welfare (Washington, D.C.: Government Printing Office, 1957).

Until recently the English have not been given to any extensive examining of their educational past, and aside from their numerous specialized studies, they have nothing comparable to the texts produced in our fair land on the educational history of the American people. The standard treatise in the field remains J. W. Adamson's *English Education, 1789-1902* (London: Cambridge University Press, 1930). It is a formidable volume and written somewhat stiffly, but for the reader who is willing to brave its challenge, its valuable instruction is well worth the effort. Covering a longer period and a vaster territory is Walter Harry Green Armytage's *Four Hundred Years of English Education*. Published in 1964 by the Cambridge University Press, it was given a fresh and up-to-date incarnation in 1970. Less ambitious, but excellent nonetheless, is Sir William Alexander's *Education in England*. It was published at London by the Newnes Educational Company in 1965. Other useful volumes are *History of Elementary Education in England and Wales*, by Charles Birchenough (London: University Tutorial Press, second edition, 1938); *History of English Elementary Education Since 1760*, by F. Smith (London: University of London Press, Ltd., 1931); *Education in Transition*, by H. C. Dent (London: Routledge & Kegan Paul, Ltd., 1945); *Growth in English Education, 1946-1952*, by the same author and the same publisher (1954). Dent is also responsible for *Education Act, 1944*. Put out by the London University Press in 1944, it offers the most thoroughly critical examination of the famous Butler Education Act that is currently available. The volume attained its ninth edition in 1962. More specialized but no less enlightening is William Pedley's critical phlebotomy of *The Comprehensive School in England*. A member of Parliament, Pedley has been the school's leading defender. His work bears the imprint of bookland's famous house of Pelican and was published in 1963. See also *Education in Great Britain Since 1900*, by S. J. Curtis (London: A. Dakers, 1952); *The British Educational System*, by G. A. N. Lowndes (New York: Holt, Rinehart and Winston, Inc., 1955); and *Education in Great Britain*, by W. W. L. Smith (London: Oxford University Press, second edition, 1956). To these *The British Universities*, by E. Baker (New York: Longmans, Green & Co., Inc., 1946), and *Two Hundred Years of the SPG, 1701-1900*, by C. F. Pascoe (London: The Society for the Promotion of the Gospel, two volumes, 1901), might well be added. For a quick introduction to education as it currently performs its varied service, there is *Education in Great Britain*, a pamphlet issued by the British Information Services at New York (revised edition, 1960). For those who speak only the American language there is a handy glossary of English educational terms.

Like American educational historians, though to a lesser degree, the English have become addicted to the compilation of "Readings." One of the most recent is D. W. Sylvester's *Educational Documents, 800-1816*, dealing with a period of time which takes us from the Anglo-Saxon Schools, including that of the celebrated Alcuin of York, to the much publicized monitorial seminaries of Dr. Bell and Mr. Lancaster.

Mention of the leading texts on American educational history has already been made, and there is no need to rehearse their names once more. Their collective pages abound with references to a vast assortment of specialized themes, useful and ornamental, and for anyone in need of light a study of their listings is recommended. In a class by itself is Professor Joe Park's *The Rise of American Education*, an annotated bibliography, almost teetotal in its scope and comprehensiveness. It was given to the world by the Northwestern University Press at Evanston in 1965.

On the course of thought and events during America's more recent past the literature is almost endless. The best historical introduction to this complex and crucial era is *The Transformation of the School*, by Lawrence A. Cremin (New York: Alfred A. Knopf, Inc., 1961). It is written with a knowledge that is full yet never flaunted. Its bibliographical commentary, which runs for thirty-two packed pages, offers a comfortable guidance to the important literature. Also historical in nature, but with an eye on the educational issues which fever all about us, is *Prologue to Teaching*, a combination of source materials and text, by Marjorie B. Smiley and John S. Diekhoff (Fair Lawn, N.J.: Oxford University Press, 1959). There are many general texts on the American educational system, but the one which has served the greatest audience, both here and overseas, is *American Education*, by Chris A. De Young and Richard Wynn (New York: McGraw-Hill Book Company, fifth edition, 1964). Other volumes which will be found useful are *Crucial Issues in Education*, by Henry Ehlers and Gordon C. Lee (New York: Holt, Rinehart and Winston, Inc., revised edition, 1959); *The Great Debate—Our Schools in Crisis*, by W. C. Scott, C. M. Hill, and H. W. Burns (Englewood Cliffs, N.J.: Prentice-Hall, Inc., 1959); *The American High School Today* (1959), *Slums and Suburbs* (1960), and *The Education of American Teachers* (1963), all from the pen of James Bryant Conant and published at New York under the imprint of the McGraw-Hill Book Company.

The literature on the great educators, European and American, from Rousseau on is, needless to say, tremendous. I have given it mention and some brief discussion in the sister-volume of this present work, i.e., *An Educational History of the American People*, 2d edition, 1968, pp. 455-459, and save for the appearance in 1970 of one important newcomer, the list, taking one work with another, needs no amendment. The new arrival is *Herbart and Herbartarianism: An Educational Ghost Story* by Professor Harold Baker Dunkel of the University of Chicago. Dunkel's étude not only offers a thoughtful revaluation of the long gone German, his followers and interpreters, with the usual academic flora of footnotes, documents, and bibliography; it is also sprightly written, thereby giving the lie once more to the ancient chestnut that sound scholarship and a graciousness and even gayety of utterance are incompatible.

There remain the writings of the schoolmen, whether theoretical or practical, physical or metaphysical. The significant ones have been given notice in the pages of the text itself, and some of them were even granted a dissection. It is not necessary to refer to them again—save, perhaps, to observe that where such writings have attained the stature of classics, not uncommonly they have been honored with paper backs. Such has been the distinction not only of Plato and Aristotle and Quintilian, but also of Jefferson, Franklin, Noah Webster, Horace Mann, Henry Barnard, Charles W. Eliot, Jean-Jacques Rousseau, and John Henry Cardinal Newman—even, indeed, the United States Supreme Court.